The Blue Guides

Belgium

Derek Blyth

A&C Black • London
WW Norton • New York

9th edition, June 2000

1st edition (Belgium and the Western Front) 1920
2nd edition (Belgium and Luxembourg) 1924
3rd edition 1929
4th edition 1963
5th edition 1977, by John Tomes
6th edition 1983, by John Tomes
7th edition 1989, by John Tomes
8th edition 1993, by Bernard Mc Donagh

Published by A & C Black (Publishers) Limited
35 Bedford Row, London WC1R 4JH

Maps and plans drawn by RJS Associates, © A&C Black
Illustrations © Peter Spells

A CIP catalogue record of this book is available from the British Library.

ISBN 0-7136-4832-5

Published in the United States of America by
WW Norton and Company Inc.
500 Fifth Avenue, New York, NY 10110

Published simultaneously in Canada by
Penguin Books Canada Limited
10 Alcorn Avenue, Toronto
Ontario M4V 3B2

ISBN 0-393-32012-X USA

The author and the publishers have done their best to ensure the accuracy of all the information in Blue Guide Belgium; however, they can accept no responsibility for any loss, injury or inconvenience sustained by any traveller as a result of information or advice contained in the guide.

 Cover photograph: Statue of Charles of Lorraine in the Place du Musée, Brussels, by Bernard Régent/The Hutchinson Library.

Title page illustration: Town Hall, Oudenaarde.

Picture acknowledgements: The publishers would like to thank the Musées Royaux des Beaux-Arts, Brussels, and the Museum voor Schone Kunsten, Antwerp, for permission to reproduce the illustrations on pp 43, 44, 46, 96, 97, 232.

Derek Blyth has lived in the Low Countries since 1980. He has written travel articles on Belgium and the Netherlands for *The Independent*, the *Financial Times*, the *International Herald Tribune* and the London *Evening Standard*. He is the author of several cultural guides to the region inluding *Flemish Cities Explored*, *Amsterdam Explored* and *Brussels Explored*. He currently lives in Brussels with his wife and four children.

Printed and bound in England by Butler & Tanner Ltd., Frome and London.

Contents

Maps and plans

Introduction

When the first edition of this guidebook was published in 1920, much of the country was in ruins. The fields around Ypres were strewn with the wreckage of four years of trench warfare. Many historic towns had been largely reduced to rubble, including Ypres, Leuven, Diksmuide, Nieuwpoort, Dendermonde and Namur. The tourists who travelled with the first edition of the Blue Guide to Belgium and the Western Front would have no doubt agreed with James Howell, who in 1640 described this region as 'the cockpit of Europe'.

Even today, the visitor to Belgium is often reminded of the almost continuous history of warfare in this region of Europe. Located at the crossroads of the main trading routes across northern Europe, the country has been involved in almost all of the major European wars.

Most Belgian cities have been attacked, bombarded, besieged and sacked many times in their history. The city of Namur has suffered in so many wars that few buildings survive from before the 17C. During the First World War, Ypres and the surrounding villages were so utterly destroyed that they had to be rebuilt from scratch. The old town of Diksmuide had been bombarded with such ferocity that it was only recognisable from a wooden sign with the town's name. Many old towns in the Ardennes, such as Malmédy and Bastogne, suffered a similar fate in the Battle of the Ardennes of 1944.

This bitter history is often reflected in the population figures for Belgian towns. The town of Dinant had 50,000 inhabitants in the 14C, but has now just 12,000. The town of Tongeren has literally shrunk in size, as can be seen from the vestiges of the Roman town wall that now stand in the middle of open countryside. The city of Ypres is an even more dramatic example. Its population dwindled because of war and economic decline from 40,000 in the 13C to a mere 5000 by the 16C. By the end of the First World War, there was not a single person left in the entire city.

This tragic history of military conquest gives Belgium a character that is quite different from its neighbours. It is impossible to travel long in this country without coming upon the site of a battlefield or the ruins of former stronghold. The country is littered with the vestiges of medieval castles, ruined city walls, devastated abbeys and abandoned concrete bunkers. You can often sense something of the brutal history as you wander across the old battlefields, enter an old barn where Marlborough's soldiers were billeted, or visit the country inn where Wellington planned his strategies. A considerable part of Belgium's tourist industry has grown up around famous battlefield sites such as Waterloo, Ypres and Bastogne.

Despite its tragic destiny, this region has produced some of the great cultural treasures of the Western world. The old cities of Belgium contain countless works of art, such as the Romanesque fonts of the Meuse valley, the Begijnhofs of Flanders, the paintings of the Flemish primitives in Bruges and Ghent, the altarpieces of Rubens in Antwerp and Mechelen, the great cloth halls of Ypres and Bruges, the Art Nouveau houses of Brussels and Antwerp and the great industrial sites of the Meuse valley and Hainaut.

After centuries of conflict, it is perhaps hardly surprising that Belgium lacks the strong identity of neighbouring countries such as France and the

Netherlands. It is in fact a deeply divided country, with the Dutch speakers of Flanders engaged in a constant struggle with the French speakers of Wallonia. Yet this conflict produces a fascinating cultural diversity that we find nowhere else in Europe. It is possible, within an hour, to travel from the Hanseatic brick houses of Bruges to the cool French Neo-classicism of Brussels, or from the flat cultivated polders of West Flanders to the wild forests of the Ardennes.

The visitor to Flanders is likely to be drawn to the historical cities such as Bruges, Ghent and Antwerp. Their splendid architecture, outstanding museums and vibrant cultural life reflect a proud urban tradition that goes back to the medieval cloth guilds. Travellers who head in the direction of Wallonia are more likely to be drawn by the countryside of the Ardennes. The pleasures to be encountered here are not so much in the towns as in the old stone villages, quiet forest trails and outstanding country restaurants. Yet it is often worth taking time to explore the older quarters of the Walloon cities, where the ancient treasures, though less conspicuous, are often quite striking. The historic city of Tournai, in particular, is one of the undiscovered delights of Belgium. Liège, too, despite its rather grimy surface, is a city of secret pleasures.

Brussels, the capital, perfectly reflects the cultural diversity of the country. The administration of the city is a confusing tangle of local councils and regional authorities that baffles most foreigners. Its official bilingual structure adds to the complexity of everyday life. And yet Brussels has, almost in spite of itself, developed into a remarkably cosmopolitan and tolerant city which has welcomed the institutions of both the European Union and NATO. With a certain dogged persistence, it has successfully transformed itself from the 'cockpit of Europe' into the capital of Europe.

It is perhaps not surprising that this complex country has developed a strange and occasionally disturbing culture. This appears in the art of Bosch and Bruegel, the Surrealism of Magritte and Delvaux, the Art Nouveau of Horta and Hankar and perhaps even the modern fashion of the Antwerp School. Much of the art we find in Belgium is slightly eccentric. No other country is quite so obsessed with comic books, puppet theatres, or medieval pageants.

The pleasures of Belgium are often rather unexpected. You might come across a procession of stilt walkers, a grown man dressed as a penguin, a group of Napoleonic soldiers tramping across a field, or a café filled with statues of saints. Most visitors are likely to be pleasantly surprised by the quaint taverns, the odd local museums and the hidden medieval treasures. It is often in the most unlikely places that you find the treasures of Belgium, such as the exquisite 13C gold and silver work by Hugo d'Oignies which is locked inside a dull modern convent in Namur.

An appealing fashion emerged in this region in the 17C and 18C of naming the seven wonders of cities such as Bruges and Leuven. After exploring the country for the Blue Guide, I am tempted to draw up a personal list of the seven wonders of Belgium. My list would be the Grand-Place in Brussels, Tournai Cathedral, the Begijnhof at Leuven, the Plantin-Moretus Museum in Antwerp, the Altarpiece of the Mystic Lamb in Ghent Cathedral, the Cloth Hall at Ypres and the Groeninge Museum in Bruges. I could in fact name a hundred more sights worth a visit. In this country torn by war, an extraordinary wealth of art has miraculously survived.

PRACTICAL INFORMATION

 Planning your trip

Gathering information

Britain
The Belgian tourist office in London split in 1998 into two separate organisations. The Brussels-Flanders office provides information on Brussels and Flanders, while the Brussels-Ardennes office covers Brussels and Wallonia. The Brussels-Flanders office is at 31 Pepper Street, London E14 9R, ☎ 020 7458 0044, fax 020 7458 0045. The Brussels-Ardennes office is at 225 Marsh Wall, London E14 9FW, ☎ 020 7531 0390, fax 020 7458 2999. Office hours are 13.00–17.00. The web address is www.belgium-tourism.net.

USA
It is likely that other Belgian tourist offices will split into two separate offices in the coming years. The Belgian tourist office in New York is at 780 Third Ave, Suite 1501, New York, NY 10017, ☎ 212 758 8130, fax 212 355 7675. The Belgian tourist office in Montreal can be contacted on ☎ 514 484 3595, fax 514 489 8965.

Other tourist offices
Austria: Tourismuswerbung Flandern/Brüssel, Mariahilferstrasse 121b, 6 Stock, A-Vienna, ☎ 01 596 0660, fax 01 596 0695 (Flanders and Brussels).
France: Office Belge de Tourisme, 21 Boulevard des Capucines, F-75002 Paris, ☎ 1 47.42.41.18, fax 1 47.42.71.83.
Germany: Belgisches Verkehrsamt, Berliner Allee 47, D-40212 Düsseldorf, ☎ 0211 864 8411, fax 0211 134 285.
Italy: Ufficio Belga per il Turismo, Piazza Velasca 5 (5e ét.), I-20122 Milan, ☎ 02 860 566, fax 02 876 396.
Japan: B.T.O., Tameike Tokyu Bldg 9F, 1-14, Akasaka 1-Chome, Minato-KU, JAP-Tokyo, ☎ 3 3586 7041, fax 3 3582 3524.
The Netherlands: Belgisch Verkeersbureau, Kennemerplein 3, NL-2011 MH Haarlem, ☎ 023 534 4434, fax 023 534 2050.

Passports and visas
Citizens of EU countries must carry at all times a passport or national identity card. Citizens of the US must have a passport. Visitors intending to stay longer than three months in Belgium have to obtain an identity card from the local commune.

Currency
The Belgian franc (BF or FB) is the basic unit. Belgium and Luxembourg operate a monetary union, which permits both currencies to be used in the two countries. One Belgian franc is equal to one Luxembourg franc. Most Belgian shops and restaurants now display prices in Euros, which will become the official currency on 1 January 2002. Until then, cash payments must be made in Belgian francs, but credit card or cheque payments can be made in either Euros or

Belgian francs. Six months after Euro coins and banknotes are introduced in 2002, the Belgian franc will disappear and the Euro will become the basic unit in Belgium, Luxembourg, the Netherlands, France, Germany, Austria, Ireland, Portugal, Spain, Finland and Italy. The United Kingdom has provisionally opted to remain outside the Euro currency system.

Climate

Belgium has a changeable maritime climate similar to southern England. Winters are relatively mild and summers can be cool. Most days see some rain.

Getting there

By air

Sabena (the Belgian national airline), *British Airways* and *British Midlands* operate frequent scheduled flights from Heathrow, Gatwick and major British airports to Brussels Zaventem airport. The flight from London to Brussels takes under an hour. Several US airports have direct flights to Brussels. A 24-hour service at Zaventem gives information on flights, ☎ 02.723.23.45.

Some airlines have flights to Antwerp, Ostend and Charleroi Sud airports. The Belgian airline *VLM* operates business flights to Belgium from London City Airport. *Ryanair* offers inexpensive direct flights from Dublin to Charleroi Sud. A shuttle bus takes Ryanair passengers from Charleroi airport to the *Wild Geese* pub in Brussels, near Maelbeek metro station.

Airline offices in Britain

British Airways ☎ 0345 222 111   *British Midlands* ☎ 0870 607 0555
Sabena ☎ 020 8780 1444   *VLM* ☎ 020 7476 6677

Airline office in Eire

Ryanair ☎ 01 609 7800

Airline offices in the USA

Air Canada ☎ 1-888-247-2262   *American Airlines* ☎ 1-800-433-7300
British Airways ☎ 1-800-247-9297 *Sabena* ☎ 1-800-955-2000

Airline offices in Belgium

Air Canada ☎ 02.212.09.50   *American Airlines* ☎ 02.508.77.11
British Airways ☎ 02.548.21.22   *Sabena* ☎ 02.723.23.23

Websites

Air Canada www.aircanada.ca
American Airlines www.aa.com
British Airways www.britishairways.com
British Midlands www.britishmidland.com
Ryanair www.ryanair.com
Sabena www.sabena.com (UK) or www.sabena-usa.com (US)
VLM www.vlm–air.com

Brussels Zaventem Airport is a modern European hub with flights to most major cities of the world. It is linked to Brussels by a train which stops at Gare du Nord, Gare Centrale and Gare du Midi. Direct trains also run to Ghent and several other cities. Otherwise, it is necessary to change at the Gare du Nord for connecting train services. For information on trains, ☎ 02.555.25.25.

By train

Eurostar

The opening of the Channel Tunnel has led to the introduction of high-speed trains from London Waterloo and Ashford International to Brussels Gare du Midi. The earliest train from London arrives in Brussels at 10.02. The last train from Brussels leaves at 21.02. The journey between London and Brussels takes 2 hours 40 minutes. Seats must be reserved in advance, ☎ 0990 186 186 (in Britain), or ☎ 0900 10.177 (in Belgium), or ☎ 800 438 7245 (US). Website: www.eurostar.com

Thalys

A sophisticated network of high-speed *Thalys* trains connects Brussels with Paris, Amsterdam and Cologne. About 16 trains a day run in each direction from Paris Gare du Nord to Brussels Gare du Midi. The journey takes about 90 minutes. The earliest train from Paris arrives in Brussels at 08.28. The last train from Brussels leaves at 21.40. Thalys trains also connect Paris with the Belgian cities of Liège, Mons, Ghent, Bruges, Ostend and Antwerp.

A slower Thalys service operates on the route from Brussels to Amsterdam, The Hague and Rotterdam, and from Brussels to Cologne. Seats must be reserved in advance on all Thalys services, ☎ 0900 10.177 (in Belgium) or via the website at www.thalys.com. Booked tickets can be collected at the Railtour desk at Brussels Midi station up to 30 minutes before the departure time. Seats can be booked in Britain through the international rail centre at Waterloo Station, London, or some travel agents.

Thalys trains have disabled areas with toilets designed for wheelchair users.

Le Shuttle

Cars are taken through the Channel Tunnel on *Le Shuttle* trains which run regular services from Folkestone to Calais. The journey takes 35 minutes. The driving time from Calais to Brussels is about 2 hours. Car spaces do not have to be reserved, but it is advisable to do so at busy times, ☎ 0990 353 535 (in Britain), or ☎ 02.717.45.00 (in Belgium). Website: www.eurotunnel.co.uk

By ferry

Rapid ferry

Rapid catamaran services from Dover to Ostend are operated by Hoverspeed. The crossing takes just over 2 hours. Information from *Hoverspeed*, ☎ 0990 595 522 (in Britain); or ☎ 059 55.99.11 (in Belgium). Many tourists prefer the shorter 90 minute ship crossing from Dover to Calais operated by *P&O Stena Line*, ☎ 0870 600 0611 (in Britain), or the 30 minute hovercraft crossing from Dover to Calais run by Hoverspeed (see above). Stena Line also operate a service from Harwich to the Hook of Holland.

Night ferry

P&O North Sea Ferries operates a night crossing from Hull to Zeebrugge. The ferries leave at 18.15 and arrive 08.00 the following morning. Information from P&O North Sea Ferries, ☎ 01482 377 177 (in Britain), or ☎ 050.54.22.22 (in Belgium).

By coach

Hoverspeed CitySprint operates a coach service from London Victoria via Dover to Brussels, Antwerp and Bruges. The journey takes 5.5 hours to Bruges and 7.5 hours to Brussels.

Tour operators

Belgian Travel Service organises package tours to the main Belgian cities and coastal resorts. For bookings, ☎ 01992 456 156 (in Britain).

Several companies organise tours of the battlefields of Flanders:

Holts Tours, Golden Key Building, 15 Market Street, Sandwich, Kent CT13 9DA, ☎ 01304 612248 (in Britain), organises excellent bus tours to Ypres and other World War battlefield lasting 3–4 days.

Salient Tours, ☎ 075.91.02.23 (in Belgium), or 0385 955908 (in Britain), run by the enthusiastic Mark Horner, offers bus tours of the Salient lasting 2–4 hours, from Easter to November 11, Thursday to Tuesday, beginning at the Menin Gate in Ypres at 10.00 and 14.30. Most tour organisers will visit a particular cemetery if notified in advance.

Prospect Music and Art Tours organise art tour both to specific exhibitions and general tours, ☎ 020 7486 5705 (in Britain).

 # Where to stay

Hotels

Hotels in Belgium are normally well run and reasonably priced by northern European standards. The Belgian tourist office produces an annual list containing information on facilities and prices. Hotels are required by law to display the room rate in the room. A useful free nationwide hotel reservation service is operated by *Belgium Tourist Reservations* (BTR), Boulevard Anspach 111, Boîte 4, 1000 Brussels, ☎ 02.513.74.84, fax 02.513.92.77 or ☎ (00 32) 2.513.74.84 from the UK or ☎ (011 32) 2.513.74.84 from the USA.

A selection of hotels in different price ranges is listed for the major towns in this guide according to the following guidelines:

- £££ = Expensive. Expect to pay over 5000 BF (125 Euros) for a double room.
- ££ = Moderate. Expect to pay between 2500–5000 BF (62.5–125 Euros) for a double room.
- £ = Inexpensive. Under 2500 BF (62.5 Euros) for a double room.

Apartments and houses

Most people staying at the Belgian coast rent an apartment on a weekly basis. The apartments tend to be owned by Belgian families in large modern blocks built over the past 30 years. They are booked through agencies based in each of the coastal resorts. Holiday houses can be rented by the week at several holiday parks. The West Flanders tourist authority publishes an annual guide to holiday rentals at the coast.

Country cottages

Attractive and well-equipped country cottages can be rented in the Ardennes and rural Flanders. The Brussels-Ardennes tourist office publishes a brochure listing all the rented properties in Wallonia. They can be booked through the BTR (see under Hotels).

Bed and breakfast

Bed and breakfast accommodation (*chambres d'hôtes*) has become increasingly popular in recent years. This offers the chance to stay with Belgian families in farms or town houses. Accommodation can be booked through **Bed and Brussels** ☎ (00 32) 2.646.07.37 (from UK) or ☎ (011 32) 2.646.07.37 (from USA).

A useful website which offers information and direct booking is www.bnb-brussels.be

Camping sites

Camping sites are found along the coast and in the Ardennes. The tourist offices of Flanders and Wallonia produce an annual list of approved sites.

 # Food and drink

Eating out is one of the great pleasures in Belgium and a selection of restaurants in different price ranges is included in the various sections of this guide. The Belgian love of good cooking goes back to the Middle Ages, when the Burgundian nobles developed a fondness for lavish banquets. Local farmers and craftsmen also ate and drank copious amounts during religious festivals and village fairs. This joyful approach to eating is reflected in the village feasts painted by Pieter Bruegel the Elder, the overflowing kitchen tables of Frans Snyders, and the still-lifes of James Ensor. Whereas Dutch artists inevitably attached some stern warning to a banqueting scene, Belgian artists have always seen eating more simply as one of the good things in life. An appreciation of good food is, indeed, one of the few matters on which the Walloons and Flemings are in complete accord.

It is no longer a secret that Belgium has some of the best restaurants in Europe. Even the French are occasionally forced to concede that Belgian cuisine and beer is at least as good as their own (and sometimes better). You can eat well in country inns in the misty Ardennes, crowded tearooms on the coast, fashionable bakeries on the boulevards of Brussels, or even at one of the simple frites stands under the Belfry in Bruges.

Belgian chefs tend to make creative use of local ingredients from the different regions of the country. The rich farmland around Mechelen produces tasty chickens, plump white asparagus and the crispest chicory (Belgian endive). Tangy young boar, wild mushrooms and smoked hams come from the dark forests of the Ardennes, while the North Sea produces shrimps, Ostend sole and Zeeland mussels.

Most of the cities of Belgium have their own local specialities. Ghent is famous for its *waterzooi*, a creamy stew made from chicken or fish, and *paling in het groen* (young eels in spinach). Brussels is known for its bustling restaurants serving steaming black pots of mussels and overflowing bowls of frites. Restaurants at the coast prepare delicious shrimp croquettes, while country restaurants in the Ardennes concoct wonderful game menus in the autumn, using local venison, hare and boar. Other Belgian specialities to look out for are rabbit served with prunes, *Carbonnades flamandes* (beef cooked in beer), *Witloof gratinés au four* (chicory with ham and cheese) and *Civet de lapin à flamande* (stewed rabbit). Nor does it end there. You can eat fluffy waffles in the back streets of medieval Liège, or hunt out country taverns serving rice flan in the Ardennes.

Ten years ago, Belgian food tended to be rich and creamy. There are still some old-fashioned restaurants that will serve slabs of rare steak drenched in butter, but many places now offer lighter cooking and sophisticated foreign dishes. The Italian workers who came to Belgium in the 1950s brought Italian restaurants to the industrial south and Brussels, while Vietnamese refugees in the 1960s introduced a more exotic cuisine to the cities. The large international populations of Brussels and Antwerp have given these cities an abundance of Greek, Spanish and Italian restaurants.

Belgians love nothing better than to talk about food. They will describe in detail a memorable meal or give you precise instructions for reaching a little shop in the middle of nowhere where they swear the chocolates are the best in the world. You will even overhear school children outside the school gates knowledgeably discussing the endives in cream they were served for lunch.

The pleasure of eating is deeply embedded in Belgian society. You can appreciate the art of eating simply by strolling around a local food market or gazing in the window of a cheese shop. A cup of coffee is almost always served on a silver tray with a small biscuit; even a simple portion of frites served at a roadside van will be cooked to perfection. Details such as this make Belgium the perfect country for food lovers to visit.

Prices of restaurants in the major towns are indicated in this guide by the following symbols:
- £££ = Expensive. Expect to pay at least 2000 BF (50 Euros) per person.
- ££ = Moderate. Expect to pay between 1000–2000 BF (25–50 Euros) per person.
- £ = Inexpensive. Under 1000 BF (25 Euros) per person.

Beer and wine

Beer has been brewed in this region of Europe since the Roman era. The art of brewing was perfected in the Middle Ages by the monks in the great abbeys, notably through the introduction of hops. By the 14C the trade had spread to lay brewers, who organised themselves into guilds. The development of pasteurisation and other technical processes in the 19C led to a proliferation of breweries. Many of the smaller firms have now gone out of business, but Belgium still produces about 355 different brands of beer. The Trappist abbeys create strong dark brews, while a number of Flemish breweries produce tangy white beers made from wheat. But the strangest beers are the Lambics brewed in Brussels using a type of bacteria found only in the Senne valley. Each Belgian is estimated to drink 126 litres of beer annually. Brands to sample include Duvel, Leffe, Westmalle, Chimay and Hoegaarden.

The old vineyards that used to grow around Huy on the Meuse have gone, but a small wine-growing region survives on the hillsides above the litle red-roofed village of Torgny in the Gaume region of Luxembourg province. They produce a limited amount of delicious Clos de la Zolette, a type of Riesling. It is only available in the Gaume.

Getting around

By car

Belgian traffic laws and signs are similar to those found in other Western European countries:

- Motorways are designated A followed by a national number
- Routes which form part of the European motorway network have an E and a European number
- Other major roads are designated N (National)
- Many road signs indicate only the E route number without giving any city names, so that it is essential to know the road number. Main routes out of cities are often signed 'Ring'

The rule of priority from the right is still widely enforced in Belgium. Cars must give way to traffic coming from the right unless they are on a road with an orange lozenge sign (indicating a priority route). The rule at roundabouts is that drivers must give way to traffic already on the roundabout.

Drivers should watch out for cycle lanes, which are often indicated by a painted line along the side of the road. Cars turning right should give way to cyclists. Drivers in towns and at the coast should watch out for trams, which have priority.

Speed limits are 120km/h on motorways, 90km/h on other routes and 50km/h in town. Some major urban routes have higher limits, and residential streets may have a 30km/h limit.

The two main motoring organisations in Belgium are:

- *Touring Club Royal de Belgique* (TCB), Rue de la Loi 44, Brussels, ☎ 02. 233.22.11 (affiliated to the British Automobile Assocation).
- *Royal Automobile Club de Belgique* (RACB), Rue Arlon 53, Brussels, ☎ 02. 287.09.11 (affiliated to the British Royal Automobile Club). Members of foreign motoring organisations which have reciprocal arrangements with the TCB and the RACB can use facilities such as road patrol breakdown services.

In the case of an accident, it is wise to wait for the arrival of the police. An official police declaration may be useful in subsequent insurance proceedings.

By train

The rail network in Belgium is excellent by international standards. There are frequent trains to all major cities and local trains to many smaller towns in the Ardennes (see the map at the back of the book). The fares are not particularly expensive and several special deals are available, including half-price travel at weekends, a B-Tourrail pass valid for five days travel in Belgium and group rates.

One of the best features of the Belgian network is the train and bike scheme, which allows train travellers to reserve a bicycle at the destination station when booking a ticket. The cost of hiring a bicycle is modest. The stations where bicycles can be rented are listed in the Belgian Railway's *Excursions* booklet. The same booklet has details of special deals combining train tickets with visits to museums, exhibitions and boat excursions. For information in Belgium: ☎ 02.555.25.25 or any main station. For information in the UK, contact: **Belgian National Railways**, Premier House, 10 Greycoat Place, London, SW1P 1SB, ☎ 020 7593 2332. Website: www.sncb.be. For rail information in the US, contact the Belgian tourist office. To book rail passes contact **Rail Europe**, ☎ 800 438 7245.

By trams and buses

Public transport in Belgium is fairly efficient for getting around cities but often less reliable in rural regions. The main form of public transport in Brussels is the metro, which covers much of the city. There are extensive tram networks in Brussels, Antwerp and Ghent. Certain trams in Brussels and Antwerp run through tunnels and are known as pre-metros. Other cities such as Liège and Namur are served by buses.

The transport network in Flanders is run by *De Lijn*. A magnetic card can be bought which is valid for the entire transport network. It is stamped in machines located on trams and buses. The bus network in Wallonia is run by *TEC*, which also uses magnetic cards. Public transport in Brussels is the responsibility of Stib, ☎ 02.515.20.00. Magnetic tickets can be bought for single trips or ten trips. The tickets should be inserted into the machine to be stamped each time you enter. The ticket machine is programmed to read the card and stamp it when required.

By the coast tram

The Flemish transport authority (De Lijn) runs a scheduled tram service along the length of the Belgian coast. Known as the Kusttram, this provides a convenient means of reaching resorts that are not served by trains. It also allows you to plan walks along the beach and return by tram. For information on services, contact the Ostend office of De Lijn, ☎ 059.56.53.53.

By bicycle

The roads in Belgium are not particularly well-planned for cyclists. The best areas to explore by bicycle are the quiet rural roads around Bruges, the coast, the Kempen and the Ardennes.

By boat

Small motor launches take tourists along the canals of Bruges and Ghent, while large cruise ships run regular tours of Antwerp harbour. Boat tours are also run on the Meuse in the summer from Liège, Namur and Dinant.

Annual festivals

One of the delights of Belgium is coming upon a local festival celebrating perhaps a local saint or a historic battle. Many of these events date back to the Middle Ages, though some are modern revivals of old rites or recent inventions to draw tourists. The tourist offices of Wallonia and Flanders publish an annual list of events in the early spring which includes important festivals. The following festivals are worth catching:

Carnival A riotous early spring festival preceding Lent. Held in towns such as Binche, Malmédy and Aalst, Carnival involves street parades, masked balls, brass bands and large quantities of confetti. The towns of the German cantons celebrate on Rosenmontag (the Monday before Shrove Tuesday) in the manner of Cologne. The other Walloon towns tend to have their main procession on Shrove Tuesday.

Royal greenhouses The royal greenhouses at Laeken, in northern Brussels, are open to the public for a brief period in late April or early May. The 19C glasshouses built by Alphonse Balat for Leopold II are filled with exotic tropical plants. Opening times from the Brussels tourist office, ☎ 02.513.89.40, or 02.551.34.00 (recorded message).

Holy Blood Procession Held in Bruges on Ascension Day, this is solemn religious procession venerating a holy reliquary said to contain drops of Christ's blood. The parade features musicians, archers, horsemen and costumed actors who enact scenes from the Bible.

Ommegang This is held on Grand-Place in Brussels on two evenings in late June or early July. Originally a 14C religious procession, the Ommegang was transformed in the 16C into an exuberant aristocratic parade. Revived in the early 20C, the modern Ommegang is modelled on the parade staged in 1549 for Charles V and his son Philip. The parade features giants, flag-waving displays and a battle fought on stilts. Grandstand seats can be booked on Grand-Place.

Waterloo The anniversary of the battle of Waterloo (18 June) is celebrated every five years with a recreation of the battle. The next is due to happen in 2000.

Midi Fair Held near the Gare du Midi in Brussels in July, this is an enormous funfair stretching along the boulevards. Local restaurants put out long wooden tables on the pavement and sell Spanish and Belgian specialities.

National Day Held on 21 July, the national holiday has a military parade in front of the royal palace in Brussels, and firework displays at night.

Open Monument Days Historic monuments throughout the country are opened to the public for one weekend in September, offering a rare glimpse inside castles, Art Nouveau houses, factories, schools and other protected monuments. Organised separately and often on different dates in the regions of Flanders, Wallonia and Brussels.

Festival of Flanders A music festival featuring classical and modern works.

Held throughout Flanders in concert halls, churches and castles in September and October.

Festival of Wallonia A classical music festival held in September in towns and castles of Wallonia.

Public Transport Day Held in early October. Railway, bus and tram operators offer cheap one-day tickets. Many tourist towns organise special events such as guided tours and concerts.

Armistice The end of the First World War is commemorated at the Menin Gate in Ypres on 11 November.

St Nicholas 6 December. Children are given presents by St Nicholas.

Christmas markets Many towns organise Christmas markets in December with wooden chalets selling food and crafts. The best markets are in Brussels, Liège, Ghent and Antwerp. Another Belgian tradition is to create a Christmas crib on the main square with sometimes a stable and live animals. The cribs on Grand-Place in Brussels, Antwerp, Verviers and in the squares of many Kempen villages are particularly striking.

Major cultural festivals
Several major festivals are being organised in Belgium over the coming years. The following are likely to be interesting:

2000 Brussels is cultural capital of Europe. The annual Europalia festival is devoted this year to Brussels. Ghent celebrates the 500th anniversary of the birth of Charles V in Ghent's Prinsenhof and the Florialies Flower Show is held at Flanders Expo Centre, outside Ghent. Re-enactment of the battle of Waterloo is held every on 18 June.

2001 Europalia in Brussels focuses on Poland. Belgium takes over the Presidency of the European Union in the second half of 2001.

2002 The 700th anniversary of the Battle of the Golden Spurs is celebrated in Kortrijk and other places in Flanders. Bruges is the cultural capital of Europe. The Procession of the Golden Tree in Bruges, held every five years, recreates the magnificent procession organised in 1468 at the wedding of Charles the Bold and Margaret of York.

 Additional information

Access for disabled travellers
Belgium lags behind other countries such as Britain and the Netherlands in providing access to buildings for disabled visitors. The old towns often have narrow cobbled streets that are difficult to negotiate. Pavements in Brussels are often blocked by parked cars or building work. Most trams and buses are inaccessible to wheelchairs apart from the most recent generation of T2000 trams which have wide doors and low floors. These are gradually being introduced in Brussels, Ghent and Antwerp.

Cinemas

The Belgians take films seriously. Most large towns have a modern multiplex centre and possibly a small art cinema showing cult films. Foreign films tend to be shown in the original language in Brussels and Flanders, but most are dubbed into French in Wallonia. Film listings indicate original language films as VO and dubbed versions as VF. Cinema usherettes often expect a 20 franc fee.

Electric current

The electric current is 220V. Plugs are the standard mainland Europe variety with two round pins. Adaptors are sold at most international airports.

Embassies

Australian Embassy, Rue Guimard 6, 1040 Brussels ☎ 02.286.05.00
British Embassy, Rue d'Arlon 85, 1040 Brussels, ☎ 02.287.62.11
Canadian Embassy, Avenue de Tervuren 2, 1040 Brussels, ☎ 02.741.06.11
Irish Embassy, Rue Froissart 89, 1040 Brussels ☎ 02.230.53.37
US Embassy, Boulevard du Régent 27, 1000 Brussels, ☎ 02.508.21.11

Emergencies

Ambulance ☎ 100   Fire brigade ☎ 100   Police ☎ 101

English-language publications

The weekly *The Bulletin* contains general Belgian news, cultural features and extensive listings of plays, exhibitions, films, restaurants and nightlife. Though mainly read in Brussels, it has good coverage of other Belgian cities. It is available in most Brussels newsagents.

Health

Chemists (*pharmacie* in French and *apotheek* in Dutch) are easily found in Belgium. The shops often have a green neon cross outside. Chemists are normally open 09.00–18.00. At other times, a list of chemists open throughout the night and at weekends is posted on the shop window. An information line can also be called which gives a recorded list of local night chemists when the caller keys in their postal code, ☎ 0900 10.500.

Visitors from EU countries are entitled to free medical treatment in an emergency while in Belgium. They should obtain an E111 form at a major post office before leaving. Show the E111 to the doctor or hospital where you receive treatment.You will have to pay the bill on the spot but be given a form to reclaim costs. The form should be sent to the Ministry of Health in the UK.

Money and banks

Banks are normally open Mon–Fri 09.00–16.00. Some banks close for lunch. Most large cities have currency exchanges which have longer opening hours. Exchange facilities are available in Brussels at the Gare du Nord, the Gare du Midi and at Zaventem airport.

Cashing travellers' cheques can be expensive, as Belgian banks make a high service charge for each transaction. There is no charge for Thomas Cook or American Express cheques cashed at their own offices.

Holders of a Eurocheque card from a British bank can cash personal cheques up to the current limit at any bank showing the Eurocheque sign. Eurocheques accompanied by a Eurocard are often accepted by shops and restaurants for payments up to 7000BF.

Credit cards

The main credit cards used in Belgium are *American Express*, *Diners Club*, *Mastercard* and *Visa*. Credit cards are accepted by most hotels, some taxis and some restaurants. It is worth remembering that many small restaurants refuse to take credit cards. The list of cards accepted is usually displayed at the entrance of a restaurant, shop or hotel. Credit cards can be used to withdraw Belgian francs from bank cash machines where the credit card symbol is indicated.

All these four companies have offices in Brussels, to which the loss or theft of cards should be reported. The 24-hour emergency telephone numbers are:

American Express ☎ 02.676.21.21   Diners Club ☎ 02.206.98.00

Mastercard ☎ 070.344.344   Visa ☎ 070.344.344

Museums, galleries and churches

The cities of Belgium boast some of the greatest art museums in Europe. The visitor with time to spare can also delve into interesting local museums devoted to folklore and history, while the truly adventurous tourist can track down quirky collections such as the Hairdressing Museum in Sint Niklaas, the Wiertz Museum in Brussels and, if it is still open, the Underpants Museum in Brussels.

Most museums charge for entry. As a general rule, they are closed on Mondays. Some of the larger museums, faced with staff shortages, may rope off certain sections at other times. A large exhibition can lead to certain sections being closed or collections moving around. Some museums have cafés, but it is generally better to eat elsewhere.

Entry charges

Almost all museums in Belgium charge an admission fee. Students can sometimes obtain a reduction on producing a student card. Entry to churches is normally free, but a charge is usually made for visits to the treasury, crypt or tower, or to see important works of art.

Opening times

Opening times are listed together for large cities and towns and under the particular site. In the case of rural locations, opening times are given with the site. It is always possible that a museum or church will change its opening hours; the visitor with a special interest in a collection or site should contact the local tourist office for opening hours. It may be worth bearing in mind that some museum staff like to usher visitors out 15 minutes before the official closing time.

Most churches of interest to tourists are open throughout the day, though some may close between 12.00 and 14.00. Opening times are usually posted near the main door. Churches are usually closed to tourists during services. Saturday afternoons can also be difficult, as this is a popular time for weddings. Other churches are open only for services, but it is sometimes possible to arrange a visit by applying to the sacristan or key-holder whose address is often given on the door. Some churches are closed for restoration for lengthy periods, or because of the difficulty in finding custodians.

Tours
Thoughout this guide the tours detailed are optional unless otherwise stated.

Place names

The traveller in Belgium is likely to be baffled by the linguistic complexity of the country. The official languages are Dutch in Flanders, French in Wallonia and German in the Eastern Cantons. Brussels is officially bilingual (Dutch and French), while other towns close to the language frontier may also enjoy a bilingual status. The Blue Guide uses the English versions of place names, where these exist, such as Brussels, Antwerp, Ghent, Bruges and Ypres. We have, however, opted for Leuven, rather than Louvain, partly to avoid confusion with Louvain-la-Neuve but also because the Dutch version is becoming more widespread. In other cases, we use the local names, with alternative names in brackets. A list of the most important towns with different names in different languages is given at the back of the book.

Post offices

Post offices are usually open Mon–Fri 09.00–17.00. The smaller offices often close for lunch. Apart from the office in Avenue Fonsny, Brussels (open daily 24hrs), most post offices are closed on Sat, Sun and public holidays.

Public holidays

The main Belgian public holidays are:

New Year's Day (1 January) National Day (21 July)
Easter Monday Assumption (15 August)
Labour Day (1 May) All Saints' Day (1 November)
Ascension (6th Thursday after Easter) Armistice (11 November)
Whit Monday (7th Monday after Easter) Christmas Day (25 December)

When a public holiday falls on a Sunday, shops and banks are generally closed the following day.

Certain places may be affected by a local holiday. Shops and businesses may close in small Walloon towns during Carnival (Shrove Tuesday and the preceding days). Other local holidays include Schuman Day (9 May), EU institutions closed; French Community Festival (27 September), French community schools closed; Flemish Community Festival (11 July), Flemish community schools closed; Dynasty Day (15 November), government offices closed.

Public toilets

Public toilets are not easy to find in Belgium. They are often located at railway stations or department stores. Most toilets are run by an attendant who expects a 10 franc fee.

Telephones

Telephone kiosks tend to be located at railway stations, supermarkets and cafés. They contain a notice with instructions in several languages including English. Some telephones require phone cards, which can be bought at post offices, some newsagents and supermarkets. Credit cards can sometimes be used to make calls. The code for calling Belgium from the UK is 00 + 32 + the area code minus the initial 0.

Time

Belgium is on Central European time. This is one hour ahead of Greenwich Mean Time and six hours ahead of New York.

Tipping

Never an easy matter, tipping is not normally expected in Belgian cafés, restaurants or hotels, as service and Value Added Tax are included in the bill. You can, of course, add an additional tip if the service has been particularly good. Taxi fares also include VAT and service in the amount shown on the meter, but it is normal to round up the sum.

Cinema usherettes expect a 20 franc tip while toilet attendants can become quite upset if they are not given 10 francs. Tour guides on boats and coaches expect to be tipped about 20 francs at the end of the tour.

Tourist offices

The Belgian national tourist office is located at 61 Rue Marché aux Herbes, 1000 Brussels, ☎ 02.504.03.90, fax 02.504.02.70. It is open Jun–Sept 09.00–19.00; other months 09.00–18.00 (but on Sun Nov–Mar 13.00–17.00). The office is closed on 25 Dec and 1 Jan. It also closes 13.00–14.00 at weekends (except on Sun when it opens 13.00).

The national tourist office was split some years ago into three separate bodies covering Flanders, Wallonia and Brussels. Each authority now produces its own tourist information brochures on places of interest, restaurants and accommodation.

Tourist Information Brussels (TIB) provides detailed information on Brussels. The office is located in the Hôtel de Ville, Grand-Place, ☎ 02.513.89.40.

Other tourist offices

Each of the ten Belgian provinces has its own tourist office, which often has useful local information. They are listed in this guidebook under the relevant province. Some offices are not open to the public. For more detailed information on particular destinations, the best sources are local tourist offices, which have maps, books and lists of events. Smaller tourist offices are often closed on Sunday and throughout the winter.

BACKGROUND INFORMATION

Belgian constitution

Belgium has slowly drifted into federalism as a result of constitutional changes introduced in 1970, 1980 and 1988. The country finally became a federal state in 1992. The three regions of Flanders, Brussels and Wallonia took over much of the business of government, such as planning and environmental affairs. The national government remains responsible for defence, finance and foreign policy, though it is subject to checks and balances to ensure fair representation between the nation's communities.

Matters are made more complicated by the existence of three Communities (Dutch-speaking, French-speaking and German-speaking), which have responsibility for education and culture. The Flemish Region and Dutch Community function as one body, whereas the Walloon Region is distinct from both the French Community and German Community. Brussels is capital of Belgium and the Flemish Region, while Namur is capital of the Walloon Region and Eupen is capital of the German Community.

It seemed for a time as if the provinces would disappear, but they have clung on to their remaining powers. Originally nine in number, they became ten when the province of Brabant was split into Flemish Brabant and Walloon Brabant. A final level of government exists at the level of the communes, which control local police forces, local schools and many of the bureaucratic procedures which make living in Belgium utterly baffling.

The language issue

Belgium has long been plagued by a linguistic division, with c 60 per cent of the population speaking Dutch and c 40 per cent speaking French. This dates back to the separation in the 3C of the lands colonised by the Germanic Franks to the north and those of the Romanised Celts (or Wala) to the south. The ascendancy of the Dukes of Burgundy led to the domination of a French-speaking aristocracy, while the revolution of 1830, fuelled by anti-Dutch sentiments, added to the influence of the French-speaking class. The 19C industrialisation of Wallonia proved a further boost to the French speakers by concentrating wealth in the south of the country.

The Dutch speakers of Flanders began to assert their rights in the late 19C. The First World War led to increased bitterness in Flanders, not only because the bloodiest battles were fought on Flemish soil, but because the officer class mainly comprised French speakers. Yet it was not until the 1960s that Flemish radicals

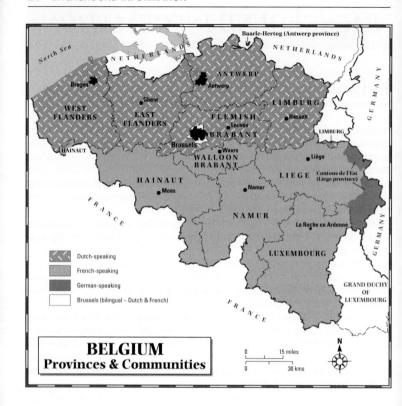

BELGIUM
Provinces & Communities

began to take to the streets in protest at the unequal status of the Dutch language.

The 'language frontier' between the two communities was officially drawn in 1962. It has been confirmed by detailed provisions in the new constitution. The language spoken to the north of the line is Dutch, albeit with some local variations and accents. French is sometimes spoken in some of the towns that lie just across the language frontier in Flanders, but it is precisely in these places that passions run high, and it is therefore unwise to assume that French will always be understood. If you do not speak Dutch, it is perhaps better to ask if English is spoken, rather than risk offending local pride. The language spoken to the south of the line is French, though again there are local accents and variations, as in the use of *septante* for *soixante-dix* and *nonante* instead of *quatre-vingt-dix*. The Cantons d'Est in the east Ardennes form a small German-speaking Community, though most people in this region are also fluent in French and possibly English and Dutch.

Brussels Region is a separate language community which is officially bilingual in all 19 communes. This is reflected in bilingual street signs, French and Dutch language schools, and films with subtitles in two languages. Most of the Belgian residents of Brussels are French speakers, though there are large Flemish communities in the centre and the northern communes.

History of Belgium

Before becoming the Kingdom of Belgium in 1831, this region of Europe was under various rulers. After forming part of the medieval Burgundian Netherlands, the territory now occupied by Belgium was known successively as the Spanish Netherlands, the Austrian Netherlands, briefly the United States of Belgium and, once again, the Austrian Netherlands. It was part of France for a time, then part of the United Kingdom of the Netherlands, before finally becoming the Kingdom of Belgium in 1831. The following brief history may help to explain this rather complicated area of Europe.

In this essay the nomenclature has generally been simplified as below.

Netherlands. The combined areas of roughly present-day Belgium and Holland, with also the Grand-Duchy of Luxembourg and parts of northern France. The term is politically valid until the de facto separation of North and South at the end of the 16C.

Spanish Netherlands. The southern part of the Netherlands from its subjection by the Duke of Parma subsequent to the Union of Arras (1579) until the Treaty of Utrecht (1713). **Belgium**. Roughly this same territory from the Treaty of Utrecht to the present day.

United Provinces. The northern and Protestant part of the Netherlands, which Parma failed to subdue and which declared its independence under the Union of Utrecht (1579). **Holland**. Roughly this same territory after the recognition of its independence by the Peace of Münster (1648). The name United Provinces in fact continued in use until the republic fell to the French in 1795. Modern Holland is officially the Kingdom of the Netherlands. The term 'Holland' as it is commonly used today is simply a popular name deriving from the ancient county, the nucleus from which the present state grew and now forming two of its provinces, and in this essay references to 'Holland' are to this county or province.

Luxembourg. Until 1815 roughly the combined area of today's Grand-Duchy and of the Belgian province of Luxembourg; after 1839 only the Belgian province. **Grand-Duchy of Luxembourg**. The independent Grand-Duchy created in 1815, but whose territories were much changed in 1839.

Roman and Frankish Period (57 BC–AD 843)

Between 57 and 50 BC the region of northern Gaul lying in the Scheldt and Meuse valleys was **conquered by Julius Caesar**. At that time the territory now known as Belgium was inhabited by Gallo-Celtic tribes (Belgae). In 15 BC these conquered lands became the imperial province of Gallia Belgica and the Roman occupation lasted until the 5C AD. During the 3C, however, as Rome began to weaken, the **Franks** (a loose federation of several Germanic tribes), began to move into the region. These early Franks were accepted by the Romans as 'foederati', or mercenaries who fought for Rome under their own chiefs. By about 431, under Chlodio, leader of the dominant Salii tribe, Tournai became the capital of the Frankish Merovingian kings, a dynasty named after Meroveus, successor to Chlodio. Meroveus was followed by Childeric I (d. 481), who threw off the Roman association. He in turn was throw off by **Clovis** who declared himself Christian, and thus gained the support of the Church. and conquered all Gaul except for Burgundy and Provence. Farther north, the eventual withdrawal of the Romans led to the completion of Frankish colonisation of the lower Scheldt and the Lys. The 'Silva Carbonaria', a belt of forest stretching from the Scheldt to the Ardennes, separated these Franks from the Wala (Walloons) or Romanised Celts, thus defining at this early stage the broad outlines of the ethnic and language frontier that persists today. On the death of Clovis in c 511, his realm splintered, and what is now Belgium became a neglected corner of Europe.

The Frankish lands developed into **two 'kingdoms'**: Austrasia (capital Metz) in the east, and Neustria (Merovingian) to the south and west. Dagobert, a child who became king of Austrasia in 623, was under the domination of Pepin I of Landen, who was 'Mayor of the Palace', the title enjoyed by the chief court official. In 629 Pepin fell out of favour, returning however on Dagobert's death in 638 and governing Austrasia until his own death the following year. Pepin II (of Heristal), son of a daughter of Pepin of Landen (possibly Begga of Andenne), led Austrasia against Neustria, in 687 winning a battle which marked the beinning of the end for the Merovingian line. The son of Pepin II, Charles Martel, became ruler in effect if not in name of all the Frankish lands. On his death in 741 he was succeeded by his younger son, Pepin III, the short, who by 751 had deposed the last Merovingian (Childeric III) and had himself crowned king of the Franks. He died in 768. One of his sons was Charlemagne.

Charlemagne, who reigned from 768 to 814, was declared by the Pope in 800 to be Emperor of the West. His empire extended from Denmark to southern Italy and from northern Spain to the Oder. 'Belgium' occupied an important position in this empire. Charlemagne's reign brought prosperity to the region, particularly through the development of waterways. However, on Charlemagne's death his lands were partitioned and in 843, after bitter fighting between his grandsons, the Treaty of Verdun divided the area of 'Belgium' between Charles the Bald and Lothair. Charles was crowned King of West Francia (most of today's France) and received the narrow strip of land west of the Scheldt (Flanders); Lothair was given the Middle Kingdom (the lands along the Rhine and the Rhône) and the remainder of 'Belgium', which later became the Duchy of Lower Lotharingia. A third kingdom to the east was known as East Francia (out of which modern Germany would grow).

Feudal and Burgundian Period (843–1482)

During the 9C and 10C the Vikings appeared, raiding and settling. Feudalism developed as a defence against the invaders. The powerful counts of Flanders emerged at this time in the west. Although nominally vassals of the kings of France, the counts took over more and more land and became virtually independent by the middle of the 11C.

The first count was Baldwin Iron Arm, who carried off and married a daughter of Charles the Bald, Judith, who had already been the wife of two English princes. In c 867 he built his great stronghold at Ghent. Baldwin II, child of this marriage, built the walls of Bruges and Ypres and married a daughter of England's Alfred the Great. The daughter of Baldwin V (1036–67), Matilda, shared the English throne with William the Conqueror. Baldwin's son married the widow of the Count of Hainaut, thus becoming ruler of that province, and the son of this marriage, Robert the Frisian, ruled over Holland and Friesland. Although Flanders became strong and unified, Lotharingia fared differently, breaking up into several minor countships and principalities.

The Monastic Age

The 10C saw the start of the monastic age proper. This received impetus from the Lateran Synod of 1059, which urged the clergy to live together as communities. During the First Crusade Count Robert II (1093–1110) was famous for his exploits, acquiring the title of 'Lance and Sword of Christendom', and Godfrey of Bouillon played a leading role in the capture of Jerusalem. He was proclaimed king, but refused the crown, adopting instead the title of Defender of the Holy Sepulchre. Count Baldwin IX of Flanders (1172–1206) led the Forth Crusade and in 1204 he became Baldwin I, the first Latin Emperor of Constantinople. His daughters, the countesses Margaret and Joanna, founded several Begijnhofs in Flanders for single women and crusaders' widows.

The monastic movement flourished in this region in the 13C–14C, exercising a considerable influence on social, commercial and artistic life. The religious houses taught agriculture to the peasants, functioned as commerical concerns, worked mines, developed forges and became skilled in metalwork. Their orders for church furnishings provided work for skilled craftsmen. Many of the monks were artists of genius, responsible for delicately illuminated manuscripts, metalwork, painting and sculpture. But the wars fought in this region led to the ruin of many religious houses.

As feudalism waned in the 12C and 13C, the cloth-making **towns** of Flanders such as Ghent, Bruges and Ypres achieved an astonishing economic prosperity and civic dignity, surpassed only by a few Italian cities. Importing most of their wool from England, the Flemish towns became the principal markets of northwest Europe and maintained an almost complete independence from France. The Flemish towns expressed their liberty by constucting tall belfries, which were practical as well as symbolic, serving as watch-towers with warning bells, refuges, meeting-places and jails. Towns in Wallonia put up columns (known as perrons) in main squares. The perrons, mainly found in Liège province, and often destroyed or carried off by new rulers, stood as focal spots for meetings, the reading of proclamations and the exercise of justice. The autonomy of towns, won and preserved only through great struggle and sacrifice, was the ancestor of today's still fiercely defended local government level of communes.

But the French were determined to reassert their authority and the nobles to regain their privileges. Although during the reign of France's Philip the Fair the towns routed the French nobility at the Battle of the Golden Spurs (near Kortrijk, 1302), by 1322 the francophile Count Louis of Flanders and Nevers had succeeded in reducing Flanders to being virtually a French province. Local rivalries, the jealousies of the guilds (protective associations which may be regarded as the ancestors of the trade unions), the tyranny of the urban oligarchy over the country people and, later, changing trade routes and the emigration of many weavers to England, all combined to bring about a long period of instability leading first to Burgundian supremacy under Philip the Good (1419) and eventually to Habsburg rule (1477). The confusing events, in Flanders and elsewhere, up to the accession of Philip the Good are summarised overleaf.

1338	Jacob van Artevelde of Ghent allied the Flemish towns with England's Edward III during the opening stages of the Hundred Years War.
1345	Death of William II, Count of Hainaut. His lands were divided between his sister, the Empress Margaret, who inherited Hainaut, and her son William, to whom went the provinces of Holland and Zeeland.
1346	Louis de Male, son of Louis of Nevers, became Count of Flanders. Like his father, he supported the French kings, which brought him into conflict with the mercantile towns.
1355	Death of John of Brabant. His daughter Joanna, and her husband, Wenceslas of Luxembourg, became rulers of Brabant and Limburg. In 1356 they were forced to sign the Joyeuse Entrée, a declaration of rights that became a form of charter for Brabant.
1357	Louis de Male invaded Brabant, acquiring Mechelen and Antwerp.
1369	Marriage between Margaret, heiress of Louis de Male, and Philip the Bold of Burgundy. This eventually brought the region under Burgundian control.
1382	Philip van Artevelde (son of Jacob) defeated Louis de Male and took Bruges, but later the same year was defeated and killed by the French at Westrozebeke (near Ypres).
1383	The English, with assistance from Ghent, unsuccessfully besieged Ypres. At Leuven the citizens surrendered to Wenceslas; as a result many weavers were forced to emigrate and, with the move of Wenceslas to Vilvoorde, Brussels began to supplant Leuven as capital of Brabant.
1384	Death of Louis de Male. Margaret and Philip the Bold of Burgundy inherited Flanders, Mechelen and Antwerp. They also owned Artois and other territories in France. Now under Burgundian control, Flanders ceased to exist as a separate state.
1390	Joanna ceded Brabant and Limburg to Philip the Bold.
1404	Philip the Bold was succeeded by John the Fearless, but in Brabant and Limburg by Philip's second son, Antoine.
1415	Antoine was killed at Agincourt. He was succeeded by John IV of Brabant who married Jacqueline, Countess of Hainaut, Zeeland and Holland.

In 1419 **Duke Philip the Good** of Burgundy (grandson of Philip the Bold) succeeded to the countship of Flanders. Ruling until 1467, he consolidated Burgundian power. He bought Namur in 1421 and inherited Brabant, Limburg and Antwerp in 1430. In 1433 he caused Jacqueline of Hainaut to be deposed and took over Hainaut, Holland and Zeeland. He bought Luxembourg in 1443. In 1456 he had his nephew, Louis de Bourbon, elected Bishop of Liège, and he also made his bastard son Bishop of Utrecht.

Philip the Good was determined to assert monarchical authority. In 1438 he forced Bruges to surrender many of its privileges, and in 1453, after an unsuccessful revolt, Ghent suffered the same fate. At the same time Philip tried to foster the towns' economic prosperity, amongst other things prohibiting the import of English cloth and encouraging the Antwerp fairs. In 1430, in Bruges, he established the Order of the Golden Fleece, partly in compliment to the Flanders wool-weavers and partly in glorification of his own house and court; and in 1465 he summoned representatives of all the provinces (or States) to a States General in Brussels.

Philip was succeeded in 1467 by his son, **Charles the Bold**. He imposed absolute rule on Liège, acquired Alsace and, by marrying Margaret of York, cemented his alliance with her brother, Edward IV of England. Disappointed in his efforts to be declared a king, he undertook a disastrous campaign in Lorraine and was killed at Nancy in 1477, leaving his lands in turmoil. His successor, his daughter **Mary**, held virtually a prisoner in Flanders, was forced to sign the Great Privilege, a charter conferring far-reaching rights on the provinces. In the same year she married Maximilian of Austria. Thus the Burgundian federation in the Netherlands, created by Philip the Good, passed to the Habsburgs.

The Holy Roman Emperors Maximilian and Charles V (1482–1555)

When Mary died in 1482, **Maximilian** became regent. He made peace with France and subdued the whole of the Netherlands. Following his election to Holy Roman Emperor in 1494, Maximilian handed the Netherlands to his son, Philip the Handsome. When Philip the Handsome died in 1506 his Burgundian lands passed to his six-year-old son Charles, for whom his aunt, Margaret of Austria, acted as governor. From 1513 to 1519 England's Henry VIII occupied Tournai in the course of his war with France. The States General declared Charles of age in 1515. He became king of Spain the following year, and Holy Roman Emperor in 1519. Ruling as **Charles V** (or Charles Quint), he succeeded to all the Habsburg dominions. Although he relinquished the Austrian territories to his brother, he still held Spain, Sardinia, Naples, Sicily and Milan, Burgundy and the Habsburg lands in Alsace and the Netherlands, which he extended to include Friesland, Utrecht and Groningen. In 1530 he appointed his sister, Mary of Hungary, as regent of the Netherlands. This region had by now become reduced to a small corner of a sprawling empire; heavy taxes were imposed to finance the wars of the absent ruler. Ghent rebelled in 1540, but the rebellion was firmly put down by Charles in person. He annulled the city's privileges and imposed a huge fine on the citizens. Charles's reign saw the rapid spread of Protestantism, particularly in the northern Nertherlands, despite severe persecution such as under the Edict of Blood which decreed death for all convicted of heresy. Charles abdicated in 1555.

The Revolt of the Netherlands

Charles V was followed by his son **Philip II of Spain**, married the previous year to Queen Mary of England. A zealous Catholic, Philip ruthlessly persecuted heretics, introduced the Jesuits into the Netherlands, and built several Spanish garrisons. This fuelled opposition and stimulated the spread of Protestantism. Much of the opposition sprang from religious and social grievances, but the nobles (some of them stadholders, or provincial governors) had more selfish reasons to rebel as they were resentful of the increasing centralisation of power into Spanish hands and of the loss of their power of patronage under Philip's plans for the reorganisation of the Church. Philip's reign also saw the separation of the North from the South (i.e. between what would become modern Holland and Belgium) and the emergence of the House of Orange.

The House of Orange

Orange, today a town and district on the Rhône in southern France, was an independent principality at the time of Charlemagne. Prince Philibert (1502–30) served Charles V and was rewarded with extensive lands in the Netherlands, lands which became more important to the family than Orange. In 1544 William I (the Silent) succeeded to the principality and to the Netherlands territories. He later became leader of the Revolt of the Netherlands and the founder of Holland. Having been seized by Louis XIV in 1672, the principality of Orange was officially transferred to France by the Treaty of Rijswijk in 1697, thereafter only the princely title surviving.

Start of the revolt (1558–67). Forced to grant a demand by the States General that all Spanish troops be withdrawn, Philip retired to Spain, leaving Margaret of Parma (natural daughter of Charles V) as governor, with, as chief councillors, Cardinal Granvelle (a French adviser to Philip, made Archbishop of Mechelen) and Berlaymont (a Walloon noble). Opposition hardened under the leadership of William of Orange, and the Inquisition was defied. Protestantism (in particular Calvinism) spread to the nobility leading to Granvelle being recalled in 1564. The following year the League of the Nobility was formed, as both a religious and a political opposition. It petitioned for moderation of the anti-Protestant edicts. Berlaymont rejected the petition, contemptuously referring to the League as 'ces gueux' (those beggars), a taunt which the leaguers turned into a proud title. The year 1566 saw the rapid growth of extreme Calvinism, with fanatics rioting and destroying Church property, particularly in Antwerp. But this development, the 'Iconoclastic Fury', split the opposition to Spain, and Margaret, seizing the opportunity to play off the popular party against the aristocratic, regained the support of many of the nobles. William of Orange and Count Egmont (governor of Flanders) attempted to steer a middle course, but failed due to a Calvinist uprising in Flanders. William retired to his estates at Nassau in Germany.

Rule by the Duke of Alva (1568–73). Determined on the absolute suppression of heresy, Philip sent the Duke of Alva and an army of 10,000 to the Netherlands. Alva promptly ushered in a period of savage suppression, setting up the so-called Council of Blood to deal with heretics and insurgents, outlawing William, and executing over 1000 people, including Counts Egmont, Hoorn and many other nobles. In Nassau, William attempted to raise an army, but he had no money and in any case gained no support from the towns, all now strongly garrisoned by Alva's troops. But in 1572 the tide began to turn when the Sea Beggars (privateers commissioned by William who had hitherto operated from England or East Friesland) captured Brielle at the mouth of the Meuse. The rebels took Vlissingen (Flushing) soon afterwards, which gave them a secure foothold in the Netherlands and was the key to their ultimate success. By the end of the year the rebels controlled most of the province of Holland and William was declared stadholder. Alva, without sea power, could do little in the North, but he put down the simultaneous uprising in the South, retaking Mons which had been seized by William's brother, Louis of Nassau. He then sacked Mechelen, while his son Frederick dealt similarly with Zutphen. But neither Alva nor his son could defeat the now thoroughly aroused northern towns. The dykes were cut, forcing Frederick to withdraw. Alva, his fleet defeated in the Zuider Zee and his army now unpaid and mutinous, left for Spain.

Separation of North from South (1573–85). Alva was replaced by Luis de Requesens and the fighting continued. The North was determined to obtain religious freedom but the South was ready for compromise. Although there were setbacks—amongst these the defeat and death of Louis of Nassau near Nijmegen — the North became virtually free from Spanish rule, to the extent that Catholicism was officially forbidden in the province of Holland. When Requesens died in 1576, William, now stadholder of the combined provinces of Holland and Zeeland, seized his opportunity and advanced into Flanders, occupied Ghent, and started negotiations with the States General. On 8 November 1576 the Pacification of Ghent was signed. The final impetus to agreement was the news of the 'Spanish Fury' in Antwerp, during which mutinous Spanish soldiers terrorised the town. The Pacification aimed at securing religious freedom and accepted in principle union between North and South.

The new governor was Philip's bastard brother, Don John of Austria, who, at the time of the signing of the Pacification, was at Luxembourg with a new Spanish army. William persuaded the States General to withhold recognition until Don John accepted the terms of the Pacification. This led to deadlock, until William's hand was strengthened in 1577 by the signing of the Union of Brussels, under which all provinces represented in the States General demanded the departure of foreign troops and the implementation of the Pacification, but at the same time recognised Philip's sovereignty. At this Don John yielded, signing the Perpetual Edict, which accepted most of William's demands. But the unity apparently achieved was shortlived—largely because the growth of Calvinism was alarming the Catholics, and especially the Catholic nobles—and confusion at once followed. Don John attacked and took Namur with a Walloon army. The States General repudiated William; and, secretly helped by southern Catholic nobles, the Archduke Mathias (brother of the emperor, and later emperor himself) arrived in Brussels and in January 1578 declared himself governor.

Philip now sent Alexander Farnese, Duke of Parma, with yet another large army, and helped by this Don John asserted his authority over much of the South. Gembloux, Leuven, Tienen, Bouvignes, Nivelles, Soignies, Binche, Beaumont and Chimay all capitulated to him before his death in 1578. Three months later the last hope for unity between North and South disappeared when the deputies of Hainaut, Artois and Douai signed the Union of Arras (5 January 1579) declaring faith in Catholicism and allegiance to Philip. The North replied with the Union of Utrecht and continued the struggle. Aided by the Union of Arras, Parma launched a campaign from 1580–85 which led to the conquest of Tournai, Ypres, Bruges, Ghent and finally Antwerp which, under Marnix van St Aldegonde, capitulated only after a two year siege. But Parma got no farther than Antwerp. The United Provinces (as the northern provinces were now termed) were supported by France and England. Philip's resources were weakened by the destruction of the Spanish Armada in 1588, and Parma had to move south to fight the French.

The Spanish Netherlands (1579–1713)

Although the southern Netherlands (Spanish Netherlands) recognised the Spanish king as their sovereign, there was no longer any question of Spanish domination. There was a Spanish governor in Brussels, but the country was virtually independent, and even if the king did control the army and foreign policy, his hands were tied because only the provinces could levy taxes. On religious matters, though, the king remained supreme. This meant that the Spanish Netherlands remained firmly Catholic.

Parma died in 1592, and Philip, just before his own death in 1598, handed over the whole of the Netherlands to his daughter Isabella (created 'archduke' in her own right) and her husband Archduke Albert, in the hope that as independent sovereigns they might be able to regain the United Provinces. This hope foundered on the insistence that Catholicism was to be the only religion, and after more years of generally indecisive fighting (during which Spain's Admiral Spinola took Ostend, still holding out for the United Provinces) the Twelve Years Truce was agreed in 1609. The 'archdukes' profited from the truce to consolidate Catholicism, in this being much helped by the Jesuits who by then were the most influencial religious power in country. The truce was also a period of intellectual and artistic brilliance, with Rubens and Moretus in Antwerp and Justus Lipsius teaching at Leuven. Many ruined abbeys were rebuilt and decorated in the 17C Baroque style.

The **Thirty Years War** broke out in 1618, and in 1621 Albert and Isabella resumed their campaign against the United Provinces, the fighting dragging on until 1648. The main events, virtually all unfavourable to Spain, are outlined below.

1621	Archduke Albert died. Isabella became governor for Spain's Philip IV.
1629 –32	Frederick Henry of Nassau took 's Hertogenbosch, Venlo, Roermond and Maastricht.
1633	Death of Isabella, succeeded as governor by the Infante Ferdinand. France concluded an alliance with the United Provinces.
1635	The United Provinces invaded Brabant, sacking Tienen.
1636	Frederick Henry took Breda.
1639	Admiral Tromp destroyed the Spanish fleet.
1644	The United Provinces captured Hulst, thus gaining control of the whole left bank of the Scheldt estuary.
1647	Frederick Henry died and was succeeded by William II.
1648	Philip IV, compelled by the need to concentrate against France, signed the Peace of Münster. Not only was the independence of the United Provinces recognised, but Philip also gave in to their insistence that the Scheldt be closed. Antwerp was thus ruined, not to recover until the re-opening of the estuary in 1795, and commercial prosperity shifted from the South to the North.

Henceforward the story of the Spanish Netherlands became that of Spain's and other countries' successive wars with France. Despite the sacrifices made under the Peace of Münster, Spain was not successful and her influence steadily declined.

Peace of the Pyrenees (1659). France gained most of Artois and several fortresses in the south of the Spanish Netherlands.

War of Devolution (1667–68). Louis XIV ascended the French throne in 1643. In 1659 he came of age, assumed power, and married the Spanish Infanta. It soon became a tenet of his foreign policy that the Spanish Netherlands should be subject to France. He used the death of his father-in-law, Philip IV (succeeded by Charles II), as the excuse to claim Flanders for his queen. Turenne conquered Flanders, but the Dutch, fearful of France as a neighbour, organised the Triple Alliance with England and Sweden. Louis partially yielded, but under the Peace of Aix-la-Chapelle nevertheless received Charleroi, Binche, Ath, Tournai and Kortrijk, which Vauban set about fortifying.

Dutch War (1672–78). Knowing that he had to eliminate the Dutch, Louis invaded Holland. But, led by William III, the Dutch cut the dykes, flooding their country, and then formed a coalition which included Spain. Louis had to withdraw, and under the Peace of Nijmegen Spain recovered Kortrijk, Charleroi and Binche, but lost Poperinge, Ypres and a number of places farther south.

Chambres de Réunion (1679–84). Under a cloak of legality Louis unilaterally annexed several places, including Luxembourg, which Vauban at once fortified.

War of the Grand Alliance (1690–97). The Dutch stadholder, William III, became the king of England in 1689, thus turning England into an active opponent of France. He formed the Grand Alliance (or League of Augsburg), embracing most of both Protestant and Catholic Europe, and war broke out in 1690. Namur was taken by Louis in 1692, but retaken by William in 1695. Under the Peace of Rijswijk, Spain recovered Mons, Luxembourg and Kortrijk.

War of the Spanish Succession (1702–13). In 1700 Charles II, the last of the Spanish Habsburgs, died childless. He willed the crown of Spain and the Spanish Netherlands to Philip of Anjou, grandson of Louis XIV. Quickly seizing his opportunity, Louis forced his grandson to hand the Spanish Netherlands over to France, whereupon, unable to accept such a threat, England and Holland, both led by William III, went to war, thus starting a drawn-out struggle which covered much of Europe. This ended when the **Treaty of Utrecht** was signed in 1713. France abandoned all claim to the Spanish Netherlands, which were placed under the sovereignty of the Emperor Charles VI of Austria.

The Austrian Habsburgs (1713–1794)

The territory was now the Austrian Netherlands, but in fact remained as independent under Austria as it had been under Spain since the Union of Arras. Under the Barrier Treaty (1715), though, aimed at discouraging any further French attacks, the Austrian Netherlands had to accept Dutch garrisons at Namur, Dendermonde, Tournai, Menen and Veurne.

Charles VI died in 1740, leaving no male heir. He had wanted his daughter Maria Theresa to succeed him, but many of the powers refused to accept her. This lead to the **War of the Austrian Succession**. This war came to the Austrian Netherlands in 1744 when the country was invaded by the French under Maurice de Saxe. The Dutch-manned Barrier Treaty forts surrendered, the English were beaten at Fontenoy (near Tournai), and Louis XV occupied the territory until the war was settled by the Peace of Aix-la-Chapelle (1748), which returned the country to Austria.

Under the Empress Maria Theresa's enlightened and popular governor, Charles of Lorraine, roads and waterways were built, agriculture modernised, and industry (notably coal and glass) encouraged. Both Charles of Lorraine and Maria

Theresa died in 1780. Maria Theresa's successor, her son Emperor Joseph II, appointed his sister Marie Christine as governor of the Austrian Netherlands. She continued to govern after her brother Leopold II succeeded as Emperor in 1790. Joseph II was well-meaning, but autocratic and impatient when faced by conservatism. He succeeded in getting rid of the Dutch Barrier Treaty garrisons, but his attempt to open the Scheldt simply by using it nearly led to war (the Dutch fired on his ships), and his plans for internal reforms—logical, humane and modern though they were—merely aroused opposition and bitterness. This was particularly the case with the Edict of Toleration (1781), recognising religious freedom, and the proposals to modernise the country's antiquated administrative system. Encouraged by the revolution in France, there was a local uprising in 1789 which defeated the Austrians at Turnhout. Within weeks the whole country was in revolt (the Brabançon Revolt) and in January 1790 the **United States of Belgium** was declared. Two Belgian factions now faced one another: the democrats who wanted a revolutionary constitution, and the nobles, supported by the clergy and the majority of the country, who wanted no significant change. Anarchy followed failure to agree, and by the end of the year the Emperor (now Leopold II) subdued the country by force of arms. Wisely, Leopold dropped Joseph's reform programme.

In 1792 war broke out between revolutionary France and Austria; the French general Dumouriez won the battle of Jemappes near Tournai and occupied Belgium. His success was shortlived and a few months later (March 1793) the Austrians defeated him at Neerwinden near Tienen. But Austrian days were numbered, and in June 1794 the French under Jourdan defeated them at Fleurus, and Belgium was again under French occupation.

Belgium annexed to France (1794–1814)

After a little over a year of military occupation Belgium was formally annexed as a part of revolutionary France (October 1795). The measures now pushed through, going far beyond anything proposed by Joseph II and ruthlessly enforced, did at least have the effect of modernising the region. The Church, hitherto so powerful, was persecuted. The religious houses were disestablished, buildings were torn down and church treasures scattered. The national administration was centralised and rationalised, ancient privileges were abolished and conscription was introduced. Local opposition to the new measures led to the Peasants' Revolt in October 1798. This was brutally suppressed by the French.

The reforms continued after Napoleon assumed power in 1799, though in a more acceptable form. A modern legal system, the Code Napoléon, was established; the metric system was introduced; industry profited from the vast market of the French empire; the Church and government became reconciled. Perhaps the most important change was the reopening of the Scheldt, which led to the revival of Antwerp. Napoleon boosted recovery of the port by constructing a new naval harbour which he described as 'a pistol aimed at the heart of England'.

But despite all their improvements the French remained unpopular, and the occupation of the country by the allies after Napoleon's defeat at Waterloo was welcomed with relief.

United Kingdom of the Netherlands (1815–1831)

The allies' main objective in 1815 was to establish a deterrent to any future French northward expansion. Therefore, paying scant regard to the wishes of the people—with their differing customs, economic outlook and religion—they amalgamated Belgium and Holland into the United Kingdom of the Netherlands under Prince William of Orange who ascended the throne as William I. William faced a near-impossible task in attempting to unite two countries with different religions and societies.

He made some progress in the beginning: industry flourished (helped by access to Dutch colonial markets), Antwerp prospered, and education advanced as new lay schools and universities were founded. But there was much that the people in the South found unacceptable, such as equality of representation in the States General when the South's population was nearly double that of the North, the wide range of powers assumed by a Protestant and foreign king, and the insistence on Dutch as the official language. The Catholic church was also unwilling to adapt to the principle of religious liberty. By 1828, the country was approaching revolution. William's continuing obstinacy and his suppression of the opposition press led to the inevitable two years later.

The **revolution** broke out on 25 August 1830 during a performance of Auber's opera *La Muette de Portici* in the old Monnaie theatre in Brussels. On hearing the duet 'Amour sacré de la Patrie', the audience left the theatre and hoisted the flag of Brabant. Similar revolts broke out simultaneously in the provinces, but the rebels were defeated at Hasselt. William sent his elder son to Brussels to negotiate. When this failed, he sent his second son Frederick at the head of an army. The Dutch were forced to withdraw after some sporadic fighting. A provisional government was formed, and national independence was declared.

Kingdom of Belgium

On 20 January 1831 the London Conference recognised Belgium as an independent and 'perpetually neutral' state. The crown was accepted by Prince Leopold of Saxe-Coburg, who became King Leopold I.

> Leopold I (1790–1865) was a son of the Duke of Saxe-Coburg-Saalfeld and uncle of Queen Victoria, over whom he long exercised a strong influence. As a youth he saw service in the Russian army, and later he fought in the campaigns of 1813–14. After Napoleon's defeat in 1815, Leopold entered Paris with the allied leaders. In 1816 he married Charlotte, only child of the Prince Regent and heiress presumptive to the British throne; she died in childbirth the following year. In 1830 he was offered but declined the throne of Greece. His second marriage (1832) was to Louise-Marie, daughter of King Louis-Philippe of the French.

However, the Dutch did not easily give way. William invaded within days of Leopold's taking the oath, and only retreated when faced by French troops, who arrived at Leopold's request. William next refused to accept the Twenty-Four Articles, which set out the terms of the separation of the two countries, and he held on in the citadel of Antwerp, which he only evacuated after assault by the French and a blockade of the Dutch ports. Only in 1839 did William finally accept defeat, the independence and neutrality of Belgium now being guaranteed by the Treaty of London (later to become historic as the 'scrap of paper'), signed by Austria, Great Britain, Prussia, France and Russia.

The new Belgian constitution ensured maximum rights for the people, the king receiving only minor executive powers. Thanks to this, and to a king who was both cultured and wise, Belgium made great economic progress, keeping clear of the general European revolutionary disturbances of 1848.

In 1865 Leopold I was succeeded by his son, Leopold II. A man of strong personality and considerable business acumen, he successfully steered neutral Belgium through the hazards of the Franco-Prussian War (1870). He helped foster the growth of commerce and transport and in 1885 established the Congo Free State in Central Africa under his own personal rule, having largely financed the exploration of the area. His reign also saw the official recognition of the Dutch language, with the founding in 1886 of the Flemish Academy and the passing of a law in 1898 giving equal importance to Dutch and French. Qualified universal suffrage was introduced as early as 1893.

Belgian Congo

Leopold II had always been interested in colonial possibilities, in particular in the Congo. In 1878 he founded the Comité des Etudes du Haut Congo, this developing into the International Association of the Congo, and the following year, at Leopold's instigation, H.M. Stanley opened trading stations and made agreements with the chiefs. In 1884–85 the powers recognised the International (but effectively Belgian) Association as an independent State, the Belgian government at the same time authorising Leopold to be sovereign but also declaring that the link between Belgium and the Congo was 'exclusively personal'. The venture brought Leopold great wealth, especially from the Domaine de la Couronne, a vast territory treated as the King's personal property. In 1890, in return for financial investment, the Belgian government was given the right of annexation, a right which it exercised in 1908 under the pressure of serious international charges of gross maladministration (seizure of native land, monopolistic exploitation and even atrocities). The Congo was granted independence in 1960.

Leopold II died in 1909. He was succeeded by his nephew Albert.

First World War (1914–1918)

Opening Phase. As war loomed in July 1914, the British government reminded France and Germany that Belgium's neutrality was guaranteed under the Treaty of London of 1839. Dismissing the treaty as a 'scrap of paper', Germany demanded that Belgium allow her troops free passage. Belgium refused on 3 August; that same night the German army crossed the frontier near Malmédy. Led by King Albert, the Belgian army made a brave if doomed stand against the mighty German army. After the fall of Liège on 9 August, the German army moved rapidly across the flat plains of Limburg and Brabant. The French were defeated near Charleroi on 23 August and the British army was forced to retreat from **Mons** on 25 August. Both armies fell back into France.

By the end of August, Namur, Leuven and Brussels had fallen to the Germans who now occupied most of central and southern Belgium. Antwerp was forced to surrender on 9 October, after which the Belgian army retreated through Flanders. By 15 October, the Allies had established a line along the **Yser**. The Belgians opened the sluices there on 29 October, creating a vast lake between Nieuwpoort and Diksmuide. The Germans took Diksmuide in November, but this was the limit of their advance; they transferred their main effort towards **Ypres**, where, despite vast superiority, they were unable to break through the small British army. Both sides dug in for the winter to create the long line of trenches that stretched from Nieuwpoort to the Swiss border.

The occupation. In the small strip of their country that was still free the Belgians established their headquarters at Veurne, while the King made nearby De Panne the 'capital'. The occupation was administered by German governors, who confiscated property and organised mass labour deportations to Germany and the front. The occupiers also seized raw materials and stripped Belgian factories of anything that might be useful in Germany. Despite strict controls on movement, thousands of Belgians escaped the country; its army maintained an average strength of 150,000 throughout the war.

Closing Phase. The tide began to turn in June 1917 when British and Commonwealth troops took the ridge at Mesen, 9km south of Ypres, though this was followed by the bloody and inconclusive Third Battle of Ypres which ended in the mud of Passchendaele. In March 1918, with troops freed by the collapse of Russia, the Germans launched their last and nearly successful offensive, but by June American troops and British reinforcements were pouring into France. The Belgian army took Diksmuide in September and by October had liberated West Flanders. On 11 November, Armistice Day, the Canadians had entered Mons while the Belgians had reached beyond Ghent.

Between the Wars (1919–1940)

Under the Treaty of Versailles, Belgium was granted huge reparations. It also received a former German region in the east Ardennes, which included the towns of Moresnet, Eupen and Malmédy. Belgium neutrality was abolished, allowing the country to sign a pact with France in 1920.

Unqualified universal suffrage was introduced soon after the war's end. One effect of this was to sharpen the Flemish question, and in 1921 Dutch was made the official language of Flanders. The same year also saw the signing of a customs, consular and railway union with the Grand-Duchy of Luxembourg.

Like other countries Belgium's economic foundations and political institutions were badly shaken by the Depression, and foreign trade, the country's main livelihood, virtually disappeared.

In 1934 King Albert, the much-loved and respected 'Soldier King', was killed in a climbing accident. He was succeeded by his son, Leopold III, whose reign started with tragedy when the following year his queen, Astrid of Sweden, was killed in car crash while Leopold was driving.

In 1936, when Germany reoccupied the Rhineland, Leopold announced that Belgium's policy was once again one of strict neutrality and he renounced all agreements on military aid.

Second World War (1939–1945)

Germany attacked Belgium and the Netherlands early on 10 May 1940. The German army swept past the Liège forts, taking bridges over the Albert Canal, and destroying the supposedly impregnable Meuse fort of Eben-Emael. As the Belgians retreated to their main line of defence between Leuven and Antwerp, the British and French moved in. The British reinforced positions between Wavre and Leuven while the French advanced to the line between Huy and Tienen. By 13–14 May, the French had been defeated at Sedan, leaving the way open to the English Channel. The Germans reached the sea near Abbeville on 20 May. Meanwhile in Belgium, despite meeting stubborn resistance, the Germans pressed inexorably forward, using their air superiority ruthlessly against both military targets and the streams of refugees now clogging the roads. The Germans took Leuven, Brussels and Antwerp; the Allies then faced the danger of being surrounded and cut off from the sea by a German pincer movement from Abbeville in the south and Antwerp in the north. An attempt was made to break out of the trap by an offensive against the still thin German line between Sedan and Abbeville, but when this failed a retreat to the coast was inevitable.

It was agreed with King Leopold that his army would cover this retreat. But the Germans broke through the Belgian line either side of Kortrijk and on 28 May Leopold surrendered. The immediate practical result was the disappearance of the Allies' northern flank. The British commander at once established his final perimeter on the line Gravelines–Bergues–Veurne–Nieuwpoort in preparation for evacuation, and, after a stand by the British between Ypres and Comines, and by an isolated French group near Lille, all the British divisions and many of the French were within this perimeter by 30 May. By 4 June the evacuation from the beaches between Dunkirk in France and De Panne in Belgium had been achieved. The Belgian government escaped first to France and then to England, but the king, considering himself a prisoner-of-war, refused to desert his army.

The **occupation** followed the same grim pattern as that of the First World War, though this time not even a corner of Belgium remained free, nor was it possible to escape over the border into Holland. Resistance again was often heroic, despite the Nazi regime of anti-semitism, concentration camps and the Gestapo. The king, a prisoner in his Brussels palace of Laeken, did what he could to help his people; he met Hitler at Berchtesgaden and negotiated the return of 50,000 prisoners and an improvement in the allocation of food supplies to Belgium. In 1941 he married Lilian Baels, a commoner who received the title of Princesse de Réthy, in 1941. When the Allies invaded France in June 1944, King Leopold was deported with his family first to Germany and then to Austria.

The closing phase. The invasion of France began on 6 June 1944. By the end of August the Allies were on the Belgian and German borders. The liberation of Belgium began in early September, the forces in the north being largely British and Canadian (under Montgomery), while those in the south were American (under Bradley). Brussels was liberated on 3 September, followed soon after by Ghent, Ostend, Bruges and Antwerp. The Americans liberated Charleroi, Mons and Namur on 3 September and, by 10 September, Liège and Luxembourg. By the end of the month, the Canadians had forced the Germans back into the Breskens corner at the mouth of the Scheldt, while east of Antwerp the British had crossed the Antwerp–Turnhout canal. By the winter, the Allied front line ran along the German frontier from Aachen to Wasserbillig in the Grand-Duchy of Luxembourg. The Allies now paused to regroup, planning to strike into Germany through Aachen in the north and through Alsace in the south. This, though, left the centre very thin, a weakness Hitler was not slow to exploit.

Hitler launched a counter-offensive on 16 December under Von Rundstedt. Known as the Battle of the Ardennes (or Battle of the Bulge) this final desperate attack was aimed at the weak Allied centre, which ran along the German border from Monschau to Wasserbillig. Hitler planned to break through here, split the Allied front, and seize Antwerp. By 25 December, an area known as the 'bulge' had been formed containing the important crossroads at Bastogne, where the 101st Airborne Division had been sent. American and British reinforcements were sent to relieve Bastogne. A major Allied air offensive was launched against the German supply lines on 23 December. By the end of the month, despite the snow and bitter temperatures, Patton's counter-attack was approaching Bastogne. Montgomery launched a second offensive from the north on 3 January. The two counter-attacks met at Houffalize on 16 January. By the end of January 1945, the Germans had been driven back beyond the Belgian frontier, having lost 120,000 men in the Battle of the Ardennes.

Post-war Belgium

King Leopold, who in the closing stages of the war had been deported first to Germany and then to Austria, was freed in May 1945 and moved to Switzerland, but found that he could not safely return to Belgium. A large sector of the population blamed him for surrendering to the Germans. He was also, though perhaps less justifiably, criticised for his relations with the Germans and his second marriage. His brother Prince Charles was appointed regent. In 1950 a referendum on whether Leopold should retain the throne gave him just 57 per cent of the vote and he abdicated in favour of his son Baudouin who ascended the throne in 1951.

Some other important post war developments are outlined below.

1958 Brussels became the provisional headquarters of the European Economic Community. This organisation grew out of the Benelux Union signed by the governments in exile of the Netherlands, Belgium and Luxembourg in London in 1944.

1960 The Congo was granted independence in 1960 and became the state of Zaire.

1962 The Language Frontier between the Dutch-speaking north and the French-speaking south was established in 1962.

1967 Brussels became the headquarters of NATO.

1992 The country changed from a centralised constitution to a federal one. Belgium became divided into the three regions of Flanders, Wallonia and Brussels. Flanders and Wallonia correspond roughly with the division of the population into Dutch-speakers and French-speakers, but Brussels, geographically enclosed by Flanders, is 85 per cent Francophone. There is also a German-speaking enclave of some 60,000 people in the east of the country.

1993 King Baudouin died suddenly in Spain. He was succeeded by his brother Albert, who was crowned King Albert II.

1996 The death penalty was formally abolished in Belgium.

1998 Since the Treaty of Maastricht in 1991, the economy has been governed by the struggle to achieve the criteria for joining the European Monetary Union in 1999. In 1991, Belgium had twice the acceptable budget deficit and crippling debts. Some years of austerity and curbs on public spending have ensured that the country will be one of the founder members.

The economy is not without its problems which reflect the polarised social structure. Flanders has become known for its high-tech industries—the Flanders Language Valley near Ypres aims to become the Silicon Valley of advanced speech and language technology—and is experiencing a growth four times that of Wallonia, where businesses are still struggling to find alternatives to the old heavy industry. Unemployment too is falling in the north but rising in the south.

1999 In the decades after the Second World War, the govenment was based on the Socialist and Christian Democrat parties, but during the last years of the 1990s this coalition was rocked by serious scandals. In the parliamentary elections of June 1999, Dutch and French-speaking Liberal, Socialist and Green parties formed a six-party coalition under the leadership of Guy Verhofstadt. The Christian Democrats were ousted from the government for the first time in 40 years.

Landmarks in Belgian culture

One of the unexpected pleasures of Belgium is the astonishing cultural richness of this small region of Europe. For example, you can spend a weekend in one of the exceptional art cities, such as Bruges, Antwerp, Ghent, Brussels and Namur or venture into the Walloon countryside to discover handsome castles and isolated pilgrimage chapels.

This region of Europe has been famous since the 15C for the outstanding quality of its painting, sculpture, tapestries and printing, although some of the greatest of its treasures have been sold abroad or pillaged by invading armies, which has left the country sadly denuded of its cultural inheritance. Several historic cities were destroyed or damaged in the two world wars, including Leuven, Ypres, Diksmuide and Ostend. A certain loss of national identity has also come from the creation of separate ministries of culture for the Dutch speakers and French speakers.

Before the 1990s, the label 'boring' was routinely applied to Belgium by newspaper headline writers. Yet, recent years have seen a remarkable resurgence of civic pride in cities such as Antwerp, Ghent and Bruges. There are countless examples of restoration and urban renewal, particularly in Brussels, Namur and Antwerp. Many of the country's museums have received major facelifts in recent years, including the Fine Arts Museum and the Musical Instruments Museum in Brussels, the Groeningemuseum in Bruges and the Fine Arts Museum in Ghent. Several major exhibitions have led a new generation of travellers to discover the extraordinary talents of Bruegel, Memling, Simenon, Horta and Magritte. The cultural identity of Belgium may remain rather bewildering, but few would dare nowadays to call it boring.

Painting

Flemish Primitives
Painting in 15C Flanders was famous for its technical virtuosity, coherent vision and painstaking attention to detail. Artists such as Dürer travelled to Antwerp and Bruges to learn from the Flemish Primitives. Most of the works from this period illustrated religious subjects, though artists sometimes experimented with miniature landscapes or distant urban views. The art of portraiture was also highly developed.

Origins of 15C Flemish art
Our knowledge of early medieval art in Flanders is limited due to centuries of critical neglect, the ravages of war and revolution, and the decay caused by the damp maritime climate. The few works that have survived from the early period of Flemish art work reveal the influence of the courts of northern France at Paris and Dijon. Outstanding examples of early fresco painting are preserved in the Bijloke Museum in Ghent, while *The Calvary of the Tanners* in Bruges is a rare case of a 14C panel painting surviving in Belgium.

The true originators of the Flemish tradition were probably the miniature painters. Masterpieces such as Jacquemart de Hesdin's *Très Belles Heures du Duc de Berry* in the Bibliothèque Royale, Brussels, reveal an early fascination with colour and detail.

The brothers **Jan** and **Hubert van Eyck** are the first artists to emerge as distinct individuals (though the biography of Hubert remains vague). It is perhaps significant that the Van Eycks originated from the Limburg region in eastern Belgium, which gave its name to the brothers who produced the famous *Très Riches Heures* at Chantilly.

Jan van Eyck was employed by John of Bavaria at The Hague in the early 1420s. He entered the service of Philip of Burgundy in 1425. From 1430 until his death in 1441, he lived in Bruges where some of his best works can still be seen. Unusually for a medieval painter, Van Eyck signed a number of paintings, perhaps because of his fame. Hubert is known primarily from an inscription on the back of the *Adoration of the Mystic Lamb* in Ghent Cathedral. The precise contribution of each brother to this extraordinary work is a matter for endless debate.

The Van Eycks, like other 15C painters, engaged in a form of 'disguised symbolism' in which they deliberately concealed religious messages within apparently ordinary scenes, though scholars disagree about the extent and nature of the symbolism. The Van Eycks perfected a complex technique of oil painting which still retains its brilliant, transparent effect after more than five centuries. Their style is notable for its minute and convincing articulation of surface and space by means of colour and light.

The **Master of Flémalle** remains a shadowy figure. He may have been Robert Campin of Tournai, who died in 1444. His work combined the realism of the Van Eycks with a concern for decorative values. Two works attributed to him can be seen in the Brussels Fine Arts Museum, though none of his greatest masterpieces remains in Belgium.

The brilliant **Roger van der Weyden** (d. 1464) worked in Tournai and Brussels. He combined the technical virtuosity of the Van Eycks with his own subjective and dramatic vision. As no artist before him had done, he exploited the emotional potential of colours and abstract form. His portraits have a nobility and spirituality which won him many aristocratic patrons. His major works are mainly outside Belgium, but there is an early copy (1440) of his *Descent from the Cross* in Leuven's Sint Pieterskerk, and other good works in the fine arts museums of Antwerp, Brussels and Tournai.

Van der Weyden's influence is evident in the work of **Dirk Bouts** (d. 1475), a Haarlem painter who settled in Leuven before 1460. His remarkable *Judgement of the Emperor Otto* hangs in the Fine Arts Museum, Brussels, while his typically Flemish *Last Supper* is in the Sint Pieterskerk in Leuven. Bouts tended to isolate elongated and angular figures within a deep but simplified space. We often find a disturbing contrast in his works between peaceful landscapes and horrific subjects such as the *Martyrdom of St Erasmus* in Leuven.

The influence of both Van der Weyden and the Van Eycks can be seen in the works of **Petrus Christus** (d. 1472) of Bruges. His *Lamentation* (in Brussels) is quietly effective.

The Ghent painter **Hugo van der Goes** was a more original artist who broke out of the conventional craftsman mould (d. 1482). The emotional intensity of his approach is conveyed by a cavalier attitude to space and scale, an ability to intimate movement, a unique palette and, sometimes, an explicit awareness of the viewers' presence. The *Death of the Virgin* (Groeninge Museum, Bruges) is one of his great masterpieces.

The technically superb paintings of **Hans Memling** (d. 1494) are balanced and rational. The bulk of his work remains in a former medieval hospital in Bruges. Their derivation from Van der Weyden is clear, but they are gentler, more idealised, more homely.

Memling's most important successor was **Gerard David** (d. 1523), who moved to Bruges from Oudewater in 1484. David's style remains solemn and reticent, but his figures have an animation and suppleness which anticipates 16C style. Some of his major works remain in Bruges, such as the gruesome *Unjust Judge* panels in the Groeninge Museum.

The rather macabre visions of **Hieronymus Bosch** (d. 1516) contrast with the gentle art of Memling and David. Although not strictly a native artist (he spent his life in the Dutch town of 's-Hertogenbosch),

Judgement of Emperor Otto: the wrongful Execution of the Count, *by Dirk Bouts, Musées Royaux des Beaux-Arts, Brussels*

Bosch is seen as a member of the Flemish tradition due to his profound influence on artists such as Bruegel and Patinir. Bosch's fantastic assemblages of grotesque motifs, all the more horrifying because they derive ultimately from natural phenomena, are still not fully understood, though they probably relate to contemporary secular and religious beliefs. Being a great favourite with the morbid Philip II, most of Bosch's major works are in Spain, but there are good works in the Brussels and Ghent fine art museums.

Flemish Renaissance

The 16C saw a curious combination of Italian Renaissance motifs with the vigorous and highly decorative traditions of northern Gothic. Many Flemish artists travelled to Italy, or assimilated Italian ideas from printed books, and this period saw an integration of certain Italian elements into the medieval Flemish tradition. The result was a distinctive, though somewhat garbled new language, which paved the way for the 17C masters.

Antwerp was the commercial and cultural centre of 16C northern Europe, taking over the role that Bruges had enjoyed in the 15C. One of the most important artists of early 16C Antwerp was **Quinten Metsys** (d. 1530), whose refined and sophisticated religious paintings sought to combine the Flemish tradition with new Italian ideas, particularly those of Leonardo da Vinci. His animated portraits and satirical genre scenes were highly influential.

The influence of Leonardo can also be seen in **Joos van Cleef**, who astutely adopted many of Metsys' formulae, though his winsome Madonnas are more frankly charming and decorative. The more vigorous **Jan Gossaert**, also known as Mabuse, returned from a visit to Italy in 1508 with an innovative approach to the monumental nude in secular, mythological paintings, such as his Venus and Cupid in Brussels.

These artists inspired the school of **Antwerp Mannerism**. Often anonymous, these artists developed a decorative and anti-naturalistic style in c 1515–25. Incorporating Italian, Dutch and Flemish elements, this style is more akin to late Gothic Brabantine architecture than to contemporary Italian art. Meanwhile, **Jan Provoost** was producing lively Flemish Renaissance works in Bruges, while the prolific **Bernard van Orley** in Brussels was working on paintings and tapestry designs in a style that borrowed from Raphael.

The preoccupation with Italy continued in the second generation of artists who called themselves **Romanists**. The artists of this group included Michiel Coxie, Pieter Coecke van Aalst, Lambert Lombard (d. 1566), who was almost a caricature of a Renaissance artist, and Lombard's immensely successful pupil Frans Floris (d. 1570). Floris reveals a broader knowledge of Italian art than Lombard, in particular familiarity with Venetian and northern Italian techniques. Among Floris' many pupils was **Martin de Vos**, whose work reflects his collaboration with Tintoretto and his intimate knowledge of Veronese.

This period saw a steady drift from religious to secular subjects. We see this reflected in the emergence of landscape painting in the Meuse region. One of the first landscape artists was **Joachim Patinir** (d. c 1524), whose strange rocky landscapes were inspired by the Meuse valley near his home town of Dinant. His airy paintings, with their unnatural bird's-eye views and high horizons, established a convention which remained dominant until the end of the century. Patinir's style is reflected in the works of Henri met de Bles, Pieter Bruegel the Elder and, later, Gillis van Coninxloo. The style was only finally abandoned by Paul Bril.

The genre of **portraiture** also flourished during this period. The fashion until

c 1530 was for extrovert half-length figures. Later in the century, artists such as Lombard, Van Heemskerk and Floris created more free and direct images. The specialist portraitists after c 1550 remained aware of Italian styles, but were no longer in awe of Italy. They produced more reticent, often three-quarter length and usually three-quarter views of bourgeois sitters. We see this in the works of Pieter

Vegetable Market, by Joachim Beuckelaer, Museum voor Schone Kunsten, Antwerp

Pourbus, Frans Pourbus the Elder, and Adriaen Key. The refined **Antonio Moro**, painter to the Habsburg court, enjoyed success throughout Europe, formulating a style that contributed to the development of the European court portrait.

Quinten Metsys' style of genre painting was followed by Jan Sanders and the Dutchman Marius van Reymerswael. The Antwerp artist Pieter Aertsen and his nephew Joachim Beuckelaer developed an innovative genre of **Flemish kitchen scenes**, which were executed broadly in the style of the Romanists.

The Bruegel family

The most significant 16C Flemish painter was **Pieter Bruegel the Elder** (c 1525–69). Painting for a limited circle of intellectual connoisseurs, Bruegel's works combine acute observation of peasant physiognomies and customs with Bosch-like fantasy and rich allegorical and symbolic content. His transparent colour, brilliant sense of design and incisive drawing serve an objective yet deeply sympathetic view of humanity.

His son **Pieter Brueghel the Younger** (sometimes known as Hell Brueghel) painted copies of many of his father's work. We know of several lost works by Pieter Bruegel the Elder through the copies made by his son. Once dismissed as a mere copyist, the son is now credited with several original works. His younger brother **Jan** (sometimes known as Velvet Brueghel) painted exquisite miniature genre works and flower paintings which were eagerly bought in 16C Flanders.

Pieter Paul Rubens

The 17C is dominated by Pieter Paul Rubens (b. 1577), an artist of prodigious energy, who also worked as an architect, scholar and diplomat. Rubens acquired his huge formal vocabulary in his twenties when he spent eight years in Italy in the service of the Duke of Mantua. He also visited Spain in 1603. His eager eye assimilated all he saw, from classical antiquity to the Carracci and Caravaggio, though it was perhaps the 16C Venetians who most impressed him.

Yet Rubens' earlier training in Antwerp, particularly in the studio of Otto van Veen (Venius), was not wasted. Reminiscences of Van Veen and other Flemings often appear in Rubens' works. More fundamentally, the enthusiastic but sometimes awkward love affair between 16C Flemish artists and the Italian Renaissance laid the ground for the synthesis achieved by Rubens in the 17C.

Even before Rubens burst upon the Antwerp scene, artists such as Abraham Janssens (d. 1632) were producing fairly sophisticated interpretations of Italian ideas which reveal knowledge of Caravaggio and the Bolognese school. But Janssens, like so many others, was ultimately swept into the tide of emulation created by Rubens' enormous success.

Rubens' early fame was established by two masterpieces executed soon after his return from Italy and now hanging in Antwerp Cathedral. The *Raising of the Cross*, rent by a fierce diagonal, is a work of tremendous passion which fully merits the label Baroque. The *Descent from the Cross* is a calmer composition of great pathos. Three *Adorations of the Magi*, also executed in the 1610s (today in the fine arts museums in Brussels and Antwerp, and the St Janskerk in Mechelen) reveal Rubens' ability to revitalise a traditional Flemish subject. Rubens' position as court painter to Albert and Isabella established him as Antwerp's leading artist. He created a large and highly efficient workshop that turned out thousands of paintings for churches and private collectors. The price of a 'Rubens'

Adoration of the Magi, *by Peter Paul Rubens, Museum voor Schone Kunsten, Antwerp*

depended on the amount of the painting executed by the master himself. The small oil sketches by Rubens from which his assistants worked have always been highly valued as 'autograph', but it is worth remembering that they were not primarily intended as independent works of art; their compositions must be visualised on a much larger scale.

Rubens was an exceptionally versatile artist. He worked on portraits, landscapes, mythological scenes, political eulogies and grand religious works. He was ideally suited to serve the 17C Church and State. Many of his works, particularly the large religious paintings, remain in Belgian churches and museums. Highlights include the splendid altarpieces painted for churches in Antwerp, the series of hunting scenes designed for tapestries to decorate Philip IV's hunting-lodge (now in the Brussels Museum) and the utterly confident portrait of Gaspard Gevartius in the Antwerp Fine Arts Museum.

Antoon van Dyck

The young Antoon van Dyck (1599–1641) collaborated so closely with Rubens in the late 1610s that connoisseurs find it difficult to separate their work. Van Dyck eventually became more exclusively preoccupied with grace, elegance and emotional sensibility. He also developed a different technique and palette from Rubens.

The two masters can be compared during the period of their closest collaboration by visiting the St Pauluskerk in Antwerp, where both artists produced works for a series devoted to the Mysteries of the Rosary. The figures in Van Dyck's *Carrying of the Cross* recall Rubens' *Scourging of Christ*, which hangs alongside. Yet the unstable composition, flickering light, elements of unrestrained pathos and rapid, sketchy technique are Van Dyck's own.

Van Dyck was in Italy from 1621–27, while his career after 1632 was pursued mostly in England, where he concentrated on portraiture. There are some excellent portraits in Belgium, such as one of the Flemish sculptor François Duquesnoy painted in Italy (in the Brussels museum). A rich collection of Van Dyck's religious works can also be found in Belgian churches, mostly painted after his return from Italy. The hypersensitive Van Dyck painted the Crucifixion many times in a manner that emphasised despair and pathos. Examples can be seen in Mechelen Cathedral, the St Michielskerk in Ghent, and the Onze Lieve Vrouwekerk in Dendermonde.

Jacob Jordaens

The Antwerp artist Jacob Jordaens (1593–1678) was a pupil of Adam van Noort (as was Rubens). He may have worked with Van Dyck in the 1610s; he was certainly commissioned to complete works left unfinished by Rubens from c 1635. Despite these close contacts, Jordaens remains a highly original artist. His early style is robust, firm, illusionistic and boldly executed. Complex influences, including Caravaggism (although he never went to Italy), 16C Flemish art and, of course, Rubens combine to produce an entirely personal approach exemplified by the *Allegory of Fertility* (1620s) in the Brussels museum. Jordaens' *Martyrdom of St Apollonia* in the St Augustinuskerk in Antwerp (1628) seems almost to burst with movement and form. Jordaens also contributed to the *Mysteries of the Rosary* series in Antwerp.

Jordaens is famed for his exuberant banqueting scenes, such as *The King Drinks* in the Brussels museum. Rather paradoxically, he converted to Calvinism when he was about fifty. His subsequent religious paintings reveal a new moderation and restraint. These works lack the energy and daring of his earlier works, particularly when he relied on the services of his large workshop.

Minor 17C artists

The presence of Rubens, Van Dyck and Jordaens meant that Antwerp, despite its relative economic decline, remained the centre of Belgian artistic production in the 17C. The works of innumerable minor Antwerp masters testify to the overwhelming influence of these three painters, though artists such as Gerard Seghers and Theodoor Rombouts were also influenced by Caravaggio and his followers. Some of the more talented 17C artists understandably preferred to work outside Antwerp, but all remained ultimately within Rubens' sphere of influence.

The Bruges painter Jacob van Oost the Elder produced sensitive works incorporating Venetian and Dutch elements, while the masterpiece of Theodoor van Loon of Brussels was the powerful, Caravaggesque decoration of the church at Scherpenheuvel. The Brussels artist Gaspard de Crayer, who received numerous commissions from Ghent churches (such as St Michiel), learnt from Rubens and Van Dyck though he always managed to retain his own identity. A relatively independent group of artists in Liège led by Gerard Douffet were influenced by Caravaggism and the paintings of Poussin in France.

Genre painting

The 17C saw a proliferation of different genres by artists known as the *kleinmeister*, who tended to seek inspiration in Dutch genre painting. The career of **Adriaen Brouwer**, a painter of landscapes and scenes from everyday life, was short but brilliant. His brushwork is direct and free, his pictures naturalistic yet lyrical. The fine arts museum in Brussels provides a good opportunity to compare Brouwer with his contemporary **David Teniers the Younger** (1610–90). The peasant scenes painted by Teniers, who was chiefly a court artist, are much more detatched and cool.

Several minor artists worked in the landscape tradition, including Joos de Momper (d. 1635), Kerstiaen de Keuninck (d. c 1632–35) and Denijs van Alsloot of Brussels (d. c 1628). The later artists Lucas van Uden and Jan Wildens were skilled interpreters of the Rubens landscape, while Jacques d'Arthois of Brussels combined baroque grandeur with the decorative charm of Van Alsloot. The more independent Jan Siberechts (1627–1700/03) achieved a bold and entirely personal monumentality in his best works.

The still-life artist **Frans Snyders** (1579–1657) developed the 16C Flemish tradition of kitchen and market paintings established by Aertsen and Beuckelaer to include hunting and game scenes. His brother-in-law Paul de Vos (1596–1678) produced similar works, while Snyders' pupil Jan Fyt (1611–61) preferred to contemplate dead game rather than evoke the frenzy of the hunt itself. His works are striking and decorative, with an impressive feeling for surface textures.

The art of flower painting was invented at the beginning of the 17C by **Jan Brueghel** and achieved greater sophistication in the work of his pupil, the Jesuit Daniel Seghers (1590–1661). Both Seghers' paintings and the still-lifes of his influential contemporary Jan Davidsz. de Heem (1616–83/84) have a symbolic as well as a decorative purpose. Among the portraitists, Cornelis de Vos (the brother of Paul) created charming and elegant representations of children while, later in the century, Gonzales Cognes achieved great success in Brussels with his fashionable conversation pieces.

18C painting

The 18C saw the continuation of 17C styles combined with the growing influence of French ideas. It was natural that many artists should hark back to the golden age of 17C religious and history painting, though the worst examples are merely pallid imitations of Rubens. The Leuven artist Pieter Verhaghen produced works in the style of Jordaens which achieved a certain vigorous originality. The slightly younger artist Andreas Cornelis Lens (1739–1822) reveals an awareness of French art in his graceful, classical pictures. The sculptural *trompe l'oeils* in the Tournai museum by Piat Sauvage were inspired by Poussin's second series of the Seven Sacraments.

Genre painting enjoyed a high status during this period. David Teniers was particularly admired by artists such as Balthasar van den Bossche and the talented Jan Joseph Horemans the Elder. Despite their aspirations to elegance, Van den Bossche and Horemans remained firmly in the Flemish tradition. Other genre artists, such as Pieter Snayers and Pieter van Angelis, drew on the art of France and Italy, while Frans Xaver Henri Verbeek and Jacob de Roore found inspiration in the Leiden School.

The increasing internationalisation of painting during this period can be traced in the development of Jan Garemijn of Bruges (1712–99), who began by painting village genre scenes in the tradition of Teniers, but later adopted a French Rococo style and finally, in c 1790, fell under the influence of the Neoclassicism which was sweeping Europe. The career of Léonard Defrance (1735–1805) likewise illustrates the gradual weakening of the native Flemish tradition. Defrance's early Neo-classicism reveals the influence of his studies in Italy and the south of France. His conversion to 17C Leiden genre painting in 1773 seems to have been partly personal conviction and partly his awareness of a lucrative Parisian market, to which he responded by introducing French elements into his pictures.

The native Flemish tradition of landscape and flower painting was also abandoned in the 18C in favour of French and Dutch styles. The landscapist Karel van Falens was inspired by the Dutch painter Wouwerman, while later in the century Henricus Josephus Antonissen and Balthasar Paul Ommeganck modelled their art on Wynants and Berchem.

19C painting

Despite gaining political independence in 1830, Belgium lost much of its national identity in painting during the 19C. Yet there were still several Belgian artists who remained part of a distinct tradition of Belgian art. They retained an eye for detail, an interest in human subjects, and a skill in depicting light and colour. A clear line of descent can be traced from the early primitives and the 17C Baroque painters to the Romantics, Symbolists, Expressionists and Surrealists of the 19C and early 20C, and even the Social Realists and Hyperrealists of recent years.

The political annexation of Belgium by France was preceded by an artistic conquest of the country. By the end of the 18C, French classicism reigned supreme in all spheres of Belgian art, though many of the artists gained their recognition abroad, such as Josef Suveé (1743–1807), Frans Jozef Kinsoen (1771–1839) and Jozef Odevaere (1775–1830).

The French painter Jacques Louis David acquired numerous Belgian pupils during his exile in Brussels from 1815–25. The leading imitator was **François Joseph Navez** (1787–1869). After training with David in Paris, Navez visited Rome before becoming director of the Brussels Academy in 1830. An outstanding portraitist, his De Hemptinne Family, in the Brussels museum, is almost the equal of David.

Historical painting

The painter **Mathieu-Ignace van Bree** (1773–1839) represents another important link with France. After training with François-André Vincent, he became head of the Antwerp Academy in 1827, concentrating on the declamatory and the naturalistic aspects of classicism. The result was a type of nationalistic history painting produced by a school of Belgian artists who worked mainly in Antwerp after the country's independence from the Netherlands in 1830. This group was led by **Gustave Wappers** (1807–74), who succeeded Bree as head of the Antwerp Academy in 1839. Other artists included Ferdinand de Braekeleer (1792–1883) and Nicaise de Keyser (1813–87). This movement dominated Belgian painting until after 1850. No longer classicist in style, their works gave Belgium a national identity through a type of romantic history painting or patriotic allegory. The past is treated in a glamorous and rose-tinted manner in works such as Wappers' *Episode during the Belgian Revolt* of 1830 (painted, rather tellingly, in 1834); De Keyser's *Battle of the Golden Spurs* (painted in 1836); Louis Gallait's *The Plague in Tournai* in 1092 (from 1857); and Emile Wauters' *The Madness of Hugo van der Goes* (from 1872). Once highly regarded, these historical paintings are now often out of sight in the reserve rooms of museums.

Romanticism

The romantic movement in Belgian painting concentrated on large-scale historical costume pieces with a rather melodramatic mood. **Antoine Wiertz** (1806–65), who trained in Antwerp, was almost a caricature of the 19C romantic artist. His passionate and sometimes hysterical paintings are reminiscent of Goya. Many of his major works hang in the Wiertz Museum in Brussels, which was specially built by the government of the time to house his immense canvases.

The murals painted by **Hendrik Leys** (1815–69) for the Antwerp town hall are calmer and less grandiose. They look back nostalgically to Flemish art before

Rubens, rather as the Pre-Raphaelites in England rediscovered medieval art. Somewhat later, the tranquil Antwerp interiors of **Henri de Braekeleer** (1840–88) were inspired by a deep empathy for 17C Dutch and Flemish interiors.

A new style began to emerge in the 1850s in the paintings of **Florent Willems** (1823–1905) and, particularly, **Alfred Stevens** (1823–1906), a pupil of Navez who spent most of his career in Paris. Willems' *Women with a Mirror* (in the Groeningemuseum, Bruges) is reminiscent of Dutch 17C genre pieces by Gerard ter Borch. Stevens' *Autumn Flowers* of 1867 (in the Brussels museum) is a delicate portrait of an elegant Parisian woman dressed in the fashion of the Second Empire. Alfred's older brother Joseph Stevens (1819–92) and Jan Stobbaerts (1838–1914) specialised in painting dogs.

The establishment of the **Société Libre des Beaux-Arts** in 1868 marked the end of the government-sponsored Academies and Salons (held triennially in Ghent, Antwerp and Brussels), and the beginning of avant-gardism in Belgium. Inspired by Courbet's *Stone Breakers*, which was exhibited in Belgium in 1851, Charles de Groux (1825–70) and Constantin Meunier launched the **Realist movement**, which concentrated on depicting the lives of the poor. Eugène Laermans (1864–1940), working almost 30 years later, continued to depict dignified workers in derelict landscapes. Many members of the Société Libre were landscape painters who wanted to escape the confines of the studio. They often exhibited alongside French painters to give the group a more European flavour. The Société Libre's members included Louis Dubois (1830–80), Alfred Verwee (1838–95), Edouard Agneessens (1842–85), Eugène Smits (1826–1912), and the notorious Felicien Rops (1833–98), who started as a landscape painter but became most famous for the erotic graphic work he produced for private collectors in Paris. A museum is devoted to Rops in his home town of Namur.

The Realists were gaining acceptance by the 1870s, when their works began to appear in the Salons. The success of Charles Herman's painting *At Dawn* of 1875 marked an important turning-point in the struggle against Neo-classical and Romantic painting. His painting of bourgeois revellers spilling out of a tavern at dawn represents the triumph of a form of an upper-class realism similar to that of Willems and Stevens.

The art of landscape painting was developed by a number of minor Belgian artists, many of them influenced by the Barbizon School, including Hippolyte Boulenger (1837–74), painter of the Ardennes and the forests of Tervuren. An early work by Emile Claus (1849–1924), *The Leie at Astene* (Groeningemuseum, Bruges), marked the transition to **Luminism**. Named after the group Vie et Lumière and influenced by the French Impressionists of the 1870s, this group was founded by Claus in 1904. Other members were A.J. Heymans, George Buysse (1864–1916) and Georges Morren (1868–1941). An interesting series of Luminist paintings of the Thames were painted by Emile Claus during his exile in London in the First World War.

The groups **La Chrysalide** (1875–81) and **L'Essor** (1876–91) succeeded the Société Libre des Beaux-Arts. The members of La Chrysalide included Louis Artan and Guillaume Vogels. Those who exhibited with L'Essor included the sculptor Julien Dillens, and the Symbolists Jean Delville (1867–1953), Léon Frederic (1856–1940) and Fernand Khnopff (1858–1921). Others artists later followed L'Essor's ideas, including Xavier Mellery (1845–1921), Khnopff's teacher William Degouve de Nungues (1867–1935), Emile Fabry (1865–1966) and, to a lesser extent, the bleak Ostend artist Léon Spilliaert (1881–1946).

The various groups disseminated their ideas through art journals founded by intellectuals and artists. Much of their success was due to the prevailing liberalism supported by Leopold I and Leopold II. French-speaking Brussels became the artistic capital of Belgium, international in its outlook and ready to absorb new ideas, while Ghent and Antwerp remained attached to their Flemish heritage, only becoming important again in the 20C.

The most famous Belgian painter of this period is **James Ensor** (1860–1949). Macabre and fantastic, he used skeletons and masks to make social comment in works such as *Christ's Entry into Brussels* of 1889 (now in the Getty Museum). Following the tradition of Bosch, these paintings still have the capacity to shock and intrigue. Even in his early works, Ensor can be penetrating, as in *Sombre Lady* (Brussels museum) and the *Oyster Eater* (Antwerp museum).

Despite being very much an individual, Ensor contributed to both L'Essor and La Chrysalide. He was one of the founding members of the group **Les XX** (Les Vingt), which flourished from 1883–94. Les XX, named because of its 20 members and 20 invited exhibitors, and its sucessor **La Libre Esthetique** (1894–1914), were, like the preceding groups, eclectic in outlook. They recognised the importance of combining every art and style. In their exhibitions, held annually, they included poetry readings and concerts as well as displays of Impressionist, neo-Impressionist, Symbolist, Art Nouveau and decorative works of art from Belgium, France and England. Seurat's famous pointillist painting *La Grande Jatte*, depicting Parisians strolling along the Seine on a Sunday afternoon, was exhibited by Les XX in 1887. It had a profound effect on several of the group's members, including Théo van Rysselberghe (1862–1926), Georges Lemmen (1865–1916), Alfred 'Willy' Finch (1854–1930), Anna Boch (1848–1933) and Henry van de Velde (1863–1957). All these artists took up pointillism, though Théo van Rysselberghe continued to paint psychological portraiture using the pointillist technique.

During his brief career, Henri Evenepoel (1872–99) was something of an individualist, painting portraits in a style inspired by Manet. Their poster-like quality anticipates the posters of Jules van Biesbroeck (1850–1920).

Flemish Expressionism

Many early 20C Belgian painters and sculptors were drawn to Surrealism and Expressionism. This was perhaps a reflection of the Flemish love of the bizarre, the exuberant and the tactile, though it may also have derived from groups such as the Symbolists who were exploring the role of imagination in art. The roots of Expressionism are found in the works of Jacob Smits (1856–1928), a Dutch artist who settled in the Kempen in 1888 and became a Belgian citizen in 1902. His paintings of peasant scenes suffused with religious symbolism were influenced by Rembrandt.

Sint Martens-Latem

The village of Sint Martens-Latem, on the River Leie near Ghent, became the centre for two schools of Flemish Expressionism. The **First Latem School** was established c 1905 by the sculptor George Minne (1866–1941) and the artists Albert Servaes (1883–1966), Valerius de Saedeleer (1867–1941), Gustave van de Woestyne (1881–1947) and Albijn van den Abeele (1835–1918), whose paintings exhibit a certain Gothic mysticism. This school was influenced by Symbolist painters and writers in Brussels, though they also drew inspiration from medieval Flemish religious painting. Minne's sculpture of *Three Marys at the Tomb*, Servaes' series of the *Stations of the Cross* and Van de Woestyne's *Crucifixion* illustrate their religious subject matter. De Saedeleer and Abeele painted Flemish landscapes with a cold stillness and contemplation that harks back to Pieter Bruegel the Elder.

The **Second Latem Group** was established c 1909 by Constant Permeke (1886–1952), a master of emotional realism, Gustave de Smet (1877–1943) and Frits van den Berghe (1883–1939). Their works betray a slight Cubist influence, though they remain figurative painters using cubic forms. Flemish Expressionism was largely independent of German Expressionism. It was more humane, evoking pathos by depicting fishermen and peasants in predominantly earthy colours. The main collections of Flemish Expressionism are at the Permeke Museum in Jabbeke, the Gustave and Leon de Smet museums at Deurle, and the Museum voor Schone Kunsten in Ghent.

Brabant Fauvism

A group of artists known as the Brabant Fauvists developed a bold use of colour modelled on the French Fauvists. One of the leading Fauvists was **Rik Wouters** (1882–1916), who died tragically young from eye cancer during the First World War. The group also included Leon de Smet (1881–1966), brother of the Expressionist Gustave de Smet, Edgard Tytgat (1879–1957), the unjustly neglected Jean Brusselmans (1884–1953) from Dilbeek, Hippolyte Daeye (1873–1952), Fernand Schirren (1872–1944), Auguste Oleffe (1867–1931), Louis Thevenet (1874–1930), Willem Paerels (1878–1962) and Henri Wolvens (1896–1977).

Belgian Surrealism

A distinctive Belgian Surrealism was launched by the art theorist Paul Nougé in 1924. Most critics regard Surrealism as a French movement, but it has something in common with the eccentric tradition in Belgian art, as seen in the works of Bosch and Bruegel. Indeed, Surrealism is so much a part of Belgian culture that major Surrealist murals have been commissioned for the Congress Palace and Bourse metro station in Brussels, and the casinos at Knokke and Ostend.

The most famous of the Belgian Surrealists was **René Magritte** (1898–1967), who was born in the industrial belt of Wallonia and lived most of his life in Brussels. His paintings use the unexpected juxtaposition of ordinary objects to create a strange dissonance. His famous painting *The Empire of Lights* of 1952 (Brussels museum) is reminiscent of Willem Degouve de Nuncques' *House of Mystery* painted 60 years before (Brussels museum). After participating in the birth of Surrealism in Paris, between 1927 and 1930, Magritte returned to Brussels.

The Surrealist **Paul Delvaux** (1897–1994) began in 1935 a somewhat obsessive career in which he produced enigmatic paintings featuring dreamy nude women, antiquated Brussels trams and skeletons. A large 1978 mural by Delvaux hangs in the Bourse metro station in Brussels. The Paul Delvaux Museum in Sint Idesbald has a large collection of his works.

Nervia

The Nervia group was established in 1928 in the industrial town of Mons. Aiming to develop a distinctive Walloon art, the group included Louis Buisseret (1888–1956), Anto Carte (1886–1954) and Leon Devos (1897–1974). Many of the works have religious, allegorical or genre images painted in a lyrical almost Graeco-Roman manner. The fine art museum at Charleroi has a good collection of Nervia works.

Other currents before 1945

Belgian art was dominated before 1945 by Expressionism and Surrealism, but a few isolated artists adopted other international styles. **Jules Schmalzigaug** (1886–1917) was touched by the Futurist style. Under the influence of the Italians Severini and Boccioni, he attempted to represent speed and light in his canvases. The Belgian Cubist Marthe Donas spent most of her life abroad.

The first experiments in abstraction were carried out between the wars by artists such as Paul Joostens (1889–1960), Jozef Peeters (1895–1960), Michel Seuphor, Karel Maes, Joseph Lacasse and Victor Severanckx (1897–1965). These artists followed developments in the Netherlands through the Belgian George Vantongerloo, who was a friend of Théo van Doesburg. Prosper de Troyer and Felix de Boeck painted abstract works that were a development from Expressionism without any structured forms.

Jeune Peinture Belge

La Jeune Peinture Belge (1945–50) was one of several art groups that emerged after 1945. Influenced in part by the lyrical and geometrical abstractions of Victor Severanckx, it paved the way for the fully-fledged abstract art of the 1950s. Its adherents included Gaston Bertrand, Louis van Lint, Anne Bonnet, Marc Mendelson, Lismonde, Jan Cox and Jo Delahaut.

Cobra

The Cobra group (1948–51) was founded in a Paris cafe in 1948 by Dutch, Belgian and Danish artists. The name Cobra was an acronym of Copenhagen, Brussels and Amsterdam. Favouring a spontaneous and often child-like art, Cobra artists questioned the distinction between painting and writing. The leading Belgian members were Pierre Alechinsky and Christian Dotremont. Their exhibition at Liège in 1951 had a profound influence on future Belgian artists.

Recent trends in Belgian art

Many Belgian artists since the 1960s have returned to social realism or hyper-realism. The most interesting figures in this development are Roger Somville and Roger Raveel. The Surrealist **Marcel Broodthaers** (1924–76) enjoyed international success in the 1960s with his quirky installations, such as his mock Museum of Modern Art, Department of the Eagles. The artist **Henri Van Herwegen** (b. 1940) creates assemblages inspired by aircraft. He works under the name Panamarenko, derived from Pan Am Airlines.

A striking trend in recent years has seen art being exhibited outside museums and galleries. The Brussels public transport authority has been incorporating works by contemporary Belgian artists in its metro stations since the 1970s. The cartoon artist François Schuiten has created imaginative stations at the Porte de

Hal in Brussels and Arts et Métiers in Paris, while the conceptual artist Benoît has redesigned Maelbeek station. The New Siru Hotel on Place Rogier in Brussels has a policy of commissioning works from Belgian artists to decorate its bedrooms and corridors. The most interesting museum curator of recent years is Jan Hoet, director of the Museum of Contemporary Art in Ghent, who created a considerable stir in 1986 by organising the Chambres d'Amis (Guest Rooms) exhibition in private homes throughout Ghent. Many Belgian cities now organise occasional Parcours d'Artistes in which local artists open their studios to the public.

Architecture

Belgian architects have tended traditionally to imitate and refine the styles of neighbouring countries such as France, the Netherlands and England. Yet this region of Europe has occasionally created innovative structures and building styles, such as the walled Begijnhof communities, municipal Belforts and 19C Art Nouveau town houses.

Merovingian and Carolingian

Little remains from the Roman period in Belgium, apart from fragments of Tongeren's town wall. The simple Merovingian chapel in the Collégiale Sainte Gertrude at Nivelles is one of the few relics of the great monastic building programme initiated after the conversion of Clovis to Christianity in the 5C.

After the **Emperor Charlemagne** established his court at Aachen, the Meuse region acquired greater importance. The circular church plan of the Palatine chapel at Aachen was copied in several Belgian churches, but all have disappeared. Excavations during the 1950s revealed that the plan of St Donatian in Bruges was inspired by the circular chapel at Aachen. The traditional basilican or hall church with aisles and apse, which had been used from ancient Christian times, also underwent radical changes during the Carolingian period, as can be seen in the church of St Ursmer at Lobbes.

Romanesque

The Treaty of Verdun of 843 divided this region of Europe along the River Scheldt. The Scaldian style (named after the Scheldt) emerged to the west of the river, while the Mosan style, named after the river Meuse, evolved in the east.

After the Meuse region became part of the Ottonian Empire (the East Frankish kingdom of Germany c 900–1050), the **Mosan Romanesque** style developed, particularly in Liège and Maastricht. Inspired by the Rhenish style of the Rhine region, Mosan architecture is characterised by simplicity, austerity and strength. Mosan Romanesque basilicas took over the typical Ottonian west fronts flanked by twin towers, known as westworks, and complex apsidal structure at the east end. The church of St Gertrude at Nivelles remains the most striking example of the Mosan basilica in Belgium. The rural churches of St Hadelin at Celles and Notre-Dame d'Hastière-Par-Delà retain fortified west ends, square piers with imposts but no bases, low transepts, flat timberwork ceilings and crypts. The rotunda was a popular Romanesque style, to be seen, for example, in the reconstructed church of St Jean in Liège.

The Scheldt valley fell under French rule, which resulted in the **Scaldian**

Romanesque style. Following Norman style, this occasionally led to the import of English Norman elements. The Scaldian style is generally more elaborate than the Mosan, largely because it blossomed in the 12C whereas the Mosan style was established in the 11C. The oldest surviving monument of this style is probably the church of St Vincent at Soignies (probably 11C), but it reached its highest expression in Tournai Cathedral in the 12C. One of the features of the Scaldian style is a tower above the crossing, though Tournai is exceptional in having five towers. The Scaldian nave is often multi-storeyed with complex piers and sometimes alternating supports. The external decoration is often more ornate towards the top, while the Scaldian westwerk, unlike the Mosan, is pierced by an entrance.

The oldest surviving secular architecture in Belgium dates from this period. The rugged stone Koornstapelhuis on Ghent's Graslei dates from the early 13C. Some parts of the Steen in Antwerp and the Gravensteen in Ghent are also relics of the Scaldian period.

The Gothic style

The earliest Gothic churches in Belgium were basically copied from northern French models. French Gothic forms were rapidly introduced at Tournai Cathedral in the choir (1243–55). The monastic orders favoured a more simple and severe Gothic, such as the ruined Cistercian abbey church of Villers-la-Ville.

Three regional styles emerged in the 13C, known as Scheldt, Mosan and Brabant Gothic. The **Scheldt Gothic**, which mainly flourished in the 13C, featured foliated 'Tournai capitals', polygonal apses, crossing towers flanked by four small stair towers, and chapels placed obliquely between transepts and choir. Outstanding examples of this style are the St Niklaaskerk in Ghent and Onze Lieve Vrouwekerk in Oudenaarde.

Churches in the **Mosan Gothic** style often featured rectilinear apses. The columns tended to be cylindrical at the bottom but polygonal at the top, with banded decoration. A high gallery above the triforium was occasionally added. The church of Notre-Dame in Huy is a good example of this rare style.

The **Brabant Gothic** style gradually became dominant in the 14C and 15C. The style originated in Leuven, capital of Brabant. The oldest buildings in this style include the Sint Pieterskerk, begun in 1425, and parts of the Groot Begijnhof, both in Leuven. The style spread throughout Brabant and the Scheldt valley, transforming into the **Flamboyant Gothic** (or late Gothic) style of the 15C. This style can be seen in the great cathedrals of Brussels, Mechelen, Ghent and Antwerp. Their tall western towers were intended to symbolise the confidence of the medieval Flemish cities. Sometimes, due to financial difficulties or structural miscalculations, these soaring towers remained unfinished, as at Leuven, Antwerp and Mechelen.

Secular Gothic architecture blossomed due to the rise of towns in the 14C and the increased influence of merchants. The new mood of civic pride was expressed in the construction of extravagant town halls, cloth halls and tall belfries. The great **cloth halls** at Ypres and Bruges date originally from the 13C, though Ypres was rebuilt after it was destroyed in the First World War. These buildings introduced elements that would repeatedly crop up in later architecture, such as a central belfry, crenellated wings and small corner turrets.

The Flemish **town halls** of the 14C–16C reflect the exuberance of secular architecture. The town hall in Bruges was begun in 1376, Brussels in 1402,

Leuven in 1448 and Oudenaarde in the early 16C. The town hall in Brussels served as a model for the 19C town halls in Munich and Vienna.

The great **commercial halls** of medieval Flanders often featured a distinctive stepped gabling which derives from the Romanesque style. This can be seen in the Groot Vleeshuis in Ghent of 1408 and the Vleeshuis in Antwerp. This style was adapted by architects working in 15C Bruges to decorate the gables of private houses. The style eventually spread from Bruges to the northern Hanseatic cities.

Early Renaissance architecture

The Brabant Gothic style continued to be dominant in the rather conservative political climate of the early 16C. But the Low Countries were now part of the Habsburg Empire, which exposed the area to the influence of Italian Renaissance art. Northern patrons who were anxious to appear fashionable commissioned architects to design buildings in Italianate style. This led to the introduction of Renaissance motifs culled from books of engravings. The style reached Bruges as early as 1515, when the decoration of the traditional triumphal arches erected for Charles V's solemn entry featured Renaissance grotesques and medallions.

The northern architects were slower to assimilate the basic principles of Renaissance proportion. Many of the designs were essentially Gothic buildings with Renaissance ornament added. The earliest of these transitional buildings tended to be built by the wealthy aristocracy who constructed new palaces or renovated old buildings in the first half of the 16C. One of the first examples of this northern renaissance is **Margaret of Austria's palace at Mechelen**. The palace of the Prince-Bishops at Liège illustrates a fondness for the grotesque Italian style.

Northern architects gained a more profound knowledge of Renaissance architecture as the century progressed. It became routine for young architects to visit Italy, while books and engravings of Italian architecture became more readily available. The town hall in Antwerp designed by **Cornelis Floris** in 1561–66 reveals a sophisticated understanding of Italian principles combined with a conscious determination to retain traditional elements. This nostalgia for the past may have been fuelled by Antwerp's stubborn resistance to Philip II of Spain.

Baroque architecture

The main developments in 17C religious architecture were due to the vigorous Counter-Reformation encouraged by the Spanish Archdukes and the Jesuits. The Jesuit church of St Carolus Borromeus in Antwerp is often considered the first Baroque church in Belgium. Begun in 1615 by the Jesuit **Pieter Huyssens**, its façade and interior were decorated by Rubens in a rich Baroque style. The destruction of Rubens' work in 1718 revealed that the basic plan remained entirely traditional. The church may be Baroque in decoration, but its spatial organisation is thoroughly old-fashioned.

Huyssens and his contemporaries Jacob Franckaert and Wenceslas Coeberger designed a number of similarly semi-Baroque churches during the first half of the century, which are often attractive and interesting in their varied solutions to the typical Belgian problem of reconciling tradition with fashion. Coeberger's church of Scherpenheuvel, near Leuven, is a brave attempt at a centralised Baroque plan, while Franckaert's façade architecture, as seen in his Begijnhof church in Mechelen, is lively and progressive. The Sint Pieterskerk in Ghent is closer to Italian Baroque, but is still characteristically Belgian in its exciting use of light and space.

The two principal figures of the second half of the century were the Jesuit **Willem Hessius** and **Lucas Faydherbe** of Mechelen. Hessius' church of St Michiel in Leuven (begun in 1650), and his Abbey Church of St Servaas in Grimbergen, illustrate a continuing tendency to produce charming but only skin-deep Baroque, while Faydherbe's church of Onze Lieve Vrouw van Hanswijk in Mechelen (begun 1663) is more bizarre than Baroque.

Refined Baroque ornamentation was applied to traditional buildings in secular 17C architecture. The Baroque house Rubens designed himself in Antwerp (restored in 1938–46) is basically a traditional Flemish building, while Jordaens' private house is rather more daring. Even at the very end of the century, the guild houses on the Grand-Place in Brussels were rebuilt after the bombardment of 1695 in a traditional tall and narrow style. This was partly, admittedly, due to the restrictions of the building plots, but there remained the possibility of innovation in the composition of the façade, rather than simply the ornamentation.

International Baroque

The 18C saw a further weakening of native architectural traditions in the face of foreign influences, aided by the transfer of the southern Netherlands from the Spanish to the Austrian Habsburgs. Built, rather symbolically, in 1700, the church of the Minimes in Brussels was the first building where traditional Belgian architecture was replaced by an international Baroque style. Nonetheless, the main examples of 18C Baroque occur in secular buildings.

A broad difference can be seen between the elegant French Baroque of the Meuse region and the more flamboyant Austrian Baroque of Flanders. The French influence of the Mosan style can be seen in J.A. Anneessens' wing for the Palace of the Prince-Bishops at Liège. The Flemish style was developed in Antwerp by Jan Peter van Baurscheit the Younger, and in Ghent by Bernard de Wilde and David 't Kindt, though the Ghent architects soon began to incorporate lighter Rococo elements into their façades.

The design of **Namur Cathedral**, begun in 1751, marks another landmark in the internationalisation of architecture in the southern Netherlands. It was designed by the Milanese Gaetano Pizzoni, who was commissioned through the Habsburg Court at Vienna. The architectural style is Italian with just a hint of international classicism apparant in the still basically Baroque interior.

Laurent Benoit Dewez (1731–1812) received an international training before being appointed chief architect to the governor, Charles of Lorraine. Working from 1766–82, Dewez was primarily responsible for the establishment of classicism. His château at Seneffe of c 1760 is a remarkable achievement reminiscent of an 18C English country house.

The urban development of Brussels towards the end of the century provided architects trained in the French classical style with several major commissions, such as the Place des Martyrs, designed in 1775 by Claude Fisco, the Place Royale and Parc de Bruxelles, begun in 1775 by Barnabé Guimard, and the Palais de la Nation, designed again by Guimard.

19C classicism

French classicism remained the dominant style in Belgium after 1815. The most important classical architect of the period was the court architect Charles van der Straeten (1771–1834), who designed the sober Palais Ducale in 1876 (now the Palais des Académies) in Brussels. The expansion of the universities during this period created opportunities for classical architects such as Louis Roelandt in Ghent and J.N. Chevron in Liège.

Castles

Due to the endless wars fought on its soil, Belgium has a long tradition of constructing castles and manor houses. The great fortresses of feudal times were mainly for defence rather than as residences. The oldest and most impressive of the great castles is the Gravensteen built by the counts of Flanders at Ghent, fragments of which date back to the 9C. Lesser nobles built private manors and farms, primarily as homes but at the same time fortified in case of attack. The fortified manors of Solre-sur-Sambre and Spontin are attractive examples of this building style. Many of the most attractive fortified farms (châteaux-fermes) are in Namur province. Most of the genuine fortresses survive only as romantic ruins, or as restored or reconstructed buildings.

The techniques of warfare changed in the 16C and made fortified castles obsolete; they were replaced by elegantly-furnished châteaux. These were either new buildings or adaptations of the old around the defensive moat and keep (donjon). A distinctive Belgian style developed in the 18C, based on a picturesque mixture of brick and stone, numerous pepper-pot turrets and often a central tower decorated with a curious onion dome. Most Belgian châteaux we see today have retained this style in defiance of subsequent French, Baroque and Neo-classical influences.

Eclecticism

Eclecticism dominated Belgian architecture from c 1830 until the end of the 19C. The rapid growth of the cities led to large-scale construction projects. Many of the buildings were banal, though there were some masterpieces, such as **Joseph Polaert**'s enormous Palais de Justice (1866–83), built on a hill overlooking Brussels. A more graceful example can be seen in **J.F. Cluysenaar**'s grand Galeries St Hubert of 1846 and his intimate Galerie Bortier of 1847, both in Brussels. The Brussels Bourse of 1873 by **Leon Suys** is another notable building, with some of the sculptures by Rodin. **Alphonse Balat** was employed on several official projects including the Musée de l'Art Ancien (1875–85), the façade and main staircase of the Palais Royal, and the royal greenhouses in Laeken. The National Bank of 1879 in Antwerp illustrates the inventive eclecticism of A. Beyaert.

Art Nouveau

By the end of the 19C, eclectic architects such as Balat were experimenting with new materials such as iron. This led to the emergence of Art Nouveau architecture, which was pioneered by Balat's pupil Victor Horta (1861–1947), Paul Hankar (1859–1901), and Henry van de Velde (1863–1957). The Belgian Art Nouveau style was partly influenced by English Arts and Crafts artists such as William Morris, Walter Crane and Aubrey Beardsley, whose works were shown in Brussels at exhibitions such as La Libre Esthétique. The Brussels architect **Victor Horta** used modern materials such as glass and steel to create extraordinary organic buildings. Many of his buildings were torn down in the 1960s building boom, including the famous Maison du Peuple with its undulating skin of glass, built in 1896–99 for the Socialist Workers' Party. His first house was the Hôtel Tassel of 1893, which has been restored to its former glory. His home and studio of 1898 in Rue Américaine is now a museum. After teaching in America during the First World War, Horta returned to Belgium with a more sober style that anticipated Art Deco. Examples can be seen in his Palais des Beaux Arts in Brussels of 1922–29, the Musée des Beaux-Arts in Tournai of 1928 and the Gare Centrale in Brussels.

Henry van de Velde was not only an architect, but also a painter, critic and interior designer. Like his contemporary Charles Rennie Mackintosh, he aimed at creating a total artistic movement. Van de Velde spent many years in Weimar as the director of the influential Arts and Crafts School, which he designed himself in 1901. This became the first Bauhaus under the direction of Walter Gropius in 1919. He returned to Belgium in 1926 to establish La Cambre School of Art and Architecture in Brussels, which still has a reputation for visual art and design. Little of Van de Velde's architectural work remains in Belgium except for the house Bloemenwerf he built himself in the Brussels suburb of Uccle in 1895. Yet Van de Velde's influence can be seen in the austerity and refinement of much early 20C Belgian architecture.

The residential districts of Brussels, Ghent and Antwerp are thick with Art Nouveau buildings. Many of the finest buildings are found around the Avenue Louise and Square Ambiorix in Brussels, and Cogels-Osylei in Antwerp. Art Nouveau furniture was designed by Gustave Serrurier-Bovy (1858–1910) of Liège.

Modernism

Following the closure of the Bauhaus in 1933, Louis Herman de Koninck (1896–1985) taught functionalism at La Cambre. One of the first Belgian Modernists, De Koninck created his own house in Uccle, where he employed his rationalist philosophy of minimum interiors with maximum spatial impact.

The work of Antoine Pompe (1873–1980) represented a new rationalised brick architecture, as can be seen in his clinic for Dr Van Neck of 1910 at Rue Wafelaerts 55 in Brussels. We can also see the clean white forms of the Bauhaus reflected in the Cité Moderne of 1922–25 built by Victor Bourgeois (1897–1962) in Berchem-Ste Agathe, Brussels, and the 1928 studio of Oscar Jespers.

Postwar individualism

Early 20C architecture in Belgium was influenced by contemporary movements in the Netherlands, France and Germany. Yet a spirit of anarchy prevailed in the postwar years, as can be seen in the imaginative new university campuses at Louvain-la-Neuve and Sart Tilman, near Liège. Whereas postwar Dutch architecture has been governed by strict planning, Belgian architecture varies between spirited individualism and dull conformity. One architecture critic has called Belgium the 'ugliest country in the world', but others have admired its freedom and variety.

The Antwerp architect Bob van Reeth, who was appointed chief architect of Flanders in 1998, retains the modernists' affection for clean white forms and nautical details, while Charles Vandenhove of Liège creates interesting urban experiments that blend old buildings with modernist details. The Louvain-la-

Neuve university campus at Woluwé-St-Pierre in Brussels has several organic buildings by Lucien Kroll, including Alma metro station, which is reminiscent of Gaudi. Other modern architects retain a vernacular attachment to Flemish brick, including Luc Schuiten, Marcel Raymaekers, Jacques Sequaris and Marc Dessauvage.

Much of the effort in recent years has been directed towards preserving the architectural heritage of Belgium. Encouraged by enormous public interest during the annual Heritage Days, the authorities are increasingly committed to preserving the old fabric of cities such as Ghent and Bruges, and finding new uses for the country's many disused castles, monasteries, factories and warehouses.

Sculpture

Romanesque sculpture

There is not much Romanesque sculpture in Belgium due to the poor quality of the local stone, which is either soft and crumbly sandstone or the exceptionally hard black Tournai marble. Some of the finest surviving works are the **Mosan ivories** dating from the 10C and 11C in the treasury of Onze Lieve Vrouw at Tongeren, the Musée Curtius in Liège, and the Musée du Cinquantenaire in Brussels. Excellent **champlevé enamel** was produced in the Meuse region in the 12C, while Godefroid de Huy produced outstanding work, such as his reliquary of Pope Alexander of 1145 in the Musée du Cinquantenaire in Brussels. High quality **metalwork** from this period also survives, including the wonderful bronze font at St Barthélemy in Liège, probably cast in 1107–18 by Renier de Huy. Its graceful figures have been seen as a revival of Classical Greek models. The font of 1149 from St Germanus at Tienen, now in the Musée du Cinquantenaire, has a more primitive vigour.

The lovely *Reliquary of Notre-Dame* at Tournai was produced by Nicolas of Verdun at the end of the 12C. Many other beautiful works by anonymous artists have survived from this period, such as the 12C Châsse St Hadelin at Visé and the 13C Châsse St Remaclus at Stavelot.

Sculptors working in wood often carved seated Madonnas known as Sedes Sapientae. The contrast between popular and aristocratic art is illustrated by the primitive but powerful Virgin from Evegnée, now in the Musée d'Art Mosan in Liège, and the more elegant and gentle image in the Musée du Cinquantenaire in Brussels. There are also simple but eloquent wooden crucifixes at Tongeren, Tancremont and Liège.

The architectural division between Mosan and Scaldian styles also applies to Romanesque sculpture. The **Mosan style** led to the mysterious iconography of the ancient doorways of Sainte Gertrude at Nivelles and the lovely Virgin of Dom Rupert originally from the Abbey of St Laurent, Liège, and now in the Musée Curtius. The Virgin portrayed suckling her child is an early example of a motif which is endlessly repeated in Flemish art. The richest source for Scaldian architectural sculpture is Tournai Cathedral, with its impressive doorways and decorated capitals.

Early Gothic sculpture

The early Gothic sculpture of this region was inspired by French examples.

Different styles evolved in the Meuse, Scheldt and Brabant districts depending on the source of inspiration (some French ideas reached the Meuse region via Germany). The direct impact of Notre-Dame in Paris can be seen in the **Scheldt Gothic** of Tournai, in works such as the reliquary of St Eleutherius of 1247 in the Cathedral Treasury, and again in the sculptures representing the Genesis story and the Prophets on the Cathedral's west front. But Tournai was by no means merely a provincial outpost of the French style; a flourishing school of funerary sculpture developed here in the 14C. Much of the work was done for export, but many reliefs can still be seen in the cathedral, such as the monument to Jean de Bos, and in the local churches. Other important works of the Scheldt region include the portal of the St Janshospitaal in Bruges of c 1270, again reminiscent of French prototypes, and the monument of Hugo II, castellan of Ghent, in Ghent's Bijloke Museum.

French developments are also reflected in the **Meuse Gothic** style after c 1250, as in the churches at Tongeren and Dinant. The lovely 13C Sedes Sapientae in the St Jean church at Liège is a good example of Romanesque iconography translated into the Gothic idiom. The French influence on Mosan sculpture becomes even more marked in the 14C, making it difficult sometimes to determine the precise origin of isolated works. The Porte de Bethléem at Notre-Dame in Huy, is, despite its international character, likely to be local work.

The two outstanding Mosan sculptors of the end of the 14C were **Jean Pepin de Huy** and **Jean de Liège**. Both artists worked mostly for French courts, illustrating once again the close ties between these regions. Mosan goldsmiths' work continued to be important, though its quality was somewhat inferior to the masterpieces of the Romanesque period. The most skilled Mosan goldsmith of the 14C was **Hugo d'Oignies**, many of whose exquisite works are displayed in the treasury of the convent of Notre-Dame at Namur. There are other important, though anonymous, reliquaries at Stavelot, Amay and in Namur Cathedral.

The **Brabant Gothic** style began to dominate sculpture as well as architecture in the 14C. The region was certainly not immune to French influence, as the Black Madonna of Halle clearly illustrates, but it transformed French Gothic into its own distinctive style. We see this in Walter Paris's Virgin in Onze Lieve Vrouw ten Poelkerk at Tienen. Carved in the 1360s, it shows hints of a new energetic realism which would later be developed by Claus Sluter.

Late Gothic sculpture

Much 14C and 15C sculpture in this region was destroyed during the Iconoclasm, though a positive glut of small carved altarpieces survives from this period. These painted wooden retables, which were produced on a massive scale by anonymous craftsmen, do not fit into normal art categories. The one fact beyond dispute is that northern French and Flemish sculptors had an international influence: the sculpture of this period was once held in the same esteem as Flemish painting.

The revolutionary work of the Dutch sculptor **Claus Sluter** (d. 1405/6) had a deep impact on Flemish sculpture. Although Sluter mainly worked at the Burgundian court in Dijon, his realistic style was felt in Flanders as a result of the political union of Flanders and Burgundy in 1384. Echoes of his vivid individual figures can be seen in the eight prophets from Brussels Town Hall (now in the Musée Communal), sculpture on the church of Onze Lieve Vrouw at Halle, and the Coronation of the Virgin in St Jacques church at Liège. The retable of the church of St Salvator in Hakendover reveals a more conservative approach, which was perhaps more appropriate to small-scale works.

It is fascinating to study the interaction between painting and sculpture in this period. Art historians have drawn interesting parallels between the few remaining early 15C alabasters and metal reliefs in Belgium and miniature paintings from the same period. It has also been established that Jan van Eyck, Robert Campin and Roger van der Weyden were employed at least to colour sculpture in polychrome, if they did not actually design it. Campin and Van der Weyden came from Tournai, a centre for the production of marble reliefs (some of which are displayed in the cathedral), which has led to the suggestion that their styles may have been influenced by the local sculpture. Van der Weyden's style in turn had an enormous impact on sculpture, as is revealed by the characteristic tension between line and volume in the Entombment in the church of St Vincent in Soignies.

Some impression of the art that has been lost from this period can be gained from the stone sculpture of St Adrian in the Musée du Cinquantenaire in Brussels, which evokes tantalising reminders of the brilliant Leiden sculptor Nicolaus Gerhaerts. The restrained and beautiful *effigy of Isabella of Bourbon*, now in Antwerp Cathedral, and the *Paschal candelabrum* of 1482–83 cast by Renier van Thienen at Zoutleeuw are further relics from this exquisite period in art. On a smaller scale, the *reliquary group of Charles the Bold* carved by Gérard Loyet of Lille in 1467 (and now in the treasury of St Paul's church, Liège) illustrates the continued vitality and refinement of goldsmiths' work.

Such sculptures contrast sharply in function and style with the countless wooden altarpieces produced in the latter half of the century, mostly in Brussels. These crowded, clear-cut and richly decorated works (often including genre elements) were designed to be appreciated in detail and in their expressive and dramatic nature show the continuing influence of Roger van der Weyden. The most impressive examples include the *Claudio de Villa retable* of c 1470 in the Musée du Cinquantenaire in Brussels, the *altar of St Leonard* of 1479 in the church of St Leonardus at Zoutleeuw, and the *altarpiece of the Passion* in St Dympna at Geel dating from c 1480–90.

The emotional grip of Van de Weyden finally relaxed at the end of the 15C, leading to an unprecedented diversity. The leading master in Brussels was **Jan Borman the Elder**, whose St George retable of 1493 (now in the Musée du Cinquantenaire) is a work of superb, if slightly impersonal technique. This work is particularly admired for the naturalistic elegance of its figures, its calm and clear composition, and the perfection of detail. The choir stalls in St Sulpitius at Diest are of a similar style. The craftsmanship in Antwerp was equally excellent, being marked here by a tendency towards vivid characterisation and anecdotal detail.

The richness of this decade is illustrated by the *Crucifixion group* in St Pieter's church at Leuven, where traditional forms and emotional values are revitalised, in stark contrast to the humour of Antwerp which anticipates the 16C. Another masterpiece of this age was the *bronze effigy of Mary of Burgundy* in the Onze Lieve Vrouwekerk in Bruges, where the exquisite decoration and freer naturalism bear witness to the two decades which divide it from the equally beautiful but more austere effigy of Isabella of Bourbon in Antwerp Cathedral.

Renaissance sculpture

The sculptors of the early 16C, like the painters and architects, were engaged in a struggle to assimilate the fundamentally alien concepts of the Italian Renaissance. This certainly produced the occasional approximation to High Renaissance classicism, but it also engendered other fruits which in their decorative extravagance and material richness both perpetuate Flemish traditions and unconsciously anticipate some aspects of the 17C Baroque.

Mass production of wooden **altarpieces** reached its apogee at the beginning of the 16C. Jan Borman and his school remained important in Brussels, producing works such as the *Auderghem altar* in the Musée du Cinquantenaire, while in Antwerp the exaggeration of the local traditions of humour and characterisation led after c 1515 to distortions of form which can be compared to the Antwerp Mannerists. The *Lamentation altar* from Averbode, now in the Vleeshuis in Antwerp, is an example of this style.

Mechelen became a new centre of production at this time due to the presence of the court, but the local style here was typically more tranquil and subdued, as in the *St Dympna altarpiece* in the church at Geel, carved by Jan van Waver). Fashionable Italianate elements were absorbed into traditional formats by the French immigrant Robert Moreau in his *Oplinter altar* of c 1530 (now in the Musée du Cinquantenaire in Brussels). The advent of the Reformation, however, destroyed much of the art market and ultimately reduced the significance of devotional wooden sculpture.

The Netherlandish court began to attract artists from further afield after the Burgundian lands were absorbed by Charles V's empire. The new artists were often imbued with Renaissance ideas and eagerly responded to their patrons' increasing preoccupation with Italy. This attitude is reflected in the presence of Michelangelo's 1506 *Madonna and Child* in the Onze Lieve Vrouwekerk in Bruges.

Conrad Meit was an outstanding sculptor from Worms (d. 1550/51). His marble *Virgin and Child* in Brussels Cathedral reveals a profound if idiosyncratic understanding of Renaissance ideas and forms. Jean Mone from Metz was another distinguished German immigrant. Mone specialised in producing alabaster objects decorated with the slender motifs of the Italian Quattrocento. His alabaster altar at Onze Lieve Vrouw in Halle is particularly ornate. The sculptor **Jacques du Broeucq** (d. 1584) was another important Italianist. His masterpiece—the decoration of the church of St Waudru in Mons—was badly damaged in 1797 but several fragments have survived to illustrate his blend of Gothic and Renaissance styles.

The most influential of the progressive sculptors was **Cornelis Floris**, who was also a distinguished architect. Floris' most exuberant work is the *tabernacle of St Leonardus* in Zoutleeuw (1550–52), which takes the form of a tall Gothic tower adorned with Italianate motifs. His tomb of Jan III Mérode at Geel and rood screen in Tournai Cathedral are much more restrained. But Floris' influence, like that of his rival Hans Vredeman de Vries was mainly achieved through his engraved designs for decorative ornament, particularly strapwork and grotesques. These designs were endlessly copied from printed books circulated in the Low Countries.

The **chimneypiece** in the Vrije Museum at Bruges illustrates many of the major themes of Flemish 16C sculpture. Commissioned by Margaret of Austria to commemorate the Peace of Cambrai (1529), it was largely executed by Guyot de Beaugrant, a foreigner from Lorraine. It thus serves as a symbol of the new internationalism of the Netherlandish court. Yet the work was produced by a team of collaborating sculptors to designs by the painter Lancelot Blondeel, which reflects a Flemish practice dating back at least to the 15C. The lavish decoration and use of contrasting materials leads to the label Mannerist being applied, though the style might equally be seen as an Italian version of the Flemish Late Gothic delight in ornament and rich effects. It also contains hints of the later Baroque style in its sheer extravagance, as well as in its political use of decoration to glorify the Habsburgs.

Baroque sculpture

After the iconoclasm and uncertainty of the second half of the 16C, artists enjoyed a period of relative calm under the Archdukes Albert and Isabella. The renewed vitality of the Catholic Church in the southern Netherlands brought particular benefit to sculptors, who relied more heavily than did painters on public and religious commissions. Several outstanding sculptors rose to the challenge of furnishing the new Baroque churches or refurbishing the old buildings.

The most influential figure to emerge was **François Duquesnoy**, the son of Jérôme Duquesnoy the Elder, creator of the Manneken-Pis fountain in Brussels. Paradoxically, he spent most of his career in Rome: only two putti (on the monument of Bishop Triest) survive by him in Belgium. François Duquesnoy achieved the remarkable feat of retaining his artistic individuality in Bernini's Rome, inspiring both his brother Jérôme Duquesnoy the Younger and the prolific Artus Quellin the Elder. Jérôme the Younger's works are rather eclectic, as can be seen in Bishop Triest's monument in Ghent (on which he worked with his brother) and the statues in Notre-Dame du Sablon and Brussels Cathedral, but they were skilfully made and in touch with contemporary trends.

Artus Quellin the Elder was a more original sculptor. He mastered the formal repertory of the Baroque, but succeeded in creating personal works characterised by a vigorous grasp of observed reality. His greatest achievement was the Baroque sculpture in Amsterdam town hall, but good examples of his sculpture can be found in Belgium, particularly in the churches of Antwerp. Quellin's nephew, Artus the Younger, was also an able sculptor with a fresh approach to the conventions of the Baroque style. He was inspired by Baroque Rome and François Duquesnoy, but his later works show signs of innovation: the *St Rose of Lima* (in St Paulus, Antwerp) anticipates the greater refinement and delicacy of the Rococo, while the dramatic *Creator* in Bruges Cathedral fully exploits the possibilities of the Baroque.

The sculptor **Lucas Faydherbe** mainly worked in Mechelen, where some of his best work can be seen in the local churches. His monument to Bishop Andreas Cruesen in Mechelen cathedral is not entirely successful. The vitality of the dead cleric contrasts rather inappropriately with the rather insipid Christ and Father Time.

The Liège sculptor **Jean del Cour** (d. 1707) produced his own interpretation of the Baroque in highly accomplished works such as the *monument of Bishop Allamont* in Ghent Cathedral (commissioned in 1667). Del Cour's figures are aristocratic and sensitive, while his beautiful draperies eventually became a recognisable mannerism. His most famous work is the *Fontaine de la Vièrge* in Liège.

Neo-classical sculpture

Sculpture, like architecture, shed its Belgian character in the 18C and followed instead the international Neo-classical style of France. This may have reflected a political shift: after being at the heart of Charles V's empire in the early 16C, the region had moved to a more peripheral role in the 18C. The number of major commissions certainly declined; several sculptors such as Gabriel Grupello were forced to move abroad in search of work.

Yet there was a final Flemish flourish in the first half of the 18C, when a series of extraordinary **wooden pulpits** were produced. They included Hendrik Verbruggen's pulpit in Brussels Cathedral, which started the trend in 1699, Michiel van der Voort's pulpit in Mechelen Cathedral of 1721–23, and Theodoor Verhaeghen's fantasy in Onze Lieve Vrouw van Hanswijk, also in Mechelen. The abundant decoration, vigour and naturalism of these works puts them firmly in the Flemish tradition.

Stone sculpture was still recognisably derived from the Quellins and the Duquesnoys at the turn of the 17C, as is seen in Grupello's numerous charming works in Brussels, but it later becomes characterised by a cool classicism. Laurent Delvaux (d. 1778) and Pieter Verschaffelt (d. 1793) both spent long periods in Rome and were fully committed to the new international style, but earlier artists such as Michiel van der Voort (d. 1737) managed to keep a foot in both the Baroque and the classical camps. Van der Voort was responsible for the Mechelen pulpit mentioned above, but his two earlier monuments in the same cathedral are distinctly classical in feeling. The ultimate triumph of classicism is represented by Delvaux's pupil G.L. Godecharle, who, significantly, later studied in Paris. Some of his work is routine, but occasionally, as in the portrait of his wife in Brussels (Musée de la Ville de Bruxelles), he achieves a more personal style.

19C–20C sculpture

The French sculptor **François Rude** lived in exile in Brussels from 1815 to 1827. His influence on Belgian sculpture was similar to David's impact on painting. This French influence returned later in the century when Auguste Rodin worked in Brussels under his master Carrier-Belleuse on the decoration of the Bourse.

Rude's emphasis on the direct observation of nature undoubtedly influenced the Belgian Willem Geefs (1805–85), whose Mausoleum of Frédéric de Mérode in Brussels Cathedral was regarded by his contemporaries as boldly realistic. The influence of eclecticism was felt in sculpture as much as in architecture and painting. With the growth of the cities, sculptors were given major commissions to decorate the façades of buildings or carve monumental statues for squares and avenues. The 19C quest for national identity led cities to put up statues of historical figures from their past. One of the most impressive of these patriotic works is Eugène Simonis' *equestrian statue of Godefroid de Bouillon*, placed in 1848 on Place Royale in Brussels. The semicircle of ten historical figures in the Parc du Petit Sablon is an appealing late 19C example of this romantic tendency.

Other works were grand allegorical groups, such as Paul de Vigne's *The Triumph of Art* and Charles van der Stappen's *The Teaching of Art*, which were added to the façade of the Musée des Beaux Arts in Brussels in the 1880s. **Thomas Vinçotte** (1850–1925) was highly acclaimed for his Belgium between Agriculture and Industry on the pediment of the Palais Royal in Brussels, while Jacques de Lalaing

(1858–1917) gained recognition for his majestic tomb to the English killed at the battle of Waterloo in the Brussels commune cemetery at Evere.

The Botanical Gardens in Brussels includes works by most of the important Belgian sculptors of the 19C, including **Constantin Meunier** (1831–1905), whose romantic sculptures of heroic workers struck a chord in industrialised Europe. Meunier based much of his work on the Borinage mining district, near Mons, where the deplorable conditions also shocked Van Gogh. We can see some of Meunier's best works in a museum in Brussels located in his former home and studio.

The Flemish sculptor **Jef Lambeaux** (1852–1908) was inspired by the Renaissance works of Giambologna, a Flemish artist whose work Lambeaux had seen in Florence. Lambeaux's exuberant nude figures often proved too sensual for late 19C tastes. His large relief of the Human Passions, carved in 1889, remains locked up in a Neo-classical pavilion designed by Victor Horta in the Parc du Cinquantenaire. Yet we can judge his exceptional talent from the *Brabo fountain* of 1887 in Antwerp's Grote Markt.

The Flemish sculptor Julien Dillens (1849–1904) created works that are Symbolist or even Art Nouveau in style. His affinity with Art Nouveau was strengthened by his use of ivory imported from the Belgian Congo in the 1890s. Another Flemish sculptor, Jules Lagae, is best known for his *Expiation* in the Ghent fine art museum, in which he captures the pathos of struggling prisoners.

Victor Rousseau produced small figures in bronze and marble based on classical forms. His works gained a greater sensibility after he encountered the works of Rodin. George Minne is best known for his elongated kneeling boys on a fountain opposite Ghent Cathedral, though he also worked as an illustrator. His use of line in his graphic work influenced his sculpture, particularly in the creation of emotive subjects.

The painter Rik Wouters (1882–1916) began his career as a sculptor. Ernest Wijnants (1878–1964) and Oscar Jespers (1887–1970) anticipated Modernism in their primitive and almost abstract forms. Contemporary trends in Belgian sculpture can be appreciated at the outstanding open-air museum of late 19C and 20C sculpture established at Middelheim, Antwerp.

BRUSSELS

Brussels is a cosmopolitan city with several outstanding museums and a fascinating architectural heritage. Known as Bruxelles in French and Brussel in Dutch, the city has been officially bilingual since 1963. All street signs and official notices are written in both French and Dutch, though French is the main spoken language of both Belgians and foreigners. English is often used in business and tourism to avoid the linguistic conflict. About one quarter of the population of just under one million are foreigners. Many work for the European Union, NATO or one of the many international companies, lobby groups and political organisations based in the city.

Brussels is the capital of Belgium, Flanders and Europe. Both the European Union (EU) and the North Atlantic Treaty Organisation (NATO) have their headquarters in Brussels. Each of these organisations has its own diplomatic representation which is quite separate from the diplomats accredited to the Belgian government. Brussels was officially recognised as the capital of Europe in 1992.

The city's ambition after the Second World War to gain recognition as an international centre has resulted in a sad disregard for the fabric of the old city. Many of the handsome tree-lined avenues have been turned into urban motorways, while distinguished residential neighbourhoods have been sacrificed to build office districts. The new Brussels Region authority established in 1988 has been less willing to tolerate such brutal destruction: after decades of neglect the city is now gradually restoring historic buildings, revitalising scarred neighbourhoods and promoting public transport. Yet there are still many derelict buildings and empty sites left over from the bad old days.

It perhaps does not help Brussels that the city is divided into 19 communes which have their own town halls and administrative structures. Some, though, would argue that this helps to give Brussels its extraordinary diversity of neighbourhoods, ranging from the Parisian allure of Rue Dansaert and the grand boulevards to the vaguely English suburbs of Uccle and Woluwé.

The visitor who explores Brussels will find attractive old streets and local markets, scintillating Art Nouveau cafés and some of the best restaurants in northern Europe. Tourists tend to spend their time in Brussels commune, which roughly covers the old town (often dubbed the Pentagon). The historic heart of the city, Brussels commune is enclosed by a belt of wide boulevards, about 8km in length, built from 1818–71 along the course of the medieval ramparts. The area within the boulevards includes the Lower Town, around the Grand-Place and the Place de Brouckère, which is the main shopping and restaurant district. The higher ground to the south is occupied by the Upper Town, where the nobility settled in the 15C. These quarters now contain the main museums and art galleries, the Palais du Roi and the Parc de Bruxelles, the huge Palais de Justice, and the European Quarter. The slopes between the Lower and Upper Towns have always proved an awkward area to develop. It is here that we find the Cathedral, central station and a terraced garden known as the Mont des Arts.

The buildings on Grand-Place and the narrow streets nearby are splendid survivals from the past and there are also handsome 18C squares and interesting districts of 19C architecture. Some of the former charm was sacrificed in the 1960s and 1970s to build high-rise blocks in the centre and along the main boulevards. A more sensitive style of architecture can be seen in the new European Parliament building near Parc Leopold, the Ministry of Foreign Affairs building in the Rue des Petits-Carmes and the twin office blocks on Place Stéphanie.

Practical information

Getting there
By air

Brussels has a large and modern international airport at Zaventem, 14km northeast of the city. Airport trains run every 20 minutes to the Gare du Nord, Gare Centrale and Gare du Midi. The journey from the airport takes about 25 minutes to the Gare Centrale. Seasoned travellers pick up taxis outside the departure hall to benefit from a slight reduction in the fare. The airport has a post office, several banks and a range of restaurants.

By car

Brussels is an unforgiving city for car drivers. Parking is difficult and roads are often jammed. Trams have priority, as do cars coming from the right and pedestrians on crossings. The city has a number of urban motorways with tunnels and slip roads which present further terrors for the novice. Despite such drawbacks, most people in Brussels continue to drive everywhere.

By train

Brussels has three main railway stations linked by an underground junction line. Most trains to Brussels stop at each of the three stations. The most important for international travel is the *Gare du Midi*, which is the terminus for *Eurostar* trains to London and *Thalys* trains to Paris and Amsterdam. The smaller *Gare Centrale* is convenient for Grand-Place and the old town. The *Gare du Nord* is close to Place Rogier and the Manhattan Centre.

Brusseis has several smaller railway stations, including Schuman, which is convenient for the European Commission, and Quartier Leopold, which adjoins the European Parliament. The stations at Gare du Midi, Gare Centrale and Schuman are linked to the metro network.

Where to stay
Hotels

Most hotels in Brussels are designed for business travellers. They often cut their rates dramatically at weekends (from Friday evening to Monday morning).

£££ *Amigo*, Rue de l'Amigo 1, ☎ 02.511.59.10, is an elegant hotel off Grand-Place built on the site of an old Spanish prison called the Amigo.

£££ *Métropole*, Place de Brouckère 31, ☎ 02.217.23.00, is a grand hotel of 1895 designed by Alban Chambon.

£££ *Radisson SAS*, Rue Fossé aux Loups 47, ☎ 02.227.31.31, is a striking modern hotel in the old town with a lofty atrium incorporating a reconstructed fragment of the 12C city wall.

££ *Ustel*, Square de l'Aviation 6, ☎ 02.520.60.53, is a comfortable hotel conveniently located 5 minutes from the Eurostar terminal. The hotel restaurant serves good French cuisine in a converted 19C pumping house.

££ *New Siru*, Place Rogier 1, ☎ 02.217.75.80, is an unusual Art Deco hotel with each room decorated by a Belgian artist.

££ *Rembrandt*, Rue de la Concorde 42, ☎ 02.512.71.39, is an inexpensive hotel in a 19C town house off Avenue Louise.

£ Lloyd George, Avenue Lloyd George 12, ☎ 02.648.30.72, is a friendly and inexpensive hotel facing the Bois de la Cambre.

£ Welcome, Rue du Peuplier 5, ☎ 02.219.95.46, is a friendly small hotel in a quiet quarter of the old town near the Eglise du Béguinage.

Eating out
Restaurants

Brussels is famous for its excellent cooking. Its restaurants range from informal corner bistros to world-famous restaurants.

£££ Comme Chez Soi, Place Rouppe 23, ☎ 02.512.29.21. One of the great restaurants of Europe. Pierre Wynants' cooking invariably lives up to expectations, and tables are often booked months in advance.

£££ Ecailler du Palais Royal, Rue Bodenbroeck 18, ☎ 02.512.87.51. An elegant old Belgian fish restaurant.

£££ Inada, Rue de la Source 73, ☎ 02.538.01.13. A stylish French restaurant with an impressive wine list.

££ Aux Armes de Bruxelles, Rue des Bouchers 13, ☎ 02.511.55.98. A traditional restaurant from 1921.

££ La Belle Maraîchère, Place Sainte-Catherine 11, ☎ 02.512.97.59. An old-fashioned fish restaurant near the former fish market.

££ Bistro du Mail, Rue du Mail 81, ☎ 02.539.06.97. One of the best new restaurants in the city.

££ De Hoef, Rue Edith Cavell 218, ☎ 02.374.34.17. A country inn from 1627 with a rustic interior.

££ Idiot du Village, Rue Notre-Seigneur 18, ☎ 02.502.55.82. An intimate restaurant with a charming interior near the flea market.

££ Jacques, Quai aux Briques 44, ☎ 02.513.27.62. Where Belgians go for copious portions of mussels and frites.

££ La Quincaillerie, Rue du Page 45, ☎ 02.538.25.53. An intriguing brasserie located in a former iron-monger's shop.

££ Rosticceria Fiorentina, Rue Archimède 45, ☎ 02.734.92.36. Utterly Italian.

££ La Roue d'Or, Rue des Chapeliers 26, ☎ 02.514.25.54. A bustling brasserie with murals in the style of Magritte.

££ Vieux St-Martin, Place du Grand Sablon 38, ☎ 02.512.64.76. An excellent brasserie offering typical Brussels dishes such as rabbit cooked in Kriek beer.

££ Vincent, Rue des Dominicains 8, ☎ 02.511.23.03. A solid Belgian restaurant with tile murals.

£ Le Cosmopolite, Avenue de Cortenberg 36, ☎ 02.280.18.70. Modern brasserie in the European Quarter with excellent salads. Open for breakfast.

£ Chez Jean, Rue des Chapeliers 6, ☎ 02.511.98.15. A traditional Belgian restaurant near Grand-Place with excellent mussels and frites.

£ Chez Léon, Rue des Bouchers 18, ☎ 02.511.14.15. Bustling restaurant famous for mussels.

£ Gallery Resto-Bar, Rue du Grand Cerf 7, ☎ 02.511.80.35. Delicate Vietnamese dishes in an airily minimalist interior.

£ Intermezzo, Rue des Princes 16, ☎ 02.351.09.37. Crowded Italian cantina next to the Théâtre Royal de la Monnaie with excellent pasta dishes. Open lunchtime Monday to Saturday and Friday evening.

£ 't Kelderke, Grand-Place 15, ☎ 02.513.73.44. Friendly basement restaurant.

£ Pacifique, Boulevard Général Jacques 115, ☎ 02.640.52.59. Popular Vietnamese restaurant in the university district.

£ Thoumieux, Rue Américaine 124, ☎ 02.538.99.09. Brussels branch of a famous Parisian brasserie offering regional specialities from central France.

Cafés

Café life in Brussels has been flourishing since the late 19C. There are several grand old cafés in the Lower Town, such as *Le Falstaff*, Rue Henri Maus 17–23, a handsome Art Nouveau café of 1904, part of which has been turned into a salsa bar, and the older but no less glittering *Le Cirio*, Rue de la Bourse 18, founded in 1886. *Le Métropole*, Place de Brouckère 31, is a grand late 19C café with signed photographs of famous former customers.

Several attractive cafés occupy the old guild houses on Grand-Place, including *La Chaloupe d'Or* at no. 24 and *La Brouette* at no 3.

Getting around
Public transport

The public transport system in Brussels works well, though it takes some time to get to grips with the network of metro routes, tram lines and buses. The *metro* is useful for reaching the Lower Town, Heysel, the European Union district, and the Erasmus House. The *tram network* provides a slower but sometimes more scenic means of getting to places such as Avenue Louise and Place Royale. The network is operated by the Société des Transports Intercommunaux Bruxellois (Stib). Single tickets can be bought on trams and buses, but it is cheaper to buy a card for ten journeys or a one-day ticket at metro stations and newsagents displaying a Stib sticker. Tickets are valid for one hour's travel on the Stib network and on trains within Brussels. The tickets are validated by insert them into the orange machine each time you board a vehicle. The machine reads the magnetic strip to determine if it is still valid. A plan of the network can be picked up at tourist offices or from the Stib offices at Porte de Namur, Rogier and Midi metro stations.

Taxis

Taxis are useful for those in a hurry though hardly necessary for most trips. The service charge is included in the price shown on the meter, but it is customary to round up the fare to a convenient sum. Bear in mind that taxi drivers often carry a minimum of change and some drivers have scarcely any knowledge of the city.

Tourist information

The **Brussels tourist office** is in the town hall, Grand-Place. It provides tourist information on Brussels only. The staff will book hotel rooms and reserve tickets for cultural events. Open daily in summer 09.00–18.00 and in winter daily 10.00–14.00. It is closed on Sundays from 1 Jan to 28 Feb. ☎ 02.513.89.40. The **Belgian tourist office** at 61 Rue du Marché aux Herbes stocks some information on Brussels (see p 22 for opening hours). It stands on the site of a meat market founded in the 12C.

Post offices

The main post office is located on the first floor of the Centre Monnaie, Boulevard Anspach and is open Mon–Sat 08.00–20.00. The office at Avenue Fonsny 48, near the Gare du Midi, is open 24 hours a day for stamps and registered letters.

Telephones

Most public telephones work with telephone cards (Telecards) sold in post offices, large supermarkets and some newsagents. The most recent phone boxes also take credit cards and bank cards fitted with a Proton chip. Some also take coins. The latest public telephones have screens providing instructions in several languages. The code for the UK is: 00 + 44 + the area code minus the initial 0. The code for the USA is: 00 + 1 + the area code minus the initial 0.

Faxes

Most hotels will send and receive faxes for guests. Many photocopy shops provide a similar service. Faxes can be sent from the main telephone office, Boulevard de l'Impératrice 13. Open daily 07.00–22.00.

Banks

Banks in Brussels are normally open Mon–Fri 09.15–15.30. Change offices are often open longer hours, but may charge a higher commission rate. It is best to check the rate before the transaction. Convenient change offices are located at Zaventem airport, the Gare du Midi and the Gare du Nord (open daily 07.00–23.00) and the Gare Centrale (open daily 08.00–21.00).
Two main banks are:
Fortis, Rue de la Colline 12, off Grand-Place.
BBL, Boulevard Anspach 2.

Churches

The English Church is at Rue Capitaine Crespel 29. The Scottish Church is at Chaussée de Vleurgat 181. The Great Synagogue is at Rue de la Régence 32. The Mosque is in the Parc du Cinquantenaire.

Organised tours

Several organisations provide guided tours of the city's art and culture. The urban action group *Arau* has been organising well-informed bus tours of Art Nouveau and Art Deco architecture since 1969. The *Arcadia* tours cover aspects of Belgian art, while Itinéraires often covers literary themes and eccentric topics such as the chocolate industry. The *De Fonderie* tours are concerned with industrial history and Pro Vélo offers cycling tours of Brussels. More conventional bus tours are operated every day by *De Boeck's Sightseeing Tours*, Rue de la Colline 8. Tours of the European Union buildings are organised by the *Visitors' Service of the European Commission*, ☎ 02.299.91.06.

Boat tours of the port of Brussels leave from the modern quay off Place Sainctelette and are organised by *La Fonderie*, ☎ 02.410.99.50.

Details of most tours can be obtained from the Brussels tourist office; some are also published in *The Bulletin.*

Media

Major foreign newspapers and magazines are widely available in Brussels. Many international residents consider the *Financial Times* as the best source of serious Brussels news. The English language weekly *The Bulletin* also covers Belgian news and culture. It has a useful listings section.

Bookshops

Several bookshops in Brussels specialise in English language books and magazines. The largest English bookshop is *Waterstone's*, Boulevard Adolphe Max 71. *Sterling Books*, Rue du Fossé-aux-Loups 38, has a good range of books and magazines at slightly lower prices. The *Reading Room*, Avenue Georges Henri 503, is a friendly bookshop with a café. *Posada*, Rue de la Madeleine 29, is an outstanding art bookshop run by a dedicated bibliophile. The *Librairie des Galeries*, Galerie du Roi 2, specialises in glossy art books. *Tropismes*, Galerie des Princes, is a French bookshop with an irresistible Parisian atmosphere. *De Slegde* bookshop, Rue des Grands Carmes 17, often has second-hand novels and remaindered academic studies in English.

Library

The **Flemish Library**, Place de la Monnaie 6, is the best public library in Brussels. It has an excellent collection of books on Brussels. Books can be consulted without joining the library. Open

Mon and Sat 12.00–17.00, Tues–Fri 10.00–20.00.

Television

The cable companies in Brussels provide more than 30 channels, including at least five French channels, four Flemish channels, three Dutch channels, three German channels, BBC 1 and BBC 2, CNN, Italian Rai Uno, Portuguese RTP and Spanish TVE. The Flemish and Dutch channels screen English programmes in the original language. The French and German channels tend to dub foreign programmes. *The Bulletin* is a useful source of television listings.

Theatre

Most plays in Brussels are performed in French at venues such as the sumptuous 18C **Théâtre Royal du Parc** and the aggressively modern **Théâtre Varia**. The grand **Koninklijke Vlaams Schouwburg** stages plays in Dutch and occasionally English.

Opera

The Théâtre Royal de la Monnaie, Place de la Monnaie, is a handsome 19C opera house with a solid reputation for the classics.

Puppet theatres

Puppet theatres opened in Brussels in the 16C after the Spanish rulers closed down the city's theatres. **Toone**, Petite Rue des Bouchers, continues to stage traditional marionette performances in Brussels dialect. Some plays are performed in English for the benefit of tourists.

Cinemas

The cinemas in Brussels offer an eclectic range of films in French, Dutch, English and other languages. The largest cinema is **Kinepolis**, a 24-screen complex with an Imax theatre. The opening of this complex in 1989 forced many of the city's older downtown cinemas to close down, yet it also prompted the **UGC De Brouckère** to modernise its 10-screen complex in the town centre. The large cinema complexes tend to concentrate on mainstream films, while smaller cinemas such as **Arenberg Galeries** and **Vendôme** offer some of the best international avant-garde films. Most films are screened in the original language with subtitles (indicated as version originale or VO), though some Hollywood blockbusters are released with French dubbing (indicated as *version française* or VF). *The Bulletin* provides a weekly listing of films.

Brussels by night

The exciting bars and clubs in Brussels are often difficult to track down. Lively venues are clustered along the Rue du Marché-au-Charbon, off Grand-Place. Friendly Irish pubs are found around the Schuman metro station, close to the European institutions.

Floodlighting

Many of the great buildings in Brussels are floodlit after dark, including the Grand-Place, the Baroque Eglise Saint Jean Baptiste au Béguinage, the Eglise Sainte Catherine, the Bourse, the Cathédrale Saint Michel, the Place Royale and the Palais de Justice. Another night attraction is Notre-Dame du Sablon's stained glass lit from inside.

Markets

Brussels boasts more than 100 regular street markets. Most of the city's communes and neighbourhoods have a weekly market. The city also has several specialised markets on fixed days.

The best local markets are held on **Place Sainte Catherine** in the city centre (daily 07.00–17.00), **Place Flagey** in Ixelles (daily 08.00–13.00), **Place du Châtelain** in Ixelles (Wed 14.00–19.00), **Place Wiener** in Boitsfort (Sun 08.00–13.00) and **Place**

St Job in Uccle (Mon 08.00–13.00). The largest general market takes place near the **Gare du Midi** on Sun (05.00–13.00).

A large flea market takes place on the **Place du Jeu de Balle** (daily 06.00–14.00). A more expensive antique market is held on the **Place du Grand Sablon** (Sat 09.00–18.00 and Sun 09.00–14.00). **Grand-Place** is the setting for a flower market (daily 08.00–18.00) and a weekly bird market (Sun 07.00–14.00).

Opening times

Most museums in Brussels are closed on Mondays, 1 January, 1 May, 1 and 11 November, 25 December and election days. The Musées Royaux des Beaux-Arts and Autoworld are accessible to wheelchairs.

Lower town

Album museum (collection of cultural ephemera) , Rue des Chartreux 25, is open Wed–Mon 13.00–18.00.

Hôtel de Ville, Grand-Place, can only be visited on a guided tour. Tours in English are Tues 11.30 and 15.15, Wed 15.15, Sun 12.15. (Not Sun Oct–Mar.) Details of tours in other languages from the tourist office on Grand-Place or the reception desk at the visitors' entrance of the town hall.

Musée de la Ville de Bruxelles (Brussels history), in the Maison du Roi, Grand-Place, is open Mon–Thur 10.00–12.30 and 13.30–17.00; Sat and Sun 10.00–13.00. It is closed on Fri.

Musée de Costume et Dentelle (Museum of Costume and Lace), Rue de la Violette 6, is open Apr–Sept, Thur–Tues 10.00–12.30 and 13.30–17.00; Oct–Mar Mon, Tues, Thur and Fri 10.00–12.30 and 13.30–16.00, and weekends 14.00–16.30.

Historium (waxwork tableaux of Belgian history), Anspach Centre, Boulevard Anspach, is open daily 10.00–18.00.

Centre Belge de la Bande Dessinnée (comic strip art), Rue des Sables 20, is open Tues–Sun 10.00–18.00.

Musée des Chemins-de-Fer Belges (history of Belgium's railways), Gare du Nord, is open Mon–Fri and on the first Sat of the month 09.00–16.30.

Upper town

Coudenberg palace (archaeological museum), Place Royale 10, is open for guided tours Wed and Sat 13.00–17.00 and Sun 10.00–14.00.

Musée des Beaux-Arts (Fine Arts), Rue de la Régence, is open Tues–Sun 10.00–17.00 (the Musée d'Art Ancien closes 12.00–13.00 and the Musée d'Art Moderne closes 13.00–14.00).

Musée des Instruments de Musique (Musical Instrument Collection). Montagne de la Cour 2, re-opens in June 2000. Tues–Sun 09.30–1700; open Thur until 20.00.

Musée de la Dynastie (Museum of the Belgian royal family), Hôtel Bellevue, Place des Palais 7, open Tues–Sun 10.00–16.00.

Musée du Cinéma (History of Cinema), Rue Baron Horta 9, is open daily 17.30–23.00.

Musée Postal (Postal Museum), Place du Grand Sablon 40, is open Tues–Sat 10.00–16.00.

National Library

The **Bibliothèque Royale Albert I** (Royal Library), Mont des Arts, Boulevard de l'Empereur, and the Chapelle de Nassau (Gothic chapel of the Nassau Mansion), are open Mon–Sat 09.00–17.00. **The Musée de l'Imprimerie** (Printing Museum), in the same building, is open the same hours. The **Musée du Livre** (manuscripts, documents and bookbinding), is open Mon, Wed and Sat, 14.00–17.00. The **Chalcography department** (engravings and prints for sale) is open Mon–Fri 09.00–12.45 and 14.00–16.45. The **Literature**

Museum is open Mon–Fri 09.00–17.00.

Cinquantenaire and Leopold parks
The Palais du Cinquantenaire in the Parc du Cinquantenaire contains the Musée du Cinquantenaire (museum of art and history), open Tues–Sun 10.00–17.00.

Musée Royal de l'Armée et d'Histoire Militaire (military history), in the same complex, is open Tues–Sun 09.00–12.00 and 13.00–16.30.

Autoworld (car collection), also in the Palais, is open daily 10.00–18.00 (closes 17.00 Oct–Mar).

Musée des Sciences Naturelles (Natural History Museum), Parc Léopold, Rue Vautier, is open Tues–Fri 09.30–16.45; Sat and Sun 10.00–18.00.

Musée Wiertz (paintings by Antoine Wiertz), Rue Vautier 62, is open Tues–Fri 10.00–12.00 and 13.00–17.00 (closes at 16.00 Nov–Mar) and every second weekend. ☎ 02.648.17.18 for details.

Heysel and Laeken park
The **Atomium** (giant model of a molecule), Parc des Expositions, Heysel, is open from Apr–Aug daily 09.00–20.00; Sept–Mar daily 10.00–18.00.

Mini-Europe (model buildings from the EU countries), Bruparck, Heysel, is open daily in Jul and Aug 09.30–20.00; Sept–Jun daily 10.00–17.00.

The **Pavillon Chinois and the Tour Japonaise** (Chinese and Japanese decorative art), Avenue Van Praet, Laeken, are open Tues–Sun 10.00–16.45.

Ixelles and Saint Gilles
Musée Horta (house of architect Victor Horta), Rue Americaine 25, is open Tues–Sun 14.00–17.30.

Espace Photographique Contretype, Avenue de la Jonction 1 (a photography gallery occupying the striking Art Nouveau town house built by Jules Brunfaut in 1902) is open Tues–Sun 13.00–18.30. It is closed mid-Jul–mid-Aug.

Musée des Beaux-Arts d'Ixelles (Ixelles Museum 19C and 20C art), Rue Jean Van Volsem 71, is open from Tues–Fri 13.00–18.30, Sat and Sun 10.00–17.00.

Musée Constantin Meunier (home of sculptor and painter Constantin Meunier), Rue de l'Abbaye 59, is open Tues–Fri 10.00–12.00 and 13.00–16.45 (and occasionally at weekends).

The **Porte de Hal** (south gate of the ancient city, exhibition of historic interiors), junction of Boulevard du Midi and Boulevard de Waterloo, is open Tues–Sun 10.00–17.00.

Anderlecht

The **Maison d'Erasme** (house once occupied by Desiderius Erasmus containing a small collection of 15C and 16C paintings), Rue du Chapitre 31, Anderlecht, and Béguinage (former nunnery, now folk museum), Rue du Chapelain 8, are closed on Tues and Fri. Both are open other days 10.00–12.00 and 14.00–17.00.

Musée Bruxellois de la Gueuze (beer brewing museum), Rue Gheude 56, is open Mon–Fri 08.30–17.00, Sat 10.00–17.00.

Musée de la Résistance (memorabilia of the Resistance), Rue Van Lint 14, is open Mon–Fri 09.00–12.00 and 13.00–16.00. Closed weekends.

Other museums

Musée David et Alice van Buuren (art collection and garden), Avenue Leo Errera 41, Uccle, is open Sun 13.00–18.00 and Mon 14.00–18.00. The garden is open every afternoon 14.00–17.30

Musée Charlier (fine art and furniture), Avenue des Arts 16, St-Josse, is open Mon 10.00–17.00, Tues–Thur 13.30–17.00, Fri 13.30–16.30. Closed weekends.

Musée Magritte, Rue Esseghem 135,

Jette, is open Wed–Sun 10.00–18.00. No more than 20 visitors are admitted at one time.

Musée Nationale de la Figurine Historique (collection of figurines representing historical scenes, also the municipal museum of Jette), Rue J. Tiebackx 14, Jette, is open Tues–Fri and on the first weekend of the month 14.00–17.00.

Musée du Transport Urbain Bruxellois (Museum of Urban Transport), Avenue de Tervuren 364b, Woluwe, is open from Apr (first Sat) to Oct (first Sun) on Sat, Sun and public holidays 13.30–19.00. Vintage trams run from Woluwé to Tervuren 14.00–18.00.

CHURCHES

The **cathedral** is open daily 08.00–18.00.

Eglise Saint Nicolas, Rue au Beurre, is open daily 08.00–18.00.

Notre-Dame du Sablon, Rue de la Régence, is open daily 08.00–18.00. Basilica Nationale du Sacré-Coeur, Avenue Charles Quint, Koekelberg, is open Mon–Sat 08.00–18.00 (closes 17.00 Nov to Easter). Cupola (view of Brussels) open 09.00–17.15 (late Apr–late Oct) and 10.00–15.45 (late Oct–late Apr).

Eglise St Pierre et St Guidon, Anderlecht is open Mon–Fri 09.00–12.00 and 14.00–17.30. Closed on Sat, Sun and during services.

OTHER SIGHTS

Palais de Justice, Place Poelaert, is open daily from 09.00–12.00 and 14.00–16.00, closed Sat, Sun and on public holidays.

Palais Royal, Place des Palais, is open daily from late July to early September 10.30–16.30.

History

Archaeological excavations have proved that the site of Brussels was occupied as long ago as neolithic times. The river Senne, which now runs through a 19C tunnel, originally formed an extensive area of marsh. After the withdrawal of the Romans, the marshes offered the Gallo-Roman inhabitants a safe refuge from the Franks. The city's name may be derived from the old Dutch word Bruocsella (Broekzele) meaning a village on a marsh.

There is a shadowy connection with the 6C Saint Géry, who is said to have built a chapel on one of the islands, on a site now occupied by Place Saint Géry. The first recorded reference to Brussels occurs in a document of 966. The village gradually grew more important, largely because it provided an easy river crossing on the old trade route from Cologne to Ghent and Bruges. The settlement passed in 977 to the dukes of Lower Lotharingia, who built a castle on an island in the Senne. A chapel on the island was dedicated to St Géry. The ducal residence was moved in 1041 to the low hill to the south known as the Coudenberg. The new castle, which occupied a site near the Parc de Bruxelles, developed into the most important palace in the 15C Netherlands. Six years after the new palace was begun, a church dedicated to St Michael was built on the heights above the lower town.

The first fortified wall was built in the early 12C. Three towers from this wall are still standing: the Tour Noire, the Tour Villers and the Tour Anneessens. Local merchants established a market in the 12C, which later became the Grand-Place. The growing power of the bourgeoisie was confirmed by the Charter of Cortenberg granted in 1312 and confirmed in 1356 on the occasion of the 'Joyeuse Entrée' of Wenceslas of Luxembourg and Joanna of Brabant.

New walls enclosing a wider area were built between 1357 and 1383. Strengthened in the 16C, these defences remained standing until the 19C, when, apart from the Porte de Hal, they were demolished to construct the ring boulevards.

As Brussels prospered, the citizens acquired a taste for luxury goods such as lace, tapestry, jewellery and retables. Work began in 1402 on the Hôtel de Ville. The Dukes of Brabant were succeeded by the ambitious Dukes of Burgundy, who favoured Brussels over their former capital of Dijon. Under their rule, the city became famous for ostentatious luxury, skilled craftsmen and dazzling banquets.

During the rule of Margaret of Austria, the capital was moved from Brussels to the quieter town of Mechelen. On the death of Margaret, Charles V transferred the capital of the Netherlands back to Brussels in 1531. He made his abdication speech in 1555 in the Coudenberg Palace. Under the repressive régime of his son, Philip II, Counts Egmont and Hoorn were executed in the Grand-Place in 1568.

The Spanish government relaxed its grip during the enlightened rule of the Archdukes Albert and Isabella (1598–1621), but disaster struck Brussels during the War of the Grand Alliance in 1695 when the French army under Marshal Villeroi bombarded the city for 36 hours, destroying 16 churches and nearly 4000 houses. Most of the buildings on the Grand-Place were reduced to rubble, but they were rapidly rebuilt over the next four years.

Brussels opened its gates to Marlborough in 1706 during the War of the Spanish Succession. When the war ended in 1713, this region was given to the Austrian Habsburgs under the Treaty of Utrecht. Six years later, the leader of the city guilds, Frans Anneessens, was beheaded in the Grand-Place for defending the privileges of Brussels against the demands of its Austrian rulers.

Although the region was occupied in 1746 by the French under Marshal Saxe during the War of the Austrian Succession, the territory was later restored to Austria. Under the rule of the cultured Charles of Lorraine, appointed governor by his sister-in-law Maria Theresa, Brussels enjoyed a period of peace and prosperity. Determined to make Brussels a northern Vienna during the second half of the 18C, Charles built the Palais du Roi, partly on the site of the old Coudenberg palace which had burnt down in 1731. The Palais de la Nation and the Place Royale were constructed at the same time.

Following the French Revolution, Brussels was demoted to the capital of the French department of the Dyle. Saved in 1815 from a further period of French occupation by the Battle of Waterloo, which was fought 20km south of the city, Brussels alternated with The Hague as the royal residence of King William I. Finally, Belgium, an unwilling partner in the United Kingdom of the Netherlands, revolted against the Dutch in 1830. The revolution began in Brussels' Théâtre de la Monnaie on 25 August.

The transformation of Brussels into a modern city began soon after Belgian independence was recognised. Keen to assert itself as the capital of an independent nation, the city embarked on a frantic period of demolition and construction. Large areas of rotting slums were cleared, to be replaced by handsome boulevards inspired by 19C Paris. The Brussels Free University was founded in 1834 and continental Europe's first passenger train service ran from Brussels to Mechelen in 1835. The Galeries Saint Hubert were opened in 1846, the Palais de Justice built from 1866–83, and the risk of typhoid was reduced by the covering of the River Senne in 1871. The ring boulevards were completed in the same year, allowing the Upper Town to develop in the direction of the Parc du Cinquantenaire and the Bois de la Cambre. The improvements were largely due to the energy of Burgomaster Anspach. The great Jubilee Exhibition of 1880 in the Parc du Cinquantenaire also led to many improvements in the eastern districts.

When the First World War broke out, Brussels was left undefended. The German army entered the city on 20 August 1914. The passive resistance of the people was encouraged by Burgomaster Adolphe Max, who was deported for refusing to co-operate with the Germans. During the war, the underground newspaper La Libre Belgique was produced in the capital.

The English nurse Edith Cavell was condemned to death in 1915 for helping fugitive soldiers to escape to the neutral Netherlands. She was shot by firing squad at the national rifle range in Schaerbeek, declaring before she died, 'Patriotism is not enough. I must have no hatred in my soul.' The following year, the Belgian heroine Gabrielle Petit was executed by the Germans for her part in the resistance.

Occupied again by the Germans during the Second World War, the citizens once again resorted to resistance. During the occupation from May 1940 to September 1944, a secret network based in Brussels helped many Allied airmen and resistance fighters to escape.

The postwar years have seen a vigorous modernisation of the city. The initial impetus came from the World Fair of 1958, when the futuristic Atomium was built on the north edge of the city. The ring boulevards were turned into a network of fast roads and tunnels to speed traffic to the exhibition site.

The bid to become a major capital paid off in 1958 when Brussels was selected as the provisional headquarters of the European Economic Community. Its importance increased further when NATO moved its headquarters here in 1967. This has turned Brussels into a cosmopolitan city which has played an important role in European politics. Despite this international vocation, Brussels has succeeded in preserving some of its historic identity and much convivial allure.

Art in the metro

The Brussels public transport authority has an imaginative policy of incorporating modern Belgian art in most of its underground stations. The works include mosaics, murals, sculpture, marble and tile designs. The authorities have continued this policy as new stations open, so that the Brussels underground now provides an intriguing insight into Belgian artistic trends over the past 30 years. The older works include a Pop Art construction by Marc Mendelson at Parc station, a Surrealist mural of old Brussels trams by Paul Delvaux (at Bourse station, and a giant mural by Roger Somville at Hankar. The newer stations tend to integrate art into the interior design. The station at Porte de Hal has a visionary city built into the fabric by the cartoon artist François Schuiten. Horta underground tram station in Saint Gilles incorporates fragments of demolished Art Nouveau buildings designed by Victor Horta. The Maelbeek station has a striking interior by the graphic artist Benoît. The Stib information offices stock free leaflets listing the works in the metro. A book has also been published (available at the Stib office, 6th floor, Galeries de la Toison d'Or).

1 • The Grand-Place

This walk begins on the Grand-Place (Grote Markt in Dutch), which is perhaps the most beautiful city square in Europe. The cobbled square is hemmed in by the Gothic Hôtel de Ville, the restored Maison du Roi and 39 Baroque guild houses. Many of the guild houses are occupied by cafés with blazing fires in winter and large pavement terraces in summer. Cars and buses have been banned from the square since 1972. A flower market occupies the square every day, and a bird market is held on Sunday mornings. The square becomes particularly romantic as daylight fades and the floodlit façades of the Hôtel de Ville and Maison du Roi turn from brown to gold.

The square provides a magnificent setting for the annual **Ommegang** held on two evenings in late June or early July. This pageant dates back to a religious procession in 1348. The current ceremony is based on the lavish Ommegang held in honour of Charles V in 1549 (see p 17).

A Baroque square

The square stands on an area of marshes bordering the River Senne which was drained in the 12C. It was originally named the Nedermerct (Lower Market), but renamed Grote Markt in 1380 (when Brussels was still a Dutch speaking town). Splendid tournaments were staged here in the 15C, including one in 1438 when Philip the Good fought in the lists. It was also the scene of public executions, including the beheading of Counts Egmont and Hoorn on 5 June 1568. The Duke of Alva, who ordered the executions, watched from the Maison du Roi.

The old square was destroyed in 1695 when Villeroi bombarded the town, but it was rebuilt within less than four years, as you can tell from the year stones on several of the guild houses. The square was the setting for another unjust execution in 1719 when the patriot Frans Anneessens was executed by the Austrians.

Hôtel de Ville

The Hôtel de Ville is one of the finest Gothic buildings in Europe. It can be visited on a guided tour beginning in the entrance hall to the right of the main courtyard. Tours in English are Tues 11.30 and 15.15, Wed 15.15 and Sun 12.15 (no Sun tour Oct–Mar). Tours are also given in French, Dutch and German.

A fragment of the porch has survived from an earlier stone building dating from c 1353; it is incorporated into the base of the tower.

History of the town hall

The present building was begun in 1402, when Jacob van Thienen built the east wing (to the left of the tower). The 96m tower was completed in 1455 by Jan van Ruysbroeck and surmounted by a figure of St Michael carved in 1455 by Martin van Rode. The statue was recently restored and regilded.

The first stone of the west wing was laid by the future Charles the Bold at the age of nine. Built from 1444–80, this wing is shorter than the other because the architect, whose name is unknown, was instructed not to encroach upon the Rue Tête d'Or.

The statues in the niches were added in the 19C. They mainly represent dukes and duchesses from the 14C to the 16C. Fragments of older sculpture can be seen in the Musée Communal opposite. A gateway under the tower leads to the courtyard, where two splendid Baroque fountains represent the rivers Meuse and Scheldt. The rear wing of the town hall was built in 1705–17 on the site of the cloth hall, which was destroyed in the 1695 bombardment.

The **Salle du Conseil Communal** was once the council room of the States of Brabant. It is hung with 18C tapestries based on designs by Abraham Janssens, who also painted the scene on the ceiling illustrating the Gods on Olympus. The **Salle Maximilienne** has portraits above the chimneypiece by André Cluysenaer depicting Maximilian of Austria and Mary of Burgundy. The walls are hung with 18C Brussels tapestries.

The **Picture Gallery** contains full-length portraits of Charles V, Philip the Handsome, Philip IV, Albert and Isabella, Charles II and Philip II. They were painted by Louis Grangé in 1718. The **Antechamber** contains interesting views of old Brussels by the late 19C painter J.B. van Moer. The **Salle Gothique** has fine woodcarving and 19C Mechelen tapestries depicting members of the guilds.

There are two paintings by Emile Wauters on the Escalier des Lions. One shows John of Brabant granting a charter in 1421, while the other depicts Mary of Burgundy swearing in 1477 to protect the liberties of Brussels. The escutcheons of the guilds are reproduced on the ceiling of the **Salle des Mariages**, while the Escalier d'Honneur is decorated with busts of burgomasters, allegorical wall-paintings by Jacques de Lalaing and, at the foot of the stairs, an 1890 fountain with a figure of St Michael by Charles van der Stappen.

The **Maison du Roi** faces the town hall. A wooden building which served as the bread market stood on this site in the 14C or perhaps earlier. Known as the Broodhuis (Bread House), it was later replaced by a stone building. The name was changed to Maison du Duc in the 16C when the Duke of Brabant used it to accommodate various officials. It was completely rebuilt in Late Gothic style for Charles V by Antoon and Rombout Keldermans and Hendrik van Pede. The new house was named Maison du Roi, though it was never a royal residence. Badly damaged during the bombardment of 1695, it was restored in 1763 but subsequently neglected until the 1870s. It was then virtually demolished and rebuilt by Victor Jamaer, who based the reconstruction on historic engravings. He also borrowed motifs from Hendrik van Pede's town hall at Oudenaarde, though the galleries on the façade and the tower are Jamaer's own inventions.

The Maison du Roi is now occupied by the **Musée de la Ville de Bruxelles**. Open Mon–Thur 10.00–12.30 and 13.30–17.00; Sat and Sun 10.00–13.00; closed Fri. This interesting museum illustrates the often turbulent history of Brussels through a well-displayed collection of paintings, plans, furniture and sculpture. One of the highlights is Pieter Bruegel the Elder's *Marriage Procession*, which shows a country wedding in the Pajottenland region west of Brussels.

The **ground floor** rooms contain 15C and 16C retables, 16C and 17C tapestries (including one based on a cartoon by Rubens), and porcelain and silver of the 18C and 19C. There are also some stone and wood carvings salvaged from old buildings, including some intriguing 14C and 15C sculptures from the town hall. The statue of St John Nepomuk dating from 1725 stood on the last surviving bridge over the Senne until it was demolished in 1868.

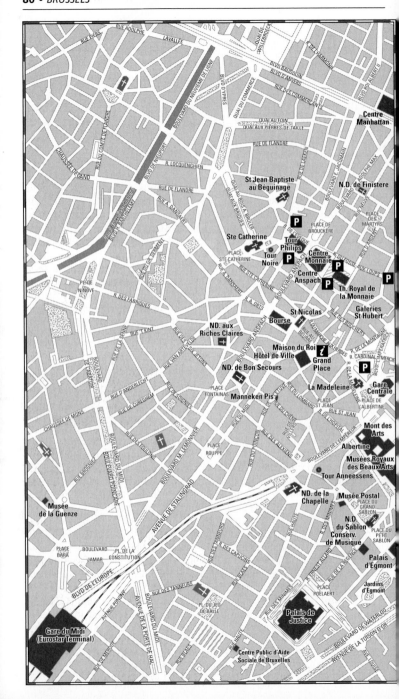

Gare du Nord

Ste Marie

BRUSSELS
CENTRE

N

Centre
Manhattan

PLACE
ROGIER

RUE DE BRABANT

BLVD ST LAZARE

RUE ROYALE

CHAUSSEE DE HAECHT

RUE DU MERIDIEN

RUE DU MOULIN

AVENUE PAUL DESCHANEL

AVENUE G-PETRE

Jardin
Botanique

BOULEVARD DU JARDIN BOTANIQUE

RUE ROYALE

Porte de
Schaerbeek

RUE TRAVERSIERE

PLACE
ARM'STEURS

RUE DES MOISSONS

RUE DE LA FEMME

RUE DE LA BLANCHISSERIE

RUE DE L'ASSOCIATION

PLACE
QUETELET

BLVD BISCHOFFSHEIM

SQ.
HENRI
FRICK

RUE DE LA FEMME

RUE VERBIST

RUE DU MARAIS

BLVD PACHECO

Cité
Administrative

Centre Belge
de la
Bande Dessinée

PLACE
DES
BARRICADES

Colonne du Congrès

Tour
Madou

RUE SCAILQUIN

CHAUSSEE DE LOUVAIN

PLACE
ST JOSSE

RUE WILLEMS

RUE DES EBURONS

BLVD DE BERLAIMONT

Banque Nat.

RUE DU CONGRES

PLACE
MADOU

CHAUSSEE DE LOUVAIN

SQ. MARIE-LOUISE

RUE STEVIN

Cathédrale
(St Michel)

RUE DE LA CROIX DE FER

RUE DE LOUVAIN

Musée
Charlier

RUE DES DEUX EGLISES

RUE DE SPA

RUE PHILIPPE LE BON

RUE DES COLONIES

RUE DE LA LOI

Palais de la Nation

BOULEVARD DU REGENT

AVENUE DES ARTS

RUE JOSEPH II

Gare
Centrale

RUE ROYALE

RUE DE LA LOI

Parc
de
Bruxelles

RUE DE LA LOI

Berlaymont (European Commission)

RUE RAVENSTEIN

Musée du Cinéma
Palais des Beaux Arts

Musée de la Dynastie

PL. DES PALAIS

SQ.
FRERE-ORBAN

RUE DE LA SCIENCE

RUE DE TREVES

RUE D'ARLON

Gare
Schuman

PLACE
ROYALE

St
Jacques

Musées
Royaux des
Beaux Arts

Palais
Royal

Pal. des Académies

BOULEVARD DU REGENT

AVENUE DES ARTS

RUE BELLIARD

RUE DE CHAMPAGNE

RUE MONTOYER

RUE BELLIARD

RUE DE NAMUR

RUE DE MAYLIR

RUE BREDERODE

PLACE DU
TRONE

Palais
d'Egmont

BOULEVARD DU WATERLOO

AVENUE MARNIX

RUE DU CHAMPS DE MARS

Porte de
Namur

SQ. DE
LUXEMBOURG
MEEUS

PLACE DU
LUXEMBOURG

RUE DU TRONE

RUE DE TREVES

RUE WIERTZ

European
Parliament

Parc
Leopold

BOULEVARD DE WATERLOO

AVENUE MARNIX

GALERIE
TOISON D'OR

RUE DE LA PAIX

CHAUSSEE D'IXELLES

RUE DE DUBLIN

CHAUSSEE DE WAVRE

Gare Luxembourg

RUE CARDDY

RUE GODECHARLE

Inst. des Sciences
Naturelles

RUE DES DRAPIERS

Musée
Camille
Lemonnier

RUE DU TRONE

Musée
Wiertz

CHAUSSEE DE WAVRE

RUE DU VIADUC

0   300 yards

0   300 metres

The large neo-Gothic room on the **first floor** contains an outstanding collection of plans, models and maps of Brussels. An intriguing series of illustrations recalls several spectacular late 19C schemes to link the lower and upper districts by an elevated arcade (1898) and a soaring funicular (1890). A stained-glass window on the staircase leading to the top floor glitters with the arms of the far-flung possessions of Charles V.

A room on the **top floor** contains the bizarre Wardrobe of the Manneken-Pis. This contains a small sample of the over 600 suits donated to the famous Brussels statue. One of the first costumes was presented by Louis XV in 1747.

The guild houses

The fanciful Baroque guild houses on Grand-Place were mostly rebuilt after the bombardment of 1695. Many have their names given in Dutch, which was then the dominant language in Brussels.

Nos 1–2 The double house at nos 1–2 was built by Jan Cosyns in 1697. Now a café, it was originally the Guild House of the Bakers. It is known as the Maison du Roi d'Espagne (King of Spain) after a statue of Charles II on the façade. A bronze bust of St Aubert, patron saint of the bakers, decorates the dome.

No. 3 The Guild House at no. 3 once belonged to the tallow merchants. They built a stone house here in 1644, which was damaged during the bombardment and restored in 1697 by Jan Cosyns. The house is known as the **Maison de la Brouette** (The Wheelbarrow). A statue of St Gilles, patron saint of the tallow merchants, stands on top of the gable.

No. 4 The house at no. 4 is known as the **Maison du Sac** (The Sack). It was built in 1644 for the Guild of Joiners and Coopers. The guild moved to this site in the 15C after their earlier guild house was razed to make way for the new town hall. The gable was rebuilt in 1697 by Antoon Pastorana, a furniture-maker by trade.

No. 5 The **Maison de la Louve** (The She-wolf) at no. 5 was owned by the archers' guild. Built in 1691 by Pieter Herbosch, it miraculously survived the bombardment four years later.

No. 6 The splendid House of the Boatmen at no. 6 is known as the **Maison du Cornet** (The Horn). It was rebuilt in 1697 by Antoon Pastorana. The curious gable is modelled on the stern of a 17C ship.

No. 7 The **Maison du Renard** (The Fox) at no. 7 was the Guild House of the Haberdashers. A 14C wooden building on this site was acquired by the guild in the 15C. The stone building we see now was constructed in 1699. Charming bas-reliefs by Marcus de Vos and Jan van Delen represent the trading activities of the haberdashers. The statue on the top represents St Nicolas, patron saint of merchants.

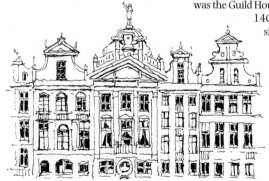

Guild houses on the Grand-Place, Brussels

No. 8 Then follows a splendid row of houses to the left of the town hall, beginning with **L'Etoile** (The Star) at no. 8. One of the oldest and most interesting houses on the square, its name goes back to the 13C. Destroyed in 1695, it was rebuilt soon after, but was then demolished in 1850 to widen the narrow lane beside the house. Enraged at this act of vandalism, Burgomaster Charles Buls had the house rebuilt over a pedestrian arcade in 1897.

A memorial was placed in the arcade to commemorate the 14C Brussels alderman Everard 't Serclaes, who led the guilds in their struggle against Louis de Male, the Count of Flanders. The count's allies launched an attack from Gaasbeek Castle in 1388 and murdered Everard in L'Etoile. According to a local tradition, it brings good luck to stroke the arm of the bronze figure. Another memorial honours Charles Buls, who died in 1914. In addition to restoring L'Etoile, Buls saved many other historic buildings in the late 19C.

No. 9 The **Maison du Cygne** (The Swan) at no. 9 was rebuilt in 1698 by C. van Nerven for Pieter Fariseau, a founder of the Brussels opera. It became the house of the butchers' guild in 1720. It was later occupied by a workers' café frequented by Karl Marx during his stay in Brussels. The Belgian Labour party was founded here in 1885.

No. 10 The **L'Arbre d'Or** (Golden Tree) at no. 10 is commonly known as the Brewers' House. Surmounted by a statue of Charles of Lorraine, it was rebuilt in 1698 by Willem de Bruyn. It now contains a small museum of brewing and a 17C basement tavern

Nos 11 and 12 The houses at nos 11 and 12 are known as **La Rose** (1702) and the **Maison du Mont-Thabor** (1699). Both were private houses. The name La Rose is a play on the name of the owners, the Van der Rosen family.

No. 13 Next is the splendid **Maison des Ducs de Brabant** at nos 13–19. This mansion takes its name from the busts of the dukes of Brabant on the façade. Built by Willem de Bruyn in 1696–98, the building has a pilastered front, rounded pediment and three pairs of steps. It was divided at an early stage into six houses. The narrow house at no. 13 takes its name from the figure of Fame above the door.

Nos 14 and 15 **L'Hermitage** at no. 14 was used at different times by the wine and vegetable merchants, while La Fortune at no. 15 belonged to the tanners.

Nos 16–19 The **Moulin à Vent** at no. 16 takes its name from a stone tablet decorated with a windmill. The Pot d'Etain (Pewter Pot) at no. 17 belonged to the Guild of Cabinet Makers. **La Colline** (The Hill) at no. 18 was the Guild House of the Masons, while La Bourse at no. 19 was a private house.

No. 20 The houses to the right of the Maison du Roi are less grand. The house at no. 20, known as **Le Cerf** (The Stag), has a carved stone giving the date of construction as 1710.

Nos 21 and 22 The double house at nos 21 and 22 is known as the **Maison Joseph et Anne**.

No. 23 The Baroque house at no. 23 known as **L'Ange** (The Angel) was rebuilt by Willem de Bruyn, who gave it Ionic and Corinthian columns.

Nos 24 and 25 The house at no. 24 was named **The Mole** after it was owned by the De Mol family, and no. 25 is called **La Chaloupe d'Or** (Golden Boat). These two houses were joined by Willem de Bruyn in 1695 to form the Guild House of the Tailors. The figure at the top is the guild's patron saint.

Nos 26–27 The double house at nos 26–27 is known as the **Maison du Pigeon**

(The Pigeon). It was built on the site of the Guild House of the Painters, which was destroyed in 1695. The site was sold by the painters' guild to the architect Pierre Simon, who probably designed the present building. A plaque recalls that Victor Hugo lived in a hotel in this building in 1852. The house at no. 28 is known as the 'Ammanskamerke' (Magistrate's Room).

Nos 34–37 Six simpler buildings, mostly private houses, stand to the left of the Maison du Roi. The Helmet at no. 34 was rebuilt in 1695 and The Peacock at no. 35 was completed in 1697 according to the stone tablet at the top. The next two houses, known as The Little Fox at no. 36 and The Oak at no. 37, were rebuilt in 1696 behind a common façade.

Nos 38 and 39 The house at no. 38 is known as St Barbara or The Crowned Blackberry Bush, while no. 39 is known as The Donkey.

2 • The Lower Town

The Lower Town is a fascinating district to explore, with its ancient cobbled streets, dark baroque churches and broad Parisian boulevards. The crowded medieval quarters largely disappeared in the second half of the 19C when the River Senne was covered over, the slums cleared and the long axis of Boulevard Adolphe Max and Boulevard Anspach laid out. Several elegant 19C shopping arcades were built at this time in an attempt to give Brussels the allure of Paris. Yet you can still find the occasional relics of an older, more Flemish Brussels in the streets around Grand-Place.

The Steenweg

The Steenweg was the city's main street from at least as early as the 10C. It formed part of the medieval trade route which linked the Rhine with Ghent and Bruges. You can still follow the course of this ancient way through the old town. On reaching Brussels from the east, the Steenweg split into two roads. One route entered the city at the Porte de Schaerbeek, then continued past the cathedral to the Rue de la Montagne, while the other road entered by the Porte de Namur and descended the Mont des Arts to the Rue de la Madeleine. The two sections met in the Lower Town at the east end of the Rue du Marché aux Herbes, which at that time bordered a rivulet that rose in the Coudenberg and joined the Senne somewhere near the modern Bourse. Flanked by stalls and markets, the Steenweg crossed the Senne near the town wharf, which remained here until the 16C. It then followed the line of the Rue Sainte Catherine and the Rue de Flandre to the Porte de Flandre.

Leave Grand-Place by the Rue Charles Buls, which runs between the Hôtel de Ville and no. 8. This leads to the Rue des Brasseurs, where a plaque marks the hotel where Rimbaud was staying when he was shot by Verlaine in July 1873.

The nearby **Musée de Costume et Dentelle** at Rue de la Violette 6 has a collection of Belgian lace and period costumes. Open Apr–Sept Thur–Tues 10.00–12.30 and 13.30–17.00; Oct–Mar Mon, Tues, Thur and Fri 10.00–12.30 and 13.30–16.00, weekends 14.00–16.30.

Rimbaud and Verlaine

After quarrelling with Paul Verlaine in London, the 19-year-old French poet Arthur Rimbaud took a room in Brussels at the Hôtel La Ville de Courtrai. Verlaine followed him here, and they quarrelled again. After Rimbaud threatened to terminate their relationship, Verlaine bought a pistol in the Galeries St Hubert and returned to the hotel to shoot Rimbaud. Although his friend was only lightly wounded, Verlaine was sentenced to six months in Mons prison for attempted murder.

The busy Rue de l'Etuve brings you to the famous fountain of the **Manneken-Pis**. This bronze statuette of a nude boy urinating was designed in 1619 by Jérôme Duquesnoy the Elder. Stolen in 1817, it was later found smashed, but the fragments were pieced together to form the mould from which the present figure was produced. The Manneken-Pis (or Petit Julien, as he is affectionately called) soon became part of the folklore of Brussels. He is famous for his elaborate wardrobe which was begun in 1698 when the Elector of Bavaria presented a costume. Another early benefactor was Louis XV, who in 1747 gave a costume and conferred a decoration on the Manneken in compensation for the ill-treatment he had suffered at the hands of the French soldiers. The costumes, which now number over 600, are kept in the Musée Communal. A notice attached to the railings gives details of forthcoming ceremonies involving the Manneken-Pis.

Now go left up the Rue du Chêne and right down the Rue de Villers to reach the **Tour de Villers**, one of the few surviving fragments of the city's 12C walls. Returning to the Rue du Chêne, continue to the Place Saint Jean where a memorial in the centre of the square honours Gabrielle Petit, who was shot by the Germans in 1916. Endowed with a photographic memory, she was active in the resistance movement. When condemned to death, she was told that if she appealed she would almost certainly be reprieved. This she refused to do, proudly replying that she would show her captors how a Belgian woman could die.

Jacques Brel

The Fondation Jacques Brel in Place de la Vieille Halle aux Blés was set up by France Brel to commemorate her father, the singer Jacques Brel, who was born in Schaerbeek in 1933. The son of a prosperous factory owner, Brel became famous as a cabaret singer in Paris in the 1960s, singing emotional songs about death, bourgeois Belgium and the Flanders coast. He later directed films, though none was successful. After undergoing surgery for lung cancer, Brel spent his final years on a yacht in the Pacific. He died in 1978 in a Paris clinic.

Go down the Rue des Eperonniers to reach the Rue du Marché aux Herbes, where a bronze statue commemorates *Burgomaster Charles Buls*. It is decorated with miniature copies of several buildings he saved from destruction. A Neo-classical entrance opposite leads into the **Galeries St Hubert**, an impressive complex of three iron and glass arcades decorated with marble columns, lamps and statues. Named Galerie de la Reine, Galerie du Roi and Galerie des Princes, these Neo-classical arcades were built by J.P. Cluysenaer in 1846. Among the earliest arcades in Europe, they contain shops, restaurants, cafés, a cinema, a theatre and apartments.

The arcades cross the **Rue des Bouchers**, a narrow lane lined with lively restaurants serving mussels and *frites* and other Belgian specialities. If you go down this lane and turn left into the Petite Rue des Bouchers, you will find the **Toone Puppet Theatre** down a narrow lane on the left. Founded in 1835 by Antoine Toone, the theatre continues a tradition that goes back to the period when Spain ruled the Netherlands. Incensed by open criticism and insults from the stage, the Spanish authorities closed down all the theatres. The locals promptly resorted to puppet theatres as a way of reviling the foreign rulers. Based on classics such as Hamlet, Carmen and the Passion, the plays are normally performed in the Brussels dialect known as Vloms, though occasional performances are staged in French or English. The dialogue is packed with allusions to local and national politics. The theatre has a café and a small museum (open during intervals).

Cathedral of St Michel

Leave the Galeries Saint Hubert at the far end and turn right up Rue d'Arenberg to reach the Boulevard de l'Impératrice. This broad road marks the line of the rail tunnel built to link the Gare du Nord and Gare du Midi. Begun in 1911, this major engineering project was finally completed in 1952 with the opening of the Gare Centrale. Cross this road to reach the Cathedral of Saint Michel on the slopes above the lower town. This is the national church of Belgium.

History of the Cathedral

The first in a succession of chapels was built on this site in Carolingian times. One of the earliest was dedicated to Ste Gudule, a young local girl from the Pepin family who refused to be diverted from her prayers by the devil. He would amuse himself by blowing out her candle as she crossed the Senne marshes to pray. Her body was brought in 1047 to a church on this site dedicated to St Michael. This Romanesque building appears to have burnt down in 1072. By the 12C, the church on the site was dedicated to both Ste Gudule and St Michael.

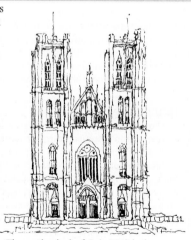

The cathedral of Saint Michel, Brussels

The construction of the present building began under Duke Henry I of Brabant, while work on the choir started in the early 13C. The church was finally completed in the 15C, but a good deal of rebuilding occurred later. The splendid double towers were built in the 15C, in part by Jan van Ruysbroeck. The church became the setting for the glittering chivalric ceremonies of the

Order of the Golden Fleece organised by Philip the Good and Charles the Bold.

The body of Ste Gudule disappeared during the religious troubles of the 16C. The church suffered further damage after the French Revolution. Wishing perhaps to make amends, Napoleon made the first donation towards its restoration. When the church became a cathedral in 1961, its name was simplified to St Michel. A new carillon of 49 bells was installed in 1975.

The **nave** was built in the 14C and 15C, beginning with the south side. The statues of the Apostles on the piers were added from 1634–54 by Lucas Faydherbe, Jan van Mildert, Jérôme Duquesnoy the Younger, and Tobias de Lelis. The Baroque pulpit was carved in 1699 by Hendrik Verbruggen for the Jesuit church at Leuven. It was transferred here in 1776 when the Order was suppressed. It illustrates the *Fall of Adam and Eve*. The Renaissance stained glass window above the west door depicts the *Last Judgement*. It was designed by an unknown Antwerp master in 1528.

Steps near the west end lead down to the **crypt** (entry charge), where archaeologists have unearthed the remains of a Rhenish-Mosan Westwork added c 1200 to an existing 11C Romanesque church. The foundations, which are well displayed, include the bases of two round towers.

The **transepts** were built in the late 13C and early 14C (south transept) and the late 14C (north transept). The stained glass windows were made from designs by Bernard van Orley. The south window shows Louis of Hungary and his wife Mary, sister of Charles V, with their patron saints. The north window depicts Charles V and his wife Isabella of Portugal. There are also two triptychs painted by Michiel Coxie at the age of 89 and 92.

The **choir** was built in 1215–65, and the triforium added in 1273. It contains the tombs of Duke John II of Brabant (d. 1312), and his wife Margaret of York (d. 1322), the daughter of King Edward I of England. The windows above the high altar glorify the Habsburg dynasty. The three in the centre, by Nicolas Rombouts, depict Maximilian of Austria and Mary of Burgundy, flanked by their son Philip the Handsome and his wife Joanna of Castile (on the left) and their grandsons Charles V and Ferdinand of Austria (on the right). The outer window on the left is by Jan Ofhuys and shows Philip III of Spain and his wife Margaret of Austria. The window on the right by Nicolas Mertens shows Philibert of Savoy and Margaret of Austria, aunt of Charles V.

The **high altar** dates from 1887. Behind it is the mausoleum of the Dukes of Brabant, surmounted by a lion in gilt copper cast in 1610 from a design of Jean de Montfort, and the Mausoleum of Archduke Ernst of Austria (d. 1595). Both were carved by Robert de Nole from designs by Josse de Beckberghe.

The early 13C **ambulatory** has an apsidal chapel added in 1282. This was reconstructed in 1675 by Leo van Heil. Its main feature is an alabaster retable of 1538 by Jean Mone, which was originally in the Abbaye de la Cambre. A memorial added in 1957 on the north side of the ambulatory commemorates the painter Roger van der Weyden, who is buried somewhere in the cathedral.

Two large chapels flank the choir. These were built in the 16C and 17C on the site of seven smaller chapels. The **Chapelle de Notre-Dame de la Délivrance** to the south was built in 1649–55 from drawings by Jérôme

Duquesnoy the Younger. The windows, executed by Jan de la Baer of Antwerp from designs by Theodoor van Thulden, depict, on the upper level, scenes from the life of the Virgin and, below, the donors. The chapel also contains the tomb of Count Frédéric de Mérode by Charles Fraikin and a retable of 1666 by Jan Voorspoel which contains a painting of the *Assumption* by J.B. de Champaigne.

The **Chapelle du Saint Sacrement de Miracle** to the north of the choir was built in 1534–39 to commemorate an anti-Semitic 14C legend which has now been disproved by historical research and was officially declared unfounded in 1968. The story, which dates back to 1369, concerns a Jew living in Enghien who arranged for the theft of a consecrated Host. After he was murdered, his wife fled to Brussels, bringing the Host with her. Gathering in the Synagogue in Brussels on Good Friday, the Jews stabbed the Host with their daggers, whereupon blood spurted forth. In fear of their lives, they ordered a woman to get rid of the Host, but instead she returned it to the church. It became a precious relic which drew large crowds of the devout. The chapel was added in the 16C to display the relic.

The chapel window on the west side was executed by Jan Haeck from designs by Bernard van Orley. The centre window was designed by Michiel Coxie to illustrate the legend (upper levels) and the six donors (John III of Portugal and Catherine of Aragon, Louis II and Mary of Hungary, Francis I of France and Eleanor of Austria). The three women were all sisters of Charles V. The east window was donated by Ferdinand, brother of Charles V, and Anna of Poland.

The window above the altar, which shows the *Adoration of the Sacrament*, was made in 1848 by J.B. Capronnier. It is a good copy of a window by Bernard van Orley which was destroyed in 1772. Behind the altar, which dates from 1849, we can see a fragment of the beam in which the Host was hidden during the turbulent years of the 16C. The crypt contains the tombs of Archduke Albert, Archduchess Isabella, and Charles of Lorraine.

On leaving the cathedral, descend the Rue de la Banque, which leads back to the Boulevard de l'Impératrice. On the far side turn right and follow the boulevard until you come to a large sculpture of *Gaston*, a Belgian comic book character. This stands at the top of a flight of steps leading down to the Rue des Sables. The **Centre Belge de la Bande Dessinée** at no. 20 occupies a former Art Nouveau department store built by Victor Horta in 1903–6. Expertly restored, the building is now a centre of Belgian comic strip art. Fans of Tintin, the Smurfs, Lucky Luke and other Belgian cartoon creations can admire original plates, sketches, albums and models. The centre has a library, bookshop and Belgian brasserie. Open Tues–Sun 10.00–18.00.

Continue down Rue des Sables and turn left along Rue du Marais, then right into Rue du Persil. This brings you to the quiet **Place des Martyrs**, a harmonious Neo-classical square designed by Claude Fisco in 1775. A monument in the centre of the square stands above the graves of the patriots who fell in the revolution of 1830. Other memorials in the square commemorate Count Frédéric de Mérode, who died at Berchem in the 1830 revolution, and Jenneval, author of the words of the Belgian national anthem.

The national anthem

The first French language version of the Belgian national anthem was written in August 1830 by the Frenchman L.A. Dechet. Better known as Jenneval, he was an actor at the Théâtre de la Monnaie, where the 1830 revolution began. Fighting on the side of the revolutionaries, Dechet was killed at Lier some six weeks later. François van Campenhout, a violinist at the same theatre, composed the music. He named the song 'La Brabançonne' since it was in Brussels in the province of Brabant that the revolution started. For the same reason the national flag uses the black, gold and red colours of the Brabant flag. The French version currently sung was written in 1860 by Charles Rogier. The Dutch version dates from 1938.

Cross the square and continue to Rue Neuve, a distinguished address in the 17C but now a pedestrianised shopping street. The little church of Notre-Dame de Finistère was built on this street in 1708. The Baroque interior contains a popular statue of *Notre-Dame du Bon Succès* brought here from Aberdeen in 1625.

The Duchess of Richmond's Ball

A run-down street behind the City 2 shopping centre on Rue Neuve was the setting of the famous ball held by Charlotte Gordon, Duchess of Richmond, on the eve of the Battle of Waterloo. The house where the ball took place on 15 June 1815 stood at the corner of the Rue de la Blanchisserie and the Rue des Cendres. Byron, in the stanzas in *Childe Harold* beginning 'There was a sound of revelry at night' perpetuated the story that Wellington had been taken by surprise by Napoleon's advance. It seems likely that Wellington had received the news beforehand but chose to attend the ball with many of his officers so as to allay any panic in the city. Many French-speaking Belgians had fought for Napoleon and the Allies were anxious that they should not join him again. Wellington, on hearing that the French were already at Quatre-Bras, is said to have calmly finished his supper before asking his host 'Have you a good map in the house?'. Nothing remains of the house, not even the commemorative plaque that was once attached to a wall.

The 19C Passage du Nord links Rue Neuve with the Place de Brouckère, a 19C square dominated by the *Métropole Hotel* of 1895. The square is named after Charles de Brouckère (1796–1860), a government minister who founded the Banque Nationale and served as burgomaster of Brussels from 1848–60. The modern Tour Philips and Centre Monnaie have robbed the square of much of its original charm. Named after the city mint which once stood here, the Centre Monnaie contains the city administration, the main post office, shops, a metro station and an underground car park.

Walk through the Centre Monnaie to reach the **Théâtre Royal de la Monnaie**. Mainly used for performances of opera and ballet, the present theatre was built by Joseph Poelaert on the site of an older theatre destroyed by fire in 1855. The old theatre was where the signal for the revolution of 1830 was given during a performance of Auber's La Muette de Portici. On hearing the words of the duet *Amour sacré de la Patrie, Rends-nous l'audace et la fierté*, the audience rushed into the street and hoisted the Brabant flag above the town hall.

The guns of Waterloo

The diarist Fanny Burney (1752–1840) lodged for some time in June 1815 in a house in the Rue d'Assaut, near the Monnaie theatre. Convinced, as were most of her friends, that Napoleon would soon enter the city, she had tried, without success, to find a barge to take her to Antwerp. Later, hearing cries of '*Bonaparte est pris! Le voilà*', she saw from her window 'a general in the splendid uniform of France', a prisoner tied to his 'noble war-horse'. This turned out to be General George Mouton, Comte de Lobau, one of Napoleon's generals.

There is another shopping centre on the square overlooking the theatre. The Centre Anspach contains the rather enjoyable **Historium**, a waxworks museum which charts important episodes in Belgian history using wax figures in lifelike tableaux. Open daily 10.00–18.00. The commentary is provided by headphones. Go through the Centre Anspach to reach Boulevard Anspach, named after the 19C burgomaster who promoted the modernisation of Brussels by covering the Senne and laying out the broad boulevards.

Turning left, you reach the Bourse, built by Léon-Pierre Suys on the site of a convent and completed in 1873. Auguste Rodin carved some of the figures on the side facing Café Falstaff during his stay in Brussels. The **Bourse metro station** contains a large mural by Paul Delvaux entitled *Our Old Brussels Trams*.

The **Scientastic Museum**, located in the underground concourse at Bourse metro station, is an imaginative hands-on science museum where children can conduct 70 different experiments involving optical illusions, sound, smell and touch. Opening hours: Mon–Sun 14.00–17.30.

The archaeological site **Bruxella 1238** stands next to the Bourse on Rue de la Bourse. The underground complex contains the foundations of the 13C Eglise des Récollets. The site can only be visited by guided tour on Wednesday beginning at Maison du Roi, Grand-Place, at 10.15, 11.15, 13.45, 14.30 and 15.15. Stout shoes are recommended.

Go up the Rue de la Bourse to reach the **Eglise St Nicolas**. Situated in the heart of the medieval merchants' district, the church is dedicated to the patron saint of merchants and children. The exterior is almost entirely surrounded by small shops. Built on the site of an ancient church, the present building dates from the 14C–15C, while the choir is from 1381. The façade was replaced during a major reconstruction in 1955, when a striking modern blue window was added over the west porch. The church contains works by Bernard van Orley and Antoon Sallaert as well as one attributed to Rubens. Its main treasure is the *Vladimir Ikon* of 1131.

3 • Saint Géry and Sainte Catherine

The oldest quarter of the city lies to the west of the grand boulevards, around Place Saint Géry and Place Saint Catherine. Begin on Grand-Place and walk down the Rue du Marché au Charbon to reach the 17C church of **Notre-Dame de Bon Secours**, built by Jan Cortvriendt in Baroque style. Continue to Place Fontainas, one of three

Neo-classical squares in this neighbourhood. A brief detour down Boulevard Lemonnier brings you to Place d'Anneessens, where a statue by Vinçotte commemorates the Brussels guild leader executed by the Austrians. The Rue de Tournai leads from here to the Place Rouppe. This square is named after N.J. Rouppe (1769–1839), who opposed the French during the annexation, played a leading role in the revolution of 1830 and served as the first post-revolution burgomaster of Brussels. The bus for Waterloo starts from Place Rouppe and some of the finest cooking in Europe is concocted in the kitchens of *Comme Chez Soi* at no. 23.

Back on Place Fontainas, cross the boulevard and continue down the Rue de la Grande Ile to **Notre-Dame aux Riches Claires**, a Flemish Baroque church designed by Lucas Faydherbe in 1665 and enlarged in the 19C. You then reach Place Saint Géry, generally accepted as the site of the island on which Saint Géry founded a chapel in the 6C. The Dukes of Lower Lorraine built a residence and chapel here in 979. These were replaced by a church in the 16C, which was demolished in 1798. The **Marché Saint Géry** was built here in 1881. A plaque at the east end of the market illustrates the probable appearance of the island in the past. The market currently contains an interesting exhibition on the history of Brussels. Open Tues–Fri 10.30–19.00, weekends 14.00–17.00.

Leave the square by Rue Plétinckx and turn right down Rue St-Christophe to reach the Rue des Chartreux, where the **Album Museum** occupies a restored 17C house at no. 25. Set up by an enthusiastic Frenchman, this engaging museum contains an eclectic collection of material on Belgian culture, including magazines, cartoon books, films, family photographs and 3-D views of the 1958 World Fair. Children are made to feel at home. The cost depends on the length of the visit. Open Wed–Mon 13.00–18.00.

Continue down this street and turn left on Rue Dansaert, then right down Rue du Vieux Marché aux Grains to reach Place Sainte Catherine, where a fruit and vegetable market is held every day. The church of **Ste Catherine** was built in 1854 by Joseph Poelaert in a typical mixture of styles. The belfry of its 17C predecessor stands on the south side. Just east of the church is the little **Tour Noire**, a rare relic of the 12C town walls.

Two parallel streets running north from the church, the **Quai au Bois à Brûler** and the **Quai aux Briques**, were once busy quays on either side of a harbour. Now flanked by small houses dating mainly from the 19C, the former harbour has been turned into an open square with basins and fountains. The harbour may have gone, but the quarter still has several fish shops and elegant restaurants specialising in seafood.

The *Cheval Marin* restaurant at the north end of the Quai aux Briques occupies a handsome building from 1680. Several old alleys lead from the Quai aux Briques to the Rue de Flandre. Once part of the old Steenweg running from Ghent to the Rhine, the Rue de Flandre has one surprising building at the end of a passage at no. 46. The **Maison de la Bellone** is a handsome patrician house of the late 17C where the Ommegang committee once met. It is now used for exhibitions on French language theatre. The house takes its name to the figure above the door of Bellona, the Roman goddess of war.

Returning to the Quai aus Bois à Brûler, go down Rue Populier to reach the church of **St Jean Baptiste au Béguinage**, built in 1657–76 by Lucas Faydherbe. The Baroque façade composed of three gables is one of the finest in Belgium, especially when floodlit at night. The church contains works by

Theodoor van Loon and a *Crucifixion* by Gaspard de Crayer. Most of the old Béguinage houses had disappeared by the mid 19C.

4 • The Upper Town

The Upper Town developed into an aristocratic quarter after the Dukes of Burgundy settled on the heights to the south of the Grand-Place in the 15C. Interesting for its Gothic churches, Neo-classical squares and landscaped parks, this quarter also contains several museums including the outstanding Musées Royaux des Beaux-Arts.

Beginning on the **Grand-Place**, walk up the Rue de la Madeleine past book-shops and art galleries. The Gothic church of **La Madeleine** on the left dates from the 15C. It was rebuilt on this site in 1958 after the underground rail tunnel was completed. The Baroque façade of the Chapelle Sainte Anne, which once stood in the nearby Rue de la Montagne, was rebuilt on the south side of La Madeleine.

The quarter around La Madeleine was once a densely populated district of small houses and shops. The buildings were torn down from 1911 to allow the construction of an underground rail tunnel linking the Gare du Nord, Gare Centrale and Gare du Midi. Known as the 'Jonction'project, this dragged on until Gare Centrale was finally completed in 1952.

Mont des Arts

Now cross the busy Boulevard de l'Empereur to reach the Mont des Arts. Also known as the Albertine, this Art Deco complex was begun in 1934 as a memor-ial to King Albert, killed that year in a climbing accident. Delayed by the Second World War, the buildings were finally completed between 1954 and 1965. The modern underground extension of the Musées Royaux des Beaux Arts was added in the 1980s.

The Mont des Arts represents the most recent attempt to link the Lower Town and the Upper Town. The sloping site was formerly occupied by terraced gardens created in 1894 on the site of the steep Rue Montagne de la Cour. These were replaced in 1958 by formal gardens with fountains designed by René Pechère. A statue of King Albert on horseback stands at the bottom of the gardens, facing his wife, Queen Elizabeth, on the far side of the busy boulevard.

The street to the left passes under an arch with a clock and carillon on the rear façade. Created in 1964, the clock is decorated with small figures representing figures from Belgian history. The elegant gentleman on the top strikes the hour with his stick.

The **Bibliothèque Royale Albert I** is on the right. Open Mon–Sat 09.00–17.00. This severe Art Deco building contains the national library and several specialised museums. The **Musée de l'Imprimerie**, open Mon–Sat 09.00–17.00, located in the library corridors, has an interesting collection of old printing presses, books and bindings. The **Musée du Livre**, open Mon, Wed and Sat 14.00–17.00, displays a selection of manuscripts, documents and book bind-ings. It also contains reconstructed studies of Michel de Ghelderode and other Belgian writers. The **Literature Museum**, open Mon–Fri 09.00–17.00, has documents, tapes and videos of interest to scholars of French Belgian literature and theatre. The **Chalcography Department**, open Mon–Fri 09.00–12.45 and

14.00–16.45, entered at Place du Musée 1, has a collection of more 5000 engravings and prints which are on sale.

The library stands on the site of the 15C Hôtel de Nassau, of which all that remains is the **Chapelle de Nassau**. Dedicated to St George, the chapel was built in c 1500 in Brabant Late Gothic style. The chapel is now embedded in the fabric of the library. The outer wall can be seen from the elevated terrace. A bas-relief nearby, carved by Georges Dobbels in 1969, shows the Nassau palace in the 15C. The stepped Gothic windows are a reminder of the steep incline of the Rue Montagne de la Cour, which once ran past the building. The chapel is occasionally used for exhibitions of manuscripts and books from the library's collection.

A final flight of steps leads to the Coudenberg. Up the steps to the right, next to a statue of Charles of Lorraine, is a rather deserted courtyard. Once known as the **Ancienne Cour**, this 18C Neo-classical complex was built by Jan Folte on the site of the demolished Hôtel de Nassau. The former palace buildings are now occupied by the **Musées Royaux des Beaux-Arts**. The modern paintings are displayed in a gallery sunk below the courtyard and concealed by a parapet. The door at no. 1 leads to the Protestant Chapel, where Charlotte Brontë worshipped every Sunday during her stay in Brussels.

The Nassau palace

The Nassau family obtained the 14C Duvenvoorde mansion on the Rue Montagne de la Cour through marriage in 1404. Englebert of Nassau rebuilt the house and the private Chapelle Saint Georges at the close of the 15C. Destroyed and subsequently rebuilt, the Nassau mansion became the property of William III of England. Marlborough lived here in 1706. After the Coudenberg Palace was burnt down in 1731, the Hôtel de Nassau became the official residence of the Austrian governors. It was almost entirely rebuilt after 1756 by Charles of Lorraine and renamed the Ancienne Cour. It was here, in 1763, that the eight-year-old Mozart performed before the governor. Charles of Lorraine's apartments, with a monumental staircase and sculpture by Laurent Delvaux, have been restored. A small museum is due to open in 2000 in the former apartment of Charles of Lorraine, devoted to 18C intellectual life.

Turn down the lane on the left to reach the last surviving stretch of the Rue Montagne de la Cour. The **Old England Department Store** at no. 2 was built by Paul Saintenoy in 1899 in Art Nouveau style. It is now occupied by the outstanding **Musée des Instruments de Musique**, which owns a unique collection of 7000 musical instruments from all over the world. Visitors are equipped with special headsets to allow them to hear different musical instruments as they tour the collection. Performances on historic musical instruments are given every Thursday evening in the concert hall. The museum will reopen in June 2000. Opening hours Tues–Sun 09.30–1700; Thurs until 20.00.

The **Place Royale** is an elegant Neo-classical square modelled on Place Stanislas in Nancy. Built from 1772–85 by Barnabé Guimard, it stands on the site of the Coudenberg Palace, which was destroyed by fire in 1731. A plaque on the wall of the Hôtel Bellevue shows the site of the old palace buildings.

A statue of Charles of Lorraine stood in the middle of the square until the French Revolution. His place is now occupied by a statue carved in 1848 by Eugène

Simonis showing Godfrey of Bouillon raising the standard for the First Crusade.

The Neo-classical church of **St Jacques sur Coudenberg** was built in 1776–85 on the site of the chapel of the duke's chaplains. The interior contains sculptures by Laurent Delvaux and Gilles Godecharle.

The ruins of **Coudenberg Palace** have been preserved below Place Royale as an archaeological museum. The underground site includes the crypt of the ducal chapel, several cellars and the remains of the Rue Isabelle. The site is entered at Place Royale 10. Visits are by guided tour only (Wed and Sat 13.00–17.00 and Sun 10.00–14.00). A new entrance to the underground complex was being created via the Musée de la Dynastie at the time of writing.

Musées Royaux des Beaux-Arts

Now turn right along the Rue de la Régence to enter the Musées Royaux des Beaux-Arts. This outstanding art collection combines the Musée d'Art Ancien and the Musée d'Art Moderne.

Musée d'Art Ancien

The Musée d'Art Ancien, open Tues–Sun 10.00–12.00 and 13.00–15.00, occupies a Neo-classical building built in 1875–85 by Alphonse Balat. The four massive Scots granite pillars at the entrance support four statues by Guillaume de Groot representing the arts of Painting, Sculpture, Architecture and Music. There are busts of Rubens, Giambologna and Van Ruysbroeck in medallions above the doors. On either side of the entrance, large allegorical groups represent Art Instruction (on the left) and the Coronation of Art (on the right).

History of the collection

The Old Masters collection originated at the end of the 18C, when a number of inferior works of art left behind by the French were exhibited in some rooms of the former Cour Ancienne. This became the Musée du Département de la Dyle established by Napoleon in 1801. The collection was subsequently boosted by two consignments of paintings from the Louvre, which included a number of French and Italian paintings and four altarpieces by Rubens.

The first curator, G.J.J. Bosschaert (1737–1815) made strenuous efforts to recover the works that had been taken to France. He obtained three more altarpieces by Rubens after the fall of Napoleon. The collection was further boosted in 1873 when forty paintings from the collection of Duke Englebert of Arenberg were bought by the museum. It received other gifts over the years, including paintings by Van Dyck, sketches by Rubens, Bruegel the Elder's Winter Landscape and a magnificent collection of 4250 drawings by Rembrandt and other Dutch masters.

The Museum of Old Masters now has a large collection of paintings from the 14C to the 18C. The collection of Flemish paintings includes major works by Roger van der Weyden, Dirk Bouts, Pieter Bruegel the Elder and Pieter Paul Rubens. Its collection of foreign artists, though limited, includes some outstanding works by Rembrandt and Jacques Louis David.

Getting around the collection

The museum has been organised into four colour-coded circuits. The **Blue Route**, on the first floor, covers paintings of the 15C and 16C (rooms 10–34). The **Brown Route**, on the second fl oor, takes the visitor around the 17C and 18C collection (rooms 50–62). The **Yellow Route**, in an 18C town house reached by an escalator, contains 19C paintings on five floors (levels minus 2 to 3). The **Green Route** guides you round the Musée d'Art Moderne. The museum **café** is in an 18C town house on Place Royale.

In the **main hall**, 19C sculptures are displayed, including one of the *Burghers of Calais* by Auguste Rodin. There are also several large paintings, among them Jan Verhas' *School Procession* of 1878, and Léon Frederic's odd triptych *The Stream*, which is dedicated to Beethoven.

The Blue Route

The Blue Route ascends up one floor to the collection of 15C and 16C paintings. One of the oldest works in the museum hangs in **room 10**. Painted by an Early Netherlands Master, the *Retable of the Life of the Virgin* dates from c 1400. Despite considerable damage, especially on the right side, this remains an extra-ordinary work from the early period of Flemish painting, revealing a typical fascination with fabrics and faces.

There is a beautiful *Annunciation* by the Master of Flémalle in **room 11**. Set in a Flemish interior, it is a loving study of 15C objects. The same room contains Roger van der Weyden's deeply-moving *Lamentation*. His *Portrait of Anthony of Burgundy*, illegitimate son of Philip the Good, expertly uses light and shadow to bring out the man's features. Anthony is wearing the collar of the Golden Fleece, which suggests that the painting dates from 1456 when Anthony was elected to the order. Van der Weyden's *Portrait of Laurent Froimont* is part of a diptych. The other panel, depicting the Madonna, is in Caen.

The influence of Flemish painting can be seen in the Master of the Aix Annunciation's *Prophet Jeremiah*, which bears the motto Noli Me Tangere on the reverse. A *Lamentation* by Petrus Christus offers an intriguing glimpse of 15C Flemish costumes. Hugo van der Goes' painting of the *Madonna and Child* with St Anne and a Franciscan donor is an early work that precedes his mental breakdown.

Dirk Bouts' *Judgement of the Emperor Otto* (see p 43) is in **room 13**. These two large paintings were part of a series of four works commissioned for the town hall in Leuven. The first painting shows the *Punishment of the Innocent Count*, while the other depicts the *Ordeal by Fire*. Bouts died while working on the first panel, which was completed by his workshop. The two works illustrate a legend in which Emperor Otto executed a nobleman after he was falsely accused by the Empress. Appealing to God to prove her husband's innocence, the widow endured the ordeal by fire. Convinced that he had made a mistake, Otto sent the Empress to the stake.

There is an interesting painting by the Master of 1473 in **room 14**. Dated 1473, the *Triptych of Jan de Witte* depicts a leading citizen of Bruges and a matching portrait his wife. It was probably commissioned to celebrate their marriage. The same room contains Hans Memling's *Martyrdom of St Sebastian*, painted c 1470 for the archers' guild of Bruges. Memling also painted the *Portrait of Willem Moreel*, burgomaster of Bruges, and a matching portrait of his wife. Completed c 1478, they were commissioned by Moreel for a hospital where he sat on the board of governors. There is another portrait of Moreel and his wife painted in 1484 in the Groeningemuseum in Bruges. A puzzling painting dated 1494 by Jean Hey bears the inscription *Ecce Homo*. This artist was active in the Val de Loire. An inscription on the reverse that reads per m. Jo. hey. teutoni. cu had led some scholars to suggest that he came from the Southern Netherlands.

There are works by several anonymous Flemish artists including the Master of the Legend of St Barbara, named after his painting of Scenes from the life of St Barbara. The Master of the Vue de Sainte Gudule was a Brussels artist who painted Brussels Cathedral in one of his works, though the painting here features a view of the south transept of Notre-Dame du Sablon, Brussels. The Master of the Life of Joseph is represented here by his portraits of **Philip the Handsome** and **Joanna the Mad**. Two panels from Carlo Crivelli's Montefiore dell'Aso Polyptych depict the **Virgin and Child Enthroned** and **St Francis of Assisi**. The polyptych originally comprised 23 panels which are now dispersed in ten different museums.

In **room 17** is a curiously restrained **Crucifixion** by Hieronymus Bosch. Some scholars have identified the city in the background as 's Hertogenbosch in the Netherlands, where Bosch was born. There is also an early copy of Bosch's **Temptation of St Anthony**. The original version of this strange and disturbing work is in Lisbon.

Several paintings by Lucas Cranach the Elder hang in **room 18**, including a **Portrait of Dr J. Scheyring**, an **Adam and Eve**, and a **Venus and Cupid** illustrating the legend of Cupid and the bees.

Madonna with the Porridge Spoon, *by Gerard David, Musées Royaux des Beaux Art, Brussels*

A charming painting by Gerard David in **room 21** is known as the **Madonna with the Porridge Spoon** because of the domestic scene it illustrates. Quinten Metsys' **Triptych of the Life of Holy Kindred** is in room 22. Dated 1509 and signed, this was commissioned for the Chapel of the Holy Kindred in the Sint Pieterskerk at Leuven. An unknown Netherlandish artist painted the tender study of a **Child with a dead Bird** in the same room. All that is known of the girl is that she is wearing a 16C dress.

The influence of the Italian Renaissance can be seen in the **Venus and Cupid** by Jan Gossaert (Mabuse) in **room 25**. Gossaert was one of the first Netherlandish artists to study in Italy. He returned to the north with exciting new ideas on the use of mythological subjects and the female nude. His unconventional **Portraits of Two Donors** are the wings of a triptych whose centre panel has been lost. The man's eyes are defiant and challenging, while the woman's expression is proud and disdainful. It is a long way from the contemplative calm of the Flemish Primitives.

In the same room is Bernard van Orley's **Portrait of the Physician, George de Zelle**, who lived in the Place Saint Géry, Brussels. This room, or the next one, contains Van Orley's **Triptych of the Virtue of Patience**, based on on a poem by

Margaret of Austria. When the triptych was closed, it showed the story of Lazarus, but it now remains permanently open, revealing the trials of Job.

The ***Temptation of St Anthony*** was painted by Lucas van Leyden when the artist was aged about 17–22 (scholars disagree on his date of birth). As well as the usual demons, Lucas van Leyden has added frogs and a chained pig.

The next three rooms are dominated by 16C works by Antwerp Mannerists. The Cook, painted in 1559 by Pieter Aertsen, revels in the robust figure of a Flemish kitchen maid preparing to roast a chicken.

Next is the outstanding collection of paintings by Pieter Bruegel the Elder in **room 31**. The most famous painting is ***Landscape with the Fall of Icarus***. A poignant study of human indifference to suffering, it shows Icarus disappearing into the sea as a shepherd guards his flock, a fisherman casts his line, a peasant ploughs his land, and a ship sails past. A recent analysis of the panel has raised serious doubts as to whether it was in fact painted by Pieter Bruegel.

Also here is Bruegel's ***Fall of the Rebel Angels***, painted in Antwerp in 1562. The ***Census at Bethlehem*** was painted four years later, after Bruegel had moved to Brussels. The biblical episode is set in a Flemish village, probably to the west of Brussels in the Pajottenland. Some scholars have seen it as a veiled condemnation of the repressive régime that governed the Spanish Netherlands. The delightful little ***Man Yawning*** is

The Census at Bethlehem, *by Pieter Breugel, Musées Royaux des Beaux Art, Brussels*

thought by some to be a representation of sloth from a lost series of paintings on the Seven Deadly Sins. It is now believed to be the work of Pieter Brueghel the Younger.

A change of name

Pieter Brueghel the Elder has caused untold confusion by his decision in 1559 to change the spelling of his surname to Bruegel. All his paintings are signed BRVEGEL in capitals. His sons Pieter and Jan reverted to the old spelling of Brueghel. Pieter Brueghel the Younger, who mostly copied his father's works, was known as Hell Brueghel, while his brother Jan was called Velvet Brueghel.

In **room 32** are some interesting works by 16C Flemish artists, including two eccentric ***Anthropomorphic Landscapes*** by an anonymous southern Netherlandish artist, in which the faces of a man and woman are cunningly concealed in the landscapes. There is also an evocative ***Winter Scene with View of Tervuren Castle*** by the 17C court painter Denijs van Alsloot.

The Delporte Bequest is displayed separately in **rooms 37–45**. Gifted by Dr Franz Delporte, who died in 1973, the collection includes paintings, sculpture and ceramics from the 13C–18C. Most of the paintings are European, but there are ceramics and objets d'art from Persia, Egypt, Mexico, China, Japan and West Africa. The collection includes Pieter Bruegel the Elder's *The Bird Trap*, painted in a Pajottenland village on an icy winter day. There is also Pieter Brueghel the Younger's *Village Wedding*, copied from a lost work by his father.

The Brown Route

The Brown Route, which covers 17C and 18C painting, is reached by climbing up one floor. This includes an outstanding collection of paintings by **Pieter Paul Rubens**. Several of his smaller works are in **room 52**, including twelve sketches made for the royal hunting lodge of King Philip IV near Madrid. One of the sketches shows *The Fall of Icarus* in a style quite different from Bruegel's version of the story. Rubens's dramatic sketch of *The Martyrdom of St Ursula* is also utterly unlike traditional versions of the legend, such as on Memling's St Ursula Shrine in Bruges.

The astonishing *Four Negro Heads* shows an African man from four different angles. The same model appears in Rubens' *Adoration of the Magi* in the next room, and again in Antoon van Dyck's *Madonna with Forget-me-nots*. This room also contains *Landscape with the hunt of Atalanta*, painted by Rubens near his country house at Elewijt. Landscapes such as this one had a profound influence on 18C English landscape artists such as Gainsborough and Constable.

This room also contains several portraits, including *Archduke Ernst*, Governor of the Netherlands, and Peter Pecquius, chancellor of Brabant. One portrait shows Rubens' second wife, *Hélène Fourment*, who married in 1630 at the age of sixteen and posed as a model in numerous works, such as the *Carrying of the Cross* in the next room. The two portraits in this room of the *Archdukes Albert and Isabella* were painted in 1635 for one of the triumphal arches erected when the Infante Ferdinand made his entry into Antwerp.

Several large canvases by Rubens hang in **room 62**. These originally hung in Catholic churches in Belgium. The dramatic *Carrying of the Cross* was painted in 1636–37 for the abbey of Afflighem. It was executed towards the end of the artist's life when he suffered from rheumatism in his right hand. The *Martyrdom of St Livinius*, another great dramatic work of the same period, was commissioned for the Jesuit church in Ghent. The *Adoration of the Magi*, an earlier work from 1620, was painted for the church of the Capucines at Tournai.

There are several paintings by Frans Snyders in room 54. His painting of *The Pantry* shows a plump Flemish maid amid piles of oysters, gleaming fruit and a dead swan.

A tranquil painting of *The Card Players* by David Teniers the Younger contrasts with the baroque exuberance of other Antwerp 17C painters. His *Flemish Fair* shows an aristocratic couple strolling past a jovial country fair. It is possible that the couple portrayed are Teniers and his wife, Anna, who was the daughter of 'Velvet' Brueghel. Teniers was one of the most successful artists of the 17C. The castle in the background has been identified as a country house owned by Teniers called De Drie Torens. The house is still standing near Perk, 3km east of Vilvoorde.

There are also several scenes of Flemish inns by Adriaen Brouwers. Admired by Rembrandt and Rubens, Brouwers was imprisoned in Antwerp in 1633, perhaps for bad debts. His painting of *Seated Drinkers* looks as if it may have been inspired by the experience.

The long gallery overlooking the hall (**room 53**) contains several portraits by Antoon van Dyck, including *A Genoese Lady and her Daughter*, painted during a stay in Genoa. The sketch of *Rinaldo and Armida* is a preliminary version of a painting now in Baltimore. The *Portrait of the Artist and his Family* by Cornelis de Vos shows a successful artist's family in 1621.

An interesting painting by Hieronymus Francken the Younger (same room) shows *Jan Snellinck's Art Shop* in Antwerp in 1621. It reveals a Flemish interior crammed with paintings, books and antiques. The large painting above the chest is Frans Floris' *Adam and Eve*.

The Della Faille Bequest is hung in **rooms 55 and 56**. Presented by Count della Faille in 1942, it includes three portraits by Antoon van Dyck. One of these portraits shows *Jean Charles della Faille*, a distinguished Jesuit and professor of mathematics at Madrid. It was painted in 1629 after Van Dyck was appointed official court painter by Archduchess Isabella.

There are several appealing works by Jacob Jordaens in **room 57**, including his gloriously sensual *Allegory of Fertility* of c 1625. Considered one of his finest works, it shows nymphs and satyrs making their offerings to Pomona. Jordaens turned to the fables of Aesop for the two versions of *Satyr and Peasant* here. His gloriously irreverent *The King Drinks* represents a bawdy Flemish scene during the religious feast of Epiphany when the revellers declaim *De Koning Drinkt*.

The long gallery (**room 60**) contains works by 17C Dutch artists. The *View of Dordrecht* by Jan van Goyen vividly conveys a feeling of wind and cold. A painting by Nicolas Maes of *Old Woman Dreaming* is a touching study of old age. The jovial *Three Children and a Cart drawn by a Goat* by Frans Hals is the right section of a larger painting of a family in a garden. The other part of the canvas, which depicts the parents and a further seven children, is in a British collection.

In the same room is Rembrandt's *Portrait of Nicolaas van Bambeeck*. This portrait of a wealthy Amsterdam merchant was painted in 1641 while Rembrandt was working on *The Night Watch*. A matching portrait of Van Bambeeck's wife now hangs in Buckingham Palace.

A small collection of French paintings hangs in **room 61**. They include Philippe de Champaigne's *Presentation in the Temple*, painted for the church of St Honoré in Paris in 1648. Born in Brussels in 1602, De Champaigne went to Paris where he became Richelieu's favourite painter. You will also find Claude Lorraine's *Aeneas hunting the stag on the coast of Libya*. This subtly-lit mythological work illustrates an episode from Virgil's Aeneid in which Aeneas kills seven deer to feed his companions. The wistful *Fountain and Colonnade in a Park* was painted in 1775 by Hubert Robert after a stay in Rome.

The paintings in room 50 are by Spanish and Italian artists. The Spanish artist Ribera painted *Apollo flaying Marsyas* in 1637 after he had settled permanently in Naples. The Venetian painter Francesco Guardi painted *The Doge in St Mark's* in 1763. This is one of twelve Venetian scenes painted by Guardi to celebrate the coronation of the Doge. A sketch by Giovanni Battista Tiepolo of *The Three Theological Virtues* served as a preliminary study for a fresco in the church of Santa Maria de l'Ospedale della Pietà in Venice. The painting by Il Guercino of the *Donor presented to the Virgin by Four Saints* was painted for the church of Sant'Agostino in Cento in c 1616.

Returning to the landing, turn right to reach a small room with various 17C views of Brussels, including a spectacular *Panoramic View of Brussels* painted by Jan Baptist Bonnecroy in c 1665. Bonnecroy painted a similar view of Antwerp now in the National Maritime Museum in Antwerp, and a view of Amsterdam in the Musée Communal in Ixelles.

The Yellow Route

From the hall the Yellow Route is reached by an escalator. On the way you pass through a room with several interesting paintings of 17C sieges by Peter Snayers.

The 19C collection occupies five floors of an 18C town house on Place Royale renovated in 1998. It begins with Neo-classicism and Romanticism on level minus 2. The famous painting of The *Assassination of Marat* by **Jacques Louis David** shows the revolutionary leader murdered in his bath by Charlotte Corday. David fled to Brussels in 1815, living in a house at Rue Léopold 5 until his death. His last painting, completed in 1824, is the sensual *Mars disarmed by Venus* which now hangs in the main hall of the museum. David died the following year and was buried in Brussels Cemetery.

There are several luminous works by David's most famous Belgian pupil, **François Joseph Navez**, in the same room. His sombre depiction of *Agar and Ishmael in the Desert* was painted in 1820 during a stay in Rome. There is also a portrait by Navez of *Jacques Louis David*, and a *Portrait of Simonne Bucheron* at the age of three by Louis Gallait. The seductive *La Belle Rosine* by Antoine Wiertz was recently moved here from the Wiertz Museum.

The rooms on **level minus 1** are devoted to 19C Realism. Here are the somber *Saying Grace* by Charles de Groux, and a curious, almost Symbolist painting of *The Storks* by Louis Dubois.

The romantic Historicism of the 19C is reflected in Emile Wauters' haunting depiction of *Hugo van der Goes at the Convent* after he had gone mad. The interiors by Henri de Braekeleer reveal his obsessive nostalgia for 16C Antwerp. *The Wreck* by Louis Artan was painted on the Brittany coast in 1871. The Brussels artist Joseph Stevens devoted himself to painting dogs, such as *The Dog with a Fly* and *Dog Market in Paris*. There are also several paintings by Alfred Stevens, brother of Joseph. He specialised in portraits of elegant Parisian women of the Second Empire, such as *Autumn Flowers* of 1867.

The rooms on **level 1** contain some outstanding works by the Realist **Eugène Laermans**, such as *Strike Night* of 1893 and *The Corpse* of 1904. Here are also paintings and sculptures by **Constantin Meunier**. One of the most prolific and famous 19C Belgian artists, Meunier depicted the dignity and pathos of manual labour in the industrial heartland of Wallonia. Many of his works are displayed in the Constantin Meunier Museum in Ixelles.

The Belgian Impressionists are hung on the same floor. *The Man in Red* by Henri Evenepoel shows the influence of Manet. The portrait of *Henrietta with the Large Hat* was one of Evenepoel's last paintings before he died at the age of 27.

Paintings of the mysterious Symbolist Movement are on **level 2**. The enigmatic Fernand Khnopff idealised his sister in several paintings such as the *Portrait of Marguerite Khnopff* of 1887. She also appears in seven different poses in *Memories of Lawn Tennis* of 1889. His painting *Abandoned City* of 1904 was modelled on a postcard of the Memlingplaats in Bruges, where he spent his early childhood.

Several works by Théo Rysselberghe also hang here. His *Arabian Fantasia* was painted when he was 22. He became versatile in various 19C styles, as can be seen in his *Portrait of Octave Maus*, a work inspired by Whistler, and the later *Portrait of Madame Charles Maus*, painted under the influence of Seurat's pointillisme.

Jean Delville's *The Treasures of Satan* of 1895 represents the radicalism of the Belgian Idealist Movement. Examples of Luminism can be found in the gentle landscapes of Emile Claus. Several works by the First Latem School also hang here, including a sombre *Lamentation* by Albert Servaes and a *Crucifixion* by Gustave van de Woestyne.

Several works by the eccentric Ostend painter James Ensor are hung on **level 3**. Early works such as *The Russian Music* of 1881 were set in somber bourgeois interiors, but Ensor's style suddenly turned wild in 1883, as is seen in works such as *Odd Masks*.

On this floor there is also a small collection of French paintings, including Sisley's *Bank of the Canal of the Loing*, Gauguin's *Portrait of Suzanne Bambridge*, Seurat's *The Seine at La Grande-Jatte*, and Bonnard's beautiful *Nude against the Light*.

Musée d'Art Moderne

From level minus 2 the Green Route passes into the Musée d'Art Moderne, which can also be entered from Place Royale 1, open Tues–Sun 10.00–13.00 and 14.00–17.00. Completed in 1984 below Place du Musée, this underground museum descends through eight levels. Some of the rooms receive natural light from a semicircular sunken glass well. The museum has an outstanding collection of 20C Belgian and international art, including the world's largest collection of Magritte paintings.

Descend to **level minus 3**, where several little rooms contain contemporary installations such as Dennis Oppenheim's *Attempt to Raise Hell*, and Vic Gentils' *Rua de amor*, inspired by a segregated red-light street in Brazil. This level also has Francis Bacon's *Pope with Owls*, one of his 35 Pope paintings, and a tall *Diana in wood* by Ossip Zadkine.

The rooms on **level minus 4** are devoted to early 20C Belgian artists. One room has several works by Rik Wouters in his appealing Brabant Fauvist style. His wife Nel posed for *Lady with Yellow Necklace* and again in the bronze statue *Household Cares*. Ferdinand Schirren's *The Woman at the Piano* reveals the Fauvists' love of colour.

The melancholy Symbolism of Leon Spilliaert occupies a room of its own. His *Self-Portrait* of 1904 is an astonishing study of anxiety. His style became more mellow after he married in 1916. Notice that Jean Brusselmans' *In the Garden* is painted in the garden of the painter Auguste Oleffe, as is Oleffe's painting *August 1909*.

This level also has works by French painters, such as Matisse's *Still Life*, *Venice Red Interior*, Raoul Dufy's *View of Marseille*, and Picasso's *Guitar and Fruit Dish*.

Beyond here (still level minus 4) are the Flemish Expressionists, or Second Sint Martens-Latem School. Constant Permeke's *The Stranger*, painted in 1916, launched Flemish Expressionism. His *Potato Eater* was painted in the large studio he built at Jabbeke, near Bruges.

Frits van den Berghe was another artist who settled in Sint-Martens-Latem, painting idyllic rustic scenes such as *Sunday of 1924*. His friend Gustave De Smet was drawn to circuses and fairgrounds, where he painted works such as *The Dressing Room* of 1928.

Most of **level minus 5** is devoted to the enigmatic Surrealism of **Paul Delvaux**. His painting of *Le Musée Spitzner* was inspired by a visit in 1932 to a travelling waxworks museum that featured nude wax models afflicted by venereal disease. The eerie *La Voix Publique* reveals Delvaux's obsession with city trams, while *Pygmalion* reinterprets the legend of the King of Cyprus (who fell in love with a female statue) by reversing the roles.

The **Magritte Room** is at **level minus 6**. Recently boosted by a gift from his wife Georgette, the collection is the largest in the world. It includes a portrait of the critic *Paul Nougé* from 1927, the enigmatic *Empire of Lights* of 1954, and the *Arnheim Estate* of 1962. Several glass cases contain Surrealist documents and photographs.

The next room (same level) contains works by other Surrealists, such as Giorgio de Chirico's *Melancholy of a Beautiful Day* from 1913, and Salvador Dali's disturbing version of *The Temptation of St Anthony* of 1946. Also here are exuberant works by the postwar Cobra group, including Pierre Alechinsky's *Sometimes it's the Opposite*, and Corneille's *New Dawn Full of Birds*.

The artists who banded together briefly as Jeune Peinture Belge are found on **level minus 7**. Shunning artistic dogma, these artists developed their own styles from 1945–48. Louis Van Lint's *Still Life, Lamp Glass* reveals his deep interest in colour, while Marc Mendelson's *Portrait of Mia* is a strangely enigmatic portrait of a young artist.

The space in **level minus 8** is given over to contemporary art. One section is devoted to the entertaining Surrealist assemblages of Marcel Broodthaers, including his *Red Pot of Mussels* and various mock museum cabinets containing quirky exhibits.

Also here are Christian Boltanski's eerie *Shrine: Murders*, featuring photographs of Spanish murder victims lit by spotlights. *The Green Curtain* by Michelangelo Pistoletto reveals his obsession with mirrors, while Bernd Lohaus' *Wall Sculptures* uses driftwood salvaged from the Scheldt at Antwerp. The French artist Roman Opalka has spent his life painting consecutive numbers on identical canvases. This work is *Detail Nos. 1556343–1574101*.

Return to the entrance hall where the **Orange Route** leads down to the **Sculpture Gallery** in the basement. This well-displayed collection of 19C sculpture includes Guillaume Geefs' statue of *Frédéric, Count of Merode*, who was killed during the 1830 revolution, Antoine Wiertz's *The Light* (from his Four Ages of Mankind), and George Minne's *Mother Weeping for her Dead Child*.

A small open-air sculpture garden occupies the slope to the west of the museum.

5 • The Parc de Bruxelles and the Parliament quarter

This walk takes you into an elegant quarter where Charlotte Brontë lived from 1842–43. Beginning at **Grand-Place**, climb the Rue de la Madeleine to reach **Gare Centrale**. Designed by Victor Horta as part of the rail tunnel between the Gare du Nord and Gare du Midi, the station was eventually completed in 1952. The curious reliefs on either side of the main entrance depict some of the old buildings that were demolished to construct the tunnel. The booking hall is decorated with a large mural by J. Hayez. A subway leads from here to the Galerie Ravenstein, a modern arcade with a rotunda, restaurants and cafés.

The Brontës in Brussels

Charlotte and Emily Brontë travelled to Brussels in 1842 to study French. They stayed for nine months at the Pensionnat Heger in the Rue Isabelle, returning to Yorkshire after their aunt died. Charlotte came back to Brussels alone the following year to teach at the Pensionnat, where she became infatuated with Monsieur Heger. Years later, Charlotte based two novels, *Villette* and *The Professor*, on her Brussels experiences. Nothing now remains of the Pensionnat Heger, which was torn down in 1909 to make way for the Palais des Beaux-Arts. Yet diligent Brontë fans can still track down sites that feature in her novels, such as the flight of steps at the end of the Rue Baron Horta, the Parc de Bruxelles and the Protestant chapel where Charlotte worshipped.

The **Palais des Beaux-Arts** stands on the site of the Pensionnat Heger where Charlotte and Emily Brontë stayed. Built by Victor Horta in his Art Deco style, it has an oval concert hall, exhibition rooms, a bookshop and café. The building height was restricted to one storey to avoid obstructing the view from the royal palace above.

The picturesque 15C **Hôtel Ravenstein** next to the Palais des Beaux-Arts in Rue Ravenstein is the only surviving artistocratic town house from the Burgundian period. It is now occupied by a restaurant and several cultural organisations.

Go up the Rue Baron Horta, passing the **Musée du Cinéma**, open daily 17.30–23.00. The museum has a fascinating collection of early cinema apparatus, including Edison's 1894 Kinetoscope, several 1895 Mutoscopes, and a Phenakistoscope made by Joseph Plateau of Brussels in 1832. Classic films are screened every day on the cinema's two screens. Silent films are accompanied by live piano music. A monthly programme is posted outside the museum entrance.

The steps at the end of Rue Baron Horta are described by Charlotte Brontë in her Brussels novels. They lead up to the **Parc de Bruxelles**, which also features in Charlotte's novels. This formal park was laid out in French style in 1776–7. It occupies the site of the ducal park and part of the Coudenberg Palace. Some of the fiercest fighting of the 1830 revolution took place outside the park gates as the Belgian rebels tried to oust the Dutch troops. The park is dotted with Neo-classical statues, including a Diana by Gabriel Grupello and a monument by Vinçotte to the sculptor Godecharle.

The **Palais Royal** is sited to the south of the Parc de Bruxelles. It occupies the position of the Coudenberg Palace which burned down in 1731. The Coudenberg was the residence of the Dukes of Brabant and later rulers such as Philip the Good and Charles V, who signed his abdication here in 1555. The original palace, built between 1740 and 1827, was transformed in 1904–12 from plans by Jean Maquet. The pediment sculpture of Belgium between Agriculture and Industry is the work of Vinçotte. The palace is the sovereign's official town residence. It is open to the public for several weeks in the summer when the royal family is away on vacation.

Royal Family

King Albert II, born 1934, was crowned in 1993 after the sudden death of his elder brother, King Baudouin. Albert is married to the Italian Princess Paola Ruffo di Calabria. Their three children are Philippe, Astrid and Laurent. Baudouin is survived by his wife, the Spanish noblewoman Fabiola de Mora y Aragon.

The **Hôtel Bellevue**, to the right of the palace, was built in the 18C as a hotel. Annexed by Leopold II to the royal palace, it became the residence of Leopold III and Queen Astrid when they were Duke and Duchess of Brabant. Now occupied by the **Musée de la Dynastie**, open Tues–Sun 10.00–16.00, it contains mementoes of the Belgian royal family, including photographs, maps, uniforms and toys. The inner courtyard was converted in 1998 to house the King Baudouin Memorial. Created in memory of the popular king who died suddenly in 1993, it contains a reconstructed office, dolls' house and other personal mementoes.

The **Palais des Académies**, at the south end of the Rue Ducale, was built in 1823 for the Crown Prince of Orange. It became the seat of the Académie Royale de Belgique in 1876.

The Rue Ducale is lined with former aristocratic town houses now used as offices. The house at no. 51 was occupied by Byron in 1816. He wrote the Waterloo episodes of *Childe Harold's Pilgrimage* here. The commemorative plaque records that he had left England where his genius was unrecognised. It fails to add that he had been ostracised for leaving his wife.

The **Palais de la Nation** at the east end of the park was built in 1783 for the States of Brabant from plans by the French architect Barnabé Guimard. The pediment was carved by Gilles Godecharle. During the Dutch period (1815–30), it alternated with the Binnenhof at The Hague as the seat of the States General of the United Kingdom of the Netherlands. One wing was used as a residence for the Crown Prince of the Netherlands (the future William III of the Netherlands), who was born here in 1817. It has been the meeting-place of the Belgian Parliament since the revolution of 1830. Edith Cavell was tried here as a spy in 1915.

Now turn right along the Rue Royale to reach the **Colonne du Congrès**. The 47m high column was designed by Joseph Poelaert. It is surmounted by a statue of King Leopold I carved by Willem Geefs. The column was erected between 1850–59 to commemorate the National Congress of 1831, which proclaimed the Belgian constitution following the revolution. The bronze figures at the angles represent Freedom of the Press, Freedom of Education (both by Jan Geefs), Freedom of Association (by Charles Fraikin), and Freedom of Religion (by Eugène Simonis). The two lions were carved by Simonis. An eternal flame burns beside the tombs of the Belgian Unknown Soldiers from the First and Second World Wars.

There is a good view of the Lower Town from the square behind the column. Various government departments occupy the modern buildings nearby known as the Cité Administrative. Continuing along Rue Royale, you reach **Le Botanique**, open daily 10.00–22.00. The botanical gardens were established here in 1926, but most of the plants were moved in the 1950s to Meise, north of Brussels. All that remains are the former 19C greenhouses and a small landscaped garden with sculptures by Constantin Meunier and other 19C artists. The greenhouses are used as a cultural centre for the French-speaking Community. The complex includes a theatre, exhibition hall, French bookshop and café.

Rue Royale ends at **Ste Marie**, an unusual octagonal church in Byzantine style built in 1844 by Hendrik van Overstraeten.

Descend through the botanical gardens to reach Place Rogier, where several grand hotels survive from the 1920s. The square is named after Charles Rogier, a leader of the 1830 revolution. He became a government minister responsible for creating Belgium's railway system. He also negotiated the freedom of navigation on the Scheldt. A statue of Rogier stands on the Place de la Liberté, not far from the Colonne du Congrès.

The quarter to the north of here is dominated by the controversial **Manhattan business district**, which was begun in 1970s but abandoned after the oil crisis led to a slump in demand for office space. The district, which is now finally nearing completion, has modern office buildings occupied by the Belgacom telecommunications company and the government of Brussels Region.

The Rue du Progrès leads to the Gare du Nord. This street was formerly lined with 19C hotels, including the Hôtel Liégois where the poet Verlaine often stayed on his frequent visits to Brussels.

The **Musée des Chemins-de-Fer Belges**, open Mon–Fri and the first Saturday of every month 09.00–16.30, is located in the Gare du Nord. It contains a collection of paintings, photographs, models and uniforms. An interesting series of paintings by James Thiriar show 19C railway workers in the uniforms of the time; and there is also a painting of the first train from Brussels to Mechelen.

The first train on the Continent
Belgians are rather proud of the fact that the first passenger train service on the Continent ran from Brussels to Mechelen on 5 May 1835. Some 900 passengers travelled on three trains from the Allée Verte station (disappeared) to Mechelen. The third train was pulled by a steam engine called L'Eléphant, which is now in the railway museum.

---

6 • The Sablon

This short walk goes through an attractive aristocratic district which developed on the heights above the old town. Begin at the church of **Notre-Dame du Sablon**, which stands on the site of a chapel built in 1304 by the Guild of Crossbowmen. The guild often held shooting competitions on the square in the 17C. At one such event in 1615 the governor Isabella succeeded in shooting down the guild's target bird from the church spire. She commissioned a painting by Antoon Sallaert to illustrate her feat (in the Musée des Beaux-Arts).

The legend of Our Lady of the Sablon
Béatrice Soetkens was a pious girl who prayed regularly before a neglected statue of the Madonna in Antwerp. She had a vision of the Virgin in 1348 in which she was told to take the statue to Brussels. Brought by boat, the statue was installed in the Sablon chapel. It soon attracted so many pilgrims that the crossbowmen decided to build a new church, which developed into the present building. The statue was carried in procession every year in a ceremony known as the Ommegang. It was destroyed by the Calvinists during the 17C religious troubles.

Notre-Dame du Sablon
This splendid Gothic church was largely built in the the 15C and 16C, though the two great piers which support the crossing date from c 1400, and the choir was added about ten years later. The slim choir lancets are particularly beautiful. The

church served the aristocratic families who lived in this district of Brussels in the 17C, as the splendid family memorials and paintings in the church bear witness.

A curious skeletal monument of Claude Bouton, chamberlain to Charles V, who died in 1556, is found at the west end of the south aisle. The most impressive monuments are the two Baroque funerary chapels on either side of the choir. They commemorate the Tour et Taxis family, which had a virtual monopoly on the European postal system from the early 16C until the French Revolution. The chapel on the left contains sculptures by Jérôme Duquesnoy the Younger and Gabriel Grupello. There is also a triptych by Michiel Coxie in the south transept.

The church stands above the **Place du Grand Sablon**, an elegant square surrounded by restored 17C and 18C houses. Many of the buildings are occupied by antique shops and restaurants. The name Sablon recalls that this was once a sandy slope on the edge of the marshes. The square is occupied on Saturday and Sunday by an attractive if pricey antique market.

A fountain of 1775 by Jacques Bergé was paid for by Thomas Bruce, 3rd Earl of Elgin, 2nd Earl of Ailesbury and friend of James II. A Jacobite exile, he lived here from 1696–1741. He installed the fountain in gratitude to the people of Brussels.

The **Musée Postal**, open Tues–Sat 10.00–16.00, occupies a handsome town house at no. 40. It contains an interesting collection of postage stamps, old post office relics and telecommunications equipment.

Now cross the Rue de la Régence to reach the seductive **Place du Petit Sablon**. The exquisite formal garden in the middle of this square was laid out in 1890. It is decorated with ten statues of 16C dignitaries, including William of Orange and Ortelius. A fountain is surmounted by a statue of Counts Egmont and Hoorn, which once stood on Grand-Place near the spot where the two nobles were beheaded on the orders of the Duke of Alva. The garden is surrounded by an elegant wrought-iron balustrade with 48 statuettes representing the medieval guilds.

The **Conservatoire de Musique**, on the corner of the Rue de la Régence and the Place du Petit Sablon, was built by J.P. Cluysenaer in 1876 on the site of the Tour et Taxis mansion. Plaques in French and Dutch recall that it was here that Prince François de Taxis founded the first international postal system in 1516.

The large **Palais d'Egmont** stands above the garden. The original palace was built c 1548 for Françoise of Luxembourg. She was mother of the Count Egmont whose statue stands in the garden below. Voltaire met and quarrelled with Rousseau in the Egmont Palace in 1722. Later known as the **Palais d'Arenberg** from the family that owned it in the 18C, the palace was rebuilt in 1750 and again after a fire in 1891. Sold to the state in 1964, it is now used by the Ministry of Foreign Affairs. It was here that Great Britain, Ireland and Denmark signed the agreements on 22 January 1972 under which they became members of the EEC. The best view of the palace is from the Parc d'Egmont, a secret urban park which can be entered from the Rue aux Laines, on the right. Other entrances are off the Boulevard de Waterloo and the Rue du Grand Cerf. Now rather dominated by the Hilton Hotel, the park contains a replica of Frampton's Peter Pan statue in Kensington Gardens, London.

Continue up the Rue aux Laines to reach the immense **Palais de Justice**, which was built in bold eclectic style by Joseph Poelaert from 1866–83. It stands, rather symbolically, on the site of the medieval Galgenberg (gallows hill). The dome, over 100m in height, was rebuilt after it was gutted by fire in 1944. The figures around the colonnade represent Justice, Law, Mercy and Strength. The portico, flanked by Doric colonnades, leads to two open vestibules between which a stairway ascends to the great hall, which occupies the centre of the building. On the right of the stairs are statues of Demosthenes and Lycurgus, on the left of Ulpian and Cicero.

A monument in the middle of Place Poelaert, in front of the Palais de Justice, commemorates the Belgian infantry. Another memorial, beyond the tram lines, was unveiled in 1923 to record Britain's gratitude for help received from Belgium during the First World War.

The terrace, which has an orientation table and telescopes, commands a fine view of the Lower Town. The curious Baroque tower to the right belongs to the church of the Minimes, built in 1700–15. The convent of the Minimes, which has now vanished, was partly built on the site of the home of the anatomist Andreas Vesalius, who was born in Brussels in 1514.

A modern lift is due to be built in 2000 to link Place Poelaert with the Marolles. The district can also be reached by a monumental ramp next to the Palais de Justice.

7 • The Marolles

This walk explores a dense urban district with a strong Brussels character. Some of the older people in this quarter still speak the curious Brussels dialect, which contains elements of Dutch, French and Spanish. Crowded with small shops and local cafés, the Marolles is currently yielding to a slow gentrification.

Beginning on the **Place du Grand Sablon**, go down the steep Rue de Rollebeek, past a remnant of the 12C fortifications known as the **Tour Anneessens** (or Tour d'Angle). Turn left to reach the church of **Notre-Dame de la Chapelle**. A chapel founded here in 1134 was replaced by the present church. Erected between 1210 and c 1300, the church is a mixture of Romanesque and Gothic elements. The nave and aisles were destroyed by fire in 1405, but later reconstructed. The tower, badly damaged by the French bombardment of 1695, was rebuilt by Antoon Pastorana in 1708. The 19C bas-relief of the Trinity in the tympanum of the main portal was carved by Constantin Meunier.

Pieter Bruegel the Elder married here in 1563; six years later he was buried in the third chapel off the south aisle. The memorial was erected by his son, Pieter Brueghel the Younger, and later decorated with a painting by Rubens (now in a private collection). The pulpit was carved in 1721 by Pierre Plumier, who also carved the Spinola family memorial in the Chapelle du Saint Sacrement. The same chapel contains a monument of 1834 to the patriot Frans Anneessens, who is buried in the church. The 19C choir stalls retain their original stone seats.

Now walk down Rue Haute. Pieter Bruegel the Elder lived at no. 132. His reputation was such that he was exempted from the duty of providing billets for Spanish troops. His great-grandson, the painter David Teniers, died in this house.

The Place du Jeu de Balle, off the parallel Rue Blaes, is occupied every morning by a chaotic and charming flea market known as the **Vieux Marché**.

The **Centre Public d'Aide Sociale de Bruxelles** occupies some rooms in the Saint-Pierre Hospital at Rue Haute 298A. This forgotten museum contains art treasures from charitable institutions, including gold and silverware, furniture, and 15C–18C paintings. Open Wed 14.00–16.00.

The **Porte de Hal**, open Tues–Sun 10.00–17.00, at the end of Rue Haute is all that remains of the city's 14C defences. The other city gates were torn down in the early 19C to buid the ring boulevards, but the Porte de Hal was spared because it was being used as a prison. Rebuilt in the 19C in a neo-Gothic style, it is now used as a museum. It is due to re-open in autumn 2000 as a museum of decorative art, with furnished interiors in Gothic, Renaissance and Baroque styles.

The Ring Boulevards

The ring boulevards were constructed between 1818 and 1871 along the line of the 14C city walls. They were converted into urban motorways and tunnels in the late 1950s mainly to speed traffic to the site of the 1958 World Fair at the Heysel in north Brussels. The ring is interrupted by a number of squares often on the site of the old city gates, such as Place Rogier, Place Madou, Porte de Namur, and Place Louise. Recent attempts to turn these busy traffic intersections back into pleasant urban squares have achieved a modest success.

Turn left along the Boulevard de Waterloo to the Place Jean Jacobs where a memorial honours the victims of the wreck in 1908 of the first Belgian training ship.

8 • The Parc du Cinquantenaire

The Parc du Cinquantenaire was laid out for the exhibition of 1880, which celebrated the 50th anniversary of the founding of the Belgian state. A road tunnel runs under the park to link the Rue de la Loi and the Rue Belliard with the Avenue de Tervuren. Take the metro to Mérode and follow signs marked Musées.

The dominant feature of the park is the **Palais du Cinquantenaire**, two large halls which originally formed the centrepiece of the 1880 exhibition. The wings are linked by a triumphal arch by Charles Girault surmounted by a quadriga carved by Thomas Vinçotte. Statues at the base of the arch symbolise eight of the nine provinces of Belgium. Brabant, the final province, is represented by the quadriga.

Musée Royal de l'Armée et d'Histoire Militaire

In the north wing wing of the Palais is the interesting Musée Royal de l'Armée et d'Histoire Militaire, open Tues–Sun 09.00–12.00 and 13.00–16.30. The entrance hall contains some relics of Waterloo. The **Historic Hall** is devoted to the Belgian army from 1831 to 1914. This admittedly dusty collection contains some fascinating relics, including uniforms, photographs, medals, and portraits of Belgian generals. Relics of the tragic Mexican Expedition of 1864–67 are displayed in cases 34 and 35.

The two large halls on the right hold a large collection of **First World War weapons and uniforms**. The exhibits include uniforms, helmets, weapons, artillery, tanks, medical equipment and gas masks. A cabinet contains mementoes of Gabrielle Petit, a Tournai woman shot by the Germans in 1916. A door leads into the courtyard where Second World War tanks are displayed.

An impressive new section devoted to **Resistance and Deportation** occupies the upper level of the large 19C Bordiau Hall. It includes a reconstructed Belgian street with shop windows and a newspaper kiosk, and a domestic interior from the Occupation. You can follow eyewitness accounts of Nazi victims on video screens and headphones. The **Air Museum** displays a large collection of historic aircraft in a separate 19C hall.

The **Arms and Armour Room** contains an interesting collection of medieval armour and weapons. Do not leave without looking at the Titeca Collection of 19C uniforms, which occupies a room above the triumphal arch. You can then go out onto the roof of the arch for a splendid view of the European Quarter.

A 19C exhibition hall opposite contains **Autoworld**, open daily 10.00–18.00. This outstanding private collection of vintage cars and trucks includes two Minervas owned by King Albert I and the Cadillac in which President John F. Kennedy was driven through Berlin in 1963. An interesting collection of 18C and 19C carriages was recently moved here from the Musée du Cinquantenaire. One of the highlights is a superb Louis XVIII Coupé de Gala with painted panels in the style of Boucher.

Musée du Cinquantenaire

The other buildings in the south wing of the Palais are devoted to the Musée du Cinquantenaire, open Tues–Sun 10.00–17.00. This contains a vast collection of decorative art from all over the world. Once a rather neglected museum with awkward opening hours, the Musée du Cinquantenaire has improved immensely in recent years. It can still happen that a section of the collection is closed, but the staff at the information desk are generally able to gain admittance to a particular room if a visitor is interested. The museum has a reference library, a collection of more than 70,000 slides, a museum for the blind, an art bookshop and a restaurant. An unusual 19C plaster cast workshop is located at the rear of Autoworld. Visitors can order plaster casts of statues in the collection.

Plans exist to create an entrance on the esplanade next to the triumphal arch, but visitors at present have to go around to the front of the building to enter by the **Albert-Elisabeth entrance**. This leads into a rotunda with an information desk. The door to the right leads into a late 19C wing containing a remarkable collection of **European decorative art** dating from the Middle Ages to the 20C.

The main hall in this wing is hung with a series of eight tapestries illustrating *The History of Jacob*. These were woven in Brussels in 1528 by Willem de Kempeneer after designs by Bernard van Orley. A door off this hall leads into a 19C cloister (room 71), which contains an interesting collection of sculpture, including Mosan baptismal fonts, stained glass from the Cathedral of Brussels and funerary monuments.

The building on the opposite side of the cloister garden is a 19C copy of the 15C Nassau chapel on the Mont des Arts. It contains an outstanding collection of metalwork from Dinant known as **dinanderie (room 73)**.

Rooms 54 to 70 contain Flemish tapestries, furniture and retables. The cradle in room 62 is said to have belonged to Charles V. A collection of amateur cinematograph cameras and projectors is displayed in **room 75**. It is said to include every model sold between 1922 and 1987.

The **Salle aux Trésors** in the basement (reached from the tapestry hall) contains a strikingly-lit collection of reliquaries, wooden statues and ivories, including several outstanding examples of the Mosan Art style, which flourished in the Meuse valley in the 11C and 12C. The most celebrated works in the collection are the portable altar from the Abbey of Stavelot from c 1160, the *reliquary of Pope Alexander* of 1145 and a polychrome wooden statue of the *Virgin and Child* (a Sedes Sapientiae) of 1070.

The section on **Belgian Archaeology** in **rooms 1–9**, on this floor, contains a striking collection from the Palaeolithic, Neolithic, Bronze and Iron Ages and the Gallo-Roman period. Objects include a Bronze Age spear imported from Britain, a La Tène drinking horn with gold filigree decoration, a Roman processional standard surmounted by a figure of Serapis and several bronze and silver gilt Merovingian buckles.

Return to the rotunda and go through the door opposite. After passing the bookshop, turn right to enter a series of rooms containing **18C and 19C furnished interiors**. **Room 46** incorporates a reconstructed Art Nouveau shop interior designed by Victor Horta. The glass cabinets contain an outstanding collection of Art Nouveau and Art Deco objects, including works in silver by Philippe and Marcel Wolfers and Henry van de Velde, ceramics by Paul Gauguin, Gallé, and Lachenal and textiles by Morris, Liberty and the Wiener Werkstätte.

Go back to the bookshop and turn right to reach another rotunda. The door on the left leads into an Art Deco wing built after the original 1880 hall was destroyed by fire. Occupying four levels, this wing is devoted to the ancient civilisations of Greece, Rome and China. The Ancient Rome collection in rooms 22–25 contain works from Etruria, North Africa, Syria and Asia Minor. Among the highlights are several Etruscan bronze candelabra and tripods, busts of Augustus and Septimus Severus from the Republican and Imperial periods, a wallpainting from Boscoreale and several uninhibited, lustful reliefs on Dionysian sarcophagi. A detailed scale model of Rome in the 4C AD in **room 20** can be viewed from the balcony one floor up.

Room 25 contains works excavated by Belgian archaeologists excavating the ruins of the ancient city of Apamaea ad Orontem in Syria from 1930–38. Some of their discoveries, including a reconstruction of the 2C AD Grand Colonnade and several splendid mosaics, are displayed in the museum. The collection includes a mosaic of *Therapenides* on the subject of Neoplatonism, several geometric mosaics from the synagogues, and a large 4C AD mosaic showing hunting scenes, which once decorated the house of the governor of Syria.

There are several Roman copies of Greek sculptures, including the *Venus of Cnidus* by Praxiteles, a *Bacchus* (style of the Westmacott Ephebe) by Polycleitus, a pensive *Daphnis*, from the group Pan and Daphnis sometimes attributed to Heliodorus of Rhodes and, from a famous Hellenistic group, an exultant *Satyr* full of fierce pagan joy.

The **Ancient Greece collection** in **rooms 108–116** includes Cycladic idols and a Mycenaean gold cup. Vases from the Archaic, Geometric, Orientalising and Classical periods include an archaic (late 6C BC) black figure Attic amphora depicting the departure of the warriors; an archaic red figure amphora of the archer; a 6C BC red figure stamnos signed by Smikros depicting a banqueting scene; and a late 5C BC kantharos of Hercules and the Amazons signed by Douris.

One floor up, the vast **Ancient Egyptian collection** occupies **rooms 123–139**. The collection includes prehistoric vases, the stele of Den, the reconstructed mastaba of Neferirtenef, an archaic female statue known as *La Dame de*

Bruxelles, Middle Empire reliefs, models and the bust of an unidentified pharaoh, a limestone relief of Queen Tiy, sarcophagi, coffins, mummies, figurines and scarabs from various periods. A colossal diorite head is believed to be that of *Ptolemy VIII* from Nubia. There is also a basalt statue of the *vizir Bakenrenef*, the bas-relief of *Petamenope*, a head (possibly of Ptolemy VIII) and several funerary portraits on wood and cloth from the Ptolemaic and Roman periods.

Room 21 contains **Islamic art**, including ceramics and textiles from Central Asia, India, North Africa, Syria, Turkey, Spain, Sicily and Iran. They include vessels and wall tiles from Iznik and Kadjar, elaborately decorated with floral and geometric patterns and representations of the human figure. The textiles, some richly embroidered, others recording ancient legends, are mainly from Iran and Turkey.

Rooms 78–87 contain works from **India and Southeast Asia**. Masks, theatre marionettes, lamps, statues, temple columns, reliefs, bronzes, paintings and ceramics are combined in a dazzling display. Rooms 79–82 are devoted to the art of **Ancient China**. This rich collection has artefacts from every dynasty, including a magnificent 19C wooden statue of the Bodhisatva, some 7C and 8C stone heads from Tianlongshan, bronzes, carved ivories, mirrors, ceramics, ritual vases, costumes and examples of delicate calligraphy.

Rooms 27–36 were recently modernised to display the art of **Pre-Columbian America**. Terracotta figurines, mosaics, stelae, vases, gold and silver statuettes, textiles, cult masks, musical instruments, tools and feather headdresses provide a fascinating record of the civilisations which flourished between Alaska and Tierra del Fuego.

Rooms 37–41 are devoted to the art of **Polynesia and Micronesia**. The Galerie Mercator contains a magnificent collection of archaeological and ethnographical artefacts from New Zealand, the Fiji Islands and Easter Island. Other sections are devoted to weaving, stone and wood working, fishing, farming, house building, furniture making and warfare. The collection includes material collected by the 1934–35 Franco-Belgian expedition to Easter Island, including a large statue of Pou Hakanononga, the God of Tuna Fishing.

The **Parc du Cinquantenaire** contains a Neo-classical temple known as the Pavilion of the Human Passions, built by Victor Horta in 1889. It contains a relief by Jef Lambeau which caused such outrage when it was unveiled that the city authorities promptly closed the building. It remains locked to this day. A memorial nearby was carved in 1921 by Thomas Vinçotte to celebrate Belgium's exploration of the Congo. The Brussels mosque occupies a building in the corner of the park which originally contained a 19C panoramic painting of Cairo.

The church of St Gertrude, off the Place van Meyel, contains a beautiful late 15C statue of St Gertrude which was found in the loft in 1935.

9 • The European Quarter

The main offices of the European Union are located around Rond Point Schuman and Place du Luxembourg. This walk begins by taking the metro to **Rond Point Schuman**, a square named after the French politician Robert Schuman who promoted the 1951 plan to pool Europe's steel and coal resources. The European

Coal and Steel Community led to the creation of the European Econimic Community, established in the Treaty of Rome of 1957 signed by Belgium, France, Germany, Italy, the Netherlands and Luxembourg. The United Kingdom, Ireland and Denmark joined the communities in 1972, Greece in 1981, Spain and Portugal in 1985, and Austria, Finland and Sweden in 1995.

The main administration of the European Commission is based in the **Berlaymont** office on Rond Point Schuman, a distinctive star-shaped building designed in 1967 by L. de Vestel, J. Gilson and A. and J. Polak. It takes its name from a monastery which once stood on the site. The European Parliament is located nearby on the edge of the Parc Léopold.

Walk down Rue Archimède to reach Square Ambiorix, one of three connected squares designed in 1875 by Gédéon Bordiau. The elaborate Art Nouveau **Maison de Saint-Cyr** at no. 11 was designed by Gustave Strauven in 1903. Descending to the Square Palmerston, Victor Horta's innovative Art Nouveau **Hôtel Van Eetvelde** is at no. 4. The lowest square, Square Marie Louise, has eclectic 19C mansions overlooking an artificial pond. Now turn left along Chaussée d'Etterbeek to reach Parc Léopold.

Parc Léopold

The Parc Léopold at the end of the street is an attractive 19C landscaped park on a sloping site with a small lake. Originally a zoo, the park was redeveloped by Léopold II as a scientific centre. Several learned institutes were built in the park, including the *Musée de l'Institut des Sciences Naturelles*, open Tues–Fri 09.30–16.45, Sat and Sun 10.00–18.00, at the top of the hill. Follow small signs illustrated with a dinosaur to reach the museum entrance on Rue Vautier. The museum was opened in 1891 to display a collection of minerals, insects and fossils, including nine 250-million-year-old **fossil iguanodons** discovered in 1875 in a coal mine at Bernissart in Hainaut and painstakingly reassembled in the Nassau chapel by the Belgian palaeontologist Louis Dollo. The museum also has a mammoth from Lier, skeletons of Stone Age miners, whale skeletons and a collection of prehistoric tools.

Musée Wiertz

Almost opposite, at Rue Vautier 62, the curious Musée Wiertz, open Tues–Fri 10.00–12.00 and 13.00–17.00, and every second weekend, occupies a house and studio built by the Belgian government for the romantic painter Antoine Joseph Wiertz (1806–65). Convinced that he was the equal of Rubens, Wiertz toiled on enormous canvases illustrating macabre themes such as *Hunger*, *Madness and Crime*, *The Vision of an Executed Criminal* and *Premature Burial*. The former studio is dominated by these paintings, which Wiertz bequeathed to the state in exchange for the studio, but the side rooms contain rather more appealing Italian scenes from his stay in Rome.

The European Parliament occupies a striking 1993 glass building at the foot of Rue Vautier. Built on the site of an old brewery, it accommodates 626 European members of parliament and their staff.

Returning to Porte de Namur by the Chaussée de Wavre, you pass the former home of the Belgian writer Camille Lemonnier (1844–1913) at no. 150. It contains a small museum with various documents and books (open only on request).

The Gare Léopold and the European Parliament, Brussels

10 • Ixelles

The commune of Ixelles developed during the late 19C in the rolling countryside to the south of the Porte de Namur. Located close to the fashionable Avenue Louise, it became popular with 19C artists, intellectuals and foreign residents. The commune has several museums, some striking Art Nouveau houses and numerous fashionable restaurants.

Universities of Brussels

The university quarter lies in Ixelles, though the university campus is technically in Brussels commune. The Université Libre de Bruxelles (ULB) was founded in 1834 in the Ancienne Cour (now the Musée des Beaux-Arts), but moved later to a site on Avenue Franklin Roosevelt. A statue of 1865 on the campus commemorates its founder, Theodoor Verhaeghen. The university was split in 1970 into a French-speaking university, which retained the original name, and a Dutch-speaking university, the Vrije Universiteit Brussel (VUB). The university has several specialised museums on the campus. The Museum of Mineralogy and the Museum of Zoology are open to the public at certain times.

The walk begins at **Place Louise** and goes down **Avenue Louise**, a broad tree-lined avenue built in 1864 to link the Upper Town with the Bois de la Cambre. An interesting quarter of Art Nouveau houses lies to the west of the avenue. Victor Horta's **Hôtel Tassel** of 1893 at Rue Paul-Emile Janson 6 is considered the earliest example of Art Nouveau architecture. Paul Hankar's private home at Rue Defacqz 71 was built in the same year.

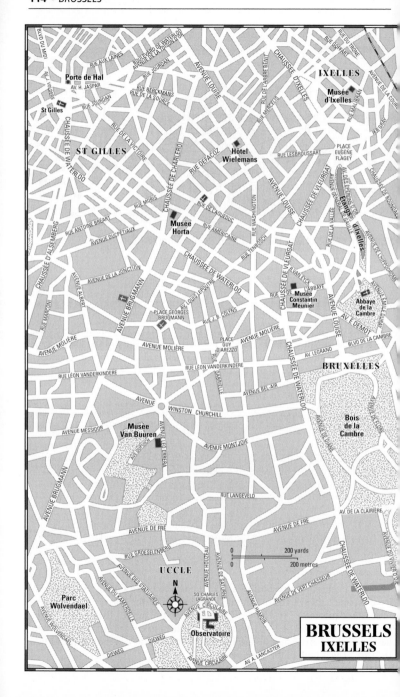

BRUSSELS
IXELLES

The **Hôtel Wielemans** at Rue Defacqz 14 was built by Adrien Blomme in 1925. Inspired by the Alhambra at Granada, it is decorated with almost 5000 traditional tiles imported from Spain. Restored in 1998, it is now used for art exhibitions and conferences.

Back on Avenue Louise, turn right down the Rue du Bailli to reach the **Eglise de la Sainte Trinité**. This incorporates the Baroque façade of an Augustinian church designed by Jacob Franckaert in 1642 which formerly stood on the Place de Brouckère.

Musées Horta and Meunier

Continuing beyond the west end of the church, you come to Rue Américaine, where the Musée Horta, open Tues–Sun 13.00–18.00, occupies the house and studio of Victor Horta at no. 25. The Art Nouveau interior contains some exquisite details. The museum has an interesting collection of photographs, plans and models of Horta buildings. Returning to Avenue Louise, Victor Horta's **Hôtel Solvay** is at no. 224, built in 1894–98.

A short detour west down Rue de l'Abbaye leads to to the **Musée Constantin Meunier** at no. 59, open Tues–Fri 10.00–12.00 and 13.00–16.45. This interesting museum occupies the 19C home and studio of the sculptor Constantin Meunier. It contains an impressive collection of 170 sculptures, 120 paintings and drawings, and some personal relics of the artist.

Abbaye de la Cambre

The Abbaye de la Cambre (Camera S. Mariae) is concealed in a hollow east of Avenue Louise. Founded by a Brussels noblewoman named Gisèle in 1201, it was originally occupied by Cistercian nuns. The church dates in part from the 14C, with a north transept added in the 15C. It contains the shrine of St Boniface of Lausanne, who died in 1265. A pupil of the nuns, he retired from his see at Lausanne to end his days as chaplain at La Cambre. A painting by Albert Bouts hangs in the nave.

The **cloister** was built in the 13C and 14C, but destroyed in 1581 during the

Wars of Religion. It was rebuilt in 1598 and restored from 1922–34. The modern windows are decorated with the arms of the abbesses, including Mary Scott of Buccleuch, Scotland, and murals of 1957 by Irene van den Linden, which tell the story of Ste Adelaide. A nun of La Cambre, Ste Adelaide was afflicted with blindness, leprosy and paralysis. Segregated from the other nuns, she prayed for souls in purgatory and experienced visions in which they reached paradise.

The adjoining buildings, grouped around two quadrangles, date mainly from the 18C. The gardens were restored to their 18C style in 1930. The La Cambre art school and the Belgian Geographical Institute are based in the former abbey buildings.

The **Bois de la Cambre** is just south of the abbey at the end of Avenue Louise. Once part of the Forêt de Soignes, it was acquired by the city in 1862 and landscaped in romantic style by Edouard Keilig. It has an artificial lake with a small wooded island reached by ferry, a roller-skating rink and several cafés. A lawn called the Pélouse des Anglais (near the roller-skating rink) gained its name after British troops played cricket there on the eve of the Battle of Waterloo.

Return to the Abbey de la Cambre and follow Avenue Général de Gaulle around the edge of two ponds known as the **Etangs d'Ixelles**. The steep streets to the west such as Rue de Belle-Vue and Rue Vilain XIIII contain interesting Art Nouveau houses. At the end of the second lake, a romantic monument celebrates Charles de Coster (1827–79), who wrote a popular 19C version of the legend of Till Eulenspiegel while living in Ixelles.

Musée des Beaux-Arts d'Ixelles

In Place Flagey a lively market is held every Sunday morning. Continue up the Chaussée d'Ixelles and turn right along Rue Jean Van Volsem to reach the Musée des Beaux-Arts d'Ixelles at no. 71, open Tues–Fri 13.00–18.30, Sat and Sun 10.00–17.00, which occupies a former abattoir of 1892. This museum has an outstanding collection of sculpture and paintings from the 16C to the 20C, including works by Dürer, Henri de Braekeleer, Théo van Rysselberghe, Jacob Smits, Delacroix, Courbet and Joshua Reynolds. The museum also has a large collection of 19C advertising posters, including an almost complete set of works signed by Toulouse-Lautrec.

11 • Anderlecht

Anderlecht was a village outside Brussels when Erasmus stayed there in 1520. It developed in the 19C into an industrial suburb with many breweries and a large abattoir. It has a famous football team which plays at a stadium beside the Parc Astrid.

Take the metro to **St Guidon**. On leaving the station, cross the Place de la Vaillance and go down Rue du Chapitre. The **Maison d'Erasme** (open daily, except Tues and Fri, 10.00–12.00 and 14.00–17.00) at no. 31 is an attractive Flemish Renaissance house built in 1515 as a guest house for the chapter of Anderlecht. While recuperating from an illness, the humanist Desiderius Erasmus stayed here in 1520 as a guest of his friend Canon Pieter Wijkman. The rooms have been carefully furnished in the style of the 16C. They contain books, documents, reproductions of paintings and curious modern ephemera connected with Erasmus. The museum also owns a small collection of 15C and 16C paintings, including a triptych of the *Epiphany* by Hieronymus Bosch. The garden has been replanted in the style of a medieval herb garden.

Erasmus of Rotterdam

Desiderius Erasmus (1466–1536) was born in Rotterdam or perhaps Gouda. He was a Renaissance humanist and theologian with a passion for learning, who applied reason and common sense to human affairs. He rejected the pedantic attitude of the schoolmen, exposed the abuses of the church and engaged in controversy with Luther, Von Hutten and the scholastic theologians of the Sorbonne. Attacked by those on both sides of the religious divide, he was unjustly accused of being lukewarm to Catholicism and even of being sympathetic towards Luther. He enjoyed a succession of generous patrons and spent long periods in England where he was an intimate friend of Thomas More. He came to Flanders in 1516 as adviser to the young Charles V and later lived in the university town of Leuven where he helped to establish the Collegium Trilingue. He was then at the peak of his fame and conducted witty and erudite correspondence with admirers all over Europe. He left Leuven in 1521 as the religious climate became more extreme. After spending six years in Freiburg, he settled at Basle in Switzerland. His considerable literary output included an annotated edition of the New Testament, the *Enchiridion Militis Christiani*, and his satirical *Encomium Moriae*. He also left a considerable amount of correspondence. More than 3000 letters, including several written from this house, provide a unique chronicle of 16C Europe.

The remarkable Collegiate Eglise St Pierre et St Guidon is near the Erasmus House. One of the most interesting churches in Brabant, it was founded some time before the 11C. The present church was built between 1470 and 1515 by Jan van Ruysbroeck and Hendrik de Mol. The tower, designed in 1517 by Mathias Keldermans, was never completed, but a spire was added in 1898.

The dark interior is decorated with some restored 15C murals. The Romanesque **crypt**, one of the oldest in Belgium, contains the 11C–12C tomb of St Guidon or St Guy. A native of Brabant, he was known as the 'Poor Man of Anderlecht'. At one time sacristan of Notre-Dame de Laeken, he spent seven years as a pilgrim in the Holy Land. After returning to Brussels, Guidon was admitted to the public hospital at Anderlecht, where he died. Some time later, a horse that stepped on Guidon's gravestone was struck down dead and St Guidon soon became revered as the patron saint of horses.

All that remains of Anderlecht's **Béguinage**, open daily, except Tues and Fri, 10.00–12.00 and 14.00–17.00, are four 17C houses to the north of the church at Rue du Chapelain 8. Founded in 1252 by the Dean and Chapter of Anderlecht, the Béguinage was occupied by single women until the 18C. The tiny houses now contain an entertaining collection of local folklore.

Anyone interested in traditional brewing techniques should visit the **Musée Gueuze** at Rue Gheude 56, open Mon–Fri 08.30–17.00, Sat 10.00–17.00. This atmospheric old Brussels brewery still produces typical Brussels beers like Lambic, Gueuze, Kriek and Faro. Brewery tours end with a glass of the house brew.

The Musée de la Résistance at 14 Rue Van Lint recalls the courage of the

Belgian resistance movement during two world wars. Open Mon–Fri 09.00–12.00 and 13.00–16.00. Closed weekends.

The northern suburbs and environs

Heysel

The northern suburbs contain several interesting buildings, including the Basilique de Koekelberg, the Atomium, Laeken church and the royal palace. The Heysel plateau was first developed in 1935 when the large Palais du Centenaire was built for an International Exhibition held to celebrate the centenary of Belgian independence. It is now used for annual trade fairs. The nearby Brussels International Trade Markt was built by John Portman in 1975.

The striking **Atomium**, open daily Apr–Aug 09.00–20.00, Sept–Mar 10.00–18.00, was built by Eugène Waterkeyn for the 1958 World Fair. This 120m high aluminium structure represents the nine spheres of an iron molecule enlarged 165 billion times. A fast lift takes you to the top sphere, where there is a panoramic view of northern Brussels. Escalators link the other spheres, which are used for exhibitions.

A large memorial at a nearby roundabout on Boulevard du Centenaire commemorates Burgomaster Adolphe Max. It is inscribed with his calm, defiant words to the Germans after they occupied Brussels in 1914.

The **Bruparck** contains various entertainment complexes, including the 24-screen Kinepolis cinema complex, the Océade tropical swimming pool and a mock Flemish village containing restaurants and cafés. You can also visit **Mini-Europe**, open daily Jul and Aug 09.30–20.00, Sept–Jun 10.00–17.00, an attractive landscaped park containing scale models of some 300 monuments from countries of the European Union.

The rather forgotten **National Planetarium** is a short distance from the Bruparck at Avenue de Bouchout 10.

Laeken

The Domaine Royal in Laeken contains the **Palais Royal**, home of the Belgian royal family. The palace is closed to the public, but the 19C hothouses, the Serres Royales, are open for a few weeks in late April or early May.

The governors Maria Christina of Austria and Albert of Saxe-Teschen commissioned the architects Louis Montoyer and Antoine Payen to build the palace at Laeken in 1782–84 on the site of an old manor. It was restored in 1802 by Napoleon, who signed the fateful order for the advance of his armies into Russia here. The palace was largely rebuilt in 1890 after a disastrous fire.

The **Parc de Laeken** contains a neo-Gothic monument to Leopold I designed by Louis De Curte in 1880. It stands on a low hill where there is a good view of the royal palace. The **Villa Belvédère** below the monument is the residence of the heir to the throne. There is a curious cluster of buildings from the age of Leopold II to the north of the park. The *Fontaine de Neptune* at the end of the Avenue du Parc Royal is a replica of the 16C fountain by Giambologna in Bologna's Piazza Nettuno.

The **Pavillon Chinois**, open Tues–Sun 10.00–16.45, on the far side of the road was built for Leopold II in 1906–10. Originally intended as a restaurant, this exotic building now provides a sumptuous setting for a collection of Chinese porcelain.

A pedestrian tunnel leads under the main road to the **Tour Japonaise**, open

Tues–Sun 10.00–16.45. This mock Japanese pagoda was bought by Leopold II at the Paris Exhibition of 1900. The tower is used for exhibitions of Japanese art. A small Japanese garden has been created in the grounds.

The **Eglise Notre-Dame de Laeken** was built by the architect Joseph Poelaert in 1870 in memory of Louise-Marie, the first Queen of the Belgians. The royal crypt (closed to the public) contains the tombs of Leopold I, Leopold II, Albert I and Queen Astrid. A monument outside the church commemorates Marshal Foch. Another memorial nearby was unveiled in 1927 to a French Unknown Soldier.

The choir of a 17C church stands in **Laeken cemetery**. This grand 19C cemetery contains the elaborate tombs of Belgian generals and politicians. Many of the funerary monuments were carved in the Salu workshop next to the cemetery entrance. A foundation hopes one day to turn the 19C workshop into a museum of funerary art.

Koekelberg

The northern commune of Koekelberg takes its name from a hill where several 17C artists painted views of Brussels. The summit is now dominated by the vast **Basilique Nationale du Sacré-Coeur**, open Mon–Sat 08.00–18.00. Begun in 1905 to celebrate 75 years of Belgian independence, it was originally planned by P. Langerock as a grandiose neo-Gothic church with six 90m high towers. The original plan was abandoned in 1914, and a new plan was later drawn up by A. van Huffel and P. Rome for an Art Deco basilica. Finally completed in 1970, the basilica is dedicated to the Sacred Heart of Jesus. Now a national war memorial, it has an impressive interior decorated with red brick, Algerian onyx, Congolese copper, stained-glass and terracotta tiles. The 92m high dome is surmounted by a stainless steel cross lit at night with red neon. Visitors can climb the dome for a panoramic view of northern Brussels.

Jette

The northern commune of Jette is mainly residential. The 18C abbot's palace at Rue Jean Tiebackx 14 is all that survives of the Abbey of Dieleghem, a Premonstratensian house founded in 1100. The palace now contains the **Musée Communal**, a local history museum, and the **Musée Nationale de la Figurine Historique**, open Tues–Fri and the first weekend of every month 14.00–17.00, a curious collection of historic tin soldiers.

Magritte in Jette

The painter René Magritte was born at Lessines, Hainaut, in 1898. The family moved to Charleroi in 1913 after Magritte's mother committed suicide. Following art studies at the Brussels Academy, Magritte married Georgette Berger and worked briefly in a factory designing wallpaper. The couple spent three years in Paris, before settling in Brussels in 1930. They lived at Rue Esseghem 135 in Jette from 1930–54, before moving up in the world to Boulevard Lambermont and finally Rue des Mimosas 97 in Schaerbeek. The **Musée René Magritte** opened in 1999 in the couple's house in Jette. The rooms have been lovingly refurnished in their original bourgeois style. None of the paintings are original. The museum is open Wed–Sun 10.00–18.00. No more than 20 visitors are admitted at one time.

Molenbeek-Saint-Jean

Molenbeek-Saint-Jean is a dense 19C industrial commune to the north of the old town. French artillery commanded by Villeroi bombarded Grand-Place from the Molenbeek ridge in 1695. The fortified farm of Karreveld at Avenue J. de la Hoese 3 dates back to the 13C. The present buildings were constructed in the 16C and 17C. Some Brontë experts believe that Karreveld served as the model for La Terrasse in *Villette*.

Evere

The small commune of Evere to the northeast of the city was mainly developed after the Second World War. The headquarters of the North Atlantic Treaty Organisation (NATO) moved here in 1967 after the organisation was forced by the French President Général de Gaulle to move from Paris.

Meise

The **National Botanic Gardens** are situated in the Flemish suburb of Meise, just north of Brussels. Known in Dutch as the Plantentuin, the gardens are famed for their superb trees and lawns. The gardens are open daily 09.00–17.00 (18.00 on Sunday). The Plantenpaleis of 1966 has several large hothouses, including one devoted to tropical water plants. The 18C Orangery now serves as a restaurant and lakeside café. The Plantenpaleis (entry charge) is open from Easter–Oct daily 13.00–16.30, Sun 13.00–18.00.

The gardens occupy the ancient estate of Bouchout. The 13C castle was much altered during the 17C (not open). It became the residence of the widowed Empress Charlotte of Mexico after her residence in Tervuren burnt down in 1879. Charlotte never fully recovered her reason after husband was executed by Mexican freedom fighters. She died here in 1927.

The village church at **Wolvertem**, 2km from Meise, has interesting Baroque confessionals. The Baroque pulpit is decorated with a vivid illustration of the story of St Hubert. A courtier of Pepin of Heristal, Hubert was converted while hunting after a stag at bay turned to him bearing an image of Christ crucified between its antlers.

Grimbergen

The town of Grimbergen, just north of Brussels, is famous both for its local beer and for the huge Baroque **Abbey Church of Sint Servaas**. Founded here in 1128, the original abbey was destroyed in 1579. After the return of the monks in the following century, Brother Gilbert van Zinnik began work on the present church. The towering high altar of 1701 is by Frans Langhermans. The monument of Philippe-François, lord of Grimbergen, who died in 1704, was carved by Theodoor Verhaeghen.

The four confessionals and the transept altars are by Hendrik Verbruggen. The pulpit may be by Verhaeghen or Verbruggen. The sacristy is a Rococo design of 1763. Between it and the church, several Romanesque arches have survived. (Access is possible for wheelchairs.)

An unusual monument beside the road to Meise commemorates Frans Hemerijckx (1902–69) who worked among lepers.

Southern suburbs

Uccle

The commune of Uccle is a pleasant suburb south of the centre with many interesting Art Deco and Modernist houses. The main attraction is the **Musée David et Alice van Buuren** at Avenue Leo Errera 41, open Sun 13.00–18.00 and Mon 14.00–18.00, which occupies an elegant villa built for a Dutch banker. The house contains a remarkable collection of paintings, drawings, sculpture and Delftware. The most famous work is a version of the Fall of Icarus, formerly attributed to Pieter Bruegel the Elder but now believed to have been painted after his death. There are also paintings by Fantin-Latour, Patinir, Ensor, Permeke, Rik Wouters and Van de Woestyne. The garden, open every afternoon, was planted by René Pechère with a maze and secret garden.

A monument in the Rue Edith Cavell commemorates the British nurse shot by the Germans in 1915. It stands next to a private hospital named the Institut Medical Edith Cavell in her honour.

The **Chapelle Notre-Dame des Affligés** is in the Rue de Stalle. Also known as Notre-Dame du Bon Secours or simply as the Chapelle de Stalle, this simple pilgrimage chapel dates from the 14C and 15C.

The abandoned **Dieweg cemetery**, near the Parc de Wolvendael, has been deliberately left as a wilderness. It has some striking 19C and 20C tombs, including many Jewish memorials. The cartoonist Hergé was buried here in 1983.

Hergé in Uccle

Georges Rémy, the inventor of Tintin, was born in Brussels in 1907. He began his career drawing cartoon strips in a Boy Scout magazine, and, adopting the name Hergé, drew the first Tintin book in 1929. Working from an office on Avenue Louise, he produced a steady stream of cartoon books describing the adventures of the boy reporter and his dog Snowy. Hergé died in 1983 and is buried in Dieweg Cemetery, not far from his Uccle home.

Forest

The industrial commune of Forest to the southwest of the city contains the impressive **Abbaye St Denis**. Established in 1238 as a retreat for noblewomen, it later became a Benedictine foundation. Rebuilt in the 18C, it is now used for exhibitions. The adjacent early Gothic **St Dionysius** church dates from the 13C–16C. A 12C Romanesque chapel to the south of the choir contains the tomb of Ste Alène. She was a noble lady whose conversion to Christianity so enraged her father that he cut off her arm. The severed limb worked so many miracles that eventually he too was converted.

The Flemish suburb of **Drogenbos** to the southwest of the city contains the modern **Museum Felix de Boeck** at 222 Grote Baan. This displays some 60 canvases by De Boeck, who was born in 1898. His work represents many of the artistic trends of the 20C.

Eastern suburbs and environs

St Josse

The commune of St Josse is a crowded 19C quarter near the Parc de Bruxelles. The **Hôtel Charlier** (open Mon 10.00–17.00, Tues–Thur 13.30–17.00, Fri 13.30–16.30) at Avenue des Arts 16 is an elegant little museum in a 19C mansion once owned by the sculptor Guillaume Charlier. Converted in 1890 into a museum, it contains Charlier's private collection of furniture, 19C silver and paintings (including works by Constantin Meunier, James Ensor, Emile Claus, Fantin Latour and Henri de Braekeleer). It also has some sculpture by Charlier himself.

Schaerbeek

Schaerbeek is an interesting 19C commune to the east of the old town with broad avenues, a large park and some Art Nouveau houses. The Dutch-language and French-language television and radio broadcasting authorities share a building off Place Meiser.

Execution of Edith Cavell

The **Enclos des Fusillés** is reached down a lane off Rue Colonel Bourg in Schaerbeek. A small cemetery contains the graves of Nurse Edith Cavell and other patriots shot here by the Germans in the First World War. Edith Cavell (1865–1915) was head of a large school for nurses which she had founded with Marie Depage, who was drowned when the Lusitania was torpedoed by a German U boat. After war broke out in 1914, Nurse Cavell helped fugitive soldiers to escape to the neutral Netherlands. Arrested, she was held at the prison of Saint Gilles before being tried in the Palais de la Nation. She was sentenced to death as a spy and shot on 12 October 1915. Her calm words, 'Patriotism is not enough', are inscribed on her memorial in London's St Martin's Place.

Woluwé Saint Lambert

Woluwé Saint Lambert is a residential commune to the east of the old town. The mournfully named **Chapelle Marie la Misérable** in Avenue Emile Vandervelde was built in memory of a pious girl of the 13C who refused the advances of a nobleman. He took his revenge by hiding a valuable cup in her hovel and accusing her of stealing it. She was condemned to death and buried alive. After the grave became the scene of several miracles, a chapel was built on the site and her body was placed under the altar (open daily from 07.30–17.30).

Woluwé Saint Pierre

Woluwé Saint Pierre is an elegant commune to the east of the old town popular with European Union employees. The broad Avenue de Tervuren was built by Leopold II at his own expense in 1897 to connect the Parc du Cinquantenaire with the Congo Museum in Tervuren. The **Parc de Woluwe** is a 19C romantic park with rolling lawns, a boating lake and a tavern.

Auderghem

Auderghem is a residential suburb to the east where many EU and NATO employees have settled. The estate of **Val Duchesse** occupies the site of the first Dominican community in the Low Countries, founded in the 13C. The

Romanesque **Chapelle Sainte Anne** in the Avenue Valduchesse was built in the 12C (open Wed from Jul–Sept 14.00–17.00 and on 26 July, the saint's feast day).

Diegem
The **Eglise Ste Catherine** at Diegem, just east of Brussels, has a striking 'wedding cake' tower, which dates from 1654. The church contains the shrine of St Cornelius with a 1643 painting of the saint by Jan van Houbraken. The small 15C restored **Châtelet** of the former manor house stands below the church.

Zaventem
The town of Zaventem, east of Brussels, has given its name to Brussels'airport. The village church contains a painting of *St Martin* by Antoon van Dyck. Van Dyck is said to have stayed in a local café (now the *Café van Dyck* on the main square) in 1624. He fell in love with one of his host's daughters, but his request for her hand was refused. The church also has a work by Gaspard de Crayer.

Vilvoorde
Vilvoorde, just northeast of Brussels, is an industrial town on the Willebroek canal. Its 14C–15C church has an unusually broad yet well-proportioned interior. The Baroque choir stalls of 1663, amongst the best in Belgium, are from the former abbey of Groenendael. The pulpit of 1665 was carved by Artus Quellin the Younger for the church of Sint Joris in Antwerp. Among the many paintings in the church are works attributed to P.J. Verhaghen and Michiel Coixe.

> ### An English martyr
> The Protestant **William Tyndale** was martyred at Vilvoorde in 1536. Strongly influenced by Luther, he translated the New Testament into English and in 1531, while living in Antwerp, he published the Pentateuch. This work contained many marginal glosses in which he violently attacked the pope and the bishops. Henry VIII dispatched his agents to capture Tyndale, but he successfully evaded them for several years. Tyndale published a revised version of his translation of the New Testament in 1534. Denounced to the authorities as a heretic, he was arrested in Antwerp in 1535 and imprisoned in the castle of Vilvoorde. Tried there in 1536 and sentenced to death, he was strangled and burnt at the stake in Vilvoorde castle on 6 October. Antonie van Straelen (1521–68), the burgomaster of Antwerp who supported William of Orange, was also executed at Vilvoorde. The castle was later torn down later to make way for a gaol.

WATERLOO

Waterloo was a village of little importance until 18 June 1815 when a furious battle was fought in the fields to the south. The battle involved an estimated 140,000 troops, out of which 39,000 are thought to have died. The hospitals in Brussels were so overcrowded that the wounded had to be tended in private houses. The site of the battlefield is now a major tourist attraction, with museums, cafés and souvenir shops. Yet there are quiet fields and isolated farmhouses nearby where you can still sense something of the atmosphere.

The Battle

Some months before the battle, on 1 March 1815, Napoleon landed in France after escaping from Elba. He rapidly reassembled his troops and marched north to Paris. The only two armies which posed any threat to his ambitions were both based in Belgium: Blücher's Prussians and Wellington's joint force of British, Belgians, Dutch and Germans.

Determined to separate his opponents, Napoleon crossed the frontier near Charleroi on 15 June and the next day mauled Blücher at Ligny. Wellington stood at Quatre-Bras, while Blücher fell back towards Wavre, forcing Wellington to retire to the area just south of Waterloo, which he had already chosen for his defence of Brussels. Early in the morning of 18 June, Wellington received an assurance from Blücher that he would join him as soon as he could. In the event he was not able to reach the battlefield until the early evening, which meant that Wellington stood alone against the superior French attack for most of the day.

Napoleon had about 72,000 men and 246 guns in the field, whereas Wellington had about 68,000 men (24,000 of them British) and 150 guns. As well as being outnumbered, Wellington was apprehensive about the courage and loyalty of some of the foreign troops under his command. On the eve of the battle, the two armies were drawn up only some 1,500m apart. The French faced north along a line with the farm of La Belle Alliance at the centre. Wellington occupied the ridge facing south, along the road that now runs from the Butte du Lion to Papelotte farm.

It rained constantly during the night of 17–18 June. The sodden ground favoured the defenders, as the attacking French had to advance uphill over mud, even though Napoleon had postponed his main attack from dawn until early afternoon in the hope that the ground would dry. The battle began at 11.30 and ended at 20.00. The fighting took place in four distinct phases.

Late morning. The French attacked Hougoumont farm at about 11.30. This walled farm was vital for the defence of Wellington's right. The attack failed and did not force Wellington to divert reinforcements for its defence. Hougoumont remained under fierce attack throughout the day. Meanwhile, the Prussians reached the area of Chapelle St Lambert, 6km northeast of La Belle Alliance, at about 14.00. Napoleon sent Lobau to counter this threat.

Early afternoon. After a half-hour artillery barrage, the French infantry attacked Wellington's left (east of the road to Charleroi) at about 14.00. The Scots infantry charged and engaged the French hand-to-hand. The British cavalry then charged through the infantry, and the French broke. The cavalry continued too far and were driven back by French cavalry.

Mid afternoon. Led by Marshal Ney, the French cavalry attacked Wellington's centre (towards and just west of the Butte) at about 16.00, but failed to break Wellington's infantry squares and were driven back down the slope by Allied cavalry. Further French cavalry waves met the same fate. Meanwhile, the Prussians forced Lobau back through Plancenoit at about 16.30, but failed to hold the village after Lobau was reinforced by Napoleon's Young Guard.

Early evening. The French stormed and took La Haye Sainte at about 18.00, but only after the Hanoverians had run out of ammunition. Only 41 of the 350 defenders survived. The French Imperial Guard attacked Wellington's centre at about 19.30, struggling up the slope which had been churned to mud by earlier cavalry assaults. Met by devastating fire from Allied infantry, who remained lying down and hidden until the last moment, the Guard broke and fled for the first time in its history. Meanwhile, the Prussians finally defeated Lobau. The French troops fled and Wellington met Blücher at about 21.15 at La Belle Alliance inn.

After the battle, Wellington handed over the pursuit to the Prussians. Napoleon, fleeing in his coach, reached Genappe, where he just had time to change to a horse. He reached Charleroi at 05.00 the next day and fled to Paris. He abdicated a second time, attempted unsuccessfully to obtain sanctuary in America or England, and finally ended up in exile on St Helena, where he died in 1821.

Practical information

Getting there

The battlefield of Waterloo is 20km south of Brussels on the N5 Charleroi road. The town of Waterloo is 3km north of the battlefield on the N5. A bus (number W) leaves about every half-hour from Place Rouppe in Brussels. It stops in Waterloo town and at the battlefield (at the Gordon stop). The battlefield can also be visited on coach excursions from Brussels. But the most convenient way to visit the battlefield sites is by car. Parking is generally not a problem at the Lion Mound.

Where to stay

Le 1815, Route du Lion 367, 3km south of Waterloo town, ☎ 02.387.00.60, occupies a restored building on the edge of the battlefield. Its rooms are decorated with mementoes of the battle. It has a restaurant, garden and mini-golf course modelled on the battlefield.

Cafés

Cafés and restaurants are clustered around the Lion Mound. *Le Cambronne*, Route du Lion 325, is a rustic tavern filled with military relics.

Tourist information

The Waterloo tourist office, next to the Wellington Museum at Chaussée de Bruxelles 149, has extensive information on the battlefield. ☎ 02.354.99.10.

Opening times

Musée Wellington is open daily 09.30–18.30 (Apr–Sept); and 10.30–17.00 (Oct–Mar).
Visitors Centre, the **Lion Mound** and the **Panorama of the Battle** are open 09.30–18.30 (Apr–Sept); 09.30–17.30 (Oct); 10.00–17.00 (Mar) and 10.30–16.00 (Nov–Feb).
The **Musée de Cires** is open daily Easter–Oct 09.00–18.30; Nov–Easter daily 10.15–16.45.
The **Ferme du Caillou** is open Tues–Sun 10.00–18.30 (Apr–Oct); Tues–Sun 13.00–17.00 (Nov–Mar). Museums and sites are closed on 25 December and 1 January.

Tickets

Combined tickets are sold for the Visitors' Centre (film and model battlefield), Lion Mound and Panorama. The Visitors' Centre has a good military bookshop.

Waterloo town

Wellington chose the small town of Waterloo as his headquarters. He spent the night of 17–18 June in a local inn before riding off to the battlefield. The building where he stayed is now occupied by the outstanding **Musée Wellington**. The old rooms of the 18C inn are filled with a fascinating collection of sabres, military maps, 19C paintings and other relics of the battle.

You can see the bed in room 4 where Alexander Gordon, Wellington's aide-de-camp from Peninsular days, died from his wounds. The museum also has his bulky correspondence box. Wellington occupied room 6, where there is a copy of Lawrence's famous portrait of the Duke. The role of the Dutch is described in room 7, while the Prussian army is covered in room 8. The French room (no. 10) contains some souvenirs of Napoleon. The efforts of the Belgian government to preserve the battlefield site are described in room 11.

The **Musée de Waterloo** occupies four small rooms of the inn. It covers the history of the town, including the interesting story of the local labourers who paved many of the 19C roads in Belgium.

Lord Uxbridge's leg

A curious monument in the museum garden was put up by Lord Uxbridge, commander of the British Cavalry, in memory of his amputated leg. The monument was originally erected in the garden of a house opposite where the leg was sawn off on the kitchen table. The monument was moved here after the house (no. 214) was threatened with demolition.

The Baroque **Chapelle Royale** opposite the museum was built in 1690 by the Marquis of Castanaga. It contains 27 memorial plaques put up after the battle by British and Dutch regiments.

The battlefield

The battlefield lies 3km south of Waterloo on the N5. The large Mont-Saint-Jean farm just outside Waterloo served as a field hospital after the battle. Then comes the crossroads known as **Waterloo-Gordon** from the memorial to Sir Alexander Gordon, Wellington's aide-de-camp who died of wounds in the Waterloo inn. The top of the mound on which the monument stands marks the original height of the ridge before the earth was removed to build the Butte du Lion to the right. Two other memorials at the crossroads commemorate the Belgians and Hanoverians. A tree planted in the southwest corner replaces the original elm which was bought in 1818 by a English businessman to turn into souvenirs. The tree marks the position of Wellington's command-post.

The **Butte du Lion** on the right was only built in 1824. At the time of the battle, this site was open farmland. The earth to build the mound was excavated from the battlefield, destroying most traces of the narrow sunken lane which ran behind the ridge and provided Wellington's troops with protection. The fields were planted with rye, which was allowed to grow much higher in the 19C, providing the Allied troops with useful cover at the start of the battle.

The road to the left marks the line of Wellington's left flank. A monument on the ridge commemorates Sir Thomas Picton, who rode into battle wearing his top-hat. A cobbled lane beyond leads to **Papelotte farm**, which was defended by

Dutch troops. The road to the right of the crossroads leads to the Butte du Lion, a conical mound built by the government of the United Netherlands in 1826 on the spot where the Prince of Orange was wounded.

The Butte is surrounded by an untidy cluster of museums, cafés and souvenir shops. The oldest attraction is the **Musée de Cires**, a now rather dusty wax-works museum created in 1818 by a veteran of the battle. A large circular paint-ing known as the *Panorama de la Bataille* occupies the rotunda opposite. Painted by the French artist Louis Dumoulin in 1912, it is one of the last surviv-ing panorama paintings in the world.

A new **Visitors' Centre** was opened in 1990 to provide a modern interpreta-tion of the battle. The centre has a theatre equipped with an electronic map of the battlefield and a cinema where the short film Waterloo 1815 is screened. The film incorporates extracts from Sergei Bondarchuk's epic 1970 movie of Waterloo. You can then climb the 226 steps to the top of the Butte du Lion for a good view of the battlefield.

Down the cobbled lane behind the Panorama are the sloping fields where the Imperial Guard floundered in the mud. The lane leads to the farm of **Hougoumont** (signs point to Goumont), a fortified Brabant farm which lay north of a wood in 1815. Most of the farm buildings were burnt down during the fighting and little remains of the wood apart from a few blighted trees.

Returning to the Waterloo-Gordon crossroads, turn right to reach the farm of **La Haye Sainte** just to the south on the busy N5. This was defended by Hanoverian troops during the battle. The French are said to have crept along the wall beside the road and seized the rifle barrels poking out of the loopholes.

The road continues south to **La Belle Alliance**, a former inn which has changed little since 1815. It was here that Napoleon reviewed his troops on the morning of the battle. Towards the end of the day, Wellington and Blücher are said to have met here.

A minor road runs to the left to Plancenoit, passing a spot marked as **Napoleon's Viewpoint**, where he is said to have stood from mid afternoon onwards. A **Prussian Monument** of 1818 stands near Plancenoit church.

Back on the main road to Charleroi is a 1956 monument on the left com-memorating Victor Hugo, who wrote a stirring account of the battle in Les Misérables. The **Wounded Eagle Monument** on the other side of the road was cast in bronze in 1905 by Jean Jérôme to commemorate the French troops.

Napoleon's headquarters was about 2km south of here at the **Ferme du Caillou**. He ate his breakfast here off crested silver plate, boasting that the fight-ing would amount to no more than a cannonade and a cavalry charge, after which he would lead the Imperial Guard against the English. The 1757 farm is now a museum with a collection of weapons, paintings, etchings and plans. There is also Napoleon's bed and the table on which he spread out his maps.

Other sites linked to 1815

The busy **Brussels to Charleroi road**, which crosses the battlefield, was the scene of several troop movements on 15–19 June 1815. Wellington lead his troops down this road to Quatre-Bras and then withdrew them to Waterloo. Napoleon's army marched along the same route confident that they would soon be in Brussels, and fled down it after the battle in the direction of Paris, pursued by Blücher's Prussians.

The small town of **Genappe** was the scene of a fierce skirmish on 17 June 1815. During a violent thunderstorm, Wellington's cavalry retreated through the narrow streets pursued by French lancers led by Napoleon. The following night, Napoleon was back in Genappe, but this time in flight. He changed from his carriage to a horse, narrowly avoiding capture by the Prussians. Wellington spent some hours during the night of 16–17 June at the *Auberge du Roi d'Espagne*. A plaque records that General Duhesme, commander of Napoleon's Young Guard, died here on 20 June.

The battles at Quatre Bras and Ligny on 16 June 1815 set the stage for Waterloo the following day. On learning that the French were approaching Quatre-Bras, Wellington left the Duchess of Richmond's ball in Brussels in the early hours of 16 June. He ordered his army to concentrate at Quatre-Bras, where he arrived at 10.00. At this moment, though neither side was aware of it, Marshal Ney's force before Frasnes, 3km to the south, had a vast superiority in both men and guns.

Wellington rode to **Ligny** at about noon to confer with Blücher, who was there with his Prussian army. Looking across the small river, Wellington and Blücher had a clear view of Napoleon and his massed troops. Wellington observed that Blücher would be 'damnably mauled', with his men drawn up as they were on an exposed forward slope. The battle raged for five hours in the narrow village streets of Ligny. The **Ferme d'en Haut**, marked by a plaque in the village, was a typical defensive point. Blücher narrowly avoided capture as he led a dashing but useless final cavalry charge. He fell and was twice ridden over, probably being saved by his aide-de-camp, who covered the field marshal's medals to hide his identity. Blücher was carried to Mellery, 7km to the north, where for several vital hours he lay semi-conscious.

Wellington was back at **Quatre-Bras** by about 14.30. He heard cannon shots signalling the start of the fighting at Ligny. Allied reinforcements were now arriving at Quatre-Bras, allowing Wellington to hold Ney. The Duke of Brunswick was killed during the fighting at Quatre-Bras. A monument was put up to his memory. Wellington narrowly escaped capture, jumping his horse clear over the Gordon Highlanders lining a bank. By 21.00, the battle had petered out.

Early next morning, 17 June, Wellington sent his aide-de-camp, Alexander Gordon, to find out what had happened at Ligny. Gordon returned with the grim news that the Prussians had been defeated and had fallen back on Wavre. Wellington had no choice but to order a retreat to the position he had already selected south of Waterloo.

Wavre

Wavre was the scene of a fierce battle between the French and the Prussians on the same day as Waterloo. The battle began as Marshal the Marquis de Grouchy, who was in command of Napoleon's right flank, pursued Blücher's Prussians as they retreated from Ligny to Wavre. Adhering rigidly to ill-drafted and contra-dictory orders, Grouchy pressed on to Wavre instead of turning west towards Waterloo, a manoeuvre which would have allowed him to cut off the Prussians and bring Napoleon badly needed support. Because of this tactical error, Grouchy was later held partly responsible for the French defeat at Waterloo. He was court-martialled and exiled for a time.

Early history

Wavre is an old and pleasant town on the Dyle known in Dutch as Waver. It stands on a site known to have been occupied since prehistoric times. The present town developed in the 11C as a trading centre located at an important crossroads and river crossing. It was granted a charter in 1222. The town was pillaged and burnt down in 1489 after it rebelled against Maximilian. It suffered again in the late 16C and early 17C, this time at the hands of the Spanish. It was subsequently sacked by the Dutch in 1647. The town suffered further damage in May 1940 when 150 houses and the Hôtel de Ville were destroyed by bombing. Part of the town centre has been rebuilt in the old style.

Tourist information

Hôtel de Ville, Rue Nivelles 1.
☎ 010.23.03.52.

The **Hôtel de Ville** occupies a former Carmelite friary. Built between 1715 and 1726, the friary was appropriated in 1797 by the invading French revolutionaries. The friary church continued to be used until 1856, after which it served as a public hall. Largely destroyed in 1940, the building was carefully restored and officially reopened in 1961. The window on the soaring façade shows the lords of Wavre handing over the keys of the town.

The **Eglise St Jean-Baptiste** in Rue Haute, opposite the Hôtel de Ville, dates from c 1476. It has been damaged by fire three times; first in 1489 during the uprising against Maximilian; then in 1582 during the wars of religion, and finally in 1604 by mutinous Spanish soldiers. The tower, striped in white stone, was built in stages between the 15C and 17C. A French bullet fired in 1815 remains lodged in one of the pillars inside the church.

The **Musée Historique et Archéologique** at Rue de l'Ermitage 23 (open Wed and Sat 14.00–16.00) has material from a Roman villa excavated near Basse Wavre in 1904.

Wavre environs

The village of **Bierges**, 2km west of Wavre, saw heavy fighting on the afternoon of 18 June 1815 as the French tried to cross the river. A memorial by the mill records that the French General Gérard was wounded here. The huge **Walibi** amusement park nearby is attractively arranged around a large lake. It has roller-coaster rides, roundabouts and a tropical swimming pool. Many of the rides are based on Belgian cartoon characters such as Tintin.

The 18C church at **Basse Wavre**, 2km northeast of Wavre, contains a copper-gilt reliquary given by the Archbishop of Mechelen in 1628 to replace one destroyed by Iconoclasts in 1580. It contains the relics of several saints and martyrs. The high ground to the northwest of the railway line was the site of a Roman settlement. The Musée Historique et Archéologique in Wavre has relics from a villa which once stood on the slope. No trace of the settlement survives at the site.

The village of **Walhain**, 10km southeast of Wavre, was reached by Marshal Grouchy on the morning of 18 June 1815. He arrived here in time for a late breakfast, which was disturbed by the sound of the opening cannonade at Waterloo. Although urged by his staff to 'march to the guns', Grouchy refused, obstinately sticking to Napoleon's woolly instruction that he should 'head for Wavre'.

The Rue du Château leads south from Walhain to the overgrown ruins of a castle believed to date from the 13C. The hamlet of **Baudeset**, just beyond, is thought to stand on the site of a Roman fort.

TERVUREN

The old Flemish town of Tervuren, 13km east of Brussels, has been a favourite aristocratic retreat since the 13C. Former residents include the Dukes of Brabant, the Archdukes Albert and Isabella, the Prince of Orange, and Leopold II's sister Charlotte. Leopold II chose Tervuren as the site for the Congo section of the 1897 Exhibition, building a pavilion to display the art and natural resources of the Congo. The broad Avenue de Tervuren was built by Leopold to link the exhibition site in the Cinquantenaire Park with the Congo Museum. Tervuren is now a leafy residential town popular with British expatriates. The town centre retains much of its old Flemish character.

Tourist information
Markt 7. Closed Sat and Sun.
☎ 02.769.20.81.

The main route to Tervuren is along Leopold II's avenue, past the rolling Woluwé Park. A tram (no. 44) runs to Tervuren, beginning at the underground station below Square Montgomery. A statue of Field Marshal Montgomery stands in the middle of the square. The tram passes, on the right, the **Hôtel Stoclet** at Avenue de Tervuren 291, a striking town house built in 1905–10 by the Austrian architect Joseph Hoffman. An example of the Wiener Werkstätte style, the façade is clad in white marble framed with gilded mouldings.

A former tram depot at no. 364 is now occupied by the **Musée du Transport Urbain Bruxellois**, open Apr–Oct Sat and Sun 13.30–19.00. This museum contains a nostalgic collection of old Brussels trams and buses. Vintage trams run at the weekends from the museum to Tervuren. Trips are also organised through Brussels on certain Sundays.

The **Africa Museum**, is open Tues–Fri 10.00–17.00, Sat and Sun 10.00–18.00; wheelchair access is possible. The museum is near the tram terminus in Tervuren and contains an outstanding collection of art and artefacts from Central Africa. Originally named the Musée du Congo, it was established by Leopold II in 1897. The museum moved in 1910 to the present building, designed by the French architect Charles Girault. In 1960, the year of the Congo's independence, the museum extended its scope to cover Central Africa.

The Africa Museum is famous for its collections of insects, masks and sculpture. Arranged around an open courtyard, its 21 rooms still retain their original decor, including frescos illustrating African scenes (room 17) and a frieze of 19C photographs (room 16). The entrance is by a large rotunda (room 1), which contains a bookshop and several statues from the 1897 Exhibition symbolising Belgium's colonial aspirations. A long gallery to the left contains an interesting ethnography collection, including exhibits from Zaire, northern Angola, Rwanda and Burundi (room 21). A small room beyond has dioramas of African wildlife. Room 17 is devoted to insects, while room 16 has fish and reptile specimens.

Room 13 has several large zoological dioramas of the northern Savannah, equatorial forest and southern Savannah.

From there a small hall leads to the café. The room beyond (no. 10) has samples of natural resources including varieties of tropical wood. The Memorial Hall (room 8) covers colonial wars and the abolition of slavery, while the Ruwenzori Room (no. 9) has dioramas made for the 1958 World Fair in Brussels showing the mountain wildlife of Ruwenzori. Some interesting cabinets in room 7 display relics of European explorers, including old maps, Dr Livingstone's suitcase and mementoes of Stanley. There are African sculptures in room 4 and elaborate tribal masks in room 2. The museum park to the south was landscaped in formal French style by Lainé.

The Belgian Congo

Leopold II had wanted since adolescence to create a Belgian colony. He began to realise his dream in 1878 when he formed the Comité des Etudes du Haut Congo, which developed into the International Association of the Congo. The following year, Leopold employed the dashing Henry Morton Stanley to open trading stations and enter contracts with tribal chiefs. The European powers recognised the International (but effectively Belgian) Association in 1884–85 as an independent state. The Belgian government authorised Leopold to rule as king, while at the same time declaring that the link between Belgium and the Congo was 'exclusively personal'. The venture brought Leopold enormous wealth, especially from the vast territory known as the Domaine de la Couronne which was treated as the King's personal property. In 1890, in return for financial investment, the Belgian government was given the right of annexation. It exercised this right in 1908 after Leopold was accused of gross incompetence, including seizure of native land, monopolistic exploitation and even massacres. The Congo was granted independence in 1960.

Moving on to the town, the ducal **Eglise Saint Jean** (13C–15C) stands in the main square. It contains a reconstructed choir-gallery of 1517 attributed to Mathias Keldermans. The graves of seven Congolese who died during the 1897 Exhibition stand in the churchyard.

On the edge of the lake, the overgrown remains of **Tervuren Castle** are visible. Founded in the 13C as a hunting-lodge of the rulers of Brabant, it was rebuilt by Archdukes Albert and Isabella as a Renaissance palace. After Charles of Lorraine died here in 1780, the castle was torn down by his uncle, Emperor Joseph II. The castle **chapel of St Hubert**, designed by Wenceslas Coeberger in 1617, is still standing on the edge of the lake. It is said to occupy the spot where the saint died in 727. St Hubert was a courtier of Pepin of Heristal. Converted while hunting, he succeeded St Lambert as bishop of Maastricht. The patron saint of hunters, his emblem is a stag bearing a crucifix between its horns.

Tervuren environs

The **Geographical Arboretum of Tervuren** was planted to the south of Tervuren in 1902 on land gifted by Leopold II. The trees are planted according to geographical regions.

The town of **Duisburg**, 3km east of Tervuren, is the centre of a grape-growing district. Many of the farmers have been forced out of business in recent years; most of the greenhouses are now derelict. The church in Duisburg has a 13C nave and choir.

The town of **Overijse** occupies a steep hillside site above the valley of the IJse on the southern edge of the grape growing district. The main square is named Justus Lipsiusplein after the distinguished scholar and classical historian who was born in 1547 at Isidoor Taymansstraat 10 (behind the Stadhuis). Lipsius taught at Leuven, Jena, Cologne, Antwerp and Leiden.

The 16C **Stadhuis** is attributed to Antoon Keldermans. The former castle, now a school, dates mainly from the 17C. Of the Begijnhof, which was founded before 1267, all that survives is the restored 15C chapel.

The village of **Huldenberg**, 3km northeast of Overijse, has a church built between the 11C and 14C. The interior contains statues dating from c 1400 of the Virgin, St Catherine and St Barbara, and an Assumption attributed to Gaspard de Crayer. The castle was built in 1514, but has been greatly altered.

The main Belgian broadcasting transmitter stands on a hill outside the attractive village of **Tombeek**, 3km southeast of Overijse. The **Ferme des Templiers**, signed off the N4 just east of Tombeek, occupies an estate given to the Templars in c 1180 by Godfrey III of Brabant. After the suppression of the Order in 1312, the property passed to the Knights of Malta. It remained in their hands until the French Revolution. A chapel survives from 1643. The other buildings date from the 18C and 19C.

FORÊT DE SOIGNES

The Forêt de Soignes (Zonienwoud in Dutch) forms a green belt around the south edge of Brussels, from the Brussels commune of Uccle to the Flemish town of Tervuren. This majestic woodland is all that survives of the ancient Silva Carbonaria which once covered much of the country. Originally an oak forest, it was replanted with beech trees under Austrian rule in the 18C. It is popular for walking, cycling and horse riding.

Eating out
The village of Jezus-Eik has several popular country restaurants:
Istas, Brusselsesteenweg 652, ☎ 02.657.05.11, is a bustling Belgian restaurant with old-fashioned charm.

Tourist information
Flemish Brabant tourist information office, Leopold Vanderkelenstraat 30, Leuven, ☎ 016.26.76.20.

The cobbled Rue du Rouge Cloître in the commune of Auderghem, Brussels, leads from the Chaussée de Tervuren to the remains of the 14C **Abbaye du Rouge Cloître**. The surviving buildings include the south wing, now a restaurant, and parts of the farm. A plaque on the wall of the restaurant recalls that the painter Hugo van der Goes spent the last years of his life in the abbey after suffering a mental breakdown. A small information centre for the Forêt de Soignes is located in an outbuilding.

The **Kasteel van Groenendaal** lies deep in the forest on the Duboislaan (in

Flemish Brabant). Now a restaurant, this 18C priory was the successor to an Augustinian foundation of c 1340. The former priory carp ponds have survived. The **Groenendaal Arboretum** is planted with about 400 species of trees.

A medallion attached to a bench near the ponds commemorates the mystic Jan van Ruysbroeck (1293–1381). Born in Ruisbroek, near Brussels, he was vicar of St Gudule in Brussels and later prior of Groenendaal. His mystical writings earned him the title of the Ecstatic Doctor. His lucid works had a profound influence on 16C mystical writers such as the Dutch preacher Gerhard Groote. His most famous book is *The Spiritual Marriage*.

FLANDERS

Flanders is a fascinating region with its own distinctive culture and architectural style. Occupying the low plain between Brussels and the North Sea, this area was settled by Frankish tribes after the fall of the Roman Empire. The inhabitants of the region were originally Dutch speaking, whereas those who settled to the south of Brussels spoke French.

The region began to acquire a distinctive identity under the powerful counts of Flanders. Though nominally subject to the kings of France, the counts were virtually independent by the 11C. They encouraged the early development of the great medieval Flemish towns of Ypres, Bruges and Ghent. Much of the wealth came from the cloth trade, which relied on imported wool from England. The Flemish towns still retain some splendid buildings from the Middle Ages, such as cloth halls, belfries and town halls. Many also have distinctive walled communities known as **Begijnhofs**, founded in the early Middle Ages for the widows of Crusaders and single women.

Flanders lost its independence in 1384 when the region was inherited by Philip the Bold of Burgundy. It also began to lose its Germanic linguistic roots as French replaced Dutch as the language of the ruling class. Until the early 20C, lectures in Flemish universities were still being given entirely in French. Flemish nationalism began to assert itself in the late 19C, growing more insistent during the First World War when the officer class was almost entirely composed of French speakers.

Dutch speakers have now gained equal rights in the Belgian state, but the **language issue** remains a touchy subject in Flanders. Bitter feuding continues in several regions, such as the Flemish communes around Brussels, where French speakers are in the majority, and the Voeren region of Limburg province, where French is again the dominant language. The simmering language conflict leads to bilingual signs being obliterated and other inconveniences, though it has never escalated to extreme violence.

Flanders is now a separate region within the federal state of Belgium. The capital is Brussels, though Brussels is itself a separate region with its own government. The Flemish Region comprises the provinces of West Flanders, East Flanders, Antwerp, Flemish Brabant and Limburg.

The majority of visitors to Flanders are attracted by the ancient cities of **Bruges**, **Ghent** and **Antwerp**. These cities have preserved their historic quarters, winding canals, and magnificent churches. They also offer countless museums filled with art treasures, including outstanding paintings by Flemish Masters such as Van Eyck, Van der Weyden, Bouts and Rubens.

It is also enjoyable to explore the smaller towns of Flanders, which tend to have a lively market place, a Begijnhof and a local museum with at least something of interest. The old university town of **Leuven** is well worth a visit for its town hall and Begijnhof. The rather forgotten town of **Mechelen** has many handsome buildings, including a spectacular cathedral tower. The medieval town hall of Oudenaarde is impressive, while Kortrijk combines old buildings with fashionable shops. The lovely town of Lier has an extraordinary astronomical clock; Diest contains a beautiful Begijnhof and an interesting museum housed in medieval cellars, and Tongeren's Gallo-Roman museum provides an intriguin-ginsight into the history of this old Roman town.

The lively **beach resorts** on the North Sea coast continue to attract many tourists. Some of the resorts are busy ports such as Nieuwpoort, Zeebrugge and Ostend. Others were developed in the 19C and 20C near inland villages such as Oostduinkerke and Koksijde. Most of the towns have long sandy beaches, inland dunes and rather overscaled apartment blocks. They can be counted on to have good fish restaurants, friendly cafés and excellent attractions for children.

The main resort is Ostend, with its long beaches and excellent museums. The quiet resort of De Haan retains its picturesque 19C buildings, while Knokke-Het Zoute strives to be fashionable. A **tram** runs the length of the coast from De Panne to Knokke, offering occasional glimpses of the sea. The historic towns such as Bruges, Ypres and Veurne lie near the coastal resorts.

Just inland of the dunes lies the beautiful **polder** landscape. This low-lying region was reclaimed in the Middle Ages when canals and dikes were dug. It remains a rural area with large white farms, straight roads bordered with trees, and scattered church steeples marking small villages. One of the most attractive polder districts lies between Bruges and the Dutch border. Another largely unspoilt area is found around Oostduinkerke village. Many of the old cottages have been converted into gastronomic restaurants. The quiet roads, often bordering canals, are ideal for cycling trips.

The **battlefields of the First World War** attract an increasing number of visitors every year. The historic town of **Ypres**, which was totally rebuilt after the war, makes a good centre for exploring the battlefields and war cemeteries. It has good restaurants, inexpensive hotels and an outstanding war museum. The old towns of Diksmuide, Poperinge and Nieuwpoort are also worth visiting.

The rural districts of Flanders, away from the large cities, are popular with hikers, campers and cyclists. The **Kempen** is an attractive area of moorland and pine forests that covers much of Antwerp and Limburg province. The area has several historic abbeys such as Averbode, Postel and Tongerlo (which has a famous copy of Da Vinci's Last Supper by one of his pupils). The region contains several large parks with attractions for children.

The **Waasland** district, near Sint Niklaas, is an exceptionally fertile area of sand and clay. Its straight roads are lined with poplars and irrigation ditches. The rolling countryside of Flemish Brabant has some attractive countryside, particularly around Tervuren, Leuven and the Zonienwoud (Forêt de Soignes in French). The Flemish Brabant tourist office publishes several excellent guides to walking trails and cycle routes in the province.

The Cities of Flanders

BRUGES

Bruges is a historic Flemish city with old brick houses overlooking narrow canals. One of the great trading cities of the 15C, it is sometimes described as the Venice of the North. The meandering cobbled lanes and overgrown canals still retain their medieval appearance, while the churches and museums are filled with 15C paintings and sculpture. Despite its apparent antiquity, it is misleading to consider Bruges as a perfectly preserved medieval city, since many of the houses in fact date from the 17C or 18C. Other rather fanciful buildings were designed in the late 19C and early 20C by British and Belgian neo-Gothic architects. The town is linked by canals to Zeebrugge and Damme, and Sluis in the Netherlands. With a population of about 120,000, Bruges (Brugge in Dutch) is the capital of West Flanders province.

Canal in Bruges

Practical information

Where to stay
Hotels

£££ **Oud Huis Amsterdam**, Spiegelrei 3, ☎ 050.34.18.10, is an elegant canalside hotel in the former 17C trading house of the Dutch merchants.

£££ **Die Swaene**, Steenhouwersdijk 1, ☎ 050.34.27.98, is a tastefully decorated small canalside hotel.

££ **Egmond** , Minnewater 15, ☎ 050.34.14.45, is a small hotel in a neo-Gothic mansion decorated in traditional Flemish style.

££ *Adornes*, Sint Annarei 26,
☎ 050.34.13.36, is an attractive canal-side hotel.

£ *Groeninghe*, Korte Vuldersstraat 29,
☎ 050.34.32.55, is a well-run small hotel.

£ *Jacobs*, Baleistraat 1,
☎ 050.33.98.31, is a friendly hotel in a traditional gable house opposite the St Gilliskerk.

£ *Ibis*, Katelijnestraat 65a,
☎ 050.33.75.75, is an inexpensive modern hotel which welcomes children.

Eating out
Restaurants

Bruges has many attractive restaurants which often serve local specialities pre-pared with beer.

£££ *De Karmeliet*, Langestraat 19,
☎ 050.33.82.59, offers outstanding modern cooking.

£££ *De Snippe*, Nieuwe Gentweg 52,
☎ 050.33.70.70, serves delicious fish dishes in a handsome 18C interior.

££ *Huyze Die Maene*, Markt 17,
☎ 050.33.39.59, offers good brasserie cooking in an informal interior.

££ *Pieter Pourbus*, Pieter Pourbusstraat 1, ☎ 050.34.11.45, is a traditional Flemish restaurant in a 17C house once owned by Pieter Pourbus.

££ *Spinola*, Spinolarei 1,
☎ 050.34.17.85, is a convivial restaurant in a narrow canalside house.

£ *'t Koetse*, Oude Burg 31,
☎ 050.33.76.80, is a traditional Flemish restaurant with a blazing fire.

£ *Brasserie Raymond*, Eiermarkt 5,
☎ 050.33.78.48, is a bustling brasserie.

£ *Lotus*, Wapenmakerstraat 5,
☎ 050.33.10.78 is an attractive vegetarian restaurant open at lunchtime only.

Cafés

Brugs Beertje, Kemelstraat 5, is a specialised beer café run by an amiable enthusiast known for his erudite beer seminars.

Vlissinghe, Blekerstraat 2, is an historic Flemish tavern established in 1515.

Getting around
Public transport

Direct trains run to Bruges from Brussels. High-speed Thalys trains run directly from Paris to Bruges. The station is 1.5km from the Markt on the south edge of the old town. De Lijn runs buses to the town centre and suburbs, though the main sights can easily be reached on foot.

Cars

Bruges is trying to develop a rational transport policy that discourages cars from the old town. A large car park has been built next to the station, about 15 minutes walk from the centre. The car park fee is relatively inexpensive. The car park ticket can be used to obtain a free bus ticket allowing all the occupants of the vehicle to travel on De Lijn local services. Those staying at a hotel should ask for a map giving directions for reaching the hotel by car and advice on parking.

Cycling

With cars discouraged from the centre, Bruges has become an ideal city to explore by bicycle. Sturdy bikes can be rented at 't Koffieboontje, 4 Hallestraat, or Eric Popelier, 14 Hallestraat. The railway station also rents out bicycles. Train travellers can claim a discount if they reserve a bicycle when buying the train ticket.

Tourist information
The tourist office is at Burg 12, ☎ 050.44.86.86. Open daily 09.00–19.00 (closed at weekends 13.00–14.00). Closes at 18.00 Oct–May. The tourist office sells some attractive souvenirs, including a reproduction of Marcus Gerards' 1562 map of Bruges.

Banks and post office

Main banks are:
BBL, Markt 18.
Kredietbank, Steenstraat 38.
The main post office is at Markt 5.

Carillon concerts

The carillon in the Belfry is played mid-Jun–Sept Mon, Wed and Sat 09.00–10.00, Sun 14.15–15.00; Oct–mid-Jun Wed, Sat and Sun 14.15–15.00.

Children

The Boudewijn Park, located in the suburbs to the south, is a large theme park with a modern dolphinarium, an astronomical clock and roller-coaster rides (open daily Easter–Sept 10.00–18.00).

Bookshops

The best bookshops for English novels, guide books and magazines are De Reyghere Boekhandel at Markt 12 and Boekhandel De Meester at Dijver 1.

Guided tours

Guided walking tours normally depart from outside the tourist information office on the Burg in July and August at 15.00.

Tours by horse-drawn carriage lasting about 35 minutes leave from the Begijnhof Mar–Nov.

Several operators run canal tours lasting about 35 minutes. Boats leave from several locations along the Dijver. Tours are run daily Mar–Nov 10.00–18.00. Guides expect to be tipped. Longer boat excursions run to Damme and Ghent from Apr–Sept.

Opening times
Museums

Most museums in Bruges are closed on 1 January, Ascension Day afternoon and 25 Dec.

Brangwyn Museum (works of Frank Brangwyn and applied art), Dijver, open daily Apr–Sept 09.30–17.00; Oct–Mar Wed–Mon 09.30–12.30 and 14.00–17.00.

Groeninge Museum (outstanding collection of paintings), Dijver 12, open daily Apr–Sept 09.30–17.00; Oct–Mar Wed–Mon 09.30–12.30 and 14.00–17.00.

Gruuthuse Museum (painting, decorative arts and lace), Dijver 17, open daily Apr–Sept 09.30–17.00; Oct–Mar Wed–Mon 09.30–12.30 and 14.00–17.00.

Memling Museum (works by Memling), Sint Jans Hospitaal, Mariastraat 38, is open daily Apr–Sept 09.30–17.00; Oct–Mar Thur–Tues, 09.30–12.30 and 14.00–17.00.

Museum of the Holy Blood (church treasures, 15C and 16C paintings), Burg, is open Apr–Sept daily 09.30–12.00 and 14.00–18.00; Oct–Mar daily 10.00–12.00 and 14.00–16.00. It is closed on Wed afternoons.

Brugse Vrije Museum (Renaissance carved chimneypiece), Burg, is open Apr–Sept daily 09.30–12.30 and 13.15–17.00; Oct–Mar daily 09.30–12.30 and 14.00–17.00.

Potterie chapel and museum (tapestries, 16C paintings), Potterielei, are open Apr–Sept daily 09.30–12.30 and 13.15–17.00; Oct–Mar Thur–Tues 09.30–12.30 and 14.00–17.00.

Museum voor Volkskunde (folk arts), Balstraat, is open from Apr–Sept daily 09.30–17.00; Oct–Mar Wed–Mon 09.30–12.30 and 14.00–17.00.

Kantcentrum (Lace Centre), Peperstraat, is open Apr–Sept Mon–Sat 10.00–12.00 and 14.00–18.00 (17.00 on Sat). It is closed on Sun.

Guido Gezellemuseum (memorabilia of Flemish priest and poet), Rolweg 64, is open Apr–Sept daily 09.30–12.30 and 13.15–17.00; Oct–Mar Wed–Mon 09.30–12.30 and 14.00–17.00.

Churches

Onze Lieve Vrouwkerk, Dijver, is open Mon–Sat 10.00–11.30 and 14.30–17.00, Sun 14.30–17.00 (16.30 in winter). The Mausoleums close half an hour earlier than the church in the afternoon. Closed during services.

Kathedraal Sint Salvator, Steenstraat, is open Apr–Sept on Mon, Tues, and Thur–Sat 10.00–11.30 and 14.00–17.00, Sun 15.00–17.00. Closed Wed and mornings from Oct–Mar.

Jeruzalemkerk, Peperstraat, is open from Apr–Sept Mon–Sat 10.00–12.00 and 14.00–18.00 (17.00 on Sat). Closed mornings from Oct–Mar.

Other buildings

Belfry (13C bell-tower), Markt, is open from Apr–Sept daily 09.30–17.00; Oct–Mar daily 09.30–12.30 and 13.30–17.00.

Stadhuis (Gothic town hall), Burg, is open Apr–Sept daily 09.30–17.00; Oct–Mar daily 09.30–12.30 and 14.00–17.00.

Guild House of St Sebastian (archers' guild) Carmersstraat 178, is open Apr–Sept Mon, Tues, Thur and Fri 10.00–12.00 and 14.00–17.00.

Guild House of St George (guild of crossbowmen), Stijn Streuvelstraat 59, is open Apr–Sept Mon, Tues, Thur and Fri 14.00–18.00.

Sint Janshuysmolen (windmill), Kruisvest, is open daily from May–Sept 09.30–12.30 and 13.15–17.00.

History

Bruges developed under the protection of a castle built in 865 by Baldwin Iron Arm, the first Count of Flanders, to defend his land against the Vikings. The settlement grew rapidly prosperous because of its proximity to the Zwin estuary. This reached as far as the port of Damme, which was connected to Bruges by the Reie. Bruges became more wealthy still in the 13C from the manufacture of cloth. Its annual fair was one of the most important in Flanders.

Philip the Fair of France began to interfere in the affairs of Bruges in the early 14C to settle the conflict between the Counts of Flanders, who supported France, and the merchants, who saw more profit in an alliance with England. Philip made a triumphal entry in 1301 with his consort Joanna of Navarre. 'I imagined myself alone to be queen, but I see hundreds of women here whose attire vies with my own,' she exclaimed.

The French occupation provoked an uprising in 1302 led by Pieter de Coninck and Jan Breydel. The rebels massacred the French on 18 May 1302 in a revolt known as the **Bruges Matins**, slaying anyone unable to pronounce the shibboleth *Schild en Vriend* (shield and friend). Six weeks later, the soldiers of Bruges played a prominent part in the defeat of the French nobility at the Battle of the Golden Spurs near Kortrijk.

The citizens surrendered many of their privileges in the 14C and 15C when the Dukes of Burgundy ruled the region. The period under Philip the Good brought enormous wealth into Bruges, largely because it was the main market of the **Hanseatic League**. Established to suppress piracy and promote commercial treaties, this association of northern European cities flourished from the 14C to the 17C. Bruges became an important banking and trading centre. Its colony of foreign merchants traded in silk from Italy and the Orient, furs from Russia and the Balkans, metals from Hungary, Poland and Bohemia, wool, cheese and coal from England and Scotland, fruit from Spain,

Arabian spices and Rhenish wines. The population rose to 80,000 and sometimes as many as 150 vessels entered the port in a single day.

This flourishing city attracted some of the greatest artists of the day, including Jan van Eyck from Maaseik and Hans Memling from Seligenstadt, near Frankfurt-am-Main. These artists found patrons among the wealthy merchant class and the nobility. Philip the Good established the **Order of the Golden Fleece** in Bruges in 1430 in recognition of the skills of the Flemish weavers. It was in Bruges that the **States General** of the Netherlands first met in 1464.

The death of Philip in Bruges in 1467 marked the beginning of a period of slow decline. This was due to a combination of factors, including the silting of Het Zwin estuary, a general recession in the cloth industry, and the development of new trade routes, but it was possibly local opposition to Habsburg sovereignty that contributed most to the economic decline. Angered at the loss of their privileges, the citizens of Bruges recklessly imprisoned Archduke Maximilian of Austria for three months in 1488. After his release, Maximilian encouraged the development of Antwerp, which replaced Bruges as the official Hanseatic capital in 1545.

To make matters worse, Bruges was frequently attacked and besieged from the 16C to the 18C. The economy only began to pick up with the digging of the Boudewijn Kanaal and the development of the port of Zeebrugge from 1895 to 1907. The town also began to see the arrival of the first tourists at the end of the 19C.

Bruges in literature

Bruges (or 'Brugges') is mentioned frequently by Chaucer and other early English writers. Wordsworth wrote of its quiet streets while Longfellow mused on its towering belfry. The 19C novelist Georges Rodenbach created a vogue for visiting Bruges through his melancholy novel Bruges-la-Morte. The modern Scottish author, Dorothy Dunnett, has based several historic novels in 15C Bruges.

1 • Markt and Burg

This walk begins on the Markt, a typical Flemish square surrounded by restaurants and cafés. One of the more traditional is **Craenenbourg** at Markt 16 although it is not as old as it looks. It was built in 1956 in the style of the demolished 15C Florentine Lodge. The café takes its name from a building on this site where Maximilian was imprisoned by the reckless citizens of Bruges for three months in 1488.

The **Huis Bouchoute** at no. 15 is older. It was built in the late 15C with a brick screen front that gives it a deceptive height. The octagonal windvane on the front was added in the 17C. The exiled King Charles II of England lived here in 1656–57.

Many of the buildings on Markt are interesting examples of Bruges neo-Gothic. De Maene at no. 17 was built in 1950 in the style of 15C Bruges Gothic. The **Provinciaal Hof** opposite, where the government of West Flanders meets, was built in 1887–1921 by Louis Delacenserie of Brussels in a flamboyant neo-Gothic style.

The monument in the centre of the square was designed by Paul de Vigne in 1887 to commemorate Jan Breydel and Pieter de Coninck the leaders of the Bruges Matins uprising in 1302.

The 13C **Halle** was once the main market hall. Built around a quadrangle, it could be reached by canal up the the 18C. Laws were promulgated from the balcony above the entrance until 1769.

Belfry

Many cities in Flanders and Hainaut built tall towers known as **belforts** from the 11C to the 15C. Cities competed with one another to construct the tallest tower as a symbol of municipal power and prestige. The towers were used to store the municipal privileges and, from the 17C, to hang the town carillon. The oldest Belfry in northern Europe was built at Tournai in 1192. The Belfry at Bruges, one of the finest of its kind, is the most prominent architectural feature in the city. Built in the 13C to replace a wooden tower burnt down in 1240, the 83m tower can be seen from far off. Other impressive Belfries are found at Ghent (91m), Mons (87m) and Tournai (72m).

The Belfry rises from the main wing of the Halle. Its two lower storeys date from 1282–96 while the octagonal upper tier was added in 1482–87. It was surmounted by a spire, but this burnt down in 1493 and again, after being rebuilt, in 1741. It was replaced in 1882 by a neo-Gothic parapet. The tower leans 1.19m to the southeast.

You can climb the 366 steps to the top for a superb view of the town and the surrounding polders. The first stop is at the **Treasure Room**, though this can only be seen through the door grille. The town charters were once kept here. The fine vaulting dates from 1285. The elaborate wrought-iron was fashioned by Nicolaas Grootwerc in the early 14C.

On reaching the 172nd step, you enter a room where there is an impressive view looking upwards. At the 220th step, a blackboard allows visitors to write their names rather than add to the graffiti left by previous generations. From the 333rd step, the **carillon** is visible with its

The Belfry, Bruges

huge drum and the works of the clock designed in 1748 by Antonius de Hondt. The carillon is programmed to play a folk tune every 15 minutes. Open Apr–Sept daily 9.30–17.00; Oct–Mar daily 9.30–12.30 and 13.30–17.00.

A lane behind the Halle known as Karthuizerinnenstraat recalls the Carthusian nuns who lived here. Their chapel, built in 1632, was restored in 1927. The crypt (open Nov 1 and May 8) is a **war memorial** with a white

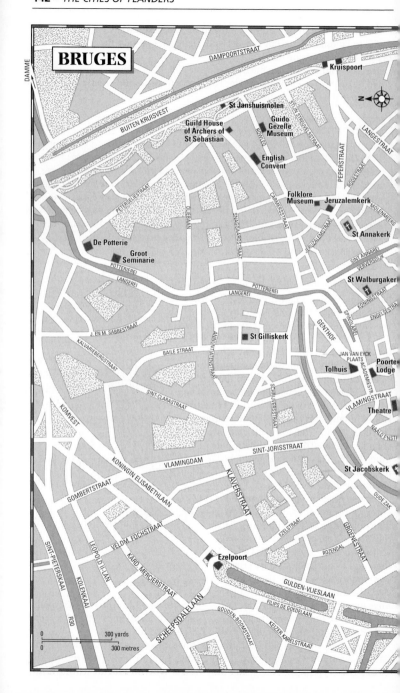

BRUGES

DAMME

DAMPOORTSTRAAT

Kruispoort

St Janshuismolen

Guild House
of Archers of
St Sebastian

Guido
Gezelle
Museum

BUITEN KRUISVEST

LANGESTRAAT

PEPERSTRAAT

RODESTRAAT

English
Convent

ROLWEG

SINT-STRUISTSTRAAT

PETERSELIESTRAAT

OLIEBAAN

SNAGGAARDSTRAAT

CARMERSSTRAAT

Folklore
Museum

Jeruzalemkerk

MOLENMEERS

JERUZALEMSTRAAT

St Annakerk

SINT-ANNAREI

De Potterie

Groot
Seminarie

VERVERSDIJK

St Walburgakerk

POTTERIEREI

LANGEREI

LANGEREI

POTTERIEREI

LANGEREI

GENTHOF

SPINOLAREI

KONINGSTRAAT

ENGELSESTRAAT

J. EN M. SABBESTRAAT

KALVARIEBERGSTRAAT

BAILE STRAAT

ANNUNTIATENSTRAAT

St Gilliskerk

JAN VAN EYCK
PLAATS

KONVEST

SINT-CLARASTRAAT

SCHRIJVERSSTRAAT

Tolhuis

ACADEMIESTR.

Poorters
Lodge

VLAMINGSTRAAT

Theatre

NAALDENSTR.

VLAMINGDAM

SINT-JORISSTRAAT

KONINGIN ELISABETHLAAN

KLAVERSTRAAT

St Jacobskerk

GOMBERTSTRAAT

OUDE ZAK

VELDM. FOCHSTRAAT

GROENESTRAAT

SINT-PIETERSKAAI

LEOPOLD II-LAN

KARD. MERCIERSTRAAT

EZELSTRAAT

ROZENDAL

KOLENKAAI

Ezelpoort

R30

SCHEEPSDALELAAN

GOUDEN-BOOMSTRAAT

GULDEN-VLIESLAAN

FILIPS DE GOEDELAAN

KEIZER KARELSTRAAT

0 ___ 300 yards
0 ___ 300 metres

N

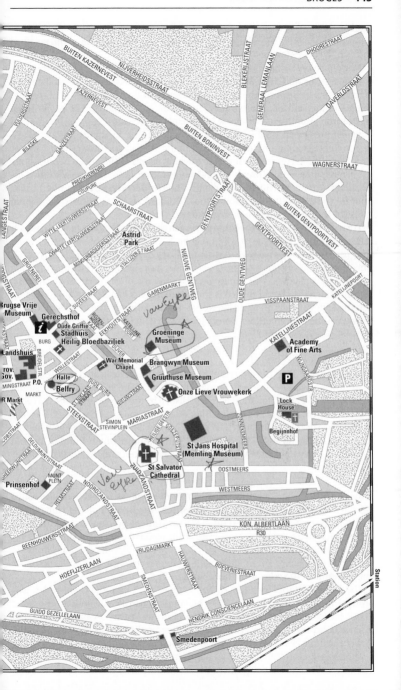

marble tomb of a recument figure modelled on a local soldier who died at Langemark in 1918. The chapel also contains the ashes of victims who perished in Dachau concentration camp.

Now go down Wollestraat, which runs next to the Halle. The house at no. 28 is known as **In de Grote Mortier**. Built in 1634, it is decorated with damaged stone tablets illustrating the relief of Bruges from the siege of 1631. Cross the bridge at the end of Wollestraat. The statue on the parapet is of **St John Nepomuk**. A native of Nepomuk in Bohemia, he became canon of Prague and chaplain to Queen Sophie, the second wife of the dissolute Wenceslas IV. According to tradition he was thrown into the Moldau and drowned in 1383 or 1393, because he refused to reveal to the king details of the queen's confession.

Turn left now along Rozenhoedkaai, an attractive quay, then go left into a little square known as Huidevettersplaats. The **Huidevettershuis** at nos 11 was built in 1630 and the extension at no. 12 added in 1716. Formerly the guild house of the tanners, it is now a restaurant.

Turn right at the end of the square to reach the **Vismarkt** (fish market), which retains a Doric colonnade of 1821. Go back a short distance along the canal, then turn right across a bridge to enter the **Burg** by the narrow Blinde Ezelstraat. This leads under the arch of the Oude Griffie, past the site of the old south gate (marked by a plaque). This square occupies the site of the original 9C fortress. The building opposite on the left is the **Landshuis**, a late Renaissance building designed in 1664 by F. van Hillewerve. It was formerly the residence of the Provost of the church of Sint Donatian, of which barely a trace remains.

The vanished cathedral

Begun in the 10C, the church of Sint Donatian was dedicated to a 4C Bishop of Rheims whose relics were brought to Bruges in the 9C. Elevated to a cathedral in 1559, Sint Donatian was demolished by the French in 1799. A reconstructed fragment of the choir with a small scale model of the apse is the only evidence of this great church. A statue of the painter Jan van Eyck, who was buried in the church, stands nearby. The paintings which hung in the old cathedral are now mostly in the Groeninge Museum and the Kathedraal Sint Salvator.

From the site of the church, a splendid row of buildings is visible on the south side of the square. The **Heilig Bloedbasiliek**, the Basilica of the Holy Blood, stands in the corner on the far right. It is named after a precious relic in the basilica, which is said to contain some drops of the blood of Christ. The building comprises a sombre lower chapel from the 12C and a more airy upper chapel from the 15C or 16C. Reached by an elaborate late Gothic staircase of 1523, the upper chapel contains the relic of the holy blood.

The **Lower Chapel** was built to house a relic of St Basil the Great which was brought from the Holy Land c 1099 by Count Robert II of Flanders. The same Count brought the relic of the True Cross now at Veurne. St Basil (c 330–79) defended Christianity against the Arians. He is revered in the Eastern Church as the first of the three Holy Hierarchs, and in the West as one of the four Great Doctors.

The chapel, rebuilt in 1134 by Count Thierry of Alsace, was restored in the 19C. The sober and shadowy interior is one of the purest Romanesque buildings in Flanders. Once accustomed to the gloom, you can admire a 13C or 14C figure of the Virgin, protected by part of its original iron enclosure. The chapel also contains an **altarpiece** of 1530 and a 12C bas-relief illustrating either the baptism of Christ or perhaps St Basil.

The holy blood

The holy blood is said to have been given by the Patriarch of Jerusalem to Dirk of Alsace, Count of Flanders, in 1147, during the Second Crusade. It was a reward for the bravery the Count had shown in fighting the Saracens. The coagulated blood, in a rock-crystal phial which dates from the 11C or 12C, has been preserved intact since its arrival in Bruges. The first reference to the relic occurs in a document dated 1256. Some historians, however, believe that the relic came from Constantinople as part of the treasure stolen by the Crusaders after they had attacked and captured the city in 1204. An account by a French knight, Robert of Clari, who was present at the siege and who witnessed the subsequent looting, states that a number of sacred relics were found by the Crusaders in the chapel of the Bucoleon, the imperial palace of the Byzantine emperors. These included two large sections of the True Cross, the lance and nails which had pierced Christ and 'a crystal phial which contained a good quantity of his blood'.

Baldwin of Flanders, who was elected the new emperor of Byzantium, presumably had the pick of the ill-gotten gains. He would have sent the relics he found for safe keeping to his daughters Margaret and Joanna, who ruled in Flanders during his absence. Famous for the many religious and charitable foundations which they established during their reign, Margaret and Joanna would have had no difficulty in finding suitable locations for their new treasures. Supporters of the Constantinople theory point out that the rock crystal phial is cut in a style that suggests it was produced in Constantinople.

The relic of the Holy Blood is kept in the **Upper Chapel**. Originally Romanesque, the current chapel is 15C–16C Gothic in style, but has been much altered, most recently in 1934. The stained-glass windows of 1847 are decorated with portraits of the dukes of Burgundy based on 15C originals. The pulpit was carved from a single piece of oak by Hendrik Pulincx in 1728. It represents a terrestrial globe.

Displayed in a silver reliquary presented by Albert and Isabella in 1611, the relic is venerated every Friday between 08.30–11.45 and 15.00–16.00. It is carried through the old town in the solemn Procession of the Holy Blood on Ascension Day.

The **Museum of the Holy Blood**, open Apr–Sept daily 9.30–12.00 and 14.00–18.00; Oct–Mar daily 10.00–12.00 and 14.00–16.00, is a small, single-room museum beside the chapel where church treasures and paintings are exhibited. A Flemish tapestry of 1637 depicts the *Translation of the body of St Augustine*. A case below contains 15C chasubles and a number of manuscripts. There is also an exquisite reliquary of the Holy Blood in gold, silver and precious stones. This was made by Jan Crabbe of Bruges in 1614–17. It is flanked by two exceptionally beautiful shutters from a triptych by Pieter Pourbus. Painted in 1556, it depicts *Members of the Brotherhood of the Holy Blood*.

The museum also contains a triptych of the *Crucifixion* attributed to Van Dyck, a 15C *Life of St Barbara* by the Master of the St Barbara Legend, and several small paintings within an illustrated frame of the *Life of the Virgin* by an unknown artist of c 1500. Other works include a triptych of the *Descent from the Cross* painted in 1620 by the Master of the Holy Blood, and an *Adoration of the Magi* by Van Dyck.

The **Stadhuis**, open Apr–Sept daily 09.30–17.00; Oct–Mar daily 09.30–12.30 and 14.00–17.00, dates from 1376–1420 and is the oldest Gothic town hall in Belgium. It provided a magnificent setting for the first meeting of the States General of the Netherlands in 1464. The façade has three graceful octagonal turrets, while the niches between the windows contain statues of the counts and countesses of Flanders. These are copies of the original figures, which were destroyed by the French in 1792.

The entrance hall has a joisted ceiling resting on four stone pillars. A broad passage off the hall is hung with large 19C historical canvases illustrating the *Death of Mary of Burgundy* (painted by Camille van Camp in 1878), and *Rubens at the deathbed of Brueghel* (by Bruno van Hollebeke).

The great **Gothic Hall** on the first floor was the scene of the meeting of the first States General. The superb wood ceiling, with a double row of six hanging painted arches, dates from 1385–1402. The 12 vault-keys are carved with scenes from the New Testament, while the 16 corbels represent the months and the elements. The walls are hung with 12 historical paintings by Albert and Julien Devriendt. Painted in 1895, they provide a romantic history of Bruges. The **Maritime Hall**, opening off the Gothic Hall, is devoted to the harbour of Bruges and the Boudewijn Canal (which links the city with Zeebrugge). One of the highlights is the 1562 map of Bruges by Marcus Gerards printed on ten copper plates in astonishing detail.

The **Oude Griffie** stands next to the town hall. This ornate Renaissance building was designed in 1537 by Christian Sixdeniers, and decorated with symbolic sculptures by Willem Aerts. Originally the Recorder's House, it was used as a local magistrates' court until 1983.

The **Gerechtshof**, formerly a court of law, is now occupied by the Bruges tourist office. The building here was constructed in 1722 on the site of the palace of the Brugse Vrije (Liberty of Bruges). This was an independent jurisdiction with authority that extended as far as Dunkirk, though it excluded Bruges itself. Fragments of the original 15C building survive, including part of the Schepenzaal where the magistrates of the Liberty tried cases.

The Schepenzaal is now occupied by the **Brugse Vrije Museum**, open from Feb–Dec, Tues–Sun 10.00–12.00 and 13.30–17.00. The main reason for visiting here is to admire the extraordinary **Renaissance chimneypiece** made from black marble and decorated with oak carvings. This was executed in 1529 by various artists working under the direction of Lancelot Blondeel. The wooden statues were carved by Guyot de Beaugrant. Charles V is in the centre, with Maximilian of Austria and Mary of Burgundy to his right, and Ferdinand of Aragon and Isabella of Castile on the left. The princes wear the chain of the Order of the Golden Fleece.

Leave the Burg by the Hoogstraat, then turn right down a narrow street that leads back to the canal. Cross by the oldest bridge in the city, the **Meebrug**, which was rebuilt in 1390, then turn left along Steenhouwersdijk. The next stretch of canal, known as Groene Rei, is overlooked by a row of almshouses called **De Pelicaan**, founded in 1708. You can walk to the end of this canal and cross by the bridge just around the corner. Look back down Groene Rei for a seductive view of the old town.

2 • The Groeninge Museum and Gruuthuse Museum

This walk takes you along the main canal and into two superb museums. Begin on **Markt** and go down Wollestraat to reach Dijver. The corner house with the small turrets was built in c 1480. It was used as a hiding place for the Holy Blood from 1578 to 1583 to protect it from Protestant iconoclasts. Now follow the Dijver, where an antique market is held along the water's edge on Saturday and Sunday afternoons (Mar–Oct).

Groeninge Museum

Turn through an arch at Dyver 12 to reach the **Groeninge Museum**, open daily Apr–Sept 09.30–17.00; Oct–Mar Wed–Mon 09.30–12.30 and 14.00–17.00. Occupying a walled garden, the museum stands on the site of the ancient abbey of Eekhout in an quarter named Groeninge in the 13C because of its greenery. Built from 1929–30 to display paintings from local churches and private collections, the museum owns an outstanding collection of Flemish Primitive paintings displayed in rooms modelled on medieval chapels. It also has notable Bruges Renaissance and Baroque works, 19C Neo-classicism and a stimulating 20C collection.

Jan van Eyck's extraordinary *Madonna with St Donatian, St George and Canon van der Paele* in **room 1** was commissioned for the vanished cathedral of St Donatian in 1436. The tiny *Portrait of Margareta van Eyck*, the artist's wife, painted in 1439, bears Van Eyck's motto *als ich can* (the best I can do). The influence of Van Eyck can be seen in the *Crucifixion* by the Master of the Strauss Madonna, a Bavarian artist who painted this work c 1445.

In **room 2** is a striking triptych painted in c 1468 by Dirk Bouts and Hugo van der Goes. It depicts the *Martyrdom of St Hippolytus*, a priest of Rome martyred in 235. The right panel, by Dirk Bouts, shows the Emperor Decius, notorious for his persecution of Christians, trying to persuade the saint to deny his faith. The centre panel, also by Bouts, shows Hippolytus being torn apart by four horses. The donors in the left panel were painted by Van der Goes.

The same room contains a good 15C copy of Roger van der Weyden's *St Luke painting the Virgin*. The painting of *Philip the Good* is also a 15C copy of a work by Van der Weyden. The Portrait of *Louis of Gruuthuse* (same room) is by the Master of the Court Portraits. The frame, which is original, bears Lodewijk's motto, *Plus est en Vous*. The man portrayed here was a wealthy 15C arms dealer who built a palace in Bruges that is still standing. Two panels from a 1452 triptych by Petrus Christus depict the *Annunciation* and the *Nativity*. The view through the open window in the Annunciation shows a town similar to Bruges.

Hugo van der Goes' *Death of the Virgin* in **room 3** was painted in c 1470 in muted colours like stained-glass. It once hung in the Abbey of the Dunes in Koksijde. The eight panels by the Master of the Legend of St Ursula come from a polyptych that once hung in the convent of the Black Sisters in Bruges. The scenes illustrate the legend of St Ursula and her 11,000 virgin companions, all of whom were believed to have been martyred by Maximian at Cologne. A reliquary by Memling in the Sint Jans Hospitaal illustrates the same legend.

Hanging in the same room, the Master of the Lucy Legend's *St Nicholas* shows the saint wearing a richly decorated cope. Painted between 1486–93, it includes the familiar spires of Bruges in the background.

Room 4 contains several works by Hans Memling, including two *grisaille* panels from a triptych painted for the Abbey of the Dunes in c 1467–70. The striking *Moreel Triptych* was commissioned in 1484 by Willem Moreel, burgomaster of Bruges. Painted for the altar of Saints Maurus and Giles in the St Jacobskerk, it includes portraits of Moreel, his wife Barbara van Vlaenderberg and their 16 children. Memling painted an earlier portrait of Moreel and his wife in 1478 (now in the Musée d'Art Ancien in Brussels).

In **room 5** is Gerard David's *Baptism of Christ triptych*. Painted in 1508, this is one of David's finest works. It includes portraits of the donor Jean des Trompes, his son and St John the Evangelist (on the left wing), and the donor's first wife, Elisabeth van der Meersch, her four daughters and St Elizabeth of Hungary (on the right wing). The backs of the wings are painted with a Virgin and Child, and a portrait of the donor's second wife with her daughter and St Mary Magdalene. Probably also in this room, David's two panels on the *Judgement of Cambyses* illustrate the story told by Herodotus of the corrupt judge Sisamnes who was flayed alive. Painted in 1498, the panels were commissioned to hang in the town hall. The first panel shows the corrupt judge, who had accepted a bribe, being sentenced by Cambyses. The second panel depicts the execution in all its gruesome detail. The scene in the background shows Sisamnes' skin hanging over the judicial seat, which is now occupied by his son.

> ### Pieter Lanchals
> Pieter Lanchals, a city treasurer, was beheaded in Bruges in 1488 for opposing the imprisonment of Archduke Maximilian. The magistrates of Bruges atoned for the unjust execution in 1498 by commissioning David's panels of the *Judgement of Cambyses*. They also introduced swans to the canals of Bruges in memory of Lanchals, whose name literally means 'long neck'. There is a chapel in memory of Lanchals in the Onze Lieve Vrouwkerk.

A fascinating *Last Judgement* probably by Hieronymus Bosch illustrates the hell on earth that precedes the last judgement. Two early 16C altarpiece wings (in room 5) by an anonymous Bruges artist reveal a similar morbid imagination. The eight scenes are rare illustrations of the *Martyrdom of St George*, who was broken on a wheel and boiled in a cauldron before being beheaded.

The rich Renaissance style of 16C Flanders is revealed in **room 6** in works such as Ambrosius Benson's *Rest on the Flight to Egypt*, and Abel Grimmer's animated *Carrying of the Cross*. Adriaen Isenbrant of Bruges reveals the influence of Italy in his *Triptych with the Virgin and Child, St John and St Jerome*. But Jan Provoost was perhaps the most original Bruges artist of the period. His *Last Judgement*, painted for the town hall in 1525, is reminiscent of the Bosch in room 5. The elaborate frame was perhaps designed by Lancelot Blondeel. An even more elaborate frame surrounds Blondeel's *St Luke Painting the Virgin's Portrait*, executed in 1545 for the chapel of the artists' guild.

The works in **rooms 8** and **9** no longer dwell on religious themes, but turn to family portraits, landscapes and historical subjects. There is a double portrait of *Archdukes Albert and Isabella* by Frans Pourbus the Younger, and a *Portrait of Lady Anne Rushout* by Marcus Gheeraerts, who was court painter in London. The interesting Pieter Pourbus painted a remarkable *Last Judgement* in 1551 inspired by Michelangelo's Sistine Chapel. He also painted an intriguing double portrait of *Jan van Eyewerve and Jacquemyne Buuck* with a view of the crane on the Kraanplein in Bruges behind the husband.

Next is the new **museum bookshop** and an attractive semi-circular conservatory with a view of the spire of Onze Lieve Vrouwkerk. The next two rooms occupy the **Xavier Wing**, a 19C neo-Gothic assembly hall restored as a museum extension in 1995. A glass corridor leads to **room 10**, where 18C and 19C paintings are hung on deep red walls. Jacob van Oost the Elder's *Portrait of a Bruges Family* of 1645 shows a contented aristocratic family on a country estate outside Bruges. A close study of the painting is required to spot the ages of the different people concealed in fabrics and objects. Jan Garemijn's astonishing *Digging of the Ghent Canal* of 1753 shows hundreds of workers excavating the canal between Bruges and Ghent. There is also a large painting of *Bruges harbour* in 1665 by Hendrik van Minderhout and a painting by an anonymous artist of the *Garden of the Willaeys-Vleys family at Groeninge* in 1759, which shows the spire of Onze Lieve Vrouwkerk and the Belfry. The museum was built on the site of the apple orchard in the right of the painting.

A spiral staircase with glass walls leads up to the Neo-classical collection in **room 11**. Joseph Suvée's intriguing *Invention of the Art of Drawing* of 1791 shows the daughter of the Greek potter Butades drawing her lover's shadow on a wall. A large 1817 painting by François Kinsoen shows the *Death of Belisarius' Wife*. Another romantic work by Joseph Odevaere shows *Lord Byron on his Death-Bed*. An interesting *View of the Grote Markt* in Bruges painted by August van de Steene in 1826 shows the Neo-classical building that once stood on the east side of the square.

The final section of the attic is devoted to Symbolism. Henri le Sidaner's *The Quay* captures the foggy melancholy of the Lange Rei in Bruges. Fernand Khnopff's *Secret-Reflet* of 1902 affirms Bruges' identity as a dead city. The lower panel shows the Sint Jans Hospitaal reflected in the Dijver. The end wall of this room is entirely filled by Jean Delville's ghostly *L'Homme-Dieu* of 1903 which was, astonishingly, a preliminary study for a much larger work intended for the Eglise de la Chapelle in Brussels.

Go back downstairs to reach **room 12**, which includes paintings by Emile Claus and James Ensor and a bronze figure titled *Household Cares* by Rik Wouters. **Room 13** is dominated by the extraordinary *Last Supper* by Gustave van Woestyne, dated 1924 and set in a wooden frame designed by the artist.

Gustave de Smet (same room) used strong red tones in the appealing *Shooting Gallery* of 1923 and the *Couple with a Rose* of 1932. The more earthy colours of Constant Permeke's art are seen in his *Farm in Flanders* and *The Angelus*. The reclusive Jean Brusselmans in **room 14** revels in the colours of objects in his *Nude with Conch* of 1945 and his *Still Life with Fan* of 1948. The same room contains René Magritte's enigmatic *The Assault* of 1932 and Paul Delvaux's *Serenity* of

1970, which was inspired by medieval Flemish paintings of the Annunciation.

The astonishing diversity of contemporary Belgian art is seen in **rooms 15–18**. Roger Raveel reveals the humour of Flemish Pop Art in his *Your World in My Garden* of 1968, featuring two mirrors and an empty bird cage. The Broodthaers Cabinet in room 18 contains an engagingly odd collection of Surrealist works by Marcel Broodthaers. His drawing of the *Bone of a Belgian*, painted the colours of the Belgian flag, is delightfully eccentric.

On leaving the museum, go straight ahead to enter the romantic **Arentspark** next to the Dijver. The two stone columns here once supported the 15C Water Hall on Markt. The building was raised above the canal to allow boats to sail inside and discharge their cargoes.

The **Brangwyn Museum**, open daily Apr–Sept 09.30–17.00; Oct–Mar Wed–Mon 09.30–12.30 and 14.00–17.00, occupies a 19C mansion known as the **Arentshuis**. The museum owns several private collections, including paintings, drawings and etchings gifted to the city by Frank Brangwyn (1867–1956). Born in Bruges, Brangwyn was the son of a British neo-Gothic architect who settled in the city. The museum also has a collection of pewter, brass, porcelain and topographical views of Bruges. The former coach house opposite now contains a collection of carriages and sleighs from the Gruuthuse Museum.

The British colony

A large British colony settled in Bruges in the 19C, including retired civil servants and army officers who found that their pensions went further in Belgium. The expatriates had their own church services, school, orphanage, club and tea rooms. Several British residents were neo-Gothic architects who played a leading role in the restoration of medieval Bruges and the development of a Flemish Gothic Revival style in harmony with the 15C architecture. The British architect Robert Chantrell was responsible for the spire of the St Salvator Cathedral.

A tree-shaded path leads through the Arentspark to the **Sint Bonifaciusbrug**, a picturesque bridge which looks medieval but was in fact built in 1910. Its name derives from St Boniface, an English martyr whose relics are kept in the nearby church of Onze Lieve Vrouw. A bust of **Juan Luis Vives** (1492–1540) stands in a shady spot next to the bridge. A Spanish scholar and friend of Erasmus, Vives edited St Augustine's *Civitatis Dei* and dedicated it to Henry VIII. A tutor to Princess Mary, he later became a fellow of Corpus Christi at Oxford. He was briefly imprisoned for his opposition to Henry's divorce from Catherine of Aragon. On being released, he moved to Bruges, where he introduced a system of public assistance.

Now cross the Sint Bonifaciusbrug and go through a passage to the right of the church to reach the vast courtyard of the **Gruuthuse Museum**, open daily Apr–Sept 09.30–17.00; Oct–Mar Wed–Mon 09.30–12.30 and 14.00–17.00, which is paved with its original stones. The lofty 15C house is decorated with elaborate turrets, chimneys and windows. A coat of arms with the motto *Plus est en Vous* surmounts the entrance arch.

The wing overlooking the canal dates from 1420, but the main part of the mansion was built c 1465–70 by Louis de Bruges, lord of Gruuthuse and lieutenant-general for Charles the Bold of Holland, Zeeland and Friesland. Louis, whose portrait hangs in the Groeninge Museum, provided a temporary refuge for England's fugitive Edward IV and his brother Richard in 1470–71. On regaining his throne, the grateful Edward conferred the earldom of Winchester on Louis. The title was renounced by his son, John, in 1500.

Gruit

The Gruuthuse mansion takes its name comes from *gruit*, a mediaeval mixture of dried herbs and flowers which was added to barley to improve the taste of beer. The *gruit* was stored in a warehouse known as the gruithuis that once stood here. The Van der Aa family was awarded the right to levy tax on *gruit* in the 14C. The family later gained the title of Lords of Gruuthuse. When brewers began to use hops rather than *gruit* in the 14C, the warehouse was converted into a toll house for collecting taxes on hops.

The museum's 32 rooms are furnished in period style and filled with a remarkable collection of antiquities, including paintings, sculpture, tapestries, coins, musical instruments, silver, ceramics, lace and arms. Begin in the **Great Hall**, which has a fine chimneypiece and several windows decorated with the arms of the guilds. A celebrated polychrome terracotta bust of *Charles V*, carved in c 1520 by the German sculptor, Konrad Meit, shows Charles wearing a large flat hat carved from oak. The solemn 20-year-old is realistically portrayed with a Roman nose and the famous Habsburg chin. Wearing the collar of the Order of the Golden Fleece, he looks away from the viewer rather disconcertingly.

Descend now to the kitchen, which is equipped with a wonderful collection of gleaming cooking pots. There are two works attributed to Peter Pourbus in **room 7**, a painting of the *Battle of 's Hertogenbosch* by S. Vranckx in **room 8** and a spinet of 1591 in **room 11**.

A curious **Oratory** is reached by a covered bridge off **room 17**. Built into the choir of Onze Lieve Vrouw, this elaborate chapel allowed the lords of the Gruuthuse to worship without leaving their mansion. The museum displays an impressive collection of Flemish lace in **rooms 18–20** including lace-making tools, pattern blocks and a magnificent altar cloth owned by Charles V.

Room 22 contains a collection of arms and weapons, and a secondhand guillotine bought in Hazebrouck in north France. After being tested on a blameless sheep, the guillotine was used by the city to execute two criminals a few days later.

Onze Lieve Vrouwkerk

Leave the museum by the gate on Dijver. A statue of the Flemish poet Guido Gezelle (1830–99) stands in the square opposite. Now turn left to enter the Onze Lieve Vrouwkerk, open Mon–Sat 10.00–11.30 and 14.30–17.00; Sun 14.30–17.00 (16.30 in winter), passing the graceful north portal of 1465. This is known as Paradis, which has nothing to do with Paradise but comes from the French word parvis, meaning a small square in front of a church.

Onze Lieve Vrouwkerk originated as a 10C chapel. Little is known of the early building, which burnt down in 1116. Nor do any traces remain of its successor. The oldest surviving structure dates from c 1220. This forms the central section of the church. The north aisle was added in the 14C and the south aisle in the 15C. The most impressive feature of the church is the tower which rises to 122m. Built in 1250–1350, it is one of the highest brick structures in Europe. The spire was added in 1440 while the pinnacles at the angles are a neo-Gothic embellishment of 1872.

The church has an exceptional collection of paintings and sculpture. Beginning in the **nave**, there are statues of the Apostles carved 1618, and a baroque pulpit of 1722 based on a sketch by Jan Garemijn. At the west end of the **south aisle** is an *Adoration of the Magi* painted in 1630 by Gerard Seghers. Lower down, on the second pillar, is a *Virgin, Child and St Joseph* by Gaspard de Crayer.

An outstanding *Virgin and Child* by Michelangelo sits on the altar in a **chapel** at the east end of the south aisle. Commissioned in 1505 by Jan van Moescroen, a merchant of Bruges, this tiny white marble statue was given to the church in 1514 or 1517. It was stolen by the French in 1794 and again by the Germans in 1944. Michelangelo's sketch for the head of the Virgin is in the Victoria and Albert Museum in London.

A tomb with black marble statues stands in the right-hand corner of the chapel. Carved in 1560, it commemorates the Sire de Haveskerke and his two wives. There is also a painting of *Christ at the House of Simon the Pharisee*. Dating from 1628, it was painted by Frans Francken the Younger.

The **choir** (entrance fee) is separated from the nave by a black and white marble rood-screen of 1722. The high altar and stalls date from 1770–79. The painted armorial bearings of the Knights of the Golden Fleece hang above the stalls. They belonged to the knights who attended the eleventh chapter held here in 1468.

The choir contains the **Mausoleums of Charles the Bold and Mary of Burgundy**. The mausoleum of Charles the Bold was constructed in 1559–62 from designs by Cornelis Floris of Antwerp. The mausoleum of Mary of Burgundy, which is considered superior, was constructed by Pieter de Beckere of Brussels in 1495–1502. Both works are festooned with magnificent heraldic decoration.

The riddle of the corpse

Charles the Bold was killed while laying siege to Nancy in 1477. Found in a frozen pond, the body was later buried. It was not until 1550 that Charles V ordered the remains to be brought to Bruges. This order so angered the authorities in Nancy that some scholars doubt whether the body removed was that of Charles or simply one of his knights. It took several years to bring the body to Bruges; it remained for three years in Luxembourg. By the time it reached Bruges, Charles V had abdicated and it fell to Philip II to order the construction of the mausoleum.

The **mausoleum of Mary of Burgundy** was commissioned by her husband Maximilian in 1495. The statue on top was probably carved by Jan Borman of Brussels, but the coffin is a 19C replacement after the original was plundered. It conceals a box containing the heart of her son Philip the Handsome. The other three tombs in the choir commemorate canons of the late 13C and early 14C.

The choir also contains a large triptych of the *Crucifixion and Passion*, begun by Bernard van Orley, and completed by Marcus Gerards in 1561. It was restored by Frans Pourbus the Younger in 1589.

The **south ambulatory** contains a painting by Caravaggio depicting the *Disciples at Emmaus*, two works by Jacob van Oost the Elder and two wings of a triptych with portraits of the donors by Pieter Pourbus. The work at the east end is the centre panel of a triptych by Gerard David, painted c 1520, and side panels with donors and children by Pieter Pourbus from c 1573.

The **Lanchals Chapel**, off the ambulatory, contains a monument to Pieter Lanchals and some c 14C tombs. There is also a *Last Supper* by Pieter Pourbus (1562), an outstanding *Madonna of the Seven Sorrows* (1518) by Adriaen Isenbrant, which is rich in fascinating detail, and a *Crucifixion* (1626) by Antoon van Dyck.

A reliquary of St Anthony stands behind the high altar. St Anthony was frequently invoked against plague, especially that scourge of the Middle Ages, the Black Death.

The Gothic **oratory** of the Gruuthuse family is in the north ambulatory. This was added in 1474 to communicate with the Gruuthuse mansion. Several interesting paintings hang nearby, including large works by Gaspard de Crayer, Jacob van Oost the Elder, and Louis de Deyster. A triptych of the *Adoration of the Shepherds* painted by Pieter Pourbus in 1474 hangs at the east end.

3 • The Cathedral and the Memling Museum

This walk takes in two further collections of art. Leave **Markt** by Steenstraat, a busy street with several interesting houses. The building at **no. 25** was built as a guild house for the masons in 1621. *De Lam* at **no. 28** dates from 1654. The house with the golden boot on the façade at **no. 40** was built as the guild house of the shoemakers in 1527, while **no. 90** was built somewhat later in 1570.

This leads to **Simon Stevinplaats** a lively square with a statue of the Flemish scholar **Simon Stevinus** (1548–1620). Born in Bruges, Stevin is credited with using the decimal point in mathematics for the first time. He also wrote on fortifications, town planning and book-keeping. He was an expert in the use of sluices for war purposes and invented a carriage propelled by sails.

A short detour to the right up Zilverstraat leads to a house at **no. 38** dating from 1468. This was the home of Juan Vasquez, secretary of Isabella of Portugal, the third wife of Philip the Good.

Kathedraal Sint Salvator
Just off Steenstraat is the Kathedraal Sint Salvator, open Apr–Sept Mon, Tues, and Thur–Sat 10.00–11.30 and 14.00–17.00, Sun 15.00–17.00, closed Wed; also closed mornings Oct–Mar.

History of the cathedral
This Gothic church was mainly built in the late 13C on the site of a 9C Romanesque church. Traces of early 12C masonry are still visible at the base of the west tower, though the neo-Romanesque top was only added in 1844–71 by the British architect Robert Chantrell.

The west part of the choir and part of the transepts are from the end of the

13C. The nave and south transept were rebuilt after a fire in 1358. The Flamboyant Gothic ambulatory and apsidal chapels were designed by Jan van der Poele in 1480–1530. The garden contains 18C statues of St Peter and St Paul by Pieter Pepers.

Originally a parish church, Sint Salvator became a cathedral in 1834. It replaced the old cathedral of St Donatian on the Burg, which was torn down by the French in 1799. Many of the paintings and treasures of the old cathedral were moved here, though the most valuable are displayed in the Groeninge Museum.

The cathedral currently has a rather dilapidated air, especially in the rooms of the cathedral museum. Indeed, the church museum has become so run-down that the more valuable paintings have now been moved to the Groeninge Museum. Until the old fabric is restored, a certain gloomy pleasure may be derived from poking around the dusty chapels and dark ambultory.

Begin in the room below the **tower**, where glass panels set in the floor allow you to see six medieval painted tombs. A fragment of the Romanesque portal has been reconstructed here. During the restoration of the adjoining 14C Sint Jacobskapel, several frescos from the 14C to the 16C were uncovered.

Now enter the **nave**, where there is a pulpit carved by Hendrik Pulincx in 1778–85. An elaborate 17C baroque rood-screen of bronze, wood and marble stands at the west end. It is crowned by a figure of God carved in 1682 by Quellin the Younger.

Down the **south aisle** is a *Resurrection* painted by Pieter Claessins in 1585. Crossing over to the north aisle, there is an interesting painting in the baptistry by Hendrik van Minderhout. Dating from c 1672, it depicts the *Battle of Lepanto* of 1571 in which a Christian fleet under the command of Don John of Austria defeated the Turks.

The **Chapel of the Shoemakers** is entered off the north transept. It is decorated with a Gothic screen of 1430 and a 14C crucifix from the Abbey of Eeckhoutte. The ubiquitous emblem of the guild, a boot surmounted by a crown, appears on the altar, chairs and doors.

Crossing over to the **south transept**, there is an *Adoration of the Shepherds* by Jacob van Oost the Elder and a Gobelins tapestry. The handsome bench with carved horses and a bust of St Eloi was once the property of the Guild of Waggoners.

The 13C **choir** has curious 15C misericords on the stalls depicting Flemish crafts, proverbs and scenes of everyday life. The armorial bearings above the stalls are those of the 13th chapter of the Order of the Golden Fleece, which was held here in 1478.

The two episcopal tombs on either side of the high altar were carved by Hendrik Pulincx in 1749–58. The painting of the *Resurrection* on the altar is by Abraham Janssens. The brass lectern in the form of an eagle dates from 1605. The six tapestries are copies of paintings by Jan van Orley. Originally eight in number, they were woven in Brussels in 1731.

There is now a series of five chapels off the ambulatory. Beginning on the right side, the **Chapel of Our Lady of Loretto** contains three paintings illustrating the legend of Loretto. A retable above the altar dating from c 1500 shows the family tree of St Anne.

The **Chapel of Our Lady of Seven Sorrows** has a 17C statue of the Mater Dolorosa holding a red plague staff, which was donated by a certain Father Melchior in gratitude for having been spared from the plague. The funeral brass set in the floor commemorates members of the Confraternity of Our Lady of the Seven Sorrows.

The **Chapel of the Blessed Sacrament** in the middle contains an 18C statue of the Virgin by Pieter Pepers, and two paintings by Jacob van Oost the Elder of St Peter and St John.

The **Chapel of the Holy Cross** was restored in 1998. Decorated in 19C neo-Gothic style, it contains a 15C retable with scenes from the Passion. It is closed off by a glass screen surmounted by four modern stainless steel figures representing the Evangelists.

The last **chapel**, formerly dedicated to St Barbara, has a curious stained-glass window made in 1903 using glass fragments salvaged from a window of 1531, which was destroyed by Protestant iconoclasts. The alabaster mausoleum of 1549 commemorates Jean Carondelet, Archbishop of Palermo and Provost of the Canons of St Donatian's Cathedral.

Just beyond here are two more small chapels. The first was formerly the guild chapel of the coachbuilders, and has a symbolic wheel incorporated into the Renaissance door. The other chapel has a memorial stone set in the floor in 1942. It commemorates Charles the Good, Count of Flanders, who was murdered in the old cathedral on Burg in 1127.

The **Cathedral Museum** is off the south transept. Added in 1912, the cloister-style museum is in desperate need of restoration. Some of its treasures have always been kept in this church, while others came from the old cathedral. Most of the important paintings were recently transferred to the Groeninge Museum, while others have been removed for restoration, yet the museum still has a certain dusty charm.

The first corridor contains a series of six **funerary brasses** of 1387–1555. One commemorates Jacob Schelewarts, a 15C priest of St Salvator's Cathedral who taught theology at the University of Paris. Another celebrates Adriaan Bave, a 16C burgomaster of Bruges. The tombs have to be studied closely to identify them as the labels have disappeared.

The **first alcove** formerly contained a triptych by Dirk Bouts, but this now hangs in the Groeninge Museum. The **second alcove** has vestments dating from the 15C, an 18C reliquary of St Barbara and a 17C crozier which belonged to the 32nd Abbot of Eeckhoutte Abbey. The **third alcove** contains the silver shrine of St Donatian, made in 1835 with 12C and 13C silver and ornamentation, and a 13C crozier-head in Limoges enamel. This shows St Martial (died c 250), the first bishop of Limoges, receiving the heart of St Valeria, a saint whose existence is now questioned. According to a legend popular in the Middle Ages Valeria was converted by St Martial and later beheaded for her faith.

Next follows a series of rooms containing miscellaneous treasures. **Room 1** has some damaged tombstones of 1380 which were found under the floor of the church. A cabinet contains a rare 6C ivory crozier and other relics. **Room 2** has four more 14C tombstones from the cathedral and an ornate reliquary of St Eloi carved by Jan Crabbe in 1612. The popular St Eloi (588–660) was a skilled metal-worker from Limoges who was ordained in 640. Appointed a bishop, he spent the rest of his life converting Flanders to Christianity.

Room 3, where the canons once met, contains church vestments, an early 16C woodcarving showing the consecration of a bishop, and a 17C cloth antependium of 1642 rescued from the destroyed Eeckhoutte Abbey. It shows the Virgin surrounded by the Doctors of the Church. A triptych by Anthony Claessins of the Descent from the Cross is one of the last paintings still on display in the museum. A cabinet in **room 4** contains a 6C ivory crozier of St Maclou. A model of the cathedral (same room) shows the spire added in the 19C.

On leaving the cathedral, go down Heilige Geeststraat to reach the **Sint Jans Hospitaal**. This ancient hospital dates back to the 13C. The tympanum of the old porch on Sint Katelijnestraat is decorated with 13C reliefs representing Death and the Coronation of the Virgin. This door is no longer used and you now enter by a passage at **Mariastraat 38**. A door to the right of the corridor leads to the 15C Dispensary, which was in use up until 1971. It now contains antique pharmacists' equipment, including a number of attractive pharmacy jars. An interesting painting shows the dispensary in use at the beginning of the 19C. The room beyond, formerly used for meetings of the hospital board, contains two fine chests with carvings of hospital scenes, a 14C Christmas cradle, and a collection of Delft tiles depicting a series of children's games.

Next is the vast 13C–14C **Hall**, which was formerly a huge hospital ward. A painting by Jan Beerblock shows the ward in 1778. At the end of the main hall is a copy of the 13C reliefs above the outer porch.

Memling Museum
The small but outstanding Memling Museum is located in the hospital chapel. Built in the 15C, the chapel is decorated with wood panelling and marble. The extraordinary *Reliquary of St Ursula* was carved in 1489 in the shape of a Gothic chapel and decorated with a series of miniature paintings. This legend of early Christian times is represented with engaging freshness and precision. The participants wear the clothes of Memling's time and the buildings of Cologne are faithfully reproduced. On one end is the Virgin with two nuns, while the other end has St Ursula sheltering ten maidens beneath her cloak. The top is adorned with six medallions, possibly the work of a pupil. The story of St Ursula and the 11,000 virgins is depicted on the sides.

> ### The legend of St Ursula
> The medieval legend of St Ursula exists in several versions. Memling relied on the version in which Ursula, daughter of a Christian king of Britain or perhaps Brittany ('in partibus Britanniae' the text says), was asked in marriage by the son of a pagan king. She consented, on condition that he embraced Christianity and sent 11,000 virgins with her on a three year pilgrimage to Rome. The reference to 'thousand' may be due to a misreading of an early manuscript, but it has added much to the charm of the tale. The cult of St Ursula was removed from the Church Calendar in 1969.

The **first scene** on Memling's reliquary depicts Ursula and the virgins arriving in Cologne and shows the unfinished cathedral, the church of St Martin and the Bayenturm. The **second scene** shows the entry into Basel, where the party disembarks in order to cross the Alps. By the **third scene**, Ursula is being welcomed in Rome by the Pope. She receives the Sacrament and her companions are baptised. The **fourth scene** shows the party returning to Basel, accompanied by the Pope who has been instructed in a vision to travel with them. The **fifth scene** represents the return to Cologne and the massacre of the virgins by pagans. The **sixth scene** depicts the pagan prince, moved by Ursula's beauty, offering to spare her life if she will marry him. She refuses with an expressive gesture and is killed by an arrow.

Memling's large triptych of *The Mystical Marriage* of St Catherine was painted in 1479 to hang in this chapel. It is dedicated to St John the Baptist and St John the Evangelist, the patron saints of the hospital. The middle panel depicts the Mystic Marriage of St Catherine, while the inner wings illustrate the Beheading of St John the Baptist and the Vision of St John the Evangelist at Patmos. The donors and their patron saints appear on the outer shutters. The signature 'Opus Johannis Memling, 1479' was added at a later date.

Another triptych by Memling is the *Adoration of the Magi*, painted in 1479. The donor Jan Floreins and his brother, possibly, are on the left. The inner wings show the Nativity and the Presentation in the Temple, while the outer shutters depict St John the Baptist and St Veronica. The *Portrait of the donor Martin van Nieuwenhove*, painted in 1487 when the sitter was twenty-three, is one of Memling's finest portraits. Another triptych, a *Pietà* of 1480, has St Barbara and the donor, Brother Adriaan Reyns, with St Adrian on the inside panels and the empress Helena and St Mary of Egypt on the outside.

A curious painting of 1480 known as the *Sibylla Sambetha* or Persian Sibyl takes its name from the inscription on a cartouche added in the 16C. Scholars once thought that the young woman portrayed was Maria Moreel, one of the daughters of Burgomaster Willem Moreel. It is rather disappointing to find that she bears little resemblance to any of the 11 daughters in Memling's *Moreel Triptych* in the Groeninge Museum.

On leaving the hospital, turn right down St Katelijnestraat. An alley at **nos 8–18** leads to an old almshouse. Turn right down a narrow lane further down the street to reach Walplein, a quiet square where the **Huisbrouwerij Straffe Hendrik** at **no. 26** continues to brew traditional Bruges ales. The brewery runs excellent guided tours, which include a view from the roof terrace and a complimentary glass of house beer.

Turn right at the end of the square to reach the Wijngaardplaats, a canalside square where horse-drawn carriages wait for tourists. A bridge crosses to a baroque portal dated 1776. This leads into the **Begijnhof**, which is much older than the gate would suggest.

This tranquil religious retreat was founded in c1235 and granted a charter by Margaret of Constantinople ten years later. It was absolved from dependence on the city magistrates in 1299 by Philip IV of France and allowed to use the title Béguinage princier de la Vigne. The Vigne is believed to refer to the vineyard which occupied the site of the original enclosure. The Begijnhof served as a place of refuge in the 16C. The church was accidentally burnt down in 1584 while some peasants were sheltering there. Rebuilt in 1605, it retains its original Romanesque doorway on the north side. The complex is now occupied by a small community of elderly Benedictine nuns.

Enter through a large courtyard shaded by lime trees. The surrounding buildings mainly date from the 17C though some go back to the 15C. A house next to the entrance has been turned into a small museum furnished in the austere style of the Beguines.

A town within a town

The Begijnhof in Bruges is one of several communities founded in the Low Countries for single women. The name possibly derives from St Begga, the daughter of Pepin of Landen, but more probably comes from Lambert le Bègue, a Liège priest who died in 1187. While caring for the bereaved families of Crusaders, he encouraged widows and other women to form pious communities that were not bound by strict vows. Lambert is thought to have established the first of these communities at Liège in c1189. The countesses Margaret and Joanna, daughters of Baldwin I of Constantinople, established similar communities in Flanders some years later.

The movement soon spread around Europe, notably in the Rhineland and the Netherlands, but it later came under the influence of the various religious orders and fell into disrepute. It was abolished in Protestant countries during the Reformation, but continued to flourish in Flanders. Some 24 Begijnhofs survive in the towns of Flanders and another two exist in the Netherlands (at Amsterdam and Breda). Some Begijnhofs constitute a 'town within a town', with a network of small streets, while others surround a courtyard or green. The communities generally had a church, and perhaps an infirmary and weaving centre. Most of the women lived in individual houses with their own gardens.

A few Begijnhofs are still occupied by religious and charitable communities, but most are now used as almshouses, municipal housing or university residences. Each Begijnhof has a particular charm, but the most impressive are those in Kortrijk, Lier, Leuven, Ghent and Bruges. Seven Flemish begijnhofs were listed by Unesco in 1998 as World Heritage Sites.

The Begijnhof overlooks the Minnewater, a quiet lake which was the busy inner dock of the harbour during the Middle Ages. The attractive **Lock House** at the north end of the harbour was built in the 15C and restored in 1893. The **Poedertoren**, or powder magazine, at the south end of the harbour dates from 1398. It originally formed part of the city wall.

Now turn left along the Begijnenvest and follow the canal to the St Katelijnestraat. Along this street is the **Academy of Fine Arts** at no. 94, which occupies the site of a former orphanage. The Hertsberge almshouse at nos 79–85 was founded c 1335 and the **Generaliteit** at no. 87–101 was added next door in 1572. Turn right along the Oude Gentweg and left into Kroezenstraat to find another cluster of old almshouses. The **Our Lady of the Seven Sorrows** at no. 2–7 was founded in 1654. Turning the corner into Nieuwe Gentweg, you pass **St Joseph's** at no. 24–32, founded in 1634, and the attractive **De Meulenaer** at no. 8–22, which was founded in 1613.

The Nieuwe Gentweg leads to the Astridpark, a romantic 19C park largely untouched by tourism. The iron bandstand dates from 1859.

4 • The Merchants' Quarter

This walk explores a fascinating and relatively forgotten quarter populated by merchants in the 15C and 16C. Leave the **Markt** by the St Amandstraat, then turn left on Geldmuntstraat. The vaulted **Muntpoort** was rebuilt in 1961. A narrow lane on the right leads to a forgotten square called **Muntplein** after the city mint that once stood here. A gabled building bears the bust of Marc Houterman (1537–77), organist at St Peter's in Rome. The 19C neo-Gothic convent on the north side of the square stands on the site of the 15C **Prinsenhof** where Philip the Handsome was born in 1478 and Mary of Burgundy died in 1482. The marriage of Charles the Bold and Margaret of York was celebrated here in 1468 with a magnificent banquet that lasted 10 days.

Leave by the lane next to the convent and turn right along Moerstraat, a narrow street that leads to the **Sint Jacobskerk**. This church looks rather plain from the outside, but the interior is exceptional. The squat tower dates from the 13C, while the rest of the church is mainly 15C. The elaborate Baroque pulpit was carved in 1690 by Bonaventure de Lannoy.

The main delight of the church is its exceptional collection of about 80 paintings mainly gifted by foreign merchants who lived in this parish. A remarkable work of c 1480 illustrating the *Legend of St Lucy* hangs in the **St Anthony Chapel**. It was painted by an anonymous artist known from this work as the Master of the Lucy Legend. The artist has included the spires of Bruges in the background, including the belfry before the octagonal top was added.

The **De Gros Chapel** contains the curious 15C tomb of Ferry de Gros. The recumbent figure of Ferry de Gros lies next to his first wife and above his second wife. A 15C terracotta medallion of the Madonna above the altar is attributed to the Della Robbia workshop in Florence.

From the church turn off St Jacobsstraat down the narrow vaulted **Boterhuis**. Named after the vanished butter market, this lane emerges on Naaldenstraat. The **Hof van Gistel** at no. 7 has a rare 15C round brick tower. Turn left along Naaldenstraat to reach the **Hof Bladelin** at no. 19. This splendid Gothic town house with its turret and spire was the home of Pieter Bladelin. The treasurer of the Order of the Golden Fleece, Bladelin commissioned a famous altarpiece from Roger van der Weyden (now in Berlin). The house later became the residence of Tomaso Portinari, a 15C Florentine banker and agent for the Medici who commissioned an altarpiece by Hugo van der Goes that now hangs in Florence.

Turn right down Grauwwerkersstraat to reach Vlamingstraat. The **Huis ter Beurze** at no. 35 was built in 1453 by the Van der Beurze family as their home. They encouraged foreign merchants to exchange goods and money inside the house. This is considered the first stock exchange in the world. The words Beurs in Dutch and Bourse in French are thought to be derived from the Van den Beurze family. The house is now occupied by a bank.

The curious **Genuese Loge** at no. 33 dates from 1399. The bell gable was added in 1720. Originally the headquarters of the Genoese merchants in Bruges, it was used in the 16C by the serge weavers and became known as the Saaihal. The Florentine House once stood at no. 1.

Dante on Bruges

A plaque on the site of the Florentine House quotes three lines from Dante's Divine Comedy in which Bruges is mentioned (Inferno, canto XV, verses 4–6):

> *Quale i Fiamminghi tra Guizzante e Bruggia*
> *temendo il fiotto che 'nver lor s'avventa*
> *fanno lo schermo perch, 'l mar si fuggia*

> (Just as the Flemings between Wissant and Bruges /In terror of the tide that floods towards them /Have built a wall of dykes to drive back the sea).

Dante is thought to have visited Bruges in the early 14C. The dyke mentioned ran along the North Sea coast.

The **Schouwburg** on the nearby Beursplein was built in 1869 in neo-Renaissance style and roundly condemned by the 19C art critic James Weale as 'a shapeless pile of stones'. The walk continues down Academiestraat, which leads to the quiet **Jan Van Eyckplaats**. The canal here formerly continued to the Markt square. The statue of Van Eyck was carved by Henri Pickery in 1878.

The **Poorters Loge** at Academiestraat 16 was where the local Bruges merchants (poorters) gathered. Regarded as privileged citizens, they were subject to a different jurisdiction from those who lived outside the city walls (who fell under the jurisdiction of the Brugse Vrije). The original 14C building was destroyed by fire in 1755, leaving just the tall, slender turret which appears in the background of David's *Judgment of Cambyses* in the Groeninge Museum. The building was at one time the meeting-place of an exclusive society known as the White Bear. A bear known locally as the 'Beertje van de Loge' can be seen in a niche at the base of the tower. Carved in 1417, it is said to be the oldest citizen of Bruges.

The splendid **Pynderhuis** was built in 1470 in Flamboyant Gothic style as the Guildhouse of the Free Porters. The **Tolhuis** at Jan van Eyckplein 1 was built as the customs house in 1477 and restored in 1878. The tall house known as **Roode Steen** at Genthof 1 was built in the mid-16C and restored in 1977.

Now turn up **Genthof**, past a 15C house with a wooden front at no. 7, and continue to the **Woensdagmarkt**, a small square formerly known as Hans Memlingplaats. The statue of Memling was carved by Henri Pickery in 1871. The tall 15C turret is a relic of the House of the Smyrna Merchants.

A lane at the far end of the square leads to the **Oosterlingenplaats**, named after the consular house of the Easterlings or Hanseatic Merchants. The Hotel Bryghia at no. 4 occupies the last vestiges of the Hanseatic trading house built in 1478. You then come to the Spaanse Loskaai, an attractive quay where you should turn left to reach the **Spanjaardstraat**. Several Spanish merchants lived here in the 16C.

Return to the canal and cross by the Augustijnenbrug, then turn right to reach the Sint Gilliskerkstraat. This leads to the **Sint Gilliskerk**, a hall-church founded in 1277 by Walter de Marvis, bishop of Tournai. Enlarged in the 15C, it contains paintings by Jacob van Oost the Elder, Louis de Deyster and a polyptych by Pieter Pourbus the Elder. A series of 18C paintings by Jan Garemijn illustrate the work of the Trinitarian brothers, who ransomed Christian slaves.

Ignatius Loyola in Bruges

Ignatius Loyola stayed several times from 1528–30 at a house called De Pijnappel at Spanjaardstraat 9. The young ecclesiastic, who was studying in Paris, was the guest of Gonzalo de Aguilera from Biscay. Loyola went on to establish the Society of Jesus, or Jesuit Order, in Spain in 1540. This austere intellectual Order became involved in preaching and education, producing many notable scholars and scientists. Rigorous and often ruthless, the Jesuits were sent to the Netherlands by Philip II. The Order became highly influential under the Archdukes Albrecht and Isabella, who profited from the Twelve Years Truce (1609–21) to consolidate Catholicism in the Spanish Netherlands. The Order was suppressed in 1773, but restored in 1814.

The artists'quarter

Many 15C and 16C artists lived in the Sint Gilliskerk neighbourhood, including Jan van Eyck, who lived in the street now called Gouden Handstraat until his death in 1441. Hans Memling owned a house at Sint Jorisstraat 20 while Pieter Pourbus bought a house in the parallel Jan Miraelstraat in 1552. Gerard David lived in his father-in-law's house, which is still standing at Vlamingstraat 51, and Lanceloot Blondeel had a house in the Sint Jorisstraat. Many artists were buried in the Sint Gilliskerk churchyard, including Memling, Provoost, Blondeel and probably Pourbus the Elder.

Turn down **Sint Gilliskoorstraat** to reach the Langerei and turn right there to cross the canal at the first bridge. After continuing down the opposite side, go left down St Annakerkstraat to reach the **Sint Annakerk**. Founded in 1496, the original church was demolished in 1581 by the Sea Beggars, but rebuilt from 1607–21. The spire was added in 1624. The poet Guido Gezelle was baptised in this church. The interior is decorated in a rich Baroque style, with fine wooden panelling, 17C stalls, confessionals and pulpit. The **rood-screen** of 1628, in marble and porphyry, is by Jan van Mildert. The church contains paintings by Louis de Deyster, Jacob van Oost the Elder, and a large *Last Judgement* by Jan Baptist Herregoudts.

Go back now along Sint Annakerkstraat and cross the canal, then continue down the crooked Kandelaarstraat to reach Boomgaardstraat. The **Sint Walburgakerk** stands on the Sint Maartensplaats. Built in 1619–40 by Pieter Huyssens for the Jesuits, it was the first church to be dedicated to St Francis Xavier, whose statue appears on the imposing façade. Sint Walburgakerk became the parish church after the suppression of the Jesuits. It is decorated with a **marble communion-rail** carved by Henri Verbruggen in 1695, a **pulpit** of 1667 by Artus Quellin the Younger, a marble **retable** of 1643 and an 18C painting by Joseph Benoît Suvee.

Continue along Koningstraat to reach a bridge. The Neo-classical school opposite at no. 13 stands on the site of the 15C English trading house.

William Caxton in Bruges

Bruges once had a large colony of English merchants who traded in English wool. William Caxton (c 1422–91) served as Governor of the English Nation in Bruges from 1462–70, presiding over the English Merchant Adventurers. While living here, Caxton 'practised and learnt at great charge and dispense' the art of printing. He set up a printing press in Bruges in partnership with the local printer Collaert Mansion. The Recuyell of the Historyes of Troye, published in Bruges c 1475, was the first printed book in the English language.

---

5 • The ramparts

For those with time to spare, an interesting walk can be done around the old ramparts, beginning at the Smedenpoort in the southwest and ending at the site of the Dammepoort in the northeast. From the **Markt**, walk down **Zuidzandstraat** past some old, if restored, façades, notably **no. 41** of 1570, **no. 40** of 1630, with interesting stone carving, and **no. 18** of 1703. This street ends at 't Zand, a square with several 19C hotels which once faced the 19C railway station before it was dismantled and rebuilt at Ronse. The present station was built in 1931 to the south of here.

A brief detour can be taken into a peaceful quarter where several almshouses were built. Go down Smedenstraat and turn right into **Kammakersstraat**, where Canon Jan van Paemel founded a small almshouse for the blind in 1669 at **nos 7–11**. Marius Voet established a similar almshouse at **nos 13–17** in 1672. The **Godshuis Onze-Lieve-Vrouw van Blindekens** at **nos 19–31** is believed to have been founded in 1305 by Count Robert van Béthune after the Battle of Pevelenberg. If you turn left along Lane and again left into Greinschuurstraat, you find another almshouse founded in 1687 at **nos 17–23**.

Almshouses

Bruges has some 52 almshouses dating from the 14C to the 20C. Known as Godshuizen, they are mostly found in the south of the city near the old walls. Generally built around a courtyard or garden, these idyllic institutions were founded by private individuals or guilds to accomodate elderly, blind or poor citizens. The oldest surviving almshouse dates back to 1305. The most recent almshouse was built in 1958 by a former Congo administrator.

Back on Smedenstraat, turn right to reach the **Smedenpoort**, one of four town gates that have survived from the original seven. The Ezelpoort or Oostendepoort is to the northwest and the other two are on the east side of town. Now walk south along a path which follows the landscaped ramparts. On reaching the station, cross the busy ring road and continue along the path to the right, following the old moat along Begijnenvest.

This leads to the **Gentpoort**, an impressive city gate built in 1407 by Jan van Oudenaerde and Maarten van Leuven. From there, head into the city by the Gentpoortstraat and turn right along Schaarstraat, which skirts the 19C Koningin Astridpark. After crossing the canal Coupure, turn right to return to the moat and follow the path to the **Kruispoort**. This was built as a city gate in 1402 by the same architects as the Gentpoort.

Now go into town along the Peperstraat to visit the curious **Jeruzalem-Kerk**, open Apr–Sept Mon–Sat 10.00–12.00 and 14.00–18.00 (17.00 on Sat); closed mornings Oct–Mar.

A private chapel

This was originally the private chapel of the Adornes family from Genoa, one of several foreign merchant families who settled in Bruges during the 13C. The chapel was replaced c 1427 by the present church, which was built by the brothers Pieter and Jacob Adornes after their return from a pilgrimage to Jerusalem. Modelled on the Church of the Holy Sepulchre in Jerusalem, it is still owned by the descendants of the family.

It is a curious and slightly mysterious church, with a choir reached by a flight of stairs, and a gloomy crypt containing a copy of Christ's Tomb. The 15C and 16C stained-glass is some of the finest in Bruges. Perhaps the most interesting feature is the black marble **tomb of Anselm Adornes**, who died in 1483, and his wife, Margaretha van der Banck, who died 20 years earlier. The dog and lion lying at their feet are conventional symbols of fidelity and strength. Anselm Adornes, a burgomaster of Bruges, was the son of Pieter Adornes. While serving as an ambassador to Scotland, he was brutally murdered in Linlithgow Palace. The church is now cared for by nuns who live in the former Adornes mansion next door. Ring the bell to visit.

The nearby **Kantcentrum** (lace centre), open Apr–Sept Mon–Sat 10.00–12.00 and 14.00–18.00 (17.00 Sat), is devoted to the local lace-making industry. The craft of making bobbin lace is still taught here. Gone are the days when elderly lacemakers could be seen on their doorsteps working on lace tablecloths. Most lace now sold locally is manufactured, but the dedicated buyer can still find the occasional shop that sells hand-made lace. Working with bobbins, Bruges lacemakers were known for designs such as the flower pattern, rose lace and the witch-stitch. Good lace collections are displayed in the Gruuthuse Museum and the Kantcentrum.

Now turn up Balstraat to reach the **Museum voor Volkskunde**, open Apr–Sept daily 09.30–17.00; Oct–Mar Wed–Mon 9.30–12.30 and 14.00–17.00. Situated in the **Godshuis van de Schoenmakersrente**, an almshouse for aged shoemakers, it has some interesting old Bruges interiors, including a school room and a tavern with wooden racks of clay pipes.

The **Guido Gezellemuseum**, open Apr–Sept daily 9.30–12.00 and 12.45–17.00; closed Tues Oct–Mar, is near here at Rolweg 64. The Flemish priest and poet Guido Gezelle was born here in 1830. Director of the English Convent in Bruges, Gezelle translated Longfellow's *Song of Hiawatha* into Dutch. He died in the nearby English Convent in 1899. The museum contains documents, photographs and other memorabilia.

In Carmersstraat, parallel to Rolweg, there is a 17C chapel surmounted by a dome at **no. 85**. Founded by nuns in 1629, this is known as the **English Convent**. It contains a relic of St Thomas More, the English scholar executed by Henry VIII. The relic was presented by Mary More, a descendant of More, who was prioress here from 1766–1808. Charles II visited the convent in the 1650s. Queen

Victoria also called here during her visit to Bruges in 1843. She was apparently moved by the warmth of the sisters. The convent chapel is open to visitors. Ring the bell.

Charles II was a regular visitor at the **Guild House of St Sebastian** at no. 178, open Apr–Sept Mon, Tues, Thur and Fri 10.00–12.00 and 14.00–17.00. Built in 1565, this was the meeting place of the town archers. The exiled Charles II, who fled to Bruges in 1656, was elected King of the Archers'Guild of St Sebastian. It was while he was exiled here that Charles II founded the regiment of Grenadier Guards. The guild house owns a portrait by Van Boeckhorst of *Henry, Duke of Gloucester*, the brother of Charles II. It also has interesting paintings by Van Dyck, a collection of gold and silverwork, and guild documents dating back to 1416. Members of the guild still occasionally demonstrate their archery skills in the garden.

A short detour to the south leads to the **Guild House of St George** at Stijn Streuvelstraat 59, open Apr–Sept Mon, Tues, Thur and Fri 14.00–18.00, where the crossbowmen met. The building contains an interesting display of crossbows and ancient archives.

The route, though, goes back to the ramparts and left past a windmill called the **Sint Janshuismolen**, open May–Sept 09.30–12.30 and 13.15–17.00. Built in 1770, it is one of three surviving windmills on this stretch of canal.

Turn left down Peterseliestraat and left again on Oliebaan to reach Potterielei. The **Bisschoppelijk Seminarie** (Episcopal Seminary) is on the right. It occupies a cluster of old buildings once owned by the Abbey of Ter Duinen, which moved to Bruges from Koksijde in 1627. Confiscated by the French in 1796, the buildings were later used as a military hospital, a school and an army depot. The cloister was built in c 1630 and has interesting murals. The church was rebuilt in the 18C.

Further along the canal, **Onze Lieve Vrouw van de Potterie** at no. 79 was founded in 1276 as a hospice for elderly women. The name possibly comes from the chapel which belonged to the Potters Guild, or it may have been that it was built on land once owned by the guild. Old people are still cared for here by the local social welfare department.

The three gables date from entirely different periods: the one on the left belongs to the hospital ward of 1529; the centre gable is an early church of 1359; while the one on the right is part of the chapel of Onze Lieve Vrouw, which was only added in 1623.

The **chapel**, open (with the museum) Thur–Tues 09.30–12.30 and 13.15–17.00, which gets very few visitors, contains several curiosities, including an exquisite stone statue of the Virgin from the late 13C and a modern tomb commemorating St Idesbald, who died 1167 and was originally buried at the Abbey of Ter Duinen. The rood screen in the left aisle dates from 1644. An *Adoration of the Magi* by J. van Oost the Elder can be seen behind the screen. The tombs of two Bruges burgomasters stand on either side of the altar. Nicholas Despars, on the left, died in 1597. Jan de Beer, on the right, died in 1608.

Several old **tapestries** are hung between the two aisles of the chapel from Easter to October. They include a late 15C Virgin and Child, a 16C Virgin and two saints, and a captivating series of three 17C tapestries depicting some 18 different miracles worked by the Virgin in the hospital. The stories are also illustrated in the stained-glass opposite.

The **Potterie Museum** contains an interesting collection of paintings accumulated over the centuries. The works include a triptych of the *Descent from the Cross* from 1520, a portrait of a sister of the Hospice de la Madeleine painted in 1575, and several pen and ink drawings attributed to Jan van Eyck. There are also a 16C leper's clapper in carved wood, a coloured relief of the Agony in the Garden and several illuminated missals.

The old harbour lay at the end of **Potterierei**. Not much remains here, yet it is perhaps interesting to glance at the basin where ships once moored. You can then return to the town centre along the Langerei.

Bruges environs

There are attractive whitewashed cottages and brick castles in the flat polder landscape around Bruges. The old port of **Damme** makes a particularly enjoyable trip from Bruges.

Kasteel Tillegem is a large castle with a moat, 3km southwest of Bruges. Founded in the 9C, it was rebuilt in the 13C and again at the end of the 19C. The castle is currently occupied by the West Flanders tourist office, and the grounds have been turned into a provincial park.

Fanny Trollope's tale

The writer Fanny Trollope rented a country villa called the Château d'Hondt outside Bruges in 1833. No longer standing, the house lay beyond the Smeedenpoort in the hamlet of Sint Baafs. Struggling to make money after her husband became bankrupt, Fanny intended to publish a successful travel book on Belgium and Germany. Her son Henry died in Bruges of tuberculois in 1834, and her husband Thomas also died here the following year. Father and son are buried next to one another in the **Stedelijk Kerkhof**, south of the Gentpoort, in the Protestant section of the cemetery near the main gate. Anthony Trollope, another son, recalled episodes of his Belgian childhood in several novels.

The Benedictine abbey of **Zevenkerken**. 7km southwest of Bruges, lies half hidden in woodland at the end of a long avenue. Founded c 1100 at St Andries in the suburbs of Bruges, it was destroyed in 1793 during the French Revolution and rebuilt here in a curious Byzantine style from 1899–1902. A nearby convent is occupied by Benedictine sisters.

The castle at **Loppem**, 2km east of Zevenkerken, is an outstanding example of Flemish neo-Gothic architecture. The original designs were drawn by the English architect Edward Welby Pugin. The Belgian architect Baron Jean Béthune produced a different design in Flemish Gothic style, which was built from 1858–63 (open from Apr–Oct 10.00–12.00 and 14.00–18.00; closed on Mon and Fri).

The village of **Oostkamp**, 6km south of Bruges, has an octagonal 12C church tower, and a castle where Louis de Gruuthuse entertained the exiled Edward IV of England.

The abbey of Trudo at **Male**, 7km east of Bruges, occupies the vestiges of a medieval castle which belonged to the counts of Flanders. The 14–15C keep has been restored.

The modest polder village of **Lissewege**, 10km north of Bruges, is believed to derive its name from the Celtic word Liswege, meaning the house of Liso. It is worth climbing the 265 steps to the top of the huge brick tower of Lissewege's restored 13C **church** for the fine view across the polders.

An ancient legend is sometimes invoked to explain the presence of such a large building in a village which had fewer than 300 inhabitants. It is said that the church was built to house a miraculous statue of the Madonna. Found in a local stream called the Lisput, the statue returned to the stream every time it was removed. The villagers eventually built a chapel (and later this church) over the Lisput, which still flows underneath. A cover in the middle of the principal nave provides access to the stream.

The pulpit, organ case and rood loft were carved in the 17C by Walram Romboudt, a local craftsman. The paintings in the church include a *Visitation* by Jacob van Oost the Elder of 1652, and *Pilgrims honouring St James of Compostela*, painted by Jan Maes in 1665. The church possesses a fine cope with 14C orphreys, a red 14C chasuble and dalmatic and a violet chasuble with 16C orphreys, a monstrance of 1619 and a chalice and a ciborium of 1620, the work of the Bruges goldsmith Melchior van Blootacker. The interesting 17C funerary monuments set in the walls just inside the entrance have figures dressed in the clothing of the period.

The site of the abbey of **Ter Doest**, just south of Lissewege, lies between the main road and the canal. Founded in 1106 by Lambert de Lissewege near the chapel sheltering the miraculous Madonna, it was ruled by 38 abbots between 1174 and 1569. The abbey was pillaged and burned by religious fanatics in 1571, leaving just the great barn of c 1250. The impressive interior measures 58m by 24m. It is divided into three sections by two rows of oak piers resting on stone bases. The immense roof is covered with some 38,000 tiles. (Ask at the nearby restaurant for entry to the barn.)

The small Baroque **chapel** at the entrance to the estate dates from 1687. It was built by Abbot Martin a Colle of the abbey of Dunes at Bruges to commemorate his success in a law suit at the tribunal of Louis XIV.

The village of **Dudzele**, 3km south of Lissewege on the other side of the canal, preserves the Romanesque tower of a 12C church.

Canal near Bruges

Damme

Damme is a delightful old Flemish town surrounded by typical polder country. Only 7km from Bruges, it is sited on the ancient tree-lined canal from Bruges to Sluis (the Netherlands), near the point where it is crossed by the Schipdonk and Leopold canals. The town has attractive Flemish restaurants located in old buildings.

Damme launched itself as a book town in 1997. It now has 12 bookshops, mainly devoted to Dutch literature, and a small literary museum. A second-hand book market is held every other Sunday. Most bookshops are open daily in July and August, and at weekends from September to June.

Where to stay

De Gulden Kogge, Damse Vaart Zuid 12, ☎ 050.35.42.17. Canalside hotel with Flemish interior and good restaurant.

Eating out

The main street in Damme is lined with traditional Flemish restaurants which are particularly popular for Sunday lunches. Most restaurants have gardens or terraces.

't Vergierderke, Kerkstraat 7, ☎ 050.35.33.38, is a family restaurant in the historic centre.

Drie Zilvren Kannen, Markt 9, ☎ 050.35.56.77 is an attractive old Flemish restaurant.

Tourist office

Jacob van Maerlantstraat 3, ☎ 050.35.33.19.

Opening times

Stadhuis is open daily May–Sept 09.00–12.00 and 14.00–18.00 (opens 10.00 at weekends); Oct–Apr Mon–Fri 09.00–12.00 and 13.00–17.00, weekends 14.00–17.00.

Museum Sint Janshospitaal is open Apr–Sept Mon and Fri 14.00–18.30; Tues–Thur and Sat 10.00–12.00 and 14.00–18.00; Sun and public holidays 11.00–12.00 and 14.00–18.00; Oct–Mar at weekends from 14.00–17.30.

Tower of Onze Lieve Vrouwkerk is open daily Apr–Sept 10.00–12.00 and 14.30–17.30.

History

Damme was founded in the 12C by Philip of Alsace, Count of Flanders, on Het Zwin estuary. The new town was originally intended to serve as the port of Bruges. It was pillaged in 1213 by Philip Augustus, Philip II of France, during his war against Count Ferdinand of Flanders, but Ferdinand's English allies burnt most of Philip's fleet in Damme harbour. The port, with a population that grew to 10,000, became sufficiently important to have its own maritime law, the Zeerecht van Damme. Two dynastic marriages took place here in the 15C. Philip the Good married Isabella of Portugal in 1430, and Charles the Bold married Margaret of York, sister of England's Edward IV, in 1468. As Het Zwin began to silt up in the 15C, the fortunes of the town declined. The town was taken by Marlborough in 1706 and its fortifications were dismantled.

Till Eulenspiegel

The writer Jacob van Maerlant (c 1235–1300) lived in Damme, where he is buried. Considered the 'father of Flemish poetry', he was one of the most learned scholars of his time, being best known for his verse translations and French and Latin works, including the *Spiegel Historiae*, a history of the world. Local tradition, originating perhaps from the title of Maerlant's book, asserts that Till Eulenspiegel, the 14C peasant clown and practical joker, also lived and died in Damme. He was in fact a German folklore figure from the area around Hanover, but his putative connection with Damme was reinforced by the publication of The Legend of Tyll Owlglass by Charles de Coster in 1867.

A walk in Damme

The main sight in Damme is the **Stadhuis**, which was built 1464–1468 on the site of a trade hall of 1241. Damme was already losing its importance by this time so that the building had to be financed by a special tax levied on the barrels of herrings discharged here. The ground floor was used as a market—the four shutters belonged to small shops. The **statues on the façade**, on either side of the double stairway, commemorate historical figures connected with the town. The figures on the left are Philip of Alsace, the founder of Damme, and the countesses Joanna and Margaret of Constantinople. Margaret is bearing a model of the hospital which she is said to have established in Damme. On the right, Charles the Bold is shown giving a wedding ring to a rather bashful Margaret of York.

The turret rising from the centre of the steeply pitched roof contains a **carillon** of 25 bells. Two of the bells date from 1392 and 1398. The clock was added in 1459. The interior has a monumental chimneypiece, tiling, and some very curious woodcarving. One of the carvings shows a man and woman together in a bath. The statue of Jacob van Maerlant was unveiled in front of the Stadhuis in 1860.

The **Huis Sint Jan** at Hoogstraat 9, next to the town hall, is a patrician house of 1468. It was here that Charles the Bold and Margaret of York were married on 3 July 1468. The ceremony was conducted by Bishop Beauchamp of Salisbury.

The **Museum Sint Janshospitaal** in Kerkstraat occupies a hospital founded in c 1249 by Margaret of Constantinople. It contains a collection of furniture, liturgical objects, ceramics and gravestones.

A short walk leads to the **Onze Lieve Vrouwkerk**. This has a 45m-high square tower of c 1210–30, separated from the 14C body of the church by two ruined bays. This once impressive Scaldian Gothic church was gradually demolished as the local population declined. The transepts were demolished in 1725 and the central nave abandoned. The lower part of the 16C rood-loft now serves as a vestibule.

The church contains Baroque confessionals from the destroyed cathedral of St Donatian in Bruges, 14C statues of the Apostles, and an Assumption by Jan Maes. The 1636 altar of the Holy Cross incorporates a cross dredged from the sea by fishermen. Jacob van Maerlant was probably buried below the tower. His gravestone was sold in the 19C and replaced by a plaque. A popular tradition holds that **Till Eulenspiegel** also lies here. He is commemorated by a small statue in the garden.

GHENT

• • • • • • • •

Ghent is an old and interesting town of medieval towers, crooked canals and waterside gardens. Known in Dutch as Gent and in French as Gand, it was once the stronghold of the counts of Flanders. The city still has extensive medieval quarters, a spectacular castle and one of the finest cathedrals in Belgium. Travellers have been drawn here since the 15C to look at the extraordinary Adoration of the Mystic Lamb altarpiece by Jan and Hubert van Eyck.

The city is situated at the confluence of the rivers Lieve and Leie (Lys in French), while the Scheldt skirts the town to the south. The old quarters grew up on the numerous islands formed by the branching waterways. Its location on the River Scheldt has made Ghent an important inland port since the Middle Ages. With a population of just over a quarter of a million, Ghent is the capital of East Flanders province.

The medieval towers of Ghent seen from St Michielsburg

Practical information

Where to stay

££ *Erasmus*, Poel 25, ☎ 09.224.21.95, is a friendly hotel located in two 17C houses furnished with an odd collection of antiques.

££ *Gravensteen*, Jan Breydelstraat 35, ☎ 09.225.11.50, is an elegant hotel in 18C town house facing the Gravensteen.

££ *Novotel*, Goudenleeuwplein 5, ☎ 09.224.22.30, is an attractive modern hotel opposite the Belfry incorporating fragments of old buildings.

££ *Sint Jorishof*, Botermarkt 2, ☎ 09.224.24.24, is a comfortable hotel in a historic building with some 13C details. It claims be the oldest surviving hotel in Europe.

Eating out
Restaurants

£££ Jan van den Bon, Koning Leopold II-Laan 43, ☎ 09.221.90.85. Offers creative cooking in an elegant Ghent villa.

££ Café Theatre, Schouwburgstraat 5, ☎ 09.265.05.50. Cosmopolitan brasserie next to the Flanders Opera.

££ Le Baan Thai, Corduwaniersstraat 57, ☎ 09.233.21.41. Refined Thai cooking.

££ Het Blauwe Huis, Drabstraat 17, ☎ 09.233.10.05. Offers serious brasserie cooking in an 18th-century house with a deep blue façade.

££ De Grill, Korenlei 23, ☎ 09.225.09.74. An attractive Old Flemish waterfront restaurant.

££ Pakhuis, Schuurkenstraat 4, ☎ 09.223.55.55. A former warehouse converted into a bustling brasserie.

££ Sint Jorishof, Botermarkt 2, ☎ 09.224.24.24. A traditional Flemish restaurant with excellent cuisine.

££ Waterzooi, Sint Veerleplein 2, ☎ 09.225.05.63. One of the most creative chefs in Belgium.

£ Brooderie, Jan Breydelstraat 8. Offers generous salads and quiches in a farm-house-style interior.

£ Salon Florian, Volderstraat 13, ☎ 09.223.83.43. Elegant tea-room with tasty Flemish sandwiches served on wooden platters, closed Sun and evenings.

£ Tap en Tepel, Gewad 7, ☎ 09.223.90.00. An eccentric cheese and wine restaurant with a romantic interior.

Cafés

Bloch's, Veldstraat 60, is a traditional Alsatian tea room.

De Foyer, Sint Baafsplein 17, is an airy theatre café on the first floor of the Royal Dutch Theatre with a small terrace overlooking the cathedral.

Tolhuisje, Graslei 11, is a stylish waterfront café in a narrow house dated 1682.

Vooruit, Sint Pietersnieuwstraat 123, is a spacious theatre café in a lively student quarter.

Het Waterhuis aan de Bierkant, Groentenmarkt 5, is a friendly brown café with a waterside terrace.

Getting around
Arriving by train

The main station is **Gent Sint Pieters**, 2.5km southwest of the old town. High-speed Thalys trains leave from this station for Brussels, Lille and Paris.

Trams

1, 10, 11, 12 and 13 run from the station to the Korenmarkt and Gravensteen, passing near the Bijlokemuseum and Museum voor Schone Kunsten.

Cars

The centre of Ghent has become virtually traffic-free in recent years. Colour-coded signs marked **P** direct cars to large underground car parks within walking distance of the city centre. Parking spaces are fairly easy to find near the Museum voor Schone Kunsten and the Bijloke Museum.

Tourist information

The tourist office is in the crypt of the Belfry, Botermarkt 17A, ☎ 09.266.52.32.

Banks

BBL is at Kouter 173; Kredietbank is at Kouter 175.

Post office

The main post office is on the Korenmarkt.

Carillon concerts

The carillon in the Belfry is played on Friday and Sunday from 11.30–12.30.

Festival

The **Gentse Feesten** began in 1843 as a summer festival for Ghent's textile workers. It has grown into a sprawling ten-day summer festival featuring music, puppet theatre and art events. The main event is the Stroppendragers procession, in which men parade with nooses around their necks to commemorate Charles V's punishment of the town in 1540.

Guided tours

Two-hour **guided walks** begin at 14.30 outside the tourist office, from Apr–Jun and Aug–Sept on Sat, Sun and public holidays.

Tours by **horse-drawn carriages** lasting about 30 minutes leave from the Belfry from Apr–Oct.

Canal tours lasting 30 mins begin on the Graslei, Apr to early Nov daily 10.00–19.00.

Longer **river cruises** to Bruges and the Leie district leave from the Recollettenlei in the summer months.

Ghent **café tours** are organised occasionally by the flamboyant town crier.

 Opening times
Most museums and the Gravensteen are closed on Mondays, 1–2 Jan, and 25–26 Dec.

Museums

Museum voor Schone Kunsten (fine art 15C to 20C), Karel de Kerchovelaan, is open Tues–Sun 09.30–17.00.

Stedelijk Museum voor Actuele Kunst (contemporary art), Karel de Kerchovelaan, is open Tues–Sun 09.30–17.00.

Museum voor Industriele Archaeologie en Textiel (Museum of Industrial Archaeology and Textiles), Minnemeers 9, is open Tues–Sun 09.30–17.00.

Museum voor Sierkunst (Museum of Decorative Arts), Jan Breydelstraat 5, is open Tues–Sun 09.30–17.00.

Bijloke Museum (decorative art and history of Ghent), Godshuizenlaan, is open Sun 14.00–18.00 and Thur 10.00–13.00 and 14.00–18.00.

Museum voor Volkskunde (Folklore Museum), Kraanlei 65, is open Tues–Sun 10.00–12.30 and 13.30–17.00.

Museum Meerhem (history of Ghent), Fratersplein, is open Sun 14.00–17.00.

School museum Michel Thiery (exhibitions for schools), Sint Pietersplein, is open Mon–Thur and Sat 09.00–12.15 and 13.30–17.15, Fri 09.00–12.15.

Museum voor Stenen Voorwerpen (monumental stone carvings) in the ruins of Sint Baaf's Abbey, is open Apr–early Nov Tues–Sun 09.30–17.00.

Churches

Sint Baafskathedraal is open 08.30–18.00 but closed during services. The chapel containing the Mystic Lamb Altarpiece and the Crypt are open Apr–Oct Mon–Sat 09.30–12.00 and 14.00–18.00, Sun and holidays 13.00–18.00; Nov–Mar Mon–Sat 10.30–12.00 and 14.30–16.00, Sun and holidays 14.00–17.00. An entrance fee is charged for the Mystic Lamb and the Crypt. The ticket office closes 15 mins before closing time.

Sint Niklaaskerk, Korenmarkt, is open daily 09.00–17.00.

Other buildings

Belfort (Belfry) is open mid-Mar–mid-Nov, daily 10.30–12.30 and 14.00–17.30. It has an elevator as an alternative to climbing the stairs. It can be visited with a guide at set times or individually at any time. The carillon room can only be visited on the guided visit.

Gravensteen, St Veerleplein, is open Apr–Sept daily 09.00–18.00, Oct–Mar daily 09.00–17.00. Last ticket sold 45 minutes before closing time.

Stadhuis can only be visited on a guided tour. Tours begin at 14.00 on Mon–Thur May–Oct.

Botanic Garden

Botanic Garden at the university is open daily 09.30–12.00 and 13.00–17.00.

History

The original settlement at Ghent grew up around a 7C abbey founded by St Amand on a site known as Ganda. The abbey was later named St Baafsabdij after St Baaf (also known as Bavo or Bavon), a native of Brabant converted to Christianity by St Amand. The ruined St Baafsabdij stands on the site of the vanished 7C abbey.

A second settlement grew up around a castle built by **Baldwin Iron Arm** in c 867. Sited at the confluence of the Lieve and Leie, the castle offered protection against invading Vikings. The town was fortified and enlarged in the 11C and 12C. Large areas of land were reclaimed and the Ghent to Bruges canal was dug in the 13C.

By the end of the 13C, Ghent occupied an area larger than Paris. But fraught relations between the nobles, who were generally loyal to the French king, and the wealthy and ambitious burghers, led to constant violent clashes in the town.

Ghent was granted charters by the counts of Flanders in c 1180 and 1191. In about 1212, the **Council of Thirty-nine** affirmed the rights of the citizens and the democratic election of city officials. The growing prosperity brought an increasing assertion of independence, which culminated in 1302 when a contingent from Ghent, led by Jan Borluut, played a major role in the defeat of the French aristocracy at the **Battle of the Golden Spurs**.

When the **Hundred Years War** broke out in 1338, the count of Flanders sided with France against England, thus endangering Ghent's cloth trade, which had been the basis of its prosperity since the early Middle Ages. The aristocrat Jacob van Artevelde (1287–1345) led the merchants into an alliance with Edward III of England. Edward's third son, John of Gaunt was born in the abbey of Sint Baaf in 1340. The alliance brought prosperity to both Ghent and the wool-growers of England.

Van Artevelde was murdered in 1345 by guildsmen who mistrusted his ambition. His son Philip (1340–82) took his father's place in 1381 and inflicted a severe defeat on Count Louis de Male, who sided with the French. The following year, Charles VI of France crushed the Flemish rebels and killed Van Artevelde at the **Battle of Westrozebeke**. Two years later, in 1384, Louis de Male died. His daughter and heiress had married Philip of Burgundy, which led to the end of Flanders as a separate state and the beginning of Burgundian rule.

The people of Ghent soon rebelled against the Burgundian rulers. After five years of struggle from 1448–1453, they were defeated by Philip the Good and forced to accept a humiliating limitation of privileges. Undaunted, on the death of Philip's son Charles the Bold in 1477, the citizens held Charles' daughter Mary a virtual prisoner. They forced her to sign the **Great Privilege** which gave them a more liberal constitution. On Mary's death, Flanders passed to her husband, Maximilian of Austria, who rapidly subdued the town. His grandson, Charles V, was born in or near Ghent in 1500.

The **cloth industry** had by now been ruined by English competition, but Ghent found a new source of wealth by exporting French grain via the Leie and Scheldt. The boatmen replaced the clothworkers as the town's leading guild. A new **canal to Terneuzen** was dug in 1547 by order of Charles V, which boosted Ghent's economy at a time when Bruges and Ypres were already in decline.

Ghent supported Charles V, at the beginning of his reign, but later refused to pay taxes for his military adventures in France. Charles crushed the rising in 1540, abolished the town's privileges, filled in the moat, and built a new citadel on the site of the abbey of Sint Baaf at the town's expense. But the most humiliating measure was to force prominent citizens to walk through the town barefoot and wearing nooses to symbolise their remorse. Ever since then, the people of Ghent have been jokingly referred to as **Stroppendragers** (noose wearers).

Ghent was racked by religious disputes under Philip II, who established the bishopric in 1561. The excesses of the Calvinist iconoclasts, which followed in 1566, were ferociously punished by the Duke of Alva. Ten years later, William of Orange marched into Flanders and occupied Ghent. The **Pacification of Ghent**, which attempted to secure religious freedom and the withdrawal of the Spanish soldiery from the Netherlands, was signed in November of that year. A brief period of domination by the Calvinists was ended by the Duke of Parma, Philip II's governor, in 1585. He retook Ghent and most other Calvinist strongholds in the Southern Netherlands, and restored the Catholic faith. The Dutch rebels managed to close the Scheldt to shipping, which led to the decline of Ghent.

The treaty which ended the war of 1812–14 between England and America was signed in Ghent in 1814. The following year, the fugitive Louis XVIII, accompanied by Chateaubriand and other royalists, took refuge in Ghent during Napoleon's Hundred Days.

The industrial revolution began in Ghent in 1799 when **cotton-spinning** was introduced from England by Lieven Bauwens (1769–1822). A local tanner turned businessman, Bauwens smuggled machinery out of England and set up the first Belgian cotton-mill in Drongen abbey outside Ghent. The city's prosperity was further boosted in 1822–27 when the 16C canal to Terneuzen was replaced by a larger canal capable of taking sea-going vessels.

Born in Ghent

The theologian Henry of Ghent, Doctor Solemnis (c 1217–93), and the painter Justus van Gent were born here. Other distinguished people born in Ghent include the painter and poet Lucas de Heere (1534–84), the Dutch Renaissance scholar Daniel Heinsius (1580–1655), and the writer Maurice Maeterlinck (1862–1949), who won the Nobel prize for literature in 1911.

1 • The Historic City

This walk begins at the **Sint Baafskathedraal**, one of the most splendid Gothic churches in Belgium, where Jan and Hugo Eyck's *Adoration of the Mystic Lamb* has hung since 1432. Open 08.30–18.00 but closed during services. The **chapel** containing the Mystic Lamb Altarpiece and the **crypt** are open Apr–Oct Mon–Sat 09.30–12.00 and 14.00–18.00, Sunday and holidays 13.00–18.00; Nov–Mar Mon–Sat 10.30–12.00 and 14.30–16.00, Sunday and holidays 14.00–17.00. An entrance fee is charged for the Mystic Lamb and the crypt. The ticket office closes 15 mins before closing time.

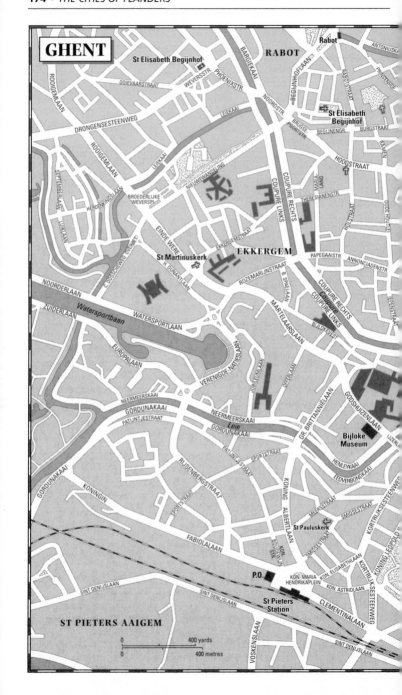

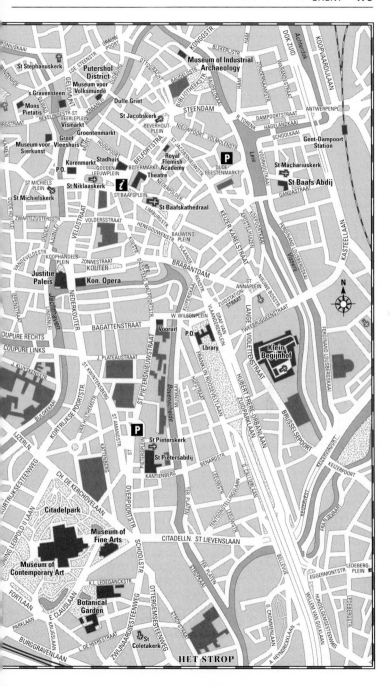

GRAAW
POORT
KONGOSTR.
BLEKERIJSTR.
HAV
DOK ZUID
ACHTERDOK
KOOPVAARDIJLAAN

St Stephanuskerk
Putershol District
Museum voor Volksmunde
OTTOGRACHT
BAUDELOSTR.
BIBLIOTHEEKSTR.
BAUDELOKAAI
HAM
ZONDERNAAMSTR.
VLAANDERSTRAAT

Museum of Industrial Archaeology

's Gravensteen
Mons Pietatis
Vismarkt
GELDMUNT
Dulle Griet
St Jacobskerk
BEVERHOUT-PLEIN
STEENDAM
NIEUWPOORT
R. TORENK.
DAMPOORTSTRAAT
HAGELANDKAAI
SCHOOLKAAI
ANTWERPENPL

Gent-Dampoort Station

Groot Vleeshuis
Museum voor Sierkunst
Groentenmarkt
VOLMOLENSTR.
VOORHOUTKAAI

St Machariuskerk

Korenmarkt
Stadhuis
MUNT
HOOGPOORT
BELFORTSTRA.
BOTERMARKT
Royal Flemish Academy
Theatre
OUDE-BEESTENMARKT
St Baafs Abdij
GANDASTRAAT

P.O.
GOUDEN LEEUWPLEIN
NEDERPOLDER
KEIZER KARELSTRAAT
KOEPOORTKAAI
VISSERIJ
FERDINAND LOUSBERGSKAAI
KASTEELLAAN

St Niklaaskerk
i
ST MICHIELS PLEIN
ST BAAFSPLEIN
St Baafskathedraal

St Michielskerk
OUDE HOUTLEI
ZWARTEZUSTERSSTR.
VOLDERSSTRAAT
LIMBURGSTR.
HENEGOUWENSTR.
BAUWENS-PLEIN
VLAANDE.

N

Justitie Paleis
VANDEVELDESTR.
KOOPHANDELS-PLEIN
ZONNESTRAAT
KOUTER
BRABANTDAM
ST ANNAPLEIN
Kon. Opera
Jacht Laven
NEDERKOUTER

BAGATTENSTRAAT
W. WILSONPLEIN
ZUIDSTATION
LANGE VIOLETTENSTRAAT
TWEEBRUGGENSTRAAT

Vooruit
GRAAF VAN VLAANDERENPLEIN
HUBERT FRÈRE ORBANLAAN
ZUIDPARKLAAN
BRUSSELSEPOORT
FERDINAND LOUSBERGSKAAI

COUPURE RECHTS
COUPURE LINKS
P.O.
Lbrary
FRANKLIN ROOSEVELTLAAN

Klein Begijnhof

J. KLUYSKENSSTR.
J. PLATEAUSTRAAT
ST PIETERSNIEUWSTRAAT
Bovenschelde
MUINKAAI
HOFBRAK.
KEIZERVEST
KEIZERPOORT

St Pieterskerk
St Pietersabdij
BENARDSTR.

Citadelpark
CH. DE KERCHOVELAAN
OVERPOORTSTR.
KANTIENBERG
LEEUWSTR.
TER PLATEN
FRA. VAS.VAAR
KEIZERVIADUKT.

Museum of Fine Arts
CITADELLN. ST LIEVENSLAAN
BELLEVUE

Museum of Contemporary Art
FORTLAAN

Botanical Garden
K.L. LEDEGANCKSTR.
SCHOOLSTR.
OTTERGEMSESTEENWEG
TER PLATEN
STROPKAAI
EGGERMONTSTR.
LEDEBERG-PLEIN

PARKLAAN
St Coletakerk
ZWIJNAARDSESTEENWEG
L. DE HEERESTRAAT

BURGGRAVENLAAN
HET STROP

Sint Baafskathedraal

A chapel dedicated to St John the Baptist stood on this site in 941. It was replaced in the 12C by a Romanesque church, which in turn was demolished at the end of the 13C to make way for the present Gothic church. All that survives of the Romanesque church is the central part of the crypt. The choir dates mainly from c 1290–1310. The transepts, nave and aisles were begun in the 15C and completed c 1550. The west tower, 82m high, was built c 1460–1554.

The seventh chapter of the Order of the Golden Fleece was held here in 1445 by Philip the Good, and the twenty-third by Philip II in 1559. Charles V was baptised in the church in 1500. In 1540, as part of his reprisals for the town's revolt, he demolished much of the abbey of St Baaf to make way for a fortress. The abbey chapter then transferred to this church, which changes its name from Sint Jans to Sint Baafs.

Philip II created a bishopric in Ghent in 1561. The Calvinist iconoclasts damaged the cathedral in 1566 and again in 1576. After their second outburst, Sint Baafskathedraal was used for Protestant worship for nearly ten years. It was restored to Catholic hands by the Duke of Parma in 1585.

The Adoration of the Mystic Lamb

People have been coming to Sint Baafs since the 15C to view the extraordinary *Adoration of the Mystic Lamb* painted by Jan and Hubert van Eyck in 1432. An outstanding work of the Early Flemish School, it hangs in a small chapel to the left of the entrance. The entry fee to the chapel includes admission to the crypt.

The large polyptych (3.65m high and 4.87m wide) contains an astonishing wealth of detail, including more than 250 figures on 20 separate wooden panels. Commissioned by Judocus Vijdt, a rich Ghent patrician, and his wife, Isabella Borluut, it was presented to the church in 1432. It is generally believed that the work was designed and partly painted by Hubert van Eyck and finished by his brother Jan van Eyck. Some scholars, however, are sceptical about the existence of Hubert van Eyck, as there are no known paintings signed by him. But the recent discovery of his tomb in the ruins of Sint Baafs Abbey lends some support to the old theory that the altarpiece was the work of the two brothers.

The altarpiece has narrowly escaped destruction on several occasions. Philip II wanted to take it off to Spain and the fanatical Calvinist iconoclasts almost destroyed it in 1566. The prudish Joseph II of Austria took exception to the naked figures of Adam and Eve, which were removed to a museum in Brussels and replaced by two panels in which Adam and Eve are clothed in bear skins. These absurd panels now hang on a column near the main entrance. The altarpiece was taken to Paris as war booty after the French Revolution, but returned to Ghent in 1815. The outer wings were then sold to a museum in Berlin. These were replaced by 16C copies made by Michiel Coxie for Philip II. The Berlin wings were returned in 1919 under the terms of the Treaty of Versailles, making the altarpiece complete for the first time since the 18C. But not for long. A thief broke into the cathedral in 1934 and stole the panel of the *Just Judges*. It was never recovered. During World War Two, Hitler ordered the altarpiece to be removed from Ghent. It was recovered by the American army in 1945 in an Austrian salt mine. Returned after the war, it was rehung in its original chapel, but moved in 1986 to a secure glass case in the baptistry.

The theft of the panel of the *Just Judges* in June 1934 remains one of the great unsolved crimes of the 20C. The thief wrote to the Bishop of Ghent demanding a ransom of one million francs, but the sum was never paid. Arsène Goedertier, a music teacher, later confessed to the crime, but died before he could reveal the location, which he claimed was somewhere in the church. The lost panel was replaced in 1941 by a copy made by Jef Vanderveken, who included the features of King Leopold III as one of the judges.

The **centre panel** illustrates the Mystic Lamb of God, who redeemed the world from sin. Adored by angels, the Lamb stands on an altar, blood flowing from its side into a chalice. A dove, representing the Holy Spirit, links the Lamb to the figure of Christ above. The Fountain of Life is in the foreground, with patriarchs and prophets kneeling on the left, and apostles and confessors on the right. The background is filled with processions of bishops, popes and virgins. The left panels show judges and soldiers defending the faith, while the right panels depict pilgrims and hermits coming to adore the Lamb.

The figure of Christ Triumphant seated in majesty appears in the **centre of the upper register**. He is flanked by the Virgin and St John the Baptist. The panels on either side contain the nude paintings of Adam and Eve which so annoyed Joseph II. Miniature monochrome pictures above show the murder of Abel and the sacrifice of Isaac.

The **landscape** is painted with astonishing accuracy. Botanists have identified more than 40 species of plants, including the lesser celandine, saxifrage and swallow-wort. The towers and pinnacles rising in the distance represent New Jerusalem. Some of the buildings have been traced to Bruges, Utrecht, Cologne and Maastricht.

The hinged panels are now kept permanently open. The backs are painted with mainly monochrome portraits showing the donors kneeling in prayer, the prophets Micah and Zachariah, the sibyls of Cumae and Eritrea, the Annunciation, and of St John the Baptist and St John the Divine.

The interior

The beautifully proportioned interior of Sint Baafs is remarkable for the richness and variety of its decoration. Particularly noticeable is the difference between the 13C–14C choir, with its grey-blue Tournai stone, and the 16C white stone in the remainder of the building.

The carved oak and marble pulpit in the **nave** was carved in 1745 by Laurent Delvaux. The side chapels in the aisles are hung with paintings by Gaspard de Crayer and Abraham Janssens.

The **choir** is decorated with sumptuous marble screens given by Bishop Triest, who did much to repair the damage caused to the church by the iconoclasts. His tomb is on the north side of the high altar. It was carved by Duquesnoy the Younger in 1657. The tomb of Bishop Allamont, who died in 1673, is by Jean del Cour. The four copper candlesticks in front were made by Benedetto da Rovezzano. Originally ordered for the tomb of Henry VIII of England at Windsor, they are decorated with the English royal arms. Bishop Triest presented the candlesticks to the church after they were sold by Cromwell. The altar is decorated with a statue of St Baaf carved by Hendrik Verbruggen in 1719.

The **ambulatory** chapels contain several interesting paintings. In the south transept one wall is covered with the hatchments of the Knights of the Golden Fleece who attended the 23rd chapter in 1559. The **first chapel** contains a masterpiece by Frans Pourbus the Elder showing *Christ among the Doctors*. It includes portraits of Charles V, Philip II, the Duke of Alva, and Bishop Jansenius, the first bishop of Ghent. Viglius ab Aytta, the chief secretary of Charles V and Philip II, also appears in the painting. His tomb is on the opposite wall.

The **second chapel** is hung with a *Martyrdom of St Barbara* by Gaspard de Crayer while the **fourth chapel** contains the tombs of two bishops. The *Adoration of the Mystic Lamb* formerly hung in the **sixth chapel**. Presented to the church in 1422 by Judocus Vijdt, it now hangs in the baptistry near the west entrance. The empty frame shows the original location of the painting.

The **seventh chapel** is closed off by bronze doors carved in 1633. It contains a *Pietà* by Gerard Honthorst. The **ninth chapel** is hung with a *Glorification of the Virgin* by Niklaas de Liemakere while the **tenth chapel** contains the *Raising of Lazarus* by Otto Venius, and the alabaster tomb of Bishop Damant who died in 1609.

Gerard Seghers' *Martyrdom of St Livinius* hangs in the **eleventh chapel** while the **thirteenth chapel** contains *The Seven Works of Mercy* by Michiel Coxie.

There is a painting of 1624 by Rubens in the **north transept**. It shows *St Baaf entering the Abbey of St Amand* after distributing his belongings to the poor. Rubens' second wife, Hélène Fourment, posed as the saint's wife, who is seen standing with two of Baaf's followers on the left. The bearded head is a self-portrait of Rubens.

Enter the **large crypt** from the north transept. Begun c 1150, it was extended laterally when the present choir was built c 1300. The crown of five chapels at the east end was added c 1400. The mural paintings, which were discovered in 1936, date from 1480–1540. Most of the Bishops of Ghent are buried here. The chapels contain the tombs of several local nobles, including Margaret de Gistel, who died in 1431.

The **Cathedral Treasury** is displayed in several glass cabinets. The treasures include illuminated manuscripts, a 10C Evangelistary, and a work on natural history illustrated with wonderful medieval monsters. The shrine of St Macarius was carved by Hugo de la Vigne in 1616, and the reliquary of the Crown of Thorns may have belonged to Mary Queen of Scots. The vestments include a 16C English Ornement de St Liéin.

A superb *Crucifixion Triptych* by Justus van Gent hangs in **chapel 8** at the east end of the crypt. There is another *Crucifixion* by Frans Francken the Elder in **chapel 10**. Elsewhere, a series of 14 paintings by Frans Pourbus the Elder illustrates the story of St Andrew.

On leaving the cathedral, cross the **St Baafsplein**. A Neo-classical statue by Isidoor de Rudder commemorates Jan Frans Willems (1793–1846), a founding father of the Flemish nationalist movement. It faces the **Nederlandse Schouwburg** (Netherlands Theatre), built in neo-Renaissance style in 1899.

The Lakenhalle and the Belfry stand opposite the cathedral. They were once surrounded by narrow streets and old houses, but this picturesque clutter was cleared away in 1913 for the Ghent World Fair. The rugged **Lakenhalle** was built as the Cloth Hall in 1425. Its vaulted undercroft is now occupied by the Ghent tourist office. A small building known as **Mammelokker** (the suckling) was added to the west side of the Lakenhalle in 1741 by David 't Kindt. Originally the town prison, it is decorated with a stone relief illustrating the legend of Charity suckling a starving prisoner.

The **Belfort** is open mid-Mar–mid-Nov, daily 10.30–12.30 and 14.00–17.30. It has an elevator as an alternative to climbing the stairs. It can be visited with a guide at set times or individually at any time. The **carillon room** can only be visited on the guided tour. The Belfry was built between 1321–1380, but has been modified several times. The spire, restored to its original form in 1913, is topped by a dragon in gilded copper. A local legend has it that the original dragon was stolen by the men of Ghent from Bruges, having been brought back from Constantinople during the Fourth Crusade by the followers of Baldwin. The present dragon dates from the late 19C. Inside the Belfort, visitors can see the remains of earlier dragons including the medieval original.

Begin in the vaulted ground-floor room known as the **Secreet**, where the charters of the privileges of Ghent were kept in an iron chest from 1402 to 1550. This room also contains dusty stone sculptures, including the sole survivor of the four stone guards attached in 1338 to the corners of the upper tier. One floor up, the **First Guard Room** contains models of the Belfort, old photographs and a rusty iron dragon that once crowned the spire. You can take the lift here to the top, or climb the steps.

The **Second Guard Room** contains the 52 bells, of which 37 were cast in 1660 by Pieter Hemony of Zutphen. Most of the others date from the 18C. The largest bell is the 6200kg Roelant Bell, which was cast in 1948. It replaces a bell cast in the 17C by Hemony, which cracked in 1913 and now lies in the garden below the Belfort. Hemony's unfortunate bell was itself the successor of a Roelant cast in 1318, which was taken down in 1540 by order of Charles V after being convicted of 'having played a very turbulent part with its tongue' during the uprising against him. The **top floor** contains a mechanical carillon installed in 1913, which is programmed to play Flemish melodies every 15 minutes. There is a good view of the city from the balcony.

The square beside the Belfry contains a fountain with bronze boys kneeling around the rim. Known as *Youth*, it was made in 1892 by George Minne. The curious **Guildhouse of the Masons** at Catalonienstraat 1 was built in 1527 by C. van den Berghe in Late Gothic style. It preserves the 13C side wall of a previous building. The six statues of morris dancers

Statues on the town hall, Ghent

on the gable are a controversial modern addition.

The **Stadhuis** can only be visited on **guided tours** which begin at 14.00 on Mon–Thur, from May–Oct. It was built on the corner of the Botermarkt and Hoogstraat in 1321 after the old town hall was torn down to make way for the Belfry. All that remains of the 14C building are two vaulted rooms in the basement. The present building has two separate wings built at different dates. The Hoogpoort façade is a fine example of Flamboyant Gothic. It was built from 1518–60 by Rombout Keldermans and Domien de Waghemakere. The Botermarkt façade was added in c 1581 in a more sober style that reflects the temper of the Calvinist regime. Further wings on the Stadhuissteeg and the Poeljemarkt were added in the 17C and 18C.

The **Pacificatiezaal**, open for guided tours as for the Stadhuis, is decorated with painted arms of the governors of Flanders and a curious maze paving. The Pacification of Ghent was signed here in 1576, bringing a temporary truce between Catholics and Protestants. Local weddings take place in the **Trouwzaal** (Marriage Room), which occupies the former chapel. The **Troonzaal** (Throne Room) contains several historical paintings, including the *Abdication of Charles V* by Gaspard de Crayer, and *William the Silent defending the Catholics brought before the Calvinist magistrates*, by M. van Bree. The **Collaciezaal**, or Armoury, was built in 1482 as an assembly hall for the representatives of the tradesmen. It was later used for storing weapons. The last chapter of the Order of the Golden Fleece was held here in 1559.

There are several attractive old houses near the Stadhuis on Hoogpoort. The building at **no. 33** was built in the 15C as the Goldsmiths' Hall. The **Sint Jorishof** at no. 58 was built in 1477 for the Guild of Crossbowmen. It was here that Mary of Burgundy was forced to sign the Great Privilege. The Sint Jorishof is now a hotel which claims to be the oldest in Europe.

Now continue along Hoogpoort. A short detour to the left leads to an attractive square called **Zandberg**, where several handsome 18C houses overlook a pump of 1810. A group of three rugged houses on Hoogpoort once belonged to the Van der Sikkelen family. The **Grote Sikkel** at no. 64 has a tall 14C double step gable. This building is now occupied by the Ghent Academy of Music. On the other side of Biezekapelstraat, the **Kleine Sikkel** at Nederpolder 2 is an impressive 13C Romanesque building with a crenellated screen wall and the Van der Sikkelen family arms above the old door. The **Hôtel van der Meersch** opposite at Nederpolder 1 is mainly 18C with a 16C corner wing. Now turn down the crooked lane Biezekapelstraat, where the **Achter Sikkel** was built in the 14C–15C at the rear of the Grote Sikkel.

You now arrive back at the Sint Baafsplein. The **Sint Niklaaskerk**, open daily 09.00–17.00, on the Korenmarkt was built in austere Scheldt Gothic style in c 1200 on the site of an 11C Romanesque church. It was restored to its original Romanesque appearance in 1992. The base of the tower and the nave walls date from the early 13C. The transepts and the west part of the choir were built after 1230, while the apse was added in 1432. The impressive tower, which was once used as a belfry, was completed c 1300. The Baroque west porch was added in 1681. Most of the 17C Baroque furnishings were removed during the last restoration to return the church to its original Romanesque austerity.

The narrow **Kleine Turkije** runs to the north of the church. A plaque on no. 4 recalls that Albrecht Dürer lodged in 1521 at the **Rode Hoed Inn**. Built in the

12C–16C, this was originally the Guild House of the Grocers. The nearby **De Fonteyne**, at the corner of Gouden Leeuwplein, was built in 1539 for a chamber of rhetoric. Its handsome Renaissance façade is the oldest surviving example in Ghent.

2 • The Graslei and the Gravensteen

Begin on the **Korenmarkt**, a lively square crowded with café terraces. Named after the medieval corn market, Korenmarkt retains several interesting buildings such as the rugged **Borluutsteen** at no. 7. Built from the 13C–15C, this fortified house belonged to the Borluut family. Jan Borluut, leader of the Ghent soldiers at the Battle of the Golden Spurs, belonged to this family.

Several old houses were demolished to make room for the neo-Gothic **Post Office**, completed in 1910. Steps beside the post office lead up to the **Sint Michielsbrug**, built over the River Leie in 1913 to provide a vantage point for visitors to the World Fair. The view from the bridge, which is particularly romantic after dark, includes the towers of Sint Niklaaskerk, the Belfort and the Cathedral. You can also see the houses along the Graslei and Korenlei and, in the distance, the fish market and Gravensteen.

The **Sint Michielskerk** is rather overshadowed by the bridge. Begun in Flamboyant Gothic style in 1440, it was completed, minus the tower, in 1648. No fewer than six plans have been drafted since the 15C to give the church a lofty tower, but all were rejected for various reasons, so that the tower remains a rather sad stump. The interior contains a *Crucifixion* by Van Dyck, and works by Gaspard de Crayer, Otto Venius and Jean-Baptiste de Champaigne. The church is not open to the public.

Go back over the bridge and descend the steps to the **Graslei**. The massive **Gildehuis der Vrije Schippers** at no. 14 was built in late Gothic style between 1500 and 1531 by C. van den Berghe. The Baroque **Gildehuis der Graanmeters** at no. 13 was built in 1698 for the Guild of Grain Weighers to replace no. 10. The tiny **Tolhuisje** of 1682 at no. 12 was originally a customs house. It was converted in 1986 into a stylish café. The **Koornstapelhuis** at no. 11 was originally a public warehouse for storing grain paid as customs duty. This austere Romanesque building of c 1200 is the oldest house on Graslei. The 16C Korenmetershuis at no. 10 was the first Guildhouse of the Grain Weighers. The **Gildehuis van de Metsers** at no. 9 was built in 1526 as the Guildhouse of the Masons. The building at no. 8 looks 15C, but it was in fact built in 1913 for the World Fair.

The Ghent World Fair

The medieval appearance of Ghent was largely the result of the 1913 World Fair. The sleepy provincial town wanted to impress visitors with its medieval grandeur. The old houses clustered around the Gravensteen and the Belfry were demolished and several neo-Gothic buildings were built to add to the medieval atmosphere, including the theatre and the post office. The house at Graslei 8 was built in 15C style to fill an unsightly gap in the Graslei waterfront and the St Pieters Station was designed in an ornate neo-Gothic style to impress visitors the moment they arrived. As a final flourish, the neo-Gothic bridge known as Sint Michielshelling was constructed to allow visitors to appreciate the 'Gothic' old town. The bridge sadly destroys much of the impact of the genuinely ancient Sint Michielskerk.

Now cross the bridge to reach the **Korenlei** quay. The fanciful Huis der Onvrije Schippers at no. 7 was built in 1740 and decorated with a gilded boat. The corner house at no. 24, originally a Romanesque building of c 1200, was altered in the 17C.

The route continues down the attractive Jan Breydelstraat. The **Museum voor Sierkunst** (Decorative Arts Museum), open Tues–Sun 09.30–17.00, occupies a mansion at no. 5 built in 1754 by David 't Kindt for a wealthy linen dealer. The old rooms of the mansion are attractively furnished in 18C styles. The rear wing was converted in 1992 to provide an airy modern interior for displaying Art Nouveau and modern decorative art.

You might pause in the café opposite at no. 8, or glance at the antique curiosities in the window of The Fallen Angel at no. 29, before continuing to the Burgstraat, where an ornate Renaissance house called De Graven van Vlaanderen (The Counts of Flanders) at no. 4 is decorated with the heads of the counts of Flanders from Baldwin of Constantinople to Philip II. The house was built in c 1560 while Philip II ruled the Low Countries.

Turn now into Reckelingestraat to reach **Sint Veerleplein**, passing the flinty grey walls of the castle rising out of the water. The portal of the former Vismarkt (Fish Market) at no. 5 is decorated with Baroque bravado. The figure of Neptune lords it over two reclining figures representing the rivers that meet in Ghent. The Scheldt is symbolised by Hercules (on the left), while the Leie is represented by Venus (on the right). Carved by Artus Quellin the Younger in 1689, the portal is all that remains of the original fish market. After the old market was destroyed by fire in 1872, a larger neo-Gothic building with an iron and glass roof was built. This called for the demolition of the 15C Hospice Wenemaer. The building was given a medieval frontage in 1913 as part of preparations for the World Fair. A curious wooden building with corner towers was added at the same time on the side where the rivers Leie and Lieve meet. The abandoned fish market was used for many years as a car park. Its future was uncertain at the time of writing.

The house to the left of the fish market occupies one of the transepts of a former church, partially demolished in 1578. The church was dedicated to St Veerle, an 8C virgin martyr of Ghent. There are several other old houses with interesting carving near the Kraanlei. Criminals were still being executed in Sint Veerleplein in the late 18C.

The **'s Gravensteen** (Castle of the Counts) is open Apr–Sept daily 09.00–18.00, Oct–Mar daily 09.00–17.00. Last ticket sold 45 minutes before closing time. It is entered through a gloomy gateway on St Veerleplein. This magnificent feudal fortress was built at the confluence of the Lieve and the Leie in c 867 by Baldwin Iron Arm. Fragments of the original castle can be seen in the cellars of the keep.

'S Gravensteen

Baldwin's castle was intended to defend the town against Viking raids, but its successor, begun in 1180 by Philip of Alsace, was expressly designed to strike terror into the unruly citizens of the town. It was stormed by the burghers of Ghent in 1302, at the time of the Battle of the Golden Spurs, and again in 1338 by Jacob van Artevelde. The building was used from 1349 until the end of the 18C for various purposes, including a prison, mint and law court. The old rooms were occupied by a textile factory from 1797 to 1887. The castle was restored between 1894 and 1913, when many old houses built within the castle walls were torn down to create a pure medieval building.

After passing through the **gatehouse**, ascend to a walkway along the **outer wall**. Crossing over the gatehouse, you can see the holes down which boiling oil could be poured on the heads of attackers. Continuing along a further stretch of wall, there are medieval latrines perched high above the water.

Now enter the **Count's Residence** to the north of the keep. The vaulted **Audience Chamber** on the ground floor was for some 300 years the meeting-place of the Council of Flanders. A group of rooms above here was once used as domestic quarters by the counts and their families. They now contain a grim exhibition of torture instruments. The **Upper Hall** has more of the same. A winding staircase leads to the roof, which commands fine views of the town and port. Descend to the **Great Hall**, where Philip the Good held a banquet of the Order of the Golden Fleece in 1445.

In the **cellars** the remains of the 9C castle and two dismal oubliettes can be seen. One cellar was used as a stable until the 14C and then as a torture chamber. Another cellar used as a refuse dump and cesspit was uncomfortably close to the well which supplied the castle with fresh water.

On leaving the castle gate, cross the St Veerleplein to reach the **Groentenmarkt**. You can recognise the **Groot Vleeshuis** from the row of tiny step gables along the side. Built in 1406–10, this was the medieval meat market. The small out-houses along one side were once used for distributing offal to the poor. They are now occupied by tiny cafés and shops. An attractive old shop at **Groentenmarkt 4** sells dark, pungent Tierenteyn mustard, made according to a secret recipe invented in 1790.

Now turn left along Lange Munt to reach the **Groot Kanonplein**. A large 15C iron mortar known as Dulle Griet (Mad Meg) stands on this waterfront square. A lane to the right leads to the Vrijdagmarkt, a large square where the medieval guilds gathered and frequently brawled. A splendid bronze statue unveiled in 1863 shows Jacob van Artevelde in rabble-rousing mood. His uprising of 1338 probably began on this square. The Toreken, a gaudily repainted building with a slender turret, was built in 1460 as the Guildhouse of the Tanners. A large market is held on the square every Friday.

The short Wijze Manstraat leads to the **Sint Jacobskerk**. Its two Romanesque west towers date from the 12C when the church was begun. The lower part of the steeple, above the crossing, was completed between the 13C and 15C.

An interesting old building stands to the north of the church at Ottogracht 2. A 19C Neo-classical portal partly conceals the 17C chapel of the **Abbey of Baudelo**. Founded in the 13C as a refuge for a Cistercian abbey, it became a full abbey in the 17C. Mozart is said to have played on the Hemony carillon in the turret.

Continue along Ottogracht and turn right down Goudstraat to reach the **Museum of Industrial Archaeology and Textiles** at Minnemeers 9, open Tues–Sun 09.30–17.00. This outstanding museum of industrial archaeology occupies a converted 19C textile factory. Begin on the **5th floor**, where an imaginative exhibition charts Ghent's industrial history from the mid-18C to 1900. Focusing particularly on women's roles, the museum displays old spinning machines, shop fronts, a schoolroom, steam engines and printing presses. There are also striking views from the factory windows looking south to medieval Ghent and north to the 19C industrial districts. The **4th floor**, which covers the 20C, contains old shop interiors, a reconstructed First World War trench, a laundry and a teenager's bedroom c 1960. The **3rd floor** is occupied by a working cotton factory. The museum also has a bookshop, **café** and medicinal herb garden.

Now cross the river Leie and turn left along the quay, then right up Rodelijvekensstraat to the **Fratersplein**. A statue on this square commemorates Pieter van Gent (1486–1572), famous for his educational work in Mexico. Erected in 1976, the statue is a copy of one in Mexico City. The convent of Sint Jan de Deo on this square was formerly a Carthusian foundation. It now contains the **Museum Meerhem**, open Sun 14.00–17.00, which illustrates the life of Pieter van Gent and charts episodes in the history of Ghent such as the founding of the textile industry.

Return down Rodelijvekensstraat and Ottogracht to reach the St Jacobskerk, then turn down a short street opposite the west end of the church to reach Kammerstraat. The painter Gaspard de Crayer died in 1669 at no. 18. At the end of this street, continue along Koningstraat, where the striking façade of the **Royal Flemish Academy** at no. 18 was built in 1746 by David 't Kindt.

Now turn right to reach Onderstraat where the attractive 16C **Ryhovesteen** is at no. 22. Restored in 1988, the house is now occupied by the Ghent department of historical monuments. A portal to the right leads into a small garden replanted in 15C style. The house retains a Romanesque rear wall from the 13C. Continue along this street to Lange Munt, then turn left to reach the Korenmarkt.

3 • The Patershol and Vrijdagmarkt

An attractive area of canals and historic buildings lies beyond the Gravensteen. Beginning on the Sint Veerleplein, go down Kraanlei, an attractive quay beside the Leie. The **Museum voor Volkskunde** (Folklore Museum) at no. 65 occupies a handsomely restored complex of 14C almshouses known as the Kinderen Alijnshospitaal, or Hospital of Alijns Children. Open Tues–Sun 10.30–12.00 and 13.30–17.00.

> ### A medieval murder
> The Kinderen Alijnshospitaal was founded as a result of a quarrel between two Ghent families, the Ryms and the Alijns. This culminated in the assassination by the Ryms of the two leading Alijns. The Ryms were sentenced in 1354 to have their houses razed and in 1362 were ordered to provide an annuity for a hospice. In a gesture of reconciliation and goodwill, the surviving Alijns offered their house in the Kraanlei. A chapel was built in 1363. Several houses were added in 1519 by Lieven van Pottelsberghe, the guardian at that time, whose portrait hangs in the Museum of Fine Arts. A new chapel was built between 1543 and 1547. The city bought the almshouses in 1940 and restored the complex as a Folklore Museum.

The museum contains a fascinating miscellany of objects that recall daily life in 19C and early 20C Ghent. A delightful collection of games and toys includes a hobby-horse made by the sculptor Laurent Delvaux for his grandchildren. Several of the tiny rooms of the almshouse contain furnished 19C interiors, including a Ghent grocer's shop, a cooper's workshop, a cobbler's shop with a water-filled glass bowl for concentrating light, a 19C tavern, a barber's salon of 1900, a baker's shop and a clog-making workshop. The museum also has a traditional **puppet theatre** which occasionally stages performances. The **chapel** contains several giant figures paraded through Ghent, while the adjoining sacristy has a graphic painting shows the Ryms murdering the Alyns.

On leaving the museum, turn left along Kraanlei to reach two interesting 17C Baroque carved fronts. The house at **no. 77**, dating from 1643, is illustrated with the Seven Acts of Charity. Its neighbour at **no. 79** is decorated with terracotta reliefs of the five senses, the virtues, a flying deer and a flute player.

Go down Rodekoningstraat to reach an old quarter known as **Patershol** where craftsmen such as the cordwainers made leather shoes. Restored in the 1980s, this district is now dotted with intimate restaurants and and galleries. Turn left along Corduwaniersstraat, right into Hertogstraat and left along Haringsteeg to reach Geldmunt.

Turn right to Lange Steenstraat, where the former **Carmelite Church** stands at no. 14. Built between the 14C and 16C, it was deconsecrated and stripped of its furnishings. The city now owns the church while the rest of the complex belongs to the provincial government. An octagonal tower from the Carmelite house founded in 1285 survives in a corner of the first courtyard.

Go straight ahead from Geldmunt down Sint Margrietstraat to reach the **Sint Stephanuskerk**. Founded in 1606, it was rebuilt in 1838 following a fire. It has a good Baroque door and altar paintings by Gaspard de Crayer. The Baroque furnishings were moved from the Carmelite Church nearby.

Now turn left down Academiestraat, past an **Augustinian Monastery** at no. 1 founded in 1296 but largely rebuilt in the 17C. This street leads us to Sint Antoniuskaai, a quiet quay beside the River Lieve with several old houses. The **Sint Antoniushof Godshuis** at no. 9 was built in 1641 for the Guild of St Anthony, whose members practised shooting arquebuses in the garden. The façade is decorated with crossed arquebuses. The building was converted into an almshouse for elderly women in 1805.

From the next bridge, the **Rabot**, a fortified sluice of 1491, is visible. The **Donkere Poort** (Dark Gate) is just across the bridge. This vaulted archway flanked by two turrets is one of the few remaining relics of the Prinsenhof palace built in 1353. It is said that Charles V was born here in 1500 but 16C records suggest that the birth took place in Eeklo. A plaque on the inner side of the gate shows the palace as it was in the 16C.

Go down the street Prinsenhof and turn right into Abrahamstraat. The Ghent city archives have occupied the **Mons Pietatis** at no. 13 since 1929. Founded in 1621 as a municipal pawnshop, the Mons Pietatis was built by the Baroque architect Wenceslas Coeberger. Inspired by the Mons Pietatis he had seen in Italy, Coeberger obtained permission from Archdukes Albert and Isabella to establish similar charitable institutions in Flanders. The 17C Mons Pietatis provided loans to people with goods to pawn. Coeberger's municipal pawnshops survive in Ghent and Antwerp.

Turn right down Bonifantenstraat to reach Burgstraat. The **Friary of the Discalced Carmelites** at no. 46 dates mainly from the 17C. The church of 1712 has three Baroque altars. A 15C fragment of the Prinsenhof can be seen in the cloister.

This street leads to the Sint Elisabethplein, where the **Sint Elisabeth**

Begijnhof was founded in the 13C. The Begijnhof was once reached through a 16C portal, but this was moved during the 19C to form the entrance to the Bijloke Museum (see walk 4). The nave of the church dates from the 15C, while the transepts were added two centuries later. The cobbled lanes around the church contain 16C and 17C Begijnhof houses once occupied by single women.

Back on Sint Elisabethplein, go down Peperstraat to reach the **Dominican Friary** at Hoogstraat 41. Founded as a medieval leper house, it was rebuilt in the 17C as a convent and school and then given to the Dominicans in 1845.

4 • Kouter and the Art Museums

The south side of Ghent was developed in the early 20C around the **Citadel Park**. The main attractions are the two art museums in the park and (if it is open) the Bijloke Museum. Beginning at the Korenmarkt, cross the St Michielsbrug and turn left down Onderbergen. This goes past **Het Pand**, the site of an ancient hospice where the Dominicans built a friary in the 13C–14C. The building is now occupied by a small museum of medicine. Turn left along Hoornstraat and cross the Leie to reach the Veldstraat. The rustic **Bloch's** tea room at no. 60 is a popular traditional café.

> ### The Treaty of Ghent
> Ghent was the setting for a major diplomatic congress in 1814 when British and American delegates negotiated the terms of the Treaty of Ghent. Signed on 24 December 1814, it brought an end to the War of 1812 and the return of all territories seized. John Quincy Adams and his staff resided in the Hôtel Schamp on the corner of Volderstraat. A plaque on the wall of no. 47 commemorates the event. The British fought one last battle near New Orleans 15 days after the treaty was signed, but were defeated by troops led by Andrew Jackson.

A short detour along Volderstraat leads to the **Aula** (assembly hall) of Ghent University, which occupies a porticoed building of 1826 designed by Louis Roelandt. The university was founded in 1816 by King William of the Netherlands. Teaching has been in Dutch since 1930. The 1642 gateway next to the Aula once led to the Jesuit college.

Back on Veldstraat, turn left past the **Hôtel Arnold Vander Haeghen** at no. 82. This 18C mansion was designed by David 't Kindt. Its salon is decorated with exceptional 18C Chinese wall hangings. The house was once occupied by a museum; this was closed indefinitely at the time of writing.

The former **Hôtel d' Hane-Steenhuyse** at nos 51–55, an 18C mansion with a Rococo façade, was the residence of Louis XVIII of France during Napoleon's Hundred Days. The house was being restored at the time of writing.

Turn left along Zonnestraat to reach the elegant square known as **Kouter**. Literally the 'ploughed field', Kouter was for centuries a popular venue for archery contests, military parades and markets. A flower market has been held on the square since 1772. It takes place every Saturday and Sunday from 07.00–13.00.

The **Handelsbeurs** (stock exchange) at no. 29 occupies a striking Rococo guard house built in 1738. The sumptuous **Hôtel Falignan** at no. 172 was built in 1755 by Bernard de Wilde. The Rococo mansion is now occupied by a private club.

Leave the square by Schouwburgstraat, which goes past the **Koninklijke Opera** built by Louis Roelandt between 1836 and 1848. The **Gerechtshof** (law courts) are now straight ahead. Built on the edge of the Leie, this impressive building was designed by Louis Roelandt in 1836–46. Julien Dillens carved the statue of Hippolyte Metdepenningen, a prominent 19C lawyer and politician, which stands in front of the courts.

Follow the tramlines down Nederkouter, but turn off to the right along Verlorenkost to reach a forgotten stretch of the Leie with gardens on one side. The leafy waterfront quay Baertsoenkaai leads past several 19C university buildings, including the curious neo-Gothic Pharmacodynamic Institute at no. 1.

Turn right at the end of the quay, past a small garden with a statue carved by G. de Vreeze in 1952 to commemorate Jan Palfijn (1650–1730), a surgeon credited with the invention of forceps. A plaque behind the statue marks the spot where Jacob van Artevelde addressed the people of Ghent for the first time in 1337.

Bijloke Museum

The exceptional Bijloke Museum, open Sun 14.00–18.00 and Thur 10.00–13.00 and 14.00–18.00, occupies the 14C–17C Abbey of Bijloke. This outstanding museum of antiquities displays an astonishing variety of objects, including old views of Ghent, guild relics, maps, 17C paintings and kitchen utensils. Many of the rooms have retained their original tiled floors and ornate fireplaces. The one drawback is that the museum is currently open only two days a week, though the situation may improve under a proposed plan to turn the ground floor rooms into a Ghent historical museum.

History of the abbey

The abbey was founded on this site as a hospice and hospital in 1228 by a group of nuns who came from the Cistercian convent of Nieuwenbosse, 3km southeast of Ghent. It suffered severely during the religious troubles of the 16C. In 1579, during the period of Calvinist rule, the construction of new ramparts led to the demolition of many of the abbey buildings, though the refectory and dormitory survived. The nuns returned in 1585 when the Duke of Parma reoccupied Ghent; the buildings were eventually reconstructed in the 17C. The nuns were expelled again in 1797, but returned in 1801. The abbey was turned into a museum in 1927.

Enter through the 1660 **portal** of the former Sint Elisabeth Begijnhof, which was moved here from its original location in c 1874. A passage behind the ticket office leads to the 17C **Room of the Governors of the Poor House**, which is decorated with a chimneypiece and panelling by Norbert Sauvage. An allegorical representation by Joos van Cleef above the chimneypiece illustrates the founding of the Poor House by Charles V. A series of 17C paintings illustrate the *Seven Works of Charity*. The **Room of the Abbots of Baudelo**, which is hung with 17C and 18C Brussels tapestries, is reached along a passage hung with various old engravings, including a 1518 plan of the Stadhuis.

Now cross the **courtyard**, from which there is a good view of the 17C House of the Abbess (far left), the 14C refectory and dormitory (middle), and part of an 18C façade rescued from Veldstraat (right). Enter a corridor and turn right into a room containing ornate woodcarvings salvaged from old Ghent houses which have been demolished.

Now go up the stairs to reach the **refectory**. This beautiful Gothic hall has a high wooden vault. A remarkable monument in the middle of the floor celebrates Hugo II, castellan of Ghent, who died in 1232. It was found in 1948 in the ruins of the abbey of Nieuwenbosse.

The wall above the entrance is decorated with a 14C mural of the *Last Supper*, with the *Coronation of the Virgin* above. The fireplace wall has figures representing St John the Baptist and St Christopher. Other exhibits include 12C Rhenish engraved copper grave-plates which were found in the Scheldt.

Climb a short flight of steps to reach the **dormitory**, another fine Gothic hall. Largely devoted to the guilds, it contains a model ship carried by the Free Boatmen in the procession of 1767 and several curious standards decorated with guild emblems.

The **upper cloister** contains medieval ceramics, Delft tile walls from old houses in Ghent, porcelain and glass, costumes of the 18C and 19C, weapons and armour, brass, pewter and ironwork, and a collection of intricate locks and keys. Perhaps the most interesting work is the large brass of Leonard Betten, Abbot of Sint Truiden, who died in 1667.

The 16C lavatorium is on the south side of the **lower cloister**. The fascinating *Panorama of Ghent in 1534* may be hanging here. The stucco ceiling of 1715 in the large hall was moved from the refectory when it was restored to its original medieval state.

Three large rooms off the **north cloister** have beautiful gilt hangings. These rooms are devoted to the shooting guilds. The first room contains guild chairs and historical pictures, while the second contains a small cannon and a painting of a meeting of the Guild of St Anthony. The **east cloister** contains the *Coronation of Christ* by Dirk Bouts.

A passage leads from the southwest corner of the cloister to the 17C **House of the Abbess**, where a series of rooms contains furnishings from old Ghent houses, abbeys and hospices. The kitchen has an interesting collection of historical cooking utensils. The last room is decorated with a fine chimneypiece by Norbert Sauvage and a painting showing aldermen meting out justice.

On leaving the Bijloke Museum, turn left along the busy Ijzerlaan and continue along Burgomaster Karel de Kerchovelaan. A fountain on the avenue commemorates Karel de Kerchove, burgomaster of Ghent from 1857 to 1881, who presided over some major improvements to the city. The fountain was designed in 1898 by Hippolyte Leroy.

Museum voor Schone Kunsten

The Museum voor Schone Kunsten, open Tues–Sun 09.30–17.00, stands on the edge of the park. This modest and yet charming museum occupies a Neo-classical building designed by Charles van Rysselberghe in 1900. The rooms, recently redecorated, have something of the atmosphere of a country villa. The collection was founded in 1798 from paintings saved from local monasteries and churches closed by the French Revolutionaries. Known for its two paintings by Hieronymus Bosch, the museum also has an outstanding collection of works by Flemish and German Expressionists.

Begin in the **large hall**, just beyond the bookshop, where five 18C Brussels tapestries illustrate the *Glorification of the Gods*. Designed by Jan van Orley and Jan Coppens, they once hung in the Gravensteen. A glass case contains some interesting photographs of the interior of the Ghent Academy pavilion at the 1913 World Fair.

The rooms to the right of the hall contain the old masters. **Room 1** has 15C works by Flemish Primitives, including a lovely *Madonna with the Carnation* by a follower of Roger van der Weyden. The background landscape in *The Family of St Anne* was painted by an unknown Ghent artist who had clearly studied the Van Eyck altarpiece in Ghent Cathedral. A strange *Ecce Homo* by a follower of the Master of Flémalle shows the risen Christ flanked by two weeping angels.

Room 2 contains two works by **Hieronymus Bosch**. *St Jerome at Prayer* is an early work showing the saint in a bizarre mountain landscape. The much later *Bearing of the Cross* conveys the horror of the Crucifixion through the grotesque faces surrounding Christ.

There is also a gentle study of the *Rest on the Flight to Egypt* by Adriaen Isenbrant. The *Portraits of Lieven van Pottelsberghe* and his wife *Livina van Steelant* c 1520, attributed to Gerard Horenbout, are thought to be the side panels of a triptych whose centre panel has been lost. Van Pottelsberghe was a noble at the court of Margaret of Austria who later became guardian of the Hospitaal der Kindren Alyns (now the Folklore Museum).

The long panel depicting *The Conquest of Jerusalem by Titus* is a remarkable 15C work by an unknown Ghent artist. Originally the predella of the *Crucifixion Triptych* by Justus van Ghent (in the crypt of Ghent Cathedral), it shows the Roman Emperor Titus attacking Jerusalem in AD 70 after a long siege. The painting depicts the terrible results of starvation on the Jews in Jerusalem. We can even see a woman roasting her dead child on a spit. The artist intended to draw a parallel with the siege of Ghent by the Emperor Maximilian in 1488.

Room 3 contains works by minor 16C Flemish artists and a 15C sculpture of *St Sebastian* by Arnt van Zwolle. The next room is dominated by Marten van Heemskerk's large *Calvary*, dated 1543 on a stone at the bottom left. This painting was once used as a door in the Rich Clares' convent in Ghent. The *Last Judgement* on the opposite wall was painted for the Ghent law courts by Raphael Coxie, son of the more famous Michiel Coxie.

There are several large works by **Rubens** in **Room 5**, including the *Stigmata of St Francis of Assisi*, and, in the next room, *The Scourging of Christ*. This was a preliminary sketch for a painting now hanging in Antwerp's Sint Paulus church. These two rooms also contain two studies for a man's head by Jacob Jordaens, a *Judgement of Solomon* by Gaspard de Crayer and Antoon van Dyck's allegorical *Jupiter and Antiope*.

Room 7 contains a copy by Pieter Brueghel the Younger of his father's *Village Wedding Feast*. Pieter the Younger spent most of his time copying works of his father, but his painting of *The Village Lawyer* (same room) is an amusing and original study of an overworked lawyer surrounded by piles of tattered documents. A bizarre painting of the *Scourges of Mankind* was discovered in the museum's storeroom in 1902. It was painted by Kerstiaen de Keuninck, an artist who was unknown until this work was found.

Three small rooms (**nos 9–12**) contain **19C and early 20C paintings**, including James Ensor's curious *Skeleton looking at Chinoiserie* of 1885 and the haunting portrait of *Marguerite van Mons* by Théo van Rysselberghe, younger brother of the architect who designed this museum. Van Rysselberghe also painted *The Poet Emile Verhaeren reading to his Friends* in 1903, a work that includes several leading French and Belgian intellectuals. One of the sculptures in the room is George Minne's *Kneeling Boy*.

The next rooms (**nos 13–15**) contain **17C Flemish and Dutch paintings**, including a Dutch marine painting by Willem van de Velde the Younger, Andries van Eertvelt's rather theatrical *Ships in Distress*, a view of a Dutch town by Jan van Goyen and Dutch still lifes by **Willem Claesz Heda**.

Next is the **sculpture hall**, which occupies a striking hemicycle. Return to the main hall to reach the rooms devoted to **Flemish Expressionism** (A to H). **Room A** contains a collection of sketches by James Ensor. **Room B** has some eccentric works by Edgard Tytgat, including a modern version of the Susanna legend called *Tragic Old Men*.

The bright **Room C** contains several paintings by Gustave De Smet bathed in warm tones of red, including *Village Fair* and the beautiful *Nude with Necklace*. Several paintings by the sadly neglected Jan Brusselmans hang in **Room D**, including the striking *Nude*.

The works by Constant Permeke in **Room E** are darker and more forbidding, but a more optimistic vision emerges in the works of the **First Latem School** hung in **Room F**. A major exhibition of Flemish Primitives in Bruges in 1902 inspired several works we see in this room, such as Gustave van de Woestyne's *Farmer* of 1910. A revival of Christian idealism can be seen in other works including Van de Woestyne's 1920 fresco *Hospitality for Strangers*, which once hung outside the front door of his house in Latem. The delicate Fauvism of Rik Wouters is seen in **Room G** in his *Woman Seated* of 1915.

The **Stedelijk Museum voor Actuele Kunst** (Museum of Contemporary Art) or Smak, open Tues–Sun 09.00–17.00, occupies a Casino built in 1913 opposite the Museum of Fine Art. Opened in 1999, the museum contains an outstanding collection of postwar international art, including works by the Cobra Group, Bruce Nauman, Sol Lewitt, Richard Long, Joseph Beuys and Marcel Broodthaers. Large works are displayed in an iron-and-glass hall constructed in the park in 1913 as an exhibition hall for the Ghent Floralies. It was originally designed as a railway station for the Belgian Congo. The museum has a bookshop and café.

The **Citadel Park** was laid out in 1871 in romantic style. It stands on the site of a fort built by the Duke of Wellington and later occupied by the Dutch. A memorial by Yvonne Serruys was unveiled near the large lake in 1926 in honour of *Emile Claus*, a leading Flemish Impressionist. Another memorial by Jules van Biesbroeck commemorates *Edmond van Beveren* (1852–94), a prominent Ghent Socialist. A third statue near the Astridlaan was carved by G. van den Meersche in 1923 in memory of *Oswald de Kerchove* (1844–1906). The son of Burgomaster Karel de Kerchove, he was a distinguished botanist and horticulturalist who helped to establish the Ghent Floralies.

Ghent Florialies

The Ghent Florialies began as a modest flower show held in a local tavern in 1809. Known since 1873 as the Florialies, this became a major flower show under the patronage of the royal family. The shows feature spectacular displays of local azaleas and begonias grown in the greenhouse belt around Ghent, particularly in Sint-Amandsberg, Ledeberg and Gentbrugge. The Florialies Palace was built in the Citadel Park for the flower show of 1913. It is now held every five years in the Flanders Expo hall (next in 2000).

The university's **Botanic Garden** is planted with over 7500 species arranged in scientific order. Landscaped around a pond, it is located to the southeast of the Citadel Park. Open daily 09.00–12.00 and 13.00–17.00,

Return to the museum and go back into town along the narrow Overpoortstraat. This leads to the large Sint Pietersplein in the heart of the university quarter. The east side of the square is bounded by the grandiose if dilapidated former abbey of **Sint Pieter**. Founded by St Amand in the 7C, the abbey was badly damaged in the Middle Ages. Work began on the reconstruction in 1584, but it was not completed until the 18C. The abbey survived after the French Revolution as it was used as public offices. The north wing, including the chapter house, has been converted into a cultural centre. The large gate at no. 12 leads to a courtyard occupied by the former hospital and guesthouse.

One wing is now occupied by the **Schoolmuseum Michiel Thiery**, open Mon–Thur and Sat 09.00–12.15 and 13.30–17.15; Fri 09.00–12.15. The museum has interesting exhibitions on natural history, geography, the evolution of man and the history of the computer. An audio-visual show is devoted to Emperor Charles V.

A gate at the far end of the courtyard leads to a grassy slope planted with apple orchards. Fragments of the old abbey buildings are visible on the hillside. The **Sint Pieterskerk** was built by Pieter Huyssens in 1629–1719. It has a fine dome in the Renaissance style. The interior, reached from the main square, has a wrought-iron choir screen of 1748 by Maniet, paintings by Niklaas de Liemakere and Theodoor van Thulden, and a porphyry cenotaph of Isabel of Austria (1501–26). The sister of Charles V, she married Christian II of Denmark. Her remains were removed to Odense in Denmark in 1883.

Continue along the lively Sint Pieternieuwstraat, past the **Vooruit theatre** at no. 23. Built in 1914 as a socialist meeting hall, it is now a centre for avant-garde theatre. Its café is popular with students and artists. An Art Deco building opposite at no. 129 was once occupied by the Vooruit newspaper office. It now has a large café on the ground floor.

Turn right to cross a bridge over an arm of the Scheldt. This leads to President Wilsonplein, where there is a cluster of modern buildings including the public library, city administration and Het Zuid shopping centre.

The long **Koning Albert Park** occupies the site of the old railway station. The park contains an equestrian memorial of 1937 to King Albert. The pedestal was designed by J.A. de Bondt while the statue is by Domien Ingels. A triangular garden at the far end of the park contains a Congo Memorial unveiled in 1936.

Leave the park on the side opposite Vooruit and go down Twee Bruggenstraat, then turn right into Lange Violettenstraat. The **Klein Begijnhof** is a little way down on the left. It was founded in 1234 by the sisters Margaret and Joanna of Constantinople. The present buildings, which date from 17C–19C, surround a quiet enclosure, where sheep can still occasionally be seen grazing peacefully. The Baroque church dates from 1658–1720. It contains an interesting polyptych, the *Fountain of Life*, by Lucas Hoorenbaut, and altarpieces by Gaspard de Crayer and Niklaas de Liemakere. Liemakere's work, the *Presentation in the Temple*, is one of his most charming paintings.

An interesting waterfront walk leads to a romantic ruined abbey (open in the summer months only). Return to the Twee Bruggenstraat and then cross two parallel channels of the River Leie by the Nieuwe Bosbrug and the Lousbergsbrug. Turn left along the Lousbergskaai to reach the **Abdij Sint Baaf** at Gandastraat 7. The **Museum voor Stenen Voorwerpen** (monumental carving) now occupies the site, open Apr–early Nov Tues–Sun 09.00–17.00.

A ruined abbey

This Benedictine abbey was founded by St Amand in the 7C. Laid waste by the Vikings in the 9C, it was rebuilt by the Count of Flanders a century later. The abbey flourished during the 12C and 13C. It was the setting in 1369 for the wedding of Philip the Bold of Burgundy to Margaret, heiress of Louis de Male. This alliance indirectly brought Burgundian rule to Flanders. The abbey was largely destroyed by Charles V in 1540. After crushing the Ghent uprising, he built a Renaissance fortress here to punish the city. The abbey church was demolished and the domestic buildings were turned into barracks and armouries. This fortress was demolished during the 19C, leaving just the abbey ruins.

John of Gaunt was born in the Abdij Sint Baaf in 1340. His father Edward III and mother Philippa of Hainaut had come to Ghent to forge an alliance with Jacob van Artevelde. John of Gaunt was the fourth son of Edward III and the brother of Edward, the Black Prince. He married Blanche, the daughter of Henry, duke of Lancaster, and inherited the title on Henry's death. John of Gaunt played a leading role in the Hundred Years War and died in 1399.

The overgrown grounds are now scattered with stone relics salvaged from old Ghent buildings and the illegible old iron labels add to the seductive charm of the place. The east wall of the Gothic cloister, partly restored, has vaulting of 1495. The octagonal 12C Lavatorium can be seen nearby.

The 13C **chapter house** has Romanesque bays. There are two curiously shaped ancient tombs, one with a head-rest. The old refectory dates from the 12C or earlier. It was used as a store from the 13C onwards. A flight of steps at the north side of the cloister leads to the large 13C refectory which has a 16C wooden ceiling and round-headed windows. This **great hall** served as the abbey chapel from 1589 to the end of the 18C, and from 1834 to 1882 as the local parish church. It now contains a **collection of architectural fragments** which includes a Romanesque font, a 12C double-tympanum from the destroyed abbey church, and a number of ancient tombstones including one said to be that of Hubert van Eyck.

From here, you can visit the neo-Gothic **Groot Begijnhof**, built in 1872 to the east of Dampoort station at Engelbert van Arenbergstraat 53. Constructed as an extension of the Sint Elisabeth Begijnhof, it has two gateways. The one on the Ghent side has a statue of St Elizabeth, while the other bears the arms of the Arenberg family, who bought the land on which it stands. A small museum at no. 64 contains objects connected with Begijnhof life.

Return to the abbey and cross the river by the bridge at the end of Gandastraat, then follow Van Eyckstraat to Reep. This broad avenue leads to the ancient **Gerard Duivelsteen**, which rises out of an arm of the Scheldt. Dating from 1245, with a fine Romanesque undercroft, this is a superb example of the private fortresses built by the Ghent nobility in the 13C. It has been used as an armoury, school, seminary, mental hospital, prison, orphanage and fire station and is now occupied by the state archives.

Return to the cathedral, passing a monument to Jan and Hubert van Eyck carved by George Verbanck for the 1913 Ghent World Fair. Another monument carved by P.P. de Vigne-Quyo in 1885 celebrates Lieven Bauwens.

Ghent environs

The suburb of **Oostakker**, 6km north of Ghent, contains the **Basiliek Onze Lieve Vrouw van Lourdes**, built in neo-Gothic style in 1877 by Baron Jean Béthune, who was also responsible for much of the painted decoration of the interior. A nearby garden has a grotto of Our Lady of Lourdes. The **Monument der Onthoofden** on Gefusilleerdenstraat commemorates 56 members of the Resistance who were executed by the Germans here. Unveiled in 1951, the monument has memorial crosses and bronze statues by George Vindevogel representing prisoners who were shot, beheaded, hung or held as hostages.

The port

Ghent has been a port since the early middle ages, when boats moored on the Graslei and Korenlei quays. A canal built in the 13C to link Ghent to Bruges is still in use. A large new canal was dug in 1547 to link Ghent with the Scheldt estuary at Terneuzen, now in the Netherlands. This route to the sea was closed by the Dutch blockade of the Scheldt from 1648 to 1795. Ghent developed into a major inland port with the opening to sea-going vessels of the 30km Terneuzen canal in 1827. The N474 follows the canal north from the port of Ghent to the industrial town of Zelzate.

The village of **Wondelgem**, 4km north of Ghent, has an imposing Baroque church of 1687. The Ghent to Terneuzen canal begins near here at the Grootdok. A memorial at **Rieme**, 13km north of Ghent, marks the site where a group of Resistance fighters were executed.

The flower district

The Bloemenstreek (flower district), just outside of Ghent, is famous for plant nurseries where begonias, azaleas, roses and orchids are cultivated. The town of **Lochristi**, 8km northeast of Ghent, is the main centre for horticulture. Other centres include De Pinte, 8km southwest, Merelbeke, 5km south, and Laarne,

8km east. The begonias are at their best from July to September. Local growers put on spectacular displays at the **Floralies festival** held every five years at Flanders Expo in the suburb of Sint-Denijs-Westrem (next in 2000).

The Leie district

The meandering River Leie (Lys in French) passes through an attractive district of small villages to the southwest of Ghent. Several Flemish artists settled here in the late 19C and early 20C to form the First Latem School and Second Latem School.

Practical information

Where to stay
Hotel

£££ *Auberge du Pêcheur*, Pontstraat 41, Sint-Martens-Latem, ☎ 09.282.31.44, is an attractive country hotel on the Leie.

Eating out
Restaurants

The former artists' colony of Sint-Martens-Latem has several attractive country restaurants:

£££ *Auberge du Pêcheur*, Pontstraat 41, ☎ 09.282.31.44, has an elegant restaurant and a more simple tavern by the river.

££ *Oude Veer*, Baarle Frankrijkstraat 90, ☎ 09.281.05.20, is a romantic Flemish restaurant in a former ferry house on the River Leie.

££ *Brasserie Latem*, Kortrijksesteenweg 9, ☎ 09.282.36.17, offers traditional French brasserie cooking.

Tourist information

The Leie district tourist office is in the Stadhuis, Gentpoortstraat 1, Deinze, ☎ 09.381.95.01.

Opening times
Museum van Deinze en De Leiestreek in Deinze is open Mon and Wed–Fri 14.00–17.30 and on weekends and holidays 10.00–12.00 and 14.00–17.00.

Ooidonk castle is open on Ascension Day, Whit Sunday and Whit Monday and Jul–mid-Sept on Sun and holidays 14.00–1800. The park is open daily.

Museum Gustave De Smet and the **Museum Leon De Smet** at Deurle are open Easter–Aug Wed–Sat 14.00–18.00 and Sun 10.00–12.00 and 14.00–18.00; Sept–Easter Wed–Sun 14.00–17.00.

MDD (formerly known as the **Museum Dhondt-Dhaenens)** at Deurle is open Tues–Fri 13.00–17.00, and weekends 11.00–17.00.

Museum Gevaert-Minne at Sint-Martens-Latem is open Wed–Sun 14.00–18.00. It is also open Apr–Sept Sat–Sun 10.00–12.00. The museum closes at 17.00 Oct–Mar.

The main town in the region is **Deinze**, 17km southwest of Ghent on the River Leie.

St Poppo of Stavelot

Deinze was the birthplace of St Poppo of Stavelot, an important 11C Benedictine monk. He began life in the army, where he led a dissolute life for several years. A pilgrimage to Rome and Jerusalem led to his conversion. A trusted adviser to the emperor St Henry, St Poppo inspired a revival of monastic discipline. He was superior-general of some of the largest and most ancient monasteries in Lotharingia and neighbouring areas.

The Onze-Lieve-Vrouwekerk in Deinze was built in the 14C in Scheldt Gothic style. The attractive modern Museum van Deinze en De Leiestreek at L. Matthyslaan 3 contains works by many of the artists who settled in the Leie district, including Emile Claus, George Minne, Constant Permeke, A. Servaes and Leon and Gustave De Smet. One of the outstanding works is La Récolte des Betteraves by Emile Claus, which was given to the museum by the artist's wife. The museum also has an interesting collection of local archaeology, history and folklore. It includes objects from the prehistoric and Roman periods, Flemish pottery and furniture.

The moated **Ooidonk castle**, 1km south of the village of Bachte-Maria-Leerne, stands in a wooded park at the end of a long avenue of copper beeches.

Ooidonk Castle

This was originally a 13C fortress which was burnt by the citizens of Ghent in 1501 after the owner supported Philip the Handsome, and destroyed again in 1578 by the Calvinists. All that now survives of the 13C fortress are the corner towers. The castle was rebuilt at the end of the 16C by Philippe de Montmorency as an elegant Renaissance residence. The interior, mainly 19C, has some good furniture, porcelain, Beauvais tapestries, and an interesting collection of royal portraits.

The abbey at **Drongen**, west of Ghent, was founded by Premonstratensians in 1138 on an earlier Benedictine site. Erasmus was a frequent visitor. Dissolved by the French at the end of the 18C, the buildings were used soon afterwards by Lieven Bauwens, an enterprising tanner turned businessman, to house Belgium's first cotton-mill. He smuggled machinery from England and lured skilled English textile workers to work in Ghent.

The abbey has been occupied since 1837 by Jesuits. The church, tower, cloister and abbot's lodgings have survived. Most of the buildings date from the 17C and 18C. The **church** of 1736 has a *Pietà* from the workshop of Roger van der Weyden. It is dedicated to St Gerulph, who died c 746. This young Flemish man, the heir to a vast estate, was killed on his way home from church by a relative who hoped to inherit his wealth. Gerulph forgave his murderer as he lay dying.

The attractive village of **Sint-Martens-Latem**, 10km southwest of Ghent, lies in woods beside the River Leie. The Symbolist painters of the **First Latem School** settled here from c 1905. The first artists' colony included George Minne and Gustave van de Woestyne. The Expressionist painters of the **Second Latem School** began to arrive c 1910. They included Constant Permeke, Gustave De Smet and Frits van den Berghe. The **Museum Minne-Gevaert** at Kapitteldreef 45 contains works by George Minne displayed in a house built in 1922 by his son-in-law.

The village of **Deurle**, 2km southwest of Sint-Martens-Latem, has several small museums devoted to the two Latem schools. The **Museum Gustave De Smet** at Gustave De Smetlaan 1 occupies a house built by the artist in 1935, where he lived until his death in 1943. Virtually unchanged since his death, it contains many of De Smet's works.

The **Museum Leon De Smet** at Museumlaan 18 has paintings by Gustave's brother Leon. The **MDD** at 14 Museumlaan, formerly known as the **Museum Dhondt-Dhaenens**, was the gift of Jules and Irma Dhondt-Dhaenens. It displays a distinguished collection of 19C Flemish paintings and often has stimulating temporary exhibitions. Open Tues–Fri 13.00–17.00 and weekends 11.00–17.00.

The Romanesque Sint Jan-de-Doperkerk in the village of **Afsnee**, 4km west of Ghent on the Leie, dates from the 12C. The octagonal tower was added in the early 13C.

Laarne

The impressive Laarne castle, 13km east of Ghent, was begun in the 12C. All that survives of the original building are the cellars and perhaps the chapel. The present moated castle dates mainly from the 13C–14C, with some 17C alterations. The castle contains unusual 16C Brussels tapestries depicting the domestic life of an aristocratic household. It also has fine 17C furniture and an outstanding collection of 15C–18C silverware. Open Easter–Oct, Tues–Thur and weekends 14.00–17.30.

ANTWERP

Antwerp is a fascinating historic city with a cosmopolitan character and a keen sense of style. Its modern port is one of the largest in Europe, yet the old town has managed to retain its intimate charm. The diligent visitor will find forgotten Renaissance courtyards, splendid works of baroque art, and countless attractive cafés. With a population of half a million, Antwerp is the largest city in Flanders and the capital of Antwerp province. Its traditional industries are shipping and the diamond trade, though the city has recently gained international recognition for its bold fashion designers. The town is known as Antwerpen in Dutch and Anvers in French.

Practical information

 Where to stay
Hotels

£££ *Rubens*, Oude Beurs 29, ☎ 03.222.48.48, is an elegant hotel incorporating a 16C Renaissance mansion near the Grote Markt. Rates drop at the weekend.

££ *Antigone*, Jordaenskaai 11, ☎ 03.231.66.77, is an attractive modern hotel on the Scheldt waterfront near the Vleeshal.

££ *Villa Mozart*, Handschoenmarkt 3, ☎ 03.231.30.31, is a comfortable hotel opposite the Cathedral.

£ *Postiljon*, Blauwmoezelstraat 6,
☎ 03.231.75.75 is a small old-fashioned
hotel in the shadow of the cathedral.

Eating out
Restaurants

£££ *'t Fornuis*, Reynderstraat 24,
☎ 03.233.62.70, is considered the best
(and most expensive) restaurant in
Antwerp.

££ *Dock's Café*, Jordaenskaai 7, ☎
03.226.63.30, is a striking modern
brasserie on the waterfront with excellent seafood.

££ *Hippodroom*, Leopold de Waelplaats
10, ☎ 03.238.89.36, is a stylish modern restaurant opposite the Museum of
Fine Arts.

££ *In de Schaduw van de Kathedraal*,
Handschoenmarkt 17,
☎ 03.232.40.14, is a romantic restaurant in a house built against the cathedral.

££ *Reddende Engel*, Torfbrug 3,
☎ 03.233.66.30, is a rustic Provençal
restaurant run by a chef from Marseilles.

£ *Pasta*, Oude Koornmarkt 32, ☎
03.233.17.76, is an Italian restaurant
on several floors of a converted house.
The top floor has a good view of the
cathedral. Closed for lunch.

Cafés

Antwerp has every style of café, from
sober Viennese coffee houses to lively
Bruegelian taverns.

Fouquets, De Keyserlei 17, is a grand
café near Centraal Station.

De Foyer, Komedieplaats 19, is a beautiful 19C theatre café with a painted
ceiling on the first floor of the Bourla
theatre.

Elfde Gebod, Torfbrug 10, near the
Cathedral, is an eccentric café filled with
19C religious statues.

De Grote Witte Arend, Reyndersstraat
18, is an artistic café with a
Renaissance courtyard .

't Hofje, Oude Koornmarkt 16, is a tea-
room in a little house with a courtyard

on a lane in the Vlaeykensgang.

Paters Vaetje, Blauwmoezelstraat 2, is
a friendly café under the cathedral tower
with a long list of Belgian beers.

Pelgrom, Pelgrimstraat 15, is an atmospheric tavern in a 15C cellar with
benches, candles and antiques.

Zuiderterras on the waterfront, is a
modern café with a striking view of the
Scheldt.

Getting around
Airport

Antwerp has a small international airport at Deurne, 5km from the centre.

Railway Stations

The main railway station is Centraal
Station, a pleasant 15 min walk from the
Grote Markt. Most international and
national trains stop here. But some international trains only stop at Berchem, to
the south. Travellers then have to
change to a train for Centraal Station.
High-speed Thalys trains from Brussels,
Paris and Amsterdam stop only at
Berchem station, where there are frequent connections to Centraal Station.

Trams

Antwerp has a good tram system. Tram
2 and 15 run through a tunnel from
Centraal Station to Groenplaats (for the
cathedral). Tram 8 runs from
Groenplaats to Leopold de Waelplaats
(for the Fine Arts Museum).

Pedestrian tunnel to the beach

A 500m long pedestrian tunnel runs
under the Scheldt from the Sint-
Jansvliet to reach the small town beach.
Known as the Sint Annatunnel, it
opened in 1933. There is a striking view
of Antwerp from the left bank.

Tourist Information
**Antwerp city tourist
information office** is at Grote Markt
15, ☎ 03.232.01.03. Infowinkel at

Grote Markt 40 has cultural information, books on Antwerp, and attractive souvenirs including facsimile copies of the 1565 Plan of Antwerp by Virgilius Boloniensis and Cornelis Grapheus. Open Tuesday to Saturday 10.00 to 18.00.

Antwerp province tourist office is at Koningin Elisabethlei 16, 2018 Antwerp, ☎ 03.240.63.98. Antwerp province includes the attractive towns of Mechelen and Lier, which are covered in other chapters. Much of the Kempen region (also covered separately) is located in Antwerp province.

Banks and post office

BBL, Lange Gasthuisstraat 20. Kredietbank, Schoenmarkt 35. Currency exchange at Centraal Station, open daily 08.00–22.00. The main post office is at Groenplaats 16. A smaller office is located at Pelikaanstraat 12 near Centraal Station.

Church services

Services in English are held in the Keizerskapel, Keizerstraat 21, on Sundays at 18.00.

Boat trips

Tours of the port of Antwerp leave from the Steenplein from May–Sept every day except Mon and Wed at 13.00, 14.00, 15.00 and 16.00. Tours are daily July, Aug, and also at weekends Apr–Oct.

Guided tours

Most guided tours leave from the Grote Markt.
A **walking tour of the old town** with an English-speaking guide begins at the tourist office at 14.00 in July and August.
Tours by 19C **horse-drawn tram** are run from April to October beginning on Grote Markt.
Tours by **motorised rickshaw** and **horse-drawn carriage** begin on

Grote Markt in the summer.
Tours by **period tram** begin on Groenplaats.
Interesting walking tours of **Jewish Amsterdam** and **the Zuid district** are given occasionally in Dutch by Antwerpen Averechts.

Markets

A flea market dating back to 1549 is held on the Vrijdagmarkt, opposite the Plantin-Moretus Museum, on Wednesday and Friday mornings. The Vogelenmarkt is a lively general market held on Sunday mornings on the Theaterplein, south of the Rubenshuis.

Carillon concerts

A carillon of 49 bells hangs in the cathedral tower. Victor Hugo described it as 'a 130 metre high piano with the cathedral as the lid'. Concerts are played mid Jun–Sept on Mon 20.00–21.00 and on Fri all year from 11.30–12.30. The best places to listen are on Groenplaats and in the lanes of the Vlaeykensgang.

 Opening times
Museums

Most museums in Antwerp are closed on Mon, and 1–2 Jan, 1 May, Ascension, 1–2 Nov and 25–26 Dec.
Plantin-Moretus Museum (printing history and art works), Vrijdagmarkt, is open Tues–Sun 10.00–17.00.
Mayer van den Bergh Museum (fine and decorative art), Lange Gasthuisstraat 19, is open Tues–Sun 10.00–17.00.
Rubenshuis (house of the painter), Wapper 9, is open Tues–Sun 10.00–17.00.
National Maritime Museum (marine history), Steen, Sukerrui, open Tues 10.00–17.00.
Vleeshuis (paintings, musical instruments) Vleeshuisstraat, is open

Tues–Sun 10.00–17.00.
Volkskundemuseum (folklore),
Gildekamersstraat 2–4, is open
Tues–Sun 10.00–17.00.
Ethnographic Museum (ethnological material), Suikerrui 19, is open
Tues– Sun 10.00–17.00.
Museum voor Schone Kunsten
(fine art), Leopold de Waelplaats, is open
Tues–Sun 10.00–17.00.
Museum of Contemporary Art,
Leuvenstraat, is open Tues–Sun
10.00–17.00.
Photography Museum (old cameras
and photographs), Waalsekaai 47.
Closed for rebuilding until April 2001.
Open thereafter Tues–Sun 10.00–17.00.
Rockoxhuis (17C museum),
Keizerstraat 10, is open Tues–Sun
10.00–17.00.
Ridder Smit Van Gelder Museum
(painting and decorative arts), Belgielei
91, is open Tues–Sun 10.00–17.00.
Diamond Museum, Lange
Herentalsestraat 31 is open daily
10.00–17.00.
Maagdenhuis (history of orphanage
and 16C and 17C paintings), Lange
Gasthuisstraat 33, is open Mon–Fri
(closed Tues) 10.00–17.00 and at weekends 13.00–17.00.
Sterckshof Zilvercentrum (decorative arts and metalwork), Deurne, is
open Tues–Sun 10.00–17.30.
Brouwershuis (water-supply house
for breweries), Adriaan Brouwerstraat
20, is only open on request.
Poldermuseum Lillo (life on the polders), Lillo, is open Easter–Oct at weekends and public holidays 13.00–18.00.

Churches

Onze-Lieve-Vrouwkathedraal
(cathedral), Handschoenmarkt, is open
Mon–Fri 10.00–17.00, Sat 10.00–15.00
and Sun and holidays 13.00–16.00.
Sint Jacobskerk, Lange Nieuwstraat
73, is open Apr–Oct on Mon–Sat
14.00–17.00.

Sint Pauluskerk, Stoelstraat, is open
May–Sept daily 14.00–17.00.
Sint Andrieskerk, Korte
Ridderstraat, is open May–Sept daily
14.00–17.00.
Sint Annakapel or **Keizerskapel**,
Keizerstraat 21, is open daily
08.30–12.00 and 13.00–17.30.
Sint Carolus-Borromeuskerk,
Hendrik Conscienceplein, is open
Mon–Sat 10.00–12.30 and
14.00–17.00 (19.00 on Sat); Sun
10.00–12.45.

Other sights

Zoo, Koningin Astridplein, is open daily
09.00–18.45 in summer and
09.00–16.30 in winter.
Middelheim Sculpture Park is open
Jun and Jul 10.00–21.00; May and Aug
10.00–20.00; Apr and Sept
10.00–19.00; and Oct–Mar
10.00–17.00.
Stadhuis, Grote Markt, is open for
guided tours on Mon–Fri (closed Thur)
at 11.00, 14.00 and 15.00; Sat at
14.00 and 15.00 (no visits during official receptions).

Charges

The Photography Museum and
Rockoxhuis are free. The Museum voor
Schone Kunsten is free on Friday.

New developments

A new Antwerp historical museum is
planned to open in the early 21C. When
completed, it will probably contain the
collections of the Maritime Museum
(currently in the Steen), the Vleeshuis
Museum and the Ethnography Museum.
The Steen will then be restored in the
style of a medieval castle, while the
Vleeshuis will contain a small museum
of musical instruments on the ground
floor. A promising plan to create a fashion centre, perhaps in an empty building at Nationalestraat 28, was being discussed at the time of writing.

The severed hand

A giant named Druon Antigonus is said to have given birth to the city. He lived in a castle on the Scheldt, cutting off the hand of anyone who failed to pay a toll. Antigonus was finally killed by Silvius Brabo, a young relative of Julius Caesar. Brabo became the first duke of Brabant, giving his name to the dukedom (and later province). Some authorities believe the name Antwerp comes from 'hand werpen' (to throw the hand). A more likely if less colourful explanation is that it comes from 'Aen de werpen', which means 'at the cast' (of the anchor) or simply 'at the wharf'. A severed hand appears on the city's coat of arms.

History

The earliest record of a settlement dates back to the 2C. The first church is said to have been built by St Amand in 660. Benedictine monks from Ireland later began to drain the nearby polders. A fortress built here was destroyed by the Vikings in the 9C. The first town walls were constructed in the 11C, when the counts of Ardennes and Bouillon were the margraves of Antwerp. **Godfrey of Bouillon** (c 1060–1100), who led the First Crusade, was one of the margraves of Antwerp.

Antwerp passed to the Dukes of Brabant in the 13C. One of the dukes, John II, who died in 1312, was married to Margaret, daughter of Edward I of England. In 1338–40, when Jacob van Artevelde of Ghent made an alliance between the Flemish towns and England, Edward III held court at the abbey of St Bernard, near Hemiksem. His second son Lionel, later the Duke of Clarence, was born there. In 1357 **Louis de Male** invaded Brabant and regained Antwerp for the counts of Flanders. The town passed to Burgundy along with the rest of Flanders in 1384.

Antwerp grew rapidly in importance in the 15C, at the expense of Bruges, which was then beginning to decline. At the same time as Het Zwin was silting up, the Scheldt was being widened considerably by flooding in Zeeland. Antwerp eventually became the chief port of the Netherlands. A thousand foreign business houses were established in the city by the beginning of the 16C.

The origins of the Flemish School of painting can be traced back to the **Antwerp Guild of St Luke**, founded in 1454 by Philip the Good for the encouragement of painting. The guild was host to Albrecht Dürer during his stay in Antwerp in 1520–21.

The prosperity of Antwerp waned during the reign of Philip II, when the city was torn by religious conflict. The cathedral was pillaged in 1566 by the Calvinists and many of its treasures were destroyed. Ten years later, the disgruntled Spanish soldiers in Alva's army went on a murderous rampage in an episode that became known as the **Spanish Fury**. The following year, 1577, William of Orange drove the Spanish out of Antwerp, leading to a ban on Catholicism for the next eight years.

The Duke of Parma began a campaign in 1580 to reconquer Flanders for Spain. Antwerp finally capitulated in 1585 after withstanding a year's siege under Marnix van St Aldegonde. This was Parma's last real success in Flanders. It meant that Antwerp's fate would be tied up with the south (later Belgium) rather than the north (later the Netherlands).

The reign of **Archduke Albert** and his wife Isabella, who made their state entry to Antwerp on 20 December 1599, inaugurated a brief interlude of peace, when the city recovered something of its former grandeur. Inspired by Rubens, Antwerp developed a Baroque school of painting that included David Teniers the Elder, David Teniers the Younger and Jacob Jordaens. A literary circle emerged at the same time around the printer Balthasar Moretus, including the poet and city secretary Gevartius, and the women poets Anna and Maria Visscher. The learned Jesuit Bollandus died in Antwerp in 1665.

The Thirty Years War ended in 1648 with the signing of the **Peace of Münster**, the terms of which forced Spain to allow the Scheldt to be closed to shipping. Antwerp was ruined while the Dutch ports to the north prospered. It was only in 1795, when the estuary was reopened, that the city began to recover its former prosperity.

By the close of the 18C, when the French ruled the region, Antwerp's population had sunk to 40,000, from a peak of about 100,000 in the 16C. Its economy began to pick up slowly under **Napoleon**, who reopened the Scheldt and constructed a naval harbour which he referred to pugnaciously as 'a pistol aimed at the heart of England'.

Antwerp suffered considerably from a bombardment by the Dutch during the **Belgian Revolution** in 1830. The Dutch garrison based in the citadel was forced to surrender in 1832 by a French force led by Marshal Gérard, who had been sent to assist King Leopold I. The port began to develop again after 1862, when the right to levy dues on Scheldt shipping, which had been granted to the Dutch in 1839, was redeemed by Belgium's payment of 36 million francs.

Antwerp played an important role at the beginning of the **First World War**. The government arrived from Brussels on 17 August 1914, pursued by the German army which besieged the city on 28 September. The ring of forts around Antwerp, which had been seen as the last word in modern defence, were quickly taken.

1 • Centraal Station and the Meir

This walk begins at Centraal Station, a monumental neo-Renaissance building designed in 1905 by Louis Delacenserie. The **Zoo** (Dierentuin), open daily 09.00–18.15 in summer and 09.00–16.30 in winter, is located next to the station on Koningin Astridplein. Founded in 1843, it is attractively landscaped in romantic 19C style, with a bandstand, statues, artificial rocks and an elephant house modelled on an Egyptian temple. Unusual features include a night house where nocturnal animals can be observed in the dark, a winter garden landscaped as a tropical jungle, and a large pool with glass walls where penguins and sea otters swim. The zoo has a large breeding estate at Planckendael, near Mechelen.

The **Provincial Diamond Museum**, open daily 10.00–17.00, is on the other side of the station at Lange Herentalsestraat 31. This interesting museum covers all aspects of the diamond industry, including mining, cutting and polishing.

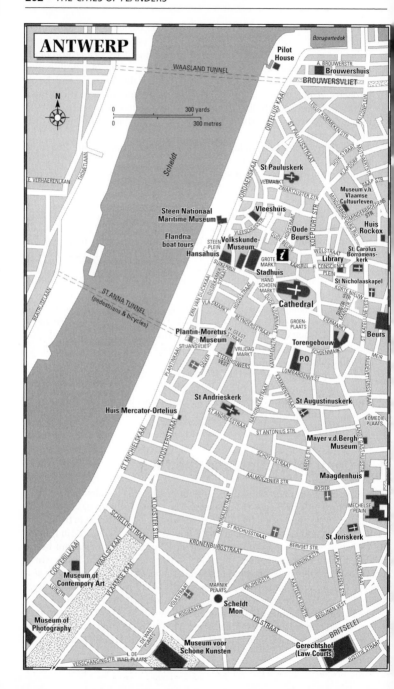

ANTWERP

WAASLAND TUNNEL

Bonapartedok

Pilot House

A. BROUWERSTR.

Brouwershuis

BROUWERSVLIET

ORTELIUS KAAI

LEGUIT KOMMEKEN STR.

FALCONPLEIN

N

0   300 yards
0   300 metres

Scheldt

JORDAENSKAAI

ST PAULUSSTRAAT

ST PAULUSSTRAAT

St Pauluskerk

VEEMARKT

ZWARTZUSTER STR.

HUI STRAAT

KLAPDORP STR.

MUTSAERTSTR.

RAAP STR.

E. VERHAERENLAAN

Steen Nationaal
Maritime Museum

Vleeshuis

MINDERBROEDERS STR.

Museum v.h.
Vlaamse
Cultuurleven

Huis
Rockox

Flandria
boat tours

Hansahuis

STEEN
PLEIN

VLEESHUISTR.

Oude
Beurs

OUDE BEURS

Volkskunde-
Museum

St Carolus
Borromens-
kerk

WOLSTRAAT

Library

H. CONSCIENCE PLEIN

St Nicholaaskapel

KORTE NIEUW STR.

GROTE
MARKT

Stadhuis

HAND
SCHOEN
MARKT

KAASRUI

SUIKERRUI

GILDEKAMER STR

HOOGSTRAAT

VLA SMARKT

Cathedral

OUDE KOORNMARKT

GROEN-
PLAATS

REYNDERSSTRAAT

EIERMARKT

ST KATELIJNE VEST

Beurs

MEIR

H. GEEST
STRAAT

KAMMENSTR

Torengebouw

P.O.

SCHOENMARKT

Plantin-Moretus
Museum

ST JANSVLIET

VRIJDAG
MARKT

STEENHOUWERS
VEST

LOMBARDENVEST

HUIDEVETTERSSTRAAT

PLANTINKAAI

LEYVER

ERN VAN DIJCKKAAI

St Andrieskerk

St Augustinuskerk

Huis Mercator-Ortelius

ST ANDRIESSTRAAT

ST ANTONIUS STR.

NATIONALESTRAAT

KAMMENSTR.

KOMEDIE
PLAATS

LANGE GASTHUISSTR.

Mayer v.d. Bergh
Museum

ST MICHIELSKAAI

KLOOSTERSTRAAT

SCHOYTESTRAAT

AALMOEZENIER STR.

Maagdenhuis

ROSIER

MECHELSE
PLEIN

SCHELDESTRAAT

KLOOSTER STR.

NATIONALESTRAAT

ST ROCHUSSTRAAT

BERVOET STR.

St Joriskerk

KRONENBURGSTRAAT

TERNINCKSTR.

KAPUCINESSEN STRAAT

LOUIZASTRAAT

Museum of
Contempory Art

COCKERILLKAAI

WAALSE KAAI

VLAAMSE KAAI

LUIKSTR.

VOLKSTRAAT

MARNIX
PLAATS

VRIJHEIDSTR.

KASTEELPLEINSTR.

BRITSELEI

Museum of
Photography

K. ROGIERSTR.

Scheldt
Mon

TOLSTRAAT

BEGIJNENVEST

L. DE WAEL
PLAATS

VERSCHANSINGSTR. WAEL PLAATS

Museum voor
Schone Kunsten

Gerechtshof
(Law Courts)

JUSTITIE STRAAT

ST ANNA TUNNEL
(pedestrians & bicycles)

BERTHASLAAN

THIJNELAAN

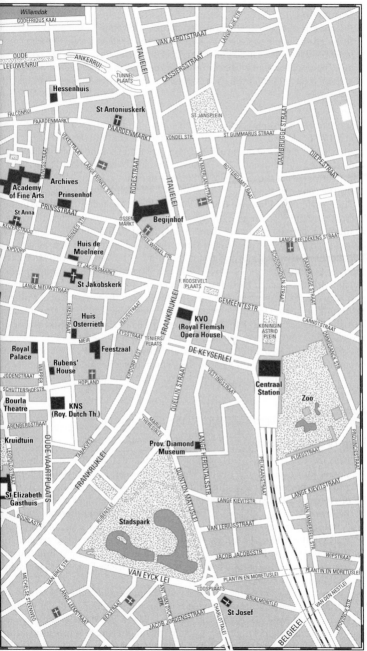

Ridder Smidt Van Gelder Museum, Koning Albertpark

> ### Diamonds
> Antwerp is the principal centre for diamond dealing in the world. The Antwerp diamond trade began in 1476 when Lodewijk van Bercken, a native of Bruges who lived in Antwerp, perfected the art of diamond polishing. The traders are now concentrated in the Pelikaanstraat, near Centraal Station. A large Orthodox Jewish population works in the Antwerp diamond trade.

The broad **De Keyserlei** runs from the station to the old town. Planned as a grand 19C boulevard, it is lined with cafés that spill out onto the pavement. You might stop for coffee at Fouquets (no. 17) or explore one of the modern shopping centres along the boulevard. The De Keyserlei soon crosses the busy Frankrijklei, which forms part of the semicircle of boulevards (*leien* in Dutch) laid out in 1859 along the course of the former 16C ramparts.

The neo-Baroque **Vlaamse Opera**, built by A. van Mechelen in 1907, is to the right. Cross the road to a small square with a 19C statue of David Teniers. Continuing down Leysstraat, there is another 19C statue commemorating Antoon van Dyck. Soon after this is Meir, originally a swamp but now an attractive shopping street with several grand 18C and 19C buildings. A. van Mechelen built the **Feestzaal** at nos 74–80 in 1908 as a shopping centre and concert hall.

The attractive Rococo **Huis Osterrieth** at no. 85 was designed by Jan Peter van Baurscheit the Younger. The same architect built the former **Royal Palace** at no. 50 in 1746. Originally owned by the Van Susteren family, this Rococo mansion was occupied briefly by Napoleon in 1811. The **Film Museum** now screens classic movies in the slightly dilapidated interior.

Turn left from Meir into Wapper, an attractive square with a fountain and benches. A gate on the right leads to the former stables behind the royal palace. Art exhibitions are held in a modern gallery attached to the stables.

Rubens House
The Rubens House, open Tues–Sun 10.00–17.00, is at no. 9.

History of the house

> Built from 1610–1617, this splendid mansion and studio gives us an impression of Rubens' immense wealth. The land alone cost Rubens 10,000 florins, which was a considerable sum for a young artist. A humanist and town clerk of Antwerp called Woverius wrote in 1620 that the mansions of Rubens and Balthasar Moretus, 'will evoke the astonishment and admiration of visitors.'
>
> Rubens spent most of his life in this house and painted many of his great works in the studio. His son was born here in 1618 and his daughter died in the house in 1624. Two years later, his frail first wife, Isabella Brant, died from the plague. His second wife, the voluptuous Hélène Fourment, moved in with Rubens in 1630.
>
> The house became a meeting-place for the noble and cultivated society of Flanders. Rubens' visitors included Isabella, the daughter of Philip II (and known, curiously, as Archduke Isabella), Marie de Medicis and George Villiers, Duke of Buckingham. A steady stream of Flemish artists visited the house and sometimes worked in the studio, including Antoon van Dyck,

Frans Snyders and Lucas Faydherbe.

After Rubens' death in 1640, the house was sold. It was the home of William Cavendish, later Duke of Newcastle, from 1649 to 1660. Cavendish had fled from England a short time before Charles I was beheaded. He established a riding school in the garden, which was visited by Charles II.

Later owners were less respectful; the mansion eventually fell into disrepair and its contents were sold off. Efforts to secure it for the city started as early as 1762, but it was not until 1937 that the mansion was finally acquired by Antwerp council, by which time little of the original fabric remained. The building was skilfully restored by Emiel van Averbeke and opened as a museum in 1946. The interiors were furnished in the style of Rubens' period, though very little comes from the artist's own collection.

Enter the building through the Italianate Baroque studio, to the right of the Flemish mansion. The ticket desk is located in the **Antechamber**, which is decorated with handsome gilt leather wall hangings. Begin in the **Great Studio** where Rubens and his pupils produced an estimated 2500 works. The largest canvases were taken out of the studio through a special high door on the right. The walls are hung with several works by Rubens, including an early *Adam and Eve* painted before 1600, and two paintings of angels from a lost altarpiece made for the church of Notre-Dame de Finistère in Brussels. The studio also has works by Rubens pupils, include a *Neptune and Amphitrite* by Jacob Jordaens.

Cross the courtyard to reach the family house which is entered by the **Parlour**, following in the footsteps of the many 17C visitors who waited here before being shown in to meet the master. The room is hung with gilt leather and decorated with several paintings, including a *Presentation in the Temple* by Jordaens and an *Adoration of the Magi* by Adam van Noort. The portrait of *Jan Wildens* is an old copy of a Van Dyck original now in Vienna. The print by Harrewijn of the Rubens House (after a drawing by Jan de Croes) was one of several old documents which Van Averbeke relied on when he restored the mansion.

Pass into the tiled **Kitchen**, which is furnished with pot hangers, ointment jars, plate-racks and a folding table believed to be early 17C Dutch. The dishes prepared in the kitchen were brought to the **Serving Room** next door before being taken into the dining room. A handsome linen press now stands in the centre of the room.

The long **Dining Room** is hung are several interesting paintings, including an elderly *Self-portrait* by Rubens which dates from c 1625–28. There is also a flower-study by the Jesuit painter Daniel Seghers and a still-life by Frans Snyders. Rubens' nephew described Rubens as abstemious at table. He apparently ate little during the day in case it affected his output. He rode his horse at five o'clock and then returned home to dine quietly with friends.

Now enter the **Art Gallery** below a 17C stone statuette of the Madonna. It was in this room that Rubens displayed the best works from his large private collection, which amounted to some 300 paintings when it was sold off after his death. The room has been restored as a picture gallery, with various paintings by 17C artists whose works Rubens owned. There are also two preliminary oil sketches by Rubens for lost paintings of the *Adoration of the Shepherds* and the *Martyrdom of St Adrianus*.

> ### *The picture gallery of Cornelis van der Geest*
> One of the most interesting paintings in the Rubens House is by Willem van Haecht. It shows the *Picture Gallery of Cornelis van der Geest* at the time of a visit by the Archdukes Albert and Isabella to the collection in 1615. One of Rubens' large circle of friends, Van der Geest was a wealthy Antwerp merchant. He is shown discussing a picture by Quinten Metsys with his visitors. There are also works by Rubens and Dürer and a lost Van Eyck in the painting.

Now enter the curious **Sculpture Gallery**, a semi-circular room where Rubens displayed a collection of Classical statues acquired during his stay in Italy. The works here include a terracotta bust of a satyr attributed to Lucas Faydherbe and an antique bust probably brought back from Italy by Rubens. Once believed to be Seneca, it is now thought to represent either the Alexandrian grammarian and poet Philetas of Cos, or the dramatist Aristophanes.

Go upstairs and turn left into the **Large Bedroom**. Rubens died in this attractive room overlooking the garden. It contains several paintings including a portrait attributed to Otto Venius of *Nicolaas Rockox*, the 17C Antwerp burgomaster who was a close friend of Rubens. There is also a *Martyrdom of St Marcus and St Marcellinus* by Veronese.

A cabinet contains a rock-crystal necklace in a gold setting which probably belonged to Hélène Fourment. The gold chain with a medallion of Christian IV of Denmark was a present to Rubens, possibly from Golnitzius, the king's secretary, who visited this house in c 1625.

Cross the landing to the **Small Bedroom**, furnished with a 17C Flemish bed. The *Portrait of Hélène Fourment* was probably painted by Jan van Boeckhorst. A tender *Portrait of a dead child in a bed* was painted by Matthijs van den Bergh, a pupil of Rubens.

The **Linen Room** contains an early 17C Antwerp cupboard. The next room, known as the **Corner Bedroom**, has the well-worn chair used by Rubens in his official capacity of Dean of the Guild of St Luke. The name 'Pet. Paul Rubens 1633' is in gilt letters on the back. The coat of arms below belongs to a chamber of rhetoric called De Violieren which had close ties with the painters' guild.

The family met in the evenings in the **Living Room** next door. The room contains several paintings, including Adam van Noort's *Sermon of John the Baptist* and Pieter Snayers' *View of Antwerp*. There are also two fascinating *Portraits* of Rubens' paternal grandparents painted by Jacob Claesz of Utrecht. Rubens' grandfather was a pharmacist and spice merchant. Dated 1530 on the back, the portraits were done soon after the couple married.

On the **Landing** is a large 17C tapestry signed by a Brussels weaver. It illustrates the *Death of Achilles*, who could only be killed by a wound in the heel. The stairs lead up to the **Private Studio**, which contains several 17C paintings and allows a good view of the garden when the windows are open. Descend to the courtyard by a handsome carved staircase modelled on the original staircase of 1617. A wooden gallery on the first floor allowed Rubens' clients to examine the paintings hung in the Great Studio.

The ornate Baroque façade of the studio can be admired from the **Courtyard**. The wall is laden with sculptures, including busts of Classical philosophers, Roman gods, and friezes illustrating Classical legends. The courtyard is divided from the garden by a splendid baroque **Portico**. Possibly designed by Rubens himself, this triple arch appears in the background of several paintings by Rubens, Antoon van Dyck and other Antwerp artists. It has survived virtually intact, though the statues on top were added in 1939 by Edward Deckers to replace the original figures of Mercury and Minerva.

There are two quotations chosen by Rubens from Juvenal's *Satires* above the **side arches**. 'Permittes ipsis expendere numinibus, quid/Conveniat nobis, rebusque sit utile nostris,/Carior est illis homo quam sibi' and 'Orandum est ut sit mens sana in corpore sano/Fortem posce animum et mortis terrore car-entem/Nesciat irasci, cupiat nihil.' The first translates as: 'Leave it to the gods to give what is fit and useful for us; man is dearer to them than to himself.' The other reads: 'One must pray for a healthy mind in a healthy body, for a coura-geous soul, which is not afraid of death, which is free of wrath and desires noth-ing.' These inscriptions remind us of Rubens' deep Classical learning and his stoicism.

The seductive **Garden** was replanted in 17C style using old prints and paint-ings by Rubens. The pergola overgrown with honeysuckle was copied from Rubens' painting of *The Walk in the Garden*, now in the Alte Pinakothek in Munich. The **pavilion** at the far end was designed by Rubens in the style of a Classical temple. It contains a statue of Hercules, guardian of the land, attrib-uted to Lucas Faydherbe. Hercules is flanked by Bacchus, who holds a bunch of grapes, and by a modern statue of Venus by Willy Kreitz. This replaces a statue of Ceres, the goddess of fertility. The figure in the niche above represents Honour holding a cornucopia. An oval monument to the right of the pavilion (behind the fountain) commemorates Rubens' brother and his son, both called Philip.

On leaving the house, turn left to reach the modern **Koninklijke Nederlandse Schouwburg** (Royal Dutch Theatre) on Theaterplein. At the time of writing, part of Victor Horta's Maison du Peuple, an Art Nouveau building demolished in 1965 in Brussels, was being rebuilt on a site next to the theatre.

Now turn right along the attractive Schuttershof to reach the beautiful **Bourla Theatre**, built in Neo-classical style by Pierre Bruno Bourla in 1834. The theatre café on the first floor is particularly grand.

An attractive little botanic garden known as the **Kruidtuin** is near here on Leopoldstraat. Our next museum is located on the Lange Gasthuisstraat, which runs roughly parallel to Leopoldstraat.

Mayer van den Bergh Museum

The Mayer van den Bergh Museum, open Tues–Sun from 10.00–17.00, at Lange Gasthuisstraat 19 is a remarkable and virtually unknown museum with an eclectic collection of medieval, late Gothic and Renaissance art including paintings, furniture, metalwork, sculpture, tapestries, ceramics and objets d'art. Small 15C and 16C stained-glass panels and medallions have been placed in some of the windows. With its 19C period rooms, large chim-neypieces and elegant furnishings, the Mayer van den Bergh rivals the best private collections in London or Paris. Its most famous work is Pieter Bruegel the Elder's *Dulle Griet* in Room 9.

A passionate collector

Emil Mayer was born in Cologne in 1824. He settled in Antwerp in 1849, became a wealthy businessman and, in 1857, married Henriette van den Bergh, the daughter of a prosperous local family. Their son, Fritz Mayer van den Bergh (1858–1901) devoted his life to the study and collection of art treasures. He acquired works by great masters, but also lesser known artists who appealed to his erudite taste. His mother provided constant artistic and financial support. After her son was killed accidentally in 1901, she established this museum in his memory. Although 16C in appearance, the building incorporates the most modern display methods of the time. On Henriette's death in 1920, the administration of the museum passed to a trust.

Begin in **Room 1**, which has interesting 17C Dutch portrait groups, including *The Family of Meyndert Sonck*, by Jan Rotius and *The Family of Willem van der Does, Burgomaster of The Hague*, by Jan Mytens.

Room 2 contains a large 15C chimneypiece from Tournai. Three 19C neo-Gothic display cases contain exquisite **miniature works** by Jan Brueghel, Hans Bol, Frans Hals and Gillis van Coninxloo. This room also has a Dutch inn scene by Adriaen van Ostade, a *Temptation of St Antony* by David Teniers the Younger and a flower painting by Daniel Seghers.

The tiny **Room 3** is decorated with two stone columns with female figures. These rare examples of French 12C Gothic sculpture come from a vanished monastery at Châlons-sur-Marne. There is also a Late Gothic portable altar of c 1500 from Mechelen and a polychromed stone *Virgin and Child* of c 1380 by an anonymous Bruges Master.

Room 4 is dominated by an outstanding *Calvary Triptych* by Quinten Metsys and a beautiful 15C embroidery with *St Mary Magdalene*. The **stairs** are hung with 16C and 17C tapestries from Bruges and Oudenaarde. A portrait of Fritz Mayer van den Bergh, painted after his death, hangs here.

The small **Room 5** contains several still life paintings by Willem Heda and Roelof Koets. The windows incorporate 15C and 16C stained glass fragments. The wood-panelled **Room 6** has an exquisite polychromed wood sculpture of *St John* resting his head on the breast of Christ. Carved in c 1300 by Heinrich of Constance, this work was described in a medieval chronicle as: 'so beautiful that it astonished everyone, even the sculptor.' The same room contains three small panels from the **Antwerp-Baltimore Polyptych** (the other panels are in Baltimore). Dating from c 1400, these tiny works are among the earliest examples of Netherlands panel painting. The scenes illustrate the story of Joseph's hose, which was cut up to provide the infant Christ with swaddling clothes.

Room 7 is mainly devoted to Renaissance works, including a *Peasant Interior* of 1556 by Pieter Aertsen, a *Landscape of 1550* by Henri met de Bles, a *Triptych* by Ambrosius Benson, an *Adoration* by Adriaen Isenbrant and a *St Christopher* by Jan Mostaert.

Stairs lead up to **Room 8**, where small sculptures from the 13C to 15C are arranged chronologically in a row of cases. One of the display cases contains some **portrait medallions**, including one of *Christina Metsys* by Quinten Metsys. This is one of the earliest portrait medallions surviving in the Netherlands.

The museum's most famous painting hangs in **Room 9**. Known as *Dulle Griet* (Mad Meg), it was painted by **Pieter Bruegel the Elder** in Antwerp. It was bought by Mayer van den Bergh in 1894 for 394 marks at an auction in Cologne. Its previous owners included the Emperor Rudolph II.

The date on the painting is partly illegible, but is thought to be either 1562 or 1564. Painted when Bruegel was still under the influence of Hieronymus Bosch, it shows *Dulle Griet* striding resolutely towards the mouth of Hell. Various interpretations have been placed on the painting. Some have seen Dulle Griet as a witch or sorceress. Others claim that she is a Flemish folklore figure used to scare the children. The figure behind Dulle Griet, who is ladling coins out of his distended anus, suggests to some scholars that the picture may be an allegory of avarice. Other authorities argue that the painting refers to the wars which devastated the Low Countries in the 16C.

The same room contains Pieter Bruegel the Elder's *The Twelve Proverbs*, painted on wooden plates in the 1560s. There is also Pieter Brueghel the Younger's meticulous copies of his father's *Census at Bethlehem* and *Winter Landscape*.

Next is the Library in **Room 10**. This evocative room hung with gilt leather contains a unique collection of Renaissance lead plaquettes made by the German Peter Flötner in the late 1530s.

The next two rooms (**nos 11** and **12**) were specially designed to incorporate 18C wood panelling salvaged from a house in Tournai. The glass cases contain Chinese and Japanese porcelain. The walls are hung with 18C French portraits by Nicolas de Largillière and Louis Tocqué.

Maagdenhuis

On leaving the museum, turn left to reach the Maagdenhuis at no. 33, open Mon–Fri 10.00–17.00 (except Tues, when it is closed) and at weekends 13.00–17.00.

This handsome Renaissance building with a courtyard and chapel is another of Antwerp's secret delights. Formerly an orphanage for girls, it has an entrance and chapel built in 1564, while the rest of the building was completed in 1636. Look out for the charming reliefs of orphan girls above the entrance and the 17C wooden figure of one of the orphans, 'Houten Klara', in the courtyard.

The building now houses a fine collection of **16C and 17C paintings** and an **archive** containing documents from the orphanage. The former **chapel** has a curious collection of 63 porridge bowls used by orphan girls in the 16C and 17C. It also contains several caps and coats worn by the orphans in 1860, some 19C orphans' tokens for bread and peat, and the token of a girl who was reclaimed by her mother in 1811. A 1232 city seal (no. 51 in the collection) is the oldest known seal of Antwerp. There is also the 1519 certificate of Election of Charles V as Holy Roman Emperor, still bearing five of the original seven seals.

The orphans' tale

The Maagdenhuis displays a revolving wooden cupboard where orphans were once deposited by their mothers for admission to the orphanage. It also has a collection of tokens which were left by parents so that they could come back at a later date and claim their child. The most widespread practice was to cut a playing card in two and leave one half with the child. The orphans were taught useful skills such as needlework.

Other rooms contain paintings by Flemish artists, including an *Orphan Girl at Work* and a *Portrait of an Old Lady before a Crucifix* by Cornelius de Vos; *The*

Multiplication of Jacob's Flocks by David Teniers the Younger; two 16C wooden statues of *St Barbara and St Anna*, a *Descent from the Cross* by Jacob Jordaens; a *St Hieronymus* by Antoon van Dyck; a 15C *Triptych of the Virgin with Saints* by Gerard van der Meire; a *Mass of St Gregory* by an Unknown Master of the late 15C; a *Last Supper* by Lambert Lombard; a *Mary Magdalen* by Jan Massys and an *Adoration of the Shepherds* by Jan van Scorel.

Other notable works include *The Wedding at Cana* by Frans Francken the Elder; a mid-16C Chasuble with scenes of the *Passion*; a *Last Supper* by Pieter Pourbus and a *Triptych of Calvary* by the 16C Master of the Antwerp Crucifixion. One of the most impressive works is *The Last Judgement, The Seven Works of Mercy and the Seven Deadly Sins* by an Unknown Antwerp Master of the late 15C. The presence of Christ identifies the Mercies, while the Devil indicates the Sins.

Your ticket to the Maagdenhuis is valid for the chapel of the **Sint Elisabeth Gasthuis**, which is reached by continuing down Lange Gasthuisstraat to **no. 45**. This hospital is the oldest foundation of its kind in Antwerp. Established c 1204 within the city walls, it was already too small by 1238 when it moved to its present site (at the time a meadow outside the city walls). The nave of the chapel dates from the 15C. The altar surround was designed by Artus Quellin the Younger, while the pulpit is by Erasmus Quellin.

Continue south to the Mechelseplein, where the neo-Gothic **Sint Joriskerk** was built in 1853. It incorporates fragments of an older 14C church where Jan Brueghel and Jan and Pieter Appelmans were buried.

Now turn down Sint Jorispoort to reach Leopoldplaats, a small square with a statue of Leopold I carved by Willem Geefs in 1867.

2 • The Cathedral

This walk begins on the Handschoenmarkt, an intimate square below the cathedral. As its name suggests, this square was once the scene of a glove market. It is surrounded by old houses occupied by cafés, restaurants and postcard shops. The painter David Teniers the Younger was born in 1610 in the house at no. 13.

A curious stone well with a graceful ironwork canopy stands in front of the cathedral. This was probably made by Quinten Metsys in c 1495. Metsys is said to have begun his career as a smith, but retrained as a painter after he fell in love with an artist's daughter. A tablet attached to the cathedral nearby refers to this old legend. 'Connubialis Amor de Mulcibre fecit Apellem' (Connubial love turned Vulcan into Apelles), it says. The canopy above the well is decorated with a small statue of Silvius Brabo holding a severed hand.

A monument stands at the base of the cathedral's unfinished south tower. Carved by Jef Lambeaux, it commemorates the architect Pieter Appelmans, who designed much of the cathedral.

Onze-Lieve-Vrouwkathedraal
The Onze-Lieve-Vrouwkathedraal is open Mon–Fri 10.00–17.00, Sat 10.00–15.00, Sun and holidays 13.00–16.00. Although it is the largest Gothic church in Belgium, it is hemmed in by old houses which give it a picturesque appearance, but make it difficult to view the building as a whole. Its most

distinctive feature is the north spire, which was for many centuries the tallest tower in the Low Countries. The cathedral contains numerous paintings including three masterpieces by Rubens.

History of the cathedral

An ancient chapel which stood here was replaced in the 12C by a Romanesque church, parts of which were discovered during restoration work in 1988–90. The present cathedral was built between 1352 and 1521. The first part to be built was the choir, which was probably completed by the early 15C. Several generations of architects worked on the construction. The overall plan was probably drawn up by Pieter Appelmans. Work on the new west front began in 1425. After the Romanesque nave was demolished, work then started on the Gothic nave. The graceful tower, 123m high, was built in several stages. The section up to the gallery beneath the clock was completed by 1431, while the octagonal top was added in c 1521 by Domien de Waghemakere.

Several bells hang in the cathedral tower. The largest, which was hoisted up in 1507, is named 'Carolus' after Charles V, who sponsored its 'baptism'. A carillon of 49 bells also hangs in the cathedral tower.

Charles V commissioned an enormous new choir in 1519 that was to have been as large as the existing church. He laid the foundation stone in 1521, but the project was abandoned in 1533 after the church was badly damaged by fire. The outline of the planned choir is marked by the curved lane that runs from the Lijnwaadmarkt to the Groenplaats. The cathedral was pillaged in 1566 by Calvinist iconoclasts. A further blow was struck in 1794, when most of the art treasures, including paintings, stained-glass and choir stalls, were removed by the French. The church was closed until 1802, when some of its treasures were returned; other churches also donated some of their works of art. A major restoration project, which began in 1965, was nearing completion at the time of writing. The exterior stonework has been restored to its original clean-cut state, while the splendid proportions of the nave and choir can again be appreciated after decades of restoration work.

Enter by the **west portal** below the unfinished south tower. A small chapel on the right is set aside for prayer. It is lit by a window with a fragment of stained glass by Abraham van Diepenbeek. This was salvaged from a 1635 window depicting the *Four Almoners*, which was destroyed by the French in 1794.

Pass the ticket office (entry charge) to enter the cathedral. A useful leaflet is sold which indicates all the works of art in the cathedral. The **nave** has seven aisles, separated by six rows of pillars. These rise, without capitals, to the vault, which was built in 1614. Turn right at the west end to look at the Baroque memorial to Bishop Capello carved in 1676 by Artus Quellin the Younger. The same sculptor carved a marble statue of Jonathan nearby in 1650–60. The painting of the *Miraculous Draught of Fishes* on the adjacent wall was painted in 1589 by Hans van de Elsburgh. The stained glass-window with St Peter and St Paul (to the right) was made by J.B. Capronnier in 1867.

Go down the south aisle, past an unusual *Stations of the Cross* series painted by L. Hendrickx and F. Vinck in 1865–66. The **Chapel of the Blessed**

Sacrament contains an altar with a painting of the *Disciples at Emmaus* painted in 1808 by W. Herreyns. The last window on the right in this chapel depicts the *Last Supper*. It was made in 1503 by L. Van Noort. The pulpit in the nave was carved by Michel van der Voort in 1713 for the abbey of Hemiksem.

At the **crossing**, look up to see a circular painting at the top of the octagonal lantern of 1535. Painted by Cornelis Schut in 1647, it shows, appropriately, *The Assumption*. There is a painting by Rubens on the same subject on the high altar. Painted in 1626, this is one of six versions of the *Assumption* by Rubens. Two of Rubens greatest works hang in the north and south transepts. Begin with the painting in the south transept (on the right).

The Descent from the Cross

The *Descent from the Cross* triptych in the south transept was painted in 1611–14 for the altar of the Guild of Arquebusiers. The central panel is perfectly composed; its restrained style reflects the lessons Rubens had learnt during his stay in Italy. Antoon van Dyck is said to have restored the canvas after it was damaged in Rubens' studio. He is attributed with painting the cheek and chin of the Virgin and the arm of St Mary Magdalene. The insides of the shutters are decorated with the *Visitation and the Presentation in the Temple*, while the outsides have portraits of *St Christopher and the Hermit*.

Several other paintings hang in the south transept, including *The Marriage Feast at Cana* by Martin de Vos, and a *Last Supper* by Otto Venius (or Van Veen) from the early 17C. There is also a 17C painting of St Francis by Murillo.

The **ambulatory chapels** are off the choir. Beginning from the south transept, the **first chapel** is painted with faded 19C murals. The **second chapel** contains a monument to the printer Jan Moretus (d. 1601) and his wife. The *Resurrection* triptych, with John the Baptist and St Catherine on the wings, was painted by Rubens in 1612. A curious early 20C altarpiece by J. Janssens opposite shows *Our Lady of Peace* tending to wounded First World War soldiers. The predella has five small paintings of burning Belgian cities. A spiral staircase next to this chapel descends to an *archaeological crypt* where you can see the foundations of the Romanesque church and five brick tombs.

The **third chapel** contains a tomb carved by Artus Quellin the Younger in memory of Bishop Capello (d. 1676). The **fourth chapel** contains the tomb of Christopher Plantin (d. 1589). The chapel contains a 1591 *Triptych of the Last Judgement* by Jacob de Backer. The left wing has portraits of Christopher Plantin, his only son and St Christopher; the right wing shows his wife, his seven daughters and St John.

The **sixth chapel** contains a polychrome *Mater Dolorosa* by Artus Quellin the Younger. The sculpture of *Christ in the Tomb*, in a niche on the left, dates from the 15C. This chapel, at the back of the high altar, contains the tomb of Isabella of Bourbon, who died in 1465. She was the second wife of Charles the Bold.

The **ninth chapel** contains six architectural models illustrating the development of the cathedral from the 12C to the 16C. The **St Anthony Chapel** is behind the 10th and 11th chapels. This has two interesting stained-glass windows of 1503. The **Burgundian window** on the left depicts Philip the Fair and Joanna of Aragon, while the **English window** on the right shows the kneeling figures of Henry VII of England and his wife. It was commissioned to commemorate the commercial treaty between Henry and Philip the Fair. A small 15C Spanish altarpiece between the windows shows St Michael and the Dragon on a gold background.

Now you come to the **north transept**, where a 16C painting by Frans Francken the Elder shows *Jesus in the Temple Confronting the Doctors*. The doctors' faces are said to be modelled on Luther, Calvin and other theologians.

The Raising of the Cross

The *Raising of the Cross* triptych in the north transept was painted by **Rubens** in 1610. Commissioned for the St Walburga church, near the Steen (demolished in the 19C), it was the artist's first major work after his return from Italy. The central panel shows the *Nailing to the Cross*; the right shutter a group of Roman soldiers with the two thieves in the background, while the left shutter shows the disciples and the holy women (including an astonishing portrait of an ugly old woman). The outside of the shutters have portraits of St Eligius and St Walburga (left), and St Catherine and St Amand (right). The work originally had an upper panel with God the Father and two Angels, and a predella. Rubens appears to have been inspired in this work by Tintoretto's great *Calvary* in the Scuola di San Rocco at Venice.

Now go down the **north aisle**, where the statues on the confessionals were carved by Hendrik Verbruggen in the 18C. A pillar at the end of the aisle has a funeral monument to the Kuerlinckx family carved by Pieter Scheemaeckers in 1688. The cathedral bookshop is just beyond here.

On leaving the cathedral, head down the narrow lane next to the south tower to reach the **Groenplaats**, a large square with several cafés that stands on the site of the town graveyard. The bronze statue of Rubens in the square was carved in 1843 by Willem Geefs.

3 • The Plantin-Moretus Museum and its neighbourhood

This walk begins on **Grote Markt** and continues down Hoogstraat, where the painter Jacob Jordaens was born in 1593 in a house on the site of nos 11–13. A short detour left along Reyndersstraat brings you to a passage at nos 4–6 which leads to the **Jordaenshuis**. Jordaens moved into an older house here in 1618 with his wife Catharina, the oldest daughter of his teacher Adam van Noort. He built the baroque mansion in 1641 and lived here until his death in 1678. After years of neglect, the mansion was restored in 1998 as an art gallery. The former coach house is occupied by an attractive coffee house called *Het Koetshuis*. The original stone drinking troughs can be seen behind the bar. The courtyard is open daily 09.00–18.00.

Back on Hoogstraat, turn left down Heilig Geeststraat to reach the **Vrijdagmarkt**, the scene of a lively flea market on Wednesday and Friday mornings.

Plantin-Moretus Museum

The Plantin-Moretus Museum, open Tues–Sun 10.00–17.00, is at no. 22. It occupies the former home and printing works of the famous printer Christopher Plantin and his successor Balthasar Moretus. This is one of the most evocative museums in Europe, still furnished with old printing presses, manuscripts and several paintings by Rubens. A visit here offers a unique glimpse of the domestic and business environment of a rich master-printer in the 16C and 17C.

The Plantin-Moretus family

Christopher Plantin (1514–89) was born in France at St Avertin, near Tours. While apprenticed to the printer Robert Macé in Caen, Normandy, he married Jeanne Rivière. He left France in 1549 and came to Antwerp, where he became a citizen and a member of the Guild of St Luke in 1550. He worked at first as a bookbinder, enjoying considerable success at this trade. While crossing the Meir one evening in 1555 he was assaulted by some drunkards, who mistook him for a man who had insulted them. He received a serious sword wound in his shoulder which forced him to give up manual work. Taking up printing instead, he soon published his first work *La Institutione di una fanciulla nata nobilmente*, a guide for the education of young ladies of good family.

Plantin made his name four years later with his sumptuous book on the funeral ceremonies of Charles V. He was appointed by Philip II as Prototypus Regis in 1570. His most famous work was the Biblia Polyglotta, an edition of the bible in Latin, Greek, Hebrew, Chaldean and Syriac, published in eight folio volumes in 1572. His good relations with the Spanish monarchy earned him the monopoly of printing missals, breviaries and other liturgical books for Spain and the Spanish empire. During the Calvinist years he continued to practise as a Catholic, but managed to maintain good relations with the Protestants. He was visited by William of Orange and became official printer to the States-General and the city of Antwerp.

Plantin was forced to moved to Leiden and then Cologne because of financial difficulties in 1583–85. He returned to Antwerp after the city had been taken by the Duke of Parma and continued his printing business here until his death on 1 July 1589. The business then passed to his son-in-law Jan Moerentorf (or Moretus). He died in 1610 and was succeeded by his son Balthasar, who ran the business until his death in 1641. Perhaps the most brilliant member of the family, Balthasar was in touch with all the principal scholars and artists of his day. He was an intimate friend of Rubens, who designed illustrations and title pages for many of his books.

The firm continued to produce books until the middle of the 19C, though it was no longer a business concern. Finally, in 1876, Edward Joannes Hyacinth Moretus-Plantin handed over the Officina Plantiniana to the city. It opened as a museum in 1877.

The museum contains an outstanding collection of more than 20,000 books, including publications of the Plantin-Moretus family, and works by other Antwerp firms and foreign printers. There are about 150 incunabula, including the only copy in Belgium of the 36-line **Gutenberg Bible**. The museum also has the **family archives**, and an impressive collection of manuscripts, drawings and paintings. The collection of printing equipment includes some 15,000 woodblocks, 3,000 copperplates and various old printing tools. The family collection of porcelain is also on display.

The entrance to the museum was only built in the 18C. When Christopher Plantin moved here in 1576, renaming the house **The Golden Compasses**, the front door was on Hoogstraat and the only access to the Vrijdagmarkt was by a narrow passage. Plantin constructed several houses along Heilig Geeststraat and, in 1579, built a large printing workshop at the south end of the garden. He also obtained permission to cover a part of the canal which ran along the south side of his property, where he built a small Renaissance house. Used as a store for some three centuries, this is now the caretaker's house.

Further improvements were made by Balthasar, who gave the inner court its handsome appearance. The **façade** on Vrijdagmarkt was added in the 18C after the family bought and demolished several small houses on the site. The bas-relief above the door was carved by Artus Quellin the Elder. It originally decorated the façade on Hoogstraat. A German V rocket exploded in the Vrijdagmarkt in 1945, causing considerable damage to the house.

The **entrance hall** contains busts of Edward Moretus-Plantin and Burgomaster Leopold de Wael who jointly negotiated the sale of the house in 1876. An 18C room off the vestibule contains mementoes of the poet Emile Verhaeren.

The intimate **Room 1** is hung with rare 16C Flemish tapestries. They depict the legend of the *Queen of the Massagetes*, who defeated and slew Cyrus the Great. The compass motif of Christopher Plantin is woven into the fabric. An old copy of Rubens' *Lion Hunt* hangs above the chimneypiece. The original is in Munich's Alte Pinakothek.

There are portraits of the Plantin family and their friends in **Room 2**. Ten of the portraits, including one of *Christopher Plantin*, are by Pieter Paul Rubens. The portraits of *Balthasar* and *Gevartius* were painted by Thomas Bosschaert. The room also contains two 17C cabinets and a silver-gilt clock in the shape of a bell-tower which is said to have been given to the family by Archdukes Albert and Isabella.

Room 3 contains more paintings, including works by Daniel Seghers and Erasmus Quellin. Several display cases contain rare manuscripts from the 9C to the 16C. The works include the 15C *Chronicle of Froissart*, an early 15C Bible of King Wenceslas of Bohemia, Sedulius' 9C *Carmen Paschale* (with Prosperus' Epigrammata), Boethius' 9C *De Consolatione*, a 16C German illustrated manual on firearms, and 15C and 16C *Books of Hours* in Flemish and in Latin.

The cases next to the windows display **drawings, title-pages and vignettes** by masters who worked for the Plantin firm, including Martin de Vos, Adam van Noort, Van der Horst, Jan de Cock, Richard van Orley, and Pieter de Joode. The ceiling is decorated with compasses (the symbol of Christopher Plantin), and stars (the emblem of Balthasar Moretus).

Next is the secluded Renaissance **courtyard**, where a vine planted in 1640 is still flourishing. The south and west wings are the oldest parts of the building. A 17C pump of bluestone occupies the centre of the Renaissance arcade. The marble busts of Plantin, Jan Moretus the Younger and Justus Lipsius are copies; the originals are displayed in the museum. The bust of *Jan Moretus the Elder* is an original of 1621 by Hans van Mildert.

The next room (**no. 4**) was once the printer's shop. It was entered by a short flight of steps from the Heilig Geeststraat. This room contains the **index of prohibited books** published by Plantin in 1569, and the city authorities' official price-list of school books and prayer books. The money-balance standing on the counter dates from the period when coin clipping was a serious problem.

The little office in **Room 5** has a well-worn cashier's desk and chair. A portrait of Jan Moretus hangs above the door. **Room 6**, formerly the drawing room, has 17C Oudenaarde tapestries, 17C patrician furniture, and portraits of Christopher Plantin and his wife.

The process of book-making is outlined in **Room 7**. The various stages are outlined from manuscript to printed copy. This room also covers the development of books from c 1450 to the 20C. The next room (**no. 8**) was the kitchen. Paper was once weighed in this room.

The lovely **Room 9** was added in 1637 as the **proof-readers' room**. The doorway was carved by Paul Dirickx. The painting of *The Proof Reader* was probably done by Pieter van der Borcht. The proof-reader is believed to be Cornelis Kiel (or Kilianus in the Latin version), the founder of Dutch philology.

The oldest part of the house where Plantin spent his days begins with **Room 10**. Originally the office, it is furnished with a desk, safe and money-balance. The barred windows confirm that the money was kept here. The walls are hung with beautiful gilded Mechelen leather. The painting of *Christ and the woman of Samaria* is by Erasmus Quellin.

Room 11 is known as the Justus Lipsius Room after the Flemish humanist and friend of the family, who often worked here. It is hung with rare 16C Spanish gilt leather. The painting of *Lipsius and his pupils* is a copy of a work by Rubens (the original is in the Palazzo Pitti in Florence). One of the pupils in the painting is Rubens' brother, while one of the figures in the background might be Rubens himself. The *Portrait of Seneca* (one of Lipsius's favourite scholars) is by Rubens.

Books, documents and memorabilia connected with Lipsius are in **Room 12**. The portraits are of scholars and humanists who were Lipsius' contemporaries. The bust was made in 1621 by Hans van Mildert and is the original of the one in the courtyard.

There is a bust of *Plantin*, also by Hans van Mildert, in the passage leading to **Room 13**. Formerly the **Type Room**, its shelves are filled with different kinds of type. There are stocks of spare letters in their original packing on the lower shelves. The 18C wooden statues above the fireplace represent Honour, Courage and Orthodoxy.

The remarkable **printing room** (**no. 14**) has been restored to its appearance in 1576. Of the seven presses, five date from the 17C and 18C. They are maintained in perfect working order. One of the presses is used to turn out souvenir copies of Plantin's sonnet *Le bonheur de ce monde*. The presses standing against the back wall, under a 17C statue of Our Lady of Loreto, are believed to date from Plantin's time. There are compartments filled with 16C type, ready to be set in the galleys by the compositors.

The next two rooms, on the first floor, are at the front of the 18C house. On the landing is a Louis XV style clock and a painting of the Carmelite Order being confirmed by the Pope. This hung in the church of the Discalced Carmelites in Antwerp until 1769.

The next room (**no. 15**) contains a leather bas-relief depicting *Christ before*

Caiaphas, probably by Justin Mathieu (1796–1864). A display case contains specimens of books printed by Plantin. There is also another portrait of Plantin by an unknown 16C master. Rubens relied on this work when he painted the portrait in room 2.

The display cases in **Room 16** illustrate Plantin's life and work, especially the famous multilingual *Biblia Polyglotta*.

Biblia Polyglotta

The *Biblia Polyglotta* was undoubtedly Plantin's greatest production. This eight folio book has been described as the most important work ever produced by a single printer in the Netherlands. King Philip II of Spain was an enthusiastic supporter of the project. He provided financial aid and sent his chaplain, the humanist Arias Montanus, as scientific director of the project. Printing began in 1568; the book was completed four years later. Printed in Latin, Greek, Hebrew, Syriac and Chaldean (an ancient Babylonian dialect), it includes sections on Greek, Syriac and Chaldean grammars and glossaries. Plantin also added studies of Hebrew customs, and descriptions of ancient measures and clothing in the Near East in Biblical times. A dozen copies of the Bible were printed on vellum for Philip II.

The paintings in this room include a *Landscape* by Lucas van Uden, *Balthasar Moretus on his deathbed* by Thomas Bosschaert and portraits of later members of the family. The furnishings include an 18C Boulle cabinet and a clock.

Now return to the 17C part of the house, beginning with the small library in **Room 17** and the Moretus Room (**no. 18**). This contains a collection of books printed by Plantin's successors, some forged books and the first known illustration of a potato plant, which dates from 1588. The bust of *Jan Moretus the Younger* once stood in the courtyard. It was carved in 1644 by Artus Quellin the Elder.

The **Rubens' Room (no. 19)** contains sketches and engravings by Pieter Paul Rubens, who worked for Plantin as an illustrator. There are several receipts here signed by Rubens. The portraits were probably by Rubens' pupils. The chimneypiece was carved by Paul Dirickx in 1622. He returned to carve the doorway in 1640.

There are books by other Antwerp printers in **Room 20**. The portraits depict various local and foreign scholars whose works were published in Antwerp. The Drawing Room (**no. 21**) is hung with rare French gilt leather. The chimneypiece of 1638 is by Dirickx, while the 17C landscape above it was painted by Pieter Verdussen. The beautiful **harpsichord** was made in 1734 by J.J. Coenen. It is rather unusual in that it combines a clavecin and a virginal. The painting inside the cover, which shows St Cecilia playing an organ, is based on a painting by Rubens of St Cecilia playing a harpsichord.

Room 22 displays licences granted to the Plantin press by Belgian and foreign sovereigns, together with various other records concerning the printing-house.

The fascinating Geography Room (**no. 23**) contains 16C atlases by Mercator and Ortelius. There is also a beautifully detailed if rather dark *Plan of Antwerp* of 1565 by Virgilius Boloniensis and Cornelis Grapheus. A detailed map of Flanders by Mercator is equally captivating and there are also several 17C terrestrial and celestial globes by A.F. van Langeren.

Room 24 is devoted to printing outside Antwerp. The collection of books includes the 36-line *Gutenberg Bible*. A large copper engraving of the *Triumphal Entry of Charles V and Pope Clement VII in Bologna* on 24 February 1530 was made by by Niklaas Hogenberg.

There is a 1879 *Portrait of Edward Moretus* by Joseph Delin in **Room 25**, while the next room is decorated in the style of a 17C patrician bedroom with Mechelen gilt leather walls. The **Illustrations Room (no. 27)** contains a selection from the 15,000 woodcuts and 3,000 copperplates owned by the museum. Plantin originally used woodblocks, but later changed to copperplate. He was a pioneer in this technique.

Pass through the Alcove (**Room 28**) to return to Room 25. The staircase leads up to the **Type Foundry (Rooms 29 and 30)**, where the print types were cast to minimise the risk of fire. The first room is a workshop, furnished with a bench, anvil, vices, files, punches, matrices and moulds. Because of the risk of fire from the smelting furnaces, the floor of the foundry was made of stone. The room contains a large collection of stamps and matrices which Plantin bought from the best specialist suppliers, mainly located in France.

Return downstairs to the **Library (Rooms 31 and 32)**. Founded by Balthasar Moretus the Elder in 1640, it contains a small selection from the 30,000 books in the museum. The larger room was used as a private chapel, where family members and workmen went to hear Mass each morning. The painting of the *Crucifixion*, attributed to Pieter Thys, served as an altarpiece. The altar has disappeared.

The **Max Horn Room (no 33)** contains rare bindings and valuable books bequeathed by the bibliophile Max Horn (1882–1953). The most precious work is displayed in Case no. 1: a 13C volume with the oldest known panel-stamp. It was made for, or perhaps by, Wouter van Duffel, an Antwerp priest. There is also a huge coloured woodcut on vellum of *Charles V and Pope Clement VII at Bologna*. This version of the episode also illustrated in room 24 was produced by the Liège artist Robert Péril.

After visiting the museum, turn left and go down Heilig Geeststraat, past the former entrance to the bookshop. Turn left down Hoogstraat and left again along Steenhouwersvest, where there are several cluttered antique shops. A right turn down Korte Ridderstraat leads to the **Sint Andrieskerk**, open May–Sept daily 14.00–17.00. Built between 1514 and 1529 and enlarged in the 18C, the church contains paintings by Gerard Seghers, Erasmus Quellin and Otto Venius.

4 • The Old Town

This walk begins on the Grote Markt, an attractive cobbled square with a large fountain known as the **Brabo Fountain**. Created in 1887 by Jef Lambeaux, it shows Silvius Brabo throwing the hand of the giant Antigonus into the Scheldt.

The square is bounded by old or restored Late Gothic and Flemish Renaissance **guild houses**. Many are now occupied by restaurants or cafés. The house In den Engel (The Angel) at no. 3 dates from 1579. The Coopers' House at no. 5 was built in 1579 and restored in 1907. The house at no. 7 was built in 1582 for the Guild of Archers. The neighbouring house at no. 9 was built in c 1500 for the Guild of Crossbowmen. The Mercers' House at no. 17 was built in c 1515. The Drapers' House at no. 38, which dates from 1615, is decorated with symbols of the trade. The Carpenters' House at no. 40 also has motifs relating the guild's activities. The sculptor Jef Lambeaux was born in 1852 at no. 44.

Stadhuis

The Stadhuis is open for guided tours Mon–Fri (closed Thur) at 11.00,14.00 and 15.00; Sat at 14.00 and 15.00. It was built from 1561–65 in early Flemish Renaissance style by Cornelis Floris, possibly working to plans by the Florentine Nicolo Scarini. Ten years later, during the 'Spanish Fury', the building was partly destroyed by the rioting Spanish soldiers, largely because it contained the city's armoury. It was rebuilt immediately afterwards.

In the centre of the **long façade** is a crowned figure of the Virgin holding the infant Christ in her arms. The **coats of arms** below belong to the duchy of Brabant (left), the margravate of Antwerp (right), and Philip II of Spain (centre). It also includes the figures of Justitia (Justice) and Prudentia (Wisdom).

A stairway inside the town hall ascends to the landing. This was an open courtyard where the city artillery was kept until it was roofed over in the 19C. A series of paintings from 1899 depict **events in Antwerp's history** from the first half of the 16C history. One series of paintings shows the economic prosperity of the city, while the other represents the arts.

The **Grote Leyszaal** is hung with four large historical paintings by Hendrik Leys, who died in 1869 before completing the planned series of six. Several other paintings by Leys from 1855, which once hung in his house, can now be seen in the Kleine Leyszaal.

The **Trouwzaal** (Wedding Room) has a 16C chimneypiece decorated with two caryatids by Cornelis Floris. The murals painted by Victor Lagye in 1886 depict Belgian wedding ceremonies over the centuries. The **Militia Room**, where young men formerly drew lots for conscription in the army, contains a painting of the town hall in 1406. The **Raadzaal** (Council Chamber), has ceiling panels by Jacob de Roore. Painted c 1715, they contain allegorical references to the Barrier Treaty, which was designed to discourage any further attempts at annexation by the French. The reliefs hint at the benefits that would come to Antwerp if the Scheldt was to be reopened.

The **Burgemeesterzaal**, arranged in the style of 1885, contains an ornate 16C chimneypiece attributed to Pieter Coecke.

Now leave the Grote Markt by the Suikerrui, then turn right down the Gildekamersstraat, a narrow street that runs behind the Stadhuis. The houses on this street were rebuilt in 1954 in the style of 16C Antwerp. The house at no. 4 is a copy of a demolished Renaissance house by Cornelis Floris. The **Volkskundemuseum** (folklore museum) at nos 2–4 contains a collection of archaeological finds, craft objects and guild relics from Antwerp and the surrounding region. Open Tues–Sun 10.00–17.00.

Turn left on Zilversmidstraat and right on Bullinckplaats. This quarter was imaginatively redeveloped in the 1970s with public housing built in traditional 16C style on the old street pattern. Turn right along Kuipersstraat, which leads into **Oude Beurs**, named after the Old Exchange (which is in fact in Hofstraat). William Tyndale, the translator of the New Testament into English, lived as a refugee from 1534–35 in a house in Oude Beurs. He was tried as a heretic and executed at Vilvoorde, near Brussels.

A fascinating house called **Den Spieghel** is concealed behind a modern building incorporating a 'Spanish' Baroque portal at no. 16. The turreted merchant's house was built in the 1490s in the style of the Vleeshuis.

Now turn left up the Hofstraat. The **Oude Beurs** at no. 15 was built in 1515 in Late Gothic style by Domien de Waghemakere. The attractive courtyard is overlooked by an octagonal tower. This building served as the exchange for just 16 years; it was replaced by the Beurs in Lange Nieuwstraat in 1531. It is now used by the local education authority (courtyard open Mon–Friday from 09.00–12.00). The painter Adam van Noort lived in a house which once stood on the opposite side of the street.

Continue to Zirkstraat, where the Renaissance corner house at no. 28 dates from c 1561. After going right a short way, go left up Stoelstraat.

Sint Pauluskerk

Turn left along Zwartzustersstraat to reach the Sint Pauluskerk open May–Sept daily 14.00–17.00.

History of the church

Built on the site of a church originally for the Dominicans in 1276, the present Gothic church was begun in 1517 and consecrated in 1571. The Dominicans were expelled seven years later by the Calvinists. The transepts and choir were substantially demolished; the rubble was then used to ballast the fireships sent in 1584 to attack Parma's barrage on the Scheldt at Kallo.

The Dominicans eventually returned to Antwerp and began reconstructing their church. The work was completed by 1639. The tower was destroyed by fire in 1679, but rebuilt soon after in the baroque style. Badly damaged during the Dutch bombardment in 1830, the church was gutted by fire in 1968. The restoration work was completed in 1993.

The church is an outstanding example of the Baroque principle of unity of iconography. Its theme is the Church of Christ as an instrument of salvation. The choir represents the Church Glorious; the central nave, the transepts and the side aisles the Church Militant; while the Calvary in the friars' cemetery the Church Suffering.

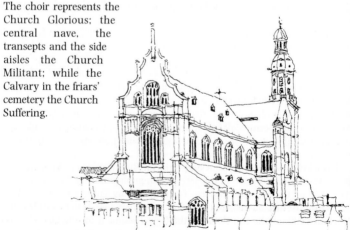

St Pauluskerk, Antwerp

The Mysteries of the Rosary

A curious row of 15 paintings in the north aisle illustrate the Fifteen Mysteries of the Rosary. These vivid Baroque works were painted in 1617–19 by leading Flemish artists. *The Visitation* is by Frans Francken the Younger; the *Nativity* and *Presentation in the Temple* are by Cornelis de Vos; the *Garden of Gethsemane* is by David Teniers the Elder; *The Carrying of the Cross* is by Antoon van Dyck; *The Crucifixion* is by Jacob Jordaens; and the *Scourging at the Pillar* is by Pieter Paul Rubens. The Museum voor Schone Kunsten in Ghent has a preliminary sketch of the Rubens painting.

The statues of the apostles in the **nave** are attributed to Michiel van der Voort, while the organ carving is by Pieter Verbruggen the Elder. The low relief of the *Soeten Naem* (Sweet Name of Jesus) was carved in 1644 by Artus Quellin the Elder. The five confessionals in the south aisle are attributed to Pieter Verbruggen the Elder.

The **south transept** contains two altars carved in 1654 by Verbruggen, who probably also did the communion bench of 1655. The *Disputation on the Nature of the Holy Sacrament* (which hangs above one altar) was painted by Rubens in c 1609 and superbly restored in 1973. The *Pietà* of c 1651 (hanging above the other altar) is by Gaspard de Crayer. The *Road to Emmaus* was painted by Erasmus Quellin in the 17C.

The **north transept** contains Rubens' magnificent *Adoration of the Shepherds*, painted c 1609. Badly damaged in the 1968 fire, it was restored and returned to the church in 1972. Other paintings include *Our Lady and St Dominic* by Gaspard de Crayer and a copy of Caravaggio's *Madonna of the Rosary* by B. de Quertemont. The original, removed by the Emperor Joseph II in 1781, now hangs in Vienna's Kunsthistorisches Museum. The 17C marble figure of *St Rose of Lima* by Artus Quellin the Younger is a masterpiece of Flemish Baroque.

The high altar in the **choir** was partly carved by Pieter Verbruggen the Elder. The altar was once surmounted by Rubens' *Vision of St Dominic* (now in the Musée des Beaux Arts at Lyon). The painting has been replaced by a *Descent from the Cross* painted by Cornelis Cels in 1807. The stalls, which bear the arms of donors, are attributed to Verbruggen. He also carved four out of the eight statues of Dominican saints: Catherine of Siena, Raymond of Pennafort, Vincent Ferrer and Anthony of Florence. The figure of Hyacinthus is by Artus Quellin the Elder, while Peter of Verona was carved by Jan Peter van Baurscheit the Elder.

The **Chapel of Lepanto** is named after four paintings of 1668 by Jan Peeters depicting the Battle of Lepanto.

A corridor off the nave leads to a bizarre Calvary in the church garden. Constructed from 1697–1747, it incorporates a grotto and an astonishing collection of 63 large Baroque statues. It was erected by the Society of the Pilgrims of Jerusalem to encourage the devout to visit Palestine. The statues illustrate the suffering of Christ, the story of Mary Magdalene, and the penitents who stayed in the Holy Land.

The curious **Brouwershuis** is a short distance from the church. Cross the Veemarkt in front of the church, turn right along the quay and again right along Adriaan Brouwerstraat. The museum is at no. 20, but at the time of writing was only open by arrangement.

The Battle of Lepanto

The Battle of Lepanto of 1571 in the Gulf of Patras was the last major naval engagment in which ships fitted with oars were used. The Ottoman Turks were defeated by a fleet of the Christian League, which comprised ships contributed by the Pope, Venice and Spain under the command of Don John of Austria. Some 15,000 Christian slaves were released. Lepanto has always been of special significance to the Dominicans, as the Christian fleet sailed under the protection of Our Lady of the Rosary and the chaplains were all Dominican friars. The battle and Don John of Austria, the natural son of Charles V, are celebrated in G. K. Chesterton's poem Lepanto:

> *But Don John of Austria is riding to the sea.*
> *Don John calling through the blast and the eclipse,*
> *Crying with the trumpet, with the trumpet of his lips,*
> *Trumpeth that sayeth ha!*
> *Domino Gloria!*
> *Don John of Austria*
> *Is shouting to the ships.*

Formerly known as the Waterhuis, the Brouwershuis was built in 1554 by Gilbert van Schoonbeke as part of a system for supplying **Antwerp's breweries** with clean water. The water was shipped by barge from Herentals in the Kempen, 28km east of Antwerp. The street behind the Brouwershuis, the Brouwersvliet, was a canal lined with breweries up to the 19C. The clean water, discharged into a cistern from the barges, was raised by a bucket-chain, at first powered by horses and later by an engine.

The stable is on the ground floor beyond the hall. The bucket-chain is behind a trap-door in the wall by the entrance to the court. The cistern, from which the water was raised, is below here. An attractively carved but rather dilapidated staircase leads to a landing where there is a painting of *Vulcan's Forge* by the Venetian Antonio Pellegrini, and a tile-picture of 1680 which was brought here in 1932. Off the landing, is the Laboratory and the Council Room, which has a fireplace of c 1660 and Mechelen leather hangings. The overmantel is decorated with the *Four Seasons* by Pellegrini and a beautiful Antwerp 16C chandelier. The brewers' insignia in carved wood hang above a cabinet of 1625.

5 • The Sint Jacobs quarter

This walk explores a historical quarter where wealthy merchants lived in the 16C. Leave Groenplaats by the Schoenmarkt (shoe market), past the 18C former **Bishop's Palace** at no. 2 and a chapel built by the Guild of Shoemakers at no. 8. The 24-floor **Boerentoren** on the left was built in 1929–32. Considered Europe's first skyscraper, it is now occupied by the Kredietbank.

Turn left up Sint Katelijnevest, then right along Lange Nieuwstraat. A narrow covered lane at no. 5 leads to the Sint Niklaasplaats, a cobbled square restored in 1958–68. The 15C Sint Nicolaaskapel overlooks the square.

Back on Lange Nieuwstraat, turn right down the short Twaalfmaandenstraat

(Twelve Months Street) where Plantin printed his first book in 1555. The Beurs stands at the end of the lane.

The Antwerp Beurs

The world's first stock exchange was established in Antwerp in the 16C. The original building was constructed by Domien de Waghemakere in 1531 in Flamboyant Gothic style. It served as a model for the Amsterdam Beurs and Gresham's London Exchange. Destroyed by fire in 1858, the Beurs was rebuilt in 16C style between 1868 and 1872 by Joseph Schadde. The large hall is decorated with world maps and the coats of arms of Antwerp merchants. The building is occasionally used for banquets, exhibitions and fashion shows, but lies empty for much of the time.

Return to Lange Nieuwstraat, where there is another chapel in a courtyard at no. 31. Known as the **Chapelle de Bourgogne**, this ivy-clad chapel was built in 1496 by Domien de Waghemakere for Jan van Immerseel, margrave of Antwerp. It takes its name from murals inside the chapel depicting four historic Burgundian marriages.

The house at **no. 43** once belonged to Sir Thomas Gresham, an English merchant who lived in Antwerp between c 1555 and 1567. Employed as a financial agent by four Tudor sovereigns, he used rather dubious schemes to raise the value of sterling on the Antwerp exchange. Gresham's ploys ensured that England's debts were paid off.

There is a good view of the tower of the **Sint Jacobskerk** from the end of the Sint Jacobsstraat. It was originally intended to be the tallest spire in the Low Countries, but was never completed.

Sint Jacobskerk

Continue along Lange Nieuwstraat to enter the church at no. 73. It is open Apr–Oct Mon–Sat 14.00–17.00.

Begun in 1491 by Herman de Waghemakere and continued after 1503 by Domien de Waghemakere, the Sint Jacobskerk was not completed until 1656. It was favoured by the wealthy families of Antwerp, who built their burial vaults, private chapels and altars here. It remains richly endowed with paintings and sculptures. More than one hundred types of marble decorate the interior.

Following a serious fire in 1967, the paintings were removed to the Museum voor Schone Kunsten for restoration. Now that the church has been fully repaired, the important paintings, church plate, vestments and statues have been returned. The main attraction in the church is the Rubens' Chapel.

Begin in the **south transept**, where there are paintings by Gaspard de Crayer, Bernard van Orley and Jan Metsys. The most interesting feature in this part of the church is the richly carved **marble communion rail** of 1696 by Hendrik Verbruggen and Willem Kerrickx in the Chapel of the Blessed Sacrament. The altar of 1670 is by Pieter Verbruggen the Elder.

The **choir** contains 17C stalls bearing the arms of benefactors. These were carved by Artus Quellin the Elder, Artus Quellin the Younger and their pupils, the

Herry brothers. The magnificent high altar of 1685 with a figure of St James was donated by the prosperous art dealer Hendrik Hillewerve. It was carved by Artus Quellin the Younger and decorated by Willem Kerrickx.

Seven chapels radiate from the **ambulatory**. The **first chapel**, known as the Trinity Chapel, was once the chapel of the doctors. It contains a *Trinity* by Hendrik van Balen based on a similar work by Rubens, and a St Peter by Jacob Jordaens.

The **second chapel** is dedicated to St Ivo, 1253–1303, a priest from Brittany who is the patron saint of lawyers. Opposite the altar are two wings of a triptych by Otto Venius. The centre panel is in the chapel of St Job off the south aisle of the nave. The **third chapel**, known as the Resurrection Chapel, was associated with the powerful merchant family of Le Candele-Vincque.

The Rubens Chapel

Pieter Paul Rubens and his family are buried in a chapel directly behind the high altar. The altar in the Rubens' Chapel is the work of Cornelis van Mildert. The figures of the Mater Dolorosa and attendant angels are by Lucas Faydherbe. Rubens painted one of his greatest works to hang here. It shows *Our Lady, the Christ Child and Saints*. Art historians generally agree that the figure of St George is a self-portrait, while the Virgin has the features of the artist's first wife. The infant Christ resembles Rubens' son, Mary Magdalene is modelled on his second wife, and the elderly St Jerome is a portrait of his father. Rubens' armorial bearings are on his tombstone in the chapel pavement. The Latin inscription gives a summary of Rubens' life and records the restoration work of 1775.

The **fifth chapel** is dedicated to St Charles Borromeo (1538–84). It is ironic that this cardinal-archbishop of Milan, an uncompromising leader of the Counter-Reformation, should have been portrayed in 1655 by the Protestant Jacob Jordaens. The painting shows the saint pleading with the Virgin on behalf of those stricken by the plague in Milan in 1576. This chapel was the gift of Jacob Antoon Carenna, whose gravestone is on the floor outside.

The **sixth chapel** is dedicated to St Peter and St Paul, while the **seventh chapel**, known as the Visitation Chapel, was gifted in 1640 by Bento Rodriguez, consul of Portugal. The altar painting is by Viktor Wolfvoet, who painted Mary with the features of Rubens' second wife.

There are some 17C confessionals nearby. A painting of the *Virgin and Child surrounded by Flowers* is by Ambroos Brueghel, the son of Jan. *The Adoration of the Shepherds* is by Hendrik van Balen.

Next is the **north transept**, where marble statues of the *Apostles John and Paul* stand at the ambulatory entrance. They were carved by Michiel van der Voort, who also sculpted the epitaph in the **Chapel of Our Lady** to the nobleman Michiel Peeters and his wife. The same chapel has a 1664 altar by S. van den Eynde, a polychrome *Pietà* by Artus Quellin the Elder (to the left of the altar), and a *St Joseph and the Infant Jesus* (on the right central pillar). The stalls are by Artus Quellin the Younger, who also carved the memorial to Jan de Gaverelle (1579–1645), an admiral, statesman and priest. The stained-glass window of the *Annunciation and the Visitation* are by Jan de la Baer.

There are three paintings high above the **north door**. They are an *Annunciation* by Gerard van Honthorst, *Jesus in the Temple* by Robert van Audenaerde and an *Adoration of the Magi* by Gerard Seghers. The west wall of the transept has an *Ascension of the Virgin* by Pieter Thys and an *Adoration of the Shepherds* by Erasmus Quellin.

There are six more chapels in the **north aisle of the nave**. The **first chapel** is known as the Robyns Chapel after its founder. It contains the last work of Wenceslas Coeberger, which shows *Constantine the Great kneeling before the Cross held by St Helena*. The figures are modelled on Joos Robyns and his wife.

The **second chapel**, known as All Saints or St Hubert, belonged in succession to the peat and the coal carriers. The latter dedicated an altar here in 1520. There is a triptych of 1608 by Ambroos Francken. The 16C window of the *Last Supper* is the oldest in the church.

The **third chapel**, dedicated to St Dympna, contains the tomb of the Rockox family. They are portrayed on the panels of a triptych by Jan Sanders facing the altar. The **fourth chapel**, known as the Three Kings Chapel, was once the chapel of the woodworkers. The altar-triptych by Hendrik van Balen shows the *Adoration of the Magi*. He also painted the two small panels below.

The **fifth chapel**, known as the Holy Name, contains the grave of the philanthropist Cornelis Lantschot, who died in 1656. There is also a carved wall-epitaph by S. van den Eynde and a portrait by Abraham van Diepenbeek.

The **sixth chapel** is dedicated to St Gertrude. It contains a macabre memorial by Pieter Scheemaeckers showing the last hours of Francesco Marcos del Pico, Spanish governor of Antwerp, who died in 1693. One of the bronze balusters in this chapel was donated by Rubens.

There are six more six chapels in the **south aisle of the nave**. The **first** chapel is dedicated to Our Lady. It contains a painting of *St George and the Dragon* by Antoon van Dyck. The tomb of Hendrik van Balen and his wife are in the nave near this chapel. A *Resurrection* by Van Balen hangs at the foot of a pillar, forming part of a stone memorial. The portraits above are also by Van Balen.

The **second chapel** is dedicated to St Anthony, portrayed here by Martin de Vos, who rather tactlessly used his wife as a model for the temptress. There is also a *Madonna* by Guido Reni.

The **third chapel** is dedicated to St Roch, who c 1337 gave his life caring for the plague-stricken in Italy. The altar with its figure of the saint, one of the finest pieces of sculptures in the church, is by Artus Quellin the Elder. The altar picture of the saint is a self-portrait by Erasmus Quellin.

The **fourth chapel** belonged to the Guild of Musicians. It is dedicated to their patron saint, St Job. The altar painting by Otto Venius is the central piece of a triptych, the wings of which hang in the chapel of St Ivo off the choir ambulatory.

The **fifth chapel**, dedicated to St Ann, contains an altar painting by Frans Floris, while the **sixth chapel**, dedicated to John the Baptist, has an altar painting by Michiel Coxie. The central panel of the triptych has a Martyrdom of St James by Martin de Vos.

On leaving the church, turn down the Sint Jacobsstraat and then right along the Sint Jacobsmarkt, past the Renaissance **Huis de Moelnere** at no. 11, built c 1544 for a city official. The twin 16C houses at **nos 16** and **18** are known as Sint Jacob Minor and Sint Jacob Maior. Now turn left down Rozenstraat to reach the small **Ossenmarkt**. A gateway off the square at Rodestraat 39 leads to the forgotten 16C **Begijnhof**. This replaced a 13C Begijnhof which stood outside the town walls.

Now go back down the Pieter van Hobokenstraat to reach the Prinsstraat. The handsome Renaissance building at no. 13 is known as the **Prinsenhof** (or the Huis van Liere). This substantial 16C building has a 17C façade. Charles V stayed here in 1520. It was occupied by English merchants from 1558 until the closing of the Scheldt in 1648. The Prinsenhof belonged to the Jesuits until 1773. It was acquired again by the Order in 1929. The St Ignatius University now occupies the building.

Turn right along Venusstraat, past the **City Archives** at no. 11. They are kept in a reconstructed 17C building, which was formerly occupied by the charitable lending bank. Next is the **Paardenmarkt**, once the site of the horse market. A detour to the right leads to the 19C **Sint Antoniuskerk**. The church faces a 16C asylum at no. 92 and an orphanage at no. 94.

Continue to the Falconrui, which runs parallel to the Paardenmarkt. The impressive **Hessenhuis** at no. 53 was built in 1562 by Cornelis Floris for the German merchants. Further along Falconrui, the impressive doorway of the 17C Lantschot Hospice is at **no. 47** and the 16C Van der Biest Hospice at **no. 33**.

Turn left at the end of Falconrui down Mutsaertstraat, then go left into Raapstraat. The 16C **Huis de Raap** at no. 27 has one of the oldest façades in Antwerp. Continuing down Mutsaertstraat, you come to the **Academie voor Schone Kunsten** (Academy of Fine Arts), which occupies part of a 15C building once owned by the Franciscans. The acclaimed Antwerp School of Fashion is based here.

Now turn down Minderbroedersstraat, past the **Museum voor het Vlaamse Cultuurleven** at no. 22. This museum has a large collection of Flemish documents, books and pictures.

Go left on Minderbroedersrui and left again into the stately **Keizerstraat**. The **Huis Delbeke** at no. 9 dates from the 17C. The handsome 16C **Huis Rockox** at no. 10 was the home from 1603 to 1640 of Burgomaster Nicolaas Rockox, a close friend of Rubens. Rockox's portrait appears on a triptych by Rubens in the Museum voor Schone Kunsten. The house is now a museum furnished in 17C style, with paintings by Rubens, tapestries and fine furniture. Open Tues–Sun 10.00–17.00.

Further along the street, the small 16C **Sint Annakapel** or **Keizerskapel** at no. 21 has a 'Spanish' Baroque doorway of 1624. The interior, recently restored, is crammed with 17C paintings and sculptures. It is open daily 08.30–12.00 and 13.00–17.30.

Turn right down a narrow lane called Jan Van Lierstraat and right again along Kipdorp. On reaching Wolstraat, go left down a small lane to reach the **Hendrik Conscienceplein**, a quiet 17C cobbled square named after the prolific 19C Flemish novelist who is best known for his historical work *The Lion of Flanders*. A statue made by F. Joris in 1883 stands behind the fountain.

The square is dominated by the **Sint Carolus Borromeuskerk**, open Mon–Sat 10.00–12.30 and 14.00–17.00 (19.00 on Sat); Sun 10.00–12.45. This impressive Baroque church was built from 1615–25 by the Jesuit architect Pieter Huyssens. It is named after St Charles Borremeo, one of the leading figures of the Counter-Reformation.

The superb west front is said to have been designed by Rubens. He also painted the ceiling of the nave and aisles. The church was struck by lightning and set alight in 1718, destroying everything except the choir, two chapels, the portal and the tower. Reconstruction by Jan van Baurscheit the Elder began the following year. He and Michiel van der Voort were responsible for much of the interior woodwork. The **Lady Chapel**, which survived the fire, is lined with the coloured marble that was a feature of the earlier building.

The Stadsbibliotheek (city library) occupies the 17C former Jesuit House at no. 4. Go through the arch and turn left to reach Korte Nieuwestraat, where the **Sint-Annakapel** at no. 22 has a handsome 17C Baroque door. Turn right on this street to return to Grote Markt.

6 • The Scheldt Quays

The Scheldt waterfront is an attractive maritime quarter with sweeping views of the bend in the river and a variety of historic and modern buildings. Two elevated walkways built in the 19C run along the quays from the Sint Jansvliet to the Veemarkt. The city embarked on a major redevelopment of the quays in 1993 during Antwerp's year as European capital of culture. This long-term plan has led to some striking modern buildings along the old waterfront.

Begin on the Grote Markt and walk down Suikerrui, past a statue by Constantin Meunier of *The Docker*. The **Ethnographic Museum** at no. 19, founded in 1864, has a large collection of wooden sculptures, masks, textiles and tools. Open Tues–Sun 10.00–17.00. The impressive neo-Baroque

The Steen, Antwerp

Hansahuis at **no. 1** was built in 1897 as an office building. It is decorated with monumental statues by Jef Lambeaux representing the rivers Scheldt, Rhine, Weser and Elbe.

Begun by Napoleon, the **quays** were completed between 1880 and 1885. They replaced the crowded old waterfront seen in many paintings by 17C artists. Napoleon's project required the river bank to be straightened, which led to the demolition of some 800 houses, and the removal of a pier which carried the town crane. The Steen fortress, at the foot of Suikerrui, was fortunately spared.

The Steen

The foundations of the Steen date from the 9C. A fortress was built here to defend the frontier established by the Treaty of Verdun between the territories of Charles the Bold and Lothair, the grandsons of Charlemagne. The oldest section of visible wall dates from c 1250. The building served as a prison later in the 13C. It was restored in 1520, during the rule of Charles V, by Domien de Waghemakere and Rombout Keldermans, and rebuilt in 1890. Further work was done on it in 1953. The present building was once the castle gatehouse and front buildings. The rest has been lost.

Lange Wapper

A figure known as 'Lange Wapper' stands at the foot of the ramp leading to the Steen. The legend of Lange Wapper is connected with a bridge over a medieval canal which brought clean water from Herenthals for use by the local breweries. The brewers built a large wooden fork with a long beam (or wapper) on the bridge to raise the barrels of water. When this landmark, known as 'Lange Wapper', disappeared, local legends grew up about a similarly shaped figure who was fond of playing pranks. He was said to be able to grow in height, which allowed him to peer in through windows. The statue was carved by A. Poels in 1963.

National Maritime Museum

The Steen is now occupied by the **National Maritime Museum**, open Tues–Sun 10.00–17.00. The collection is attractively displayed in a series of small rooms linked by narrow passages and steep stairs. The objects on display include model shops, old photographs and 17C paintings of the Antwerp waterfront.

The collection is spread over 12 rooms which are devoted to particular themes. **Room 1** covers arts and crafts, while **Room 2** contains several ship models. **Room 3**, which is devoted to religion and superstition, contains a votive ship of c 1757 and a gravestone decorated with a caravel. **Room 4** contains old photographs and other objects connected with maritime life.

Room 5 is devoted to inland navigation and contains two interesting paintings of old Antwerp by Jan Ruyten. **Room 6** covers the fishing industry. Several scale models explain methods of netting. The next room contains several more ship models, while **Room 8** has objects connected with shipbuilding, including a particularly good diorama of an Antwerp shipyard in c 1850.

The objects in **Room 9** illustrate the history of shipping from early times to the end of the 18C. There are excellent scale models of ships here, including Napoleon's state barge and several modern ships. A cabinet contains fragments of a 2C boat found in 1899 during the digging of the Bruges to Zeebrugge canal. The paintings include several works by the Dutch marine artist Willem van de Velde the Younger , including *Salute to an Amsterdam Ship*. **Room 10** concludes the history of shipping with exhibits from the 19C and 20C. The next room is often used for exhibitions.

The handsome **Council Chamber (Room 12)** is hung with several paintings of Antwerp by Bonaventure Peeters and Jan Baptist Bonnecroy. Bonnecroy specialised in panoramic views of cities such as Antwerp, Brussels and Amsterdam. His *Panorama of Antwerp* was painted from the left bank in 1658.

On leaving the Steen, you can also visit the **open-air museum** which occupies a large disused shed to the north. The collection of old barges and lighters includes the **Lauranda**, a lighter from 1928 (open the same times as the museum). Several old harbour cranes are preserved on the waterfront. A plaque commemorates the liberation of the Scheldt estuary in autumn 1944 by the 1st Canadian Army, supported by British and Polish units.

Vleeshuis

Now cross the road and walk up the short Vleeshuisstraat. This lane leads through a cut in the old town wall to the Vleeshuis. This Late Gothic building with step gables and corner turrets was constructed by Herman de Waghemakere in 1503 for the Butchers' Guild. It now contains a museum with a fascinating collection of paintings, architectural fragments and musical instruments. Open Tues–Sun 10.00–17.00.

The impressive **Ground Floor Hall** has a central row of six columns rising to a brick vault. Local butchers sold meat here until the mid 19C. It now contains a miscellaneous collection of metalwork, arms and armour, 16C–18C sculpture and woodcarving, an embroidered cope of 1525, several fine chests and 16C murals from an old Antwerp house. A remarkable collection of Renaissance carved wooden panels came from the loggia of a 1549 house called Den Grooten Sot, attributed to Pieter Coecke van Aelst.

A long, steep spiral staircase leads to the **first floor**, where there is a small kitchen with tile pictures and a huge pump. Another room contains leather wall hangings. The former **Council Chamber of the Butchers** is hung with gilt-leather and tapestries. This room contains some musical instruments, gold and silver objects, jewellery and furniture (including a 14C chest). A vivid painting on this floor by an anonymous artist depicts the *Spanish Fury* of 1576. Believed by some to be the work of an eye-witness, it is filled with lurid detail (including a scene of rape in the bottom left corner).

Another steep stairway leads to the **second floor**, where there is a small Egyptian section and an impressive collection of musical instruments. Descend to the large **basement**, which has brick vaulting. An interesting **Lapidarium** contains a collection of old carved stones from demolished churches and houses in Antwerp.

The **Burchtgracht**, which runs north from the Vleeshuis, was once the moat of the Steen, or 'burcht' (castle). Follow this lane to reach the quays. A flight of steps opposite leads to an elevated 19C **Promenade**, modelled on the harbour walkway in Genoa. The picturesque neo-Gothic **Norderterras** restaurant was built at the north end of the walkway in the 19C. Follow the promenade south, past disused 19C hangars with fine ironwork pediments and several redundant harbour cranes which now belong to the maritime museum. The quays are mostly abandoned now that the main port has moved downstream, but the occasional cruise ship still moors here. Descend to the Steenplein, where a ramp leads up to the **Zuiderterras**. The Zuiderterras restaurant at the south end of the walkway was built in 1989–91 by Bob van Reeth. There is a striking view of the river from the café. A 50m-high jet of water was installed opposite in 1998.

The steps at the end of the Zuiderterras lead to the Sint Jansvliet, a small square with the **Sint Annatunnel** entrance. Built in 1933, the 572m-long tunnel takes cyclists and pedestrians under the Scheldt to the modern districts on the left bank. Enclosed by a sharp bend in the **Scheldt**, this land was once the site of a great moated redoubt, but is now a modern residential suburb. It is worth going through the tunnel (or taking tram 2 or 15 to the Frederik van Eedenplein) for the splendid view of the old town from the other side. Near the exit from the **Sint Annatunnel**, a small maritime park is dotted with anchors, buoys and other curiosities. A short walk north, past the yacht basin, brings you to the Sint Annastrand, a beach resort with a view of a massive oil refinery on the opposite bank.

7 • The Museum of Fine Arts and the Zuid Quarter

The Museum voor Schone Kunsten lies in the **Zuid district**. Formerly off the beaten track, this quarter now has new museums, art galleries, cafés and restaurants. The district can be reached on foot in about 20 minutes from the centre, or by tram 8 from Groenplaats.

Leave Groenplaats by the Nationalestraat. One of the streets on the left is Sint Rochusstraat, where a former 17C Capuchin Chapel is located. At the end of Nationalestraat, turn left down Geuzenstraat to reach the **Scheldt Monument** on Marnixplaats. Designed by J.J. Winders in 1883, this colossal monument celebrates the lifting in 1862 of Holland's right to levy dues on Scheldt shipping. The monument stands on the site of a 16C Spanish citadel demolished in 1874. Leave the square by Zwijgerstraat, then turn right to reach the Leopold de Waelplaats. This square is named after the 19C burgomaster who negotiated the purchase of the Plantin-Moretus Museum.

Museum voor Schone Kunsten
The Museum voor Schone Kunsten (Fine Arts Museum) on Leopold de Waelplaats is open Tues–Sun 10.00–17.00.

The museum was designed by J.J. Winders, whose Scheldt Monument is nearby, and F. van Dyck. Built between 1878 and 1890, it replaced the old Antwerp art gallery located in a former Franciscan friary. The chariots on the roof were designed by the sculptor Thomas Vinçotte.

This outstanding art gallery contains an impressive collection of paintings from the 15C to the 20C. The collection includes important works by **Flemish primitives** such as Jan van Eyck, Roger van der Weyden and Quinten Metsys. The cosmopolitan spirit of Antwerp is reflected in a good number of foreign artists such as Jean Fouquet, Simone Martini and Lucas Cranach. The museum is particularly proud of its collection of works by **17C Antwerp artists** such as Rubens, Jordaens and Van Dyck. Many of the paintings in the museum were bequeathed in the mid-19C by the burgomaster and banker Florent van Ertborn. The museum has an art shop and a café.

Begin in the **entrance hall**, which is a replica of the main hall in the old museum. After passing busts of two governors of the Spanish Netherlands carved by Artus Quellin the Elder and Willem Kerrickx, climb the monumental **staircase**, which is decorated with a series of 16 paintings by Nicaise de Keyser illustrating the history of Flemish painting. Painted in 1866, these works originally hung in the art gallery of the Antwerp Academy. The large painting above the stair well shows Antwerp enthroned, surrounded by architects, artists, sculptors and engravers.

The collection of **Old Masters** occupies the 20 rooms on the first floor, which are identified by gilded Roman letters above the doors. Begin in a small room with several views of Antwerp including a panorama painted by an anonymous artist c 1600. Now go through the door on the left to reach the Flemish Primitives, beginning in **Room Q** which has Jan van Eyck's exquisite *St Barbara* of 1437 and his *Madonna at the Fountain* of 1439.

St Barbara

The legend of St Barbara arose in the 10C. The beautiful daughter of a wealthy pagan of Nicomedia, Barbara was imprisoned by her father in a tower to protect her from suitors. She converted to Christianity during her imprisonment. When she refused to renounce her faith, her enraged father had her tortured and then beheaded. Van Eyck's drawing shows the saint with a prayer-book and palm, symbols of her belief and suffering. The tower has a triple-lancet window which Barbara had installed as a symbol of the Trinity. It was this which first aroused the suspicions of her father.

Now go into **Room S**, which contains several works by Roger van der Weyden, including a *Portrait of Philippe de Croy*, a nobleman at the time of Philip the Good and Charles the Bold. This panel is thought to be the right side of a diptych. The left side, showing the *Madonna and Child*, now hangs in the Huntington Collection in New York. A curious work by the Master of Frankfurt in the same room shows the artist and his wife with a large fly on her head-dress.

Two side panels which may be hanging in this room come from a triptych painted by Gerard David in 1480–85. The panels show the *Dispute Between Pilate and the High Priest* (on the left) and the *Holy Women and St John at Golgotha*. The central panel depicting *Christ being nailed to the Cross* now hangs in the National Gallery in London.

A portrait by an anonymous artist in the same room shows *Jan Zonder Vrees* (John the Fearless), a son of Philip the Bold murdered in 1419. This portrait c 1450 was probably the work of an assistant of Roger van der Weyden. It may be a copy of an earlier portrait.

Van der Weyden's *Triptych of the Seven Sacraments* hangs in **Room T**. There is also a *Portrait of a Man holding a Roman Coin* by Hans Memling. Painted in c 1478, it is thought to show Giovanni de Candida, an Italian courtier in the service of Mary of Burgundy. Also here is Memling's curious *Christ with Angels Singing and Playing Instruments*.

Several works by **Quinten Metsys** hang in **room R**, including an exquisite little painting of *St Mary Magdalene* and a diptych of c 1505 showing the *Saviour of the World* and *Mary at Prayer*. A much larger *Lamentation Triptych* shows *Herod, Salome and John the Baptist* (on the left wing) and the *Death of John the*

Evangelist (on the right wing). Painted in 1511, this work was commissioned for an altar in Antwerp Cathedral. There is also a copy of Metsys' *Portrait of Pieter Gilles, City Secretary of Antwerp*. Erasmus commissioned this portrait and a matching one of himself as a gift for his friend Thomas More.

Room L contains a tiny painting of the *Flight into Egypt* by Joachim Patinir. This is the only signed painting by Patinir, who was born in Dinant. The three fig-ures seem lost in the strange pastoral land-scape which combines features of the Meuse valley, Brabant and Italy. Another small landscape in this room shows a *View of Huy seen from Ahin* painted c 1570 by Lucas van Valckenborgh.

View of Huy seen from Ahin, *by Lucas van Valckenborgh, Museum voor Schone Kunsten, Antwerp*

This room also con-tains one of the many portraits of *Judith* painted by Jan Metsys, son of Quinten Metsys. Jan shows the beautiful Judith after she has saved her town from siege by seducing and beheading the enemy leader Holofernes. There is also a series of portraits in this room by Pieter Pourbus, including one of *Olivier van Nieulant, alderman of Bruges*.

Many of the works in **Room M** were painted by the Brueghel family. Jan Brueghel's *Visit to the Farm* is probably a copy of a lost grisaille by his father. There is also a copy of Pieter Bruegel the Elder's *Wedding Dance*. The Flemish love of food is reflected in Joachim Beuckelaer's *Fish Market and Vegetable Market* (same room).

Room G contains the *Fall of the Rebel Angels* painted by Frans Floris in 1554. Inspired by Michelangelo's ceiling in the Sistine Chapel, this extraordinary work once formed the central panel of a triptych commissioned by the Guild of Fencers for an altar in Antwerp Cathedral. Badly damaged by Calvinist iconoclasts in 1566, it was shorn of its two wings.

There is a curious painting by Frans Francken the Younger in **Room E** of the *Picture Gallery of Sebastian Leerse*. Leerse was a wealthy Antwerp merchant who is shown with his second wife and his son. The paintings in the picture gallery include *Apelles Painting Campaspe* (signed by Francken in the bottom right corner), a *Susanna and the Elders*, probably by Jan Metsys, and a *Mountain Landscape* by Joos de Momper.

Several works by Jan Siberechts hang in **Room D**, including an attractive series of four paintings showing peasants and carts crossing water. **Room A** con-tains 17C still lifes by Frans Snyders.

Room N is devoted to foreign paintings, including a curious work by Jean Fouquet showing the *Madonna and Child surrounded by Angels*. This is believed to be the right panel of a diptych painted for Etienne Chevalier. The other panel, showing the patron, now hangs in Berlin. The figure of the Madonna is generally believed to be based on Agnes Sorel, mistress of King Charles VII of France.

There are three panels of uncertain date by Simone Martini in the same room. They show the *Annunciation*, the *Crucifixion* and the *Descent from the Cross*. Another interesting work is Antonello da Messina's *Crucifixion with the Virgin Mary and St John the Evangelist* of 1475. An admirer of Flemish painting, the artist combines a Flemish love of detail with an Italian breadth of vision.

A painting by the **Master of St Veronica** shows the *Man of Sorrows standing between the Holy Virgin and St Catherine*. The wheel and sword held by St Catherine represent the instruments of her martyrdom, while the instruments of the Passion of Christ float rather strangely behind the figures. An intriguing portrait by Jean Clouet shows the *Dauphin, son of François I*. Born in Brussels c 1475, Clouet became court painter to François in 1518.

There is also a study of *Caritas* by **Lucas Cranach the Elder** in this room, signed with the artist's mark on the tree trunk. The *Portrait of a Man* next to it is by his son Lucas Cranach the Younger.

Room P normally contains works by Dutch Masters, including Frans Hals' *Portrait of Stephanus Geraerdts*, an alderman of Haarlem, painted between 1650 and 1652. There may also be Adriaen van Ostade's *The Smokers*, and Jan Steen's *Wedding Feast* in this room.

Now return to the room at the top of the main staircase, where a door leads into the **Rubens Gallery** in **room I**. Most of the paintings here were originally altarpieces commissioned for Antwerp churches. The *Triptych of the Incredulity of St Thomas* of 1613–15 was commissioned by Rubens' patron Nicolaas Rockox to hang above the family tomb in the Franciscan church. The portraits on the side panels depict the patron and his wife.

Rockox also commissioned the large altarpiece of *Christ Crucified between the two Thieves* to hang above the main altar in the Franciscan church. Known as The Lance, this work of 1619 shows the dramatic moment when Longinus stabs Christ's side with a lance. *A Triptych of Christ on the Straw* was painted in 1618 to hang above the tomb of Jan Michielsen and his wife Maria Maes. The figures on the side panels represent the couple's patron saints Mary and John the Evangelist. Rubens' curious painting of *The Prodigal Son* of 1618 is more a study of a farmyard scene than a Biblical episode.

Another altarpiece of c 1634 shows *St Theresa of Avila obtaining the delivery of Bernardino de Mendoza from Purgatory*. Bernardino was a wealthy nobleman who donated his property to the saint to fund a new convent. He died suddenly before receiving absolution, but St Theresa interceded on his behalf. Rubens shows Christ instructing an angel to save Bernardino from the flames of purgatory.

An unconventional painting of *The Education of the Holy Virgin* dated c 1625 shows Mary as a young girl sitting with her parents in a garden. There is also a *Portrait of Gaspard Gevartius* (1593–1666), a municipal official who wrote poetry and historical works. He is shown sitting beside a bust of Marcus Aurelius which alludes to a commentary he wrote on the Roman Emperor.

The elaborate drawing of the *Triumphal Chariot of Kallo* in this room was designed by Rubens in 1638 as part of the celebrations following the Infante Ferdinand's defeat of the Dutch at Kallo, just across the river from Antwerp. The chariot is laden with symbolic details, including war booty, grieving prisoners and goddesses of victory.

Room H contains several works by **Jacob Jordaens**, including the eccentric *As the Old Sing so the Young play Pipes*. Painted in 1638, this genre piece shows a family concert. The old man in the picture is Jordaens' teacher and father-in-law Adam van Noort. There is also here (or perhaps in Room F) Jordaens' *Adoration of the Shepherds* of c 1650 and a *Group Portrait of the Nuns of the Antwerp Hospice*. Works by Antoon van Dyck are normally hung in this room, including his *Christ Dying on the Cross* painted for the Augustinian monastery.

Now go down to the first floor where the **Modern Art** collection is displayed. Begin in **room 29**, just beyond the stairs down to the museum shop, where romantic works by Gustave Wappers are hung. **Room 28** is devoted to the rather melancholy 19C paintings of Henri de Braekeleer, who painted Antwerp street scenes and interiors.

One of the delights of the museum is the collection of paintings by **James Ensor** in rooms 25 and 24. His early style can be seen in room 25 in his *Ostend Interior* and the lovely *Oyster Eater* of 1882. The following room (**no. 24**) has several works illustrating his later style such as *The Intrigue* of 1890 and the equally bizarre *Masked Figures Fighting over a Hanged Man* of 1891.

Room 23 is devoted to the strange **Symbolism** of Léon Spilliaert and Fernand Khnopff while works by the **Expressionist** Rik Wouters are found in **room 19**. The works include several portraits of his wife Nel and the *Self-Portrait with an Eye Patch* of 1915, painted the year before he died from eye cancer in Amsterdam.

Room 21 is devoted to **Belgian Surrealism**. Paul Delvaux's strange, ghostly women stare blankly in *The Pink Bow*. There is also René Magritte's *The Storm Cape*, *The Wreck*, and his macabre sculpture of *Madame Recamier*.

On leaving the museum, go down Verschansingstraat to reach Gillisplaats. A city gate known as the **Waterpoort** was moved here in 1936. Built in 1624 in honour of Philip IV, it originally stood on the Vlasmarkt. Probably designed by Rubens, it is decorated with the coat of arms of Spain carved by Huybrecht van den Eynde. The gate was moved here when the Sint Anna Tunnel was built.

Now cross to the Waalsekaai, a former quay on the edge of a filled-in 19C dock. The **Museum of Photography**, open Tues–Sun 10.00–17.00, occupies a warehouse of 1911 at no. 47. The museum has a collection of antique cameras, a reconstructed 19C photographer's studio and an impressive collection of 19C and 20C photographs.

Go along the Waalsekaai and turn left down Leuvensestraat to reach the **Antwerp Museum of Contemporary Art**, open Tues–Sun 10.00–17.00. Located in a former Art Deco grain warehouse painted pink, the museum displays international art from 1970 to the present day. Its temporary exhibitions are often worth a visit.

Back on the Waalsekaai, continue to the **Zuiderpershuis** at no. 14. This massive neo-Baroque building was constructed in 1882 as one of eight hydraulic power stations used to work the port installations. Closed down in 1977, it now contains an alternative theatre and an attractive café.

Now turn left to reach the Scheldt quays. Long neglected, this quarter is now in the throes of redevelopment. The route back to the centre passes several impressive buildings, including a striking black and white house on the corner of Goede Hoopstraat designed by Bob van Reeth in 1985.

The cartographer's tale

The **Mercator-Ortelius House** at Kloosterstraat 11–17, one block from the waterfront, was built in 1619 and extended in 1698. Its name derives from the fact that Abraham Ortelius, the Flemish cartographer, lived in this street at no. 43. Ortelius (1527–98) published the first modern atlas in 1570. Known as the *Theatrum Orbis Terrarum*, it contained 52 maps drawn to the same scale. Seven years later, the Plantin publishing house brought out a pocket-sized edition under the title *Epitome Orbis Terrarum*. Pieter Paul Rubens was another resident of the Kloosterstraat. He lodged with the Brant family from c 1610–17 after his marriage to Isabella Brant.

Antwerp suburbs

There are several grand 19C buildings on the boulevards, including the **Gerechtshof** (Law Courts) on Britselei, built by L. and F. Baekelmans from 1871–77 and the **National Bank** on Leopoldplaats, built in 1879 by Henri Beyaert.

The short Maria Henriettalei leads from the National Bank to the romantic **Stadspark**. Landscaped in English style in 1869 by Edouard Kelig, it stands on the site of a triangular bastion which formed part of the Spanish fortifications. The park contains a lake created out of the former moat, an elegant iron suspension bridge, and several sculptures. The works include a war memorial of 1935 by E. Deckers; a *Mother and Child* by George Minne unveiled in 1938 in memory of Queen Astrid; and a fountain-figure by Slojadinovic from 1954.

Now go along Charlottalei to reach the **Ridder Smidt van Gelder Museum**, just beyond the roundabout at Belgielei 91. Open Tues–Sun 10.00–17.00, but it is worth checking with the tourist office that the museum is open.

This elegant 18C mansion was presented to the city in 1949 by the Chevalier Pieter Smidt van Gelder (1878–1956). The exquisite **private collection** includes furniture, tapestry, porcelain, jewellery, objets d'art and many fine paintings. There are works by Joachim Patenir, Giovanni Paolo Panini, Van Ruysdael, Jan van Goyen, Pieter Claes, Van de Velde, Van Vliet, Abel Grimmer, Lucas van Uden, Jan van Oosten, Pieter Wouwerman and Jan ten Compe. One of the charms of the museum is that the collection reflects the informal tastes of a wealthy connoisseur. The mansion has an attractive garden.

On leaving the museum, turn left along Belgielei to reach the **Koning Albertpark**. Once the site of the Galgenveld (gallows' hill), the park was laid out by the Marquis d'Herbouville, prefect of Antwerp under Napoleon.

The **Nachtegalenpark** (Nightingale Park), south of the Koning Albertpark, was laid out in the 18C by the French architect Barnabé Guimard. A pleasance of some 120 hectares, it embraces the old estates of Vogelenzang (which has an aviary, animal enclosure and educational garden); Den Brandt (with an 18C mansion) and Middelheim.

The Middelheim Park has been a **Museum of Modern Sculpture** since 1950. The rolling lawns are dotted randomly with works by Rodin, Rik Wouters, Ossip Zadkine, Meunier and Henry Moore. Open Jun and Jul 10.00–21.00; May and Aug 10.00–20.00; Apr and Sept 10.00–19.00; Oct–Mar 10.00–17.00.

The **Cogels Osylei** (or Zurenborg) district, north of Berchem station, which can be reached on **tram 11** (which runs from Koningin Astridplein to Cogels-

Osylei), is a remarkable quarter of **late 19C eclectic architecture**. The district was planned by private developers who used some of the best Belgian architects of the day. The district contains examples of virtually every 19C eclectic style, but also several innovative Art Nouveau houses. The stately Cogels-Osylei, laid out in 1894, is lined with the grandest mansions. The complex of three houses at **nos 25–29** (The Star, The Sun and The Moon) was designed by Joseph Bascourt in a fanciful Flemish Renaissance style, while the houses at nos 65–71 are concealed behind a Venetian Gothic façade. Several Art Nouveau houses were designed by Jules Hofman, including the lovely Huize Zonneberg at no. 50.

Joseph Bascourt displayed his versatility in the Art Nouveau corner houses at the intersection of Generaal Van Merlenstraat and Waterloostraat. Named after the four seasons, they were built in 1899. There is also a handsome building modelled on a Greek temple at Transvaalstraat 23–35.

The **Rivierenhof** is a large recreational park in Deurne, east of Antwerp. The **Sterckshof Zilvercentrum**, open Tues–Sun 10.00–17.30, occupies a castle in the park dating from the 14C, but rebuilt in 1525 and restored in 1934. Its period rooms contain displays of silver, copper, pewter, iron and glassware, calico prints, coins, medals and weights and measures.

The Antwerp forts

A ring of eight massive forts was constructed in the 19C to replace the Spanish walls built by Charles V in 1542. Designed by General Brialmont, the forts were thought to be strong enough to defend Belgium against attack from Germany. Sadly for Belgium, the forts proved totally ineffective against the German onslaught in 1914. The young Winston Churchill, then the British First Lord of the Admiralty, arrived on 4 October 1914 with Royal Marines and Royal Navy reinforcements, but two days later the Germans pushed forward until they were within shelling range of the city. The government sailed for Ostend, leaving Antwerp to surrender on 10 October. Much of the population fled to the Netherlands, along with some 2,500 British troops who were immediately held in internment camps. During the **Second World War**, Antwerp was abandoned at an early stage of hostilities. In the final days of the war, it was heavily bombarded by V1 and V2 attacks

Several of the star-shaped military installations are still standing in the Antwerp suburbs. Some are still used by the army, but others can be visited. The most interesting is **Fort 5** in Edegem, southeast of the old town, which now contains a public transport museum. A nature trail runs around the old moat.

The port

Antwerp developed after the Second World War into one of Europe's leading maritime cities. Located some 90km from the sea, it can only be reached through Dutch waters. The international boundary is a short distance beyond the limits of the port area. For centuries this difficult location has had a decisive influence on Antwerp's fortunes.

It is worth exploring this vast, and still expanding, port area. **Boat tours** begin at the Steen, but it is perhaps more interesting to drive along the **Havenroute** indicated by hexagonal signs. Created by the tourist office, the route begins at the Steen and covers a total distance of some 60km, though shorter tours of 35km or 12km are possible. The entire route is described in a booklet sold by the Antwerp tourist office.

Begin by following the quays north of the Steen as far as the **Pilot House** of 1894, which serves both the Belgian and the Dutch pilotage services. The route continues north past the **Bonapartedok** and **Willemdok** (on the right). The oldest docks in Antwerp, they were constructed on Napoleon's orders from 1804–13.

The route continues north past the **Kattendijkdok**, the largest of the 19C docks. Built in 1860–81, this contains the municipal dry docks. The route now crosses two locks known as the **Kattendijksluis** and **Royerssluis**. Constructed in 1907, the Royerssluis is the first large sea lock.

Art Nouveau house, Antwerp

Now bear left past the **Hogere Zeevaartschool** (Merchant Navy College), and continue along a stretch known as Noord Kasteel after one of the city's northern fortresses which once stood here. Continue along the Scheldelaan past large oil refineries. On the opposite bank of the Scheldt, a huge industrial complex is occupied by firms such as Polysar, Union Carbide and BP Chemicals.

Follow a bend in the river, past the small **Industriedok** on the right, which is used for ship repairs, and a massive complex of Esso oil storage tanks on the left. The road then crosses the **Petroleumbrug**, which separates the Marshalldok (on the left) from a large stretch of water (on the right). Built with Marshall Aid funds in 1951, the **Marshalldok** is surrounded by petro-chemical installations, including the Société Industrielle Belge des Pétroles, Belgium's largest refinery. **The Hansadok**, which can take the biggest ships, is to the right.

Over the Petroleumbrug, there are several large jetties for supertankers on the right. The Havenroute then crosses two locks: the **Van Cauwelaertsluis** of 1928, and the **Boudewijnsluis** of 1955, which was Antwerp's largest lock until the opening of the Zandvlietsluis. There is a good view east across the main complex of docks, including the Churchilldok to the north, and the Hansadok to the south. A 1962 statue of the Universal Worker by F. Libonati faces the administrative buildings.

The route now skirts the huge Bayer Chemicals plant. It then reaches a road junction next to a windmill dating from 1745, which once stood east of here on land now submerged by Kanaaldok. The **Frans Tijsmanstunnel** and **Lillobrug** (to the right) lead to the far side of the Kanaaldok.

The picturesque village of **Lillo** is on the left beside the Scheldt. This settlement is all that remains of a much larger village, most of which was destroyed to build the Kanaaldok. The **Poldermuseum Lillo** is devoted to the local life of the Antwerp polders.

The route continues past more petro-chemical installations to the **Zandvlietsluis**, where there is a figure carved by Ossip Zadkine. Opened in 1967, this lock, 500m long and 57m wide, allows access to the port by ships of up to 100,000 dwt. Cross the lock by the great drawbridge and continue past BASF to within a few metres of the Dutch border. The road runs for a short distance beside the Rhine–Scheldt canal, built in 1975, which reduces the distance between Antwerp and the Rhine by some 40km.

Crossing the entrance to the Kanaaldok, turn south through the villages of **Zandvliet** and **Berendrecht**. Though now incorporated into the administrative district of Antwerp and surrounded by industrial developments, these settlements have tried to hold onto their character as quiet polder villages. The village of Berendrecht takes its name from the Latin *Ursipraedium* (the land of the bear). A large colony of blue herons has settled in the nearby woods of **Reigersbos** (open from mid February to the end of June).

Continue south to an intersection at the east end of the Tijsmanstunnel, which links up with the motorway back to the city. The Havenroute turns right from the tunnel approach and continues under the road to the bridge, passing a German Second World War concrete landing-ship known as Quay 526 which has been converted into a seamen's church.

Now follow Noorderlaan, which runs between the Antwerp North railway marshalling yards, and the General Motors complex, built in 1962 on the site of the polder village of Oorderen. Turn right beyond the **Churchilldok**, built in 1967 for container traffic. The church tower standing amid the container stacks is all that remains of the village of Wilmarsdonk, which was evacuated in 1962. The route then skirts the small **Graandok**, which is used by barges and coasters. These vessels carry the grain offloaded from seagoing ships berthed at the special pier equipped with grain elevators at the rear of Graandok.

The Havenroute now skirts the **Havendok no. 6**, built in 1964, with the Van Cauwelaertsluis and Boudewijnsluis opposite. The road continues along the side of the Hansadok, where the great loading bridges are used to handle ores. Rejoin Noorderlaan near the **Nieuw Entrepotcomplex**, passing bonded warehouses and the Ford complex. The **Albertdok** is on the right, which handles timber, fruit and nitrates. The network of pipes between Havendok 3 and Havendok 2 carries potassium. The road now curves south to cross the **Albert Kanaal**, returning to the old town at Noorderplaats.

Antwerp environs

The industrial suburb of **Hoboken** has an attractive town hall which occupies a mansion of 1745 built by Jan Peter van Baurscheit the Younger.

The Duke of Parma built a large fort in 1584 at **Kallo**, east of the Scheldt. He also constructed a long barrage across the river to block the port, which at that time was under siege. The star-shaped fort to the north marks the northwest limit of the fortifications built during the 19C and 20C.

The polder village of **Doel**, 8km north of Kallo, lies close to the Dutch border. It has a picturesque port and an old stone windmill overshadowed by a nuclear power station and new port installations.

There are vestiges, mainly 18C, of the former abbey of Sint Bernard at **Hemiksem**, 10km south of Antwerp. Founded in 1246, it offered accommodation in 1338 to Edward III of England, who was allied to Jacob van Artevelde. The monks of Sint Bernard founded the local brick industry in the 13C.

LEUVEN

Leuven (Louvain in French) is a historic Flemish university town with a spectacular Gothic town hall. Virtually destroyed in 1914, and bombed in 1944, Leuven was still being reconstructed in the 1970s. The town was until recently rather neglected and run-down. It is now becoming an increasingly attractive destination, with crowded cafés, friendly restaurants and elegant shops. The capital of Flemish Brabant province, Leuven has a population of 87,000.

Practical information

Where to stay

££ *Binnenhof*, Maria Theresiastraat 65, ☎ 016.20.55.92, is a comfortable hotel near the station.
££ *Holiday Inn Garden Court*, Alfons Smetsplein 7, ☎ 016.29.07.70, is a comfortable modern hotel in the city centre.
££ *Ibis*, Brusselsestraat 52, ☎ 016.29.31.11, is a modern hotel near the centre, good for children.
£ *La Royale*, Martelarenplein 6, ☎ 016.22.12.52, is a modest family hotel opposite the station.

Eating out
Restaurants

££ *De Blauwe Zon*, Tiensestraat 28, ☎ 016.22.68.80, is a striking restaurant with old stone floors.
££ *Ramberg Bistro*, Naamsestraat 60, ☎ 016.29.32.72, is an elegant bistro with rambling garden.
££ *Syre Pynnock*, Hogeschoolplein 10, ☎ 016.20.25.32, offers inventive cooking in a bright interior.
£ *Ming Dynasty*, Oude Markt 9, ☎ 016.29.20.20, offers delicate Chinese cooking.
£ *Oratorienhof*, Mechelsestraat 111, ☎ 016.22.81.05, is a striking Italian restaurant with garden.
£ *De Wiering*, Wieringstraat 2, ☎ 016.29.15.45, is an amiable student restaurant with a curious interior.

Cafés

Domus, Tiensestraat 8, is a rambling Flemish tavern serving Domus beers and traditional Burgundian cooking.
Gambrinus, Grote Markt 13, is a traditional café with wood-panelling and 19C frescos.
Het Dagelijks Brood, Parijsstraat 33, is a bakery café with a spacious farmhouse style interior.
The most lively **student cafés** are on Oude Markt.
In Den Rosenkranz, an attractive 19C tavern occupying the gatehouse of Vlierbeek Abbey, 4km northeast of Leuven. Offers good selection of Belgian beers and simple café cooking.

Tourist information

Grote Markt 9, ☎ 016.21.15.39. Closed on Sundays from November to February.

Banks and post office

BBL, Bondgenotenlaan 31.
Gemeentekrediet, Naamsestraat 11.
Main post office is at Smoldersplein 1.

Carillon concerts

The carillon in the Sint Pieterskerk is played on Saturday from 15.00–16.00. The carillon in the university library belfry is played during the university terms on Tues and Fri 19.00–19.45.

Children

The **Kessel-Lo provincial estate** is an attractive landscaped park to the northeast of Leuven with lakeside walks, adventure playgrounds, a boating lake and a small farmyard. The **Zoet Water Park**, south of Leuven on the edge of the Heverlee woods, is a popular adventure playground in pine woods with a miniature train, trampolines and a café. The nearby Zoet Water area has lakeside walks, woodland trails and several convivial Flemish taverns.

Opening times

Sint Pieterskerk, Grote Markt, is open Tues–Fri 10.00–17.00; Sat 10.00–14.30; Sun and holidays 14.00–17.00; also Mon mid-Mar–mid-Oct 10.00–17.00.

Stedelijk Museum Vanderkelen-Mertens (fine art, local archaeology), Savoyestraat 6, is open from Tues–Sat 10.00–17.00; Sun and holidays from 14.00–17.00.

Stadhuis, Grote Markt, is open for guided tours Mar–Oct, Mon–Fri at 11.00 and 15.00, Nov–Feb Mon–Fri at 15.00.

Museum Van Humbeeck-Piron (paintings by Pierre van Humbeeck and his wife Marie Piron), Mechelsevest 108, is open Wed–Mon 10.00–18.00.

History

According to a popular local tradition, Leuven was founded on a camp established by Julius Caesar. The first written reference to the settlement, however, occurs in a 9C chronicle when the area was under Viking rule. The Norsemen were eventually defeated at the end of the 9C by Arnold of Carinthia, who built a castle on the Keizersberg, on the north edge of the town.

The first Count of Leuven was named Lambert. He built a church on the site now occupied by Sint Pieterskerk in about 1000. Count Henry II of Leuven annexed the county of Brussels, assuming the title of Duke of Brabant in 1190. Leuven then became the **capital of Brabant county**.

Like other Flemish towns, Leuven prospered in the 13C through the growth of the cloth trade; the population grew to over 50,000. The 14C, marked by conflicts between the nobles and the citizens, was a key period in Leuven's history. In 1338 Edward III of England, the ally of Jacob van Artevelde of Ghent, wintered in the castle outside the Mechelen gate. In 1356, when Wenceslas of Luxembourg acquired Brabant through marriage, he was obliged to sign the '**Joyeuse Entrée**' declaration. This almost immediately led to a conflict between the citizens, who were favoured by the declaration, and the nobles. The tribune Pieter Courtercel was master of the town for a short period in 1360. The citizens in 1379 threw seventeen nobles from the windows of the Stadhuis on to the guildsmen's pikes below. This savage act brought an equally savage response from Wenceslas, who favoured the nobles' cause. The citizens were finally obliged to submit in 1383, forcing thousands of weavers to emigrate to England. The prosperity of Leuven declined rapidly. Matters were made worse when the ducal residence was removed to Vilvoorde and Brussels became the principal town of Brabant.

Leuven recovered some of its former status in the next century when a **university** was founded here in 1425 by Pope Martin V and Duke John IV of Brabant. By the early 16C it had become one of the leading universities of Europe, boasting more than 6000 students and 52 colleges.

Mercator learned his geography here, founding and running an institute of cartography until he was hounded out of the country in 1544. The young Charles V, who lived in the castle in c 1507, was educated here by Adrian

Florisz, who became Pope Adrian VI. Bishop Jansenius and Justus Lipsius also taught here. Distinguished 19C and 20C students included Father Damien, Cardinal Mercier and Emile Verhaeren.

The university was suppressed by the French in 1797. It was replaced in 1817 by the 'Collège Philosophique' founded by William I of Holland. This secular institution was bitterly resented by the Belgian clergy, who established a Catholic university at Mechelen in 1833. This was transferred to Leuven two years later.

Leuven has been a brewing town since the 14C. The oldest brewery, known as Den Horen (The Horn), was established in 1366. This brewery became the largest enterprise in Leuven in the 16C. Acquired by Sébastien Artois in 1717, it was renamed Stella Artois. Now the largest brewery in Belgium, it retains the horn emblem of its 14C predecessor.

'Walloons go home'

Controversy has raged at Leuven University during the 20C on the question of whether teaching should be done in both Dutch and French or solely Dutch. The debate was briefly silenced in 1962 by a statement from the Primate which reaffirmed Leuven as a Catholic university with teaching in both languages. This sparked off violent demonstrations in 1968 when students marched under banners proclaiming 'Walloons go home'. The government finally agreed to create a French-speaking university at Louvain-la-Neuve in Walloon Brabant. The teaching at Leuven University is now given in Dutch or English.

---

1 • The Grote Markt

The first thing you see on leaving **Leuven station** is an impressive World War One war memorial. Facing the station are several hotels and cafés which replace buildings destroyed in 1914. Now go down the Bondgenotenlaan to reach the **Grote Markt**, the main square. The handsome café **Gambrinus** at no. 13 is decorated with 19C frescos.

The **Stadhuis** on Grote Markt is open for guided tours from Mar–Oct Mon–Fri at 11.00 and 15.00, and Nov–Feb Mon–Fri at 15.00. It was built in Flamboyant Gothic style by Mathys de Layens from 1448 to 1463. Three storeys of Gothic windows are surmounted by a steep roof of dormer windows and six graceful turrets. The bases of the niches between the windows were carved with biblical themes by medieval sculptors in a grotesque and independent style.

The 230 large and 52 small niches remained empty until the exterior of the building was restored between 1828 and 1850. The 236 statues represent eminent citizens, artists, philosophers, royalty, nobility, religious thinkers, municipal institutions, municipal privileges, virtues and vices.

The richly-decorated **interior** contains sculptures and paintings by Constantin Meunier, Jef Lambeaux, P.J. Verhaghen, Gaspard de Crayer and Antoon Sallaert.

Sint Pieterskerk

The Sint Pieterskerk opposite is open Tues–Fri 10.00–17.00; Sat 10.00–14.30; Sun and holidays 14.00–17.00; also Mon from mid-Mar–mid-Oct 10.00–17.00.

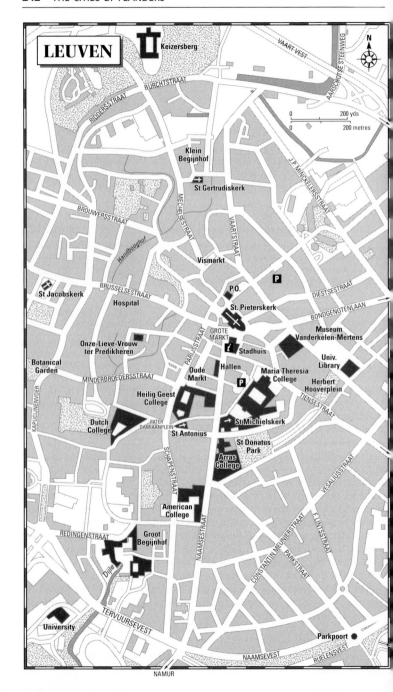

LEUVEN

Keizersberg

VAART-VEST

AARSCHOTSE STEENWEG

N

BURCHTSTRAAT

RIDDERSSTRAAT

0   200 yds
0   200 metres

Klein
Begijnhof

J.P.MINCKELERSSTRAAT

St Gertrudiskerk

BROUWERSSTRAAT

MECHELSESTRAAT

VAARTSTRAAT

Hanthooghof

Vismarkt

DIESTSESTRAAT

P.O.

P

St Jacobskerk

BRUSSELSESTRAAT

St. Pieterskerk

BONDGENOTENLAAN

Hospital

GROTE
MARKT

Museum
Vanderkelen-Mertens

Onze-Lieve-Vrouw
ter Predikheren

PARIJSSTRAAT

i   Stadhuis

Univ.
Library

Botanical
Garden

MINDERBROEDERSSTRAAT

Hallen

Oude
Markt

P

Maria Theresia
College

Herbert
Hooverplein

KAPUCIJNENVOER

Heilig Geest
College

TIENSESTRAAT

Dutch
College

PATER
DAMIAANPLEIN

St Antonius

St Michielskerk

St Donatus
Park

VESALIUSSTRAAT

SCHAPENSTRAAT

Arras
College

American
College

NAAMSESTRAAT

F.LINTSSTRAAT

REDINGENSTRAAT

Groot
Begijnhof

CONSTANTIN MEUNIERSTRAAT

PARKSTRAAT

Dijle

University

TERVUURSEVEST

Parkpoort

NAAMSEVEST

RUELENSVEST

NAMUR

History of the church

The church was built on the site of a Romanesque church which burned to the ground in 1373, leaving just the crypt. An even older Romanesque church was built on the site in c 1000, but was destroyed by lightning in 1176. The present Late Gothic building was begun in c 1425 by Sulpicius van der Vorst of Diest. After his death in 1439 the work was taken over by Jan Keldermans of Mechelen who completed the south aisle and part of the nave. Mathys de Layens is believed to have built the central nave and north aisle in 1445.

The Romanesque west towers were finally demolished in 1497. Work then began in 1507 on a Late Gothic tower designed by Joos Metsys, brother of the more famous Quinten. The foundations proved too weak to support the ambitious structure; the towers were abandoned and reduced to the level of the roof between 1612 and 1630. An impressive stone model of the planned tower is displayed in the south transept.

The nave was gutted by fire in 1914, and the choir was damaged by a bomb in 1944. The explosion exposed the Romanesque crypt, which had been filled in since the 15C.

Sint Pieters contains an impressive **collection of paintings** commissioned for the church. The most famous of these works is a *Triptych of the Last Supper* painted by Dirk Bouts in c 1464. The Last Supper is depicted as taking place in a Flemish Gothic hall. The view through the window on the left may be of Leuven's Grote Markt in the 15C, with the Stadhuis under construction. A second triptych by Dirk Bouts shows the *Martyrdom of St Erasmus*, an early bishop of Antioch and patron saint of mariners.

The church also owns a copy of Roger van der Weyden's *Descent from the Cross* made in c 1463 by the Master of the Edelheere Triptych. The original once hung in the third chapel of the ambulatory (St Aubert Chapel), but was later moved to the Escorial in Spain.

The interior is lit by 90 windows with elaborate Flamboyant Gothic tracery. The most striking feature in the **nave** is the elaborate Baroque pulpit of 1742 designed by Jacques Bergé for a church in Ninove. It shows St Norbert falling from his horse after being struck by lightning. The work features delightful details, such as a frog, a cherub holding forked lightning, a crowing rooster and several birds taking flight.

The **first chapel** on the south side contains the tomb of Dr Thomas Stapleton flanked by mourning angels. Stapleton was an Irish rector of the university who died in 1694. The baptistry opposite contains a splendid baptismal font with an iron crane to lift the cover, possibly carved by Quinten Metsys, who was born in Leuven in 1466. The rood screen dates from 1490, while the choir beyond has a tall Gothic stone tabernacle of 1450 by Mathys de Layens and a Renaissance screen of 1568 by Jan Veldener.

The **ambulatory** contains an outstanding collection of paintings and sculpture (entry charge). The **first chapel**, dedicated to St Anthony, contains the funerary monument of Duke Henry I of Brabant, Count of Leuven. Dated 1235, it is the oldest monument of its kind in Belgium. The inscription describes Duke Henry as an 'example of good morals, mirror of justice, avenger of the wicked, flower of our country, peace of the Church, shield of widows, hope of remission, crucible of fine mannners (and) protector of the poor.' His two wives Matilda, who bore him seven children, and Maria, who provided two more offspring, are also commemorated.

The **second chapel**, dedicated to St Augustine, once belonged to the Guild of St Sebastian—the guild of archers. A 12C head of Christ is displayed here. The **third chapel**, dedicated to St Aubert, contains an *Ecce Homo* by Gerard Seghers on the altar. Roger van der Weyden's *Descent from the Cross* once hung here.

The **fifth chapel**, dedicated to the Virgin of Seven Sorrows, contains a triptych of 1593 of the *Martyrdom of St Dorothea* by Joost van den Baeren. The **sixth chapel**, dedicated to the Holy Trinity, has a funerary monument of the Crucifixion carved in 1520. It shows St Luke and St James with the donor, Jacques Bogaerts, professor of medicine, kneeling below. The **seventh chapel**, dedicated to St Ann, has a triptych by Joost van den Baeren showing *St Ivo*, who defended the poor against unjust judges.

> ### Proud Margaret
> The **eighth chapel** is dedicated to St Margaret of Leuven, a local woman known as Proud Margaret who was killed in 1225. A servant at an inn, she was abducted by a gang of robbers who murdered her master and mistress. After refusing to marry one of her captors, she was slain and her body thrown into the river. There are scenes from her life on the shrine and in the adjacent **ninth chapel** (Chapel of the Last Judgement), where a series of paintings by Pieter Verhagen show the murder, the body floating in the River Dijle, the corpse being recovered and carried to the Sint Pieterskerk, and the faithful praying at her grave.

The **tenth chapel** (Chapel of the Blessed Sacrament) contains a painting of *Christ and the Disciples at Emmaus* by Erasmus Quellin and the *Martyrdom of St Ursula* by Theodoor van Thulden, a pupil of Rubens. The **fifteenth chapel**, dedicated to St Andrew, contains the tombs of Matilda of Flanders, wife of Duke Henry I of Brabant, and their daughter Mary, wife of Emperor Otto IV of Germany.

It is thought that the 12C Counts of Leuven were buried in the **crypt**, built as an extension of the early Romanesque churches. Filled in when the Gothic church was built in the 15C, it remained hidden until the bombing of 1944 revealed its existence. Vestments, reliquaries, church plate and religious sculpture are now displayed here. Some of the pillars have ancient graffiti which may date from the 11C.

Turn left on leaving the church. The **National Bank** at no. 5 occupies a faithful replica of a guild house called the Tafelronde (Round Table) built by Mathys de Layens in 1480–88. The original guild house was torn down in the 19C and a neo-classical edifice built in its place. This was destroyed in 1914, allowing the original Gothic building to be faithfully reconstructed in 1921.

The **Museum Vander Kelen-Mertens** in Savoyestraat occupies part of the Savoy College. Open Tues–Sat 10.00–17.00; Sun and holidays 14.00–17.00.

The museum contains an good collection of **Flemish paintings**, sculptures, furniture, metalwork, porcelain and tapestries. Many of the works come from destroyed churches and monasteries. The works are displayed in handsome period rooms furnished in Renaissance, Baroque, Rococo and Louis XVI style. The paintings include a *Descent from the Cross with Donors* by an unknown artist of c 1567, a superb Mosan *Sedes Sapientiae* of the 11C or 12C, the *Childhood and Passion of Christ* by a painter of the Antwerp School of c 1520, the *Holy Trinity* by Roger van der Weyden, a *Mourning over the Body of Christ* by Quinten Metsys, a *Madonna and Child* by Van Cleef and a *Temptation of St Antony*, reminiscent of Bosch, by Jan Mandyn. There is also a curious **circular calendar** by an unknown artist of c 1500, which is full of captivating medieval details. The **basement** contains an interesting new section devoted to local archaeology.

The Savoy College

The Savoy College was founded in 1545 to accommodate about 25 poor students from the Savoy region of France. The portal dates from 1650, but the building beyond, which was acquired by the Vander Kelen-Mertens family after the French Revolution, was transformed in the late 19C. Excavations in the garden have uncovered fish bones and other food remains discarded by 16C students. The family gave the house to the town in 1919 for use as a municipal museum. The garden has been planted in 15C style. The foundations of the students' lodgings can be seen near the gate.

Leave the museum garden by the back gate and turn left down Tiensestraat to reach the **University Library** on Herbert Hooverplein. Opened in July 1928, this building in Flemish Renaissance style replaces the medieval library destroyed by the Germans in 1914. It was designed by the American architect Whitney Warren, who based the design on the cloth hall at Ypres. The architect worked without a fee and the building was largely funded by American donors. The **carillon**, located in the belfry (85m), commemorates American engineers who died in the First World War.

Fire and sword

On 25 August, 1914, six days after entering Leuven, German troops set fire to Leuven. The Stadhuis and Sint Pieterskerk were badly damaged and 1200 houses were totally destroyed. The university library, located at the time in the medieval cloth hall, was reduced to a smouldering ruin. Its famous collection of books was destroyed, including 500 manuscripts, 1000 incunabula, and over 250,000 printed books. Historians are still not certain about the cause of the attack. Some believe that the German troops were thrown into confusion after a Belgian counter-attack came within 3km of the town, and panicked when a horse bolted through the streets. Others say that they were ruthlessly pursuing a military plan to strike terror into the civilian population.

After the war, Germany was required by the terms of the Treaty of Versailles to restock the library with books equal in value to those destroyed. Many universities in the United States and Britain contributed funds for the construction of the new library on Herbert Hooverplein. The names of the donors are carved in handsome calligraphy on the pillars of the arcade. Most of the destroyed houses were rebuilt in their old style in the 1920s. The reconstructions are marked by a plaque with the date 1914 and the symbol of a flaming torch and sword.

A Baroque portal at the far end of Herbert Hooverplein leads to the **Sint Donatus Park**, which follows a stretch of the old city wall. Turn right at the park entrance down Tiensestraat, past the **Kollege De Falk** at no. 41. This 18C Neo-classical building is now occupied by the law faculty. Turn left down Muntstraat and left again to reach the leafy Hogeschoolplein. The **Pope's College** at no. 3 was founded in 1523 by Pope Adrian VI, a Leuven theology professor who was appointed Pope in 1522 but died the following year. The nearby **Maria Theresia College** was established by the Empress Maria Theresa in 1778. The university assembly hall is located here.

2 • The University and Groot Begijnhof

Begin on **Grote Markt** and follow Naamsestraat, past the Stadhuis (on the left) and the **Hallen** (on the right). The Hallen (cloth hall) was built in Gothic style by the clothworkers' guild between 1317 and 1345. The building was given to the university in 1619 to accommodate the university library. A rather incongruous Baroque upper tier was added in the 17C and the rear façade on Oude Markt was rebuilt in 1723. Largely destroyed by the German army in 1914, the Hallen was rebuilt after the war. It is now occupied by the university administration.

The route now passes several old colleges on Naamsestraat, beginning with the **Heilig Geest College** at no. 40, founded in the 15C for theology students and rebuilt in the 18C. Damaged during an air raid in 1944, it has been rebuilt in its old style. Almost opposite, the **Sint Michielskerk** was built as a Jesuit church by Father Willem Hessius between 1650 and 1666. Badly damaged in 1944, it was rebuilt between 1947 and 1950. The splendid Baroque façade was considered one of the 'seven wonders of Leuven' in the 18C. The interior retains some outstanding 17C–18C woodwork.

The **King's College** at no. 59 was founded in 1579 by Philip II of Spain and rebuilt in Neo-classical style in the 18C. The **Premonstratensian College** at no. 61 was founded in the 16C by the abbeys of Parc, Ninove, Grimbergen and Averbode. It was rebuilt in Louis XV style in 1755. The 18C **Arras College** at no. 63 was founded in 1508 by Nicolas de Ruyter, bishop of Arras. If the gate is open, you can go into the courtyard to look at the replica of the bronze **celestial globe** designed by Ferdinand Verbiest in 1675 for the Kangxi Emperor in Beijing.

Next is a curious 15C Gothic house at no. 71 known as the **Huis van 't Sestich**. The **Van Dale College** is opposite at no. 80. Founded by Pieter van Dale in 1569, it is the last surviving Renaissance college in Leuven. The buildings are now occupied by student welfare offices. Further down the street, the **American College** at no. 100 was built in 1857 in neo-Gothic style to educate missionaries bound for North America.

Now turn right down Karmelietenberg to reach the beautiful **Groot Begijnhof**. Founded in the 13C on the banks of the River Dijle, this rapidly grew into one of the largest Begijnhofs in Belgium. The 70 or so houses mainly date from the 17C and 18C. Acquired by the university in 1962, the brick buildings have been sensitively restored as student accommodation. With its old brick bridges, iron water pumps and occasional gardens, the complex is one of the

Begijnhof, Leuven

most picturesque sites in Flanders. The church was constructed in 1305, though the furnishings are 17C.

Leaving the Begijnhof by the north entrance, follow the River Dijle along Redingenstraat. This leads to the Pater Damiaanplein, where you see the curious **Sint Antonius Kapel**, built in the 14C but transformed in 1961.

The **crypt** of the Sint Antonius Kapel contains the grave of the missionary priest Joseph de Veuster. Known as **Father Damien** of Tremelo, he spent years caring for the outcast lepers of Molokai, Hawaii. Damien finally contracted leprosy and died from the disease in 1889. His body was brought here in 1936. He is commemorated by a statue in the Capitol Building in Washington.

The **Irish College** opposite the chapel was founded in 1601 by Irish Franciscans. The **Dutch College** at no. 9 was founded in 1617 for educating Dutch priests. Rebuilt in 18C Neo-classical style, it is now occupied by a school. **Bishop Jansenius**, founder of Jansenism, was master here from 1618 to 1636. A lane to the right of the Dutch College leads to a waterside tower dating from 1616 which was used by Jansenius as a retreat. Known as the **Janseniustoren**, it was imaginatively restored in 1985. The tower rests on a 12C turret from the city defences.

Back on the square, go left along Parijsstraat and left along Minderbroedersstraat to reach Kapucijnenvoer. A curious brick building on the corner was built in the 18C as an anatomy theatre and later used as a studio by the 19C sculptor Constantin Meunier. A 19C Neo-classical portal opposite leads into the **Botanical Gardens**. Follow Kapucijnenvoer a short distance to the right and then turn left down Biezenstraat. This leads to the St Jacobsplein, and the sadly neglected **Sint Jacobskerk**. Built from 13C–15C, the church has been closed since 1963. A statue of Father Damien carved by Constantin Meunier stands outside the church.

Now go down Kruisstraat and turn right on Brusselsestraat. A narrow waterside lane on the left known as Handbooghof leads past the remains of the 12C city wall. Back on Brusselsestraat, there is a striking Romanesque gate at **no. 63**. Dating from c 1220, this formed the entrance of the St Elisabeth Hospice. A chapel, cloister and farm are still standing. The gate at **no. 65** leads to the vestiges of the hospice, which have been converted into a cultural centre.

Soon after the portal, turn right down the cobbled Predikherenstraat, passing on the left the 16C residence of Guy Morillon, secretary of Charles V. The portal beyond here leads to a peaceful corner of the town where the Dominicans built a monastery. All that remains is the Gothic chapel of **Onze-Lieve-Vrouw ten Predikheren**, and even that has now been converted into an exhibition centre. The Drinkwaterstraat leads from here to Parijsstraat, where the walk turns left to reach Grote Markt.

3 • The Klein Begijnhof and the Sint Gertrudiskerk

This walk begins at the **Grote Markt** and heads down the hill opposite the town hall, past the post office of 1893–95. The attractive Mechelsestraat opens into the Vismarkt, where a portal next to no. 4 leads to the remains of the **Collegium Trilingue**. The Gothic spiral staircase at no. 6D is a last vestige of Erasmus's college.

The scholar's tale
Aided by a bequest from Hieronymus van Busleyden, Erasmus founded his 'Collegium Trilingue' on the Vismarkt in 1517. Originally intended to provide a liberal Catholic education in Hebrew, Greek and Latin, Erasmus' dream was shattered by the rise of the radical Luther in Germany. The authorities took fright and strict orthodoxy was enforced. Erasmus fled to Switzerland in 1521 and never returned to his native land.

Continue down Mechelsestraat from where the **Keizersberg** can be seen in the distance. This hill is surmounted by the ruins of the castle of the dukes of Brabant and a modern Benedictine abbey (not open to the public).

Turn right down Halfmaartstraat to reach the **Sint Gertrudiskerk**, originally an abbey church. The choir was built between 1298–1310, and the nave added from 1327–1380. The **spire** (71m) was added by Jan van Ruysbroeck in 1453 and considered one of the 'seven wonders of Leuven' in the 18C. His work remained standing until the mid 19C when, because of structural weakness, the spire had to be rebuilt. The 16C choir stalls, badly damaged in an air raid in 1944, were skilfully restored by Jan van Uitvanck. Inside are interesting misericords and high reliefs of scenes from the Passion.

Through the gate to the right of the tower is a bizarre row of houses known as the **Thierry Wing**, built using architectural fragments salvaged from houses destroyed in 1914. This curious project was proposed by a canon who sat on the committee for the reconstruction of Leuven.

Return to the church and cross the road to enter the **Klein Begijnhof**, which originated as an infirmary c 1275. It was suppressed by the French in 1796, and all that remains are some 17C and 18C houses, many of them now in need of restoration.

The **Museum Humbeeck-Piron**, open Wed–Mon 10.00–18.00, is rather off the beaten track at Mechelsevest 108. This mansion contains a collection of paintings by Pierre van Humbeeck and his wife Marie Piron. The rooms contain furniture, porcelain and pictures collected by the couple.

Leuven environs

Heverlee

The town of Heverlee is an old settlement on the River Dijle, 2km southeast of Leuven. Surrounded by woodland and lakes, it is a popular district for walking and cycling. Several faculties of Leuven University are based at Heverlee near Arenberg castle.

Where to stay

The *Kasteel van Neerijse*, Lindenhoflaan 1, ☎ 016.47.28.50, is a country house hotel in a large park, 10km from Leuven.

Eating out

The woods around Heverlee are dotted with attractive restaurants and rustic inns.

De Oude Kantien, Kantineplein 3, Heverlee, ☎ 016.22.20.84, is an old Flemish inn from 1596 opposite Arenberg castle, with a large garden and children's playground.

The Renaissance castle of **Arenberg** was built in 1511 by Guillaume de Croy next to the meandering River Dijle in Heverlee. The castle, restored in the 19C, was presented by the Duke of Arenberg to the university in 1916. The architecture faculty is based in the castle. Other university departments have been established in the grounds.

The Premonstratensian abbey of **Park** was founded in Heverlee in 1129 by Godefroy I of Brabant. Closed down by the French in 1797, it was reopened in 1836. The existing abbey buildings date mainly from the 17C and 18C. Enter through a gateway of 1722 and cross the rustic farm courtyard. The farm buildings were constructed in the late 17C. The church, which is basically 13C Romanesque, was refaced in the Baroque style in 1729. It contains interesting paintings by Erasmus Quellin and Pierre Joseph Verhaghen. The east side of the cloister is 16C, the rest 17C. The magnificent ceilings in the Baroque library and refectory were decorated by Jan Hansche between 1672 and 1679. (**Guided tours** on Sun and public holidays at 16.00.).

Kessel-Lo

The remains of the **Benedictine abbey of Vlierbeek** are in the suburb of Kessel-Lo. Founded in 1127, the abbey was suppressed by the French in 1796. Some of the buildings are still standing, including the 17C abbot's residence and the former abbey church. Built by Laurent Dewez between 1776 and 1783, it is now used as the parish church (open daily 09.00–16.00).

Leefdaal

The **castle** at Leefdaal, 8km southwest of Leuven, was rebuilt after 1626. It retains two pepperpot towers which flanked the drawbridge of the older castle. The Romanesque chapel at **Sint Verone**, 1.5km northeast of Leefdaal, probably dates mainly from the 12C. The choir and tower may be as old as 1000. The church in nearby **Bertem** dates from the 11C and retains a fortified tower.

MECHELEN AND LIER

Mechelen

Mechelen (Malines in French) is an attractive Flemish town of 64,000 inhabitants on the River Dijle with a spectacular late Gothic cathedral tower. It is internationally famous for its tapestry workshop and carillon school. Mechelen has been the ecclesiastical capital of Belgium since the mid-16C. The Cardinal-Archbishop of Mechelen is Primate of Belgium. The farmland around Mechelen produces chickens, asparagus and chicory.

Practical information

Eating out
Restaurants

£££ *Hoogh*, Grote Markt 19,
☎ 015.21.75.53, is an elegant restaurant on the main square.
£ *Den Beer*, Grote Markt 32,
☎ 015.20.97.06. Modern brasserie facing the cathedral. Good Italian sandwichs and traditional Belgian dishes.

Cafés

Negrita, Désiré Boucherystraat 7–9, has been making delicious ice cream since 1890.
Royale, Grote Markt, is a traditional grand café with a good beer list.

Tourist information

Stadhuis, Grote Markt, ☎ 015.29.76.55. Closed on Sundays from November to March.

Carillon concerts

Two carillons, each with 49 bells, hang in the cathedral tower. The older of the two has bells dating from the 15C. A modern carillon was installed in 1981. Concerts are played on the carillon from Jun–mid-Sept on Mon 20.30–21.30. A small carillon hangs in the tower of the **Hof van Busleyden**. Students at the nearby carillon school practise here.

Festival

A statue of Our Lady of the Hanswijk is carried in procession every year on the last Sunday before Ascension. The procession dates from 1277, when the people of Mechelen were spared from the plague by a miraculous statue of the Virgin. The procession is one of the oldest in Belgium.

Opening times

Hof van Busleyden (municipal museum) and the **Carillon Museum**, Frederik de Merodestraat 65, are open Wed–Mon 10.00–12.00 and 14.00–17.00.
Mechelen Cathedral, Grote Markt, is open daily 09.00–12.00 and 13.00–17.00. No visits during services. Guided tours of the cathedral tower are given on Sat, Sun and public holidays at 14.15 (Easter–Sept), and on Mon at 19.00 (Jun–mid Sept).
Onze Lieve Vrouw van Hanswijk, Hanswijkstraat, is open Mon–Sat 09.00–16.00, Sun 14.00–16.00.
Onze Lieve Vrouw over de Dijle, Onze Lieve Vrouwstraat, is open in May, June and Sept Sat 14.30–17.30; in July and Aug Wed 14.00–17.00, Sat 14.00–17.30.
St Janskerk, St Jansstraat, is open Sat 15.00–15.30 and Sun 10.00–11.30.

**Gaspard de Wit tapestry work-
shop**, in the Abbey of Tongerlo,
Schoutetstraat, is open for guided tours
Sat at 10.30. Closed Jun and 25–31 Dec.

**Centrum voor Speelgoed en
Volkskunde** (toy museum),
Nekkerspoelstraat 21, is open Tues–Sun
10.00–17.00

History

Mechelen began in the early Middle Ages as a settlement in the marshy land
beside the River Dijle. **St Rombout** founded an abbey here in 756 and converted the people to Christianity. He is described in some accounts as the
bishop of Dublin and the son of the king of the Scots (which at that period
meant the Irish). St Rombout was martyred in 775 for criticising two men
about their evil ways. His body was dredged from the Dijle and a church was
built on the spot where he was buried.

The settlement became a fiefdom of the prince-bishops of Liège in the early
11C, but in 1213 sovereignty was delegated to the powerful Berthout family.
Despite disputes over ownership, Mechelen was granted charters in 1301 and
1305. The town enjoyed considerable freedom until c 1333, when it was
acquired by **Louis de Male**, Count of Flanders. Mechelen passed on his
death, along with the rest of Flanders, to the dukes of Burgundy.

Much of the town was destroyed in a fire of 1342. Its fortunes began to
improve after Charles the Bold founded the Grand Council here in 1473.
This was the supreme court of the Netherlands; its presence brought numerous lawyers and court officials to the town. After Charles died in 1477, his
widow Margaret of York, sister of Edward IV of England, settled in
Mechelen.

The **golden age of Mechelen** began in 1506, when Margaret of Austria
was appointed governor of the Netherlands, as regent for the infant Charles
V. She chose Mechelen rather than Brussels as her capital; her court attracted
some of the best scholars and artists of the early 16C, including the painters
Jan Mostaert, Jan Gossaert, Bernard van Orley and Albrecht Dürer, the
humanist Hieronymus van Busleyden and the architect Rombout
Keldermans. This period of brilliance ended with Margaret's death in 1530,
when the capital was transferred back to Brussels.

The town's fortunes revived in 1559 when Mechelen, formerly in the dio-
cese of Cambrai, was made an **archbishopric**. Antoine Perrenot de
Granvelle (1517–86), Philip II's French adviser, was the first holder of the
see. Archbishop Granvelle was created Primate of the Spanish Netherlands. A
brief interlude of Calvinist domination ended with the capture and sack of
the town by the Duke of Alva in 1572. Mechelen soon recovered; it became
famous in the 17C–18C for its **lace and Baroque wood-carving**, while its
tapestry was acclaimed in the 19C.

Mechelen was bombarded three times in 1914 before it capitulated to the
Germans. The Belgians were encouraged to resist the occupying army by
Cardinal Mercier in his famous pastoral letter *Patriotism and Endurance*. The
town was badly damaged again at the end of the Second World War by bombing and V weapons.

Mechelen was the **birthplace** of the painters Michiel Coxie in 1499, and
Frans Hals in 1580, and the sculptor John van Nost, or van Ost (fl
1686–1729). Beethoven's grandfather was also born in Mechelen in 1712.

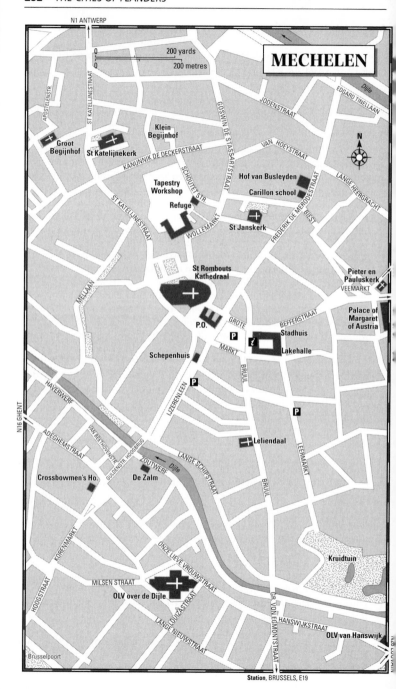

1 • Historic Mechelen

Begin on **Grote Markt**, the main square, where a statue of Margaret of Austria was erected in 1849. It is surrounded by a paved circle equal in circumference to the clock dial once on the cathedral tower. The **Stadhuis** on the east side of the square is made up of two very different wings. The right wing is the former Lakenhalle (cloth hall).

History

Begun in 1320 and modelled on the Cloth Hall at Bruges, it was badly damaged by the great fire of 1342. The tower was never completed. The octagonal turrets date from the 16C. The left wing was demolished in 1526 to make way for a new building which Charles V intended to be used as the meeting-place of the Grand Council. Designed by Rombout Keldermans, this building was begun in 1526, but work ceased in 1546, following a disastrous city fire. The unfinished building was occasionally used for various purposes, but most of the time was left to rot. A fake façade was set up for formal occasions. It was not until 1911 that the town took over the site and completed the building to Keldermans' original plans.

In a **niche**, and looking a trifle grim, sits Charles V. An arch in the Lakenhalle leads to a courtyard where there is a modern sculpture called *Mother* carved by Ernest Wijnants.

The **Post Office** stands on the side opposite the Stadhuis. It occupies an 18C house built on 13C foundations. This was the town hall until Kelderman's building was finally completed in 1911. Turn down IJzerenleen to the **Schepenhuis**. Built in 1374, this was the seat of the Grand Council from 1474 to 1618. It later served as a town hall, theatre and museum. The municipal archives were kept here up until 1991.

Sint Romboutskathedraal

The Sint Romboutskathedraal, off the Grote Markt, is open daily 09.00–12.00 and 13.00–17.00. Guided tours of the **cathedral tower** are given on Sat, Sun and public holidays at 14.15 (Easter–Sept), and Mon at 19.00 (Jun–mid-Sept).

History of the cathedral

The cathedral was begun c 1217 after the marshland near the Dijle was drained. Traces of the first church can still be seen in the crossing and transepts, the central nave and the lower courses of the choir. Dedicated in 1312, it was badly damaged by the fire of 1342. The reconstruction included the addition of a triforium and the enlargement of the choir with its ambulatory and chapels. The chapels off the north aisle date from 1498–1502. The church was completed in the 16C.

The **tower** was begun in 1452. It was probably designed by Wouter Coolman (d. 1468), though some historians believe that the plans were prepared by Jan Keldermans (d. 1445). The original plan was to build a tower with a spire reaching a height of 167m, which would have created the highest structure in the Low Countries (the spire of Antwerp cathedral is 123m). There is a model of the proposed spire in the cathedral and the architectural plans are displayed in the Hof van Busleyden. The tower was built by the Keldermans family, but financial difficulties brought construction work to a sudden halt in 1546 when it had reached a height of 97m. Having surmounted the 514 steps of the tower there is a good view of the town.

The cathedral is one of the most impressive Gothic buildings in Europe. Enter from the Grote Markt, and begin at the **Altar of St Anne** in the **south transept**, which was carved in 1699 by Jan Steen for the masons' guild. It is surmounted by a *Crucifixion* painted by Antoon van Dyck in 1630. Originally commissioned for the church of the Friars Minor, this is regarded as one of the artist's finest achievements. The decorated blind arches partly hidden behind the altar are among the oldest parts of the cathedral.

The statues of the Apostles in the **nave** date from the 17C. A Baroque Communion Bench made of white marble stands in front of the Chapel of the Blessed Sacrement in the north aisle. Attributed to Artus Quellin the Younger, it was brought here from the ancient convent of Leliendaal. The Baroque **pulpit** came from the same convent. Carved in 1723 by Michel Vervoort, it shows St Norbert being thrown from his horse.

The **Sacraments Chapel** has an impressive vaulted ceiling. A painting by Michiel Coxie of 1580 shows the *Circumcision of Christ*. A tomb by Louis Jehotte marks the grave of Archbishop de Méan, who led the church during the crisis years immediately after the French Revolution.

The **Chapel of Our Lady of the Miracle** contains an ancient image of the Virgin, which has been venerated in the cathedral since the beginning of the 16C. There is also a statue of 1688 by a local sculptor, Niklaas van der Veken, of *Christ Suffering*.

The **Chapel of Cardinal Mercier** commemorates a Belgian cardinal who took a courageous stand against the Germans during the First World War. His *Appeal to All Christian People* led to the Malines Conversations of 1921–26, which aimed at bringing about the union of the Roman Catholic and Anglican Churches. A plaque in the chapel was presented by the Church of England in 1966 to commemorate the Malines Conversations. The bronze figure of the cardinal on the marble tomb was designed by a Capuchin friar, R.P. Ephrem. The stained glass windows recall various incidents in the life of Mercier.

The **Altar of Our Lady** in the north transept was made by Frans Langhermans in 1699. It incorporates a painting of the *Adoration of the Shepherds* by Jan Erasmus Quellin. A painting on the opposite wall shows the interior of the cathedral in 1755.

The eight statues on the walls and columns of the **transept** are by Lucas Faydherbe, Theodoor Verhaeghen and Pieter Valckx. They represent Mark, Luke, Ambrose, Augustine, Charles, Gregory, Jerome and Joseph.

The spectacular **high altar** in the choir was carved by Lucas Faydherbe. It is dominated by a huge statue of St Rombout. The relics of the saint are in a reliquary protected by a grill decorated with arabesques. Lucas Faydherbe also carved the *Mater Dolorosa* which hangs above a door near the north entry to the ambulatory.

Enter the **ambulatory** (entrance fee) on the north side, where there is the tomb of the Berthout family, lords of Mechelen during the 13C–14C. A triptych on the opposite wall by Michiel Coxie illustrates the *Martyrdom of St George*. Twelve glass cases contain 15C–16C panels illustrating the *Legend of St*

Rombout. The former chapel of Our Lady of Zellaer (**first chapel**) contains a triptych of 1607 by Jean le Sayve the Elder with scenes and figures from the Old Testament; they show *David the Conqueror of Goliath*, the *Sacrifice of Abraham* and *Judith leaving the Tent of Holofernes*. The chapel also contains a Virgin and Child surrounded by Saints of 1649 by Gaspard de Crayer.

The **second chapel** has funerary monuments and grave slabs from the 17C–19C. The **third chapel**, which is dedicated to St John Berchmans, has the gravestone of Igramus van Achelen, president of the Grand Council, who died in 1604. The **fourth chapel**, dedicated to St Joseph, contains the gravestone of Arnould de Mérode, who died in 1553, and of his wife, Catherine de Gottignies.

The Chapel of the Blessed Sacrament (**fifth chapel**) is decorated with stained glass windows commemorating the first Eucharistic Congress, held in Mechelen in 1930. The **sixth chapel**, dedicated to St Engelbert, commemorates Cardinal Engelbert Sterckx, who died in 1867. The **seventh chapel** is dedicated to priests from Mechelen killed during the First World War. A 17C painting by Gaspard de Crayer shows *St Francis praying to the Madonna*.

The Chapel of the Relics (**eighth chapel**) contains a curious reliquary of the **Martyrs of Gorcum**. Murdered by Calvinists in 1572 at Gorinchem, near Dordrecht, the 19 martyrs were canonised in 1867. You can also see the hatchments of the Knights of the Golden Fleece, who met at the chapter held in the cathedral in 1491. A tombstone marks the grave of Jacques Godin, a lawyer to the Grand Council who died in 1559. The **ninth chapel** contains a painting of 1632 by Abraham Janssens showing *St Luke painting the Virgin*.

A triptych by Michiel Coxie on the **sacristy** wall depicts the *Martyrdom of St Sebastian*. A painting in the baptistry by Jean le Sayve the Elder shows the *Baptism of Christ*.

Manneblussers

The inhabitants of Mechelen have been known as 'Manneblussers' or Moon-dousers since 1687, when a citizen returning home after an evening's drinking mistook the ruddy glow of the moon on the cathedral tower for a fire and promptly roused the whole town to put it out.

Now follow Sint Katelijnestraat to reach the **Sint Katelijnekerk**, begun in the mid 14C with a portal added in the 15C. The Baroque Confessionals were carved in 1700 by Niklaas van der Veken. A 1716 statue of *St Catherine* by Piérard de Lyon stands at the entrance to the choir. The stalls have exquisitely carved 18C faces by Pieter Valckx.

The Baroque **Begijnhofkerk** lies down the lane opposite. It was built 1629–1647 by Jacob Franckaert. The two statues on the façade were carved by Lucas Faydherbe. They show St Catherine (above the porch) and God the Father (at the top). The sumptuous if slightly gaudy interior contains Flemish Baroque sculpture and paintings by Lucas Faydherbe, Jan Steen, Jerome Duquesnoy the Younger, Gaspard de Crayer, Jan Erasmus Quellin and Cornelis Cels.

The history of the two **Begijnhofs** in Mechelen is rather vague and confused, but it appears that the original settlement was founded in the 13C outside the town walls. Some of the older Beguines established a second Begijnhof, the

Klein Begijnhof, within the walls in 1562. This attractive network of cobbled lanes lined with modest houses survives to the east of the Sint Katelijnekerk. The original Begijnhof was frequently attacked and pillaged, notably by the Calvinists in 1580–85, and eventually relocated in 1595 to a new close within the town walls. Known as the Groot Begijnhof, this warren of small streets remains standing to the west of the Begijnhofkerk. It is entered by a gate at Sint Katelijnestraat 111.

After exploring the Groot Begijnhof, turn down Schoutetstraat to look at the Refuge of the **Abbey of Tongerlo**, built in 1483 and now occupied by the **Gaspard de Wit tapestry workshop** which is open for guided tours on Sat at 10.30; closed Jun and 25–31 Dec. Further along, the **Refuge of the Abbey of St Truiden** was built slightly later in c 1500.

Turn left at the end of Schoutetstraat down Goswin de Stassartstraat to obtain a striking view of the St Truiden refuge reflected in a stagnant branch of the Dijle known as Groen Waterke. The **Museum of Deportation and Resistance** occupies a former army barracks at no. 153 where more than 25,000 Jews were held before deportation. The museum, which opened in 1996, charts the Holocaust through documents, photographs and recordings. Open Sun–Thurs 10.00–17.00, Fri 10.00–13.00. Closed Sat.

A narrow lane opposite the Groen Waterke called Klapgat leads to the 15C **Sint Janskerk**, open on Sat 15.00–15.30 and Sun 10.00–11.30, which has a triptych of the *Adoration of the Magi* painted in 1619 by Pieter Paul Rubens. The artist's first wife was the model for the Virgin Mary in the centre panel. The benches and organ case at the west end of the church were carved by Pieter Valckx. The pulpit and two benches by the transept pillars are by Theodoor Verhaeghen and pupils.

The **Carillon School** occupies an attractive corner building opposite the church. Students come from all over the world to study the techniques of carillon playing here. The school is named after Jef Denyn (1862–1941), a famous Mechelen carilloneur on whose sixtieth birthday the school was founded.

> ### Carillons
> Carillon concerts are one of the most appealing aspects of the Low Countries. The ringing of bells began in medieval belfries where small bells hung in the tower were struck by a hammer to signal the passing of the hours. Most belfries originally had four bells, known as the 'Quadrilloner', which led to the name carillon. The modern carillon containing six or eight bells was developed at the beginning of the 16C. At about the same time, the mallet was replaced by a clavier. The first keyboard carillon was built at Oudenaarde in 1510. A version with pedals was introduced in Mechelen in 1583. Some belfries have installed automatic carillons programmed to play tunes on the quarter hour. About 300 carillons have survive in the Low Countries. Many of the carilloneurs receive their training in Mechelen's school.

Hof van Busleyden
The Hof van Busleyden just around the corner at Frederik de Merodestraat 65 was built in 1503–17. One wing is now occupied by the **Carillon Museum** while the remainder of the palace is occupied by the Municipal Museum. Both are open Wed–Mon 10.00–12.00 and 14.00–17.00.

This handsome late Gothic palace was probably designed by Antoon Keldermans and built by his son Rombout. It was once the home of the Flemish humanist Hieronymus van Busleyden (c 1470–1517). Wenceslas Coeberger opened a municipal pawnshop here in 1619; it remained in this building until the First World War. Damaged in World War One, the building was restored and reopened in 1935 as the municipal museum.

Hieronymus van Busleyden, a member of a noble Luxembourg family, studied at Leuven and Bologna and became a Doctor of Law. He so impressed Philip the Handsome that he was appointed counsellor to the Grand Council. A friend of Thomas More and Erasmus, he helped Erasmus establish his **Collegium Trilingue** for the study of Latin, Greek and Hebrew at Leuven. Van Busleyden was a member of the brilliant and scholarly circle that formed around Margaret of Austria. He died on the way to Spain while on a mission for Charles V.

The first object you are likely to see on entering is the mascot of Mechelen, 'Op Signoor'. The name derives from *señor*, a 16C term mocking the citizens of Antwerp for their alleged snobbery. The figure was carved in 1647 by Valentyn van Lanscroon and carried during the town's annual processions. After being kidnapped by the students of Antwerp in 1949, it was placed in the museum for safety.

The museum has some **Gallo-Roman finds** (rooms 1 and 2), an interesting plan of Mechelen in 1574 (room 6) and some paintings of the Great Council in session (room 8). The next room (room 9) contains the *Poupées de Malines*, a set of 16C handmade wooden dolls. The Hapsburg connection is covered in Room 10, which includes a statue of Margaret of Austria and two handsome terrestrial globes. Van Busleyden's former **dining room** (room 11) is decorated with murals attributed variously to Bernard van Orley and Michiel Coxie.

The upstairs rooms contain **Baroque sculptures** by Lucas Faydherbe (room 12) and **Louis XV furniture** (rooms 14 and 16). There is also the former **reliquary of St Rombout** (room 17), guild paintings (rooms 23 and 24) and works by 20C artists and sculptors, including Albert Servaes and Rik Wouters. The **Carillon Museum** contains an interesting collection of old bells, carillons and documents.

The walk continues down Biest, which begins opposite the Carillon School and ends at the triangular Veemarkt where the **Sint Pieter en Sint Pauluskerk** stands. Built between 1670 and 1677 in typical Jesuit style, the church has paintings by Jan Erasmus Quellin and others depicting the life of St Francis Xavier. A pulpit carved in 1700 by Hendrik Verbruggen symbolises the saint's missionary work.

The former 15C hall of the **Palace of Margaret of York** stands to the right of the church. A plaque attached to the octagonal tower records that she stayed here from 1477 to 1482. The **Palace of Margaret of Austria** stands directly opposite on Keizerstraat. The oldest part of the building is the late Gothic wing in the courtyard, which was built in 1507–17 by Rombout Keldermans. The Renaissance façade was designed by Guyot de Beaugrant, and introduced Italian architectural principles to the Low Countries. The palace served as the seat of the Grand Council between 1618 and 1794. It is now occupied by the local law courts.

2 • The River Dijle

Leave the **Grote Markt** by Bruul, passing the Jesuit church of **Leliendaal**, built in 1662 by Lucas Faydherbe. Just before the river, turn left into the **Kruidtuin**, or Pitzemburg Garden, where there is a statue of the botanist Rembrecht Dodoens (1517–85), a native of Mechelen. Looking across the river, there is a view of the Baroque church next on the itinerary.

The church is reached by leaving the garden and crossing the river, then turning left along Hanswijkstraat. The impressive basilica of **Onze Lieve Vrouw van Hanswijk,** open Mon–Sat 09.00–16.00 and Sun 14.00–16.00, was built 1663–1678 by Lucas Faydherbe. The inside of the dome is decorated with unusual reliefs by Faydherbe. A pulpit showing the *Expulsion* was carved by Verhaeghen. Just beyond the church, an old fulling mill stands by the river.

Now go back along Hanswijkstraat and continue straight ahead along Onze Lieve Vrouwstraat. This leads to the church of **Onze Lieve Vrouw over de Dijle**, open in May, June and Sept on Sat 14.30–17.30; in July and Aug on Wed 14.00–17.00, Sat 14.00–17.30. The nave and tower were built during the 15C, and the church completed in the 17C by Jacob Franckaert, who was working at the same time on the Begijnhof church. Damaged by artillery fire in 1914, air raids in 1944 and hit by a V weapon in 1945, the church was restored from 1962–68 by J. Lauwers.

A painting by Rubens of the *Miraculous Draught of Fishes* hangs in the south transept. This triptych was painted in 1618 for the Guild of Fishmongers. A *Last Supper* by Jan Erasmus Quellin hangs above the high altar. Seven small 17C altars representing the Seven Sorrows of the Virgin are attached to the outside walls of the church.

Return to the river down the lane 't Plein and turn left along Zoutwerf, the Salt Wharf. The wooden house **De Zalm** (The Salmon) at no. 5 was built for the Guild of Fishmongers. The façade dates from 1530. The street ends at the **Hoogbrug**, a bridge over the Dijle rebuilt in 1595 on the site of a 13C crossing. The bridge has unusual irregular arches and traces of the original guard towers.

Do not cross the bridge but turn left along Guldenstraat to look at the Renaissance house at **Korenmarkt 8**. Built as a cloth hall in the 13C, it became a private house in the 15C. The slender spire was added in 1561 by a German merchant who owned the house. In 1604 it became the **Guild House of the Crossbowmen**. The Baroque house at **no. 6** is occupied by a workshop making large clocks for towers. Now go back along Guldenstraat and turn left down Van Beethovenstraat, named after Ludwig van Beethoven's grandfather (1712–73), who was born in this street. The De Anker brewery stands on the site of the house.

Continuing along the waterfront quay known as Haverwerf, you come to three 16C–17C façades which have been repainted in their original gaudy colours. Turn right over the bridge and follow the road on the right to reach the picturesque waterfront square where the fish market was once held and several fishmongers still thrive. Return to the Grote Markt along the broad Ijzerenleen, which takes its name (Iron Avenue) from the iron railings erected in 1531 along a canal. The canal was covered over in the 17C.

Other sights

The sturdy **Brusselpoort** at the end of the Hoogstraat is the only one of Mechelen's original 12 gates to survive. Built c 1300, the gate was given a curious Baroque roof in the 17C. The **Centrum voor Speelgoed en Volkskunde** at Nekkerspoel 21 is a rambling and rather disorganised toy museum which has a certain dusty charm. It is open Tues–Sun 10.00–17.00.

Mechelen environs

Mechelen is surrounded by attractive countryside where several 17C artists including Rubens and Coxie and bought country estates.

Het Steen

Rubens' country house, The Steen or **Rubenssteen**, can be seen from the road near **Elewijt** village, 12km south of Mechelen. First mentioned in 1304, this old castle was bought by Rubens in 1635. Racked by illness and surrounded by young children, Rubens spent his last years here. The castle and surrounding fields appear in several landscape paintings, such as the *View of Het Steen in the Early Morning* (National Gallery, London, 1636). These works were eagerly bought by British collectors and inspired 18C English landscape artists such as Gainsborough and Constable. Het Steen was sold on the death of Hélène Fourment in 1681. The building was heavily restored in 1875 and 1918.

Perk

A farmhouse called **De Drie Torens** (The Three Towers) at Huinhovenstraat 16 in Perk, 4km south of **Elewijt**, was the home of Hélène Fourment, Rubens' second wife. It was bought in 1663 by David Teniers the Younger and appears in some of Teniers' paintings. Isabella de Fren, the second wife of David Teniers, is buried in the Sint Niklaaskerk. The large, turreted 17C–19C **Château Ribaucourt** stands to the southeast of the village.

Planckendael

An old country estate once owned by the painter Michel Coxie on the River Dijle has been used since 1956 as a **breeding park** for Antwerp Zoo. Animals roam in open spaces and a large colony of storks has been persuaded to settle in the trees. The park has an excellent children's adventure playground landscaped like a jungle and several cafés. A **boat** runs from Mechelen to the estate in the summer. (Leuvensesteenweg 582, Muizen-Mechelen. Open 09.00–18.15 in the summer and 09.00–16.30 in the winter.)

Ham

Ham castle, near **Steenokkerzeel**, was once the home of Charles de Lannoy who received the surrender of Francis I of France after the battle of Pavia on 24 February 1525. Francis was imprisoned for a year and obliged by Charles V to cede Artois, Burgundy, his Italian territories and Flanders. Ham castle was badly damaged in 1942 and shorn of its turrets.

Other sights

Hofstade, 5km southeast of Mechelen, is a popular **recreation park** with a large lake and inland beach. The town of **Heindonk**, 4km northwest of

Mechelen, has a town hall of 1550. **Rumst,** 6km northwest of Mechelen at the confluence of the Rupel and the Nete, is an important horticultural centre. The village church at **Reet**, 3km northwest of Rumst, has a 15C tower. The **Hof van Reet** is a 17C château.

Duffel

The town of Duffel, on the Nete, 9km north of Mechelen, was famous during the 16C for its manufacture of woollen garments. It is alleged to have given its name to the 'duffel coat'. The town was the birthplace of Kilianus (Cornelis Kiel 1528–1607, founder of Dutch philology and associate of Christopher Plantin). The castle of **Ter Elst** dates from the 16C.

Kontich

The town of Kontich, 12km north of Mechelen, originated in Gallo-Roman times. A 'fountain' from this period survives in the municipal park. The **Sint Maartenskerk** has a 12C Romanesque tower.

Willebroek

The small industrial town of Willebroek, 10km west of Mechelen, straddles the Willebroek Canal, which links Brussels with the river Rupel. The canal project was authorised by Mary of Burgundy in 1477, but bitterly opposed by Mechelen, as it would have deprived the town of toll rights by by-passing the town's waterways. The canal was finally opened in 1561. The church in Willebroek has a 12C Romanesque tower. William the Silent met Count Egmont in 1567 in an inn called Het Gulden Vlies next to the bridge.

The **Fort Breendonk**, 2km south of Willebroek, was built from 1906–1914 as an outlying fortress for the defence of Antwerp. It was used by the Germans as a concentration camp from 1940–1944. Now a **memorial museum**, the fort preserves the cells, torture room and execution site. A monument to the resistance movement by S. Jankevitsj was placed at the entrance in 1954. Fort open daily 09.00–17.00 (closes 16.00 Oct–Mar).

Sint Amands

The tomb of the poet Emile Verhaeren stands on a grassy spot near the Scheld outside the attractive river town of Sint Amands, 12km west of Willebroek. A modern sculpture titled the *Ferryman* by M. Macken stands near the tomb. Verhaeren, who wrote in French, was born in 1855 at Emile Verhaerenstraat 69. The **Verhaeren Museum** at no. 71 contains mementoes of the poet (open Jul–mid-Sept Tues–Thur, Sat and Sun 12.00–19.00; Mar–June and mid-Sept October on Sat and Sun 12.00–19.00).

Boom

The town of Boom, 5km north of Willebroek, is the most important brick-making centre in Belgium. A former brickworks at Noeveren 196 has been converted into a **museum of the brick industry** (open for guided tours from Apr–October on Sun at 14.00).

Bornem

The town of Bornem, 12km northeast of Willebroek, is important for asparagus cultivation. A monument commemorates the Peasants' Revolt of 1798, when atholics rebelled against French rule. The church has a 12C choir and lower ower. The 10C–11C crypt of a Benedictine priory church has survived.

A strange lost district of marshland lies north of Bornem, enclosed by the cheldt and the Old Scheldt (a former channel abandoned in the 13C). The ttractive village of **Weert** has a regional museum called the **Zilverreiger** with collection of local folklore (open Easter–Oct Tues–Fri 10.00–18.00, weekends nd public holidays 13.00–18.00).

.ier

ier is an appealing small town at the confluence of the Grote and Kleine Nete. It as a famous astronomical clock and attractive walks around parts of the 14C amparts.

ating out

he waterside *De Fortuin*, Felix immermansplein 7, ☎ 03.480.29.51, ccupies a striking building which was ne medieval granary. The tavern has in-xpensive dishes and a waterfront terrace.

ourist information

tadhuis, Grote Markt 57, ☎ 03.488.38.88.

Opening times

tedelijk Museum Wuyts-Van

Campen en Baron Caroly is open Apr–Oct Tues–Thur and at weekends, 10.00–12.00 and 13.30–17.30.
Zimmertoren is open daily 09.00–12.00 and 13.00–19.00 (closes 18.00 Apr, May, Jun and Sept; closes 17.00 in Mar and Oct; closes 16.00 from Nov–Feb).
Timmermans-Opsomerhuis is open Apr–Oct Tues–Thur and at weekends, 10.00–12.00 and 13.30–17.30; Nov–Mar on Sun 10.00–12.00 and 13.30–16.30.

History

Lier dates back to the 8C, when St Gummarus (717–74) settled here. A noble at the court of King Pepin, Gummarus apparently fled here to escape from his nagging wife. Lier was granted the status of a town by Duke Henry of Brabant in 1212. Philip the Handsome and Joanna of Castile were married here in 1496. Christian II of Denmark and his queen, Isabel of Austria, sister of Charles V, settled in Lier in 1523 after fleeing from Denmark.

A number of famous people were **born in Lier**. The metal sculptor L. van Boeckel (1857–1944) was born here, as was the writer Felix Timmermans (1886–1947), and the painter Baron Isidore Opsomer (1878–1967). Perhaps the most famous native is Louis Zimmer, 1888–1970, who constructed an astonishing astronomical clock in Lier.

A walk round Lier

he **Vleeshuis** on the Grote Markt dates from 1418. The Rococo **Stadhuis** was uilt in 1740 on the site of the medieval cloth hall. The preliminary plans were rawn by Jan Peter van Baurscheit the Younger. The building has more than ,500 small, bottle-green window panes. The interior contains an elaborate taircase of 1775 and a clock made by Zimmer. The attached belfry of 1369 once ormed part of the medieval cloth hall.

Go down Florent van Cauwenberghstraat to reach the **Stedelijk Museum Wuyts-Van Campen en Baron Caroly** at no. 14. This museum contains several important collections bequeathed in 1886 by the family which owned the house at that time. Other works were presented by Baron G. Caroly in 1935.

The paintings include Bernard van Orley's *Madonna with Child and Angel*, David Teniers the Elder's *Seven Works of Mercy*, and *The Alchemist*; Pieter Brueghel the Younger's *St John* and *Flemish Proverbs*; Jan Brueghel's *Madonna and Child*; Frans Floris' *The Van Berchem Family*; Antoon van Dyck's *St Sebastian* and *Portrait of a Nobleman*; Pieter Paul Rubens' *St Theresa*; David Teniers the Younger's *Jealous Wife* and *The Village of Perk*; Jan Steen's *Brawling Peasants*; and Murillo's *Bacchus*.

Back on Grote Markt, go down Eikelstraat, passing the **Eikelpoort**, which was built in c 1375 as part of the town defences, but altered in 1727. Used as a prison for many years, it is sometimes called the Prisoners' Gate.

Now go down Begijnhofstraat to reach the large **Begijnhof**, founded on the edge of the old town in c 1200. Most of the surviving buildings date from the late 17C. The Baroque chapel, which was built from 1664–1767, contains an **antependium**.

The design is attributed to Rubens, while the embroidery is thought to be the work of his daughter. The church also has a tabernacle by Willem Ignatius Kerrickx and sculpture by Artus Quellin the Younger.

Go back towards Grote Markt, then turn right into Zimmerplein, a long square which until the end of the 19C lay under water.

Begijnhof, Lier

The **Zimmertoren** at the far end of the square occupies a former medieval tower known as the Corneliustoren.

The local clockmaker Louis Zimmer built the extraordinary **Centenary Clock** on the tower in 1930–31. It features a central clock-face surrounded by 11 small dials and two spheres. The dials and spheres indicate the phases of the moon, the 19-year metonic cycle (covering the changes of the moon), Greenwich Mean Time, the signs of the zodiac, the solar cycle of 28 years, the dominical letter, the days of the week, the globe, the months with their various distinguishing features (Ice, Duck, Fish, Fool, Flower, Shearing, Hay, Harvest, Fruit, Wine, Butchering and Rest), the calendar, the seasons, the tides at Lier and the ages of the moon. A small crowd gathers below the clock at noon to watch various mechanical figures representing the Belgian national arms, the first three kings of Belgium, the arms of Lier, and the local burgomasters.

Zimmer also built an **Astronomic Studio** on the first floor of the tower. A clock with 57 dials records the subdivisions of time, the tides, the planetary system astronomical calculations, the rotation of the sun and planets, the phases of the moon and the tides, astronomical phenomena and the constellations of the northern hemisphere.

The **mechanisms** which work the Centenary Clock and the Astronomic Studio are on the **second floor**. Zimmer's astronomical **Wonder Clock** is displayed in an annexe. Exhibited at the Brussels World Fair of 1935 and New York World Fair of 1939, this 4.5m high clock has 14 automata and three large dials, each surmounting a panel of 30 smaller dials. Zimmer's workshop is also here. A small garden contains iron sculptures by L. van Boeckel.

Now cross the Kleine Nete by a small bridge just beyond the Zimmertoren. The **Timmermans-Opsomerhuis** at Netelaan 4 contains a collection of books by Timmermans and paintings by Baron Opsomer. It also has Van Boeckel's forge and some of his metal sculptures.

Turn left along Werf, once the waterside commercial quarter. The restaurant **De Fortuin** on the opposite quay occupies the medieval granary. On reaching the bridge, turn right along the Rechtestraat to reach the **Sint Gummaruskerk**. This Flamboyant Gothic church was built from 1425–1540. The base of the tower dates from the 14C, but the octagonal upper part is an 18C addition.

The **stained-glass** was restored after war damage in 1914. It includes some of the oldest and best glasswork in Belgium, dating from the 15C to the 20C. The most impressive windows include the 15C *Crowning of the Virgin* in the south aisle, the window of 1475 by Rombout Keldermans in the choir (left first row), and the group of five windows above the high altar. Three of these windows were presented by the Emperor Maximilian when he visited Lier in 1516.

The church contains some outstanding **works of art**, including a 1534 roodloft with the *Way of the Cross*. The pulpit and altar were carved by Artus Quellin the Elder. The triptych in the first ambulatory chapel on the left has wings painted by Rubens depicting *St Clare* and *St Francis*. The fourth ambulatory chapel contains another triptych of c 1516 attributed to Goswin van der Weyden. The **chapels** also contain works by Otto Venius, Martin de Vos, Michiel Coxie and Frans Francken the Elder.

The **Sint Pieterskapel** faces the north transept of the church. Founded in 1225, it was largely rebuilt after it was damaged in 1914. The Berlaarsestraat leads from here to the **Jesuitenkerk**, which has a fine Baroque façade. The church was built from 1749–54.

Lier environs

The hilltop town of **Heist-op-den-Berg**, 12km southeast of Lier, stands on a hill 45m above sea-level. This is the highest natural point in the province of Antwerp. The **Sint Lambertuskerk** of 1587 contains a marble *Madonna* by Artus Quellin the Younger.

HASSELT AND TONGEREN

Hasselt and Tongeren are attractive historic towns in Limburg province. Hasselt has an interesting genever museum, while Tongeren is worth visiting for its Basilica and Roman museum.

Hasselt

Hasselt is a small and friendly Flemish town with elegant shops and excellent museums.

Practical Information

Where to stay
Portmans, Minderbroedersstraat 12–14, ☎ 011.26.32.80, is a comfortable modern hotel in the town centre.

Eating out
Martenshuys, Zuivelmarkt 18, ☎ 011.22.96.56, is a fashionable restaurant and café with an eclectic interior and garden.
Het Dagelijks Brood, Persoonstraat 12, is a bakery and café with a farmhouse style interior and a small garden.

Public transport
Hasselt has introduced a transport policy which discourages cars from the town centre and encourages cycling and walking. A free shuttle bus service runs from the station to Grote Markt (the Centrumpendel) while another free shuttle does a circuit of the inner ring (the Boulevardpendel). The city also operates a free bicycle scheme.

Tourist information
Lombaardstraat 3. ☎ 011.23.95.40.

Carillon concerts
The carillon is played on Sun from mid-June to the end of August 15.00–16.00.

Opening times
Nationaal Jenevermuseum (gin museum) is open Apr–Oct Tues–Sun 10.00–17.00; Nov–Mar at weekends 13.00–17.00. Closed Jan.

Museum Stellingwerff-Waerdenhof is open Apr–Oct Tues–Sun 10.00–17.00; Nov–Mar Tues–Fri 10.00–17.00 and weekends 13.00–17.00.

Stedelijk Modemuseum (fashion museum) is open Apr–Oct Tues–Sun 10.00–17.00; Nov–Mar Tues–Fri 10.00–17.00 and weekends 13.00–17.00. Closed Jan.

Carillon Museum and **De Waag** are open Jun–Sept weekends and public holidays 13.00–17.00; July and Aug Tues–Fri 10.00–17.00.
Museums are closed on Mon and on 1, 2 and 11 Nov and 25 Dec.

History

The town's origins go back to the 7C when a settlement was established on the edge of a hazel wood. Hasselt was granted a charter as a town in c 1165. It was under the control of the Prince-Bishop of Liège from 1366 to 1794. Four years later, the capture of the guerrilla leader Emmanuel Rollier at Hasselt put an end to the **Peasants' Revolt**. The Belgian rebels were defeated at Hasselt by the Dutch in 1831, but the town was later liberated. Hasselt became **capital of Limburg province** in 1839 and a bishopric in 1967. Many buildings in the old town are decorated with attractive old style shop signs.

A walk round Hasselt

Begin in the **Grote Markt**, an attractive square surrounded by cafés with pavement terraces. The handsome Mosan Renaissance style house at **no. 3**, now a pharmacy, bears the date 1639 in the half timbering of the upper floor. An arm holding a sword gives the house its name **Het Sweert**.

Leave the square by the Maastrichterstraat, a narrow lane with old shop signs, and turn left to reach the **Sint Quintinus Kathedraal**. Work began in 1292 on the nave, transepts and choir. Various chapels were added in the 14C and 15C; the ambulatory and its chapels were built in the 16C, and various neo-Gothic features were added during the 19C. The curious tower comprises an 11C base, a 13C tower and an 18C spire. A small **Carillon Museum** is located in a room at the top of the tower where the town carilloneur performs.

Now turn right down Hemelrijk (east of the church) and right again on Persoonstraat. This leads to Maastrichterstraat, where the **Museum Stellingwerff-Waerdenhof** occupies a Neo-classical mansion at no. 85. Once the home of a local gin baron, the house has been converted into a striking modern museum. The eclectic collection includes old photographs of Hasselt, Art Nouveau ceramics from a defunct local porcelain factory, 19C and 20C paintings, and some amusing wrought-iron shop signs. The museum claims to own the oldest **monstrance** in the world; it was made in 1297 to display the Miraculous Host of Herkenrode.

Turn right on leaving the museum, passing at no. 100 the former refuge of **Herkenrode Abbey**, built in Brabant Late Gothic style in 1542–44. Turning left down Meldertstraat, you reach Zuivelmarkt, the dairy market, and the **Begijnhof** at no. 33. Built between 1707–62, this typical Mosan style building is now used by cultural organisations. Its church was destroyed by a flying bomb in 1944; the ruined nave is now overgrown with ivy. Several of the Beguines' gardens have been planted in medieval styles. The house at **no. 11** is occupied by a modern art gallery. The garden contains a whimsical installation by Hans Weyers titled *The Pumpkin* (1994).

Leaving the Begijnhof, turn right on **Zuivelmarkt**, where there are several interesting art galleries, and right again along Bonnefantenstraat, past the **Provincial Museum** where modern art exhibitions are organised. The small Waag Museum on the corner contains an exhibition of weighing machines. Turn right into Witte Nonnenstraat to reach the exceptional **Nationaal Jenevermuseum** at no. 19. Located in a former gin distillery that belonged to the Stellingwerff family, it contains a large collection of distilling equipment, ceramic signs and stoneware bottles. Visitors are offered a free tot of local gin in the museum's wood-panelled *proeflokaal* (gin tasting house).

Turn left on leaving the museum and continue along Gasthuisstraat to reach the **Stedelijk Modemuseum** at no. 11. This interesting fashion museum is located in two wings of a former 17C convent linked by an industrial-style covered courtyard. The collection includes clothes from the 18C to the 20C, fashion photographs and jewellery.

Now go left into Molenpoort, right on Demerstraat and right again into Minderbroederstraat. The Walputsteeg at **no. 12**, an attractive alley lined with restaurants, leads to Groenplein. Continuing straight ahead, you come to the **Stadhuis**, the town hall, an attractive 17C classical building.

Turn right along Lombardstraat and left into Zwanestraat to reach the **Onze Lieve Vrouwkerk** in Kapelstraat. Rebuilt in 17C Baroque style on the site of a 14C pilgrimage chapel, the church was hit by a flying bomb in 1944, but reconstructed in its 17C style. Most of the furnishings were brought here in 1803 from Herkenrode Abbey, including the high altar, carved by Jean del Cour, and the funerary monuments of two abbesses of Herkenrode. The monument on the right was carved by Artus Quellin the Younger for Anne-Catherine de Lamboy, who died in 1675, while the one opposite was carved by Laurent Delvaux in memory of Barbara de Rivière, who died in 1714. The church also has a miraculous 14C statue of the Virgin known as the 'Virga Jesse'.

A small **Japanese Garden** off Gouverneur Verwilghensingel was landscaped in 1992 in the style of a 17C Japanese tea garden. It has a tea house and a several hundred flowering cherry trees.

Hasselt environs

The village of **Kuringen**, 3km northwest of Hasselt, stands on the site of the **abbey of Herkenrode**. Founded in 1182, it was occupied by Cistercian nuns until its suppression by the French Revolutionaries in 1797. Its treasures were dispersed throughout Europe; some beautiful stained-glass from the abbey is now in Lichfield Cathedral. Other precious possessions, including a monstrance in which a Miraculous Host was displayed, are now in the Museum Stellingwerff-Waerdenhof in Hasselt. The surviving buildings date from the 16C to the 18C.

The town of **Kortessem**, 9km southeast of Hasselt, is mentioned as early as 741. Its Sint Pieterskerk dates in part from 1040. The town of **Bilzen**, 17km southeast of Hasselt, has a town hall dating from 1685. The attractive castle of **Alden Biesen**, 3km to the south, was founded in 1220 as a commandery of the Order of the Teutonic Knights. The order survived in Belgium until 1798. The present building, which dates from the 16C and 17C, was badly damaged by fire in 1971. Subsequently restored, it now serves as a Flemish cultural centre.

Tongeren

Tongeren (Tongres in French) is an interesting Flemish town with impressive Roman and Romanesque remains. Settled in pre-Roman times, it is the oldest town in Belgium. The streets are particularly lively on Sundays when a large antique market is held along the 13C town walls.

Practical information

Eating out
The elegant, rather pricey *Biessenhuys*, Hemelingenstraat 23, ☎ 012.23.47.09, occupies a handsome mansion with parts that date back to the 16C. It has a garden.

Tourist information
Stadhuisplein 9, ☎ 012.39.02.55.

Market
An extensive antique market is held every Sunday 06.00–13.00 on the

Veemarkt and the Leopoldwal. Its fame has spread to the Dutch town of Maastricht, 19km southeast.

Opening times
Treasury in Onze-Lieve-Vrouwbasiliek is open daily Apr–Sept 10.00–12.00 and 13.30–17.00.

Gallo-Roman Museum, Kielenstraat 15, is open on Mon 12.00–17.00, Tues–Fri 09.00–17.00, and at weekends from 10.00–18.00. Closed from 25 Dec –Jan 1.

Moerenpoort Museum is open May–Sept, at weekends and public holidays, 11.00–17.00.

History

Tongeren originated as the capital of the Eburones and the Tungri. Historians have identified it with the Atuatuca Tungrorum mentioned by Caesar. Ambiorix, a leader of the Eburones, defeated the Romans here in 54 BC. It became a **walled Roman settlement** on the road from Bavai to Cologne in c AD 70. Protected by fortifications 4.5km in length (of which 1.5km survives), the Roman settlement was considerably larger than the present town.

Following its destruction by the Franks in c 300, a shorter wall, 2.7km in length, was built. Nothing survives of this wall apart from the foundations of a tower. Tongeren was the site of the **first bishopric** to be established in Belgium. It was set up by St Maternus of Cologne, but the first bishop, St Servatius, moved to Maastricht in 382. St Hubert later moved the see to Liège in 720. Tongeren was ravaged by the Vikings in the 9C, but became a prosperous dependency of the prince-bishops of Liège during the Middle Ages. A **third protective wall** was constructed during the 13C and 14C. Tongeren was attacked by Charles the Bold in 1486, but he spared the town after the Sire de Humbercourt convinced him to show mercy. It was not so fortunate in 1677 when most of the town was burned to the ground by the soldiers of Louis XIV. Tongeren did not begin to recover until after the creation of the Belgian state in 1831.

A walk round Tongeren

Begin on the **Grote Markt**, where the Stadhuis was built from 1737–54. An impressive 18C statue of Ambiorix, the Eburones leader who defeated the Romans in 54 BC, stands in the square. The foundations and lower courses of a 4C **Roman rampart tower** are located just to the east. This is a last vestige of the second city wall, which encircled a smaller area than the first.

Onze Lieve Vrouwbasiliek

The impressive Onze Lieve Vrouwbasiliek, founded c 350, claims to be the first church north of the Alps to be dedicated to the Virgin. Parts of the 11C and 12C Romanesque building survives, but the nave and south transept were built in Gothic style from 1240, while the rest of the church was built between the 14C and 16C. The north portal of 1532 contains a few traces of the 13C building.

The **choir** is lit by four stained-glass windows of 1550. There is also an elaborate 16C retable carved with scenes from the life of the Virgin. Other works of interest include a paschal candlestick of 1372, a lectern of 1375 and four candelabra of 1392, all of them by Jehans Josès of Dinant.

The **north transept** contains a walnut statue of *Our Lady of Tongeren* dated 1479. The first chapel in the north aisle has a 15C *Man of Sorrows*, while the final chapel contains a *Pietà* of 1400. Look out for a curious antique alms box made from a tree stump, and a *Madonna and Child* of 1280 in the northwest porch.

The organ dates from 1753. A brass gate below the loft was made in 1711 by Christian Schwertfeger. The west chapel of the south aisle contains a 16C altar. The **fifth chapel** is dedicated to **St Lutgart**, a pious woman born in Tongeren in 1182. She became a Black Benedictine nun but, not wanting to be appointed abbess, she moved to a Cistercian convent. One of the outstanding women mystics of the Middle Ages, St Lutgart was blind for the final eleven years of her life.

A vestibule at the east end of the south aisle contains a remarkable **Crucifix** which is believed to date from the 11C. The vestibule provides access to the treasury and cloister. The impressive **cloister** has three walks, one of which dates from the 12C and is surrounded by small columns each crowned with a different capital. The other two were added during the 13C and 14C. The lintel of the garden doorway is late 11C. The two Gothic chapels date from the 15C.

The **Treasury** is one of the richest in Belgium. It has a number of exceptionally beautiful reliquaries dating from the 10C to the 13C, including a mid 12C triptych-reliquary of the Holy Cross; a 10C evangelistary with a 14C cover embodying an 11C ivory plaque; a 14C monstrance-reliquary of St Ursula; a 12C or 13C portable altar of porphyry; and an 11C Head of Christ.

Go down Groendreef to reach the **Gallo-Roman Museum** at Kielenstraat 15. This impressive modern museum contains an exceptional collection of sculpture, Roman coins and glassware. Most of the finds come from Tongeren and environs. They date from the Neolithic period to the Roman occupation. One of the most interesting objects is a 13C copy of the *Tabula Peutingeriana*, a 4C road map of the Roman world extending from Britain to India.

The **basement** contains an imaginative attempt to unravel 'the secret of the Dodecahedron'. This mysterious 12-sided bronze object has turned up in 90 different locations in Europe. One was discovered in 1939 buried near the Leopoldwal in Tongeren. Its significance has eluded archaeologists; visitors are invited to reach their own conclusions by wandering through an abandoned lecture theatre cluttered with dusty textbooks and old books. Concealed slide projectors and video screens add to the mysterious atmosphere. The museum has a spacious **café** with a good view of the town.

A short walk down Kielenstraat leads to the **Moerenpoort**, built in 1379 as one of the medieval gates. The gate contains a small museum with weapons and plans of the city walls. The view from the battlements is impressive. Stretches of the 13C ramparts are visible on either side of the gate. The section to the north along Leopoldwal was built on a 2C Roman base. The Sunday flea market is held along this stretch of wall.

Now go back into town to find the **Begijnhof**, just south of the Kielenstraat. This complex of cobbled lanes retains several 17C and 18C houses. The church was built in 1294 but altered during the 16C.

Going out of town on the Hasseltsesteenweg leads to the **Roman wall**. An impressive stretch of 1C and 2C Roman wall runs along the line of Legionenlaan. Another section can be seen near the **Beukenberg**, an artificial hill built by the Romans. Planted with a beech wood, the hill has several **walking trails**. The impressive **Kasteel van Betho** is nearby. The main building was built in Mosan Renaissance style in the 17C. A footpath leads from here through the Stadspark (city park) to the **Pliniusbron**, a medicinal spring known to Pliny the Elder.

KORTRIJK AND OUDENAARDE

Kortrijk

Kortrijk is a prosperous and elegant town of 77,000 inhabitants on the River Leie (Lys in French). Famed in the Middle Ages for its flax, it is now the centre of a major technology region. Known in French as Courtrai, Kortrijk is only 7km from the French frontier, yet it remains a Dutch-speaking town.

Practical information

Where to stay
The *Damier*, Grote Markt 41, ☎ 056.22.15.47, is an elegant 19C Rococo town house with a Flemish interior.

Eating out
Bistro Aubergine, Groeningestraat 16, ☎ 056.25.79.80, is an attractive bistro in the former parsonage of Onze Lieve Vrouwekerk.
Boxy's, Minister Liebaertlaan 1, ☎ 056.22.22.05, is an artistic restaurant with creative modern cooking.

Tourist information
Sint Michielsplein 5, ☎ 056.23.93.71.

Opening times
Stadhuis, Grote Markt, is open Mon–Fri 09.00–12.00 and 14.00–17.00.
Broelmuseum, Broelkaai 6, is open Tues–Sun 10.00–12.00 and 14.00–17.00.
Groeningeabdij, Houtmarkt, is open Tues–Sun 10.00–12.00 and 14.00–17.00.
Nationaal Vlasmuseum (history of flax), Etienne Sabelaan 4, is open Mar–Nov Tues–Fri 09.00–12.30 and 13.30–18.00 and weekends 14.00–18.00.

History
Kortrijk was known to the Romans as Cortoriacum (or Curtracum). It was established as a town, possibly during the 7C, but was later destroyed by the Vikings and then rebuilt in the 10C by Baldwin III . It was outside the walls of Kortrijk that the weavers of Ghent and Bruges routed the French knights under Robert of Artois at the Battle of the Golden Spurs on 11 July 1302. This was one of the first defeats inflicted by a trained infantry of yeomen and burghers on elite mounted knights. Charles VI wreaked a savage revenge in 1382 by burning the town after his victory at Westrozebeke over Philip van Artevelde. A century later, Charles VIII came to the aid of the Flemish in their struggle against Maximilian and occupied Kortrijk between 1488 and 1492.

The River Leie (Lys) is a chalk-free river which was especially suitable for flax-retting. Kortrijk became a major centre of linen making and by the 15C its population reached a peak of about 200,000. Kortrijk was taken by the French in 1793 and became the chief town of the department of the Lys.

Captured by the Germans in 1914, Kortrijk became an important military base behind the Ypres front. Between 1940 and 1945, the town suffered severely from aerial bombardment, but the damage was rapidly restored after the war. The painter Roelant Savery (1576–1639) was born here, but moved later to Utrecht.

A walk in Kortrijk

The walk begins on the irregularly shaped **Grote Markt**, where the 14C–15C **Belfry** stands. This is all that remains of the cloth hall which was demolished after being irreparably damaged by bombing in 1944. The **Stadhuis** in the northwest corner of the Grote Markt dates from 1519 but has been repeatedly enlarged and restored. The last restoration was by J. Vierin and his son Luc in 1959–62. The statues of the counts of Flanders on the façade are 20C additions.

Modern stained-glass windows and frescoes in the **Schepenzaal** on the ground floor depict events in Kortrijk's history. There is also a fine 16C chimney-piece with the arms of Ghent and Bruges, the figures of Albert and Isabella, and a wealth of renaissance detail. The **Council Chamber** upstairs has a more elaborate chimneypiece of 1527 with three rows of statuettes. The upper row represents the Virtues, below are the Vices, while the lowest level represents the torments of Hell. The enigmatic figures on brackets represent Charles V, Isabella and a personification of Justice.

Go down Rijselstraat and turn right to the **Jesuit Church of St Michael** of 1607–11. A modern Romanesque chapel on the south side contains an early 13C ivory statuette of Our Lady of Groeninge. Made in Arras, this was presented by Countess Beatrice de Dampierre in 1285 to the Abbey of Groeninge in

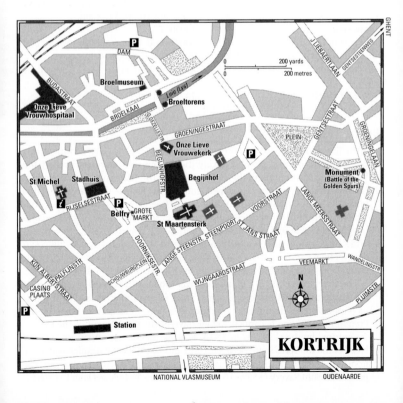

Groeningestraat, Kortrijk. A convent of the Poor Clares now occupies part of the original abbey building.

Return to the Grote Markt and go down Leiestraat to reach the River Leie. Cross the river and follow Budastraat to reach the **Onze Lieve Vrouwhospitaal**. Founded by Margaret of Constantinople in 1219, this hospital was almost entirely rebuilt in the 16C–17C. It has a Baroque-style chapel and some 13C fragments in a courtyard.

Now go back to the river and turn left along Broelkaai to reach the **Broelmuseum**. Located in an elegant 18C mansion, it has an interesting local collection of lace, period furniture, coins and paintings by local artists such as Roelant Savery. Opposite the museum, the bridge is flanked by the squat, massive **Broeltorens**, two impressive towers that once formed part of Kortrijk's ancient fortifications. The south tower dates from the 12C, the north from the 15C.

Cross the bridge and continue down Guido Gezellestraat to reach the **Onze Lieve Vrouwkerk**. Begun in the 13C in fortified style, the church was partly rebuilt in the 18C and again after it was damaged in 1944. The

Broeltorens, Kortrijk

west exterior, with a row of arches along the pavement, is unusual. Its main treasure is an alabaster statue of St Catherine of 1374–84 in the Chapel of the Counts ascribed to André Beauneveu of Valenciennes.

Founded by Louis de Male in c 1365, and restored in 1963, this chapel has an interesting collection of portraits of all the counts of Flanders and of some of their wives. Van Dyck's *Raising of the Cross* of 1631 in the north transept was one of the artist's last paintings before his departure to England. The adjoining chapel contains an *Adoration of the Shepherds* by Louis de Deyster. Another of his works hangs in the south transept. One of the chancel lecterns dates from 1695. It was made by Ignace de Cock, who is better known as a bell-founder. The other was made in 1711 by Jan Lepies.

Continue down the Begijnhofstraat to enter the attractive **B egijnhof**, an intimate community of cobbled lanes and whitewashed houses. It was founded in 1238 by Joanna of Constantinople, who is commemorated by a statue of 1891. Destroyed many times, most of the surviving houses date from the 17C. The side wall of the 18C chapel on Begijnhofstraat dates from the 15C. There is a small museum in one of the houses.

The **Sint Maartenskerk** stands just south of the Begijnhof. Begun in the 13C, the church was largely rebuilt in the 15C and restored in the 19C. It has a richly carved and gilded stone tabernacle of 1585 by Hendrik Maes and a triptych of 1587 by Bernard de Ryckere.

Continuing south from the church, turn left along the long pedestrian precinct that runs along Lange Steenstraat, Steenpoort and Voorstraat. Turn right down Sint Jansstraat to the **Baggaertshof**, a group of old almshouses with a small courtyard and a chapel of 1638. Continue along Voorstraat and turn left down Sint Niklaasstraat to the Houtmarkt. **The Groeningeabdij** was built here c 1600 by Cistercian nuns. It now contains an interesting museum of local history, damask and Kortrijk silver. A section is devoted to the Battle of the Golden Spurs. There is a small monument commemorating the battle near here in Groeningelaan.

Battle of the Golden Spurs

The Battle of the Golden Spurs was fought outside Kortrijk on 11 July 1302 between Flemish weavers and burghers under Pieter de Coninck, already famed as a leader of the Bruges Matins, and an army of French knights led by Robert of Artois. The Flemish army was drawn up facing a stream, now the Groeningelaan. Their left was protected by the River Leie (Lys), and their right by a marsh. The French knights, contemptuous of their low-born opponents, made two frontal attacks across the stream. Each was repelled by the Flemish pikemen, the French losing 63 nobles, including Robert of Artois, and 700 knights. It is said that 700 pairs of golden spurs were collected after the battle and displayed in the church of Onze Lieve Vrouw. The battle was the first in which ordinary citizens defeated mail-clad knights. This marked the beginning of the decline of chivalry.

Kortrijk environs

The history of flax is covered in the **Nationaal Vlasmuseum** at Etienne Sabbelaan 4 in the southeast outskirts of the town beyond the motorway ring. Located in a restored 19C flax farmhouse, it illustrates the story of flax from cultivation to weaving by means of tableaux set in rooms furnished in period style.

Outside Kortrijk on the Gentsesteenweg, there is a memorial in the form of a moose on the town outskirts. This commemorates Newfoundlanders who fell in Belgium in 1914–18.

The village of **Harelbeke**, 3km northeast of Kortrijk, is a centre for flax and tobacco. It has an 18C Neo-classical church with a detached 11C Romanesque tower, part of an earlier church, which was badly damaged in 1940. It was restored in 1954 and later given a 50-bell carillon. A statue opposite the old town hall of 1764 commemorates the composer, Pierre Benoît, 1834–1901. Born here, he attempted to establish a distinctive Flemish style in music.

The church at **Deerlijk**, 2km from Harelbeke, contains an early 16C altarpiece with scenes from the life of St Columba.

OUDENAARDE
• • • • • • • • • • • • • • •

Oudenaarde (Audenarde in French), is a busy textile manufacturing and brewing town on the Scheldt. Famous from the 16C to the 18C for is tapestries, it is now a somewhat forgotten Flemish town. Yet is still has considerable charm, with its striking Gothic town hall and spacious Grote Markt surrounded by cafés.

Practical information

Where to stay
The *Hostellerie La Pomme d'Or*, Markt 62, ☎ 055.31.19.00, is an attractive hotel in a former 15C coaching inn where Margaret of York once lodged.

Eating out
The restaurant of the Pomme d'Or (see above) offers good Flemish cooking.

Tourist information
Stadhuis, Markt, ☎ 055.31.72.51.

Opening times
Stadhuis, Grote Markt, is open for guided tours from Apr–Oct Mon–Fri at 11.00, 14.30 and 15.30, and weekends at 14.00 and 15.30. Tours lasts one hour.
Huis de Lalaing, Bourgondiestraat 9, is open Mon–Fri 09.00–12.00 and 13.00–17.00. Closed at weekends and public holidays.

History

The name Oudenaarde means 'old anchorage' or 'old landing place'. Situated by the river on a trade route, it is likely that there was a settlement here before Roman times. Proof of Roman occupation is provided by the discovery of coins and artefacts. According to medieval accounts St Amandus brought Christianity to Pamele, the district east of the river, in 613. Under the terms of the Treaty of Verdun of 843, the river formed the boundary between the land of Lothair, Germany, and of Charles the Bald, France.

The area fell to the counts of Flanders in the early 11C. Sheltered by the **Turris Aldenardensis** of Baldwin IV a town began to grow and prosper. Around 1030 the first meeting of the States of Flanders was held here. A charter granted by Philip of Alsace in 1193 gave an impetus to trade, especially in cloth. By the 15C Oudenaarde was famous for its **tapestry**, a craft which reached its zenith in the 16C only to die out completely in the 17C.

The town has had a turbulent history. From 1325–1382 it suffered from the revolt of the Flemish communes. From 1527–1584 it was fought over during the religious disturbances. Then followed the revolt against the Spaniards in the 16C, the wars of Louis XIV from 1658–1684, the War of the Spanish Succession, the war of Louis XV in 1745 and the two World Wars. All left their mark on Oudenaarde.

Governor of the Netherlands from 1560–67, Margaret of Parma, illegitimate daughter of Charles V and his mistress Joanna van der Gheynst, was born here in 1522. The painter Adriaen Brouwer was also born in Oudenaarde in 1605. In 1708, during the War of the Spanish Succession, Marlborough defeated the French at the Battle of Oudenaarde to the north and northwest of the town. In 1745, during the War of the Austrian Succession, the French took the town and dismantled its fortifications.

A walk in Oudenaarde
Begin in the large **Grote Markt**, the old market square. This is dominated by the strikingly beautiful **Stadhuis**, which replaced a Romanesque building burnt by a carnival mob in 1525. The present building was constructed c 1525–36 by the Brussels architect Hendrik van Pede in Flamboyant Gothic style. The sculptured façade is supported by an arcade with a projecting porch. An ornate tower with

a cupola in the shape of a crown rises from the centre. It is surmounted by the gilded figure of Hanske de Krijge (Little John the Warrior), depicted waving a banner bearing the town's arms. The fountain in front of the town hall was presented by Louis XIV in 1675. Behind the building is the Romanesque **Halle**, a 13C cloth hall with 17C alterations.

The main feature of the interior of the Stadhuis is the Renaissance carving by Paul van der Schelden, particularly the chimneypieces and the magnificent **oak doorway** of 1531 with 28 carved panels. Copies of this doorway are exhibited in the Louvre in Paris and the Victoria and Albert Museum in London. The Stadhuis and Halle also contain archives dating from 1200, tapestries, paintings (including an *Allegory of the Five Senses* attributed to Adriaen Brouwer), guild relics,

Town hall, Ouedenaarde

archaeological finds from the area, seals, coins and weapons.

The **Sint Walburgakerk** is just off the Grote Markt. It is named after St Walburga (c 710–79), the sister of St Willibald and St Wineband. A nun from Dorset, she went to Germany at the invitation of St Boniface and became abbess of Heidenheim. Her relics are preserved at Eichstätt in Bavaria.

The **choir** dates from the 12C–14C. The nave was built by Jan van Ruysbroeck in the 15C. The spire was damaged by a fire in 1804, leaving just the bell-shaped lantern.

The interior has several Oudenaarde tapestries, a triptych of the *Trinity* by the local artist Simon de Paepe, screens by Lucas Faydherbe, and a monument in the choir to four Catholic priests murdered in 1572 by Protestant fanatics.

The **Onze Lieve Vrouw Ziekenhuis** (hospital), just north of the church, was founded in the 12C. The present buildings date mainly from the 17C and 18C, but a 13C–14C chapel has survived.

The **Boudewijnstoren**, just south of the church, is a relic of the 11C–13C fortifications. It is named after Count Baldwin V, who ordered the construction of the Romanesque gatehouse. The attractive Late Gothic **Huis van Margareta van Parma** next door was built in the early 16C. It is named after the illegitimate daughter of Charles V, who may have been born here.

Leave the Grote Markt by the Voorburg, where a mellow 17C portal leads into the Begijnhof. Founded in the 13C, this peaceful enclosure is surrounded by neat whitewashed 17C houses. Continue down Kasteelstraat to the Scheldt, then turn left to cross the bridge. A quay on the opposite side named Bourgondiestraat recalls the vanished Burgundian castle built here in 1385 by Philip the Bold. Louis XI of France took refuge in this castle during his exile in c 1460. In 1572, Protestants threw four Catholic priests from the castle windows into the Scheldt, where they drowned. They are commemorated by a monument in the church of Sint Walburga.

The **Huis de Lalaing** at Bourgondiestraat 9 was built close to the law courts n c 1717. It has an Oudenaarde tapestry centre which undertakes restoration work. A collection of local artists is displayed.

Follow the quay in the opposite direction to reach the **Onze Lieve Vrouwekerk van Pamele**, which is called Pamele after the ancient name of his district. It was begun in Scheldt Gothic style in 1234 and virtually completed within just four years. The church was founded (and for the most part designed) by the monk **Arnulf de Binche**. The first master-builder in Belgium to be known by name, he is commemorated by a plaque bearing an inscription in Latin on the outside wall of the choir. The north transept dates from the 14C, while two chapels were added in the 16C. Some of the pillars and walls inside the church are tilting at alarming angles. The church contains paintings by Simon de Paepe and a magnificent triptych by Jan Snellinck. It also has the tombs of two lords of Pamele and their wives, from 1504 and 1616.

Back on Grote Markt, go down Hoogstraat to reach Tacambaroplein, where a monument of 1867 commemorates volunteers from Oudenaarde who fell in Mexico fighting for the ill-fated Emperor Maximilian, the son-in-law of Leopold I. The square also has an American war memorial, a local war memorial and a monument to the deportees of the First World War.

Oudenaarde environs

The northeast suburb of **Ename** was an early fortress of the German emperors. A prosperous trading centre and river port until the 11C, it was taken by Count Baldwin IV in 1002. When its castle was demolished by Baldwin V in 1047, much of Ename's trading activity ceased. Its people moved to Oudenaarde and found shelter under the **Turris Aldernardensis**. A Benedictine abbey built here in the 11C was destroyed in the 18C. The **Museum t 'Ename** (open Tues–Sun 09.30–17.00) uses computer technology to create a virtual reconstruction of the abbey. The nearby archaelogical park contains vestiges of the medieval port.

The coast

The Belgian coast is lined with broad, sandy beaches and windswept dunes. Hotels, casinos and private houses were built in extravagant eclectic styles up until the 1920s. Though many of the old buildings have been destroyed, a few splendid architectural relics have been preserved along the coast, particularly in De Haan and De Panne. The 13 resorts along the 67km coastline continue to attract thousands of visitors from Belgium, Germany and Britain. Most resorts are ideal for families, with their broad beaches, paved promenades, go-karts for rent, and nearby theme parks. The coastal resorts also make a good base for exploring the historic cities of West Flanders such as Bruges, Veurne and Ypres.

Some of the resorts on the Belgian coast were originally fishing villages, while others were developed by private companies in the late 19C. Despite the construction of modern apartments along much of the coastline, each of the resorts retains a distinctive character. Some are quiet family places such as Heist and Middelkerke. Others such as Blankenberge are more lively, while Knokke-Het Zoute is considered one of the most fashionable towns on the North Sea.

Practical information

Getting there
Hoverspeed runs a fast ferry service from Dover to Ostend. The crossing takes under 2 hours.

Frequent **trains** run from main Belgian stations to Ostend, Blankenberge, Knokke and De Panne.

Other resorts can be reached on the Kusttram, a **coastal tram** service that links all the resorts along the coast. Allow half an hour to take the tram from Ostend to Blankenberge or Nieuwpoort, and just over an hour from Ostend to Knokke or De Panne.

Where to stay
Most visitors rent an apartment at the coast, which can be done through a local agency, or through advertisements in Belgian newspapers, such as the Saturday edition of De Standaard. The resorts of De Haan, Knokke and De Panne have some attractive, traditional hotels. The West Flanders tourist office publishes an annual list of hotels and apartments at the coast.

Eating out
Each resort has a good supply of restaurants offering fresh fish, mussels served in big black pots and traditional Belgian steak and frites. Cafés can be counted on to serve good coffee, Belgian beers and sustaining waffles. Local butcher's shops often prepare delicious ready-to-eat dishes.

Tourist information
West Flanders tourist information office Kasteel Tillegem, 8200 Bruges. ☎ 050.38.02.96, has information on all the beach resorts.

Sports
Belgians tend to enjoy bracing walks along the broad beaches or though the rolling dunes (though some sections are closed off to prevent erosion). The flat polders inland are ideal for cycling. Several farms near Oostduinkerke offer horse riding, while an area of the beach at De Panne is set aside for sand yachting.

OSTEND
• • • • • • • • •

The oldest resort on the Belgian coast, Ostend enjoyed a golden age in the 19th century when it was a popular summer haunt of European aristocracy. The resort became thronged with British visitors after the introduction in 1847 of a regular steamship from Dover. Later known as the Queen of the Belgian Resorts, it was visited by Queen Victoria, Kaiser Wilhelm II and Albert Einstein. The architectural grandeur was mostly destroyed after the Second World War when the old hotels on the promenade were replaced by modern apartment blocks. More recently, the ferry port has gone into decline due to the opening of the Channel Tunnel. With a population of 68,000, Ostend now sees itself as an art city on the sea, wooing visitors with its antique shops, fish restaurants and museum of modern art.

Ostend, the promenade

Practical information

Getting there

A good **train** service links Ostend with Brussels. Thalys trains run direct high-speed services to Paris. The railway station is within walking distance of the town and beach. The coast tram stops opposite the station.

Ferries. Hoverspeed runs a fast ferry service from Ostend to Dover. The terminal is next to the railway station.

Airport. Ostend airport is 3km west of the town.

Where to stay

£££ *Thermae Palace*, Koningin Astridlaan 7, ☎ 059.80.66.44, is a grand Art Deco hotel on the beach.

££ *Du Parc*, Marie Joséplein 3, ☎ 059.70.16.80, is an elegant Art Deco hotel overlooking the Leopold Park.

£ *Old Flanders*, Josef II Straat 49, ☎ 059.80.66.03, is a friendly hotel near the station with Old Flemish interiors.

Eating out
Restaurants

££ *Lusitania*, Visserkaai 35, ☎ 059.70.17.65, is an elegant fish restaurant on the harbour front.

££ *Petit Nice*, Albert I Promenade 62b, ☎ 059.80.39.28, offers sophisticated cooking at moderate prices.

£ *James*, James Ensorgalerij 34, is a tavern decorated with Ostend memorabilia. Its garnaalkroketten (shrimp croquettes) are considered the best on the coast.

Cafés

Falstaff, Wapenplein, is a Flemish tavern decorated with old Ostend photographs.

Parc, Marie-Joséplein 3, is a handsome Art Deco café.

Rubens, Visserskaai 44, is an Old Flemish tavern on the harbour front.

Tourist information

Monacoplein 2, ☎ 059.70.11.99.

Bookshop

English books are sold at Internationale Boekhandel, Adolf Buylstraat 33.

Sea cruises

The Seastar runs trips along the coast from Ostend to Nieuwpoort in July and August.

Festival

Ostend's gaudy Carnival is held every year on the weekend after Shrove Tuesday. The main event is the Bal Rat Mort (Dead Rat Ball) in the Casino. This charity ball was initiated in 1896 by the Cercle Caecilia, whose members included James Ensor.

Beaches

Ostend has five official beaches: Kleinstrand (small beach) near the harbour entrance is the oldest.

Grootstrand (large beach) stretches west from the Casino to the Thermen.

The quieter Mariakerke beach runs from the Thermen to Dorpstraat.

The Raversijde beach continues beyond the town.

A fifth beach known as Oosterstrand lies to the east of the harbour entrance.

Most beaches have huts, deckchairs and showers. Swimming is forbidden when a red flag is flying. A yellow flag means dangerous conditions while a green flag means swimming is safe.

 Opening times
Most museums apart from the modern art museum close on Tuesday.

Museum voor Schone Kunsten is open Wed–Mon 10.00–12.00 and 14.00–17.00.

De Plate folk museum is open mid Jun–mid Sept and on Belgian school holidays, Wed–Mon 10.00–12.00 and 14.00–17.00. At other times of the year, Sat only 10.00–12.00 and 15.00–17.00.

James Ensor Huis, Vlaanderenstraat 27, is open at Easter and Jun–Sept 10.00–12.00 and 14.00–17.00. At other times of the year, at weekends 14.00–17.00.

Provincial Museum of Modern Art, Romestraat 11, is open Tues–Sun 10.00–18.00.

Mercator ship at the west end of the harbour is open Jan–Mar and Oct–Dec at weekends 10.00–13.00 and 14.00–17.00 (but closed on 1 Jan and 25 Dec); Apr–Jun and Sept daily (including Tues) 10.00–13.00 and 14.00–18.00, and in Jul–Aug daily (including Tues) 09.00–18.00.

Aquarium is open daily (including Tues) from Apr–Sept 10.00–12.00 and 14.00–17.00. At other times of the year, it is open at weekends at the same times.

Domein Raversijde (military complex in the dunes west of the town) is open Jul–Aug daily 10.30–18.00; Sept–Nov 11 and Apr–Jun 14.00–17.00. Closed 11 Nov–Mar.

History

Ostend began as an 11C fishing village known as Oostende-ter-Streepe (the east end of the strip), which was given a charter as a town by Margaret of Constantinople in 1267. The port rapidly grew in importance, becoming one of the main departure points for the crusades. Until the development of Zeebrugge in the 19C, it was the only major port on the Belgian coast.

During the Revolt of the Netherlands, Ostend sided with the Dutch rebels. It was finally taken by the Spanish commander Spinola in 1604, though only after a bitter siege which lasted three years. The **Ostend Company** was established by the Emperor Charles VI of Austria in 1722 to trade with China and the East Indies. Under pressure from England and Holland its charter was later revoked, but it none the less opened the way to greater prosperity.

Ostend became an important **19C port** for sailings between England and the Continent. The town first became a **royal residence** in 1834; four years later Leopold I inaugurated the Ostend–Brussels railway. The first Casino Kursaal was opened in 1852. After the dismantling of the fortifications in 1860–70, the town began to spread along the coast and inland.

At the start of the **First World War**, the Belgian government was based in Ostend from 7–13 October 1914. The Germans marched into the town on 15 October and proceeded to turn it into a destroyer and submarine base. An attempt was made by the British navy to block the harbours of Ostend and Zeebrugge on the night of 22–23 April 1918. This failed, but the crew volunteered for a second attack, which was successfully carried out on 9–10 May. The Germans evacuated Ostend on 17 October 1918 after blowing up the station and harbour facilities. During the **Second World War**, Ostend served as a German coastal fortress. The town suffered considerably from air attacks. It was liberated by the Canadians on 9 September 1944.

The Palais des Thermes was opened in 1933 and the new Casino-Kursaal in 1953. The motorway to Brussels was completed in 1958 and work on the extension of the airport has continued since 1976. The town is known in Dutch as Oostende and in French as Ostende.

1 • The town

Beginning at the **station**, cross the canal and walk straight ahead down the Leopold III Laan. This leads to the old harbour, which is now crowded with private yachts. The *Mercator* is normally moored at the west end of the harbour. A three-masted merchant training ship built in 1932, it was used on several scientific expeditions. Taken out of service in 1960, the ship retains handsome period interiors and a collection of objects acquired during its voyages to 54 different countries.

Return along the opposite quay and turn left down Dekenijstraat to reach the **Sint Petrus en Pauluskerk**. Built in 1905–07 by Louis Delacenserie, this interesting neo-Gothic church contains a curious chapel reached by a passage behind the high altar. The **chapel** contains a marble tomb carved by Charles Fraikin in memory of Queen Louise-Marie, the first Queen of the Belgians, who died in Ostend in 1850.

A solitary brick tower to the west of the church is all that survives of the old church of Sint Peter, which was gutted by fire in 1896. Known as the **Peperbus** (Peppermill), the tower has an interesting *Calvary* at the base, which is dated 1764.

Now continue down Kapellestraat, a lively shopping street, to reach the **Wapenplein.** Much of the square was destroyed by bombing in the Second World War, but an attractive 19C bandstand has survived. The modern **Feest en Kultuur Paleis** (Festival and Culture Palace) was built in 1958 on the site of the destroyed town hall. Its rather bleak façade is enlivened by a large clock with the signs of the zodiac. A 49-bell **carillon** was placed in the belfry in 1965. It is plays a folk tune automatically every half hour.

Despite its slightly forbidding exterior, it is worth exploring the Feest en Kultuur Paleis. Enter the courtyard to reach the excellent public library, which has an interesting Ostend collection and many books in English. A door at the far end of the courtyard leads to two museums. The Museum voor Schone Kunsten lost more than 400 works when the museum burnt down in 1940, but the collection has been rebuilt with works by 19C and 20C Belgian artists linked with Ostend. Occupying the second floor, the museum has paintings by James Ensor, Léon Spilliaert and Constant Permeke.

The **De Plate Folklore Museum**, one floor down, contains an immensely appealing collection of Ostend memorabilia, including Roman finds, local fishermen's costumes, a beach hut, war photographs, and an interesting section on the Dover to Ostend ferry service. The museum also has several furnished interiors including an Ostend fisherman's house, a tobacconist's and a local bar.

Leave Wapenplein by Vlaanderenstraat to reach the **James Ensorhuis** at no. 27.

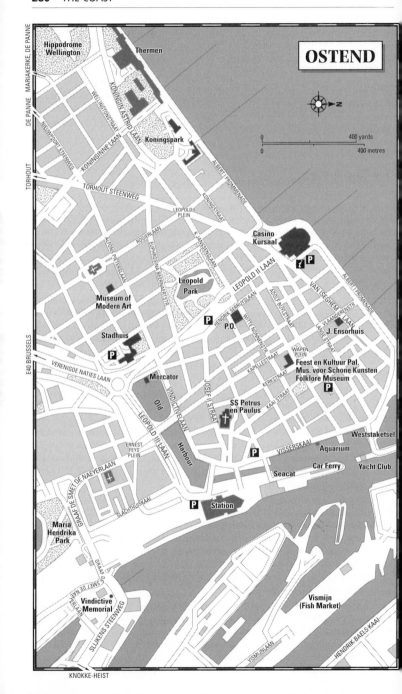

OSTEND

Hippodrome Wellington
Thermen
Koningspark

KONINGIN ASTRID LAAN
WELLINGTONSTRAAT
KONINGINNE LAAN
NIEUWPOORT STEENWEG

DE PANNE · MARIAKERKE, DE PANNE

TORHOUT

ALBERT PROMENADE

0   400 yards
0   400 metres

TORHOUT STEENWEG

LEOPOLD II PLEIN
KONINGSTRAAT

ROGIERLAAN
ALFONS PIETERSLAAN
EUFROSINA BEERNAERTSTR.
K. JANSSENSLAAN

Casino Kursaal

i P

LEOPOLD II LAAN

VAN ISEGHEM LAAN
ALBERT PROMENADE

Museum of Modern Art

Leopold Park

E40 BRUSSELS

HENDRIK SERRUYSLAAN
WITTE NONNENSTR
ADOLF BUYLSTRAAT
VLAANDERENSTR
LANGE STRAAT

J. Ensorhuis

Stadhuis

P.O.
P

WAPEN PLEIN
KAPELLESTRAAT
KERK STRAAT

Feest en Kultuur Pal.
Mus. voor Schone Kunsten
Folklore Museum

P

VERENIGDE NATIES LAAN

Mercator

Old

VINDICTIVELAAN
JOZEF II STRAAT
KAAI STRAAT

SS Petrus en Paulus †

P

Weststaketsel

Aquarium

VISSERSKAAI

LEOPOLD III LAAN

ERNEST FEYS PLEIN

Harbour

P

Seacat   Car Ferry   Yacht Club

GRAAF DE SMET DE NAEYERLAAN

SLACHTHUISKAAI

P Station

Maria Hendrika Park

GRAAF DE SMET DE NAEYERLAAN

Vindictive Memorial

S. LUKENS STEENWEG

Vismijn (Fish Market)

VISMIJNLAAN
HENDRIK BAELS KAAI

KNOKKE-HEIST

This eccentric museum was once the home of the painter James Ensor (1860–1949), who was born in Ostend of an English father and a Flemish mother. The downstairs shop where Ensor's aunt and uncle sold shells and curios has been reconstructed. The first floor has some interesting documents on Ensor, while the floor above contains a reconstruction of the artist's cluttered studio. Though none of the paintings are originals, the museum gives an intriguing impression of Ensor's oddly-furnished home, where he once received Albert Einstein.

Go back down Vlaanderenstraat and turn right along Adolf Buylstraat to reach the Leopold II Laan. This leads to the **Leopold Park**, a romantic park with a small lake, floral clock and 19C bandstand. The modern post office facing the park was begun in 1939 but only completed after the war. It is decorated with a striking sculpture by Joseph Cantré.

The **Stadhuis** (town hall) was built by Victor Bourgeois from 1956–60 at the end of Leopold II Laan. It replaced the 17C town hall on Wapenplein which was destroyed by bombing in 1940. The façade is decorated with Ostend's arms, carved by A. Michiels.

A short detour along Alfons Pieterslaan leads to the **Provincial Museum of Modern Art**, at Romestraat 11. Located in a former department store, the museum has an impressive collection of works by international painters and sculptors. It organises excellent temporary exhibitions.

The large 19C **Maria Hendrika Park** lies to the south, off the Mercatorlaan. Landscaped in romantic style, it has boating lakes and an outdoor swimming pool.

The **Vindictive Memorial** stands in a small memorial park below the Blankenberge road, near the inner docks. This striking monument incorporates the bows of the *Vindictive* and the masts of HMS *Thetis* and *Iphigenia*. The *Vindictive* was sunk across the entrance to Ostend port on 9–10 May 1918.

The modern **Vismijn** (fish market) is located east of the port at the Vissersdok.

2 • The Promenade

Begin again at the station, but this time turn right along the Visserskaai. Once the heart of the fisherman's quarter, this appealing street is lined with former bars converted into fish restaurants. The old shrimp market next to the port has been turned into a **North Sea Aquarium**, which displays fish, molluscs, crustacea, shells and algae in their natural environment.

Turn right along the Montgomery Kaai, past the North Sea Yacht Club, to reach the Weststaketsel, a long jetty that runs along the harbour mouth. The café at the end of the jetty is often battered by high winds. This is a popular place to watch the occasional fast ferry arriving from Dover. Back on the promenade, the Visserskaai becomes the rather more grand Albert I Promenade. An impressive monument was unveiled here in 1953 in memory of seamen who lost their lives during the Second World War.

Continue along the promenade to the **Casino-Kursaal**, opened in 1953 on the site of a much grander Casino that opened in 1852. Local opinion is divided on the question of whether the casino should be demolished or preserved as an architectural monument. The modern Casino has a restaurant, a night club and several gaming rooms, including one decorated with murals by Paul Delvaux. It is regularly used for concerts and opera.

Continue along a broad promenade attractively redesigned in 1998. The **Venetiaans Gaanderijen** (Venetian Arcades) on the left was built for Leopold II. Recently restored, it is now used for exhibitions. The **Koningspark** (royal park) behind the arcade once belonged to the royal family. The former royal pavilion in the park is now a hotel.

There is an impressive equestrian statue of Leopold II that was unveiled in 1932. The long Tuscan arcade beyond here was designed by Charles Girault in 1906. The Art Deco **Thermae Palace Hotel** was built alongside the arcade in 1933. The promenade ends at the **Hippodrome Wellington**, a popular venue for flat racing and trotting.

Continue beyond the racecourse to reach **Mariakerke**. The painter James Ensor is buried in the cemetery of **Onze Lieve Vrouw ter Duinenkerk** (Our Lady of the Dunes) in Dorpstraat. Built in the second half of the 14C, the simple Gothic village church is furnished in Baroque style.

Ostend environs

The **Fort Napoleon** is a 19C fort built by Napoleon to the east of the port. Imaginatively restored in 2000, it is used for exhibitions. There is a cafe in the fort.

The **Domein Raversijde** is an extensive area of dunes, just west of Ostend. This estate formerly belonged to Prince Charles, Count of Flanders, who served as Regent from 1944–1950. The former villa in Duinenstraat contains various personal mementoes. The dunes contain extensive German military installations from the two world wars including a German battery of 1915 and a section of Hitler's Atlantic Wall. The installations can be visited on 90min guided tours. The vanished 14C fishing village of **Walraversijde** is being excavated in the dunes to the S. A nature reserve created by Leopold II in 1904 lies to the east.

Bredene-aan-Zee is a modest resort established to the east of Ostend in 1902.

Knokke-Heist

The resort of Knokke-Heist includes the neighbouring beach towns of Heist, Duinbergen, Albertstrand, Knokke and Het Zoute. Once a popular 19C artists colony, Knokke has elegant shops, art galleries and villas built in English Tudor style. The adjoining resort of Het Zoute to the east is an exclusive residential district.

Practical information

Getting there

Direct **trains** run from Brussels to Heist, Duinbergen and Knokke. The station at Knokke is about 2km from the beach.

The **coast tram** terminates near Knokke railway station.

Where to stay

Britannia, Elizabetlaan 85,
☎ 050.62.10.62, is a comfortable hotel furnished in English country house style.
Locarno, Generaal Lemanpad 5,
☎ 050.63.05.60, is a comfortable family-run hotel.
Lugano, Villapad 14, ☎ 050.63.05.30, is a Normandy-style hotel with garden.
Villa Verdi, Elizabetlaan 8,
☎ 050.62.35.72, occupies a comfortable English-style villa.

Eating out
Restaurants

Jean, Sylvain Dupuisstraat 24,
☎ 050.61.49.57, is a popular
brasserie.

't Kantientje, Lippenslaan 103,
☎ 050.60.54.11, is a repected mussels
restaurant.

Open Fire, Zeedijk 658,
☎ 050.60.17.26, is a traditional fish
restaurant with a garden.

Cafés

The *Prins Baudouin*, Lippenslaan 35,
is a traditional Belgian café.

Tourist information

The Knokke-Heist tourist office is at
Zeedijk 660, Knokke, ☎ 050.63.03.80.

Festivals

The World Cartoon Exhibition has been
held in Knokke every summer since 1962.
An international fireworks festival is held
on Duinbergen beach every summer.

Casino

The Casino is to the west at
Albertstrand. Ossip Zadkine's statue of
The Poet stands in front of the casino.
The interior is decorated with murals by
René Magritte and Paul Delvaux. The
casino programme includes concerts,
ballet, theatre, films and exhibitions.

Opening times

Het Zwin nature reserve is open
daily 09.00–19.00. It closes at 17.00
Oct–Easter and on Wed Nov–Mar.

Knokke environs

Until it silted up towards the end of the 15C, **Het Zwin**, 3km east of Het Zoute,
was an estuary which brought prosperity to Sluis in the Netherlands, and to
Damme and Bruges in Flanders.

History

An important sea battle took place in Het Zwin in 1340 when the fleet of
Edward III of England, commanded by the king in person, sailed up the estuary. With his Flemish allies, Edward inflicted great destruction on the French
fleet which was assembled in the roadstead in preparation for an invasion of
England. Some idea of the size of the estuary can be gained from the fact that
the English are said to have had 250 sail and the French 200.

Most of the reclaimed land is now cultivated, but 150 ha. of dune and marsh near
the sea (including 25 ha. on the Dutch side of the border) have been preserved as
a **nature reserve and bird sanctuary**. The windswept reserve is populated by
oyster catchers, avocets, storks, greylag geese, golden orioles and collared doves.

Zeebrugge

Zeebrugge has a small beach resort and a fishing harbour with several good
restaurants, but the modern port, begun in 1895, dominates the town, dividing
the resort to the east from the old harbour to the west. The port was built to give
Bruges a link to the sea, beginning with the digging of the Boudewijn Kanaal to
Bruges and the construction from 1895–1907 of the mole built by Baron de
Maere. Passenger ferries sail nightly from Zeebrugge to Hull, but the port's main
business is container transport. Modern wind generators built on the quays gen-
erate sufficient power to operate many of the port installations.

Eating out

Several good fish restaurants can be found near the fish market, including Maison Vandamme at Tijdokstraat 7 and Le Chalut at Rederskaai 26.

Opening times

Seafront is open daily 10.00–17.00 in winter, 10.00–18.00 in spring and autumn, and 10.00–19.00 in summer. It is closed early Jan–early Feb.

History

The mole is associated with the heroic St George's Day raid on the night of 22–23 April 1918, when an attack was launched on the German submarine base at Zeebrugge. Led by Vice Admiral Roger Keyes, a task force was sent to block the harbour entrance. The vessels included the old cruiser Vindictive, two Liverpool ferries and the submarine C3. Under constant fire, the C3 rammed the wooden viaduct, which formed the first part of the mole, and was blown up. Her crew escaped by collapsible boat. The Thetis ran aground just clear of the mole, but Intrepid and Iphigenia were sunk across the channel and their crews were rescued by launches. The Vindictive and the landing party returned to Dover. Although not as decisive as had been hoped, the partial closing of the port reduced German submarine operations at a crucial time in the war.

During the Second World War, Zeebrugge was blocked in May 1940 and blown up by the Germans in 1944. The port was finally reopened in 1957 when the Thetis, the last of the 1918 blockships, was removed.

A tour of the port

Dwarfed by more recent developments in the port, Baron de Maere's mole has largely lost its identity. The 1918 raid is commemorated by the **St George's Day Memorial**, which replaces one destroyed by the Germans during World War II. It now stands at the east end of the Zeedijk promenade in the beach quarter. This is effectively the base of the mole, the first section of which is marked by a path named Sint George's Day Wandeling. The memorial incorporates a bas-relief of the plan of the raid.

A new maritime museum called **Seafront** is being developed in the old Vissershaven (fishermen's harbour) next to the fish market, to the east of the resort. Visitors can explore the Westhinder, a former Channel lightship with a 1950s interior, and, if they are agile, squeeze through the cramped quarters of a redundant Soviet submarine, *Foxtrot U-480*, which spied on the West during the Cold War. Good special effects recreate the noise of thudding engines, radio crackle and Russian pop music. It is not for the nervous. **Catamaran trips** along the coast lasting two hours (in July and August, at 11.00, 13.30, 16.00 and 18.30) leave in the summer months from the Seafront museum. **Boat tours** of the port lasting 1 to 1.5 hours (Jul–Sept at 11.00 and 14.30) leave from the opposite end of the harbour.

Blankenberge

Blankenberge was the most elegant resort on the Flemish coast at the end of the 19th century, wooing visitors from Britain and Germany with its clean water and relaxed atmosphere. A handful of eclectic buildings have survived along the dike, but most of the promenade is now lined with modern apartments. Probably the most popular resort on the Belgian coast, it has a certain gaudy charm.

Getting there
Direct trains run from Brussels to Blankenberge.

Eating out
The *Oesterput*, Wenduinesesteenweg 16, ☎ 050.42.86.77, is a vast concrete warehouse where Belgians feast on excellent mussels and crabs, oblivious of the austere surroundings.

Tourist information
The tourist office is at Leopold III Plein, ☎ 050.41.22.27.

Opening times
Aquarama is open daily Apr–mid Sept 11.00–18.00 (to 21.00 in Jul–Aug).
The **Sea Life Centre** is open daily 10.00–18.00 (to 21.00 in Jul–Aug).

A tour round the town
On leaving the **station**, the **Sint Antoonskerk** is on the left. Built in 1335–58 but much restored, the church contains interesting 17C and 18C paintings, including a *Temptation of St Anthony* by Jan Maes, *Storm and Sea* attributed to Jacob van Oost the Younger and a *Flight into Egypt* believed to be the work of David Vinckeboons.

Now head to the sea down Kerkstraat, passing the **Oude Stadhuis** at no. 31. Built in Flemish Renaissance style in 1680, this former town hall is now used for exhibitions. The **Casino** on the waterfront was built in 1934 in Art Deco style. The 350m **Art Deco Pier** from 1933 has a somewhat old-fashioned marine museum, **Aquarama**, displaying fluorescent minerals, shells and ship models. The pier is due to be renovated in 2002. The more modern **Sea Life Centre** further east (at Koning Albert I laan 116) has several large tanks containing marine life. Visitors can walk through a glass tunnel below a large tank containing sharks.

The picturesque **harbour** at the west end of the resort was built between 1862–1876. It is now used by yachts rather than fishing boats. The romantic **Leopoldpark** nearby contains the Paravang, an unusual covered promenade built in neo-Gothic style in 1908.

De Haan

De Haan (Le Coq in French) is said to have obtained its name one stormy night when some local fishermen were saved from running aground when they heard a cock crowing in the village. A beach resort was established here in the 1880s in an area of dunes planted with pines. De Haan is the only town on the coast to have resisted the spread of modern apartment blocks. Most of the 19C hotels and villas are built in English Tudor style. The quaint Art Nouveau tram station dates from 1902. The Staatsduinen (state dunes) near the town are crossed by walking trails.

Where to stay
The *Belle-Epoque*, Leopoldlaan 5, ☎ 059.23.34.65, is a comfortable hotel in picturesque Normandy style.
Rubens, Rubenslaan 3, ☎ 059.23.70.21, is a small family hotel in a quiet villa.

Eating out
Auteuil, Leopoldlaan 18, ☎ 059.23.34.13, is a traditional Flemish family restaurant, good for fish.

Tourist information
The tourist office is located at the tram station, ☎ 059.24.21.35. Open Easter–Sept and school holidays.

Middelkerke

Middelkerke was originally a 13C fishing village behind the dunes. It was developed into a beach resort from 1876, though most of the buildings are modern. The town has a casino built in 1954. The church of Sint Willibrord in the village was rebuilt in 1935, but a 17C tower has survived. This was once used as a lighthouse.

Café
The Tavern on the Beach, is an elegant café in the casino with a good sea view.

Tourist information
The tourist office is at Casselaan 4, ☎ 059.30.03.68.

Westende

The 19C resort of Westende lay just within range of the Allied guns behind the River Yser (IJzer). Most of the villas were destroyed, but the Hôtel Bellevue, designed in 1910 by Octave Van Rysselberghe, has survived at the east end of town.

Nieuwpoort

Nieuwpoort is a lively fishing port and beach resort on the left bank of the Yser estuary. The town is now divided into the beach resort of Nieuwpoort-Bad and the reconstructed old town of Nieuwpoort-Stad.

History

Named 'Novus Portus' in its charter of 1163, the 'new port' was established when the Yser silted up and the old port of Lombardsijde was abandoned. The port was besieged nine times between 13C–18C. The Dutch won a major victory here in 1600 when troops led by Maurice of Nassau defeated a Spanish army commanded by Archduke Albert on the sands to the northwest of the town. An English contingent, led by Sir Francis and Sir Horace Vere, fought on the Dutch side. The town was fortified until 1862. Throughout the First World War Nieuwpoort remained in Belgian hands, but the little that survived the Yser battle and the bombardments of the following years was destroyed in the fighting of 1918.

Where to stay
The *Duinhotel*, Albert I laan 101, ☎ 058.23.31.54, is an inexpensive family hotel with a garden.

Eating out
Au Bon Coin, Albert I laan 94, Nieuwpoort-Bad, ☎ 058.23.33.10, is a traditional Belgian restaurant. *Café de Paris*, Kaai 16, ☎ 058.24.04.80, Nieuwpoort-Stad, is an attractive brasserie near the fish market with outstanding seafood.

Tourist information
Stadhuis, Marktplein 7. ☎ 058.22.44.44.

Canal trips
Boats sail in the summer months to Diksmuide and Veurne.

Carillon concerts

Concerts are played on the carillon in Marktplein mid Jun–mid-Sept on Wed and Sat at 20.30 and on Fri at 11.15. From mid Sept–mid June the concerts are on Sun and Fri at 11.15.

A walk in Nieuwpoort

Begin on the **Marktplein** in Nieuwpoort-Stad, the old town. The **Onze Lieve Vrouwkerk** was built in 1163. Destroyed several times, it has been rebuilt in the original style. After losing a succession of towers, it was finally given a detached **belfry** in 1539. Razed in 1914, it was replaced in 1952 by a modern belfry with a chromatic carillon of 67 bells.

The **Stadhuis** on the square was built in 1922 in neo-Renaissance style. The **Halle** was also rebuilt in 1922 in the style of the corn exchange of c 1280 which once stood here.

There are several monuments from the First World War near the **Ganzepoot sluice complex** to the east of the old town. Forming an arc, the six sluices stand at the point where three waterways enter the Yser estuary. Three of the sluices allow access to canals, while the others regulate the flow of water. The striking **Koning Albert Monument** was built at the late date of 1938. An equestrian statue by Karel Aubroeck stands inside a rotunda designed by Julien de Ridder. The interior walls bear resounding French poetry by Maurice Gauchez and some lines in Flemish by Auguste van Cauwelaert. A tablet commemorates Queen Elisabeth, Albert's wife, who died in 1968. It is worth climbing to the upper gallery for a view of the polders.

A **British memorial** nearby is guarded by defiant lions. This lists the 566 men who were lost during the defence of Antwerp in 1914 and along the Belgian coast during the First World War. A **French monument** stands on the other side of the canal. The **Yser Memorial** carved by the sculptor Pierre Braecke is in the trees near the waterfront. Closer to the town, there is a memorial to the Resistance and a national memorial to Belgium's fishermen unveiled in 1958.

Nieuwpoort environs

The **Laurentiustoren** lies to the south of the sluices. Known as the 'Duivelstoren' because of a local legend in which a witch came here to meet the devil, it was originally built c 1281 as part of the Sint Laurentius church. The tower was later incorporated into a fortress built by Philip the Bold. It continued to be part of the ramparts until they were demolished in 1862. During the First World War the tower was used as an observation post and suffered much damage as a result.

A statue of a lone Belgian soldier stands near the **Uniebrug**, 3km southeast of Nieuwpoort on the N367. A tablet on the right records the gallant action here of the Belgian 14th Régiment de Ligne between 22–24 August 1914. In defending the last corner of Belgium from the Germans, the regiment lost 900 soldiers.

The old port of **Lombardsijde**, on the east side of the Yser estuary, is believed by some historians to have been established by Lombards from the lower Elbe. The river silted up during the 12C, leaving Lombardsijde high and dry. Its demise led to the foundation of Nieuwpoort, the Novus Portus, or new port.

Lombardsijde changed hands in October and November 1914. The remains of the town became the German front line for the next four years. The Allied sentry in the dunes to the west of the village was known as *l'homme de l'extrême gauche*, the first man on the Western Front, which stretched from the Belgian coast to Switzerland.

Ramskapelle, 2km south of Nieuwpoort, was a key military position on the railway line which ran immediately to the east. The rails have been lifted, but a low embankment marks the position of the historic line. After the area to the east had been successfully flooded during the night of 29 October 1914, a Belgian and a French regiment recaptured Ramskapelle by bayonet charge. This exploit is commemorated by a memorial on the village churchyard wall.

Flooded land

Much of the land east of the Yser was flooded in the First World War, including the district called **Moere Blote**, near Gistel. This former marshland was largely drained between 1620–23 by Wenceslas Coeberger. The outposts of the opposing armies were 3km apart in places and patrolling was carried out in boats. The Germans first got across the Yser in strength at Tervate, near Keiem. The lake of **Blankaart**, near Woumen, was created during the flooding of the Yser front. It is now a nature reserve.

The village of **Pervijze**, 10km southeast of Nieuwpoort, was taken by the Germans on 28 October 1914, but it was almost immediately evacuated when the Belgians flooded the area. A tower to the southeast of the main crossroads served as an observation post from 1914–1918. The tower may seem of little importance today, but, if viewed from the south, its tactical value becomes evident.

Oostduinkerke

Oostduinkerke is a pleasant family resort with a magnificent beach where Belgium's last shrimp fishermen ride out on horseback, sweeping the breakers with nets spread out on either side.

Where to stay

The *Argos*, Rozenlaan 20, ☎ 058.52.11.00, is a small hotel with a garden in a quiet setting.

Eating out

Eglantier, Albert I laan 141, ☎ 058.51.32.41, is a romantic hotel restaurant.
Florishof, Koksijdesteenweg 24, ☎ 058.51.12.57, is a snug local restaurant in a former fishermen's café

next to the National Fishing Museum.

Tourist information

Astridplein 6, off Albert I Laan, ☎ 058.51.13.89. Open Easter–Sept.

Opening times

The *Nationaal Visserijmuseum* is open Tues–Sun 10.00–12.00 and 14.00–18.00. Also open Mon in Jul–Aug (same hours).

Walk down Leopold II Laan from the beach to reach the old village, past the modern **Sint Niklaaskerk**, built by J. Gilson in 1955 and decorated with a huge crucifix by Arnost Gause. The **Nationaal Visserijmuseum** is located in the village at P. Schmitzstraat. This captivating museum of fishing contains ship models, fishing equipment, old photographs and a reconstructed fisherman's house.

Koksijde-Bad

Koksijde-Bad claims to have the highest dune on the Belgian coast. The 33m **Hoge Blekker** is part of the **Doornpanne** nature reserve, situated to the east of the town.

Tourist Information
Casino, Zeelaan, ☎ 058.51.29.10.
Closed weekends.

Opening times
Abbey of Ter Duinen is open at
Easter and Jul–Sept daily 10.00–18.00;

other months 09.00–12.30 and
13.30–17.00. It is closed in Jan.
Paul Delvaux museum is open
Apr–June and in Sept Tues–Sun
10.30–18.30; in Jul–Aug daily
10.30–18.30; and Oct–Dec Fri–Sun
10.30–17.30. It is closed Jan–Mar.

Go inland along **Zeelaan** and turn right down Jaak van Buggenhoutlaan, past the modern **Onze Lieve Vrouw ten Duinenkerk**, built by J. Landsoght in 1964. The ruins of the Cistercian abbey of **Ter Duinen** are in a nearby park. An interesting museum contains objects found in the ruins during excavations in 1949. It also has archaeological material from the region, a natural history collection and an exhibition on daily life in the Middle Ages. An arboretum and a garden of medicinal plants are nearby.

The vanished abbey

The Cistercian abbey of Ter Duinen was founded in 1108, rebuilt after a flood in 1237 and destroyed by the Dutch Sea Beggars in 1566. Some of the monks settled in 1597 in the Cistercian grange of Ten Bogaerde, 1.5km to the south. The present buildings date mainly from 1612, though part of the 12C–13C barn survives. The abbey was transferred to Bruges in 1627 and suppressed in 1796. A remarkable painting by Pieter Pourbus in the Brangwyn Museum in Bruges shows the abbey in the 17C.

A windmill to the south of the abbey ruins known as the **Zuidabdijmolen** was built in 1773 at Veurne and moved here in 1954. A **pilgrimage chapel** of 1819 beside the J. van Buggenhoutlaan marks the grave of Blessed Idesbald van der Gracht, the third abbot of Ter Duinen, who died in 1167. Born in Flanders, Idesbald spent his youth in the service of the count of Flanders. He became Canon of Veurne in 1135, but resigned to become a Cistercian at Ter Duinen.

Koksijde environs

The artist Paul Delvaux lived much of his life in **Sint Idesbald**, west of Koksijde-Bad. The **Paul Delvaux Museum** at Kabouterweg 42 contains a large collection of his enigmatic works. His view of the *Quarter Leopold Station* in Brussels, painted in 1922, reveals an early obsession with melancholy Belgian railway stations. His fixation with female nudes is revealed in other works such as *The Red Chair* of 1936 and *The Bride's Dress* of 1969. *The Sabbath* of 1962 has impressive lighting and draped cloth, while *The Procession*, painted in 1963, depicts nine solemn nude women proceeding quietly through a grove as a steam train passes.

De Panne

De Panne takes its name from its location in a slight depression (or *panne*) in the wooded dunes.

History

It was still a small fishing village when King Leopold I first set foot on Belgian soil here in 1831. The event is commemorated by a statue of the king at the west of the Zeedijk. De Panne developed into an elegant resort at the end of the 19C. During the First World War, the seaside town was effectively the capital of the small area of Belgian territory which remained unconquered. King Albert I and Queen Elisabeth lived in the Villa Maskens at the north end of the promenade. The Queen worked as a nurse in a field hospital which had been set up at Hôtel de l'Océan. De Panne played a crucial role during the evacuation of the retreating British army in May 1940. After reaching the sea at De Panne, the troops were evacuated from the beaches between here and Dunkirk in France. A memorial on the Leopold I Esplanade commemorates the evacuation. Some interesting 19C villas survive in the Demolderlaan.

Eating out
Le Fox, Walckierstraat 2,
☎ 058.41.28.55, offers good Flemish cuisine.

Tourist information
Gemeentehuis, Zeelaan,
☎ 058.42.18.18.

Children
Plopsaland (open early Apr to early Sept) is an attractive theme park with roller-coaster rides, a fairytale village and a small zoo. It is just south of De Panne on the road to Adinkerke.

De Panne environs
The **Westhoek** nature reserve lies to the west of De Panne. Some 150 hectares of dunes provide a unique habitat. The De Panne tourist office publishes a useful guide to the reserve.

Veurne

Veurne is an interesting and attractive old town with a number of 17C brick buildings constructed in a style called Spanish Renaissance. Known in French as Furnes, the town is located a few kilometres inland near the French frontier. It is mainly an agricultural centre at the junction of several canals, which form a moat along the course of the old ramparts.

Practical information

Eating out
The *Ibis*, Grote Markt 10,
☎ 058.31.37.00, is a rustic Flemish restaurant with good fish.

Tourist information
Grote Markt 29, ☎ 058.33.05.31.

estival

everal hundred penitents dressed in
rown robes drag wooden crosses
hrough Veurne during the annual
enitents' Procession. Held on the last
unday in July, the procession recalls a
pisode in 1099 when Count Robert II
f Flanders was caught in a gale while
eturning from Jerusalem with a relic of
he True Cross. He vowed, if he sur-
ived, to offer the relic to the first
hurch he saw. He prayers were
nswered and he presented it to the Sint
Walburgakerk in Veurne. A brotherhood
as founded in 1637 to honour the
elic with an annual procession (the
oete Processie).

listory

Veurne began as a fortified settlement, created at the time of the 9C and 10C
Viking raids. The town's ramparts were not demolished until 1771. During
the First World War, Veurne lay 9km behind the Yser front and served as the
Belgian military headquarters. It suffered much from intermittent bombardment during the First World War and from the fighting which took place here
in May 1940.

A walk in Veurne

egin on the **Grote Markt**, an appealing square surrounded by Flemish
Renaissance buildings. The **Stadhuis** was built by Lieven Lucas in a curious mix-
ure of Gothic and Renaissance styles in 1596–1612. The loggia was added by
érôme Stalpaert. The interior is decorated with exquisite Cordoba leather wall-
angings, 17C paintings and Flemish tapestries.

Carillon concerts

Concerts are given on the belfry carillon
Jul–Aug on Wed at 10.30 and Sun at
20.00.

Opening times

Stadhuis is open Apr–Sept daily and
Oct–Mar Mon–Sat. Guided tours lasting
45mins are given at set times.
Bakery Museum is open Apr–Sept
Mon–Thur (also Fri Jul–Aug)
10.00–12.00 and 14.00–18.00, week-
ends 14.00–18.00. It is open between
Oct–Mar Sun–Thur 14.00–17.00.

eurne

The more severe **Landhuis** at no. 29 was built in 1613–18 by Sylvanus Boullair The curious chimneypiece in the hall was designed by Jérôm Stalpaert. Kin Albert established his headquarters in this building in 1914. The **belfry** behin the Landhuis was built in 1628 in late-Gothic style. The campanile was restore after the last war. The five **Flemish Renaissance houses** at nos 30–34 wer built in 1609 and restored after being destroyed in the First World War.

Now go down the lane behind the Gerechtshof to reach the **Sin Walburgakerk**, which stands according to an ancient legend on the site of temple dedicated to Wotan. The choir of 1230–80 was rebuilt after a fire in 135. The transepts, begun c 1300, were completed together with the short nave i 1902–4. The ruined 14C tower in the park was never finished. The choir stal were carved by Osmaer van Ommen in 1596, while the pulpit was made b Hendrik Pulincx in 1727. There is also a *Descent from the Cross* attributed t Pieter Pourbus of Bruges, and a 16C reliquary of the True Cross in the sacristy.

Leave the Grote Markt by the Ooststraat. The crenellated **Spaans Paviljoe** on the corner of Ooststraat was built as a guard house in 1448 and extended ε the rear in 1530. It was the town hall until 1586 and later served as the heaε quarters of the Spanish officers based in Veurne. The graceful façade of the foi mer **Vleeshuis** is on the opposite side of Ooststraat. Built as a meat hall in 161 it now contains the public library and cultural centre.

Turn right to reach the Appelmarkt, where the **Sint Niklaaskerk** was built i the late 15C as a hall-church. The choir was added 1773. The massive bric tower has survived from the 13C. It houses a huge bell cast in 1379. Known ε **'t Bomtje**, it is one of the oldest surviving bells in Belgium. The well-lit moder interior contains a triptych of 1534 ascribed variously to Pieter Coecke an Bernard van Orley.

The appealing **Bakery Museum** at Albert I Laan 2 occupies an 18C Flemis. farm. It contains an old baker's shop and a collection of utensils.

Veurne environs

The castle of **Beauvoorde**, 7km south of Veurne, was rebuilt c 1591–161? probably by Sylvanus Boullain, on the site of an old castle which had fallen int ruin. The interior (**open** Jun–Sept Tues–Sun 14.00–17.00) contains ornat chimneypieces, including one attributed to Stalpaert, paintings, ceramics, glas and silverware.

The village of **Houtem**, 3km west of Beauvoorde, was King Albert's heac quarters from 1915–18. The **De Moeren polder**, drained in 1627 by Wencesla Coeberger using windmills, stretches north of here.

The small town of **Lo**, 12km southeast of Veurne, grew important after a Augustinian abbey was founded here in the 12C. It was demolished at the time ε the French Revolution, leaving just an attractive **dovecote** of 1710 behind th present church. This 19C–20C successor to the abbey church has baroque stal and a pulpit of 1626 by Urbain Taillebert.

The **Westpoort**, with two pepperpot turrets, dates back to the 14C. A local tra dition claims that Julius Caesar tethered his horse to the ancient yew here. Th **Stadhuis** is a restoration of a 16C building. The restored 15C–16C convent ε the Grauwe Zusters, the Grey Sisters or Poor Clares, is nearby.

Battlefields of the First World War

he peaceful countryside around Ypres was the setting for some of the worst bat-
es in human history. For four bitter years, the troops of the British Empire
ught in appalling conditions to defend the old town of Ypres from the German
rmy. Some five million troops marched through the ruins of Ypres to reach the
ne of muddy trenches that formed the notorious Ypres Salient. Within a few
juare kilometres, some 300,000 soldiers were killed and a further million were

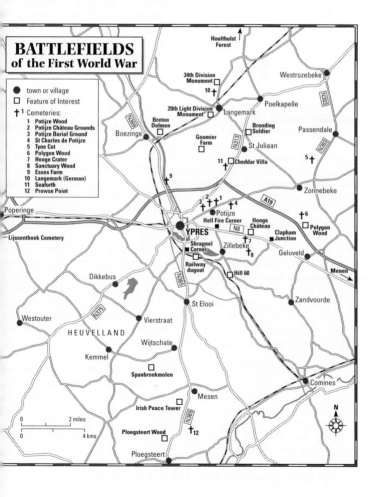

BATTLEFIELDS
of the First World War

● town or village
□ Feature of Interest
† ¹ Cemeteries:
1 Potijze Wood
2 Potijze Château Grounds
3 Potijze Burial Ground
4 St Charles de Potijze
5 Tyne Cot
6 Polygon Wood
7 Hooge Crater
8 Sanctuary Wood
9 Essex Farm
10 Langemark (German)
11 Seaforth
12 Prowse Point

Grieving Couple, Vladslo

wounded on the British side. The loss on the German side have never bee calculated, but they were probab about the same.

The area around Ypres is still dotte with the reminders of this tragic co flict. The fields contain craters, co crete bunkers, and monuments, as we as some 160 battlefield cemeterie Several museums provide a furth glimpse of the horrors endured. It now more than 80 years since the la shots were fired, yet there is somethin infinitely moving about this area. It perhaps, one of the most tragic spc on earth.

Commonwealth War Graves

The Commonwealth War Graves Commission takes care of the graves of some 204,000 Commonwealth soldiers who died in Belgium during the two world wars. Most of the graves are in the war cemeteries around Ypres. The largest is **Tyne Cot Cemetery**, Passchendaele, which has 11,900 graves. There are 175 Commonwealth war cemeteries in Belgium, but soldiers are also buried in 460 other local graveyards. More than 102,000 soldiers with no known grave are commemorated on the Menin Gate Memorial at Ypres, Tyne Cot Cemetery and several other memorials in the Salient.

Most Commonwealth war cemeteries are bounded by a low wall or hedge. Each cemetery has a Cross of Sacrifice, while larger ones also have an altar-like Stone of Remembrance inscribed with the words 'Their Name liveth for Evermore'. They are planted with trees, flowers and grass lawns to evoke the atmosphere of an English churchyard. The orderly rows of graves are marked by uniform headstones bearing the name, rank, unit and date of death of the soldier, the regimental crest, and the symbol of his faith. Some have a personal inscription chosen and paid for by the next-of-kin.

A bronze box near the entrance to each cemetery contains a register of the soldiers buried there and a book for visitors' comments. The Commonwealth War Graves Commission maintains the cemeteries and graves. Anyone looking for a particular grave can write to the Commonwealth War Graves Commission, 2 Marlow Road, Maidenhead, Berks, SL6 7DX, ☎ 01628 634 221, or to the North-West Europe Headquarters, Elverdingsestraat 82, Ieper, Belgium, ☎ 057.20.01.18. The Royal British Legion, 48 Pall Mall, London SW1V 5JG, ☎ 0345 725 725 can arrange for poppy wreaths to be laid. A small fee is charged.

Battlefield tours

Several companies organise tours of the battlefields of Flanders:

Holts Tours, Golden Key Building, 15 Market Street, Sandwich, Kent CT13 9DA, ☎ 01304 612248 (within Britain), organises excellent bus tours to Ypres and other World War battlefield lasting 3–4 days.

Salient Tours, ☎ 075.91.02.23 (within Belgium), or 0385 955908 (within Britain), run by the enthusiastic Mark Horner, offers bus tours of the Salient lasting 2–4 hours, from Easter to November 11, Thur–Tues, beginning at the Menin Gate in Ypres at 10.00 and 14.30. Most tour organisers will visit a particular cemetery if notified in advance.

Web site

The **In Flanders Museum** at Ypres has an excellent web site covering First World War topics at: www.inflanders-fields.be

Safety

Unexploded shells are still frequently unearthed by local farmers in the Ypres area. They are often stacked at cross-roads for collection by the Belgian bomb disposal unit. Many of these shells are still highly dangerous and should not be touched. Tourists should keep to **foot-paths** in the woods to avoid stepping on hidden shells.

YPRES

• • • • • •

Ypres is a friendly Flemish market town located at the south end of the Yser canal about 12km from the French frontier. Known in Dutch as Ieper, Ypres was the greatest cloth town in Flanders from the 13C to the 15C, but was reduced to rubble in 1914–18. Carefully rebuilt in the original Flemish brick style, this town (population 35,400) is now visited mainly for the monuments, churches, museums and cemeteries linked to the First World War. 'A more sacred place for the British race does not exist in the world,' Winston Churchill declared in a 1919 speech.

Practical information

Getting there

Direct **trains** run to Ypres from Brussels. The journey takes about 1.5 hours. The final stage of the journey, from Comines to Ypres, crosses a gentle slope where fierce fighting occurred in 1917. Some relics of the war can still be seen from the train, such as shell holes, pill boxes and British cemeteries.

Where to stay

The town has some small hotels which make a good base for visiting places connected with the Great War. *The Ariane*,

Slachthuisstraat 58, ☎ 057. 21.82.18, is a comfortable modern hotel within walking distance of the Grote Markt.

Eating out
Restaurants

Cyper, Grote Markt 5, ☎ 057.21.73.39, is a friendly Flemish family restaurant.

Regina, Grote Markt 45, ☎ 057.21.88.88, is a traditional hotel restaurant on main square.

Cafés

Au Miroir, Grote Markt 12, is a traditional Flemish tavern.

Old Tom, Grote Markt 8, is an old Flemish tavern with photographs of Ypres during the First World War. *Ter Posterie*, Rijselsestraat 57, is a friendly Flemish cellar tavern with over 200 beers on offer including the local Poperings Hommelbier. It has simple food.

Tourist information

Lakenhallen, Grote Markt,
☎ 057.22.85.84.

Commonwealth War Graves Commission

The Commonwealth War Graves Commission maintains some 40 British military cemeteries within 3km of the Grote Markt and 130 others around the Salient. Maps can be consulted and directions obtained at the Commission office, Elverdingestraat 82, Ypres, ☎ 057.20.01.18. Some of the cemeteries can be reached by local bus. The office is open Mon–Fri 08.30–12.30 and 13.30–17.00 (16.30 on Friday).

Cycling

The countryside around Ypres is ideal for a cycling tour. The tourist office has signposted a 45km Vredesroute (Peace Trail) for cyclists. Bicycles can be rented at the railway station or the Jeugdstadion, Leopold III-laan 16.

Bookshop

The *Standaard Boekhandel*, Meensestraat 16, stocks books on Ypres and the Salient in English.

English Church

The *memorial church of St George* is almost opposite the west door of the cathedral, at the corner of Elverdingestraat. Services are held on Sunday at 18.00.

Festival

A curious procession known as the **Kattestoet** originated in the 12C when cats were kept in the upper floor of the cloth hall during the winter months to keep down the mice. No longer needed in the spring, the cats were thrown from the belfry in a cruel custom symbolising the killing of evil spirits. Abolished in 1817, the Kattestoet was revived in 1955, but using cloth cats rather than the real thing. The procession features floats, giants and some 2000 locals dressed in cat costumes. The Kattestoet is held every three years on the second Sunday in May. The next procession is in 2003. A more modest ceremony called **Kattenworp** or cat tossing is held every year on the second Sunday in May.

Carillon concerts

Concerts are played on the carillon in the belfry Jun–Sept every Sunday (but not on the first and second Sundays of August) 21.00–22.00. The inner courtyard of the Cloth Hall is the best place to listen to the concerts.

Children

Ypres has a good **adventure playground** and mini golf course next to the camping site on Hoornwerk, 1km south of the Menin Gate. **Bellewaerde theme park**, 3km east of Ypres, is an attractive landscaped park with rollercoaster rides, a safari train, monorail, cowboy village, Mexican village, wildwater river and other attractions. The park is open from Easter to the end of September.

Opening times

In **Flanders Field Museum**, in the cloth hall, Grote Markt, is open daily Apr–Sept 10.00–18.00 and Oct–Mar daily except Mon 10.00–17.00. Closed for 3 weeks after Christmas. Tickets for In Flanders Fields include entry to the Stedelijk Museum, the Belle Godshuis Museum and the Museum of Education. **Stedelijk Museum** (municipal museum), Ieperleestraat 31, **Belle**

Godshuis Museum (paintings and history of Ypres), Rijselsestraat, and **Museum of Education**, G. de Stuersstraat, are open Tues–Sun 10.00–12.30 and 14.00–18.00. They close at 17.00 Nov–Mar. A combined ticket is sold for all three museums. **Merghelynck Museum** (Louis XV period house), Merghelynckstraat 2, is currently (2000) closed except for group visits booked in advance.

Council Chamber in the Nieuwwerk can be visited when it is not being used for council meetings, on weekdays 08.30–11.45.

Sint Maartens Kathedraal (behind the cloth hall), and **Saint George's Memorial Church**, Elverdingsestraat, are open daily, except during services.

History

A settlement grew up here in the 10C at the place where the Paris to Bruges trade route crossed the river Ieperlee. The river was navigable in those days, but now runs along an underground canal. The town became a powerful medieval centre, deriving great wealth from its **weaving industry**. It shared with Bruges and Ghent the effective control of Flanders. When the cloth hall was built in c 1260–1304, Ypres was one of the greatest cities of Europe, with a population of some 40,000. Cloth from Ypres was in great demand throughout Europe. It was sold as far away as Novgorod in the 12C.

The first of the Flemish '**Chambers of Rhetoric**' was founded here in the 14C and called Alpha en Omega. These literary societies played an important part in the life of the Burgundian Netherlands up to the 17C.

The prosperity of Ypres began to wane towards the end of the 14C. In 1383 the English, aided by 20,000 troops from Ghent, besieged the town (a painting in the cathedral illustrates the episode). Ypres held out, but the surrounding district was ravaged. The weavers were forced to leave, taking their lucrative industry with them. Chaucer's description of the skill of the Wife of Bath as surpassing that of the weavers of 'Ipres and Gaunt' dates from about this time. The **dispersion of the weavers** marked the beginning of a period of decline. Rivalries between the towns and the rigid traditionalism of their guilds hastened the recession. By the end of the 16C, the population had dwindled to 5000.

Yet in strategic terms Ypres remained an important town. It was taken and sacked by the Duke of Parma in 1584 and throughout the next century was fought over continually by France and Spain. In 1678, under the Peace of Nijmegen, Ypres became French, leading to Vauban strengthening the defences. Peace did not last long; after surviving the **War of the Grand Alliance** (1690–97), Ypres changed hands several times during the War of the Spanish Succession (1702–13); in the War of the Austrian Succession (1744–48); and again during the war of 1792 beween revolutionary France and Austria. It became a French town once more in 1794. Under the **Congress of Vienna** of 1815, Ypres was incorporated into the kingdom of the Netherlands.

On 13 October 1914 the town was occupied by German cavalry. They withdrew the next day, when the **British Expeditionary Force** arrived. Over the next four years, the town was reduced to rubble by German artillery. Lying immediately behind the front line, the routes through the town were shelled continuously long after the buildings had disappeared. The junction of the Grote Markt with the Menen road (Meensestraat) became known as 'the most dangerous corner in Europe'.

After the war, Churchill wanted to preserve the ruined city as a permanent reminder of the horrors of the war, but the plan was rejected by the Belgian government after heated debate in parliament. Many of the buildings such as the great cloth hall and the cathedral are faithful reconstructions of the pre-war buildings. The **reconstruction of the town** was completed in 1967 when the final stone was laid in place on the cloth hall.

A walk in the old town

Begin on the **Grote Markt** with the famous **Cloth Hall** or Lakenhalle. Considered the most splendid secular Gothic building in Belgium, it symbolised the wealth and power of Ypres' cloth industry. Built c 1260–1304 along the river Ieperlee, which in those days was busy with shipping, the hall was a combined market, warehouse and covered quay.

After surviving centuries of siege and warfare, the hall was completely destroyed, largely by a German artillery barrage on 22 November 1914. It remained in ruins until 1933–34 when work began on a faithful reconstruction, but it was not until 1967 that the cloth hall was formally opened by King Baudouin.

The **façade**, 125m long, is crowned by a superb square belfry 70m high. The present spire with its helmet and dragon of 1692 is an exact copy of the original. It has a carillon of 49 bells which cover four octaves.

The lower courses of the Cloth Hall incorporate part of the original 13C building. Above the **Donkerpoort** are the municipal coat of arms and a statue of Our Lady of Thuyne, the protectress of Ypres since the English siege of 1383. The statues on the right-hand side of the passage represent Earl Baldwin IX of Flanders and his consort, Mary of Champagne, who laid the first stone in 1200. The statues to the left of the belfry show King Albert and Queen Elisabeth, during whose reign the reconstruction was begun. A memorial to the right of the entrance commemorates the French victims of 1914–18.

The **Nieuwwerk**, which houses a part of the town hall, was added to the east side of the Cloth Hall. This elegant Renaissance building was constructed above a vaulted gallery between 1619 and 1624. Destroyed during the 1914 bombardment, it was reconstructed in 1962 by P.A. Pauwels, who drew inspiration from the Cloth Hall. Above the large window are the arms of Philip IV of Spain. The niches contain statuettes of Our Lady of Thuyne, patron saint of Ypres, and figures representing justice and prudence. The Council Chamber has a fine stained-glass window by Arno Brys.

The **In Flanders Fields Museum** is open daily Apr–Sept 10.00–18.00 and Oct–Mar daily except Mon 10.00–17.00. It is closed for 3 weeks immediately after Christmas. Tickets for In Flanders Fields include entry to the Stedelijk Museum. It was opened in 1998 on the upper floor of the cloth hall to replace the Ypres Salient Museum. Beginning with nostalgic photographs taken by Anthony d'Ypres at the beginning of the 20C and ending with the rebuilding of Ypres after the war, the museum uses the latest sound and light technology to create a dramatic impression of the war. It achieves an extraordinary emotional impact

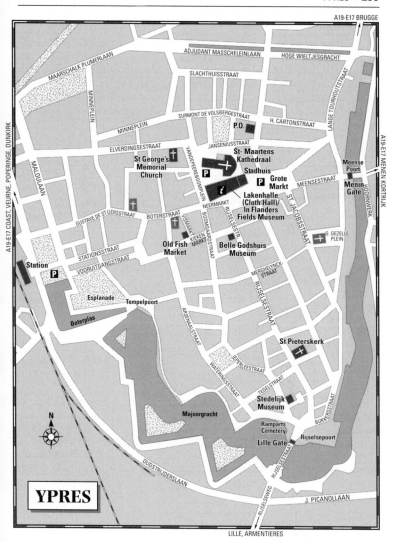

YPRES

through the use of old film footage, photographs, war poems and diaries. Recorded texts are spoken in English, German, French and Dutch, and visitors are able to follow the fates of soldiers and civilians caught up in the war using interactive computer technology. The museum has set up an internet site to collect personal details of people involved in the war.

Sint Maartens Kathedraal

Sint Maartens Kathedraal stands behind the cloth hall. It is open daily, except during services.

History of the cathedral

Built in the 13C on the site of an earlier 11C church, it was destroyed in 1914 but rebuilt in the original gothic style. The church did not originally have a spire (as you can see from old photographs and engravings displayed in the choir) but this was added during the reconstruction, using medieval plans for a spire that was never achieved. The remains of an early 12C cloister on the north side of the cathedral contain a small collection of sculptural fragments and damaged tombs.

Most of the works of art in the cathedral were lost during the 1914 bombardment, but a Flemish diptych of 1525 with scenes of the *Passion* survives on the west wall. Several interesting paintings are found in the **Sakrakapel** at the east end, including a detailed 17C picture by Joris Lybaert depicting the 1383 siege of Ypres, when the English joined forced with Ghent in an unsuccessful bid to take the town. The statue of *Our Lady of Thuyne*, who according to local legend saved the town from the besieging army, stands in a niche on the side altar to the south.

There are also three **alabaster effigies** of 17C bishops and the black marble tomb of Guillaume de Saillant, chancellor of Ypres, from 1552. Count Robert de Béthune, who died in 1322, and Bishop Jansenius (Cornelis Jansen (1585–1638) are buried in the chapel. A handsome tomb in the **south transept**, reconstructed after the war, commemorates George Chamberlain, who was born in Ghent of English parents and served as Bishop of Ypres from 1628–34.

Other **memorials** in the church recall the war years, including a monument to Abbé Camille Delaere (1860–1930), a courageous parish priest who ministered to the wounded in 1914 while the town was under heavy fire. The rose window above the south door was presented in 1935 by the British Army and the Royal Air Force in memory of King Albert I.

The British Empire Memorial in the **north transept** is one of a number of identical memorials found in churches along the 1914–18 front line. It commemorates the one million dead of the Empire 'many of whom rest in Belgium'. A copy of the poem *Ypres Cathedral 1930*, found in the papers of General H. M. Horden and probably written by him, is hung on the wall. A memorial in the **south transept** commemorates the French soldiers who fell in Belgium during

Cloth hall and Cathedral, Ypres

the Great War. The baptismal chapel at the west end incorporates sculptural fragments salvaged from the ruined church.

Cornelis Jansenius

Cornelis Jansenius, Bishop of Ypres, was a theologian who gave his name to **Jansenism**. This was a movement in the Catholic Church which was based on Jansenius' strict interpretation of the teachings of St Augustine. Jansenius argued that man could only be saved by the grace of Christ, which was given to a small number of the elect only. This belief in predestination soon brought Jansenism into conflict with the Catholic Church, particularly the Jesuits. The movement was condemned by Pope Urban VIII in the bull In Eminenti of 1642. Jansenius himself steered clear of serious trouble. He became professor of theology at Bayonne, Bishop of Leuven in 1630 and Bishop of Ypres in 1636. He died two years later from the plague, leaving a statement in which he accepted the judgement of the Church on his teachings. Supported by Pascal and the Port Royalists, the Jansenist movement continued in France for many years after his death.

A Celtic cross known as the **Munster Memorial** stands to the north of the cathedral. Inscribed in Irish, English, French and Dutch, it commemorates Irish soldiers killed in the First World War.

Almost opposite the west entrance of the cathedral is the **Saint George's English Memorial Church**, built by Reginald Blomfield in 1929. Open daily except during services. Virtually every object in the church commemorates a unit or individual soldier. The armoured figure on the font cover is a memorial to Field Marshal the Earl of Ypres, Sir John French (1852–1925), commander of the British Expeditionary Force in 1914–15.

Turn right on leaving St George's Church, past a memorial to the people of Ypres known as the **Gedenkteken**. The reconstructed building straight ahead at Neermarkt 8 was the **Vleeshuis** up until the First World War. The stone ground floor was built in 1275, while the Late Gothic brick upper level was added in 1530. It is now occupied by the offices of the local youth service. Turn right along Boterstraat to reach the Baroque gate decorated with Neptune next to no. 21. Carved in 1714 and restored in 1939, this leads to the Vismarkt (fish market). There are two covered fish stands here and a curious toll house built in 1899.

Now turn left along Kiekenmarkt to reach Boomgaardstraat, then continue down Burchtstraat and turn right down Rijselsestraat to reach the **Belle Godshuis** at no. 38, open Tues–Sun from 10.00–12.30 and 14.00–18.00. (closes at 17.00 from Nov–Mar). This almshouse was founded c 1276, but rebuilt in the 16C and 17C. It bears a plaque to its founder Jean Yperman, a local physician, and the date 1616. The house is now a museum with an interesting collection of paintings, including a *Madonna with Donors* of 1420, and a 16C *Temptation of St Anthony* in the style of Hieronymus Bosch. It also displays 17C vestments, 17C and 18C silver, furniture, city seals and interesting photographs of old Ypres. The bakery at **no. 6** has a blown-up photograph of Ypres in 1911 taken by Antony d'Ypres.

Continue down the street and turn left on Merghelynckstraat to admire the façade of the **Merghelynck Museum** at no. 2. This handsome patrician home was built in 1774 in Louis XV style, and reconstructed after the First World War. The period rooms contain a splendid collection of 17C and 18C works of art, including Rubens' *Vanity of Riches*, painted for Bishop Jansenius. It is unfortunately rarely open.

Return to Rijselsestraat and turn left past the 13C Tempeliershuis at **no. 70**, part of which survived the war. The **Little Talbot House** at no. 83 was occupied by British troops from November 1917 to April 1918. Further down the street, the **Sint Pieterskerk** on the left still has traces of the original Romanesque church in the lower course of the west tower. Begun in the 12C and largely rebuilt in the 15C and 16C in late Gothic style, the church was destroyed in 1914–18. Interesting photographs inside show the church at different periods.

Further down the street, turn right into Ieperleestraat to reach the **Stedelijk Museum**, the municipal museum, open Tues–Sun from 10.00–12.30 and 14.00–18.00 (closes at 17.00 from Nov–Mar). Located in the 16C Late Gothic wing of an almshouse founded in 1277, the museum provides a fascinating insight into the history of Ypres through old photographs, drawings, maps and paintings. A portrait by Gortzius Geldorp shows Cornelis Jansenius as a student at Leuven University. It is signed GG and dated 1604 on the clock. A 17C *Adoration of the Magi* was painted by Jan Thomas of Ypres, a pupil of Rubens.

Antony d'Ypres

Many old photographs of Ypres bear the signature Antony d'Ypres (1883–1963). These were taken by Maurice Antony from c 1909 to 1919. His early photographs show the beauty of Ypres before the war, while the shots taken during 1914–15 depict the tragic destruction of the cloth hall. A final series of photographs from 1919 show the temporary huts erected amid the rubble and the earliest battlefield pilgrims to the town. Maurice Antony later moved to Ostend to photograph the glamourous resort in the 1920s and 1930s. His photographs can be seen in the Stedelijk Museum, In Flanders Fields Museum and the Sanctuary Wood Museum.

Continue down Rijselsestraat, past a wooden gable rebuilt in 16C style, to reach the **Rijselsepoort**, or Lille Gate. The oldest surviving city gate, it was rebuilt by Vauban in the 17C, but still has two towers from 1395. The vaulted chamber on the east side was used in the 17C as a guardroom, while the chamber on the west side marks the spot where the Ieperlee enters the city by an underground canal. Most British troops marched out to the Salient through the Lille Gate as it was less exposed to shelling than the Menin Gate.

A path beside the gate leads to the **Ramparts Cemetery**, one of the most beautiful war cemeteries on the Western Front. The ashes of Rose Coombe, whose book *Before Endeavours Fade* reawakened interest in the war cemeteries, are buried in the cemetery. A rosebush marks the spot.

There is a footpath along the top of the restored **ramparts**, from the Lille Gate to the Menin Gate. Surrounded by a moat, the ramparts were largely the work of

Vauban in the 17C. During the First World War, they were protected by a trench and shelters, traces of which survive. Used by British artillery observers, the ramparts still provide a good view of the arc of ridges where the Germans dug in after the Second Battle of Ypres, running from Pilkem on the left, through Zonnebeke to Mesen on the right.

The Wipers Times

The vaulted rooms under the ramparts resisted the heaviest bombardments. They contained bedrooms, a signals headquarters, a hospital and even a cinema. They also briefly housed a makeshift printing press where the Sherwood Foresters turned out the famous *Wipers Times* in 1916. The newspaper, which ran to four editions, was full of grim humour and risqué jokes. A section of the In Flanders Fields Museum is devoted to the newspaper.

Continue along to the ramparts is the **Menin Gate**, a classical gate designed by Sir Reginald Blomfield and opened by Field Marshal Plumer in July 1927 as a memorial to the missing of the Salient who have no grave. Built on the site of an old city gate destroyed in the war, it stands at the beginning of the notorious Menin Road which led to the Salient. The memorial takes the form of a gateway with three entrances. The brooding lion above the main arch was carved by Sir W. Reid Dick. The walls of the gate are inscribed with the names of 54,896 soldiers who died in the Ypres Salient but whose bodies were never recovered. The names of a further 35,000 missing soldiers are inscribed on the rear wall of Tyne Cot Cemetery.

Last Post ceremony

One of the most moving ceremonies on the Western Front takes place every evening at 20.00 when traffic is halted briefly at the Menin Gate while buglers from the Ypres fire brigade play the *Last Post*. The plaintive bugle call was first played on 24 July 1927 at the unveiling of the Menin Gate. The ceremony has been repeated every day since, apart from the period of the German Occupation from 1940–44.

Return to the old town through the gate, passing the St Jacobstraat where a convent was founded in 1665. Occupied mainly by Irish nuns, it was destroyed during the bombardment of 1914. Among its treasures was the flag carried at the battle of Fontenoy in Hainaut in 1745 by the Irish Brigade, a famous band of exiles who served in the French Army. The Duke of Cumberland (later known as the 'Butcher of Culloden') was defeated at Fontenoy by the French under Marshal Saxe. The charge of the Irish Brigade ensured the French victory. The nuns moved from Ypres to a new home at Kylemore, Connemara.

The way back to Grote Markt leads past the **Gerechtshof** (law courts) on the east side of the square. This reconstructed early Renaissance building stands on the site of a 12C almshouse. The **Klein Stadhuis** on the north side was built in the 15C and altered in the 17C. The first floor is decorated with a row of medallions depicting the seven deadly sins.

POPERINGE

Poperinge is an attractive small town of c 20,000 inhabitants surrounded by hop fields.

Practical information

Where to stay
Poperinge is a pleasant quiet town convenient for those visiting the Salient.
Belfort, Grote Markt 29,
☎ 057.33.88.88, is a modern hotel on the main square.
Palace, Ieperstraat 34,
☎ 057.33.30.93, is a friendly hotel in a 19C mansion.

Eating out
The *d'Hommelkeete*, Hoge Noenweg 3,
☎ 057.33.43.65, is a rustic restaurant with dishes based on hops.

Tourist information
Stadhuis, Grote Markt 1,
☎ 057.34.66.76.

Opening times
Talbot House (wartime servicemen's club), Gasthuisstraat 43, is open daily 09.00–12.00 and 14.00–17.00.
Stadhuis death cells, Botermarkt, are open daily 09.00–17.30.
Nationaal Hopmusem, Gasthuisstraat 71, is open in May, Jun and mid-end Sept on Sun and public holidays 14.00–18.00, and in Jul–mid-Sept daily (same times).

History

Poperinge was once a cloth-making town, but could not compete with Ypres and so in the early 15C turned to **hops**. Troops from Poperinge helped Philip the Good in 1436 when he attacked Calais, which was then an English port. The English besieged Poperinge in revenge, burning down the Sint Bertinuskerk and killing 2500 inhabitants. The Renaissance artist Lancelot Blondeel was born in Poperinge in 1496.

Occupied by the Germans in August 1914, the town was recaptured by the British in October. Known simply as 'Pop' to the British soldiers, the town was devoted to providing recreation for troops based in the Salient. Although it was occasionally shelled from 1914–18 and bombed in May 1940, the main buildings have suffered little war damage.

A walk in Poperinge
Begin on the **Botermarkt**, the main square. The **Sint Bertinuskerk** is an outstanding example of a Flemish hall church. Dedicated to a Benedictine abbot who died c 700, it was built in the 15C to replace an older church burnt down by the English in 1436. The interior has some good woodwork (including an 18C pulpit brought from the Dominican church in Bruges), two baroque confessionals and an 18C rood-screen.

The **Stadhuis** was built in 1911 in neo-Gothic style. Several British soldiers found guilty of cowardice were shot in the courtyard. The former death cells were recently opened to the public, open daily 09.00–17.30. A plaque outside **no. 16** recalls that this was a favourite café for soldiers on leave.

The church of **Onze Lieve Vrouw**, in Kasselstraat, has a tower of c 1400, a

16C portal and splendid choir stalls of 1752 by E. Wallijn. The church of **Sint Jan** in Bruggestraat also has woodwork by Wallijn. It contains a miraculous figure of Our Lady of St John.

Now walk down Gasthuisstraat, named after an ancient hospice founded here in 1312. A sign announcing the Everyman's Club still hangs outside **Talbot House** at no. 43, open daily 09.00–12.00 and 14.00–17.00.

'Toc H'

This wartime club was named after Gilbert Talbot, the younger brother of the senior chaplain of the 16th Division, who was killed at Hooge on 30 July 1915. The house was rented from its absentee owner by the Reverend P.B. Clayton (1885–1972) as a soldiers' club and home. About half a million soldiers visited this house from December 1915 until the end of the war. It was affectionately known as 'Toc H' after the army signallers' code. The Toc H movement, founded in 1922, was inspired by Talbot House.

The house contains some fascinating photographs and other relics of the war. The chapel built by 'Tubby' Clayton in the attic has remained virtually unchanged since the war. The contents of the house were mostly saved during the Second World War by local people who hid them in their homes. The house itself was bought by Lord Wakefield for Toc H in 1929. It now serves as a centre of European reconciliation. Rooms can be rented at a modest rate.

The pharmacy at **no. 12** was once a Flemish café. During the war, it was used for a time as the advanced headquarters of Sir Douglas Haig. It later became a famous British officers' club known as Skindles.

The **Nationaal Hopmuseum** at no. 71 is open in May, Jun and mid-end Sept on Sun and public holidays 14.00–18.00, and in Jul–mid-Sept daily (same times). It occupies the former municipal weighhouse which dates from 1866. The weighbridge, which was in use from 1866 to 1966, forms part of the museum. The museum covers the cultivation of hops and their use in brewing. The visit ends with a taste of the local beer.

Poperinge in literature

Poperinge is mentioned several times in English literature. Chaucer (c 1345–1400) says that the hero of the *Rime of Sir Thopas* was born 'in Flaundres, al beyonde the sea, at Popering, in the place'. Mercutio in Shakespeare's *Romeo and Juliet* (1594) refers to the 'poperin pear', a variety which came to England from this district, while Sebastian, in *The Atheist's Tragedy* by Cyril Tourneur (c 1575–1626) describes a 'poppring pear tree'.

Poperinge environs

The **Lijssenthoek** war cemetery, 3km southwest of Poperinge, is the second largest military cemetery in the Salient. It contains some 9900 graves of soldiers, including Germans, French and one nurse. Most of the men died of wounds in the nearby casualty clearing station based in Remi farm. The farm buildings are still standing behind the cemetery.

THE SALIENT

The 'Salient' was the name given during the First World War to a projecting bulge in the Allied front to the east of Ypres. It was the scene of some of the most horrific fighting of the war, yet the enormous loss of life brought few military gains. This small corner of Belgium now contains 160 Commonwealth cemeteries.

Practical information

Getting there

• The Salient is reached from **Brussels** by taking the E40 motorway to Ghent, then the E17 to Kortrijk and the A19 to Ypres.

• From **Ostend**, take the E40 motorway towards Veurne, then turn off onto the N369 to Ypres. This route runs close to the front line for some of the way.

• To reach the Salient from **Calais**, take the E40 motorway in the direction of Brussels, and turn off onto the N8 soon after crossing the Belgian frontier. The war cemeteries in the salient are marked with green road signs.

Opening times

Streekmuseum at Zonnebeke is open from Apr–mid Nov on Wed, Sat and Sun 14.00–18.00. It is open Jul–Aug Tues–Sun 14.00–18.00.
Sanctuary Wood Museum and **Hill 60 Museum** at Zillebeke are open daily 10.00–19.00.
Hooge Crater Museum at Zillebeke is open Feb–mid-Dec 10.00–19.00.

Visiting the Salient

This is a flat and not particularly exciting land of isolated farms and neat villages. Apart from having better roads, a motorway and cars instead of horsecarts, it has changed little since the beginning of the century. In such bucolic surroundings, it is not always easy to picture the utter devastation and desolation of the war. After months of heavy shelling, many villages were reduced to heaps of rubble, often marked simply by a wooden sign standing in the ruins. The flooded, stinking trenches, crowned with entanglements of rusty wire, meandered through a nightmarish landscape of tortured trees. Thousands of young men, deafened by constant shelling, died horribly in these surroundings, many of those involved in the Battle of Passchendaele drowning in a quagmire of mud.

Visiting this area by car, bicycle or coach, you pass through places which recall the gallant enthusiasm of the First Battle of Ypres, the desperate rallies that saved the wavering British line after the poison gas attack of 1915, and the unbelievable horror of the Third Battle of Ypres. The countryside still contains battered concrete bunkers, eroded and overgrown trenches, tangles of barbed wire and areas pockmarked with mine craters. The crowded cemeteries, monuments, and old photographs in local museums help the visitor to understand what happened in the Salient.

History of the Salient

The Salient was established by the **First Battle of Ypres** in October 1914. Launched by the Allies, the attack aimed to strike at the German lines of communication across Flanders. The Germans mounted an offensive at the same time with an army that outnumbered the Allies by about three to one. During the course of the battle, the British lost Zandvoorde and Hollebeke and were forced back to the Mesen–Wijtschate ridge. The village of Geluveld was also lost. Mesen was lost on 1 November and the Wijtschate ridge fell to the Germans on 2 November. This spelled disaster for the Allies, as it gave the Germans a view over Ypres and its surroundings.

The Allied line was manned by the French from the canal at Steenstraat in the N to Zonnebeke. The British and Commonwealth troops held the Salient from Zonnebeke along the E of Polygon Wood to Hill 60 and the railway. The French occupied the line from the railway to west of Mesen, while the British held the remaining stretch from Mesen to the Lys at Frelinghien. The fighting had ceased by 22 November and the armies began to dig **trenches**.

The Salient was seriously reduced by the **Second Battle of Ypres** in 1915, and modestly enlarged by the **Third Battle of Ypres** in 1917. The key tactical feature was the range of low ridges, from Pilkem in the north to Mesen (Messines) in the south. Holding these from 1915–1917, the Germans were able to keep much of the Allied forward and rear areas under observation.

The Salient again came under attack in the **Battle of the Lys** in 1918, when the German army launched a final offensive on 9 April. The main weight of the attack fell along the River Lys (Leie) and against the Salient. By 30 April, when the battle ended, all the Allied gains of 1917 had been lost. The Allied line south of Ypres no longer reached the Lys but ran through Voormezele, Vierstraat, and Loker. The losses were regained in the final Allied offensive of August to October.

1 • The Menin Road and Tyne Cot

Leave Ypres by the N8, the Menin Road (Meenseweg in Dutch), which runs east from the Menin Gate in Ypres to Menen. This notorious road which led out to the battlefield is depicted in Paul Nash's large painting *The Menin Road* commissioned by the Imperial War Museum, London. The French spelling 'Menin', rather than the correct Menen, was commonly used during the first World War and has remained in use for the Menin Gate and the Menin road.

Less than 1km from Ypres is a roundabout known as **Hellfire Corner**, with side roads leading off to Zillebeke and Potijze. Constantly subject to German shelling, the roads here were lined with canvas screens to thwart enemy observers. The Germans reached this spot in their final attack of 1918.

Take the exit to **Potijze**, where three British cemeteries lie to the north of the village. A short detour to the south, down the road signposted to Zillebeke, leads to a blockhouse half hidden by a farm building. Known to the soldiers as **Hussar Farm**, this was a valuable Allied observation point for four years. Return to Potijze and turn right on the N332. The French flag flies over the great cemetery of **Saint Charles de Potyze**, where 4600 soldiers are buried. It contains a striking stone monument of a Crucifixion and grieving women. The British Aeroplane Cemetery is just beyond here. Cross the A19 motorway and continue to Zonnebeke.

Zonnebeke

Tourist information

Ieperstraat 5, ☎ 051.77.04.41.

History

Zonnebeke is a prosperous little town with neat brick houses lining the main road. It is difficult to imagine that this was once the scene of some of the worst fighting along the curve of the Salient. At the beginning of the war, Zonnebeke was chosen by the Germans as the base from which the Kaiser would make his triumphal entry into Ypres on 1 November 1914, but the village was defended stubbornly until May 1915. By 1917, aerial photographs of Zonnebeke show an eerie mass of grey rubble in a landscape of muddy craters and shattered trees. Recaptured by the Allies in September 1917, it was lost in April 1918, but retaken the following September.

The interesting **Streeksmuseum** is located in a quaint country house in Zonnebeke built in Normandy style in 1924. The museum has photographs of Zonnebeke before the war, army maps and some dioramas. It is open Apr–mid Nov on Wed, Sat and Sun 14.00–18.00. It is open Jul–Aug Tues–Sun 14.00–18.00.

Tyne Cot Cemetery

Take the N303 north from Zonnebeke and follow the signs to Tyne Cot Cemetery. This haunting cemetery stands on the gentle slopes below Passchendaele village where soldiers battled through the mud in 1917.

The curious name came about after soldiers of the Northumberland Fusiliers thought that the concrete pill boxes they were attacking resembled a row of Tyneside cottages. The pill boxes were eventually taken by the 2nd Australian Division on 4 October 1917. The village was lost again in April 1918 and retaken the following September. While in Allied hands, the largest of the bunkers was used as a forward dressing station.

Designed by Herbert Baker in Greek Revival style, Tyne Cot is the largest British war cemetery in the world. It has nearly 12,000 gravestones and a further 35,000 names of missing soldiers inscribed on a wall at the back. Following a suggestion of George V, the **Cross of Sacrifice** stands on top of a large bunker which was the objective of the 2nd Australian Division. A plaque on the base commemorates this attack. Two other bunkers stand near the entrance. The scattered graves near the Cross remain in the places where they were dug during the fighting from October 1917 to April 1918. The great wall of the **Memorial to the Missing** evokes the Salient in its curved shape. The central apse contains the names of the New Zealand missing of Broodseinde and Passendale from October 1917.

The spire of Passendale church can just be seen from Tyne Cot. The peaceful fields where cows graze were the scene of carnage in 1917, as the Canadians fought their way in torrential rain through a sea of mud up the valley of the Strombeek towards Passendale.

Continue north for about 2km to a memorial that commemorates the New

Zealand soldiers who lost their lives in the Battle of Broodseinde on 4 October 1917. The memorial stands on the site of 's-Gravenstafel crossroads, which the New Zealand Division assaulted and won.

Passchendaele

Turn right at the crossroads and follow a narrow road to reach Passendale. A grassy path leads to a simple stone **Canadian Memorial** which commemorates the capture of Passendale village in 1917.

The village of Passchendaele (now spelled Passendale) has entered the English language as one of the most gruelling battles in human history. Thousands of soldiers died in the 1917 offensive to capture the low ridge on which Passchendaele stands.

Passchendaele had been held by the Germans from early in the war. By the time the Canadians took it on 6 November, all that remained was a heap of rubble. Many of the soldiers were deeply moved by the contrast between the bloodied morass of water and mud on the western slope, up which they had fought, and the gentle green fields which stretched away to the east.

The main monument in Passendale is the Canadian **Crest Farm Memorial** to the west of the small town. It stands above the shallow valley where the soldiers battled through mud. A window in the north transept of Passendale church commemorates the 66th Division. One of the four plaques attached to the town hall commemorate the Belgian Grenadiers and Carabiniers, who in September 1918 took Passendale after its reoccupation by the Germans during their desperate last effort to win the war in April 1918. Two other plaques recall Passendale's role in **World War II**. It was defended in 1940 by the Belgian 43rd Régiment de Ligne and liberated in 1944 by the 1st Polish Armoured Division.

Mud

The **Third Battle of Ypres** was launched in 1917 to open the way for an offensive against the German positions along the coast. After the success of the Battle of Messines on 7 June, the main offensive began on 22 July with a ten-day artillery barrage by 2300 guns. On 31 July, in heavy rain, the infantry attacked along a 24km front. On the left, Bikschote, Sint Juliaan and the Pilkem ridge were all taken, but there was no progress in the central section by the Menen road. A second attack on 16 August brought the left flank past the ruins of Langemark, but the centre once again achieved nothing.

Fresh offensives, always in heavy rain, between 30 September and 4 October gave the largely Australian and New Zealand divisions the main ridge from Geluveld by way of Polygon Wood to Broodseinde. This was far from being enough. The 'forest' of Houthulst and the high ground behind had to be won if the coastal campaign was to be possible. Several attacks were made, but all foundered in the mud, until 4 November when the Canadians fought their way across the morass to the site of Passendale village. This marked the end of a tragic campaign seen by many as doomed from the start by the combination of German preparedness and their use of **mustard gas**. The desperate cause was made worse by the continuous rain and heavy bombardment, which turned the battlefield into a sea of mud.

The N303 runs north to the village of Westrozebeke, 4km from Passendale. This was the scene of a battle in 1382 at which Charles VI of France defeated the Flemish weavers and killed their leader, Philip van Artevelde. The battle, which is described by Froissart, was fought on the spur of Goudberg to the south of the village. This high ground also marked the limit of the 1917 Allied advance.

Take the N303 again south of Passendale. After passing Zonnebeke, a brief detour can be made down the first road on the right to look at Polygon Wood.

Polygon Wood

Polygon Wood, south of Zonnebeke, was until 1914 the home of the Belgian army's Polygon riding school. The scene of desperate fighting, the wood changed hands several times between 1914 and 1918. As a result, it became a lethal wilderness of pockmarked ground and shattered tree stumps. Now carefully replanted and skirted by the A19 motorway, it is difficult to imagine the former scenes of desolation here. Yet there are still reminders of the war, including British and German bunkers, eroded shell craters, several memorials and two cemeteries.

The **Polygon Wood Cemetery** lies behind a polygonal wall. The graves mainly belong to New Zealand soldiers. The **Buttes New British Cemetery** opposite is approached through a glade. It takes its name from a Belgian army firing range which stood here until 1870. The former butts are marked today by a large mound surmounted by a memorial to the 5th Australian Division, which retook the wood in September 1917. The **New Zealand Memorial Pavilion** records the names of all the New Zealand missing in this sector from September 1917 to May 1918.

Continue along the north edge of the wood and then turn left along the west edge to reach the **Black Watch Corner**, named after the Royal Highlanders and Cameron Highlanders who defeated the Prussian Guard here in November 1914. Turn left along the south boundary of the wood and then turn first right and cross the A19 motorway the Geluveld.

Geluveld and Zandvoorde

The village of **Geluveld** was lost, retaken and lost again on 31 October 1914 during the First Battle of Ypres. The 2nd Welsh Regiment and 1st South Wales Borderers were driven from their trenches and forced back to the château. Brigadier General FitzClarence is famous for mustering all the cooks, orderlies and anyone else he could find to relieve the Welsh and drive the enemy back. He succeeded in delaying the Germans, who might otherwise have taken Ypres and perhaps reached the Channel ports.

The village of **Zandvoorde**, 2km south of Geluveld, was the scene of a charge by the Household Cavalry on 26 October 1914. After capturing this position, they were reinforced by other units. They dug in and held on until overwhelmed. A tall, graceful monument (reached by a footpath of Komenstraat on the southeast edge of the village) commemorates the 1st and 2nd Lifeguards and the Royal Horse Guards. Its simple inscription states that they 'died fighting in France and Flanders in 1914, many of them in defence of the ridge on which this cross stands'.

Return to the N8. The town of **Menen** lies off the route, 8km southeast of Geluveld on the N8. Located close to the border with France, it is an industrial town on the Lys. It was fortified by Vauban in 1685.

The church at **Dadizele**, 6km north of Menen on the N32 to Roeselare, was built in honour of a miraculous statue of the Virgin which has been venerated since the 14C.

Continue from Geluveld down the busy N8 in the direction of Ypres, passing after c 3km two obelisk memorials on opposite sides of the road. These mark the site of **Clapham Junction**, where several tracks once met. The memorial on the south side of the road honours the 18th Division, engaged here in 1917. The one opposite commemorates the Gloucestershire Regiment, which fought around Geluveld in 1914 and again at Clapham Junction in 1915.

Hooge

A restaurant stands on the site of the notorious **Hooge Château** (Meenseweg 497, Ypres). A memorial stands next to the coach park.

Hooge Château

This old country house became the headquarters of the 1st and 2nd Divisions on 31 October 1914. Most of the staffs of these divisions were killed or gravely wounded by shelling during the fighting at Geluveld. The château was taken by the Germans after a gas attack in May 1915. Two months later, they used flame-throwers here for the first time. Bellewaerde theme park occupies the area where the King's Royal Rifle Corps fought.

The **Hooge Crater Museum** at Meenseweg 467, Zillebeke, is open from Feb–mid-Dec 10.00–19.00. Standing on the main road to Menin just east of Bellewaerde, it occupies a small chapel built in memory of soldiers who died in the Salient. It contains an interesting collection of weapons and uniforms from two private collections. The **Hooge Crater Cemetery** on the other side of the road contains 5892 graves. The Stone of Remembrance stands within a symbolic crater. The actual crater, which was created by a British mine sprung in July 1915, is now filled with water (on private land).

Sanctuary Wood

Continue down the N8 a short distance and turn left at the Canada Café down Canadalaan (which is also called Maple Avenue). This quiet road leads to the **Sanctuary Wood Cemetery**, which contains the grave of Lieutenant Gilbert Talbot MC. Talbot House at Poperinge was named in his memory.

The road continues to the interesting **Sanctuary Wood Trenches Museum**, open daily 10.00–19.00, where a stretch of muddy trenches and waterlogged craters have been preserved in the woods. The museum contains a fascinating collection of old weapons, uniforms and photographs. It also has a unique set of bioscope photographs which feature horrific 3D war scenes.

The wood probably gained its romatic name during a brief period in October 1914 when orders were given by a brigade commander that some stragglers collected here were not to be sent back into the line immediately. The wood soon became a part of the front line. The Canadians fought to capture this area from April to August 1916. A Canadian memorial stands on Hill 62, at the top of the hill just beyond the museum. The hill is sometimes known as Mount Sorrel, though this in fact lay further south.

Return to the N8 and turn left to return to Ypres through the Menin Gate.

2 • Essex Farm and Langemark

Leave Ypres on the north side by the N369 to Diksmuide. It is worth stopping at **Essex Farm Cemetery**, 3km north of Ypres, where 1088 soldiers are buried, including a boy aged 15. The concrete bunkers next to the cemetery, restored in 1995, were used as a field hospital in 1916–17. A memorial to John McCrae, carved by Pieter Boudens in 1985, stands outside the cemetery.

In Flanders Fields

One of the most famous poems of the war was written at Essex Farm soon after the poison gas attack in April 1915. The Canadian doctor John McCrae, a veteran of the Boer War, wrote the poem *In Flanders Fields* after a close friend was killed by a shell. Just three verses long, it begins with the famous lines: 'In Flanders fields the poppies blow/Between the crosses, row on row.' First published in Punch in December 1915, the poem became known throughout the English-speaking world. McCrae died of meningitis in 1919 in a hospital at Wimereux on the French coast. His poem partly led to the adoption of the poppy as a symbol of remembrance in 1919.

Follow the N369 north to **Boezinge**. This village marked the northern point of the British sector, which linked up with the French trenches on the north side of the village. A bunker with a German mortar on top stands in the village. A tall aluminium cross known as the **Cross of Reconciliation** stands on the N369 north of Boezinge. This replaces a French monument of 1929 which commemorated the first victims of the gas attack. It was blown up by the Germans in 1942 because they objected to being described on it as 'barbarians'.

Go back to Boezinge and turn left along a minor road that leads to Langemark. The road runs past the **Breton dolmen** at the Carrefour de la Rose, 1km east of Boezinge. This site became a place of pilgrimage for people from Brittany after the war. The memorial commemorates two French divisions, including many soldiers from Brittany, caught in the first German poison gas attack in the late afternoon of 22 April 1915. The Breton calvary, dolmen and menhir were brought here from different locations in Brittany. An orientation table and map outlines the gas attack. The concrete posts surrounding the site are modelled on the early wooden posts used to support barbed wire before the introduction of iron screw-pickets.

Continue on the road to Langemark. After c 1km, a short detour can be made to a bunker called **Goumier Farm** (turn left down Groenestraat and then right down Ieperstraat). After changing hands frequently, Goumier was taken by the 38th Welsh Division in July 1917. A plaque attached to a battered concrete bunker commemorates the attack.

Continue a short distance on the Langemark road to reach the **Cement House Cemetery**, named after a fortified farm which once stood here. The crossroads just beyond the cemetery were shelled constantly. Now cross a narrow brook, the Steenbeek, which was crossed by temporary bridges during the 1917 attack. The **20th Light Division Monument**, just beyond the stream, commemorates the troops who captured the ruins of Langemark in August 1917.

Poison gas

The Germans chose the Ypres Salient to test their new secret weapon—poison gas. At 17.00 on 22 April 1915, a yellowish cloud of **chlorine gas** was released from cylinders. It slowly drifted towards French trenches on the Yser Canal, next to the Canadian positions. Forced by the unknown choking gas to retreat behind the canal, they left a gap of almost a kilometre in the Front line. The Germans took Langemark and the Pilkem ridge and crossed the canal at Steenstraat.

At 04.00 on 24 April, the Germans launched a second gas attack, this time against the Canadians. After two days of fierce fighting, in which Graventafel and Sint Juliaan were lost, the British were left holding an untenable long narrow strip pointing towards Passchendaele, which they abandoned in two stages. Known as the **Second Battle of Ypres**, this German attack reduced the Allied salient from 13km to 8km in length. By the time fighting ended on 25 May, the German trenches had moved 5km closer to Ypres and were now just 4km from the town walls. The Salient now ran from south of Boezinge to Wieltje, through Hooge and Sanctuary Wood to northwest of Hill 60 and then followed the original line west of Mesen to the Lys.

Continue on the minor road to Langemark village.

Langemark

The village of Langemark was attacked as early as October 1914. Enthusiastic German student battalions were decimated in what had been expected to be a walkover. The village was finally taken by the Germans in April 1915, when lethal poison gas drifted towards the French and Canadian trenches. Retaken by the British 20th Light Division on 16 August 1917, the ruined village was lost again in April 1918. By the time it was regained the following September, Langemark had been reduced to a heap of rubble.

Take a minor road north of Langemark to a large **German cemetery** where 44,292 soldiers killed in the Salient are buried. This sombre cemetery has hundreds of flat stone slabs, each carved with several names. Some German concrete bunkers are preserved at the back of the cemetery. A sculptural group representing four mourning figures was carved by Emil Krieger. A special room at the entrance lists the young students who lost their lives in the fruitless attacks of October 1914 which became known in Germany as the Massacre of the Innocents.

After continuing on this road a short distance turn left along Beekstraat to reach the **34th Division Memorial**. It stands in front of one of the many German bunkers that survive around Langemark. The momument commemorates those 'who fought near this spot, October–November 1917'. Captured in September 1918, the bunker served for a time as a British advanced dressing station.

From Langemark, a detour can be made north on the N301 to **Houthulst Forest**. The Germans concurred with Napoleon's description of this forest as the 'key to the Low Countries'. Having overcome stubborn Belgian and French resistance by October 1914, the Germans used the forest for the next four years as a main rear concentration zone for the Salient campaigns. The Belgian army bomb disposal unit now has a base at Houthulst where thousands of tons of unexploded shells from the war are defused.

Go back to Langemark and take the minor road to **Poelkapelle**, 2km east of Langemark. This village remained in German hands for most of the war. A memorial of 1923 commemorates Georges Guynemer (1894–1917), a dashing French pilot credited with destroying 54 enemy planes. He was shot down near here on 11 September 1917. Guynemer led a squadron known as 'The Storks,' which explains the crippled stork on top of the memorial retracing the airman's last flight.

Take the main N313 from Poelkapelle to reach the **Brooding Soldier** at Vancouver Corner, 2km southwest of the village. An impressive shaft of granite is surmounted by a bust of a Canadian soldier with his head lowered and his hands resting on a reversed rifle. This moving memorial commemorates the 18,000 Canadians on the British left who bore the brunt of the first German gas attacks on 22 and 24 April 1915. Some 2000 died in the attack. The clipped trees and low bushes in the garden represent shells.

Keep on the N313 to reach the **Seaforth Cemetery**, near Sint Juliaan. This mainly contains soldiers killed in 1915. A German bunker nearby known as **Cheddar Villa** is now part of a farm. It was captured in July 1917 and used as a dressing station, but suffered heavy shelling the following month. A shell burst near the entrance, which faced the German lines, killing or wounding most of the members of a platoon sheltering inside. Continue down the N313 to return to Ypres.

3 • Hill 60 and Kemmelberg

The ridge to the south of Ypres was the scene of bitter fighting at the start of the Third Battle of Ypres. The fields are still pitted with craters and dotted with bunkers.

Leave Ypres by the **Lille Gate** (Rijselsepoort) to the south and follow the N365. Being less exposed than the Menin road, this route to the front was preferred by the troops. Yet it was not without danger; the crossroads just beyond the railway line soon became known as **Shrapnel Corner**. Turn left here along a minor road to reach the Railway Dugout Burial Ground, where there are still traces of concrete bunkers in the railway embankment.

Continue on this road to the peaceful **Zillebeke village**, where a water reservoir was excavated some time before 1300. Its appearance changed in 1914, as artillery units dug into its banks and the surrounding area became a morass. Virtually all traces of the war have vanished; the reservoir, which still supplies Ypres, is now used for angling and sailing.

Hill 60

Continue on this road for c 2km and turn left to reach Hill 60, an artificial hill made from the spoil of a 19C railway cutting. It was known before the war as the *Côte des Amants* (Lovers' Hill), but the army preferred a more prosaic name that referred to its height in metres above sea level. During the war, Hill 60 was the most dreaded name in the Salient after Passchendaele. Fought over bitterly, the hill and the surrounding area changed hands six times between 1914 and 1918. Shelled constantly, drenched in gas and shaken by massive mines, this hill of sand and clay soon lost all resemblance to its original shape.

Hill 60 was presented to the **Imperial War Graves Commission** in 1930 as a gift to the nations of the British Empire. It has been left virtually untouched since then. Two monuments stand beside the road; one is to the 14th Light Division, while the other commemorates the 1st Australian Tunnelling Company which took over responsibility for digging the mine shafts in November 1916.

The two massive mines placed here formed the north end of a line of underground mines stretching from the Messines Ridge. Their detonation on 7 June 1917 marked the opening of the **Third Battle of Ypres**. The bullet scars on the memorial bear witness to the fact that Hill 60 was fought over again in the Second World War.

As you wander around the cratered field, you should bear in mind that the war was waged as viciously below ground as on the surface. Hidden underground is a tortuous labyrinth of collapsed tunnels and mineshafts where countless soldiers were killed. The concrete blockhouse was built by the Germans, but used by both sides. The memorial to Queen Victoria's Rifles, who fought here in 1915, was badly damaged in the fighting of 1940. Rebuilt, it now also commemorates the victims of 1939 to 1945. A café nearby contains the small **Hill 60 Museum**, open daily 10.00–19.00, which contains weapons and photographs.

Now go back across the railway line and turn right and then left. This leads to the main N365 where you should turn left for **Sint Elooi**. This leads past Chester Farm and Spoilbank cemeteries.

Wijtschate

Continue up the N365 to the village of Wijtschate, 8km south of Ypres on the Messines Ridge. With its view of Ypres, this ridge was tactically vital, and changed hands several times during bitter fighting. The German trenches along the ridge were blown up by huge mines at the start of the Third Battle of Ypres in June 1917. The reverberations were felt as far away as London.

Turn right at Wijtschate along the Kemmel road and turn left after c 2km to reach the crater at **Spanbroekmolen**, 2km southwest of Wijtschate. After a memorial to the 16th Irish Division, you come to the enormous **Lone Tree Crater** created when of one of the largest of the 19 mines exploded at 03.10 on 7 June 1917. A charge of 91,000 lbs of ammonal was laid at the end of a tunnel 517m long. The site was acquired in 1930 by Lord Wakefield on behalf of Toc H. Now a quiet pond c 25m deep and hidden by trees, it is known as the Pool of Peace.

Mesen

Continue past the farm and follow the minor road to Mesen (Messines in French), 2km south of Wijtschate on the ridge overlooking Ypres. The **Sint Niklaaskerk** was originally a 12C abbey church. Destroyed in the fighting, it was rebuilt in 1930. The 12C Romanesque crypt survived the shelling. Adolf Hitler is said to have received treatment for a wounded arm in a dressing station located in the crypt. He painted several views of the ruined church. A New Zealand kowhai tree was planted next to the town hall in 1993.

Tourist information

Stadhuis, Markt 1, ☎ 057.44.50.40.

The Battle of Mesen

Launched on 7 June 1917, the Battle of Mesen was intended to capture the German salient along the Mesen–Wijtschate ridge. A fierce artillery barrage, the use of mines and the gallantry of the Australian, New Zealand, Irish and London regiments achieved the desired result. By evening the whole ridge was in Allied hands.

Mesen was taken in 1917, following the detonation of the mines, by the New Zealand Division which is commemorated in two places here. The **New Zealand Memorial to the Missing** is at Mesen Ridge Cemetery, immediately W of the town beside the Wulvergem road. The **New Zealand Park**, just to the south of Mesen, incorporates two German bunkers close to the white obelisk divisional memorial, which records the capture of the ridge and an advance of 2000 yards beyond.

The **Irish Tower**, just south of Mesen on the N365 to Ploegsteert, was unveiled by the Irish President and Queen Elizabeth on Armistice Day, 1998. Modelled on an ancient Irish round tower, it commemorates Irish Protestants and Catholics who died in the Salient.

The village of **Ploegsteert**, 4km south of Mesen, was famous for its wood, which was nicknamed *Plug Street* by the soldiers. Now overgrown and privately owned, the wood covers the crest above Ypres. This was a relatively quiet area of the Salient for much of the war. Just beyond the wood, the N365 passes the striking rotunda of the **Ploegsteert Memorial**, which commemorates 11,447 missing soldiers. Many were killed in France. Hyde Park Corner Cemetery lies opposite.

A minor road runs along the edge of the wood to **Prowse Point Cemetery**, just west of the village of Saint Yvon. It is named after Major Prowse who fought here in October 1914 and died on the first day of the Somme in 1916. Many of the soldiers buried here came from the 2nd Dublin Fusiliers and 1st Royal Warwickshire, who defended this sector in the following month. The pond below the Cross was once part of the front line trench. Mud Corner Cemetery and three other small cemeteries are located in the nearby wood. They can only be reached on foot along a farm track.

The Christmas truce

An unofficial ceasefire occurred on Christmas Day in 1914 on a section of the Salient near Ploegsteert Wood. It apparently began after German soldiers put up Christmas trees and started to sing carols. Soldiers eventually left the trenches and exchanged tobacco and gifts in No Man's Land. The military authorities were apparently furious.

A minor road leads east of Ploegsteert to **Comines**, 10km to the east. This town, known in Dutch as Komen, lies in an enclave of the Walloon province of Hainaut. It stands on the River Lys, which forms the border with France. A French town of the same name stands on the opposite bank.

The French historian
Comines was the birthplace of Philippe de Comines (c 1445–1509). A French statesman, biographer and historian, De Comines entered the Burgundian court in 1463, but later joined the service of Louis XI in 1472. Richly rewarded, he became one Louis' closest advisers. After Louis' death in 1483 he fell from grace, lost many of his possessions and was imprisoned for eight months in an iron cage. He later regained favour and accompanied Charles VIII to Italy, where he met Machiavelli. His Mémoirs of 1524 are considered one of the best studies in medieval history.

Go back to Mesen and continue along the N314 to reach **Nieuwekerke**, 6km to the west. This important road junction was lost in 1918, but only after a party of the Worcestershire Regiment had held out for some time in the town hall while the Germans occupied the rest of the town. Turn right here to reach an attractive district known as the Heuvelland.

Heuvelland
The Heuvelland is an area of low hills south of Ypres formed by sandbanks left by the retreating sea. It is dotted with attractive little villages such as Westouter and Kemmel. The wooded Kemmelberg (159m) was a popular tourist destination before the war. Devastated in the fighting, the woods have been replanted and a new belvedere built. The main town of the area is Kemmel, 10km southwest of Ypres.

Where to stay
The *Hostellerie Kemmelberg*, Berg 4, Kemmel, ☎ 057.44.41.45, is a comfortable hotel built in 1954 in Swiss chalet style with a panoramic view of the plains of Flanders.

Tourist information
Reningelststraat 10, Kemmel, ☎ 057.45.04.55.

History
By the close of the 1918 German Spring offensive, the Allied troops had fallen back to a line that ran from Vierstraat to Méteren in France. A line of small hills along the French border, including Rodeberg (Mont Rouge) and Zwarteberg (Mont Noir) became vital for Allied observation after the loss of Kemmelberg.

The **Kemmelberg**, 1km west of Kemmel, was for much of the war an invaluable Allied stronghold. Its loss by the French in April 1918 gravely endangered communications along the important Ypres–Poperinge road. The hill was recaptured by the British on 31 August.

The belvedere (open Apr–Sept) was reconstructed in a different style from the original, which was destroyed in the 1914–18 war. An interesting collection of photographs in the Belvedere tavern show the original 19C belvedere, maze and castle. An orientation board in front of the tavern pinpoints the spires of Ypres and other local landmarks. The Kemmelberg woods still show traces of trenches and shell holes, though the evidence is gradually being eroded.

Continue past the hotel to reach a **French monument** that stands at the top of a steep cobbled lane. It commemorates all the French soldiers who died in

Belgium, particularly those killed here in 1918. Unveiled by General Pétain in 1932, the monument is decorated with a Winged Victory. It used to be surmounted by a French helmet until lightning struck in 1970.

The lane descends to the **Ossuaire Français**, a French memorial incorporating a pyramid surmounted by a French cockerel. This marks the spot where 5294 soldiers were buried, mostly during the fighting in April 1918. Only 57 bodies were ever identified.

The N331 back to Ypres passes Vierstraat, where a simple **American memorial** recalls 'the services of American Troops who fought in this vicinity 18 August–4 September 1918'. The Brussels Art Nouveau architect Ernest Blérot built the curious Elzenwalle Castle, off the N331 near Voormezele, after the First World War.

A short detour (turn left at Vierstraat and right on the N375) leads to **Dikkebus** village, 5km southwest of Ypres. A lake near the village was created in 1320 by damming the Kleine Kemmelbeek. Medieval Ypres was supplied with water channeled through oak pipes. The lake still supplies Ypres, though the water now passes through a filtration station. The **Vauban Tower** was built in 1684 to regulate the water supply by means of a sluice gate. The 36 hectares lake is now popular for rowing and fishing. Return to Ypres by the N375.

THE BELGIAN FRONT

The flat land to the north of Ypres is dotted with small Flemish towns. Much of this land was flooded in the First World War. It is now a popular area for cycling.

The battles

The Belgian front line ran for 35km from Nieuwpoort on the North Sea to Steenstraat on the Yser canal. This line was established during the **Battle of the Yser** in October 1914. Fighting at the same time as the British launched the First Battle of Ypres to the south, the Belgian army heroically resisted the Germans for two days. The Germans finally managed to get a force across the Yser at Tervate on the night of 21–22 October and reinforced their position the following night in the face of gallant Belgian counter-attacks. On 24 October a major German offensive broke through the front at this point, only to find that the Belgians, now supported by a French division, had retired and were strongly deployed along the embankment of the Nieuwpoort to Diksmuide railway line.

The Germans then turned their attention to **Diksmuide**, where they set fire to the town and attacked through the rubble at midnight on 24–25 October. This attack and another the following night were repulsed. Exhausted and running out of ammunition, the Belgians decided to flood the flat polder land by opening the **Veurne canal sluices** at high tide on 27, 28 and 29 October. The result was disappointing, so they decided to open the sluices of the Noordvaart, which now lay in No Man's Land. A daring operation was launched on the night of 29 October. The sluices were opened and sea water flooded the land, creating large lagoons in the flat meadows between the river and the railway. The three German divisions which had taken Ramskapelle and Pervijze were forced to retreat. The Battle of the Yser was over.

Diksmuide

Diksmuide was, like Ypres, rebuilt after the war in the old Flemish style.

Tourist information
Grote Markt 28, ☎ 051.51.91.46.

Opening times
Dodengang is open daily Easter–Sept 09.00–12.00 and 13.30–17.30.

IJzertoren is open daily Mar–11 Nov 09.00–17.00 (18.00 in summer).
Stedelijk Museum is open daily Easter–mid Sept 10.00–12.00 and 14.00–17.00.

Diksmuide began as a 9C settlement. By the middle of the 16C, it had grown into a small town with a Spanish garrison. It was one of several places arbitrarily annexed by Louis XIV in 1680. During the 1914 battle of the Yser, Diksmuide bore the brunt of the German attacks. Defended courageously by the Belgian army, it remained part of the Belgian front line; it was so devastated by German artillery that little remained apart from a wooden sign bearing its name.

A walk in Diksmuide

The spacious **Grote Markt** has a number of houses rebuilt in their original style. Above them rises the tower of the **Sint Niklaaskerk**. A 14C foundation, it was rebuilt in the 17C and again after both World Wars.

The **Stedelijk Museum** has a small collection of local paintings, folklore, photographs from 1914–18 and fragments of buildings destroyed in the war.

The **Begijnhof** is approached by an alley from the canal bridge which bears the name of St Thomas. This recalls a tradition that Thomas à Becket once stayed there. The Begijnhof was founded in the 13C and remained occupied by Beguines up until the First World War. It has been carefully rebuilt in its old style.

Diksmuide environs

The **IJzertoren**, 1km west of Diksmuide on the N35, was built in 1930 by Flemish nationalists as a war memorial and peace monument, but was blown up in 1946 by unknown extremists. The ruins were later turned into a gate known as the Paxpoort (Peace Gate). A new tower was built near the ruins of the original bearing the letters AVV and VVK (All for Flanders and Flanders for the King). The crypt contains memorials to Flemish patriots, while the museum contains an exhibition on Flemish patriotism and the First World War.

There is a lift to the top of the tower which offers a fine view of dunes, polders, farmland, and woods. The towers and steeples of Nieuwpoort, Veurne, Ypres and Bruges rise vaguely in the distance as in a painting by Memling or Van der Weyden.

The **Dodengang** (Trench of Death), 2km northwest of Diksmuide, is a stretch of Belgian trench preserved by filling old sandbags with concrete. The building at the entrance displays some interesting 1914–18 photographs, while the upper floor provides an impressive view of the trench system on the River Yser. Some visitors, however, find the trenches too neat and tidy to ring true.

The nearby **OLV Hoekje** marks an exposed and remote part of the Belgian front. Flat, bleak and bare, this area contains a number of poignant reminders of

1914–18. They include a bunker, some regimental memorial stones set around a monument, and a plaque honouring a Franciscan friar turned artillery officer who set up his observation post in the ruins of an old chapel. Just beyond the chapel, an inscription on a demarcation stone recalls that the German invaders were halted here. The chapel contains stained-glass windows decorated with war scenes and a number of rapidly deteriorating wartime pictures and maps.

The impressive **Vladslo Cemetery**, 5km east of Diksmuide, contains 25,664 German graves. The statue of *Grieving Parents* by the German artist Käthe Kollwitz was carved in 1932 in memory of her son Pieter, who was killed in October 1914 during the desperate German attack on Diksmuide. The statue did not please the Nazi regime.

The **Käthe Kollwitz Tower** in Koekelare, 15km northeast of Diksmuide, contains a collection of graphic work by Kollwitz.

The historic port of **Nieuwpoort** stood at the north end of the Western Front. It is described under The Coast, p 286.

The Kempen

The Kempen is an extensive area of heath, dunes and pine forests in eastern Flanders. The old towns of Lier, Aarschot and Diest lie on the edge of the Kempen. Several great Flemish abbeys were established in the Middle Ages in this remote region, including Westmalle, Averbode, Tongerlo and Postel. With walking trails, cycle routes and recreational parks, the Kempen is an attractive and popular tourist region.

Where to stay

The *Priorij Corsendonk*, Corsendonk 5, Oud-Turnhout, ☎ 014.46.28.00, is a comfortable country hotel in a restored 14C Augustinian abbey.

Tourist information

The Kempen tourist office, Grote Markt 44, Turnhout, ☎ 014.43.61.11, covers the Kempen region.

The Antwerp province tourist office has information on the area of the Kempen in Antwerp province. Koningin Elisabethlei 16, Antwerp, ☎ 03.240.63.73.

Christmas cribs

Every year in early December, Christmas cribs featuring Nativity scenes appear in churches and on village squares throughout the Kempen region. Built in the style of local farm buildings, the outdoor cribs often contain live farm animals. The Antwerp province tourist office publishes an annual guide in Dutch to cribs in the Kempen.

Westmalle

The Trappist abbey at Westmalle half-way between Antwerp and Turnhout on the N12, was built in 1794. The neo-Romanesque church was added in 1886. The abbey is famous for its Trappist beer, which can be sampled in the local cafés.

Trappists
Westmalle is one of six Trappist abbeys in Belgium. The order was founded in 1664 after Armand de Rancé, abbot of the Cistercian abbey at La Trappe in Normandy, introduced austere reforms in the **Cistercian Order**, including a vow of silence. A group of 20 Trappist monks settled in Switzerland after the French Revolution; the Order spread from there throughout Europe. The six Trappist abbeys in Belgium are Chimay, Orval, Rochefort, St Sixtus Achel, and Westmalle. They are famous for their potent ales and cheeses.

The **Sint Laurentiuskerk** in **Oostmalle** replaces an older church of 1683 which was destroyed by a tornado in 1967. All that remains of the 17C church is the tower. The unusual modern church, built in 1973, contains some of the old furnishings and a striking ironwork representation of Christ Crowned. The church at **Vlimmeren**, 3km east of Oostmalle, dates from the 14C–15C, but the tower was added in the 18C.

Hoogstraten

Hoogstraten, 12km north of Oostmalle on the N14, is an interesting Kempen town with several impressive buildings. The attractive main square is planted with old lime trees.

Tourist information
Stadhuis, ☎ 03.340.19.55.

The impressive **Sint Katharinakerk** on the Vrijheid square was built in Late Gothic style by Rombout Keldermans from 1524–46. The lofty 105m tower is a striking example of brick architecture. The church was blown up by the retreating Germans on 23 October 1944. Much of the building, including the tower, was rebuilt after the war. The church contains striking marble and alabaster tombs of the founders, Count Antoine de Lalaing (d. 1540) and his wife Elisabeth of Culemborg (d. 1555). These were probably carved by Jean Mone in 1529. The 16C stained-glass windows depict Charles V, Margaret of Austria and members of the Lalaing family. The pulpit was carved by Theodoor Verhaeghen.

The **Stadhuis**, adjoining the church, was also built by Rombout Keldermans in Late Gothic style. Destroyed in 1944, it was rebuilt in the 1950s. The **Begijnhof**, just north of the church, was founded in the 14C, but largely destroyed by fire in 1506. The present buildings date from the 17C and 18C. The Baroque church was built in 1687. A sensitive restoration of the Begijnhof reached completion in 1999.

Hoogstraten environs

The church at **Meerle**, 11km north of Hoogstraten, has a nave and lower section of tower dating back to the 13C. The Dutch border lies 3km to the north.

Baarle-Hertog

The village of Baarle-Hertog, 18km northeast of Hoogstraten, is an intriguing political curiosity in which several small Belgian enclaves have survived within the Dutch village of Baarle-Nassau.

Where to stay

The small *Den Engel*, Singel 3, ☎ 0031.13.507.93.30 (from outside the Netherlands), is a comfortable modern hotel in the centre of Baarle-Nassau.

Cafés

The *Brouwershuis*, Molenstraat 42, Baarle-Hertog, is a Belgian beer hall which doubles as a museum of smuggling. The shop sells 700 varieties of potent Belgian beer. The café *De Pomp* in Baarle-Nassau is a friendly Dutch brown café.

Tourist information

The tiny tourist office is in the Dutch village of Baarle-Nassau, ☎ 0031.13.507.99.21 (from outside the Netherlands). It provides information on both countries.

The village's unusual situation dates back to 1479 when the village of Baarle was divided into two parts for inheritance reasons. One part ended up owned by the Duke of Brabant (Baarle-Hertog), while the other went to the Lord of Breda (Baarle-Nassau). Under the Treaty of Münster in 1648, Baarle-Hertog remained part of the Spanish Netherlands while Baarle-Nassau passed to the independent Dutch Republic.

This odd state of affairs saved Baarle-Hertog from German occupation during the First World War. The Belgians who lived in Baarle-Hertog established a radio station within their territory in October 1915. The Dutch, who remained neutral during the war, put up a barbed-wire fence around the Belgian enclaves, but the village still managed to serve as an important centre of Allied espionage. It is now popular with tourists from both countries.

The town has two post offices and two town halls. Every house has a small metal flag attached to indicate whether it is Dutch or Belgian. The market square belongs to the Dutch, but one tavern is on Belgian soil. The café **Het Hoekske** has the international border running through it, while the Camp pharmacy in Nieuwstraat has a living room in Belgium and a bedroom in the Netherlands. The old church is firmly within Belgium.

Turnhout

Turnhout, 45km northeast of Antwerp, is a lively industrial town in Antwerp province famous for the manufacture of playing cards.

Tourist information
Grote Markt 44, ☎ 014.44.33.55.

Opening times
Museum Taxandria, Begijnenstraat 28, is open from Tues–Sat 14.00–17.00, Sun 11.00–17.00.

Museum van de Speelkaart, Druivenstraat 18, is open Tues–Sat 14.00–17.00, Sun 11.00–17.00.

The town of Tourhout belonged to Brabant from the 14C–16C. It was then given by Charles V to his sister Mary of Hungary. Following the Treaty of Münster in 1648, it briefly belonged to the House of Orange before passing to Brandenburg in 1753. The Belgians defeated the Austrians at Turnhout in 1789 during the Brabançon Revolt. This led to the creation of the short lived United States of Belgium.

A walk in Turnhout
Begin in the **Grote Markt**, where the **Sint Pieterskerk** was built in the 12C on the site of an older wooden chapel. Little has survived of the 12C structure apart from the lower part of the tower. The apse was built in 1486 and further additions and alterations were made up until the 18C. The interior contains fine baroque stalls. The confessionals were carved by Jan Peter van Baurscheit the Younger. The 19C pulpit by H. Peeters is decorated with a striking *Miraculous Draught of Fishes*.

The Begijnenstraat leads to the moated **Kasteel**. Constructed in c 1110, it was originally the residence of the dukes of Brabant and later of Mary of Hungary. The castle was rebuilt during the 17C for Amalia von Solms, wife of Prince Frederick Henry of Orange-Nassau.

The **Taxandria Museum** occupies a 16C house at Begijnenstraat 28. It contains an interesting local collection of archaeological finds, historical relics, lace, furniture and paintings. Continue up the same street to reach the **Begijnhof**. First mentioned in 1372, this enclosed religious community was completely rebuilt during the 17C. The church dates from 1665. The **Museum van de Speelkaart** (Playing Cards Museum) is south of the Grote Markt at Druivenstraat 18. It contains a large collection of playing cards manufactured in Turnhout.

Turnhout environs
The church in **Oud-Turnhout**, 3km east of Turnhout, contains a *Last Supper* painted in 1698 by Jan Erasmus Quellin.

The town of **Retie**, 11km southeast of Turnhout, has a Tree of Justice in front of the church. The town is surrounded by woods, heath and dunes. The **Prinsenpark**, northeast of Retie, is an attractive nature reserve.

The Premonstratensian abbey of **Postel**, c 7km northeast of Retie, is located in an area of woods and marshes. Founded in 1140 by monks from Floreffe as a hospice for pilgrims, it became an abbey in 1621. Suppressed in 1797 by the French Revolutionaries, it was returned to the monks in 1847.

The Romanesque church was built in c 1190 from tufa brought from the Eifel region in Germany. It was much altered in the 16C and 17C, but a beautifully decorated 13C doorway survives beside the cloister. The domestic buildings date from 1631, with additions of 1713 and 1743. The **library** has a rich collection of incunabula, 16C books, etchings and old atlases. The belfry of 1610 has a 40-bell carillon installed in 1947.

Herentals

Herentals in Antwerp province, 18km southwest of Turnhout, has been an important town since the 14C. During the Middle Ages, fresh water was sent from here by barge to Antwerp, 30km west, for use in the city's breweries. The sculptor Charles Fraikin was born in Herentals in 1817.

Tourist information
Grote Markt 41, ☎ 014.21.90.88.

The town
The **Stadhuis** on the Grote Markt was built c 1400 as a cloth hall. Destroyed by fire in 1512, it was rebuilt two years later, and substantially reconstructed in 1880. It has a belfry from 1590 with a 49-bell carillon. The **Sint Waldetrudiskerk**, south of Grote Markt, was built in Brabant Late Gothic style. It contains an early 16C retable by Pasquier Borremans and paintings by Frans Francken the Elder.

The Hofkwartier leads north from Grote Markt to the **Begijnhof**. Built from the 17C–18C, it replaced a complex founded c 1266 on a different site which was destroyed by the Calvinists in 1578. The church was built in 1595–1614. The horizontal courses of white stone were brought from the previous Begijnhof.

Two of the town's old gates survive: the 14C **Zandpoort** on the road to Lier, and the **Bovenpoort** of 1402 on the road to Geel.

Herentals environs
The village of **Grobbendonk**, 13km west of Herentals, has a **Diamond Museum** which covers mining, cutting and polishing (**open** Mon–Fri 09.00–16.30; also Jun–Sept on Sat 10.00–15.00, Sun 10.00–16.00).

The village of **Vorselaar**, 2km northeast of Grobbendonk, has a pillory dating from 1759. A fine avenue of limes leads to an imposing moated castle, which in the 13C belonged to the van Rotselaar family, the chief stewards of the dukes of Brabant. It was rebuilt in neo-Gothic style during the 19C (not open to the public).

Geel

Tourist information
Stadhuis, Markt 1, ☎ 014.57.09.50.

History
Geel, c 10km east of Herentals, is known internationally for its humane system of treating the mentally ill. Patients are boarded out among the townspeople so that they can enjoy a home environment, some measure of freedom, and the opportunity to find work. Officially supervised by doctors since

c 1850, the system was originally linked to 13C pilgrimages to the shrine of **St Dympna**. The patron saint of the insane, Dympna was an Irish princess who fled to Geel to escape from the unwelcome attentions of her crazed and incestuous father. Dympna and her confessor, St Gerebernus, were caught and executed, reputedly on the site of the Sint Dimpnakerk.

The **Sint Dimpnakerk** was built from 1344 to 1492. It contains the reliquaries of the two saints as well as other treasures. The tower dates from the 16C. Cornelis Floris designed the beautiful mausoleum of 1554 in memory of Jean III, Count of Mérode, and his wife Anne de Ghistelles. The church contains several outstanding retables, including a **Passion Retable** of c 1490 attributed to Goswin van der Weyden. A second retable by Jan van Waver carved in 1513 tells the story of St Dympna. A third retable of 1350 carved in sandstone depicts the Apostles. The *Sieckencamere*, sick room, is where the mentally afflicted pilgrims made their novenas.

A 15C chapel near the church at Gasthuisstraat 1 contains the **Sint Dimpna en Gasthuismuseum**. This has a special section devoted to the saint (**open** Tues–Fri and Sun 14.00–17.30.

The **Sint Amandskerk**, near the Markt, was built from 1490–1531. It has one of the finest Baroque interiors in Belgium. The high altar is by Pieter Verhaghen. Pieter Valckx and W. Kerrickx did much of the carved work.

Tongerlo Abbey

The abbey of Tongerlo c 8km southwest of Geel, was founded by Premonstratensian monks in 1130 in a desolate area of the Kempen. Dissolved in 1796, the abbey was restored to the monks in 1840 and is once again flourishing. The abbey is approached along a stately drive lined with 300-year-old lime trees. The large inner court is entered under two Romanesque arches built in the 12C–14C. The building on the right is the **Prelaatshuis**, built by Willem Ignatius Kerrickx in 1726. The Guest House of 1547, with its elegant turret of 1479, is also interesting.

The main attraction of Tongerlo Abbey is the **Da Vinci Museum**, reached by crossing the abbey garden. Opened in 1956 in a small theatre, the museum contains a copy of Leonardo Da Vinci's *Last Supper*. This was painted from 1506–1507 by the artist's pupil Andrea del Solario. It was apparently commissioned by Pope Clement VII for Henry VIII of England. Bought by the abbey in 1545, the painting was admired by Rubens and Van Dyck. Open Easter vacation and from May–Sept daily 14.00–17.00; also in Mar–Apr and Oct on Sun 14.00–17.00.

Premonstratensians

Tongerlo is the largest Premonstratensian abbey in Belgium. The Premonstratensians (or Norbertines) are not monks but an austere order of Augustinian Canons founded in 1120 by St Norbert at Prémontré in northern France. Norbert (1080–1134) was a German aristocrat who underwent a dramatic conversion. He preached in Antwerp against the theories of Tankelin, who believed that wives should be held in common. Several churches in Belgium have Baroque pulpits carved with the scene of St Norbert's conversion.

Tongerlo environs

The town of **Westerlo**, 2km south of Tongerlo abbey, is pleasantly situated on the Grote Nete. Its main attractions are the **Kasteel van Gravin J. de Mérode**, a neo-Gothic building of 1911 now used as a municipal and cultural centre, and the older **Kasteel de Mérode** built from the 14C to the 19C. The surrounding countryside is popular with walkers and cyclists.

The 14C–15C Sint Martinuskerk in **Tessenderlo**, 16km east of Westerlo, has a good rood-screen of c 1500 depicting the life of Christ.

Mol

Mol is a straggling town in Antwerp province 8km northeast of Geel, set in a typical Kempen landscape. The **Sint Pieter en Pauwelkerk**, rebuilt in 1852, has a tower of 1492 with a 49-bell carillon. The church contains a thorn from Christ's crown. Two statues on the transept pillars are attributed to Artus Quellin the Elder. A monument nearby commemorates the Peasants' Revolt of 1798. The square contains part of an old pillory.

Mol environs

The village of **Achterbos-Sluis**, 3km north of Mol, attracted the Kempen painter Jacob Smits A small museum at Sluis 155 in Mol, the **Oude Pastorie**, is dedicated to Smits (open Wed–Sun from 14.00–18.00; also Tues during school holidays).

A provincial park at **Zilvermeer**, 8km northeast of Mol, contains a boating lake and adventure playground. The **Keiheuvel** park, east of Mol, has an open-air swimming pool, adventure playground and woodland walks. The hamlet of **Scheps**, 3km southeast of Mol, was the birthplace of St Odrade. This 8C saint is invoked to bring fine weather.

The town of **Leopoldsburg**, 13km southeast of Mol, is a garrison town linked to the military base at Beverlo, 4km to the south. The base was founded in 1850 by Leopold I.

The church at **Oostham**, 6km west of Leopoldsburg, was rebuilt after it was burnt down in 1940. The curious 11C tower has bricks laid in a herringbone pattern.

The town of **Hechtel**, 8km east of Leopoldsburg, lies at the centre of an extensive area of dunes, heath and woodland. There are **nature reserves** at In de Brand, to the northwest, and Begijnenvijver, to the southeast. The **Park der Lage Kempen**, north of Hechtel on the N715, has signposted walks and picnic areas.

Set in a typical Kempen landscape, the town of **Lommel**, 13km north of Leopoldsburg, has an attractive main square planted with trees. The town belonged to the Netherlands from 1648–1839. The **Sint Pieterskerk** was built in neo-Gothic style in 1900–2. Its brick Gothic west tower dates from c 1500. The **Museum Kempenland** at Dorp 16 has a collection of local archaeology (open from Tues–Fri 09.00–12.00 and 14.00–17.00, weekends 14.00–17.00) The **Kattenbos** woods and heath, to the south, is a popular nature reserve. The reserve has a restored windmill of 1805 and a large German war cemetery.

Houthalen-Helchteren

Houthalen-Helchteren , 10km north of Hasselt, is a popular tourist area with several recreation areas. The **Molenheide** park, 3km to the north, has walks, an animal enclosure and an adventure playground (open daily from 10.00); **Hengelhoef** has walks, an animal park, a subtropical swimming pool and an adventure playground (open daily); and the **Domein Kelchterhoef** has lake swimming, an adventure playground an a 19C farm (open daily Apr–Oct).

The former mining town of **Beringen** is c 7km west of Houthalen. The Sint Theodardskerk, built in 1939–43 and named after a 7C Bishop of Liège, is known as the 'Miners' Cathedral.' The tower is detached because of the danger of subsidence.

Genk

Genk is an expanding industrial town to the east of the region c 13km northwest of Maastricht, with woods and heath to the south and east. The **Villa van Doren**, at H. Decleenestraat 21, is a local history museum located in the former home of the 19C landscape artist Emile Van Doren. The museum contains paintings by Van Doren (open on Wed, Sat and Sun from 10.00–12.00 and 15.00–18.00).

The **Europlanetarium** at Kattevennen 19 is a modern planetarium with impressive special effects (open Tues–Fri, and Sun, ☎ 089.30.79.90 for details of screenings).

Bree

Bree, 20km north of Genk in the east of the Kempen, was once the main town of a district which prospered from the wool trade from the 14C–16C. Its former wealth is reflected in the grandeur of the Gothic **Sint Michielskerk**, built in 1452, and enlarged in 1901. This church replaced a Romanesque edifice which was itself built on the site of a 7C chapel. A small **museum of local history** in the old town hall exhibits a model of the town in 1700 (open on the first Sun of the month from 10.00–12.00 and 14.00–17.00).

> ### Limburg Gothic
> The churches in Bree and the surrounding villages reflect the wealth generated by the medieval wool trade. Many are built in a local style known as Limburg Gothic. The walls tend to be built from local marl, which is also used in the vaulting (often featuring diagonal ribbing). Other parts of the church are built from bluestone. Many contain ancient statues of saints. The best of the Limburg Gothic churches are at Neeroeteren, 9km southeast of Bree; Gerdingen, 1km northwest; Beek, 2km north; Opitter, 4km southeast; Neerglabbeek, 6km south; and Opglabbeek, 11km south.

The impressive Limburg Gothic church at **Neeroeteren**, 9km southeast of Bree, was built in the 15C. It remains virtually unaltered apart from the addition of the tower in 1719. The church contains an outstanding collection of early 16C statues of saints, including the patron St Lambert, St James and St Christopher. The **Marianum** (a representation in wrought and painted iron of Our Lady in a garland of roses) is one of only two in Belgium. The other is at Zoutleeuw, near Sint Truiden.

Maaseik

Maaseik is a pleasant small town on the Maas with several interesting museums. The river forms the border with the Netherlands, which gives the town a strong Dutch character.

Tourist information
Markt 1, ☎ 089.56.63.72.

Opening times
Museactron is open daily Jul–Aug 10.00–17.00; Sept–Jun Tues–Sun 10.00–12.00 and 14.00–17.00. Closes 12.00–14.00 Oct–Mar.
Van Eyck Exhibition and the **Treasury of the Sint Catharinakerk** are open daily in Jul–Aug 13.00–17.00; Apr–Sept, Tues–Sun 13.00–17.00; Oct–Mar Sat –Sun 13.00–17.00

> The town grew up around an 8C convent built by a Frankish noble for his two daughters. Maaseik became an important cloth town in the 14C. A wall was built in 1386, but destroyed in the 15C. New fortifications were built by Vauban at the end of the 17C, but these, too, were demolished by the Dutch.

The **Markt** in Maaseik is one of the most attractive squares in the country, with its lime trees and scattering of 17C and 18C houses. The 18C pharmacy at **no. 46** is the oldest pharmacy in Belgium. A monument was unveiled in 1864 in honour of Jan and Hubert van Eyck, who were probably born at Maaseik. Jan was born c 1390, while Hubert, if he existed, was 20 years older.

The **Museactron** at Lekkerstraat 5, just off the Markt, is an imaginative hands-on museum complex. It incorporates an archaeological museum, an 18C bakery and the interior of the 18C pharmacy at Markt 46.

The **Van Eyck Exhibition** at Boomgaardstraat contains copies of several paintings by the Van Eyck brothers, including the *Altarpiece of the Mystic Lamb* in Ghent Cathedral.

The Bosstraat, off the Markt, has some attractive 17C and 18C façades. The **Katharinakerk**, in Grote Kerkstraat, has an important Treasury containing an early 8C evangelistery known as the *Codex Eyckensis*. The oldest book in Belgium, it is believed to have once belonged to St Relindis and St Herlindis, who founded a Benedictine convent nearby at Aldeneik in c 750.

Maaseik environs
A stone church at **Aldeneik**, just east of Maaseik, was built in 870 and restored in the 11C. Additions were made in the 13C, by which time the nuns had been replaced by a community of monks. Further restoration and alterations were carried out in the 19C. The central part of the Romanesque nave, with its 13C frescoes, dates from the 11C or 12C. The west part is early 13C and the choir late 13C. The neo-Romanesque aisles and the tower are 19C additions.

Off the beaten track

FLEMISH BRABANT
• • • • • • • • • • • • • • • • • • •

The province of Flemish Brabant is a region of historic towns, white stone churches and rolling countryside. Its capital is the old university town of Leuven. The old Flemish Brabant towns of Diest, Aarschot, Tienen, Zoutleeuw and Halle are all interesting to explore. The main regions of Flemish Brabant are the Hageland, the Haspengouw, the Dijle valley, the Zenne valley, and the Pajottenland. The region of Flemish Brabant bordering Brussels is covered in Brussels environs. A separate chapter is devoted to Leuven.

Tourist information
Flemish Brabant tourist information

office, Diestsesteenweg 52, Leuven, ☎ 016.26.76.20.

Halle

Halle (Hal in French), c 16km southwest of Brussels, owes its fame to the huge Gothic basilica built between 1341 and 1409. This has long been a place of pilgrimage because of its famous 13C 'black' Virgin, which was originally venerated in a chapel on this site.

Tourist office
Grote Markt 1, ☎ 02.356.42.59.

Onze Lieve Vrouwbasiliek
The exterior of the Onze Lieve Vrouwbasiliek is rather odd due to the heavy 18C tower and curious 'balloon' above the octagonal baptistry. A 15C group of the Virgin and musician angels decorates the south portal. A recess to the right of the porch contains some 33 cannon balls which were aimed at the church during a siege of the town in 1580. According to a pious local tradition, these were caught by the Virgin in her robe. Another tradition asserts that the black colour of the famous statue was caused by gunpowder. It is more likely that the darkening of the statue was caused by centuries of candle smoke and the oxidisation of the silver which once covered it.

A **chapel** off the north aisle was built by Gilles de Trazegnies in c 1647. It contains an alabaster reredos of 1533 carved in pure Renaissance style by a local sculptor, Jehan Mone. The carvings show St Martin dividing his cloak, the evangelists Mark and Luke, and a representation of the Seven Sacraments. The statues of the Apostles in the choir date from 1410.

A tiny black marble effigy stands in a niche in the **Lady Chapel**, to the left of the choir. Carved in 1460, it depicts Joachim, the Dauphin of France and son of Louis XI. A naive painting nearby shows a dramatic rescue, which was attributed to the intervention of the Virgin. The octagonal **baptistry**, with stained-glass of 1408, contains a brass font of 1446 by Jean de Febvre of Tournai. The crypt, which is supported by a single column, houses the **Treasury**. The treasures include a silver monstrance presented by Henry VIII of England after the capture of Tournai by his army in 1513.

Pajottenland

The Pajottenland is a rural region west of Brussels where Pieter Bruegel painted many of his most famous landscapes in the 1560s. Critics have identified Dilbeek village church in Bruegel's *Haymaking*, now in Prague, and the church at Sint-Anna-Pede in the background of *The Parable of the Blind*, which hangs in Naples. A **Bruegel trail** beginning from the church in **Sint-Anna-Pede**, just south of the N8 to the west of Brussels, leads to a dilapidated windmill that appears in Bruegel's melancholy *The Magpie on the Gallows*, in Darmstadt. (A booklet describing the Bruegel Route can be obtained from the Flemish Brabant tourist office in Leuven.)

Gaasbeek

Gaasbeek, 12km southwest of Brussels and 5km south of Sint-Anna-Pede, is an impressive Renaissance castle. The original 13C building was destroyed by the citizens of Brussels after the murder of Everard 't Serclaes in 1387. The castle was rebuilt and converted into a château in 1545. Further additions and restorations were made during the 18C and 19C. The castle became the property of the state in 1921 and contains several notable **tapestries** from Brussels (16C and 17C), Tournai (15C), and England (17C). The rooms also contain period furniture, 15C and 16C ceramics and a large number of valuable objets d'art. The collection of **Flemish paintings** includes a *Tower of Babel* by Martin van Valekenborgh, which once belonged to Rubens, and a portrait of the *Countess of Dorset* by Van Dyck. The castle is surrounded by landscaped grounds with lakes, woods, a chapel and pleasure pavilion. Open from Apr–Oct, from Tues–Thur and at weekends, 10.00–17.00 and Mon in Jul–Aug. Much of the park is accessible to wheelchairs.

Eating out
Oud Gaasbeek, Kasteelstraat 37, is a rustic tavern opposite the castle entrance with an attractive garden and a good children's playground. It serves local Greuze beer and Flemish open sandwiches, made from bread baked in a 19C clay oven.

Beersel

The impressive ruined castle of Beersel, 10km south of Brussels, lies in the valley below Beersel village.

Dating from the 14C, the castle was much damaged in 1489, when the owners, the Wittem family, supported Maximilian in his struggle against the towns. Rebuilt soon afterwards, it was abandoned after 1544 and suffered much from neglect. It came into the care of the Association Royale des Demeures Historiques in 1932 and has subsequently been carefully and sympathetically restored.

Surrounded by a moat, the castle retains its medieval appearance. Its three towers, linked by solid walls, look down on a circular courtyard. The moat is crossed by a small drawbridge. For defence purposes, the towers are rounded on the outside, but have typical Flemish step gables on the side facing the courtyard. Open

Mar–mid-Nov Tues–Sun 10.00–12.00 and 14.00–18.00; mid-Nov–Dec and in Feb, weekends only 14.00–18.00; closed Jan.

The 15C church in **Alsemberg**, 12km south of Brussels, contains some interesting murals and a pulpit of 1837 by F.J. van Geel and J.B. van Hool. The pulpit is decorated with carvings of Christ teaching the people. It is worth looking closely at the various figures, which include a mother with her two children, one of whom is pulling away from her to catch a tortoise. The church also contains a 12C font, a *Descent from the Cross* by Theodoor Rombouts and a 13C figure of the Virgin.

The attractive provincial estate at **Huizingen**, c 12km southwest of Brussels, has beautiful rose gardens, a deer enclosure, boating lake and several adventure playgrounds. The 19C neo-Renaissance château is now used as a restaurant.

The village of **Onze Lieve Vrouw Lombeek**, c 14km west of Brussels, has a 13C–14C church. It contains an outstanding Brabant retable of the Virgin carved in 1512–16, and a 15C rood.

The **Musée du Tram** at **Schepdaal**, 10km west of Brussels. occupies a steam tram depot built in 1888 on the old line from Brussels to Schepdaal. The museum contains a nostalgic collection of 30 trams which once ran on rural routes in Belgium. Open Apr–mid-Oct on Sun and public holidays 14.00–18.00; also Saturdays in July and August (same hours).

The town of **Hekelgem** in northwest Brabant, 5km southeast of Aalst, was once famous for the Flemish folk art of 'Zandtapijts' (sand carpets). Weeks of meticulous work are required to build up a 'carpet' on a board divided into squares. The artist produces an outline of a picture and then lays down sand in different colours. The pictures can be original works or copies of famous paintings.

The **Abbey of Afflighem**, north of Hekelgem, was founded in the 11C, but almost completely destroyed in 1796. All that survive are one wall of the church nave and some 17C buildings, including the entrance lodge. The Benedictines returned to the abbey in 1869 and began reconstructing the buildings. The main church was completed in 1972. Godfrey of Leuven and his daughter Adeliza were buried at Afflighem. The second queen of Henry I of England, Adeliza died in 1151.

Diest

Diest is an ancient town on the River Demer in the northeast of Brabant, c 28km northeast of Leuven, with old ramparts and an attractive Begijnhof. Ruled by the House of Orange from 1499 until the French occupation of 1794, the town still has buildings connected to the Orange-Nassau family.

Where to stay

The *Hotel De Fransche Croon*, Leuvensestraat 26, ☎ 013.31.45.40, is a comfortable hotel in the town centre.

Eating out
Restaurants

Nieuwe Haan, Grote Markt 19, ☎ 013.33.51.06, is an old inn on the main square specialised in French cooking.

Proosdij, Cleynaertstraat 14, ☎ 013.31.20.10, offers Provençal cooking in a handsome 17C building behind the church.

Café

The Gasthof 1618, in the Begijnhof, is

an attractive historic tavern with inter-esting local cooking.

Tourist office
Grote Markt 1, ☎ 013.35.32.71.

Opening times
The Stedelijk Museum is open daily 10.00–12.00 and 13.00–17.00.

A walk round the town

Begin on the **Grote Markt**, an irregular square surrounded by 17C and 18C buildings which are now mainly occupied by cafés and restaurants. The **Stadhuis** was built in 1735 by Willem Ignatius Kerrickx on the site of several older buildings. The Gothic cellar of the former aldermen's house of c 1320 and the 13C Romanesque cellar, with its original well, of the house of the lords of Diest, are all that remain of the earlier structures. These buildings are now occupied by the **Stedelijk Museum**, which contains several curiosities, including 17C silver, a small frame-reliquary full of meticulously labelled sacred relics, a marble statue of the Virgin of 1345 (a replica of an original in the Metropolitan Museum of Art, New York), paintings by Theodoor van Loon, and a dramatic *Last Judgement* by an unknown artist of c 1420–50.

The nearby **Sint Sulpitiuskerk** was built from 1321–1534 and dedicated to the 7C Bishop of Bourges. The colours of the stone record the successive stages in its construction. Excavations have revealed the remains of two earlier churches. The older dates from the 11C, though it is believed that a wooden chapel stood on this site as early as the 7C.

The choir stalls of Sint Sulpitiuskerk date from 1491. Notice the appealing figures on the misericords. The church has an interesting treasury, some fine 15C–16C stained-glass, a 13C *Sedes Sapientiae*, and the tomb of Philip of Nassau, who died in 1618. The son of William the Silent, Philip was lord of Diest.

A 15C cannon called 'Holle Griet' stands near the church. The best view of the nearby **Halle**, the 14C cloth hall, is from its east end. The oldest part of Diest is to the east of this area. Go down Guido Gezellestraat to reach the **Sint Barbarakerk** which has an impressive 17C Baroque façade.

Turn left along Kattenstraat to the **Warande Stadspark**, once a hunting ground of the princes of Orange. The cemetery in the far corner of the park contains the ruins of a 14C church.

Return to the Grote Markt. The abbeys of Tongerlo and Averbode had refuges inside the walls of Diest, just off Demerstraat to the north of the Grote Markt. The 16C refuge and grain warehouse of Tongerlo Abbey is down a lane on the right. The 15C refuge of Averbode Abbey is at Refugiestraat 6.

Return to the Grote Markt again and take the Koning Albertstraat to reach the 13C **Onze Lieve Vrouwkerk** in Begijnenstraat. This replaced an earlier chapel. Further down the Begijnenstraat, a Baroque portal of 1671 leads into the beautiful **Begijnhof**. With its cobbled streets and neat white houses, this is one of the most attractive Begijnhofs in Flanders. Founded in 1252, it was largely reconstructed from 1538–1575 by the chaplain Nicolaas van Esch. Most of the houses date from this period. The interior of the 14C Gothic church was restored in Rococo style.

Return to the Onze Lieve Vrouwkerk and turn right down Schaffensestraat to reach the **Schaffensepoort**. This impressive vestige of the 19C town defences consists of a narrow fortified tunnel that crosses two arms of the river Demer.

The provincial park **Halve Maan** occupies a former bastion beyond the moat near the Begijnhof. It contains a large open air swimming pool created in the 1930s, an adventure playground, a small farm and a rustic restaurant.

Aarschot

Located on the River Demer at an important crossroads c 16km northeast of Leuven, the small town of Aarschot is a centre for agriculture and light industry. According to one tradition, the town derives its name from the fact that the Romans kept their eagles (or standards) here. Another legend has it that Julius Caesar shot an eagle in the neighbourhood.

Prosperity came to the town with the cloth trade in the 13C. Aarschot was attacked by Charles the Bold and sacked in 1489 by Maximilian of Austria. It was pillaged several times and burnt by the Spanish in the 16C. Joseph II razed the town's fortifications in 1782, which led many of the inhabitants to support the Brabançon Revolt a few years later. The town was the scene of German brutality in 1914 when 400 houses were burnt and 149 citizens were murdered, including the burgomaster.

Tourist office
Demervallei 14, ☎ 016.56.97.05.

A walk round the town
A good view of Aarschot can be gained from the **Orleanstoren**, a relic of the 13C walls on the hill above the town. The Gothic **Onze Lieve Vrouwkerk** stands near the river. This has a 13C–14C choir, a 15C nave and a tower 85m high. It contains paintings by Gaspard de Crayer, a chandelier by Quinten Metsys and lively misericords on the choir stalls carved by Jan Borchman in 1500.

> ### The Mystic Winepress
> A naive painting in Onze Lieve Vrouwkerk by an unknown Flemish artist of c 1525 illustrates the curious notion of the 'Mystic Winepress'. The lower part of the painting depicts the Seven Sacraments, while the upper part shows Christ on the 'press' of the Cross shedding blood as if it was wine. The image is continued on the left, where Peter and the other Apostles press the grapes. The Four Evangelists take the grape juice to the church, where the barrels are closed by the Pope, Emperor, Cardinals and Bishops and then placed in the cellars. Priests are shown offering the wine of Christ to the faithful.

A large Renaissance mansion west of the church was once the home of a burgo-master. The remains of the **Begijnhof** are just beyond here. Founded in the 13C, it was largely destroyed during the two World Wars and by postwar town planning. Several houses have been restored in 17C–18C style. They are now occupied by municipal offices, old people's homes and a local museum.

A small statue of a lacemaker opposite the museum recalls a vanished local skill. Straddling the river just beyond is the **'s Hertogenmolens**, built in the 13C–16C as ducal mills.

Aarschot environs

The attractive **Horst** castle is at Sint Pieters-Rode, 6km south of Aarschot. The tower and keep are all that survive of the original medieval castle of the 13C–15C. The rest of the building, which dates from the 15C–17C, has remained unaltered since it was last occupied in the 17C. Surrounded by water, it is an excellent example of a 17C seigneurial home. Despite being long abandoned, the castle has been well maintained. The most interesting feature of the interior is the late 17C ceiling in the great hall, which is decorated with scenes from Ovid's *Metamorphoses* by Jan Hansche.

The missionary priest Father Damien was born at **Tremelo**, 7km west of Aarschot, in 1840. After devoting his life to the leper outcasts on the Hawaiian island of Molokai, he died of the disease there in 1889. His body was brought to the chapel of St Antonius in Leuven in 1936. The house in which he was born is now a museum (open Jul–Aug, Tues–Sun 14.00–18.00; Sept–Mar Sun 14.00–17.00; Apr–Jun at weekends 14.00–17.00).

A high fortified tower stands at **Rotselaar**, 10km southwest of Aarschot. Its origins are unknown, but it is thought to have been rebuilt during the 15C.

Scherpenheuvel

The town of Scherpenheuvel, 16km east of Aarschot, is the scene of Belgium's most important annual pilgrimage on the Sunday after All Saints.

Pilgrimage

The procession arose after a miracle in c 1514 when a shepherd found a statue of the Virgin and the Child Jesus attached to an oak near Scherpenheuvel. He tried to remove it, but became fixed to the spot. On discovering his missing servant, the master took it as a sign that the Virgin wanted to be honoured in this place. He therefore built a chapel for the statue. The Duke of Parma prayed here in 1578 before laying siege to Zichem, 3km to the north. Two years later, the statue was destroyed by the Iconoclasts. Albert and Isabella vowed in 1601 to make a pilgrimage to Scherpenheuvel if their commander Spinola forced the United Provinces army to retreat. After Spinola finally took Ostend, Archduke Albert kept his vow. He had the town of Scherpenheuvel built in 1607 in the shape of a seven-pointed star.

The circular **Basilica** was completed by Wenceslas Coeberger, the court architect, in 1627. It is based on the design of St Peter's in Rome. The seven windows in the lantern turret symbolise the seven Sacraments. A copy of the original miraculous statue stands above the tabernacle on the high altar. The church contains numerous gifts left by pilgrims, including a brass font of 1610, a *Head of Christ* carved by Frans Duquesnoy presented by Albert and Isabella, six paintings by Theodoor van Loon given by Isabella, and an *Assumption* attributed to Martin de Vos. (Access by **wheelchair** is possible.)

Scherpenheuvel environs

The old town of **Zichem**, 3km north of Scherpenheuvel, has a church of c 1300 with stained-glass windows dating from 1387. The **Maagdentoren** near the river marks the site of the 14C ramparts. The town has a small museum containing memorabilia of the writer Ernest Claes, who was born here in 1885.

The Premonstratensian **Averbode Abbey**, 4km north of Zichem, stands on the watershed between the valleys of the Demer and the Nete at a point where the provinces of Antwerp, Brabant and Limburg meet. Founded in 1134, the abbey was closed down and sold at the time of the French Revolution. It was reopened in 1833. Access to the inner court is by a 14C gatehouse. The courtyard is overlooked by the vaulted 17C cloisters and the 18C abbot's house. Most of the domestic buildings were rebuilt after a fire in 1942. The large Baroque church, by D. van der Ende (1664–72), has an unusual choir which is longer than its nave. (Access by **wheelchair** is possible.)

Tienen

Tienen (Tirlemont in French), c 18km southeast of Leuven, is an ancient town at the centre of a beet-growing district. It is best known in Belgium for its sugar industry, which produces the wrapped sugar cubes found in most Belgian cafés. The sugar refinery, which was established in the 19C, is on the outskirts of the town on the N3 to Liège.

Tourist office
Grote Markt 4, ☎ 016.80.56.86.

Opening times
The **Museum Het Toreke** is open

Mon–Fri 09.00–12.00 and 14.00–16.30; weekends 14.00–18.00, but closed the weekends before Christmas and after New Year.

History

The earliest evidence of human occupation dates from the late neolithic period (c 2500 BC). A decorated vase of the La Tène period (c 250 BC) and many Gallo-Roman remains are evidence of later peoples in this region. Tienen was awarded town status in 1194. It was sacked in 1635 by a joint French and Dutch force. The town suffered atrocities for three days, including the destruction of more than 600 houses, the convents of the Carmelites and other religious orders, the town hall and hospital.

The ring road around the north of the town follows the course of the fourth and last fortifications, which were erected in the 16C and 17C.

A walk round the town

The huge **Grote Markt** is the second largest in Belgium, after the main square in Sint Niklaas. The **Onze Lieve Vrouw ten Poelkerk** (Our Lady of the Pool) stands on the east side. Built from 1345–1460, but with later additions, this church replaced a 13C chapel which was a popular place of pilgrimage. Many cures were claimed for a nearby miraculous spring, which dried up in the 18C. Several notable architects worked on the church, which does not have a nave, including Sulpicius van der Vorst, Jan Keldermans and Mathys de Layens. The

west portal of 1360 has small figures on the pedestals of the empty niches. It opens onto the transepts. The statue of the Virgin above the main door is a copy of the 1365 statue by Walter Paris above the high altar.

The Neo-classical **Stadhuis** was built in 1836 on the south side of the square. A stone star opposite marks the position of the pillory and guillotine. The **Gerechtshof** was added in 1846 on the north side of the square. It stands on the site of the medieval cloth hall. There are two memorials in the northeast corner of the square. One statue by Jef Lambeaux commemorates the volunteers who fought in the 1830 Revolution. The other is a memorial to those who lost their lives in Belgium's struggle for independence in 1830 and 1831 and during the two World Wars.

The **Museum Het Toreke** on the Grote Markt is reached through the court-yard of the Gerechtshof. It has an interesting collection of Gallo-Roman coins, Romanesque fonts and medieval sculptures. A sculpture of St Martin may be by the studio of Jan Borman (fl. 1479–1520).

Now take the Peperstraat and Wolmarkt, which lead up the hill. This is known in Celtic as *dunen*, which some believe gave Tienen its name. Several 17C houses in the Wolmarkt were built to replace dwellings burned down in 1635. The **Sint Germanuskerk** was founded in the 9C, but rebuilt several times. Parts of the choir, the west façade and the main tower date from the 12C. Further recon-struction was undertaken c 1535 by P. van Wijenhoven, architect to Charles V, and again a century later after the sack of the town by the French and Dutch. The interior contains a 15C copper **pelican lectern** and some rather theatrical 16C and 17C sculptures in the southeast chapel.

Descend from the Wolmarkt by the Grote Bergstraat to reach the site of the **Begijnhof**, most of which was destroyed by air raids in 1944. Only a few of the old houses survived the attack.

Tienen environs

A detour down Pastoriestraat, turning left off the N3 just beyond the sugar refin-ery, leads to the cemetery chapel of **Sint Pieter** in Grimde. This has an 11C tower and nave. The chapel has been made into a mausoleum for 140 Belgian soldiers who fell near here on 18 August 1914. Returning to the N3, you pass a short path on the right leading to three large c 2C **Gallo-Roman tumuli**.

The 14C–16C church at **Oplinter**, 4km northeast of Tienen, contains a poly-chrome statue of Christ which once belonged to a nearby Cistercian abbey. The abbey was converted into a farm in the 19C, but some of the original buildings survive.

The church at **Hakendover**, 2 km east of Tienen, dates from the 13C–16C. Its tower is Romanesque. The interior contains an outstanding oak retable of 1430 depicting an old legend on the construction of the church.

The construction of Hakendover church

The story goes that some pious virgins attempted to raise a church near Tienen. They were dismayed to find that each day's work was pulled down dur-ing the night. They later had a vision in which angels instructed them to build the church near a hawthorn (a hagedoorn in Dutch). This turned out to be an instant success. Twelve local workmen completed the task with the help of a thirteenth labourer (The Saviour). The church is dedicated to the Salvator.

Zoutleeuw

This small town in the Hageland district c 12km notheast of Tienen was at its most prosperous in the 13C and 14C. Decline set in during the 18C when the town was bypassed by the main Brussels to Liège road. Zoutleeuw's fame now rests on an outstanding collection of religious art displayed in the Sint Leonarduskerk.

Tourist information
Grote Markt, ☎ 011.78.12.88.

Opening times
The **Sint Leonarduskerk** is open
Easter–Sept on Tues–Sun 14.00–17.00.

A walk round the town

The **Sint Leonarduskerk** was the only important Belgian church to escape the fury of the Calvinist iconoclasts in the 16C and the destruction that came in the wake of the French Revolution. It thus provides a unique insight into the rich artistic heritage that was destroyed by pillaging armies.

The church tower, west front and apse date from the 13C, while the nave was added in the 14C. Extensions were built onto the chapels in the 16C. The church's treasures include retables, triptychs, furniture and vestments. Some of the vestments in the chapels are protected by curtains.

There is a *Marianum* hanging high up in the **nave**. This representation of the Virgin surrounded by a garland of roses is probably a Rhenish work. It was made of wrought and painted iron in 1533. The only other *Marianum* in Belgium is at Neeroeteren, near Maaseik.

The **choir** has a handsome triforium and a magnificent six-branched candelabrum made in 1483 by Renier van Thienen. It is surmounted by a Crucifix and statuettes of the Virgin, St John and St Mary Magdalene. The work is particularly admired for the drapery, attitude and expression. The huge wooden cross of 1483 which hangs in the choir arch is by Willem van Goelen.

The **ambulatory** contains a series of statuettes dating from the 12C to the 18C. These include a 12C *Sedes Sapientiae* and a 16C *St Mary Magdalene*.

Sedes Sapientae

A *Sedes Sapientiae* is a statue of the Virgin seated with the Child Jesus on her left knee. She sometimes holds a staff in her right hand. Usually made of wood, the statues were often clothed in richly embroidered garments or covered with silver or gold plate. Many date from 1000 or earlier.

An exquisite stone tabernacle in the **Chapel of the Blessed Sacrament**, off the north transept, was made by Cornelis Floris between 1550 and 1552 for Marten van Wilre, lord of Oplinter. The spire, 18m high, is in seven tiers and has several groups of figures. The tomb opposite commemorates Van Wilre, who died in 1558, and his wife, who died in 1554. This was also carved by Cornelis Floris. To the left of the altar, the *Baptism of Christ Triptych* was probably painted by Frans Floris, the more famous brother of Cornelis.

A chapel dedicated to St Leonard in the **south transept** is decorated with murals of 1490 of the *Last Judgement*. It also contains an altarpiece of 1478 by

Arnold de Maeler depicting the life of St Leonard. There is also a statue of the saint, painted and studded with precious stones, which dates from c 1300.

The **Stadhuis** was built in 1539 to plans by Rombout Keldermans. The **Hallen** (cloth hall) next door was built between 1316 and 1320, when the town was evidently enjoying a period of early prosperity.

WEST FLANDERS

The province of West Flanders is an attractive low-lying region bordering the North Sea. The province includes the ancient towns of Bruges and Kortrijk, the Belgian coastal resorts and the battlefields of the First World War. These are covered in separate chapters.

Tourist information
West Flanders Tourist Information Office, Kasteel Tillegem, 8200 Bruges, ☎ 050.38.02.96.

Torhout

The town of Torhout, 20km southwest of Bruges, is the centre of the Houtland district. Destroyed in both World Wars, the **Sint Pieterskerk** has been rebuilt in its original Romanesque style. The church contains a *Martyrdom of St Sebastian* by Van Dyck. The **Stadhuis** of 1713 contains a small local museum with a collection of pottery.

Where to stay
The *Hostellerie 't Gravenhof*, Oostendsestraat 343, Wijnendale, ☎ 050.21.23.14, is a comfortable hotel facing Wijnendale castle. It has a good restaurant and a garden.

Tourist information
Kasteel Ravenhof, Torhout, ☎ 050.22.07.70.

Opening hours
Stadhuis museum is open weekdays 10.00–12.00 and 14.00–17.00.
Wijnendale castle is open mid-May–mid-Sept on Tues, Wed and Sun 14.00–18.00.

Torhout environs
The historic 12C castle at **Wijnendale**, 4km northwest of Torhout, lies in the Houtland district. It contains a museum with tableaux illustrating episodes in its history.

The most famous event occurred in 1292 when the Count of Flanders Guy de Dampierre, son of Margaret of Constantinople, received an ambassador from Edward I of England asking for the hand of his daughter for Edward's son. Largely because of this request Guy's suzerain, Philip the Fair, who wished the future Edward II to marry his own daughter, had Guy imprisoned in France and forced him to cede Flanders.

It was while hunting in the park that Mary of Burgundy fell from her horse and later died (the tragedy is illustrated in the Stadhuis at Bruges). This castle was also the scene of the final meeting in 1940 between Leopold III and his prime minister, Pierlot, during which Leopold decided to surrender. The armistice with Germany was also signed here.

The church at **Zedelgem**, 9km north of Torhout, has a 12C font of Tournai marble.

The Sint Jacobskerk at **Lichtervelde**, 3km southeast of Torhout, has a late Romanesque font.

Roeselare

Roeselare, c 28km south of Bruges, was the headquarters of the German forces facing the Ypres Salient. The **Sint Michielskerk**, built in 1497–1504, contains some interesting woodwork, including an elaborately carved 18C pulpit from the Carmelite church in Bruges. It has some interesting paintings including a *Scourging of Christ* by Abraham Janssens (1575–1632), in which the figures are dressed in 17C clothes.

Roeselare environs

The attractive red-brick **Rumbeke Castle** is just south of Roeselare (open to groups). The building dates mainly from the 16C, though some parts are older. The Sterrebos park, laid out in 1770 by F. Simoneau, is now a provincial recreational estate. A monument opposite the castle commemorates soldiers of the 1st Grenadier Guards who died near here on 17 May 1940.

The small town of **Izegem**, 10km southeast of Roeselare, has been known for centuries for its brush and shoe industries. The town has a **museum of brushes** at Wolvenstraat 2 and a **museum of shoes** at Wijngaardstraat 9 (both open on Sat 10.00–12.00).

The town of **Ingelmunster**, 3km east of Izegem, has an 18C castle. This replaced the medieval castle where Philip the Fair of France received the keys of Bruges in 1301. A battle fought near here in 1580, following the signing of the Union of Arras, was one of Parma's first successes against the Protestants.

Tielt

Tielt, c 16km northeast of Roeselare, has long associations with textiles and shoemaking. It was the birthplace of Olivier le Daim, an itinerant barber who achieved great power as confidant of France's Louis XI. He was hanged one year after the King's death in 1484. During the First World War, Tielt was for a time the German headquarters on the Flanders front. The Kaiser narrowly escaped death from a bombing attack by British aircraft here on 1 November 1914.

Tourist information

Tramstraat 2, ☎ 051.42.60.60.

Tielt has an ancient **belfry** in the Markt square, built in 1275, with a spire added in 1620. The **Halle** (cloth hall) in the same square dates mainly from the early 17C. The coats of arms below the windows belong to local lords. A plaque on the south façade commemorates the Peasants' Revolt of 1798.

The **Stadhuis** mainly dates from the 19C, but a wing on Tramstraat partly belonged to a 13C convent hospice. The **Sint Pieterskerk**, just west of the Markt, was founded in the 11C. It has a tower of 1646 and interesting furnishings including a Rococo-style pulpit of 1857. A lane off the Minderbroedersstraat, south of the Markt, leads to the **Minderbroederskerk**, which has splendid Baroque altars and 17C cloisters which belonged to the Franciscan monastery. The **Onze Lieve Vrouwkerk**, at the end of Minderbroedersstraat, is a large modern church built in 1937. It is decorated with striking sculpture and bronze Stations of the Cross.

The **Stockt Chapel** in Oude Stationsstraat is a 1949 copy of a 17C chapel built by a Spanish noble who was spared from the plague. Four stained-glass windows illustrate the ravages of the plague.

Tielt environs

> ### The Flemish Vasari
> **Meulebeke**, 6km southwest of Tielt, was the birthplace of the Flemish portrait painter Karel van Mander (1548–1606). Known as the Flemish Vasari, Van Mander is famous for his collection of short biographies of painters from the Netherlands. The *Schilderbouck* is a key source book for the history of art in the Low Countries.

The village of **Aarsele**, 6km east of Tielt, has a Romanesque church and a restored windmill.

Oudenburg

At one time on an arm of the sea, the village of Oudenburg, 19km west of Bruges, stands on the site of a prosperous medieval port. The remains of a large Roman coastal fortress and necropolis have been excavated, but little remains visible above ground. The considerable finds, which include fibulae, pottery, glass, coins, spearheads, combs and a fine ivory plaque bearing a representation of the *magister militum* Stilicho, are preserved in the **Gemeentelijk Museum**, Markstraat 25 (only open on request).

There are also some 17C buildings from a Benedictine abbey founded in 1084 by St Arnulf of Soissons. Born in Flanders, Arnulf served in the armies of Robert and Henry I of France. He became a Benedictine monk and lived as a recluse for a number of years. Appointed bishop of Soissons in 1082, he later retired to Oudenburg where he died in 1087.

Gistel

The town of Gistel, 12km south of Ostend, is an old settlement whose name may be derived from the stables (*stallingen*) of the counts of Flanders. The church, which dates from c 1500, contains the shrine of St Godeleva (Godliva). Married at a young age to Bertulf of Gistel, Godeleva was abused by him for several years and finally strangled on his orders.

Gistel environs

The abbey of **Ten Putte**, 3km west of Gistel, is a 19C foundation built on the site of a Benedictine convent established soon after St Godeleva's death. It is said to stand on the site of the castle where she was strangled. The **St Godelieve Museum** in the abbey has an interesting historical and iconographical collection (open daily Easter–Sept 10.00–12.00 and 13.30–18.00).

Jabbeke

The **Constant Permeke Museum** in Jabbeke, 10km east of Gistel, occupies a house built by the Flemish Expressionist Constant Permeke (1886–1952) in 1929 (open Tues–Sun 10.00–12.30 and 13.30–18.00, but 17.00 Nov–Mar). Named 'Les Quatre Vents' because the façades look to the four cardinal points, the house had a large studio. The museum owns 80 canvases and sketches, together with almost all of Permeke's sculptures. The paintings include *Au Sujet de Permeke*, *La Moisson*, *Paysage Breton*, *L'Adieu* and *Le Pain Quotidien*. Among the sculptures are *Niobé*, *Le Semeur* and *Marie Lou*.

The recreation area **Klein Strand**, just northwest of Jabbeke, has a beach and a lake with water-skiing shows in summer.

EAST FLANDERS

East Flanders is a province of historic towns and rich farmland. The capital of Ghent and the historic town of Oudenaarde are covered in separate chapters.

Tourist information
East Flanders tourist information office,

Woodrow Wilsonplein 3, Ghent, ☎ 09.267.70.20.

Aalst

Aalst is a textile and brewing town on a canalised stretch of the river Dender, midway between Brussels and Ghent. It was a seat of the court of the counts of Flanders from the 13C and an assembly-place of the States-General until the end of the 15C. The town was badly damaged in both World Wars.

Tourist information
Belfort, Grote Markt, ☎ 053.73.22.70.

Carillon concerts
Concerts are played on the 52-bell carillon during the summer.

Opening times
The **Museum Oud Hospitaal** is open Mon–Thur 10.00–12.00 and 14.00–17.00; on Sat 14.00–17.00 and on Sun 10.30–12.00 and 14.00–18.00.

A walk in the old town

Begin on the irregular **Grote Markt**, where a statue by Jan Geefs of 1856 depicts the humanist Dirk Martens (c 1450–1534). The first Belgian printer, Martens published his work *Speculum Conversionis Peccatorum* at Aalst in 1473.

The **Schepenhuis** on Grote Markt was once the town hall. Of the original building of c 1225, only the left and rear façades and something of the lower part survive. Most of the present building dates from the early 15C.

The **belfry**, completed in 1466, is decorated with statues of a knight and a citizen, symbolising municipal power and freedom. Proclamations were once read from the Flamboyant Gothic corner gallery of 1474. The five 19C statues represent Justice; Charles V; Dirk, Lord of Aalst; the Renaissance painter Pieter Coecke van Aalst (1502–1550), and Cornelis de Schrijver (1482–1588), secretary of Antwerp.

The 1831 **Stadhuis** by Louis Roelandt preserves in its courtyard the façade of the Landhuis of 1646, seat of the States of Flanders when Aalst was the provincial capital.

The arcaded building on the left, now a restaurant, was originally the **Vleeshuis**. It later became the meeting-place of the Barbaristes, the literary guild of St Barbara. It burnt down in 1743, but was rebuilt five years later.

The **Sint Martinuskerk**, off the Grote Markt, is a large Gothic building of 1480–1638. It is based on the designs of Jan van der Wouwe, and Herman and Domien Waghemakere (the father and son who built the cathedral at Antwerp). The church remained unfinished because of the religious wars of the 16C, though a Baroque portal was added in 1730.

The church contains a celebrated painting by Rubens in the **south transept**. It shows *St Roch receiving from Christ the gift of healing plague victims*. St Roch (1350–80) was a native of Montpellier in France who devoted his life to tending victims of the plague. He is often depicted with a dog licking a plague spot on his leg. Rubens' large and highly decorative composition is in a contemporary carved wood frame, which also encloses some minor works from the painter's studio. Carried off to Paris in 1794, the painting was returned in 1816, largely through the efforts of the Duc de Berri, who had been a refugee in Aalst.

The next **chapel** contains a painting of *St Simon Stock* by Gaspard de Crayer. Simon Stock was one of the first English members of the Carmelites; he became the sixth general of the order in 1247 and was largely instrumental in establishing Carmelite houses in many European university cities, including Cambridge in 1248, Oxford in 1253 and Paris in 1260. His relics are kept in the Carmelite Priory at Aylesford in Kent.

The fine marble **tabernacle** of 1605 is by Jérôme Duquesnoy the Elder. Several of the guild chapels are decorated with vault paintings, the oldest and best of which dates from 1497. The **first ambulatory chapel** on the right contains an *Adoration of the Shepherds* by Otto Venius. The **fourth chapel** contains the tomb of the printer Dirk Martens, who died in 1534. The epitaph on the tomb was penned by Erasmus.

A narrow lane leads east of the church to the former hospital of **Onze Lieve Vrouw** at Oude Vismarkt 13. The restored 15C–17C buildings provide an attractive setting for the **Museum Oud Hospitaal**. This has an interesting collection of objects from Aalst and environs, including some Roman antiquities.

Now go down Pontstraat, which runs south from the church. An entrance on the left leads into the **Begijnhof**. The Neo-classical church dates from 1787. The small houses around the church were built by the local council in 1952 on the site of the Beguines' homes.

Aalst environs

The town of **Moorsel**, 4km east of Aalst, has a 13C–14C church and a moated castle built in 1646.

The industrial town of **Zottegem**, 18km southwest of Aalst, was once a fief of the counts of Egmont. The vault below the church contains the tomb of Count Egmont, who was executed on Grand-Place in Brussels on the orders of the Duke of Alva. His wife and two sons are also buried here. The family castle was largely rebuilt in the 19C.

The castle of **Leeuwergem**, 2km north of Zottegem, was built in 1724 on the site of a 12C castle (only open to groups).

The Waasland

The Waasland, east of Ghent, is one of the most productive agricultural districts of Europe. Until about the 12C this was a virtually uninhabitable tract of swamp and undrained forest. The development of the district began when it came under the rule of the counts of Flanders. The hermit settlements gradually developed into religious communities, whose members cleared the land and built the first dykes. Peat-cutting grew as an industry and a network of small waterways was dug to serve both for drainage and for transporting the peat. Sheep were introduced to meet the wool demands of Ghent. Villages and towns sprang up. Although the reclaimed land was largely of sand and clay, it has been made increasingly fertile by the addition of rich soil and the development of scientific farming skills.

Sint Niklaas

The lively and prosperous market town of Sint Niklaas, mid-way between Ghent and Antwerp on the N70, is the main centre of the Waasland district. Its roughly triangular market square is the largest in Belgium, covering an area of more than 3 hectares. The site was given to the parish of St Niklaas in 1248 by Margaret of Constantinople, Countess of Flanders.

Tourist information
Grote Markt 45, ☎ 03.777.26.81.

Opening times
The *Stedelijk Museum* is open Apr–Sept Tues–Sat 14.00–17.00, and on Sun 10.00–17.00.

The walk begins on the **Grote Markt**. The **Sint Niklaaskerk** partly survives from 1262, though most of the building dates from the 16C and 17C. The Baroque side altars were designed in 1664 by Hubert and Norbert van den Enden of Antwerp. The *Descent from the Cross* above the high altar was painted in 1836 by Pieter Thys. The monumental statues of *St Peter* and *St Paul* nearby were carved in the 17C by Lucas Faydherbe. The church also has a Baroque pulpit from 1706 and confessionals carved in 1707–10.

The **Stadhuis** stands on the far side of the square. A pleasingly proportioned 19C rebuilding of its 17C predecessor, it has a tower with a carillon. The interior is decorated with some interesting paintings, including Jozef Odevaere's painting of *William I Taking the Oath*.

The neo-Byzantine church of **Our Lady of Succour of the Christians** is behind the Stadhuis. Built in 1844, it is crowned with a 6m-tall statue of Our Lady. The work of a local sculptor, Fr. van Havermaet, the statue was brazed in copper and gold-plated.

Go up Stationstraat and turn right on Dr Verdurmenstraat to reach the **Stedelijk Museum** at Zamanstraat 49. The museum has several interesting collections, including local archaeology from the prehistoric, Roman and Frankish periods. It also displays some fine Flemish and Dutch paintings of the 17C to 19C, including a canvas attributed to Rubens and attractive works by Belgian artists from 1850–1900.

The striking **Mercator Room** displays a fascinating collection of works by the the geographer Gerardus Mercator, who was born in the Waasland town of Rupelmonde in 1512. The collection includes some 40 atlases, a terrestrial globe of 1541 and a celestial globe of 1551. Another section of the museum displays a quirky collection of antique hairdressing equipment, including a furnished salon of the 1920s.

The Parklaan runs south from Grote Markt to the **Walburghof**, a park created in 1550 on the orders of William van Waelwijck.

Sint Niklaas environs

The old shipbuilding town of **Temse** stands 8km southeast of Sint Niklaas on the Scheldt. An old legend tells of St Amelberga, the niece of Pepin of Landen, who escaped from an importunate suitor by crossing the river on the back of a giant sturgeon. St Amelberga is commemorated by a procession on Whit Tuesday. The town has a small **Municipal Museum** at Kasteelstraat 16 (open Sat 14.00–19.00 and Sun 10.00–12.00 and 14.00–19.00) and a **Museum of Heraldry** at Kasteelstraat 74 (open Apr–Oct Sat 14.00–18.00 and Sun 10.00–12.00 and 14.00–18.00).

The town of **Rupelmonde**, 5km east of Temse, stands at the confluence of the Rupel and the Scheldt. This town was the birthplace of the cartographer Mercator (1512–94). He was born Gerhard Kremer in a house at Kloosterstraat 54. A statue was unveiled in 1871 in the square. The waterfront still preserves something of the atmosphere of a fishing village. A ruined tower is all that survives from a 13C castle.

The church at **Bazel**, 2km north of Rupelmonde, stands within a pleasant close which has some interesting old façades. The moated **Kasteel van Wissekerke** occupies the site of a 10C fortification. A 16C octagonal tower survives, but the rest of the building is 19C. The park is landscaped in English style.

The small town of **Kruibeke**, 4km north of Bazel, has a church of c 1300, which is decorated with exceptionally rich Baroque woodwork of 1711–45 carved by members of the Kerrickx family.

The town of **Beveren**, 15km northeast of Sint Niklaas, has a 15C church with Baroque furnishings and silverware.

Lokeren

The pleasant town of Lokeren, mid-way between Ghent and Sint Niklaas stands on the small river Durme. It has several attractive 17C–18C buildings, including the town hall. The 18C church has a carillon and a pulpit of 1736 by Theodoor Verhaeghen. A small **museum** at Grote Kaai 1 contains a collection of local folklore.

Lokeren environs

The church at **Daknam**, 2km north of Lokeren, dates from the 11C and 12C. The town of **Overmere**, 12km southwest of Lokeren, was the scene of the first skirmish in the Peasants' Revolt of 1798, when locals rebelled against the anti-clerical policies of the occupying French. A monument commemorates the battle. The **Donkmeer**, 2km east of Overmere, is the largest lake in Flanders. An abandoned arm of the Scheldt, the lake was formed during the 16C by the flooding of peat diggings. It has rowing boats, an animal park and a duck decoy.

The **Domein Puyenbroeck**, 12km northwest of Lokeren, is a provincial park in typical Waasland countryside (open daily 09.00, but closed Mon Nov–Easter). The park has a swimming pool, boating lake, horse riding, a small zoo and a **mill museum** (open daily May–Sept 10.00–12.00 and 13.00–18.00; in Mar, Apr and Oct, open on Sun 14.00–17.00).

Dendermonde

Dendermonde, c 26km east of Ghent, is a pleasantly old-fashioned town near the confluence of the Dender and Scheldt rivers.

Once of great strategic importance, the town has been invaded many times. Incorporated into the county of Flanders in the 13C, Dendermonde was the first town captured by Maximilian in 1484 when he subdued the Netherlands. Louis XIV was forced to withdraw his troops from here in 1667 after the inhabitants flooded the entire district. Marlborough took Dendermonde in 1706; it was later occupied by the Dutch under the Barrier Treaty of 1713. The town was looted and largely burnt down in 1914 by the German army.

Café

The friendly *Den Ommeganck* at Grote Markt 18 serves Pauwel Kwak, a local brew served in a glass with a bulbous base.

Tourist information

Stadhuis, Grote Markt, ☎ 052.21.39.56.

Festivals

An **Ommegang** procession is held every ten years to commemorate a local legend involving the four sons of Aymond, Lord of Dendermonde, who fled the town on the horse Bayard after killing Charlemagne's son. The next parade is scheduled for May 2010.

Opening times

The **Oudheidkundig Museum** is open Apr–Oct Tues–Sun 09.00–12.30 and 13.30–18.00.
Onze Lieve Vrouwkerk is open Easter–Sept at weekends 14.00–16.30; July–Aug daily 14.00–16.30.
The **Stadhuis** is open Mon–Fri and Sun 10.00–12.00 and 14.00–16.00; also Easter–Sept Sat 10.00–12.00 and 14.00–16.00.

The **Stadhuis** on the Grote Markt occupies the former cloth hall, built in the 14C and 16C. The building was gutted in 1914, leaving just the belfry and the outer walls. It was restored to its original appearance from 1921 to 1926.

The **Vleeshalle** was built on the Grote Markt in 1460 with a late Gothic octagonal turret. The building is now occupied by the **Oudheidkundig Museum**, a museum of local antiquities. The massive **Justitiepaleis** was built nearby in 1924.

Follow Kerkstraat to reach the **Onze Lieve Vrouwkerk**. Built on the site of an earlier church, this Gothic edifice dates mainly from the 14C–15C. Its tower was badly damaged when Dendermonde was attacked by Ghent in 1379. According to a local legend, six cartloads of stones were removed by the defenders and used as ammunition. The reconstruction was not completed until c 1468, when Margaret of York, wife of Charles the Bold, visited the town.

The church contains two important paintings by Antoon van Dyck. His *Crucifixion* hangs in the baptistry and an *Adoration of the Shepherds* is in the north aisle. The baptistry also contains a 12C font in Tournai marble decorated with the *Last Supper*. A painting by Gaspard de Crayer in the north ambulatory shows a donor at prayer before the Virgin. The north transept and choir contain early 15C murals.

Now cross the River Dender to the south of Grote Markt and continue down Brusselsestraat. A narrow cobbled lane at no. 38 leads to the picturesque **Begijnhof**, where whitewashed 17C houses overlook a triangular green with grazing sheep and stray chickens. The community dates back to 1288. The church was rebuilt in the 1920s on the original foundations.

Two gates from the 17C town walls are still standing near the station.

Ronse

A pleasant town best known for its textile industry, Ronse (Renaix in French) lies along the line of hills known as the Flemish Ardennes, 10km south of Oudenaarde. It lies just inside East Flanders province, but the border with Hainaut is barely 1km away. Like Brussels, Ronse is officially bilingual.

Where to stay
The *Shamrock*, Ommegangstraat 148, Louise-Marie, 7km northeast of Ronse, ☎ 055.21.55.29, is a small country hotel built in Tudor style with an attractive garden landscaped by Jacques Wirtz.

Tourist information
Hoge Mote, De Biesestraat 2, ☎ 055.23.28.16.

Opening times
The **crypt of the Sint Hermeskerk** is open daily Tues–Fri 10.00–12.00 and 14.00–17.00.
The **Stedelijk Museum** and **Textiel Museum** are open Easter–Oct Tues–Fri 10.00–12.00 and 13.30–17.00, Sat, Sun and public holidays 10.00–12.00 and 14.30–17.30.

A walk in Ronse
Begin in the **Markt**, where an obelisk was erected in 1815. It was originally surmounted by the initial W for William I of the United Kingdom of the Netherlands. Removed during the revolution of 1830, the carved letter W is now

kept in the Stedelijk Museum. Its place has been taken by the Hapsburg eagle and the arms of the town.

The **Stadhuis** was rebuilt in 1953 by Frank Blockx in 16C Spanish style. Leave Markt on the north side along the Hospitaalstraat and continue into Priesterstraat, to the **Sint Hermeskerk**, a late Gothic building of the 15C–16C with a high west tower.

> The church is named after Hermes, a Roman exorcist executed in c 117. His relics were given by Pope Leo IV in c 855 to Lothair of Lower Lotharingia. Lothair donated them to Ronse where they attracted many pilgrims. They were once thought to provide a cure for lunacy. The richly embroidered 17C reliquary of the saint represents an equestrian figure leading a chained demon. It is kept in the south choir chapel, where a life-size statue repeats the motif. The iron rings on an old bench in a niche opposite the altar were used to secure the demented while they waited for exorcism. The church has a large Romanesque crypt dating from 1089. Restored in 1267, enlarged and again restored in 1518, it is still used for worship.

Outside the church, beside the north wall, a fragment has survived from the foundations of the church of **Sint Pieter**. Built c 1100 and enlarged in 1510, it was demolished in 1843. The outline of the cloister is marked by a hedge.

The town's two museums are in the nearby Bruul Park. The **Stedelijk Museum** occupies several late 18C houses which were once the canons' residences. The museum contains period rooms with paintings by local artists, memorabilia of distinguished citizens of Ronse and environs, guild relics, prehistoric objects, archaeological finds, a folklore section, and objects connected with old crafts such as weaving, basket making, clogs, shuttle making and printing. The **Textiel Museum** offers an interesting survey of the local textiles industry from 1800–1950.

The **railway station** to the south of the town originally stood on 't Zand at Bruges. It was demolished and rebuilt here when a new station was built in Bruges. The figure in front of the station is known locally as 'Bonmos'. He symbolises the local 'Fools' Monday' carnival held in Ronse on the Saturday after Epiphany.

Flemish Ardennes

A range of low hills known as the Flemish Ardennes runs through Ronse, south of Oudenaarde. The summits give extensive views of the Flanders plain to the north, with Hainaut and northern France visible to the south. The N425 north of Ronse passes two of the highest visible points: the 140m **Kluisberg** and the 150m Hotondberg. The **Hotondberg** has a useful orientation table. The 141m **Mont de l'Enclus** is another summit with extensive views.

Geraardsbergen

Geraardsbergen (Grammont in French) is a small town of considerable antiquity situated below the Oudeberg, c 20km east of Ronse. This hill of 113m has a steep slope known as **De Muur** (la Mur de Grammont in French) which provides a gruelling challenge in cycle races.

Tourist information

Markt 1, ☎ 054.41.41.21.

Festival

The **Krakelingenfeest** (Pretzel Festival) on the last Sunday in February is an ancient pagan festival during which the revellers drink wine containing dead fish.

Opening times

The abbey of **Sint Adriaan** is open Apr–Sept Mon–Fri 09.30–11.30 and 13.00–16.30, Sun 14.00–18.00. Closed Sat.

The museum of the **Manneken-Pis** is open daily 09.00–17.00.

The **Stadhuis** in the Markt, 14C in origin, dates mainly from the 18C. A faithful copy of the **Manneken-Pis** presented by Brussels in 1745 stands outside the town hall. A small **museum** in the Stadhuis contains a collection of some 70 costumes worn by the Manneken-Pis. The 15C Marbol (a stone fountain) and the 15C market cross stand opposite.

The **Sint Bartholomeuskerk**, built in the 15C but much altered since, has a chapel attached which is dedicated to Our Lady of the Market. Formerly a separate building, the lower part of the chapel dates from the 13C. The church contains a marble work of 1770 by Pieter Pepers, a painting of the *Martyrdom of St Bartholomew* by Gaspard de Crayer, and confessionals and a pulpit carved in the 18C.

Signs from the Markt point north to the former abbey of **Sint Adriaan** on the slope of the Oudeberg. The grounds have been converted into public gardens and a children's playground. The abbey buildings contain a **museum** where artefacts from the area and portraits of the abbots are displayed.

Ninove

The **Onze Lieve Vrouwkerk** in Ninove, 24km west of Brussels on the east border of East Flanders, is all that survives of the abbey of St Cornelius and St Cyprian. Founded in 1137, and closed by the French in 1796, its domestic buildings were demolished in 1822. The baroque church dates from 1660–1723, with a tower added in 1844. It is famous for the richness of its interior. The furnishings were carved by three outstanding 18C sculptors: Theodoor Verhaeghen, J.B. van der Haeghen and Jacques Bergé. The choir stalls date from the mid 17C.

The **Koepoort** in Vestbaan is the town's only surviving 14C gate.

Eeklo

Eeklo, 16km northwest of Ghent, is an important agricultural and textiles centre. It is the principal town of the **Meetjesland**, the land of little meadows. The 19C Flemish poet Karel Ledeganck (1805–47) was born in Eeklo. Charles V may also have been born here.

The town has an early 17C **Stadhuis** with a belfry. The **Folklore Museum** is located in Het Leen provincial park, 2km to the south of Eeklo. Its collection covers local folklore, natural history and trade (open daily from 10.00–17.00; closed Mon morning, and 12.00–14.00 at weekends).

Eeklo environs

The town of **Kaprijke**, 4km northeast of Eeklo, has an attractive 17C–18C town hall. The town of **Watervliet**, 6km north of Kaprijke, is near the Dutch border. Its 15C church was restored in 1893, when the tower was built, and again in 1973 after war damage. The altar was carved by the workshop of Lucas Faydherbe, the pulpit and other woodwork is by Hendrik Pulincx, and a 15C *Descent from the Cross* is attributed to Quinten Metsys.

LIMBURG PROVINCE

Limburg province is an attractive region of eastern Flanders with small towns and extensive areas of woodland and heath. The attractive town of Hasselt is the provincial capital. Hasselt, Tongeren and the Kempen district are dealt with in separate chapters.

Tourist information

Limburg tourist information office,

Universiteitslaan 1, Hasselt,
☎ 011.23.74.50.

Domein Bokrijk

Domein Bokrijk is a wooded country estate, near Genk and 7km northeast of Hasselt. Named after a medieval beech estate, Bokrijk belonged to the abbey of Herkenrode until 1797. It was subsequently privately owned, then purchased in 1938 by the Province of Limburg. The main attraction is the Openlucht Museum, an open-air folk museum occupying part of the estate, but there is also a large park with a rose garden, a children's adventure playground, an arboretum, and deer reserve.

Getting there

Direct trains run from Brussels to Bokrijk station, 15 minutes walk from the museum.

Eating out

The *museum* has several old Flemish taverns with shady gardens. *In den Dolphin* is a former country inn from the Veurne region, West Flanders. It offers excellent regional dishes and local beers.

Tourist information

There is a single telephone number for the park and the museum,
☎ 011.26.53.00.

Opening times

The **Openlucht Museum** is open daily Apr–Sept 10.00–18.00.
The **park** is open daily 10.00–dusk.

The **Openlucht Museum** was established in 1958 as an open-air folk museum. Expanded over the years, it now displays over 100 traditional reconstructed-farmhouses, mills, cottages, chapels, town houses and village inns. The buildings are clustered by province to evoke traditional village squares, farmyards or city streets. Many of the houses have reconstructed interiors furnished in period style. Demonstrations of traditional country crafts are staged by locals dressed in blue smocks at weekends and on holidays. A similar museum near St Hubert has farmhouses and industrial buildings from Wallonia.

Sint Truiden

The ancient town of Sint Truiden, 16km southwest of Hasselt, (Saint Trond in French) is named after the Benedictine abbot St Trudo.

Ordained by St Clodulphus of Metz, Trudo founded an abbey in c 660 on his father's estate. Ruled by the prince-bishops of Liège from the 13C, the town has a Walloon perron to symbolise its liberty, but also a Flemish belfry which serves the same role. Sint Truiden is now the principal town of the Haspengouw district (the Hesbaye in French), which is famous for its spring blossom.

Tourist information
Stadhuis, Grote Markt,
☎ 011.70.18.18.

Opening times
Begijnhof church is open from Apr–Oct Tues–Fri 10.00–12.30 and 13.30–17.00, and at weekends 13.30–17.00.
Brustemporch (old town gate) is open Easter–Sept on Sat, Sun and holidays. Guided tour (compulsory) begins at 14.00.
Festraets Studio is open Apr–Oct Tues–Sun. Demonstrations are given at 13.45, 14.45, 15.45, and 16.45.
Sint Franciscusmuseum is open Tues–Fri 10.00–12.00 and 14.00–17.00, and at weekends 14.00–17.00.

A walk in the old town
Begin on the south side of the large **Grote Markt**, where there is a fine view of the towers of Sint Truiden's three principal buildings: the former Abbey to the west, the Stadhuis in the centre and the Onze Lieve Vrouwkerk to the east. The **Stadhuis** dates from the 18C, but the attached Spanish-style **Belfry** was built in 1606 after the old belfry was blown down in a gale. The **Perron** at the foot of the belfry dates from 1361.

The first church on the site of the **Onze Lieve Vrouwkerk** was consecrated in 1058, but destroyed by fire in 1186. The present church is a Gothic building erected from 14C–16C. The tower, which was repaired many times, collapsed in 1668. It was later rebuilt in 1854 by Louis Roelandt. The church contains a reliquary of St Trudo.

The **St Trudo Abbey** became one of the great houses of the Benedictine order, but suffered much damage during the French Revolution. The 11C tower was given a new spire in the 18C. The gateway at the base dates from 1655. The main gatehouse of 1779 provides access to the principal courtyard. The abbey is now a seminary.

The story of **St Trudo** is told in a delightful carving above the main entrance to the church. Every time St Trudo attempted to put up a building, it was pulled down by an interfering woman. Reduced to despair, the saint prayed for help. His prayers were finally answered when the woman was struck down with paralysis.

Leave the Grote Markt by the Minderbroedersstraat to reach the Neo-classical Minderbroederskerk. Built for the Franciscans in 1731, its lofty roof is ingeniously supported on 50 pillars. The Sint Franciscusmuseum at no. 5 contains medieval statuary and some interesting paintings and drawings, including an etching by Rembrandt and paintings attributed to Rubens and Cranach.

The **Brustemporch** stands at the end of Luikerstraat. This is the undercroft of a gateway which once formed part of the 15C ramparts. It contains several medieval guard rooms. The **Sint Pieterskerk** on Naamsesteenweg is an impressive Romanesque building of the late 12C. It contains the tomb of Wirik, an abbot of c 1180.

The **Begijnhof** is on the north edge of town, just beyond the cattle market. Founded in 1258, it remains a peaceful enclosure surrounded by small houses dating from the 17C and 18C. The houses overlook a 13C church with a remarkable series of 38 murals on the walls and pillars dating from the 13C to the 17C.

The **Festraets Studio** nearby contains a remarkable astronomical clock built in 1937–42 by Kamiel Festraets.

St Truiden environs

The town of **Brustem**, 2km southeast of St Truiden, was the scene of a victory by Charles the Bold in 1467 during his campaign to suppress Liège. It is now the site of a military airfield.

The striking Baroque church of Onze Lieve Vrouwbasiliek at **Kortenbos**, 5km northeast of Sint Truiden, is said to have been founded by a wealthy widow who owned land which was being constantly attacked by a band of brigands. In 1636, as a deterrent, she placed a figure of the Virgin in a hollow oak tree that grew on her property. Her act of faith apparently had the desired result.

A church was built from 1641 to c 1665 to replace the simple chapel where the statue of the Virgin was kept. It contains fine Baroque furnishings and paintings by Gaspard de Crayer and A. van Diepenbeek.

The village of **Neerwinden**, c 12km southwest of St Truiden, was the scene of an important battle in 1693 when the army of the Grand Alliance under William III of England was defeated here by Marshal Luxembourg. The Jacobite and romantic Irish patriot Patrick Sarsfield, Earl of Lucan, was killed in this battle. In a second battle on this site, the Austrians defeated the French under Dumouriez in 1793.

Pepin, the founder of the Carolingian dynasty, died in **Landen**, 2km southeast of Neerwinden, in 640. Before being removed to Nivelles, his body lay beneath a hill which still bears his name.

The 15C Sint Genovevakerk in the village of **Zepperen**, 2km east of Sint Truiden, has a Romanesque tower. The interior is decorated with fascinating 15C murals depicting the Last Supper and the lives of St Christopher and St Genevieve. A mansion of 1655 near the church belonged to the provost of Sint Servaas at Maastricht, the Netherlands. This village was formerly ruled by the provost. A large castle at **Rijkel**, 2km south of Zepperen, dates from c 1600, with some later additions.

Boorgloon

The small town of Borgloon, c 10km east of Sint Truiden, (known as Looz in French), is the centre of a fruit-growing area. It was the chief town of the county of Looz in the 11C. Outside the **Stadhuis,** which dates from 1680, are the old stocks where petty criminals were punished. The **Sint Odulfuskerk**, which dates in part from the 11C, contains interesting 15C murals. The tower was built in 1406, while the nave was altered in 1900 in neo-Romanesque style. The church is named after St Odulfus, a 9C native of Brabant who helped St Frederick to convert Frisia to Christianity. His relics were apparently stolen in 1034 and taken first to London and later to Evesham abbey.

Klooster Marienhof

The Cistercian convent of Klooster Marienhof is 2km north of Borgloon at Kerniel (open Mon–Fri between 10.00–11.30 and 15.00–18.00). It contains a reliquary of St Odile, traditionally thought to be one of St Ursula's 11,000 virgins. Dating from 1292, the **reliquary** is one of the oldest examples in Belgium of painting on wood. It was seriously damaged in the 19C by a carpenter who tried to force it into a niche. The convent also has a 12C Romanesque choir stall, paintings by the 18C artist Martin Aubé and 18C church furnishings.

The town of **Herk-de-Stad**, 15km north of Sint Truiden, was the birthplace in 1872 of Pauline Jeuris, a missionary martyred in China in 1900. Beatified in 1946 as the Blessed Amandina, her life and work are remembered in a small museum.

Hendrik van Veldeke, the first Netherlands troubadour, was born in the 12C in the village of **Spalbeek**, 4km to the east. An old chapel has an unusual horseshoe-shaped 12C choir and 14C murals.

The small town of **Halen**, 4km west of Herk-de-Stad, has a pleasant square of 18C and 19C houses. A monument commemorates a victorious charge by the Belgian cavalry in August 1914. The church of **Donk**, 4km southeast of Halen, contains a 16C recumbent statue of the Virgin which is said to cure sterility.

WALLONIA

Wallonia is an attractive upland region with a culture and architecture that is heavily influenced by France. Located to the south of Brussels, this area was settled by the Wala, a Celtic tribe colonised by the Romans. The inhabitants of Wallonia speak French, though the inhabitants of the small Ostkantone (Cantons de l'Est) region have German as their mother tongue.

Wallonia is one of the oldest industrial regions of Europe. The cities prospered in the 19C due to coal mining and steelworks. These old industries have now virtually collapsed, bringing unemployment and poverty to the once booming towns of southern Belgium. The hardship is particularly severe in the areas around Mons, Charleroi and Liège. Many of the 19C relics of the industrial past have recently been turned into impressive museums or cultural centres.

The economic recovery is now in the hands of the regional government of Wallonia. Its capital is Namur, a pleasant if unassuming town on the River Meuse. The region of Wallonia comprises the provinces of Hainaut, Walloon Brabant, Namur, Liège and Luxembourg.

Wallonia's main tourist destination is **Waterloo** battlefield, just south of Brussels. The centre of the battlefield is occupied by a cluster of museums, cafés and souvenir shops. Much of the rest of the battlefield has remained virtually unchanged since the armies clashed in 1815. The area around Waterloo is thick with mementoes of the battle, including old inns, monuments and museums.

The **old cities** of Wallonia have suffered greatly from war and industrialisation. Yet they still possess impressive buildings, excellent museums and fine restaurants. The main problem the tourist faces is a severe lack of good hotels in Liège, Namur and Mons. It is often much easier to find an attractive country hotel outside an old town or in the nearby Ardennes.

Deep in the Meuse valley, **Liège** is an interesting and appealing city. Its attractions, admittedly, require some effort to discover, but the more adventurous tourist can discover some remarkable churches, paintings and sculpture. The town of **Mons** also bears industrial scars, yet its old centre has some pleasing buildings and interesting museums. The Battle of Mons in 1914 is recalled by an war museum and several monuments outside the town. Charleroi is surrounded by a grim industrial landscape, yet the town itself is a cultured place, with an excellent art gallery and photography museum.

Namur occupies a spectacular location at the confluence of two rivers. It has an interesting old centre with many good restaurants. The ancient town of **Tournai** was once a Roman staging post and later capital of the Franks. It has one of the finest cathedrals in Europe and a good art gallery.

Most tourists are drawn by the rivers and forests of the **Ardennes**, which lie to the south of the River Meuse. Known to the Romans as Arduenna Silva, the Ardennes covers much of the provinces of Namur, Liège, and Luxembourg. The landscape consists of pine forests, wild moors and winding river valleys. The region is popular for hiking, kayaking, hunting and camping. Local tourist offices often have guides to walking trails in the area.

The Wild Boar of the Ardennes

The nobleman William de la Marck (1446–85) became known as the Wild Boar of the Ardennes after he was banished from Liège for murdering the bishop's secretary. Occupying strongholds at a number of places in the Ardennes including Amblève, Franchimont, Aigremont and Logne, he became a notorious robber baron. He captured Liège and murdered the bishop in 1482. The new bishop invited him to a feast, seized him and had him executed.

The Meuse Valley links the old towns of Dinant, Namur, Huy and Liège. The stretch between the French frontier and Namur is the most appealing, with riverside towns, craggy cliffs and elegant châteaux. The stretch from Namur to Liège is of more interest for its industrial archaeology, though the town of Huy is worth a stop. Boats run in the summer from Namur and Dinant. Kayaking down the Lesse near Dinant is popular in the summer.

The German-speaking Ostkantone is an attractive upland region of dense forests, wild moors, lakes and reservoirs. The Hohes Venn (Hautes Fagnes) is a bleak upland moor that rises to the Signal de Botrange at 694m, the highest spot in Belgium. Down in the valleys, the towns of Eupen, Malmédy, and St Vith are lively places.

The old watering town of **Spa** was a favourite resort of the 18C aristocracy. It has declined somewhat in recent years, yet still has grand buildings and attractive woodland walks.

Much of the eastern Ardennes was devastated in 1944 during the fierce Battle of the Ardennes. Several towns that bore the brunt of the fighting have museums, memorials and other relics. The main places of interest to understand the battle are at Bastogne and La Roche-en-Ardenne.

The deep **Semois Valley** follows a winding route along the French frontier. The most beautiful stretches are around the historic fortress town of Bouillon and farther east near Florenville. The winding **Ourthe Valley** passes attractive towns such as La Roche-en-Ardenne and Durbuy.

Tourists have been fascinated since the 19C by the many grottoes in the Ardennes. Several of these **cave complexes** were occupied in prehistoric times. The largest and most popular complex is at Han-sur-Lesse, where the guided tour includes an underground boat trip. Other impressive grottoes are located at Remouchamps, Goyet, Rochefort and Dinant.

The Four Sons of Aymon

The legendary Quatre Fils Aymon have links with several Ardennes castles. Renaud, Guichard, Alard and Richard were the sons of Aymon of Dordogne, a vassal of Charlemagne. The emperor knighted the brothers and gave them the fabulous horse **Bayard**, which could carry all four of them at the same time. They later fell out of favour and were outlawed. Their romantic adventures and perilous feats while being pursued by the emperor are chronicled in a 13C poem, one of the most popular romances of the Charlemagne cycle. William Caxton printed *The Foure Sonnes of Aymon* in English. The brothers also feature in poems by Tasso, Boiardo and Ariosto.

The upland region north of the Meuse contains some attractive landscape. Much of Hainaut and Brabant-Wallon province is taken up by a rolling, placid, fertile landscape which is devoted to agriculture. The Botte du Hainaut, south of Chimay, is a sparsely populated, wooded enclave of great charm. Elsewhere in Wallonia, there are numerous old castles and great abbeys in isolated locations.

The cities of Wallonia

LIÈGE

The ancient city of Liège strikes many visitors as a rather grim industrial town. 'The great blast furnaces of Liège rose along the line like ancient castles burning in a border raid,' Graham Green wrote. Yet the ancient heart of Liège has a surprisingly southern spirit, a rambling provincial charm and even a hint of Parisian elegance. Spread along the valley of the Meuse, this town of just under 200,000 inhabitants offers visitors several outstanding museums, ancient Romanesque churches and an elegant shopping district. The town is the capital of Liège province. It is named Luik in Dutch and Lüttich in German.

Though the area around Liège is heavily industrialised, much of the rest of the province is pleasantly rural. The regions of the province are covered in the Liège environs section below, and in the chapters on Spa and the Eastern Cantons, the Meuse Valley, Vesdre Valley and Ourthe Valley.

Practical information

Getting there
The main railway station is Gare des Guillemins, 2km south of the centre. High-speed *Thalys* trains run from Brussels, Paris and Cologne to Guillemins station.

 Where to stay
££ *Bedford*, Quai St Léonard 36, ☎ 04.228.81.11, is an elegant hotel in a former 17C convent overlooking the Meuse.
£ *Simenon*, Boulevard de l'Est 16, ☎ 04.342.86.90, is an inexpensive hotel in an Art Nouveau town house in the Outremeuse district. The bedroom interiors are inspired by the crime novels of Georges Simenon.

 Eating out
Restaurants
Many of Liège's most popular restaurants are found in the lively Carré quarter.
££ *Au Mamé Vî Cou*, Rue de la Wache 9, ☎ 04.23.71.81, a typical Liège establishment, is a handsome and convivial restaurant in the medieval quarter near the Eglise Saint Denis. It serves local specialities such as white sausage (*boudin*) and rabbit in prunes.
£ *Duc d'Anjou*, Rue Guillemins 127, ☎ 04.252.28.58, is an outstanding

Belgian brasserie close to the station which is open long hours every day.

Cafés

A Pilori, Place du Marché 5, is a rambling old tavern with oak beams and huge fireplaces.

Taverne Saint Paul, Rue Saint Paul 8, is a handsome café dating from 1881. It occupies a former coaching inn where Trotsky once stayed.

Tourist information

The main tourist office is located in a handsome 17C building at En Féronstrée 92, near Place Saint Lambert, ☎ 04.221.92.21. The tourist office publishes a useful printed list of official opening hours of museums and churches. It also provide interesting free folders on Georges Simenon, Historic Liège, Churches and Baptismal Fonts. The Province of Liège tourist office is at Boulevard de la Sauvenière 77, Liège, ☎ 04.232.65.10.

Banks and post office

BBL, Boulevard Avroy 136.
Main **post office** is on Rue de la Régence 61.

Opening times
Museums

Most museums, except the Musée Curtius, and the Musée de Zoologie, are closed on Mondays, and also on 1 January, 1 May, 8 May, 1–2 November, 11 November, 15 November, 24–26 December and 31 December.

Musée de la Vie Wallonne (museum of local life), Cour des Mineurs, is open Tues–Sat 10.00–17.00, Sun 10.00–16.00.

Musée d'Art Religieux et Mosan (religious art), Rue Mère-Dieu, is open Tues–Sat 11.00–18.00, Sun 11.00–16.00.

Musée de l'Art Wallon (Walloon art), Rue St Georges, and the **Musée d'Art Moderne**, Parc de la Boverie, are open Tues–Sat 13.00–18.00, Sun 11.00–16.30.

Musée d'Ansembourg (18C house with period furnishings), En Féronstrée 114, is open Tues–Sun 13.00–18.00.

Musée Curtius (archaelogy and decorative arts), Quai de Maestricht 13, is open Mon and Wed–Sat 10.00–13.00 and 14.00–17.00, Sun 10.00–13.00.

Musée d'Armes (museum of weapons), Quai de Maestricht 8, is open Tues–Sat 10.00–13.00 and 14.00–17.00, Sun 10.00–13.00.

Musée de Zoologie et Aquarium Quai van Beneden, is open Mon–Fri 10.00–12.30 and 13.30–17.00, weekends 10.30–12.30 and 14.00–18.00.

Musée de la Métallurgie (iron and coal industries), Boulevard R. Poincaré 17, is open Mon–Fri 9.00–17.00, and weekends 14.00–18.00. Closed weekends Nov–mid-March.

Maison Grétry is open Tues and Fri 14.00–16.00, and on Sat 10.00–12.00.

Musée Tchantchès (marionettes), Rue Surlet 56, is open Tues and Thur 14.00–16.00. It is closed in July.

Churches

Cathédrale Saint-Paul, Rue Saint Paul, is open daily 08.00–12.00 and 14.00–17.15.

Eglise Saint-Barthélemy is open Mon–Sat 10.00–12.00 and14.00–17.00, Sun 14.00–17.00.

Eglise Saint Jacques Rue Saint Rémy, is open daily in the summer 10.00–12.00 and 14.00–18.00, and daily in the winter 08.00–12.00.

History

Liège probably derives its name from the Légie brook, a tributary of the Meuse that now runs underground. The town owes its origin to a chapel built here in 558 by St Monulphus, Bishop of Maastricht. A later Bishop of Maastricht, St Lambert, was murdered in this area in 705, traditionally because he had accused Pepin of Herstal of incest. His successor, St Hubert, built a basilica in his memory and shortly afterwards, in 720, moved his see to Liège. For more than 1000 years, Liège was a **centre of ecclesiastical power**, occupying a commanding political and geographical position between the spheres of influence of France, the Netherlands and the Holy Roman Empire.

Already a centre of learning in the 9C, Liège enjoyed a golden age under the vigorous **Bishop Notger**, who was appointed in 972. Having raised the see to a position of real territorial power, he was nominated Prince-Bishop by Otto I. This title was passed on to his successors for almost 800 years. Under Bishop Notger, Liège was fortified and trade encouraged.

The first bridge across the Meuse was built soon after his death in 1008. The present Pont des Arches is the seventh bridge to cross at this spot. The history of Liège is rife with quarrels between prince-bishops, municipal authorities, wealthy merchants, landed gentry and tradespeople. It was only the threat of invasion that brought an end to the squabbles, as in 1213, when the Liégeois defeated Duke Henry II of Brabant, and again in 1343 when the people supported Bishop Adolphe de la Marck against Brabant. In return they demanded and were granted the representative council of XXII.

Coal mines were already being exploited in the hills around Liège in the 12C. This led to the development of one of Europe's oldest metallurgical industries. Social conditions improved, but the rise of the **dukes of Burgundy** proved fatal to the development of civil liberty in Liège. John the Fearless crushed the Liégeois at Othée in 1408 and Philip the Good defeated them again at Montenaken in 1465. After winning the battle of Brustem in 1468, Charles the Bold sacked the city, annulled civil liberties, and carried off the Perron to Bruges. Nine years later, Mary of Burgundy restored the city's privileges; over the next three centuries the principality preserved a neutral stance in the wars between France and the Habsburg Empire.

William de la Marck, the '**Wild Boar of the Ardennes**', captured and killed Bishop Louis de Bourbon in 1482. His successor, Bishop Jean de Hornes, invited William to a feast, seized him and sent him to Maastricht for execution. The story provided Sir Walter Scott with the inspiration for *Quentin Durward*.

Liège maintained its neutrality during the religious wars. The citadel was stormed by Marlborough in 1702, while Dumouriez captured Liège for revolutionary France in 1794, expelling the last prince-bishop, Antoine de Méan, and destroying the cathedral.

Liège occupied a vital strategic position at the outbreak of the **First World War**, guarding the gap between the neutral Netherlands and the Ardennes. Commanded by General Leman, the city's ring of 19C fortresses put up a stubborn resistance from 5–14 August. During the German occupation, the workers employed in the city's small-arms factories refused to produce weapons for the enemy. The town was badly damaged at the end of the **Second World War**, when the bridges were blown up by the retreating Germans and the city was hit by more than 1500 flying-bombs and rockets.

The completion in 1939 of the **Albert Canal**, linking Liège and the Meuse to Antwerp and the Scheldt, helped Liège to develop into the third largest inland port in western Europe (after Paris and Duisburg). The port installations stretch through the city from Herstal in the northeast suburbs to Chokier in the southwest suburbs. The main port area is downstream at Monsin, where a memorial to King Albert (incorporating a 45m tower and a 14m statue of the king) marks the beginning of the Albert Canal. Hit by economic decline after the Second World War, the town is currently struggling to rebuild its economy.

Born in Liège

Liège was famous in the 14C for its Song School which supplied most of the singers for the refounded Sistine Chapel. Charlotte, the only daughter of Prince Charles Stewart, the Young Pretender, was born in Liège in 1753. Several 18C and 19C musicians were born here, including André Grétry, César Franck and the violinist Eugène Ysaye. The writer Georges Simenon was also a native of Liège.

1 • The historic quarter

Begin on the busy **Place Saint Lambert**, which was being redeveloped at the time of writing after almost 20 years of heated debate on its future.

A vanished cathedral

Excavations have shown that mesolithic people lived here at least 6000 years ago, as did their neolithic successors. Traces of a Gallo-Roman villa have been uncovered. Following the adoption of Christianity, a chapel was built on this site, perhaps by St Lambert. This was followed by a sanctuary built by St Hubert for St Lambert's relics. Bishop Notger then constructed a 10C cathedral which burned down in 1185. From the 13C to the 18C, the great Gothic Cathedral of St Lambert covered most of the area in front of the palace of the prince-bishops. Destroyed in 1794 as a symbol of the old and discredited order, the cathedral ruins served as a building quarry for 30 years.

The imposing **Palais des Princes-Evêques** (Palace of the Prince-Bishops) stands on the north side of Place Saint Lambert.

A Renaissance palace

Bishop Notger's original building was burned in 1505 and the palace was rebuilt from 1526–1533 by Bishop Erard de la Marck in Late Gothic style. The new building was damaged by another serious fire and the south façade was reconstructed in 1737. The entire building was restored from 1848–1883 and a west wing added for the provincial government. The two 16C court yards can be entered through the portal at no. 18. The Renaissance columns in the first courtyard are carved with unusual grotesques in various styles. The second, smaller courtyard is reached by a passage off the first courtyard. This rather secret courtyard has grass and a fountain. A curious collection of sculpture and architectural fragments forms the Galerie Lapidaire. The buildings are now occupied by law courts labelled in quaint Gothic lettering.

The short Rue du Bex leads from Place Saint Lambert to the **Place du Marché**. The **Hôtel de Ville** on the south side was built in 1718. The building is sometimes referred to as 'La Violette' because the municipal authorities met in the 13C in a house near here bearing that name. The present building contains statues by Jean del Cour and rich 18C furnishings.

Perron

Perrons are often found on the main square of towns in Liège province. Symbols of civic independence, they served as meeting places and venues for reading proclamations and carrying out punishments. The Perron in Liège has stood in the centre of the Place du Marché since 1697. It replaces an older Perron destroyed in a storm. The group of the Three Graces was carved by Jean del Cour.

The domed **Bourse** on the north side of the square was formerly a church of 1722 dedicated to St Andrew. The **Fontaine de la Tradition** at the east end of the square was built in 1719. It has an armorial door of 1719 and bronze reliefs depicting Liège folklore characters added in 1930.

Turn left at the end of the Place du Marché, following the Rue des Mineurs to reach the Cour des Mineurs. A Franciscan friary on this site was destroyed by a flying bomb in 1945. Painstakingly reconstructed, the building is now occupied by the delightful **Musée de la Vie Wallonne**, open Tues–Sat 10.00–17.00, and Sun 10.00–16.00. This museum of local Walloon life has furnished interiors, curious superstitious relics, old stereoscopic photographs of Walloon scenes and a collection of wooden marionettes.

The **Musée d'Art Religieux et Mosan**, open Tues–Sat 11.00–18.00, and Sun 11.00–16.00, occupies a handsome building in the Rue Mère-Dieu, which runs below the raised Cour des Mineurs. This rather forgotten museum has an extensive collection of Mosan religious art, including a beautiful painting of c 1475 known as the *Virgin with the Donor and St Mary Magdalene*. Attributed to the Master of St Gudule, it includes a captivating view through a window to a medieval garden and a distant city.

Montagne de Bueren

A flight of steps known as the Montagne de Bueren was named after a local hero who defended Liège in 1468 against Charles the Bold's army. No two guidebooks agree on the number of steps; the previous edition of this book had 407 steps, but the tourist office claims 373 and the present author counted 571. The steps, however many in number, lead to the former Citadel, the site of which is now occupied by a hospital, public park and war memorial.

A more interesting ascent can be made by turning left at the foot of the steps up the Impasse des Ursulines, passing the former Béguinage du Saint-Esprit on the right, built in Mosan Renaissance style. A gate (open 09.00–18.00) gives access to the Sentier des Coteaux, a narrow flight of steps that leads to a grassy terrace with a splendid view of the old town. Steps descend from the terrace to an old 12C tower known as the **Tour des Vieux Joncs**. You then continue upwards by the Rue du Péry to reach the summit. The descent can be made by the Montagne de Bueren.

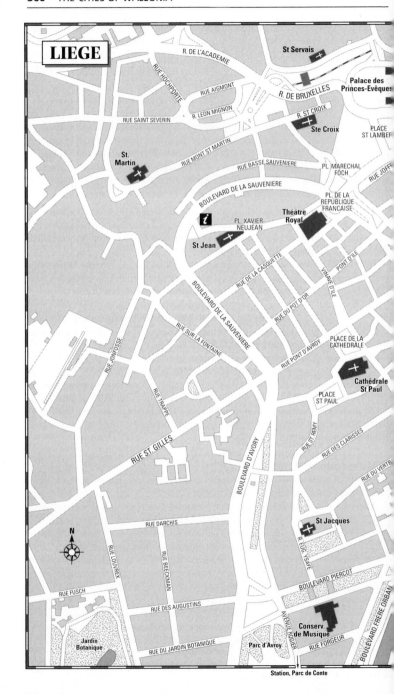

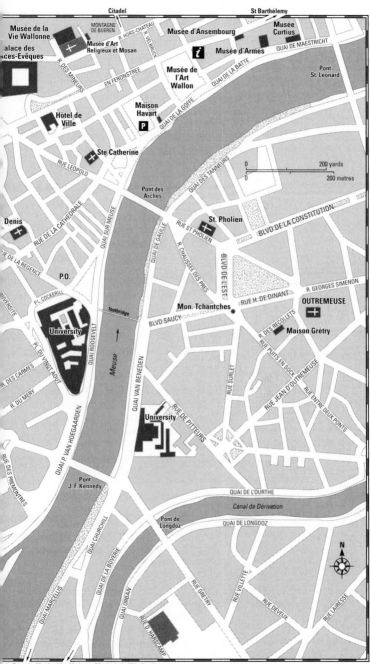

Citadel
St Barthélemy

Musée de la
Vie Wallonne

Musée
Curtius

MONTAGNE
DE BUEREN

R. HORS-CHATEAU
R. VIELBRUCK

Musée d'Ansembourg

alace des
ces-Evêques

Musée d'Art
Religieux et Mosan

i
Musée d'Armes

QUAI DE MAESTRICHT

R. DES MINEURS

EN FERONSTREE

Musée de
l'Art
Wallon

QUAI DE LA BATTE

Pont
St. Leonard

Hôtel de
Ville

Maison
Havart

P

QUAI DE LA GOFFE

Ste Catherine

RUE LEOPOLD

Pont des
Arches

QUAI DES TANNEURS

0   200 yards
0   200 metres

Denis

RUE DE LA CATHEDRALE

RUE ST PHOLIEN

St. Pholien

BLVD. DE LA CONSTITUTION

QUAI SUR MEUSE

QUAI DE GAULLE

R. CHAUSSEE DES PRES

BLVD. DE L'EST

JE DE LA REGENCE

P.O.

P.L. COCKERILL

footbridge

Mon. Tchantches

RUE H. DE DINANT

R. GEORGES SIMENON

OUTREMEUSE

University

BLVD. SAUCY

R. DES RECOLLETS

Maison Grétry

Meuse

QUAI VAN BENEDEN

QUAI ROOSEVELT

RUE SURLET

RUE PUITS EN SOCK

RUE JEAN D'OUTREMEUSE

RUE ENTRE DEUX PONTS

N. DES CARMES

R. DU MERY

University

RUE DE PITTEURS

RUE DES PREMONTRES

QUAI P. VAN HOEGAARDEN

Pont
J. F. Kennedy

QUAI DE L'OURTHE

Canal de Dérivation

Pont de
Longdoz

QUAI DE LONGDOZ

QUAI CHURCHILL

N

QUAI MARCELLIS

QUAI DE LA BOVERIE

QUAI ORBAN

RUE DE HAISCAMP

RUE GRETRY

RUE VILLETTE

RUE DEVEUX

RUE LAIRESSE

Turn left at the foot of the steps along the narrow **Rue Hors-Château**, where a number of old alleys and courts survive, such as the picturesque *Impasse d'Ange* next to **no. 43** and the vaulted *Impasse de la Vignette* next to **no. 79**. The modest houses in these alleys were once occupied by servants employed in the mansions on Hors-Château.

A sensitive urban restoration was carried out by Charles Vandenhove in the 1970s at **nos 108–114**, where a row of old Mosan Renaissance houses was carefully restored. The modern Ionic columns at no. 114 mark the entrance to a secret square by Vandehove called **Place de Tikal**.

Cross the Place de Tikal and emerge on En Féronstrée (Ironworkers Street). Settled since the 10C, this neighbourhood is considered the historic heart of Liège. The **tourist office** occupies a traditional Mosan Renaissance house at no. 92. A gate at **nos 94–96** leads into a seductive 18C courtyard.

The **Musée d'Ansembourg** occupies the handsome mansion at no. 114, open Tues–Sun 13.00–18.00. Built between 1735–1741 for a banker, it retains sumptuous rooms furnished in their original 18C décor. This provides a fitting setting for a collection of fine furniture, chandeliers, porcelain, tapestries, Mechelen leather, Delft and Liège tiles. Concerts are occasionally given in the 18C music room.

The impressive **Eglise Saint Barthélemy**, open Mon–Sat 10.00–12.00 and 14.00–17.00, and Sun 14.00–17.00 (entry charge), stands in a square on the left. The exterior retains its austere 12C Romanesque appearance, but the interior, apart from the narthex, was completely changed at the beginning of the 18C.

A Romanesque font

The church has a splendid bronze **font** of 1118 attributed to Renier de Huy. This was commissioned by Hellin, abbot of Notre Dame aux Fonts, for his church, which at the time was the only church in Liège where baptisms were authorised. The church was demolished by the French revolutionaries, but the font was hidden from them. Following the conclusion of the concordat of 1804 between the Vatican and France, it was placed in its present position. Resting on ten half-figures of oxen, it is decorated in high relief with baptismal groups. It is considered one of the seven wonders of Belgium.

On leaving the church, go down Rue St Barthélemy and turn left along En Féronstrée to reach the narrow Rue des Aveugles, which leads down to the **River Meuse**.

Musée Curtius

A right turn along the Quai de Maestricht leads to the Musée Curtius at no 13, open Mon and Wed–Sat 10.00–13.00 and 14.00–17.00, on Sun 10.00–13.00. This interesting museum occupies a splendid Mosan Renaissance mansion with a distinctive high-pitched roof and tower. The mansion was built c 1600 for the wealthy merchant Jean de Corte, who adopted the Latin name Curtius.

Opened in 1909, the museum displays a fascinating and diverse collection of objects covering regional archaeology, prehistory, Belgo-Roman and Frankish history, numismatics, Mosan art from the 11C to the beginning of the 13C, medieval decorative art, furniture from 16C–18C, tapestries, miniatures, European ceramics from 16C–19C, and a collection of funerary monuments from the Middle Ages to the end of the 18C.

The **archaeological section** displays several small objects which were found in the Place Saint Lambert. It also has Roman glass, pottery, bronze and terra-cotta figurines, enamelled fibulae, Roman and Frankish ornaments from tombs in the Hesbaye district, and Gallo-Roman bronzes from the Liège suburb of Angleur.

The **medieval collection** includes an English alabaster statue of the Virgin of c 1400, a 16C *Pietà* from Eben-Emael, 15C German carved wooden groups of the *Death of the Virgin* and the *Last Supper*, Byzantine ivories and icons, the 11C or 12C *Arenberg Evangelistery*, statues of *St Anne* and the *Virgin and Child*, sculpture from the destroyed cathedral of St Lambert, a *Sedes Sapientiae* from Xhoris, Bishop Notger's *Evangelistery*, a 10C manuscript with a binding of ivory, Mosan enamels of c 1170, the *Virgin* of Dom Rupert, and an unusual profane work depicting the *Mystery of Apollo*.

Other exhibits of interest are 17C and 18C Liège woodwork and tapestries, the **Moxhon Collection** of paintings and 18C silver, an astonishing late 18C six-face clock by Hubert Sarton of Liège, weapons, coins, medals, seals, and a series of old plans of Liège which clearly show the Maison Curtius. The impressive **Renaissance chimneypieces** are decorated with the arms of Bishop Erard de la Marck. Reliefs in the museum courtyard show three earlier versions of the Pont des Arches.

The **Musée du Verre** is entered from the courtyard. This rich collection of glass includes examples of Roman, Byzantine and Islamic specimens, Venetian ware and modern Liège glass. The collection of Art Deco and Art Nouveau glass is particularly impressive.

The **Musée d'Armes** is a few doors down at no 8, open Tues–Sat 10.00–13.00 and 14.00–17.00, on Sun 10.00–13.00. This outstanding collection of weapons occupies a mansion of c 1775 which served as the French prefecture of the Ourthe from 1800–1814, and then as the seat of the Dutch governor from 1815 to 1830. Napoleon stayed here in 1803 and again in 1811. His visits are commemorated by a portrait by Ingres. Blücher was another famous guest in this mansion.

Founded in 1885, the museum boasts that it owns the most **complete collection of small-arms** in Europe. It has more than 12,000 pieces, of which only a small proportion are on display. The weapons made for the nobility are particularly ornate.

A tile-plaque on the wall of one of the houses on the Quai de Maestricht recalls that diligences left from here in 1750 for Brussels, Antwerp, Verviers, Germany, Switzerland and Italy.

Marché Dominical de la Batte

A lively market takes place every Sunday morning on the Meuse waterfront along the length of the Quai de Maestricht, Quai de la Batte and Quai de la Goffe. Visitors come from as far afield as Maastricht and Aachen to wander past stalls selling food, antiques, pets, cheap jewellery, Ardennes cheeses, clothes, and household gadgets. This area of Liège was settled by cloth workers from the 12C or 13C, though until the early 16C the waterfront was little more than a waterlogged meadow. The area began to improve in the mid 16C when a trading quay was built and commercial activity started to pick up. The cattle market moved here in 1561, followed by a vegetable market and a horse market. The three quays were known collectively as la Batte (local Walloon dialect for quay) until 1863. The area has long been famous for its strolling players, quacks, hawkers and other colourful characters.

Turn right up Rue St Georges, where the medieval scale is disrupted by the modern Îlot St-George. The Musée de l'Art Wallon is entered from the elevated square on the left.

Musée de l'Art Wallon

This interesting modern museum of Walloon art displays paintings on bare concrete and painted wood walls. It is open Tues–Sat 13.00–18.00, and Sun 11.00–16.30. The adjoining Salle Saint Georges is used for special exhibitions.

Begin on the **fourth floor**, which looks out on a hidden roof garden. This level is devoted to 16C artists such as Joachim Patinir and Henri met de Bles, whose landscapes were inspired by the Meuse valley north of Dinant. There are also several works by Lambert Lombard, including a *Self Portrait*.

Descend by a spiral route past two plaster casts of statues carved by **Jean del Cour** for the tomb of Bishop Allamont in Ghent Cathedral. There are also some curious 18C views of Liège factories by Léonard Defrance. The realist **Constantin Meunier** painted a dramatic view of the *Blast Furnaces at Ougrée* in 1880 while the grandiose ambitions of **Antoine Wiertz** are reflected in his enormous painting of *The Greeks and the Trojans Fighting over the Body of Patroclus*, an early work painted in Rome in 1836. There are also some views of the industrial landscape around Charleroi by Pierre Paulus and a curious work by Anto Carte of the *Archers of St Sebastian*, set as a modern Belgian scene.

The museum has several Surrealist works by **Paul Delvaux**, including a painting called *The Man in the Street* of 1940 which shows a businessman in a bowler hat strolling unaware past two nudes. The collection also includes Magritte's *The Forest*, and Marcel Marien's playful *The Haunted House* which features a mock Belgian front door.

Back on the waterfront, the route passes the largely wooden façade of the 16C **Maison Havart** on the Quai de la Goffe. The nearby **Vieille Boucherie**, set back from the river, was built as the meat market in 1545.

Turn right up the Rue de la Cité to reach the **Pont des Arches**, which was opened in 1947 on the site of a bridge destroyed in the Second World War.

The Pont des Arches

Seven successive bridges have crossed the Meuse at this spot, the oldest completed in 1026. The name recalls the seven arches of the early bridges. It is thought that the medieval Pont des Arches appears in the background of Jan van Eyck's *Virgin with Chancellor Rolin* (now in the Louvre in Paris). Reliefs showing the earlier bridges can be seen at the Musée Curtius. The statues on the present bridge represent resistance to invaders (upstream, right bank), Liège's struggle against the Burgundians (upstream, left bank), the revolutionary spirit of 1789 and 1830 (downstream, right bank), and the emergence of Liège as a regional power at the time of Bishop Notger (downstream, left bank).

2 • The Cathedral quarter

The Cathedral district is an attractive area to explore on foot, with cobbled pedestrian streets, elegant small shops and glass-roofed arcades. The district is enclosed by the Meuse and an arc of boulevards (de la Sauvenière and d'Avroy) which follow the course of a former branch of the river. Several old plans of Liège in the Musée Curtius show the development of this quarter.

Begin on **Place Saint Lambert** and walk down Rue Léopold, where a plaque on **no. 24** marks the house where the novelist Georges Simenon was born in 1905. The domed Eglise Sainte Catherine on the left was rebuilt in 1691 in French Baroque style.

A right turn along Rue de la Cathédrale leads to the mysterious **Eglise Saint Denis**. Dedicated to the first bishop of Paris, this was the second church founded in Liège by Bishop Notger in the 10C. It looks very curious indeed from the outside, with its rugged 10C Westwork and soaring 15C apse. Enter the church from the Rue de la Cathédrale through an 18C cloister. The interior is a curious mixture of styles, with a Romanesque Westwork, a pale yellow Baroque nave and a lofty Gothic apse. An ornate early 16C **Brabant retable** is carved with five scenes from the life of St Denis. Several paintings by Lambert Lombard are also devoted to the saint. The composer André Grétry sang here as a choirboy. You can leave by a door leading out on the shady Place St Denis.

Leave the square by the lane to the west and turn left along Rue de la Régence to reach the **Post Office**, a curious building constructed near the river in 1901 in 16C Gothic style. The building opposite belongs to **Liège University**, which was established in 1817 by King William I. Built from 1820–1824, it incorporates part of the former Jesuit church. Cross the river by the Passerelle (a footbridge) and turn right along the Quai van Beneden, to the **Musée de Zoologie** which has a good aquarium. It is open Mon–Fri 10.00–12.30 and 13.30–17.00, and weekends 10.30–12.30 and 14.00–18.00.

Crossing back to the left bank by the Pont J.F. Kennedy, the walk passes the **Maison de la Culture Chiroux**, a curious modern rotunda containing the public library. Turn right along the attractive Rue Saint Paul to reach the **Cathédrale Saint Paul**. It is possible to avoid the crowds by turning left down Rue Bonne Fortune and entering by the door at no. 6, which leads into the cloister. The cathedral is open daily 08.00–12.00 and 14.00–17.15.

History of the Cathedral

Originally a parish church, Saint Paul was elevated to a Cathedral in 1801 to replace the Cathédrale Saint Lambert torn down in 1794 by French revolutionaries. The first church on this site, founded in 971, was demolished in the 13C. The present Gothic edifice was built between the 13C and the 19C. The apse, the lower part of the tower and the aisleless choir are 14C, while the 13C nave and 15C aisles were rebuilt at the beginning of the 16C. The upper part of the tower was completed with masonry salvaged from the ruins of Saint Lambert in the 19C. The cathedral has several sculptures by Jean del Cour. The inside roof is painted with arabesques of 1570, which are all that 19C restorers left of the original decoration.

The **Treasury** in the 15C cloisters is entered from the south transept. It has a doorway incorporating early 13C wrought iron. Its treasures include a silver-gilt reliquary of 1505 containing the skull of St Lambert, a 10C Byzantine painting of the *Virgin* and a 9C book of the *Gospels* bound with an ivory plaque in high relief.

The north door leads out onto Place de la Cathédrale, formerly the Place Roi Albert, where you see the **Fontaine de la Vierge** of 1695 by Jean del Cour. The street Vinâve d'Ile leads from here into the lively **Carré** quarter, where there are shops selling Antwerp fashions, elaborate floral bouquets and cooking equipment. The Passage Lemonnier, an elegant 19C arcade, runs to the right off Vinâve d'Ile. Turn left beyond the arcade along the Rue du Pot d'Or and left again down Rue d'Amay, where the Mosan Renaissance mansion at **no. 10** dates from c 1520. The interior, now occupied by a tavern, contains a splendid 17C fireplace decorated with Delft tiles.

Return to the Cathedral by the Rue Pont d'Avroy and turn right into the pleasant little Place Saint Paul, to see the **Monument Jean del Cour**, erected in 1911 in memory of the sculptor who produced the memorial to Bishop Allamont in Ghent cathedral and the Fontaine de la Vièrge in Liège. He died in Liège in 1707.

Now follow the winding Rue Saint Rémy, glancing at the hidden **Cour St Rémy** at no. 10, where several 18C houses were recently restored including one in the corner with a tablet dated 1761. The street leads to the **Eglise Saint Jacques**, open daily in the summer 10.00–12.00 and 14.00–18.00, and daily in the winter 08.00–12.00.

History of St Jacques

The church formerly belonged to a Benedictine abbey. Being independent of the bishops' jurisdiction, the abbey was charged with guarding the town's charters and administering the burgomasters' oath of office. The abbey was closed c 1750 at the request of its own monks.

Considered by many the most beautiful church in Liège, Saint Jacques combines several styles. It has a Romanesque façade of 1170, which lost both its towers. One was struck by lightning and the other was demolished. The stone columns change colour at window level: the work was begun in the 15C but halted in 1421, and subsequently resumed in Flamboyant Gothic style from 1518 to 1538 using a different type of stone.

The Renaissance north portal was designed in 1558 by Lambert Lombard of Liège. It leads into a Gothic vestibule with a *Coronation of the Virgin* of 1380 above the far door. The 15C vaulted rib roof is very elaborate. The stalls are carved with curious 14C grotesques, while the rood-screen dates from 1600. A stair provides access to the Burgomasters' Gallery where the oath of office was administered.

The Rue du Vertbois leads towards the river, past the ochre Baroque buildings of a former hospice for incurables and penitent girls at **no. 13**. Established in 1701, the institution was recently restored and is now occupied by the economic department of the Walloon government. Then turn right down the Rue des Premontrés to reach the **Evêché** (Bishop's Palace), which has an impressive 18C Baroque church designed by Barthélemy Digneffe (not open). Round the corner is the Boulevard Piercot, where a formal garden is dotted with the busts of musicians. The building on the left is the **Conservatoire de Musique**, built in 1881 and containing a monument of 1922 to César Franck.

Continue to the end of the garden to reach the **Parc d'Avroy**, a romantic 19C park with an equestrian statue of *Charlemagne* of 1868 by Louis Jehotte and bronze reproductions of antique sculptures including the Borghese *Gladiator* and *The Faun and the Child* (both from the Louvre), the *Wrestlers* and *Perseus holding up the head of Medusa* (both from Florence), and the *Death of Laocoön and his Children* (from the Vatican).

Turning left in the park, and continue to the **Monument National à la Résistance**, designed by P. Etienne and L. Dupont and unveiled in 1955. The figures on the left represent armed resistance, while those to the right symbolise intellectual resistance.

Cross the Avenue Rogier to reach the **Terrasses**, a formal garden containing a popular sculpture of the *Bull Tamer* by Léon Mignon. A huge, nude male figure is shown bringing a struggling bull to its knees. The Liégeois call the group *Li Tôore*, the bull, and generations of local students have turned their appreciation of its rampant virility into a bawdy cult. The traditional call *Av vèyou l'Tôre?* (Have you seen the bull?) has long been a familiar rallying cry in the city.

Now cross the Meuse by the Pont Albert I and turn right to reach the **Parc de la Boverie**, a romantic park laid out for the 1905 Liège exhibition. Continue past the Palais des Congrès of 1958 to reach the **Musée d'Art Moderne**, which occupies a Neo-classical building from the 1905 exhibition. The museum is open Tues–Sat 13.00–18.00, and Sun 11.00–16.30 and contains a small, but interesting collection of 20C art, including works by Kokoschka, Picasso and Ensor. Many of the works were removed from German art galleries in 1938 after Hitler pronounced them 'degenerate'. Put on sale in Switzerland to raise money for the Nazis, they were bought by a group of Liège collectors.

Go back through the park and turn right across the Pont des Vennes, to the **Musée de la Métallurgie** at Boulevard R. Poincaré 17, open Mon–Fri 9.00–17.00, and weekends (mid-March–Oct) 14.00–18.00. This unusual museum devoted to the iron and coal industries contains a 17C Walloon forge with a waterwheel which once worked the enormous bellows. The museum owns a magnificent display of ironwork, including some elaborately patterned and illustrated firebacks, one of which dates from 1584. The collection also includes models, locks and keys (including some from the Roman, Merovingian and Carolingian periods), and several interesting paintings of industrial scenes.

3 • The western slopes

This walk covers the interesting old quarter west of Place St Lambert. Begin at the **Place de la République Française**, where the **Théâtre Royal** stands on the site of a Dominican convent. The theatre was built in 1818 using masonry salvaged from the convent and two demolished churches. Eight marble columns, which now decorate the façade of the theatre, come from the church of the Carthusians. Willem Geefs carved the statue of André Grétry (1741–1813) in front of the theatre. The heart of the composer, who was born in Liège, is buried in the plinth.

Go down the Rue Hamal and cross Place Xavier-Neujean to the **Eglise Saint Jean**. Founded c 997 by Bishop Notger, the plan of this church is modelled on the Carolingian basilica at Aachen. The tower, which was not finished until 1200, is all that survives of the early church, although the 18C nave and choir rest on 10C foundations.

There is a good view of the tower from the 16C and 17C cloister on the west side. The **entrance porch** contains two 13C polychrome wood figures of the *Virgin* and *St John* and there is a *Sedes Sapientiae* of c 1200 inside the church. The doors of the treasury date from the 14C.

Continue to the Boulevard de la Sauvenière, cross it, then turn right. A short flight of steps on the left leads to the Rue Basse Sauvenière. Turn left and climb the Rue des Bégards to the **Eglise Saint Martin**. This church stands on the Publémont, a hill where coal was first extracted in the Liège district. The church was founded in 965 by Bishop Eracle after he prayed at the tomb of St Martin to be cured of a serious illness. A series of paintings in the choir illustrate the miracle. The original church was burned down in 1312. The present church dates from the 16C, though the tower is 15C.

> ### Corpus Christi
> The festival of Corpus Christi was first celebrated in Liège in 1246. Robert de Torote, bishop of Liège, was persuaded to institute the feast by Blessed Juliana (1192–1258), prioress of the convent of Mont Cornillon near Liège, who experienced a vision while venerating the Holy Sacrament. The feast was first celebrated in the church of St Martin. It spread throughout the Catholic world after Jacques Pantaléon, archdeacon of Liège, was appointed Pope Urban IV. The feast is celebrated on the Thursday after Trinity Sunday.

Now descend the streets Mont St Martin and Rue St Hubert to reach the **Eglise Sainte-Croix**, a rare Belgian example of a hall church with the nave and aisles of equal height. The tower and baptistry were built in the late 12C, and the remainder in the 14C, though traces of a wall from 979 survive. The baptistry, which forms a kind of west apse, contains a 15C polyptych. The **Treasury** displays a key given by Pope Gregory II to St Hubert in 722. Such keys were presented by the Pope to distinguished visitors to Rome as a symbol of their right of entry to the crypt of St Peter. Only two of these keys survive in Europe, the other being kept in Maastricht.

On leaving the church, turn right along Rue Saint Pierre, where the composer César Franck was born at **no. 13** in 1822. Go back to the church and descend by the steep Rue Haute-Sauvenière, past the **Maison de la Presse** at no. 19, which occupies a former refuge founded in the 8C by Charlemagne.

The walk continues up the Rue du Palais, an old street with Mosan Renaissance houses which climbs the hill behind the Palace of the Prince Bishops. Turning left along the Rue Fond St Servais leads to the rather forgotten **Eglise Saint Servais**, a 13C church much altered in the 16C. If it is open, you can admire the Renaissance stained-glass, 13C figure of *St Servatius* and 14C *Visitation*. The Rue des Anglais ascends from here to a gate at no. 38, which leads to the Escalier des Capucins. The 16C steps lead up a grassy slope to the appealing **Chapelle de Banneux**.

4 • Simenon's Liège

The novelist Georges Simenon was born in Liège in 1903 at 24 Rue Léopold. A plaque gives the date as 13 February, though his superstitious mother always claimed that he was born the previous day. The family later moved to the Outremeuse district, living in the street now named Rue Simenon. It was while working as a journalist on the Gazette de Liège that Simenon wrote his first novel. He left Liège at 19, settling in Paris where he wrote more than 300 novels, including the Inspector Maigret series. Simenon died in 1989.

This walk explores the **Outremeuse** district, on the right bank of the Meuse, where Simenon spent his youth. Cross the Pont des Arches to reach the **Eglise Saint Pholien**, built in 1914, where a corpse was found hanging from a gargoyle in Simenon's *Maigret and the Hundred Gibbets*. Now turn right down the Boulevard de l'Est, past the **Hôtel Simenon** where rooms are decorated with scenes from Simenon's crime novels. The figure on the **Monument Tchantchès** on Place Saint Nicholas represents the 'spirit of Liège'.

There are several *potales* in the streets of Outremeuse. These street shrines containing a statue of the Virgin mainly date from the 17C. The tourist office publishes a detailed guide to the Liège *potales*.

Continue down the Rue Puits-en-Sock and turn left into Rue des Récollets. The **Maison Grétry** at no. 34 occupies the house where the composer lived as a young man. 'It is like the houses you see in paintings by the Flemish Primitives,' Simenon wrote in his memoirs.

Return to Rue Puits-en-Sock and turn right down Rue Roture, a lively nocturnal street much loved by Simenon. It leads to the **Musée Tchantchès** at Rue Surlet 56, which contains an interesting collection of traditional Liège marionettes. The museum is open on Tues and Thur 14.00–16.00. It is closed in July.

Liège suburbs

The **Parc de Cointe** sprawls over a hillside to the south of the Gare des Guillemins and affords one of best views of Liège and its suburbs. A useful orientation table stands next to the road to the north of the sports grounds. The **Basilique du Sacré-Coeur** and the 83m high Allied War Memorial of 1936 stand in the park.

The **Pont de Fragnée**, southeast of the park at the junction of the Meuse and the Ourthe, has four piers which survived the destruction of 1944. It is the only

Liège bridge to have been rebuilt to its pre-war design. A little garden where the two rivers meet contains a monument of 1905 by Vinçotte to Zénobe Gramme, the inventor of the dynamo. Gramme worked in Liège from 1849–1855.

The university campus at **Sart-Tilman** occupies a wooded site south of the city. The campus grounds are dotted with interesting works by modern Belgian sculptors. The university botanic gardens are also here. The university hospital at Sart- Tilman was designed by Charles Vanderhove in 1969.

Liège environs

The Brialmont forts

Liege was surrounded by a ring of 19C forts designed to protect the country in the event of invasion. Considered virtually impregnable, the forts were bombarded into submission in August 1914 by heavy German artillery. Several forts, some of them bearing the scars of 1914, have been preserved as monuments. They can sometimes be visited on guided tours, usually at weekends.

A memorial at **Fort Loncin**, 6km northwest of Liège, commemorates the Belgian force under General Leman which made a brave stand here against the Germans in August 1914. General Leman was found unconscious beneath the ruins. In a chivalrous gesture, his sword was returned to him by the commander of the German forces. A memorial across the road commemorates a Royal Air Force crew who died here in July 1943.

The fort at **Eben-Emael**, 17km to the north of Liège, was considered impregnable. Despite a gallant defence, it was rapidly taken by German paratroops during the invasion of 1940. The fort can be glimpsed from the memorial just to the east of the village. It is occasionally open to visitors.

The industrial towns

Liège is the centre of a mining district rich in coal, lead, zinc and iron. This forms the basis of a vast metallurgical industry whose origins can be traced back to the 12C. The 19C saw great expansion and the firm establishment of heavy industry. Among the most important factories were the Cockerill works in Liège and at Seraing, the blast furnaces at Ougrée painted by Constantin Meunier, the ironworks at Sclessin, and the Usines de la Vieille-Montagne at Angleur. Other industries in the area include armaments, glass, electronics and petrochemicals.

The former Cistercian abbey at **Val Saint Lambert**, 10km west of Liège, was converted into a glassworks in 1826. Founded in 1202, the abbey sheltered the younger brothers of Louis XVI—the Count of Provence (later Louis XVIII), and the Count of Artois (later Charles X)—when they fled from France at the time of the Revolution. The abbey was suppressed in 1796 and glassworks later set up in the mainly 18C buildings.

Seraing, 6km southwest of Liège, is the home of the huge Société Cockerill which was founded here in 1817 by John Cockerill as an extension to the works founded at Liège in 1807 by his father William, a mechanic from Lancashire. The Seraing works were the first on the Continent to build locomotives, in 1835. They were also the first outside Britain to use the Bessemer process in the production of steel, in 1863.

The village of **Neuville-en-Condroz**, 18km southwest of Liège, has a 16C manor house. The American Ardennes Cemetery here contains over 5000 Second World War graves and a monument to the Supply Services. Wall maps in marble illustrate the 1944 campaign.

The village of **Othée**, c 10km northwest of Liège, was the site of a battle in 1408 where John the Fearless crushed the citizens of Liège. The church in **Hannut**, c 34km west of Liège, has an impressive, large 14C statue of St Christopher.

NAMUR

Namur is an old and appealing town of cobbled lanes, second-hand bookshops and dusty Baroque churches. The settlement originated as a fortress built on the heights above the confluence of the Meuse and Sambre rivers. The town's strategic location meant that Namur has been besieged countless times. This tumultuous history has led to the destruction of most of its medieval buildings, though much survives from the 17C and 18C, due in part to the edicts of 1687 and 1708 which prohibited the construction of wooden houses or thatched roofs. Now with a population of just over 100,000, the town has pleasant cafés on shady squares and several good restaurants. Known as Namen in Dutch, the town is the capital of Namur province and Wallonia region.

Practical information

Getting there
High-speed *Thalys* trains run from Paris to Namur in just over 2 hours. Trains from Brussels take 40 minutes.

Where to stay
££ *Beauregard*, Avenue Baron de Moreau 1, ☎ 081.23.00.28, is a comfortable hotel on the Meuse waterfront.
££ *Les Tanneurs*, Rue Tanneries 13, ☎ 081.24.00.24, is an unusual hotel in former 17C tannery. It offers a good choice of room styles and prices.

Eating out
£ *Brasserie Henry*, Place St-Aubain 3, ☎ 081.22.02.04 is a friendly bustling brasserie with a conservatory and garden.
£ *Grand Café des Galeries Saint-Loup*, Rue du Collège 27, ☎ 081.22.71.46 is a large brasserie in a converted 19C auction room.
£ *La Maison des Desserts*, Rue Haute-Marcelle 17, offers wicked cakes.

Cafés
The *Taverne Alsacienne*, Place du Marché-aux-Légumes, is a friendly café on a shady square filled with tables in the summer.

Shuttle bus
A bus runs from Place du Grognon to the citadel, daily in July and August. It replaces a cable car, which no longer operates.

Tourist information
The main tourist office is on Square Léopold, near the station, ☎ 081.24.64.49. Open daily 09.30–18.00.
A small tourist office is open from Easter–Sept at Place du Grognon, beside the Meuse (same hours).

Banks and post office
BBL, Rue Godefroid 5.
Fortis, Place d'Armes 2.

Main **post office** is on Boulevard Ernest Mélot.

Meuse cruises

Boat trips from Namur on the Sambre and Meuse rivers run daily from early April to mid-September. Tours last 45 minutes. Longer trips are run in July and August, daily to Wépion (3 hours), and on Sundays to Dinant (9 hours). Contact the tourist office for information on times and booking.

Markets

A large flea market is held on Sunday mornings along the banks of the Meuse in the suburb of Jambes, near the Pont de Jambes.

Festivals

Namur en Mai is an appealing festival of traditional fairground shows, including fortune tellers, roundabouts, street musicians and a flea circus. It is held in late May or early June.

Beer

The local beer is known as Blanche de Namur after the daughter of Marie d'Artois and Jean I, Count of Namur. Blanche became Queen of Sweden in the 14C.

Opening times

Most museums close on Monday.

Citadelle (Domaine Fortifié 'Terra Nova') is open Jun–Sept daily 11.00–17.00; Easter–May on weekends and public holidays 11.00–17.00; closed Oct–Easter.

Hôtel de Groesbeeck de Croix (local art and decorative art), Rue Saintraint 3, is open Tues–Sun 10.00–12.00 and 14.00–17.00. It is closed 23 Dec–3 Jan.

Musée Archaéologique (local archaeology), Rue du Pont 21, is open Tues–Sun 10.00–17.00.

Musée des Arts Anciens du Namurois (artworks from local churches), Rue de Fer 24, is open Tues–Sun 10.00–18.00 (closes 17.00 early Nov–Easter). It is also closed 23 Dec–3 Jan.

Musée Diocésain (Treasury of the cathedral), Place du Chapitre 1, is open Easter–Oct daily 10.00–12.00 and 14.30–18.00; Nov–Easter daily 14.30–16.30.

Musée Félicien Rops (house of the artist), Rue Fumal 12, is open Tues–Sun 10.00–18.00 and also on Mon Jul–Aug.

Treasury of the Priory of Oignies Rue Julie Billiart 17, is open Tues–Sat 10.00–12.00 and 14.00–17.00 and Sun 14.00–17.00. It is closed on public holidays and 11–27 Dec.

History

Namur has been identified, on rather tenuous grounds, with the stronghold of the Aduatuci mentioned by Caesar. It enters documented history in the Merovingian period as **Namurcum Castrum**. At that time it consisted simply of the citadel and the spit of land below, which lies between the Meuse and Sambre rivers. It rapidly became an important commercial centre, and developed into a feudal holding by the 10C. Its rulers styled themselves counts. Count Jean III de Dampierre sold the County of Namur to Philip the Good of Burgundy in 1421.

The town has been besieged many times in its history. It fell to Don John of Austria in 1577, and in 1692 it was taken by Vauban for Louis XIV, an event celebrated by Boileau and Racine. It was recaptured by William of Orange in 1695, which inspired the martial spirit of *Tristram Shandy*. Seized by the

French revolutionaries in 1792 and 1794, it was, until 1814, the capital of the **French department of Sambre-et-Meuse**. Grouchy's rearguard made a gallant stand here in 1815 during Napoleon's retreat from Waterloo.

The fortifications were dismantled by Joseph II between 1782 and 1784, but rebuilt in 1816 after the establisment of the United Kingdom of the Netherlands. They were again razed to the ground in 1862–65 and replaced by boulevards and gardens. Namur became an important fortress again in 1887 when an ring of nine modern forts was built around the town. Like those around Liège and Antwerp, the Namur forts were believed to be impregnable, but the German army proved otherwise when it captured the forts within three days in August 1914. The soldiers then burned and looted parts of the town. Namur suffered more damage, particularly to its bridges, during the Second World War. In April 1975, after about 2000 years of military occupation, the last army unit left the citadel and the keys were handed over to the town.

Born in Namur

Charles de Berlaymont (1510–78), councillor to Margaret of Parma, was a native of Namur. He was the first to call the Netherlands League of Nobility *'ces gueux'*, 'those beggars'. The painter and engraver Félicien Rops (1833–98) was also born here.

1 • The old town

Beginning at the station, cross Square Léopold and continue down the attractive Rue de Fer. This street contains several 18C mansions, including the **Hôtel de Ville** on the left at no. 42. Further down the street, the Hôtel Gaiffier d'Hestroy at no. 24 is occupied by the **Musée des Arts Anciens du Namurois**. This attractive museum is open Tues–Sun 10.00–18.00 (closes 17.00 early Nov–Easter). It is also closed 23 Dec–3 Jan.

The museum contains a collection of Mosan art, medieval statues and 16C retables from local churches and abbeys. It also has a small collection of paintings including works by Henri met de Bles and two curious works of 1594 by **Jean de Namur the Elder**. Illustrating *January and February*, and *March and April*, they form part of a series commissioned by Archduke Ernest of Austria.

The **Eglise Saint Joseph** opposite dates from 1650. Continue down the Rue de l'Ange (a continuation of Rue de Fer) to the Place de l'Ange, where there is a fountain of 1791. Now turn right down a lane that leads to the quiet Place du Marché-aux-Légumes, which is filled with café tables on summer evenings. Overlooking the square is the **Eglise Saint Jean Baptiste**, which has vestiges of a 13C church, though most of the building is 16C. It was restored and modified in 1616 and 1890. All that remains of the medieval furnishings is the font.

Leave this square by the Rue Saint Jean and turn right along Rue du Président to reach the Baroque **Eglise Saint Loup**, where Baudelaire suffered a stroke in 1866. 'Saint Loup is a terrible and delicious hearse,' he wrote afterwards. The church was built for the Jesuits by Father Pieter Huyssens from 1621 to 1645. It is exuberantly decorated with coloured marble and carved sandstone vaulting. The **altar** is made of wood painted to look like marble. The Jesuits adopted

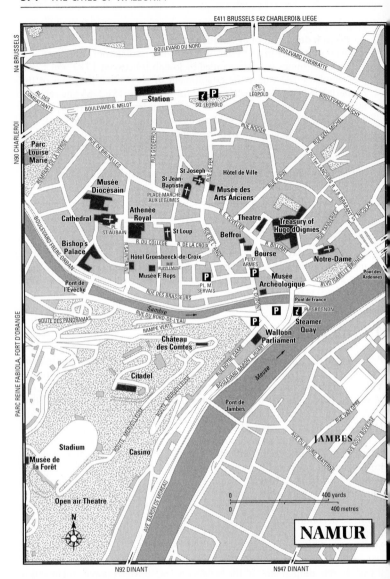

NAMUR

this solution after the ship bringing the marble altar from Italy was wrecked off the coast of Calais. The altar was salvaged and placed in the church of Notre-Dame in Calais.

Now turn down the Rue du Collège, past the pink façade of the **Athénée Royal** at no. 8. This was built by the Jesuits in 1614 as a college. The street leads to the

Place Saint Aubain, where the Namur province offices occupy the former episcopal palace, built from 1726–1740. Opposite is the **Cathédrale Saint Aubain**, an impressive Neo-classical design built by Gaetano Pizzoni from 1751–1767. The oldest church on this site was completed in the 3C. A later church was demolished in 1751, leaving only the tower behind the apse, which was built in 1388 and raised in height in 1648.

The rather bare interior has stucco decoration by the Moretti brothers and paintings by the Jesuit priest J. Nicolai and Nicolas Roose, both pupils of Rubens. There is also a *Calvary* attributed to Antoon van Dyck and works by Jacques Baudin and Gaspard de Crayer. A memorial tablet behind the high altar marks the place where the heart of **Don John of Austria** is buried. He died in his camp at Bouge, to the northeast of Namur, soon after capturing the town in 1577.

The Cathedral's treasures are displayed in the **Musée Diocésain**, on the north side of the building, which is open Easter–Oct daily 10.00–12.00 and 14.30–18.00; Nov–Easter daily 14.30–16.30. Here are found a magnificent 13C **golden crown-reliquary** containing two thorns from the Crown of Thorns, a 12C portable altar with 11C ivory panels and a silver-gilt reliquary arm attributed to Hugo d'Oignies.

The museum also has a 14C silver-gilt statuette of St Blaise, a physician who became bishop of Sebaste in Armenia. He is said to have saved the life of a boy who had choked on a fish bone. This led to the custom of invoking St Blaise for protection against infections in the throat. He was martyred in c 316 after his flesh was ripped apart with iron combs. Blaise thus became the patron saint of woolcombers; he is often portrayed with a comb.

The **Bishop's Palace** is at the end of the Rue du Séminaire, which begins behind the Cathedral. The palace occupies the former refuge of the abbey of Malonnes. Now go left along the Rue de l'Evêché, which skirts the high wall of the palace garden.

This leads to the 18C **Hôtel Groesbeeck-de-Croix** at Rue Saintraint 3, open Tues–Sun 10.00–12.00 and 14.00–17.00. It is closed 23 Dec–3 Jan. This handsome 18C mansion stands on the site of the 17C refuge of the abbey of Villers. The house now contains a **collection of 18C arts and crafts** from the Namur region, including furniture, portraits, paintings of the 1695 siege of Namur, flower paintings by **Joseph Redouté**, sculpture and porcelain by Jacques Richardot, Vonèche glass, Namur clocks, sculpture by Laurent Delvaux, Andenne porcelain and a delightful 18C game of Lotto with cards illustrating trades of the period. The fireplace in the kitchen is a relic from the original refuge.

Now head towards the river and then turn left along the Rue des Brasseurs, past an attractive Mosan Renaissance house at **no. 169** dated 1621. Then go left into the Rue Fumal. The **Musée Félicien Rops** occupies an 18C mansion at no. 12 once owned by Rops' parents-in-law. It is open Tues–Sun 10.00–18.00 and also on Mon Jul–Aug. Reviled by many as a pornographer, Rops was praised by Baudelaire as: 'the only true artist I have found in Belgium'. The collection includes witty caricatures of eminent Belgians, illustrations made for Charles de Coster's *Ulenspiegel*, and erotic drawings produced in Paris between 1874 and 1898.

On leaving the museum go straight ahead along Rue Rupplemont, then right into Rue du Président, where a plaque on **no. 33** marks the house where Rops was born in 1833. Then go left along Rue des Brasseurs, past the Place Maurice Servais. On reaching the Rue du Pont turn left into the attractive Place d'Armes. The **Bourse** opposite stands on the site of the 19C Hôtel de Ville, which was burnt down in 1914. The tower looming behind the Bourse is known as the **Tour Saint Jacques** (or Beffroi). A rare vestige of the late 14C walls, it was equipped with a bell chamber in 1746. Now go down the street to the right of the Bourse to reach the Place du Théâtre, where the Neo-classical **Théâtre Royal** stands.

Turn down the Rue de la Tour to the south of the square, past a small tower from the city wall known as the **Tour Marie Spilar**. At the end of the street, go left along the Rue Bas-de-la-Place and left again into the Rue Julie Billiart. The Maison des Soeurs de Notre-Dame at no. 17 contains the exquisite **Treasury of the Priory of Oignies**, open Tues–Sat 10.00–12.00 and 14.00–17.00 and on Sun 14.00–17.00. It is closed on public holidays and 11–27 Dec. Considered one of the Seven Wonders of Belgium, this collection of precious religious objects was hidden in a farm when French revolutionaries sacked the priory in 1794. It was moved to a convent in Namur in 1818, and hidden again during the Second World War (when the convent was destroyed). The collection contains several early 13C works by **Hugo d'Oignies**, including an evangelistery cover, a silver-gilt chalice, a reliquary for a rib of St Peter, and two magnificent double-crosses. Ring the bell at no. 17 to enter.

Go back to the end of the street, where a portal dated 1647 is all that survives from the refuge of the abbey of Floreffe. Now turn left along the Rue de Gravière to reach the **Eglise Notre-Dame**, built in 1775 by Franciscan Recollects on the site of several earlier churches. The church, which is closed indefinitely, contains a figure of St Anthony by Laurent Delvaux and a high altar by Denis Bayart. An inscription to the left of the altar records the burial here of two Counts of Namur, William I who died in 1391, and William II who died in 1418. The old façade of the **Hospice d'Harscamp**, formerly a Franciscan convent, stands next to the church.

Go along the Rue Saint Nicolas through an ancient red-light district where a few brothels survived at the time of writing. Some of the houses on the north side of the street have been imaginatively restored as part of the Hôtel Les Tanneurs de Namur. Another positive sign is the opening of the **Musée des Traditions Namuroises** at no. 6. This enjoyable museum contains furnished interiors, local costumes and quirky folklore mementoes.

Turn right down the Rue J. Brabant to reach the river. The **Pont des Ardennes**, built in 1957, is decorated with a striking modern sculpture by Olivier Strebelle illustrating the legend of the Quatre Fils Aymon and their horse Bayard. Now go right along the Boulevard Isabelle Brunell, which is named after the founder of the 19C hospital on the right. The founder's statue, which stands in the garden, was carved in 1872 by Willem Geefs.

The walk soon reaches the Pont de France, which is overlooked by the modern **Palais de la Culture** of 1961 (used for temporary exhibitions). Go down the steps to the left of the building to reach the Baroque **Porte de Sambre-et-Meuse**, designed by the local sculptor Denis-Georges Bayart in 1728.

A covered flight of steps on the right leads back up from the quayside to the **Ancienne Maison des Bouchers**. This former meat hall built in 1590 now contains the **Musée Archéologique**, open Tues–Sun 10.00–17.00; 10.40–17.00. The museum displays objects found locally in prehistoric graves,

Roman villas, Gallo-Roman burial grounds and Merovingian sites. The collection includes superb pottery, amphorae, bronze tools, seals, statuettes, jewellery, coins, a rare glass oil lamp, fibulae and buckles. There are also reconstructions of a Frankish tomb and a 2C Roman tomb complete with cinerary urn and grave goods. The museum recently acquired a copy of the **scale model of Namur** made for Louis XV by the engineer Larcher d'Aubancourt. This remarkable model was originally intended for military use.

2 • The Citadel

The old town is dominated by a massive citadel built on a spur at the confluence of the Meuse and Sambre rivers. The oldest buildings, including the scant remains of the Château des Comtes, stand on the steep spur high above the point where the two rivers meet. The plateau known as the Terra Nova to the west has later buildings. The opening hours, Jun–Sept daily 11.00–17.00; Easter–May on weekends and public holidays only 11.00–17.00, refer to the Domaine Fortifié 'Terra Nova', whose entrance is opposite the sports stadium near the summit. The rest of the hill is freely accessible at all times.

The Citadel can be reached by various routes, all of which begin at the **Place du Grognon**, just south of the Rue du Pont. There is a minibus service from the Place du Grognon which stops at several points of interest. Those with a car can drive up the steep **Route Merveilleuse**, which winds up the south flank of the hill from the casino to a large car park at the summit. An alternative route for cars winds up through the woods on the north flank of the hill. Perhaps the most enjoyable way of discovering the Citadel is to hike up the **Grande Randonnée** route marked with red and white stripes, which begins beside the former cable car station.

Cross the Sambre to the Place du Grognon, where an equestrian statue of King Albert I stands at the point where the rivers meet. The confluence of the Sambre and the Meuse is celebrated by two statues and some Walloon verses. Boat tours leave from a quay to the south on the Meuse.

The imposing ochre building facing the Place du Grognon is the former 17C **Hospice Saint Gilles**. The restored building has been occupied by the Walloon Parliament since 1998. Now climb to the Citadel by the flight of old steps opposite. This leads to a grassy plateau with a panoramic view of the town, and, soon after, a cluster of old buildings. The gateway straight ahead leads to the **Porte Bordiale** of 1766, the only surviving town gate.

Continue upward past the former 18C castle chapel. Now occupied by the **Espace Archéologique Saint-Pierre**, it exhibits archaeological finds from the Citadel. Steps lead up from here to a former military building now occupied by the **Parfumerie Guy Delforge**. Perfumes are manufactured and matured in ancient vaults which once formed part of the vanished Château des Comtes. A shop sells the finished products.

A panoramic view of the Meuse valley can be enjoyed from the nearby terrace. Just below here, the road passes between two round towers which are all that remain of the **Château des Comtes**. Continue to the summit, where there is a café with a panoramic view, an open-air theatre and a curious building in the style of a hunting lodge. Constructed in 1910 on the site of a former fort, it now contains the **Musée de la Forêt**. The museum explains the ecology of Belgian forests through the use of excellent dioramas and a vivarium. It is open Sat–Thurs April–Oct 09.00–12.00 and 14.00–17.00.

The **Parc Reine Fabiola**, just to the west, contains a well-equipped children's playground. Just beyond the park are the remains of the **Fort d'Orange**. Constructed in 1690, this was largely demolished by the Dutch in 1816 when they rebuilt the whole citadel. Little has survived apart from the foundations.

Descend to the Meuse, where the **Casino** stands on the waterfront. Return to the old town past the Pont de Jambes, a modern bridge replacing one blown up in 1944. The earliest bridge was built on this site in the 11C.

DINANT

Dinant occupies a striking site on the River Meuse below a sheer grey cliff surmounted by a 19C citadel.

Practical information

Where to stay
££ *Mercure*, Route de Walzin 36, Anseremme, 3km southwest of Dinant, ☎ 082.22.28.44, is a comfortable country hotel in a wooded estate. It has an indoor pool and a children's playground.
£ *La Couronne*, Rue Sax 1, ☎ 082.22.24.41, is a traditional Ardennes hotel next to the Eglise Notre-Dame in the town centre.

Tourist information
Rue Grande 37 (next to the Casino), ☎ 082.22.28.70.

Boat excursions
River boats leave in the summer from the quay just south of the bridge. Boats sail to the former 19C artists' colony at Anseremme, southwest of Dinant, daily from Apr–Oct, every 20 minutes. The return trip takes 45 minutes.
Trips lasting 1 hour 45 mins are organised to Freyr, daily from May–Aug, departing at 14.30.
Longer trips lasting 3 hours are organised to Hastière on Sun in June and daily in Jul–Aug, departing at 14.00.

Boats also run to Namur on Sat in Jul–Aug. The boat departs Dinant at 15.30 and arrives at Namur at 19.00. The trip is one way only.
For bookings and schedules of boat excursions, ☎ 082.22.43.97.
Day trips to Givet are organised by Bateau Bayard, Quai de Meuse, ☎ 082.22.30.42, on Wed and Thur in Jul–Aug. Boats leave at 10.00 and return at 19.00. The trip includes a 3 hour stop in Givet.

Descent of the Lesse
Kayaks can be rented to make a descent of the River Lesse, southeast of Dinant. The lower river winds through wooded hills for 21km from Houyet to Anseremme, where it joins the Meuse. One of the best firms for kayak rental is Kayaks Ansiaux, Rue du Vélodrome 15, Anseremme, ☎ 082.22.23.25. The descent can be made from Houyet to Anseremme (about 5 hours) or from Gendron to Anseremme (about 3 hours). Several cafés are located along the route; the complex at Anseremme has showers and a hotel. A local train runs up the valley from Anseremme to Houyet. The

season runs from mid-Mar–Oct. Kayaks should be booked in advance. The most impressive stretch is from Gendron to Anseremme, where the river passes beneath the rocky slopes of Furfooz National Park and the 13C castle of Walzin, which was rebuilt in 1581.

Opening times

Citadel is open 10.00–18.00 (closes 16.30 out of season). It closes on Fri Oct–Mar and in Jan. The citadel can only be visited by guided tour, which lasts 1 hour 30mins. Expect long queues in the summer.

Château de Vevês, c 7km east of Dinant, is open Apr–Oct, Tues–Sun 10.00–18.00; also Mon in Jul–Aug.
Furfooz National Park, 6km south-east of Dinant, is open daily mid-Mar–mid-Nov 10.00 to two hours before sunset.
Grotte de Montfort is open Easter–Oct 10.00 to about 18.30.
Mont-Fat chair lift and park are open Apr–Aug 10.30–19.00 and in Sept at weekends 11.00–18.00.
Grotte de la Merveilleuse is open daily Apr–Oct 11.00–17.00 (10.00–18.00 in Jul–Aug).

History of Dinant

The town, which was occupied by the Romans, is thought by some to derive its name from Diana, the Roman goddess of the hunt. It grew into a prosperous medieval town famed for producing ornate metalwork known as '**dinanderie**'. These objects made from copper, brass or bronze were used in wealthy households and churches. During the 14C, about 7,500 persons were employed in the dinanderie industry out of a population of about 50,000. The industry began to decline in the 19C, though attempts have been made recently to revive it. The Musée du Cinquantenaire in Brussels has an outstanding collection of dinanderie.

A **fortress** was built on the clifftop above the town in c 1050. Dinant was frequently at war with neighbouring towns, particularly Bouvignes to the north. The town was pillaged and burnt by Charles the Bold in 1466 after it rebelled against Burgundian rule. Charles brought his aged father, Philip the Good, to observe the punishment he inflicted on the inhabitants. More than 800 townspeople were bound back to back in couples and thrown into the Meuse. Dinant was sacked again in 1554 by the French during the war between Charles V and Henry II. The French returned once more in 1675, when Louis XIV attempted to bring the Spanish Netherlands under his control.

After the **First World War** broke out in August 1914, the French rushed to the aid of Dinant. They fought valiantly to defend the citadel on 15 August, but the Germans forced them to surrender eight days later. Alleging that their troops had been fired on, the Germans executed 674 citizens, deported 400 to Germany and set fire to the town. A plaque in the Rue Daoust, south of the town centre, marks the site of the massacre. Dinant was also the scene of bitter fighting in May 1940, and again in September 1944, when the town was shelled by American artillery for three days to dislodge the Germans from the Citadel.

Born in Dinant

The painter **Joachim Patinir** (c 1475–1524) was born in Dinant. His paintings often feature strange mountain landscapes inspired by the Meuse valley north of Dinant. The romantic 19C painter **Antoine Wiertz** (1806–65) also came from Dinant. His studio in Brussels is now a museum.

Adolphe Sax was born in Dinant in 1814. The son of a musical instruments maker, Adolphe studied at the Brussels Conservatory, where he invented the saxophone in 1840. He moved to Paris in 1842 and patented his invention in 1846. Sax developed a total of 14 instruments including the saxhorn, saxo-tromba and saxtuba. Involved in costly lawsuits to protect his patents, he died in Paris in abject poverty in 1894.

A walk round the town

The main town is located on the right bank of the Meuse under the steep cliffs. The first bridge across the Meuse was built here by monks from Waulsort in 1080. This was blown up in 1914, and its replacement was destroyed in 1944. Some of the original 11C piers are displayed in the Citadel.

The town is dominated by the **Eglise Notre-Dame**. Completed in 1240, it has been destroyed several times, but always rebuilt in the original style. It is said to stand on the site of a chapel founded by St Maternus in 320. It was succeeded by several other chapels, the last of which was destroyed by a rock fall in 1227. Parts of this chapel are embedded in the present structure, including a sandstone arch on the outside north wall and a porch with three carved Romanesque arches in the baptistry to the right of the entrance.

The tomb of **Gérard de Blancmoustier**, who died in 1306, is in the north transept. Two paintings by **Antoine Wiertz** hang in the south transept. The church has a fine modern window by Perot. A cable car ascends to the Citadel from the station next to the church.

Now follow the narrow Rue Grande, which runs parallel to the river. It has attractive taverns, tea rooms and shops selling Ardennes hams. This leads to the 17C **Hôtel de Ville**, which was rebuilt after 1918. A small garden on the left contains an allegorical group called *La Triomphe de la Lumière* by Antoine Wiertz. A prehistoric cave known as the **Grotte de Montfort** is buried in the hillside nearby. It is open from Easter–Oct from 10.00 to about 18.30. A chair lift runs from here to the **Tour de Montfort**. Built in the 14C on the crags above Dinant, the tower was restored in 1910. The clifftop site has been turned into a children's playground and hanging gardens.

The Citadel

Perched more than 100m above the Meuse, the citadel offers magnificent views of the town and surrounding countryside. It can be reached by cable car from the station next to the church or by climbing the 408 steps cut by the French in 1577. (It is also possible to drive up and park, 3km by winding road).

Historians believe that a fortification stood here as early as the 4C. Destroyed by the Vikings in the 9C, it was replaced by a fortress built by the Bishop of Liège in 1051. Several other fortresses were built and destroyed over the centuries. Most traces of the old citadels were demolished by the French in 1707. The present buildings were essentially built by the Dutch in 1818–21.

The **guided tour** takes in part of the casemates, the gallery in which trapped French soldiers held out against the Germans for five hours in 1914, a memorial commemorating the French and German dead of 1914, prison cells from the period of Dutch occupation (now containing a guillotine and torture instruments) and the Dutch forge, kitchen and bakery. There are other interesting historical relics, including the piers of the 11C Meuse bridge built by the monks of Waulsort (which were dredged from the river in 1952), a small **museum of arms** from the 17C–19C, the carriage of Madame de Maintenon, who stayed at Dinant in 1692 while Louis XIV was besieging Namur, and several historical dioramas (including one depicting Madame de Maintenon's visit). The citadel has a **café** with a terrace.

The **Grotte la Merveilleuse** lies on the left bank of the Meuse, about half a kilometre from the bridge. Filled with white stalactites, it is considered one of the most beautiful caves in Belgium. It is open daily Apr–Oct 11.00–17.00 (10.00–18.00 in Jul–Aug).

A tour of Dinant environs

There is an impressive 60m high rock pinnacle known as the **Rocher Bayard**, just south of Dinant on the right bank. Named after the horse of the Quatre Fils Aymon, it was said to have been dislodged by the horse's hoof as he leaped across the river. The road beside the rock was cut by Louis XIV when he prepared to attack Dinant in 1675. A plaque records King Albert's climb of the Rocher Bayard in 1933, one year before he died in a climbing accident.

The road continues to **Anseremme**, 3km southwest of Dinant, a small resort at the mouth of the Lesse where a colony of 19C Belgian artists spent their summers. The Lesse is crossed by a 16C bridge, while the Meuse is crossed by a railway bridge with a footpath. The valley is also spanned by a concrete viaduct carrying the N97.

Turn inland up the Lesse valley to reach the **Furfooz National Park**, 7km southeast of Dinant. This attractive park occupies a rocky promontory in a loop of the Lesse once occupied by the Romans. A Roman bath has been reconstructed on the original foundations. There are also earthworks and other remains of a Roman camp. The site is pitted with deep holes known as *trous*, including one known as the **Trou du Frontal** where the bones of a Mesolithic man were uncovered. A signposted trail lead to a clifftop viewpoint high above the Meuse. The park is open daily mid-Mar–mid-Nov 10.00 to two hours before sunset.

A minor road leads to **Château de Vêves**, 4km east of Furfooz village (open Apr–Oct Tues–Sun 10.00–18.00, also Mon in Jul–Aug). Perched dramatically on a ridge above Celles village, the castle dates from the 15C or 16C, though the site is thought to have been fortified from c 640. There are striking 17C half-timbered balconies around the court.

The Comte de Beaufort, who owned the castle in the 18C, moved to the small manor house of Noisy in 1770. But his grandson, the Comte de Liedekerke Beaufort (1816–90), found this too modest a residence and built himself the much grander **Château de Noisy** in the Scottish-Baronial style. The turrets can be glimpsed in the distance on the other side of the valley.

The village of **Celles**, 2km northeast of Vêves, contains an outstanding fortified Romanesque church. The **Eglise Saint Hadelin** was built in Mosan style in c 1035. It is named after St Hadelin, a Merovingian courtier who c 670 decided to withdraw from the world. He established a hermitage here which grew into a monastery. Four centuries later the monks built the present church out of local stone. St Hadelin's reliquary is in the Eglise St Martin at Visé. The **13C stalls** are among the oldest in Belgium. The church also contains the splendid 16C **tombstone of Louis de Beaufort** and his wife, and a 13C stone lectern. The building has two crypts; one dates from the 11C, while the other smaller crypt below the tower is possibly from the 8C.

Celles narrowly escaped destruction in 1944. The Von Rundstedt offensive was stopped at the crossroads outside the village in December 1944. Most of the villages to the east of here were destroyed, but Celles preserves its ancient stone houses.

The village of **Foy Notre-Dame**, 2km northwest of Celles, was also spared in 1944. A stone on the road to Ciney (behind the church) marks the limit of the German advance in December 1944. The village is entered through an arch formed by old houses.

> The church was built in 1623 after the **Virgin of Foy**, a small figure carved in local stone, was found in 1609 by a woodsman inside an oak he had felled on this site. Several miracles were attributed to the Virgin; the Archdukes Albert and Isabella, rulers of the Spanish Netherlands, made a pilgrimage here in 1619. This event led to the church being built. The lime tree in front of the building is said to have been planted on the site of the legendary oak. The original 14C or 15C statute of the Virgin is now rarely seen. After being stolen in 1974 and later recovered, it has been replaced by a copy.

The church contains a curious panelled ceiling with 147 individual portraits. It was carved by the 17C Dinant artist Michel Stilmant, a pupil of Rubens, who also designed the church and much of its woodcarving.

TOURNAI

Tournai is an old and interesting town on the River Scheldt in Hainaut province. Situated close to the border with France, just 20km from Lille, it remains a rather forgotten town. Yet it possesses perhaps the most beautiful cathedral in Belgium and an excellent Musée des Beaux-Arts. Tournai has been known for centuries for the quality of its sculptures, tapestries, gilt bronzes and porcelain. Its Dutch name is Doornik.

Practical information

Where to stay
££ *Holiday Inn*, Place St-Pierre, ☎ 069.21.50.77, is an attractive modern hotel with reasonable rates.
££ *Hotel d'Alcantara*, Rue des Bouchers St-Jacques, ☎ 069.21.26.48, is an attractive and friendly hotel in a grand 18C mansion restored in 1991. Close to the cathedral, it has large rooms and an attractive blue lounge. A personal favourite.

Eating out
££ *Carillon*, Grand-Place 64, ☎ 069.21.18.48, is an elegant Belgian restaurant on the main square.
££ *Taverne du Beffroi*, Vieux-Marché-aux-Poteries, ☎ 069.22.13.94, is a

simple Walloon restaurant specialising in mussels and *lapin à la Tournaisienne*.

£ *Trois Pommes d'Orange*, Rue de la Wallonie 28, ☎ 069.23.59.82, occupies a handsome gilded 17C mansion off Grand-Place once owned by Empress Maria Theresa. It is currently a modest pizzeria.

Cafés

Ecu de France, Grand-Place 55, is a comfortable Belgian tavern in a reconstructed 17C building.

Pâtisserie Quénoy, Place Crombez 2, near the station, is famous for its gateaux.

River trips

River boats leave from the Pont des Trous, May–Aug Tues–Sun at 11.00, 14.30 and 16.15. Trips last one hour.

Tourist information

The tourist office is near the Belfry at Vieux-Marché-aux-Poteries 14, ☎ 069.22.20.45.

 Opening times **Cathédrale de Notre-Dame** is open daily 09.00–12.00 and 14.00–18.00 (closes 16.00 Nov–Mar). The Treasury is open Mon–Sat 10.15–11.45 and 14.00–17.45 (closes 15.45 Nov–Mar), Sun 14.00–16.45 (closes 15.45 Nov–Mar).

Museums

All the museums open Wed–Mon 10.00–12.00 and 14.00–17.30. Closed on Tues, 1 Nov, 24–26 Dec, 31 Dec and 1–2 Jan.

Musée d'Armes (collection of weapons), Avenue Leray.

Musée des Arts Décoratifs (decorative arts), Rue Saint Martin 50.

Musée des Beaux Arts (fine art), Rue Saint Martin.

Musée de Folklore, Réduit des Sions 36.

Musée d'Histoire et d'Archéologie, Rue des Carmes 8.

Musée de la Tapisserie (Tournai tapestries), Place Reine Astrid 9.

History

The town began as the settlement of Tornacum on the important Roman road from Boulogne to Cologne. Its inhabitants were converted to Christianity by St Piat (or Piaton), who came from Benevento in south Italy. Sent by the Pope to convert the areas around Tournai and Chartres, Piat was probably martyred at Tournai during the persecutions of Maximian in c 286.

Tournai had become a **Frankish royal city** by the end of the 4C. Clovis may have been born here in 465; Childeric almost certainly died here in 481 (his grave was unearthed in 1653). The Tournai-born St Eleutherius was appointed bishop in c 486; he built the town's first church c 501 and was beaten to death in front of it by a local mob of fanatical Arian heretics in 532.

After belonging in turn to the counts of Flanders and Hainaut, Tournai came into the hands of the French kings in 1187. It remained faithful to France during the **Hundred Years War** and withstood a siege by Edward III of England in 1340. The siege was raised after Edward and Philip VI of France signed a treaty at Esplechin, 6km southwest of Tournai.

Henry VIII of England captured Tournai in 1513 during his war against France and gave the bishopric to **Cardinal Wolsey**. The town was occupied by the English from 1513–18, but was sold back to the French five years later, largely at the instigation of Wolsey, who hoped to gain favour with the French through this action. After a month-long siege, the town was taken by the

army of Charles V in 1521 and so became part of the **Spanish Netherlands**.
The town was captured in 1667 by Louis XIV and fortified by Vauban.
During the War of the Spanish Succession, Tournai was retaken by allied
forces under the command of Marlborough in 1709. Under the terms of the
Treaty of Utrecht, Tournai was ceded to Austria in 1713. It fell to the
French after the defeat of the English at the Battle of Fontenoy in 1745, but
returned to Austrian rule three years later. It was retaken by the French from
1792 to 1794.

Tournai suffered some damage in November 1918 when the retreating
German army blew up the bridges over the Scheldt. The town was heavily bombarded by the Luftwaffe in May 1940 while refugees crowded the streets. Most
of the old houses in the Grand-Place were destroyed. Tournai became the first
Belgian town to be liberated after British troops entered in September 1944.

The old town is encircled by boulevards which were constructed in the mid-
19C along the line of the **13C ramparts**. The ancient fortifications are still
visible in many places. Up until recent years, Tournai still bore many scars
from the 1940 bombardment. The authorities have carefully reconstructed
many of the old buildings to their original state. The old squares such as
Grand-Place and the cathedral quarter have also been attractively repaved.

Born in Tournai

The painters **Robert Campin** (sometimes known as the Master of Flémalle),
and Roger van der Weyden were natives of Tournai. The 18C trompe l'oeil
painter Piat Sauvage and the 19C painter Louis Gallait also came from Tournai.
The First World War heroine Gabrielle Petit was born in Tournai in 1893.

The English pretender **Perkin Warbeck** was born in Tournai in c 1474.
The son of a Tournai official, he was persuaded by the Yorkist faction to imper-
sonate Richard, Duke of York (the son of Edward IV and the younger of the
two princes murdered in the Tower). Landing in Cornwall in 1497, Warbeck
was proclaimed King Richard IV, but the rebellion fizzled out and this youthful
pretender to the English throne surrendered to Henry VII after being promised
a royal pardon. Despite this guarantee, Warbeck was imprisoned and executed
in the Tower of London in 1499 after he allegedly tried to escape.

1 • The old town

On leaving the **station**, cross to the park where there is an interesting statue to
Jules Bara, a 19C government minister, in Place Crombez. The Art Nouveau base
is by Victor Horta and the figures were carved by Guillaume Charlier.

The Rue Royale leads directly to the cathedral, but a brief detour right is possible down Avenue Leray to look at the massive **Tour Henri VIII**. This cylindrical
keep has 7m thick walls and a conical roof with a brick vault. The tower is all
that remains of a citadel built in 1513–18 by Henry VIII of England for his garrison. The rest of the building was torn down by Louis XIV. Two floors inside are
occupied by a **Musée d'Armes**, which displays an interesting collection of
weapons, munitions and uniforms. The oldest object is a late 14C bombard. A
section of the museum is devoted to the Resistance movement in Tournai during
the last war. The museum is open from Wed–Mon from 10.00–12.00 and

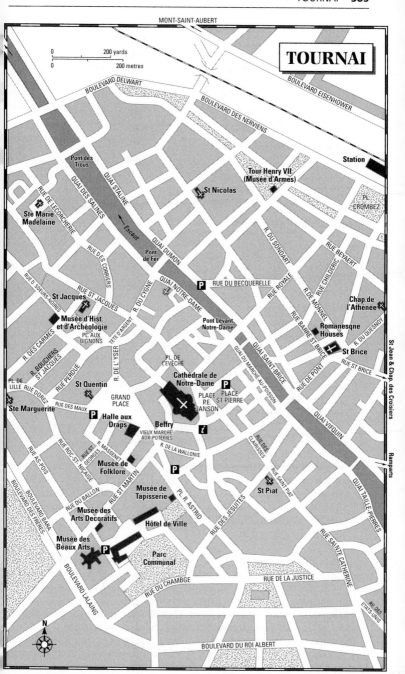

MONT-SAINT-AUBERT

TOURNAI

0 — 200 yards
0 — 200 metres

BOULEVARD DELWART

BOULEVARD EISENHOWER

BOULEVARD DES NERVIENS

Pont des Trous

QUAI SALINE

QUAI DES SALINES

RUE DE L'ÉCORCHERIE

Ste Marie Madeleine

Station

PL. CROMBEZ

Tour Henry VII (Musée d'Armes)

St Nicolas

Escaut

QUAI DUMON

Pont de Fer

RUE DES CORRIERS

RUE D. SOEURS-NOIRES

RUE ST JACQUES

St Jacques

Musée d'Hist. et d'Archéologie

PL. AUX OIGNONS

R. DES CARMES

R. BOUCHERS

ST JACQUES

PL. DE LILLE

RUE DOREZ

Ste Marguerite

RUE PERDUE

R. DE L'YSER

TÊTE D'ARGENT

R. DU CYGNE

QUAI NOTRE-DAME

RUE DU BECQUERELLE

RUE ROYALE

R. DE MONNEL

RUE BEYAERT

RUE CHILDÉRIC

Chap. de l'Athénée

Romanesque Houses

St Brice

R. DU QUESNOY

RUE ST BRICE

Pont Levant Notre-Dame

RUE BARRE ST BRICE

PL. DE L'ÉVÊCHÉ

St Quentin

GRAND PLACE

RUE DES MAUX

Cathédrale de Notre-Dame

QUAI DU MARCHÉ-AU-POISSON

QUAI SAINT BRICE

RUE DE PONT

QUAI VIFQUIN

QUAI TAILLE-PIERRES

PLACE P.E. JANSON

PLACE ST PIERRE

Halle aux Draps

Beffry

VIEUX MARCHÉ AUX POTERIES

R. DE LA WALLONIE

RUE ST GEORGES

R. MASSENET

RUE BALLON

RUE ROC ST-NICAISE

Musée de Folklore

RUE ST MARTIN

Musée de Tapisserie

PL. R. ASTRID

RUE DES JÉSUITES

RUE DES CLARISSES

RUE SAINT PIAT

St Piat

Musée des Arts Decoratifs

Hôtel de Ville

BOULEVARD DES FRÈRES

RUE AS POIS

Musée des Beaux Arts

BOULEVARD LALAING

Parc Communal

RUE DU CHAMBGE

RUE DE LA JUSTICE

RUE SAINTE CATHERINE

AV. DES ÉTATS-UNIS

BOULEVARD BARA

N

BOULEVARD DU ROI ALBERT

St Jean & Chap. des Croisiers

Ramparts

14.00–17.30. The **Eglise Saint Nicolas** stands near here in the Rue du Château. Completed in 1213, it stood inside the English citadel walls.

Return to Rue Royale and head towards the cathedral. Cross the Scheldt by the Pont Levant Notre-Dame, which is occasionally raised to allow barges to pass. The Rue de l'Hôpital-Notre-Dame leads to the small Place Paul Emile Janson, named after a Tournai councillor murdered in Buchenwald in 1944. The square contains a sculpture group of *The Blind* carved in 1908 by Guillaume Charlier. The 12C Romanesque cloister stood on this site.

Cathédrale de Notre-Dame

There is a striking view of the Cathédrale de Notre-Dame from the Place Paul Emile Janson. The cathedral is open daily 09.00–12.00 and 14.00–18.00 (closes 16.00 Nov–Mar). The Treasury is open Mon–Sat 10.15–11.45 and 14.00–17.45 (closes 15.45 Nov–Mar), Sun 14.00–16.45 (closes 15.45 Nov–Mar).

History of the Cathedral

Considered by many art historians to be the finest cathedral in Belgium, this stone edifice is built in a rugged Romanesque and early Gothic style. A church was built on this site in c 501 by St Eleutherius. This was replaced in the 9C by a Carolingian basilica, which was badly damaged by Viking raiders in 881. The present building was consecrated in 1175. The oldest part is the great Romanesque nave, which was probably completed by 1150.

The apsed and aisled transepts, the most original feature of the cathedral, were constructed mainly between 1150–1171. They were not completed until 1200, when the vault was built by Bishop Etienne. Between 1245 and 1255, Bishop Walter de Marvis, who had a reputation as a great church-builder, reconstructed the choir in a pure northern French style. Much damage was done to the interior by Protestant iconoclasts in 1566 and again by French revolutionaries in 1797. The upper part of the Gothic west front was rebuilt in a neo-Romanesque style in the 19C.

The cathedral's most distinctive external feature is its **five towers**, which are known to the locals as *les chongs clotiers*. The oldest, 80m high, is in the centre. The two on the east are 12C Romanesque, while the northwest tower (which once housed the chapter prison), is 12C to 13C Transitional, and the southwest tower is 13C Gothic. The great bell of the bishop, the Marie-Gasparine (sometimes called the Marie-Pontoise), weighs 8000 kilos. Cast in 1842, it hangs in the southeast tower. The oldest of the other four bells is called Marc. Cast in 1617, it weighs 250 kilos. The pyramidal spires were added to the towers during the 16C.

Enter the cathedral from Place Paul Emile Janson by the **Porte Mantile**, the north door, which is named after a man called Mantilius who was cured of blindness by St Eleutherius. The exceptional carvings around the door depict the Virtues and the Vices. Virtue struggles with Vice, while Avarice, weighed down by his purse, is carried off by the Devil. Though badly mutilated, these are the most important 12C Romanesque decorative sculptures in Belgium.

The proportions are impressive. Measuring 134m by 66m, the cathedral occupies an area of 5120 square metres. The 22m high **nave** was vaulted over in brick in 1774. It is the same length as the choir, while the triforium is almost the same height as the main arcade. Above the triforium is a smaller gallery and a plain clerestory. The **intricately carved capitals** were once painted in glowing colours. The sculptors based the carvings on illuminated manuscripts, local flora, oriental tapestries, Byzantine ivories and pictures of fabulous beasts.

Henry VIII had his throne placed in the **north transept**. An altar now stands on the spot. The wall above is decorated with late 12C or early 13C **murals** which are considered the most important Romanesque works of this kind in Belgium. A vibrant blue colour has survived in many of the scenes, which tell the story of St Margaret, a shepherdess of Antioch in Pisidia, who was martyred under Diocletian. On confessing her faith to the local governor, she was whipped. Refusing to sacrifice to the gods, she was tortured and beheaded. An angel then carried her head away. The red Lancastrian rose in the fourth picture was added on Henry's orders in c 1513.

The splendid Renaissance rood-screen in front of the **choir** was carved in 1572 by Cornelis Floris. The daringly slender piers in the choir, which were inspired by Soissons Cathedral, have had to be doubled in thickness, though those in the apse have been left untouched. The high altar of 1727 was brought from the vanished abbey church of St Martin at Tournai in 1804.

Now enter the **north ambulatory**. A painting by Rubens of the *Souls Delivered from Purgatory* hangs on the wall to the left. The ambulatory chapels contain several 15C Tournai memorial sculptures. Some of these were brought from other churches, often after having been mutilated by the French at the time of the Revolution. A monument behind the high altar commemorates the bishops of Tournai. It is decorated with the effigy of Bishop Villain de Gand, who died in 1644, and attractive sculptures from other 17C tombs. The painted walls, pillars and roof in this part of the ambulatory are particularly attractive.

Tournai marble

The slate-coloured Tournai marble has been used since Roman times for architectural detail and sculpture. Tournai's masons enjoyed an international reputation in the 14C and 15C. Fonts of Tournai marble are to be found in many English churches, and the cathedral of Pamplona in Spain possesses a fine monument by a Tournai artist. Many works remaining in Tournai were damaged by Calvinist fanatics in the 16C and by the French revolutionaries in the late 18C, though a few examples have survived in the cathedral.

Enter the **treasury** (small entry charge) from the south ambulatory. This room contains some exceptional works, including an 9C ivory diptych of St Nicasius, a 13C ivory Madonna, a 6C or 7C Byzantine cross-reliquary lavishly decorated with gems and pearls, a mid 13C reliquary of St Eleutherius, an Arras tapestry of 1402 depicting the stories of St Eleutherius and St Piat, 16C Brussels and Tournai tapestries, 12C, 13C and 14C psalters, a 13C missal, a chasuble worn by St Thomas à Becket shortly before his martyrdom, and a cope made from a mantle worn by Charles V at the 20th chapter of the Order of the Golden Fleece. The most impressive work is the glittering **Shrine of the Virgin** made by the goldsmith Nicolas of Verdun in 1205. This has been considered one of the 'Seven Wonders of Belgium'.

The chapels in the **south ambulatory** contains some interesting paintings. The Chapel of St Piat has a *Raising of Lazarus* by Pieter Pourbus and *Our Lady of the Seven Sorrows* by Wenceslas Coeberger. The last chapel before the transept is closed off by an iron grille. It contains a 16C Bruges silver reliquary.

The 16C **stained glass** in the principal window of the **south transept** was made by Arnoult de Nimègue. The glass panes illustrate events in Tournai's history, beginning with the unsettled period between c 570 and 615 following the death of Clotaire, the successor of Clovis (illustrated in the lower panes).

A divided kingdom

The Frankish realm was divided between Clotaire's sons: Sigebert was given Austrasia in the east, while Chilpéric received Neustria to the west. Tournai belonged to Neustria, which had its capital at Soissons.

The brothers married Brunehaut and Galswinthe, the daughters of the king of the Visigoths. Shortly after her arrival at court, Galswinthe was murdered by Chilpéric's mistress, Frédégonde. Determined to avenge her sister, Brunehaut urged her husband Sigebert to go to war (first panel). He won (second panel) and Chilpéric fled to Tournai (third panel). But Frédégonde would not accept defeat and armed Chilpéric's soldiers with poisoned daggers (fourth panel). They stabbed Sigebert to death (fifth panel), and Chilpéric, the victor, conferred temporal powers, symbolised by a key, on the bishops of Tournai (sixth panel). As a result, the magistracy had to swear loyalty annually (seventh panel).

The upper part of the window shows how the bishops made use of their new powers. One panel makes it clear that a tax was levied on every head of cattle that crossed the river. Taxes on wine and beer, weights and measures are shown on other panels.

Now enter the Romanesque **nave**. The pulpit was carved in 1740 with statues of *Faith, Hope* and *Charity* by François Gillis, founder of Tournai's academy of design. The **Chapelle Saint Louis** off the south aisle was built in 1299 to commemorate a visit to Tournai in 1257 by St Louis IX, king of France. It is lit by restored stained-glass windows incorporating 14C and 15C fragments. A *Crucifixion* by Jordaens hangs in the chapel. Another chapel off the south triforium is decorated with 13C murals depicting the *Legend of St Catherine* and the *Crucifixion*.

Leave the cathedral by the Porte du Capitole, opposite the Porte Mantile. This leads into the small Place du Vieux-Marché-aux-Poteries, where a sculptural group is based on Roger van der Weyden's painting of *St Luke painting the Virgin*. Now go through the dark archway on the right known as the **Fausse Porte**. The vaulting, which is among the earliest Gothic work in Belgium, dates from 1189. The archway is surmounted by a small 12C chapel dedicated to St Vincent. This links the bishop's palace with the cathedral.

There is a fine view of the **west front** of the cathedral from the Place de l'Evêché. The west front was rebuilt in the 13C and given a portico in the 14C. The upper part contains a fake Romanesque rose window which was altered in the 19C. The façade is decorated with some remarkable **sculptures**. The lowest row, which dates from the 14C, includes the figures of Adam and Eve, the prophets and the early fathers of the church. The 16C reliefs above illustrate the history of the see of Tournai, while the top row features 17C figures of apostles and saints flanking a 14C statue of Notre-Dame des Malades. The heads of the Virgin and the Child were restored in 1609.

The **Evêché** (Bishop's Palace), on the left, was rebuilt after being destroyed by fire in 1940. It has Romanesque cellars and a slender turret of 1643. It stands on the site of the Merovingian royal residence. Turn left up the Rue des Orfèvres, past the 18C façade of the former Palace of the State of Tournai. This leads to the **Grand-Place**, where a statue of 1863 celebrates the heroic *Christine de Lalaing*, Princess of Epinoy. The wife of the governor of Tournai, she led the townspeople in a brave but doomed stand against the Duke of Parma in 1581. The square is dominated by the oldest **Belfry** in northern Europe. This detached stone tower, 72m high, was completed in 1192. It contains a carillon with 43 bells which were cast between the 16C and 19C.

The gilded **Halle aux Draps**, on the south side of the square, was designed in Renaissance style in 1611 by Quentin Ratte. It was rebuilt after being destroyed in the 1940 bombardment. The adjoining **Maison Tournaisienne** has a fine façade from 1677.

The Romanesque **Eglise Saint Quentin**, opposite the Belfry, was begun c 1200 on the site where a church had stood since the 7C. The choir was extended in 1464. It has an unusual interior with a transept composed of two round chapels. This contains the tomb of Jacques Kastangnes, a provost of Tournai who died in 1327. A short detour down the Rue des Maux leads to a building at no. 10 built in 1633 as a tithe barn of the vanished abbey of St Martin, which once stood south of Grand-Place.

Back on Grand-Place, an arch at no. 63 leads to the attractive lane Réduit des Sions. A curious modern bronze door on the right is decorated with four masks. It was designed by the architect Henri Lacoste. The **Musée de Folklore** occupies a handsome Renaissance building at no. 36, restored in 1949, and an adjoining hospice founded in 1690. It is open Wed–Mon 10.00–12.00 and 14.00–17.30. This appealing local history museum contains a collection of old Tournai tools, furnished kitchens and reconstructed workshops. It also displays a fascinating copy of the **relief model of Tournai** commissioned by Louis XIV after his troops took the town in 1667.

There are four towers near Grand-Place which once formed part of the first defensive walls erected in the 11C and 12C. The **Tour du Cygne** is in an alley off Rue du Cygne, the **Tour St Georges** is in Rue Saint Georges and the others are in Rue Perdue, and off the Place Reine Astrid.

2 • The Musée des Beaux-Arts

Beginning at the Belfry, follow the Rue Saint Martin to the **Musée des Arts Décoratifs** at no. 50 which contains a collection of Tournai porcelain, including a set ordered for the Duc d'Orléans c 1790. It is open Wed–Mon 10.00–12.00 and 14.00–17.30. A Neo-classical gate at no. 52 leads into a large courtyard overlooked by the **Hôtel de Ville**. This is the site of the Abbey of St Martin, an important Cluniac abbey founded in 1095.

A vanished abbey

This had become one of the wealthiest abbeys in western Europe by the 13C. Most of the abbey buildings were demolished at the time of the French Revolution, apart from the abbot's palace, built by Laurent Dewez in 1763. This Louis XIV building has been occupied by the town hall since 1809. Destroyed by German bombing in 1940, the building was restored after the war.

A building on the left side of the courtyard has been occupied by a small **natural history museum** since 1828. The long brick building was designed by Bruno Renard in Neo-classical style. It contains animal specimens and natural dioramas.

Musée des Beaux-Arts

A Neo-classical arch to the right of the town hall leads to the Musée des Beaux-Arts. This impressive collection of painting and sculpture occupies an attractive museum designed by the Belgian Art Nouveau architect Victor Horta from 1903–28. It is open Wed–Mon 10.00–12.00 and 14.00–17.30. The organic motifs at the bases of the columns are typical of Horta's style. Guillaume Charlier carved the sculptural group on the roof, which illustrates *Truth inspiring the Arts*.

The collection includes works by Campin, Gossaert, Snyders, Rubens, Jordaens, Watteau, Manet, Monet, Seurat, Van Gogh and Ensor. Many of the paintings were bequeathed in 1904 by the discerning collector and painter Henri Van Cutsem (1839–1904), including two outstanding works by Manet. Van Cutsem bequeathed his mansion in Brussels to the painter Guillaume Charlier and most of his art collection to the Musée des Beaux-Arts in Tournai.

Begin in the **sculpture hall**, a bright oval room from which the other rooms are reached. The hall contains various 19C sculptures, including works by Guillaume Charlier, whose former home in Brussels is now a museum.

Now turn left into **room A**, an octagonal room with blue walls hung with small paintings by **Flemish Masters** from the 15C–17C. There are two exquisite miniature landscapes by Jan Brueghel, no larger than postcards but filled with exquisite detail. Also in this room are a *Portrait of a Gentleman* by Adriaen Key, two *Mountain Scenes* by Joos de Momper, a *Virgin and Child* by Roger van der Weyden, and a *Baptism of Christ* set in a typically bizarre landscape by Joachim Patenir.

Room B contains several large 17C Flemish paintings, including a version of Jacob Jordaens' boisterous *The King Drinks*, a tender painting of *Jesus with Martha and Mary* set in a typical Antwerp interior and an *Adoration of the Shepherds* by Gaspard de Crayer.

There is an interesting collection of 18C *trompe l'oeil* paintings by **Piat Sauvage** in **room C**, a tiny room with red walls. The works include several *grisailles*, a self-portrait, and a realistic painting of a bronze crucifix. An octagonal room with yellow walls (**room D**) contains a collection of **French 18C paintings**, including a charming *Village Fête* by Watteau.

The **Ideal Museum** in the next room contains full-size photographs of all the paintings of **Roger van der Weyden**, from 18 different collections (including museums in Brussels, Antwerp and Leuven). The rooms beyond here are occupied by works collected by Van Cutsem.

Another yellow room (**room H**) is devoted to **Belgian Realism**. It includes Charles de Groux's *Pilgrimage at Diegem* and several Antwerp interiors by Henri de Braekeleer, including an interesting *Artist's Studio*.

The small **room G** displays a collection of drawings acquired by Van Cutsem, including a view of olive trees at Montmajour by Van Gogh, Fernand Khnopff's *The Roses* of 1912, and a striking 1890 *Study of a Woman* by Louis Anquetin.

The octagonal **room F** has four paintings of dogs by Joseph Stevens, who specialised in this limited genre. It also has a view of the *Borinage* by Constantin Meunier and several disturbing paintings by **Belgian Symbolists**. The long **room I** has several large works painted at the Belgian coast by Theodore Verstraete including Blankenberge jetty.

An interesting painting by Guillaume Van Strydonck in **room J** shows Van Cutsem and his friends (including Guillaume Charlier) at his villa in Blankenberge in 1890. This room also contains a portrait of his wife by Emile Claus, a *Still Life* by James Ensor, a View of the Pointe du Cap Martin by Claude Monet, and a view of the garden of Alfred Stevens (brother of the dog painter). There are also two outstanding works by **Edouard Manet**: *Argenteuil* of 1874 shows a couple in a boat on the Seine in the summer of 1874; the other is an appealing café scene from 1879 called *At the Père Lathuille*.

A final room to the left of the entrance (**room E**) contains paintings by Louis Gallait, including two huge historical canvases illustrating *The Plague in Tournai* in 1092 and the *Abdication of Charles V*. A smaller historical work depicts the *Last Rites over the bodies of Counts Egmont and Hoorn*.

On leaving the museum, turn right past a building (no. 18) designed by Henri Lacoste in 1935. A concrete relief attached to the side wall shows a plan of the Abbey of St Martin. Some of the stones used in the construction were salvaged from the ruins. Then turn left to reach the **Parc Communal**. A fragment of the 15C Gothic abbey cloister can be seen incorporated into the rear wall of the town hall. An arch leads to a small garden with a bronze statue of the painter *Louis Gallait* carved by Charlier in 1891.

Descend past two basins to reach the **Place Reine Astrid**, an attractive Neo-classical square laid out by Bruno Renard in 1822–37. This architect designed the handsome former concert hall on the left. This features a colonnaded apse originally occupied by a market. The building is now home the **Conservatoire**. The colonnade to the left of this building is decorated with six modern bronzes representing Tournai's ancient trades (painting, tapestry, music, gold work, dinanderie and porcelain). The **Tour de la Loucherie**, just to the right of the Conservatory, is a vestige of the 11C and 12C wall. The **Musée de la Tapisserie** opened in 1990 in a Neo-classical building at no. 9. It contains Tournai tapestries from the 15C and 16C and some modern designs. It is open Wed–Mon 10.00–12.00 and 14.00–17.30.

Leave the square on the side opposite the Conservatoire, then turn left along the Rue des Jésuites, past the former Jesuit church of 1603 (on the right) and a house belonging to the order, which was erected from 1619–1672. The **Eglise Saint Piat** in the same street stands on the site of a 6C church, traces of which were discovered during restoration work in 1971. A plaque and model inside the northwest door illustrate the findings. The tower of the present church dates from the 12C; the choir was added in the 13C and the apse is from the 14C. The lectern dates from 1403. The *Crucifixion* above the high altar is attributed to J. van Oost the Elder.

Walk 3 • The St Brice Quarter

There is an interesting old quarter on the left bank of the Scheldt around the Eglise St Brice. Beginning at the **Belfry**, go down the Rue de la Wallonie and turn left down the Rue de la Tête d'Or and the Rue des Puits-l'Eau to reach the river. On the other side, the Rue de Pont leads to the **Eglise Saint Brice**, which is dedicated to the disciple and successor of St Martin of Tours. Forced to flee after 20 years in office because of his arrogance and licentiousness, Brice went to Rome where he repented. He returned to Tours and was reinstated in his see. Such was the change in his life and manner that he was proclaimed a saint after his death. The nave of the church dates from the 12C, and the choir was extended eastwards in 1405. A 12C crypt was discovered in 1941. A silver-gilt fibula from the tomb of Childeric is kept in the sacristy.

Now turn left along the Rue Barre-Saint-Brice where two remarkable houses at **nos 12** and **14** date from between 1175 and 1200. They are among the oldest private houses still standing in Western Europe.

A Frankish royal tomb

A plaque at Place Clovis 8, just north of the church, marks the site where the tomb of the Frankish king Childeric I, who died in 481, was discovered in 1653. The tomb contained Childeric's sword and other relics including the 'golden bees' which are believed to have been used to ornament the royal robes. Adopted as a symbol by Napoleon in preference to the fleur-de-lys, they are now kept in the Bibliothèque Nationale in Paris.

To the east of the church is a memorial to the heroine **Gabrielle Petit**. A native of Tournai, she was shot by the Germans in 1916. A detour along the Rue du Quesnoy, north of the church, brings you to the **Chapelle de l'Athénée**, which has a façade of 1612.

Back at St Brice, take the Rue Saint Brice and the Rue des Moulins to reach the **Eglise Saint Jean**. Rebuilt in 1780, it retains its graceful tower of 1367. Turn left along the Rue des Croisiers to the Chapelle des Croisiers, the Chapel of the Crutched Friars, which dates from 1466. Continue along the Rue des Croisiers towards the ring boulevard then turn right along the Avenue de Craene to reach some well-preserved sections of the 13C ramparts surmounted by two towers known as Marvis and Saint Jean. The fortifications extend down to the river.

4 • The St Jacques Quarter

There are some handsome mansions in the district around the Eglise St Jacques. Beginning on Grand-Place, follow the Rue de l'Yser, the Rue Tête d'Argent and the Rue du Cygne to reach the river. A tower known as the **Tour du Cygne** dates from the 12C–13C wall. Turn left on reaching the Scheldt quay. An avenue planted with chestnut trees leads downstream to the impressive Pont des Trous, a 13C bridge of three arches guarded by towers. Once part of the 13C ramparts, it had three portcullises which could be lowered to block the river. River trips leave from the nearby jetty.

Now turn left up the Rue des Foulons to reach the **Eglise Sainte Marie Madeleine**, which was built by Bishop Marvis in 1252. The church contains a sculptured Annunciation of 1482 by Jean de la Mer, which has polychrome painting by Robert Campin.

Now turn left along the Rue de la Madeleine to reach the **Eglise Saint Jacques**. This has a 12C tower, a 13C nave and a 14C choir. The southeast chapel contains a monument, in the form of a bas-relief with faint traces of colour, to Colart d'Avesnes, who died in 1404. The lectern dates from 1411.

Now go right up the handsome Rue des Carmes. The **Musée d'Histoire et d'Archéologie** occupies a Renaissance building with a slender round tower at no.8. It is open Wed–Mon 10.00–12.00 and 14.00–17.30. This was originally the Mont de Piété, a municipal pawnshop built in 1622 by Wenceslas Coeberger. The old-fashioned museum contains artefacts from the Gallo-Roman period, including local and imported pottery, jewellery and a number of reconstructed graves. It also has medieval archaeological finds, such as stelae of Tournai marble from the 12C, sculptures, decorated capitals and local documents relating to trade and administration. There is also a good collection of coins, dies and casts of ancient seals.

The **Eglise Sainte Marguerite** at the end of the street was built in 1363 and reconstructed in 1760. A monument on the Place de Lille commemorates French soldiers who died in 1832 outside Antwerp. The Avenue de Gaulle leads from here to the attractive little **Chapelle de la Ladrerie du Val d'Orcq** of 1163.

Tournai environs

The **Mont Saint Aubert**, 5km north of Tournai, is an isolated hill of 147m, which has a commanding view of the Scheldt valley. Its name recalls a 7C bishop of Cambrai-Arras, who founded numerous monasteries in Hainaut and Flanders. A modern leisure centre on Mont Saint Aubert has a swimming pool, restaurant and cafés.

The village of **Esquelmes**, 6km north of Tournai, has a little Romanesque church. The village of **Pecq**, 3km farther on, has a ruined castle and a 13C church. The village of **Templeuve**, 8km northwest of Tournai, is believed to be the birthplace of St Eleutherius.

A memorial at **Hertain** on the French border, 7km west of Tournai, marks the place where British troops entered Belgium on 3 September 1944 during the liberation.

MONS

• • • • • •

The town of Mons and Charleroi, in Hainaut province, tend to be overlooked by tourists, yet they are lively and interesting places to visit briefly.

Mons is a lively, compact Walloon town built on a hill near the French frontier. With a population of 90,000, it is the capital of the province of Hainaut. This interesting town has an outstanding church, several good museums and lively pavement cafés on the Grand-Place. It is known in Dutch as Bergen.

Practical information

Where to stay
The *Château de la Cense au Bois*,
Route d'Ath 135, Nimy,
☎ 065.31.60.00, is an elegant 19C
country house 4km northeast of Mons.

Eating out
The *Alter Ego*, Rue Nimy 6,
☎ 065.35.52.60, is an attractive modern restaurant off the main square.

Tourist information
The Mons tourist office is located in a
handsome 17C Baroque building at
Grand-Place 22, ☎ 065.33.55.80.
The Hainaut province tourist office
occupies a 16C town house at Rue des
Clercs 31.

Lumeçon Festival
Every Trinity Sunday, the Car d'Or is
dragged by six horses through Mons in a
ceremony that probably dates from
1348. A spectacular battle is staged on
Grand-Place between St George and a
dragon affectionately known as Doudou.

Opening times
Museums in Mons are closed on
Mondays. A combination ticket can be
bought for entry to most of the town
museums. The first five museums listed
here (up to and including Hôtel de Ville)
are open Tues–Sat 12.00–18.00, and
Sun 10.00–12.00 and 14.00–18.00.
Musées du Centenaire (war

museum, archaeology and coins),
Grand-Place.
**Musée du Folklore et de la Vie
Montoise** (folklore), behind Musee des
Beaux-Arts.
Musée des Beaux-Arts (fine art),
Rue Neuve 8.
Musées Chanoine Puissant (collection of church furniture and decorative
art owned by Canon Puissant), Rue
Notre-Dame-Débonnaire 22.
Hôtel de Ville, Grand Place, is open
for guided tours only daily Jul–Aug, at
14.30. At other times, group tours may
be booked in advance.
Mundaneum (collection of ephemera
of 19C philanthropist Paul Otlet), Rue
de Nimy 76, is open Tues–Fri
10.00–18.00, weekends 12.00–20.00.
Musée François Duesberg (porcelain and clocks) Square Roosevelt 12, is
open on Tues, Thur and weekends
14.00–19.00.
**Treasury of the Collégiale Sainte
Waudru** is open Tues–Sat
13.30–18.00 and Sun 13.30–17.00. It
is closed Nov–mid-March and in early
June.
**Centre de Recherche et
d'Information sur la Protection
de la Nature** (natural history
museum) Rue Galliers 7, is open
Mon–Fri 08.30–12.00 and
13.00–17.00.
Maison Van Gogh in Cuesmes is open
Tues–Sun 10.00–18.00.

History of Mons

Mons probably began as a **Roman military post** on a hill just east of the
road from Bavai to Utrecht. A settlement grew up in the 7C around a hermitage founded by Waudru, the daughter of Count Walbert of Hainaut and
wife of St Vincent Madelgar of Soignies. There is a local tradition that men
from Mons fought on the English side at the battle of Crécy in 1346.

The tragic **Jacqueline of Hainaut** surrendered to Philip the Good at Mons
in 1433. The town prospered in the 16C under Charles V, when it was famous
for the quality of its cloth. Captured in 1572 by Louis of Nassau, Mons was
rapidly retaken by the duke of Alva. It was captured by Louis XIV in 1691,

Marlborough in 1709 (after the Battle of Malplaquet), the Prince de Conti in 1746 (after the Battle of Fontenoy) and Dumouriez in 1792.

The Angel of Mons

At the opening of the First World War the British army moved to Mons to support the French offensive. By the morning of 23 August 1914 it was in position. One flank faced northeast between the town and the river Sambre, while the other faced north along the line of the Canal du Centre, which runs west from Mons. This long front of some 45km proved impossible to hold against a German superiority of twenty to one, particularly after the French withdrew on the right flank. By early afternoon the town had to be evacuated, and on the following morning the historic retreat to Le Cateau and the Marne was under way. Some soldiers claim that at a critical point in the fighting an angel appeared in the sky. This gave courage to the flagging British army and forced the Germans to retreat. The legend of the 'Angel of Mons' is depicted in a painting in the Hôtel de Ville, but recent research suggest that the story was deliberately fabricated by a journalist.

During the Second World War, French troops entered Mons on 10 May 1940. The Germans launched several air attacks the following week, hitting the Collégiale Sainte Waudru twice. The French withdrew and the inhabitants fled, so that the town was virtually empty when the Germans took it over on 19 May. Mons came under severe air attack again in 1944, this time by the Allies. The town was liberated on 2 September by American forces which had driven straight through from Meaux near Paris. There followed two days of fierce fighting to the south as a German rearguard attempted to isolate the Americans, but the fighting ended with the taking of 27,000 German prisoners.

Born in Mons

Philippa of Hainaut (c 1314–69), the wife of Edward III of England, was born in Mons. The 16C musician and rival of Palestrina **Orlando di Lasso**, sometimes known as Roland de Lassus (1532–94), came from Mons, as did **Louise de Stolberg**, Countess of Albany (1752–1824) and wife of the Young Pretender.

A walk in Mons

Beginning at the **station**, take the Rue de la Moussière to reach Square Roosevelt, where the **Musée des Arts Décoratifs François Duesberg** occupies a former 19C bank at no. 12. The museum has a remarkable collection of 18C and 19C pendulum clocks. It also displays a large collection of porcelain bequeathed by Henri Glépin, a wealthy citizen of Mons who died in 1898. It is open on Tues, Thur, and weekends 14.00–19.00.

Cross the square to enter the **Collégiale Sainte Waudru**, one of the finest examples of the Late Gothic style in Belgium.

The church takes its name from St Waudru, a hermit who built a primitive chapel on this site during the late 7C. No trace remains either of this building or the three others that followed over the next 800 years. It is known that a Romanesque church stood here in 1450, the year in which work on the present building began. The original architects were Jean Spiskin and Mathys de Layens. The choir was completed in 1502, the transepts by 1527, and the nave by about the end of the 16C.

Plans were drawn up in 1547 to build a tower which, at 190 metres, would have been higher than the planned Mechelen cathedral tower. Work stopped c 1570 on the death of the architect, Jean de Thuin. The authorities decided in 1686 that the tower should remain in an unfinished state.

The vast interior (115m long, 32m wide, 24m high) is remarkable for its structural simplicity and stylistic unity. There are exquiste **sculptures** by the local

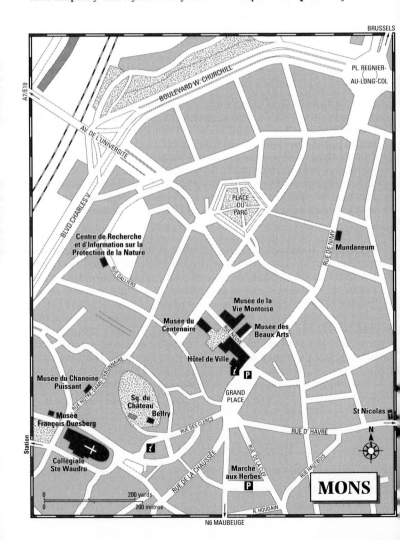

artist Jacques du Broeucq (c 1505–84), including fragments of the great **rood-loft** carved in 1535–39 and broken up in 1797. The relics of this masterpiece include reliefs of the *Resurrection*, *Ascension* and *Descent of the Holy Ghost* in the north transept. Look out for the sculptor's signature near the right foot of Christ on the *Resurrection* relief.

The **south transept** contains reliefs of the *Flagellation of Christ*, and the *Bearing of the Cross*. Du Broeucq also carved the statues surrounding the choir, and the reliefs on the high altar and in the chapels. Look out for the unusual and effective rendering of the *Last Supper* in the fourth ambulatory chapel on the north side of the church. The sculptor's memorial in the south transept is decorated with three medallions on the themes of the *Creation*, the *Triumph of the Church* and the *Last Judgement*.

Three adjoining **chapels** off the north aisle contain some beautifully preserved 15C funerary reliefs. The east chapel of the south aisle contains a heraldic painting of 1577 which sets out the genealogy of St Waudru. The choir stalls of 1707 from the church of St Germain (demolished) are surmounted by medallion-heads from the abbey of Cambron-Casteau. The chariot parked in front of the choir is known as **Car d'Or**. Made in 1780, it is used to carry the shrine of St Waudru in solemn procession through the town on Trinity Sunday. The **Treasury**, in the former chapter house, has the ring, cross and brooch of St Waudru, and a 13C reliquary of St Vincent attributed to Hugo d'Oignies.

Leave the church by the north door and continue down the Rue Notre-Dame-Débonnaire to reach the **Musées du Chanoine Puissant** at no. 22, open Tues–Sat 12.00–18.00, and Sun 10.00–12.00 and 14.00–18.00. One of the two museums occupies the 16C Le Vieux Logis, formerly a refuge of the abbey of Ghislenghien. The other museum is located in the 13C Chapelle Sainte Marguerite. **Le Vieux Logis** contains 16C chimneypieces, furniture, weapons and ironwork. The **chapel** contains 15C to 17C wooden statues, church furnishings and plate, vestments, books, manuscripts, textiles and lace. The two collections were amassed by Canon Edmond Puissant (1880–1934), who was granted special dispensation to be buried in the chapel.

The nearby **Centre de Recherche et d'Information sur la Protection de la Nature** at Rue Galliers 7 is an interesting natural history museum. Its most curious object is the skeleton of Julius Koch, who died in 1902 aged 30. Known as Giant Constantin, he measured 2.59m and may well have been the world's tallest man. The museum is open Mon–Fri 08.30–12.00 and 13.00–17.00.

Return to the Collégiale and turn up the steep lane leading to the Square du Château. A Gothic gate leads to a park, open May–mid-Sept Tues–Sun 10.00–20.00; mid-Sept–Apr Tues–Sun 10.00–18.00. The castle of the counts of Hainaut stood here until it was demolished in 1866. Turn right to the **Chapelle Saint Calixte**, built in 1051 by Richilde, Countess of Hainaut, to house the relics of St Calixtus. She was given these by her aunt, abbess of a convent near Cologne. St Calixtus was a Christian slave who became pope in 217. Famed for his lenient attitude to repentant sinners, he was probably martyred c 222. The chapel is, at least in part, the oldest building in Mons. It contains murals recreated in 1951 from records and drawings of the 11C or 12C originals (now destroyed), which were discovered in 1872. A small collection of engravings, maps and armour is displayed in the chapel.

The **crypt** contains two effigies dating from the 12C–14C which were transferred here from Saint Ghislain and Cambron-Casteau. The much damaged 12C figure represents Gilles de Chin, a famous knight and Grand Chamberlain of Hainaut. A nearby **underground cellar** used during World War Two as a bomb shelter can be visited (the custodian of the Chapelle Saint Calixte has a key for the cellar). The chapel is open Tues–Sat 12.00–18.00 and Sun 10.00–12.00 and 14.00–18.00.

The park also contains a small tower, a relic of the 11C ramparts, and the 12C basement of the castle. The summit is crowned by the impressive Baroque **Belfry** built from 1662–1672 by the local architect Louis Ledoux. The belfry is 87m high and can be seen from 30km away. It contains a 47-bell carillon. Panoramic views of the Battles of Mons in 1914 are attached to the upper balcony. A ceremony was held in 1935 in which soil taken from the graves of every British and Canadian soldier killed in the Mons area during the two World Wars was scattered at the foot of the belfry. The **British and Canadian War Memorial** stands on the edge of the park. Designed by Sir Edwin Lutyens, the monument was unveiled in 1952 by Field Marshal Lord Alexander, who had fought here in 1914.

Descend the steep Rue des Clercs to reach **Grand-Place**, an attractive square with a market on Friday mornings. The ornate Brabant Gothic **Hôtel de Ville** was built here in 1458 by Mathys de Layens, architect of Leuven's town hall. The Baroque bell tower was added in 1718. Historians remain baffled about the purpose of the 15C iron monkey to the left of the entrance. Known as the 'Grande Garde', it may once have formed part of a children's pillory. The monkey is believed to bring good luck to those who stroke its head. An elaborate iron lock on the main door represents the town's demolished castle. It is a copy of the original which is kept inside the building.

There are several **memorials** inside the porch, including one to the 5th Royal Irish Lancers, another commemorating the Canadian liberation of Mons in 1918, and a third expressing gratitude for food sent to Belgium by America during the First World War. The town hall contains some early chimneypieces and several 17C and 18C tapestries. A painting of 1934 by Marcel Gillis depicting the legend of the *Angel of Mons* hangs in the mayor's office (not open to visitors). The Hôtel de Ville is open for guided tours only daily Jul–Aug, at 14.30. At other times, group tours may be booked in advance.

Go through the gate into a courtyard and then through the passage straight ahead to reach the **Jardin du Mayeur**. The courtyard to the right is overlooked by the former 16C charitable lending bank, which still has its original barred windows. The **Musées du Centenaire**, open Tues–Sat 12.00–18.00, and Sun 10.00–12.00 and 14.00–18.00, now occupies this impressive building. The ground floor rooms are devoted to an interesting if dusty display of weapons and uniforms from the **First World War**, including two

Mons, detail of lock in town hall door

Allied guns which fired the last shots of the war, and several mementoes that recall the courage of the Belgians in resisting the Germans. One room on the first floor contains a large collection of old European **coins and medals** donated by Henri Glépin and an interesting collection of historical engravings. The other rooms are filled with prehistoric, Gallo-Roman and Frankish finds. The top floor has a large collection of weapons and uniforms from the **Second World War**. A prehistoric menhir stands in the garden outside the museum.

Now go back to Grand-Place and turn left to reach the Rue Neuve. The **Musée des Beaux-Arts** at no. 8 opened in 1913 to display works bequeathed by Henri Glépin. It is open Tues–Sat 12.00–18.00, and Sun 10.00–12.00 and 14.00– 18.00. Enlarged and modernised in 1970, it has an interesting collection of **Flemish paintings** by Cornelis de Vos, Jan Gossaert, Jan Metsys, Paul Bril, Antoino Moro and Otto Venius. The museum also has 17C to 19C works by French, Dutch and Italian artists, but it is perhaps best known for its collection of **modern paintings** by the Mons School, the Hainaut Five, the Nervia group and Paul Delvaux.

A lane beyond the museum leads to the **Musée du Folklore et de la Vie Montoise**, open Tues–Sat 12.00–18.00, and Sun 10.00–12.00 and 14.00–18.00. Occupying a former convent built in 1636 (see the date on the four iron wall anchors), the museum has an interesting collection of local folklore. An exhibition in the basement covers the Lumeçon festival in Mons. An overgrown garden in front of the museum is filled with fragments of sculpture saved from demolished buildings.

Return to Grand-Place again and turn left down the Rue de Nimy. The **Mundaneum** at no. 76 occupies a former Art Deco department store. A fascinating exhibition in the restored building charts the utopian ideals of Paul Otlet, a Brussels lawyer who founded the Mundaneum in the 1890s as a universal library. The museum displays a reconstruction of Otlet's study and a selection of documents from the vast collection of memorabilia, including old posters and American magazine covers. It is open Tues–Fri 10.00–18.00, weekends 12.00–20.00.

Go back towards Grand-Place and turn left down the Rue Clesse, right along Rue Damoiseaux and straight ahead down the narrow Ruelle de l'Atre. This leads to the **Eglise Saint Nicolas**, a dilapidated 17C Baroque church filled with gloriously gaudy 18C woodcarvings. These are laden with angels, saints and gilded swags.

Continue along the Rue d'Havré to the Place de Flandres where an equestrian statue represents Count Baldwin of Flanders (1171–1205). One of the leaders of the Fourth Crusade, Baldwin was elected Emperor of Constantinople in 1204. The following year he was taken in battle by the Bulgarians and died in captivity.

Mons environs

First World War battlefields
The countryside around Mons was the scene of desperate fighting in 1914 as the British Expeditionary Force attempted to stall the German advance. The Mons tourist office sells a useful guide to local sites linked to the First World War.

The **Supreme Headquarters of Allied Powers in Europe** (SHAPE) is located on the N6, 8km northeast of Mons. This is the military headquarters of NATO. Both NATO and SHAPE were originally located near Paris, but were told by General De Gaulle to leave France in 1967.

A **memorial** on the N6 near the SHAPE headquarters commemorates the first shot fired by a British soldier in Belgium. Corporal Thomas of the 4th Royal Irish Dragoon Guards fired the shot at daybreak on 22 August 1914. His target was the outpost of the German 4th Cuirassiers. Just over four years later, Canadian troops halted at this same spot after the cease-fire was declared at 11.00 on 11 November 1918.

The hillocks of **Mont Panisel** and the **Bois de Mons**, just southeast of Mons, were the scene of fierce fighting on the afternoon of 23 August 1914, when three British battalions held an entire German corps here. This allowed the main British force to retreat. A memorial stands at **La Bascule**, a busy cross-roads on the N90 and N40. More than four years later, on 9 and 10 November 1918, German rearguards held out on these hillocks against the attacking Canadians.

The beautiful military cemetery at **Saint-Symphorien**, 6km southeast of Mons, contains the graves of British and German soldiers killed in the fighting. The cemetery was begun by the Germans in 1914 on the spoil heaps of an old potash mine.

The town of **Villers-Saint Ghislain**, 7km southeast of Mons, was the headquarters in August 1914 of General Allenby, commander of the British cavalry. The first important cavalry action of the war was fought on 22 August on the rise to the west of **Péronnes**, 7km east of Villers-Saint Ghislain.

A memorial at **Jemappes**, 2km west of Mons, commemorates a French military victory in 1792 when an army led by Dumouriez defeated the Austrians. The British 9th Brigade made a stand here on 23 August 1914 to delay the German army crossing the canal.

The canal crossing at **Saint Ghislain**, 9km west of Mons, was also defended by the British in 1914. The town was largely rebuilt after the First World War. It takes its name from St Gislenus, a 7C Frankish recluse who founded the Benedictine abbey of St Peter and St Paul to accommodate his followers.

The 9th Lancers made a gallant charge in 1914 at **Audregnies**, 4km southeast of the border town of Quiévrain. Captain Grenfell, who later died at Ypres, won the Victoria Cross here. The Château de la Haie at **Sars-la-Bruyère**, 18km southwest of Mons, was the British headquarters before the first Battle of Mons.

Borinage

The Borinage is a densely populated district southwest of Mons where coal has been mined since the 13C. The local mines have now closed, forcing the area to turn to other industries.

Van Gogh in the Borinage

Vincent van Gogh lived at Wasmes, 7km southwest of Mons, from 1878–1879. He preached to the miners who worked in the nearby Borinage. After working briefly as an evangelist in Pâturages, 4km south of Wasmes, he was appointed to an official post in Wasmes. Van Gogh lived in poverty, gave away his clothes, and nursed the victims of typhus. He was eventually dismissed for urging the mine owners to improve the lot of the miners. His missionary and philanthropic endeavours are commemorated by a monument at Wasmes by Ossip Zadkine. After his dismissal, Van Gogh moved to Cuesmes, 3km south of Mons, in August 1879 and stayed there until October 1880. The small house in which he had his first studio stands in a wood on the northern edge of Cuesmes.

The **Grand-Hornu** complex, 9km west of Mons, is an outstanding example of an early 19C miners' township. Founded in 1810 by the French industrialist Henri de Gorge, it was built by Bruno Renard from 1820–32. The Neo-classical complex has been sensitively restored as an industrial archaeological site (open Tues–Sun 10.00–18.00; closes 16.00 Oct–Feb). A museum of contemporary art was being built here at the time of writing.

The **Parc d'Aventures Scientifiques** is a stimulating science park which opened in 2000 on the site of a former coal mine at Rue de Mons, Frameries, 5km southwest of Mons. Designed by the French architect Jean Nouvel, the park incorporates an extensive industrial site including the former machine house, mine-shaft, railway line and slag heap. Imaginative hands-on exhibitions allow visitors to explore concepts of science, geography and industrial history. The centre will eventually include a brasserie and bookshop. Opening hours: school terms, Mon, Tues, Thur, Fri 09.00–1700. Sat & Sun 10.00–1800; school holidays, daily 10.00–1800; July and Aug, daily 10.00–19.00.

The town of **Boussu**, 2km west of Hornu, was ruled by Maximilien de Hennin (1542–79). Known in Dutch history as 'Bossu' (the Hunchback), De Hennin served the States General between 1576 and 1577 in their struggle against Don John of Austria.

The border village of **Roisin**, 13km south of Quiévrain, was the home of the poet Emile Verhaeren (1855–1916). His house was burnt down in 1914, but it has been restored as a museum (open Sat–Thur 10.00–12.00 and 14.00–18.00).

The ruined abbey of **Bélian**, just south of Mons, served as the headquarters of Louis XIV in 1691 and Marlborough in 1709.

The **Cheval Blanc** cross-roads, 6km south of Mons where the N6 crosses the N546, was the scene of heavy fighting in the **Second World War** in September 1944 when the Germans tried to cut off the Americans who had reached Mons. The Americans established their headquarters in the Château de Warelles, west of the road about halfway between Cheval Blanc and Bois-Bourdon. Almost surrounded here, the American commander's call for help brought massive air support. The short stretch of Roman road which runs west from Bois-Bourdon to Goegnies-Chaussée was blocked by over a thousand destroyed German vehicles. A memorial to the American 1st Infantry Division stands by the road at **Bois-Bourdon**, 5km south of Cheval Blanc on the N6.

Neolithic flint mines known as the Camp à Cailloux have been found in fields west of **Spiennes**, 2km southwest of Saint-Symphorien.

The village of **Malplaquet**, where Marlborough and Prince Eugene defeated the French marshals Villars and Boufflers on 11 September 1709, lies just across the French border, c 16km southwest of Mons and 8km south of Sars-la-Bruyère.

CHARLEROI

Charleroi is an unexpectedly pleasant town in the heart of Belgium's 19C industrial region. Though surrounded by steelworks and slag heaps, the town (population 212,000) has remained untouched by industrialisation. Originally a 16C hilltop fortress, Charleroi is divided into an upper town, where the barracks once stood, and a lower town near the River Sambre. The lower town is especially attractive with its shopping arcades, bookshops and cafés. The main sights are the Musée des Beaux-Arts and Musée du Verre, both in the upper town.

Practical information

Getting there

Charleroi Airport (officially known as *Brussels South Charleroi*) is at Gosselies, 6km north of Charleroi. The main station in Charleroi is *Charleroi-Sud*. The station is five minutes on foot from the town centre.

Where to stay

££ *Socatel*, Boulevard Tirou 96, ☎ 071.31.98.11, is a comfortable hotel in the lower town.
££ *Piersoulx*, Rue Grand Piersoulx 8, Gosselies, 6km north of Charleroi, ☎ 071.35.66.87, is a comfortable hotel with a good restaurant.

Eating out

Mirabelle, Rue Marcinelle 7, ☎ 071.33.39.88, is an excellent fish restaurant off Place Albert I.
Café
The best cafés tend to be found around Place Albert I. The *Prince Baudouin*, Place Albert I 17, is an attractive modern café on the main square.

Tourist information

Square de la Gare du Sud, ☎ 071.31.82.18.

Public transport

The **Musée de la Photographie** is a short bus ride from Charleroi-Sud station. Take no. 70, 71 or 170.

Opening times

Musée des Beaux-Arts (fine art), Hôtel de Ville, Place Charles II, and the **Musée du Verre** (museum of glass), Boulevard Defontaine, are open Tues–Sat 09.00–17.00.
Musée de la Photographie (19C photographer's studio, cameras and photographs), Mont-sur-Marchienne, is open Tues–Sun 10.00–18.00.
All museums are closed on public holidays.

History

Charleroi was established as a **hilltop fortress** by the Spaniards in 1666 and named in honour of King Charles II of Spain. Following its capture nine months later by Louis XIV, the town was encircled with **ramparts designed by Vauban** (which were torn down in 1868 to create a ring of boulevards). Charleroi was besieged four times by the French in 1794. Twenty-one years later, Napoleon led his troops across the Sambre at Charleroi, driving out the Prussians and advancing up the roads to Quatre-Bras and Ligny. The Charleroi region became heavily **industrialised** during the 19C when steelworks and coal mines were developed. In August 1914 French troops vainly attempted to defend the Sambre bridgehead against the mighty German army. The town was captured by the Germans in May 1940 and remained under occupation until it was **liberated by the Americans** on 3 September 1944. Charleroi's heavy industry declined catastrophically in the post-war years, yet the city retains its dynamic spirit, now pinning its hopes on the development of the Gosselies airport (known rather grandly as Brussels South Charleroi).

A walk in Charleroi

The walk begins at the **station**, crossing the Sambre by a modern bridge with 19C statues of workers by Constantin Meunier. Turn right along the Quai de Brabant, past an interesting modernist building at **no. 5** built in 1935 by Marcel

Leborgne for Pianos De Heug. A left turn down Rue du Canal leads to the Passage de la Bourse, a covered arcade built in 1890–93. At the far end, turn right along Rue de Collège to reach Place Albert I.

Cross the square and ascend the cobbled Rue de la Montagne to reach **Place Charles II** on the hilltop. The star-shaped street pattern survives from the period when the summit was occupied by a Spanish fortress. The yellow Baroque façade of the **Eglise Saint Christophe** was built in 1667, but transformed in 1956 by the addition of a modern nave and dome. The **Hôtel de Ville** occupies a triangular site where Spanish barracks once stood. Built in 1936 in Art Deco style, it has a modern Belfry and a concert hall.

The **Musée des Beaux-Arts,** open Tues–Sat 09.00–17.00, was opened in 1980 on the second floor of the Hôtel de Ville. It owns a good collection of works by artists from the Charleroi region, including **René Magritte** who went to school in Charleroi. One room is devoted to François Joseph Navez, a Neoclassical painter born in Charleroi in 1787, who studied under Jacques Louis David in Paris. But the most impressive works in the collection are by **Pierre Paulus**, an Expressionist who painted the grim industrial region around Charleroi in a style that recalls Manet's studies of the Gare Saint Lazare. Paulus captures the bleak landscape of Belgium's Black Country in works such as *Jeunesse* (Youth) of 1911, which shows a courting couple strolling along an industrial canal. His mother cradling a child (*La Berceuse*) has the tenderness of a medieval Madonna. The museum also has works by **Constantin Meunier**, who visited the Black Country to paint and sculpt the workers.

The museum has a small collection of **Surrealist paintings**, including Paul Delvaux's *Annunciation*, and René Magritte's *La Liberté de l'Esprit*. A metal staircase leads to the **Musée Jules Destrée** in the attic, which contains interesting mementoes of a local lawyer and art critic who campaigned on behalf of the working class and argued in 1912 for the creation of a separate Walloon state.

A short walk from Place Charles II leads to the **Musée du Verre**, which occupies a modern building in the Boulevard Defontaine. The collection features **ancient and modern glass**, including fine examples of Roman, Chinese, Islamic, Byzantine, Venetian and Bohemian glassware. The museum also describes the manufacture and decoration of glass. It is open Tues–Sat 09.00–17.00.

Charleroi environs

The outstanding **Musée de la Photographie** occupies a 19C red brick convent in the suburb of Mont-sur-Marchienne (see public transport). The collection includes a 19C photographer's studio, a room of Belgian family portraits, several hundred antique cameras and a display of international photographs. An imaginative discovery area on the first floor allows children to find out the secrets of photography. The museum has a photography bookshop and a small café. It is open Tues–Sun 10.00–18.00.

René Magritte lived in the small town of **Châtelet**, 3km east of Charleroi, from 1904 to 1917. A plaque is attached to the Maison Magritte at Rue des Gravelles 95 where the family moved in 1911, having previously lived at no. 77 in the same street. Magritte was living here when his mother committed suicide in the River Sambre in 1912.

The village of **Trazegnies**, 10km northwest of Charleroi, has a small château.

Originally built in the 12C, it was rebuilt from 16C–17C, and enlarged in 1854. The 13C church has the tombs of the lords of Trazegnies, including one carved by Lucas Faydherbe.

The town of **Fleurus**, 12km northeast of Charleroi, is believed to be the site of Julius Caesar's crushing defeat of the Nervii in 57 BC, though the village of **Presles**, 12km southeast of Charleroi, also claims to be the site of the battle. Fleurus was the scene of another battle in 1690 when the French under Marshal Luxembourg defeated the Germans and Dutch. A third major battle was fought here on 26 June 1794, when the French revolutionary army under Marshal Jourdan defeated the Austrians, led indifferently by the Prince of Coburg.

The hamlet of **Frasnes-lez-Gosselies**, 14km north of Charleroi, has an interesting church built between the 13C and 17C.

The Rivers of the Ardennes

THE VALLEY OF THE MEUSE

The Belgian Meuse flows through a remarkable landscape of limestone cliffs, fortified towns, historic castles and industrial works. The towns along the Meuse share a picturesque architectural style known as Mosan renaissance which combines grey stone and brown brick.

The French border to Namur

The Meuse enters Belgium at Heer-Agimont, 3km north of Givet in France. Keeping to the left bank, which is the more attractive, first stop is the town of **Hastière**. The town is divided into Hastière-Lavaux on the left bank and Hastière-par-delà on the right bank. The **Grottes du Pont d'Arcole** (open daily Apr–Sept 10.00–16.00; Jul–Aug 09.00–19.00; Oct–Mar on Wed, Thur, Sat, Sun 10.00–16.00) are on the left bank. On the opposite bank is a mixed Romanesque and Gothic **church**. This once belonged to a priory which was subordinate to Waulsort. The present church, much restored, was built from c 1033–1260. The crypt is the oldest part of the building. Some of the misericords of the stalls in the apse date from the 13C. The church contains the tomb of the 13C Abbot Allard who was responsible for much of the later construction work. There is also a striking triptych of 1914 by Auguste Donnay depicting the martyrdom of St Walhere, and an interesting *Stations of the Cross* from Vietnam.

The church at **Onhaye**, 4km north of Hastière, contains the tomb of St Walhere, a local priest who was murdered after he reproached a colleague for his dissolute life.

A 17C château at **Waulsort**, 4km east of Hastière on the Meuse, occupies the site of the abbey established c 962 by the Irish missionary bishop St Forannan. The monks from Waulsort built the first bridge across the Meuse at Dinant in 1080. The château at **Freyr**, 3km north of Waulsort, dates mainly from the 18C. It has attractive formal gardens planted in the French style with orangeries and a maze. Castle open May–Sept on Sun 14.00–18.00.

After passing the Rocher Bayard and Anseremme on the right bank, the river arrives in Dinant, which is described in a separate chapter. Beyond Dinant, there is a choice of roads on the left or right bank. The narrow and winding road on the right bank is the more picturesque, but the main sights are on the left bank.

Bouvignes

Leaving Dinant by the left bank, the first town is Bouvignes, 2km north. Now something of a backwater, it is a rather interesting town with a long history.

History

First mentioned in 882, a fortress built here in the 11C by the Count of Namur was strengthened by town walls in 1176. The castle of **Crèvecoeur**, now a ruin, was built above the town in 1320. This obsession with fortifications was due largely to a deep enmity and commercial rivalry between Bouvignes, which belonged to Namur, and Dinant, which belonged to Liège. The rivalry, accentuated by the grant of a charter to Bouvignes in 1213, was not finally resolved until 1964 when Bouvignes was transferred to the old enemy of Dinant. Yet an inscription above the entrance to the Musée de l'Eclairage gives an idea of local resentment: '*1213 Bouvignons nous étions. 1964 Bouvignons nous resterons.*'

Both towns were **sacked and burnt by the French** in 1554. It was during this attack that three women of Crèvecoeur are said to have fought the French until they ran out of ammunition. Preferring death to dishonour, they leapt hand-in-hand from the battlements.

Bouvignes may have been the birthplace of **St Walhere**, a priest murdered by a dissolute colleague and buried in Onhaye church. The artist **Henri met de Bles**, who painted in the style of Joachim Patinir, was born in Bouvignes in 1480.

The 16C Hôtel de Ville in the main square contains the unusual **Musée de l'Eclairage** (open May to early Oct Wed–Mon, 13.00–18.00). The museum traces lighting techniques from prehistoric times to the present day. It contains over 300 exhibits including lamps, accessories and documents. The **Eglise Saint Lambert** dates from c 1200 but was altered in the 15C, again after the French siege of 1554 and yet again during the 18C. After war damage in 1914, it was restored to its 15C appearance. It contains an outstanding early 16C polychrome Antwerp retable, which features a lively representation of the Passion with more than 50 figures clad in costumes that are a curious mixture of Eastern and Western styles. The church also has a poignant early 16C wooden *Bon Dieu de Pitié*.

The main town gate flanked by two small fortified towers lies to the north of the church.

The town of **Anhée**, 6km north of Dinant on the left bank, is an attractive small resort at the foot of the picturesque **Molignée Valley**. It is worth making a detour to explore this narrow, winding valley. The route passes a large farm on the left, 2km from Anhée, which was formerly an abbey. The ruined castle of **Montaigle** clings precariously to a spur of rock 6km from Anhée (open Mar–Oct Tues–Fri, 11.00–16.00, weekends 11.00–19.00; daily Jul–Aug 11.00–19.00). Built in the 13C by Guy de Dampierre, it belonged to the Counts of Namur. The French blew it up in 1554. A **museum** contains several scale models of the castle.

The imposing neo-Gothic buildings of the Benedictine abbey of **Maredsous**, founded in 1872, stand high above the Molignée valley. The large, austere monastic church is very impressive (open daily 09.00–18.00).

A large fortified farm of 1670 at **Falaën**, 10km southeast of Maredsous, contains an exhibition on monastic brewing and bread-making (open daily Jul–Aug 13.00–20.00; at weekends Apr–Jun and Sept, and Sun only Mar, Oct and Nov).

The Benedictine convent at **Maredret**, 1km southwest of Maredsous, was built in 1891. It produces liturgical prints, miniatures, ceramics and embroidery. It also offers traditional monastic hospitality. The **Musée du Bois** in Maredret village has an interesting exhibition of 18C to 20C woodwork (open Thur–Tues 09.30–12.30, 14.00–18.00; also Wed in Jul–Aug).

Return to the Meuse at Anhée and cross the river to reach **Yvoir**, 8km north of Dinant on the right bank. This attractive riverside resort lies at the foot of the winding Bocq valley. The **Domaine de Champalle** contains large tropical greenhouses where exotic fish and butterflies are bred. The **Ile d'Yvoir** is a small island in the Meuse reached by a ferry (operates May–Sept from 10.00). It has a restaurant, children's playground and paddling pool. A footbridge crosses the Meuse beside the railway, 1km south of the road bridge.

A short detour south leads to the ruins of the castle of **Poilvache**, 4km southeast of Yvoir. The castle, which is 125m above the Meuse, offers some fine views. The extensive ruins include oubliettes and a rock-well. Tradition claims that it was built by the Quatre Fils Aymon. It certainly existed in the 10C and served as a stronghold for the Counts of Namur and John the Blind of Luxembourg. It was destroyed by the Liégeois in 1430. The curious name Poilvache (cow's skin) comes from a successful assault by besiegers who disguised themselves in skins and hid among the cattle.

A footpath ascends from **Houx**, 2km south of Yvoir on the right bank, to the ruins of Poilvache castle. Further south of Houx on the road, there is a good view across the Meuse to the ruins of Crèvecoeur Castle above Bouvignes.

The abbey of **Leffe**, 6km south of Yvoir on the right bank of the Meuse, was founded in 1152 by the Premonstratensian order. It was dissolved in 1794, but restored to the Church in 1902. The surviving buildings date from the 17C to the 20C. The abbey is famed for its Leffe beers.

Returning to the left bank, the château at **Annevoie**, 5km north of Yvoir, is famed for its outstanding water gardens laid out in 1775 in a mixture of French, Italian and English styles. The gardeners plant attractive floral displays which vary according to the season. The château is 18C but with a 17C tower. It has interesting stucco work by the Moretti brothers. The gardens are open Apr–Oct daily 09.30–18.30.

The resort of **Profondeville**, 3km north of Annevoie on the left bank, is a pleasant town facing picturesque cliffs. The town traces its origins back to

Roman times. The monks of Fosses-la-Ville are said to have hidden the relics of St Foillan here when their abbey was sacked by the Vikings.

Cross the river at Profondeville to reach the **Rochers de Frênes** on the right bank. The road climbs to a belvedere and café with a splendid view of the Meuse. There is a small grotto nearby.

Back on the left bank, the village of **Wépion**, 5km south of Namur, is famous among Belgians for its delicious strawberries. The village has a small **museum of strawberries**. Namur and its environs are described in a separate chapter.

From Namur to Huy

Follow the left bank from Namur to pass below the **Rocher du Roi**, where King Albert I fell to his death in 1934 while climbing the rocks on his own. The tragedy is commemorated by a cross on the road 3km east of Beez. A small museum contains some souvenirs of the King.

The straggling village of **Marche-les-Dames**, 1km northeast of the Rocher du Roi, is said to owe its name to the crusaders' wives who settled here in the 11C. These women may have founded the abbey situated on the road to Gelbressée. Now a school, its buildings date mainly from the 18C, though the church, which has a 13C figure of Our Lady, is from about the 14C. The nearby château of Arenberg, rebuilt in 1917, is used by the army.

A brief detour may be made up the **Gelbressée valley** to the north, which was the scene of heavy fighting in 1914. The village of Gelbressée has a Romanesque church. Just north of the village is the attractive moated château of **Franc-Waret**, rebuilt in 1748 but retaining its early 17C tower. The interior has period furniture, Brussels tapestries from designs by Bernard van Orley, and Flemish paintings. (Open Jun–Sept at weekends and public holidays 14.00–17.30.)

Back on the Meuse, cross the river at **Namêche**, 2km southeast of Marche-les-Dames. The village of **Samson**, on the right bank roughly opposite Namêche, lies below a group of rocks crowned by fragments of a 13C ruin. This was once the residence of Sibylle de Lusignan, the mother of Baldwin V, King of Jerusalem.

A pleasant road ascends the **Valley of the Samson** to the south, past an animal park where beavers can be watched. The road continues to the **Grotte de Goyet**, 3km south of the Meuse near Mozet. This complex of caves is considered one of the most important archaeological sites in Europe. Excavations began here in 1868. Archaeologists have uncovered the remains of 255 bears, 12 mammoths, 6 lions and 8 rhinoceroses. A guided tour explores the series of caves inhabited by Neanderthal and Cro-Magnon man. Several reconstructed scenes evoke prehistoric life in the caves. The **museum** contains human remains, tools and prehistoric weapons. Excellent guided tours are given in English, French, Dutch and German. (Open Mar–Nov Thur–Tues 10.00–17.00.)

The road continues below an extraordinary turreted folly of 1870 which stands on 10C foundations at **Faulx-les-Tombes**, 3km south of Goyet. The remains of the Cistercian abbey of **Grand-Pre**, now a large farm, are about 1km further. The village of **Wierde**, 4km west of Faulx-les-Tombes, has an 11C Romanesque church with unusual loopholes in the tower.

Andenne

Back on the Meuse, the largely industrial town of Andenne owes its origin to a convent founded here c 690 by St Begga, who died in 698.

St Begga

The daughter of Pepin of Landen and St Ida, she married Angisilus, the son of St Arnulf of Metz. Her son Pepin of Heristal founded the Carolingian dynasty. One day, while hunting, he found a hen protecting her seven chicks from his hounds. Regarding this as a sign from Heaven, Begga built her convent and seven churches. Nothing survives of this ancient foundation. The **Collégiale Sainte Begge** was built in the 18C by Laurent Dewez in the south of the town against the hill. It contains the tomb of St Begga and a bust-reliquary.

The **Musée de la Céramique** at Rue Charles Lapierre 29 (open May–Sept Mon–Fri 09.00–12.00 and 13.00–16.30, weekends 14.00–17.00) has an interesting collection of porcelain and kilns from the 2C to the 20C. It also has an 18C scale model of Andenne. On the eastern outskirts of the town, in the suburb of Andenelle, the Romanesque **Eglise Saint Pierre** dates from 1100.

Huy

Huy is a fascinating old town tucked below a steep outcrop at the confluence of the Meuse and the Hoyoux. Much admired by Victor Hugo, the town has handsome Mosan renaissance houses, steep cobbled lanes and old-fashioned tailors' shops. The main buildings of interest are the late Gothic Collégiale Notre-Dame and the citadel.

Roller-skates

The inventor of roller-skates was a musical instrument-maker from Huy called **Joseph Merlin** (1735–1803), who adapted a pair of ice skates by adding wooden rollers. After demonstrating his invention in Liège in 1760, Merlin was invited to a masked ball at Mrs Cornelys' assembly rooms in Soho Square, London. He is reported to have played a violin while roller-skating through the ballroom. The performance ended after Merlin collided with a large mirror. The mother of William the Conqueror, **Arlette of Huy**, also came from here.

Practical information

Eating out

The *Auberge des Chats qui Rient*, Quai de Compiègne 62, ☎ 085.25.00.51, is an elegant restaurant in a waterfront Mosan Renaissance house.

Tourist information

The tourist office occupies the 16C former Hospice d'Oultremont at 1 Quai de Namur, next to the Collégiale Notre-Dame, ☎ 085.21.29.15.

Boat trip

The Val Mosan tour boat leaves from the quay next to the tourist office, several times daily in July and August.

Opening times
Treasury of the Collégiale Notre-Dame, Rue du Pont, is open daily except Fri and during services 09.00–12.00 and 14.00–17.00.
Musée Communal, Rue Vankeerberghen, is open every day

Apr–mid-Oct 14.00–18.00.
Citadel is open at Easter and May–Sept Mon-Fri 10.00–17.00 and weekends 10.00-18.00; Jul–Aug to 19.00. The cable car runs at weekends May, June and Sept, and daily Jul–Aug 10.00–19.00.

A walk in Huy

The old town is dominated by the **Collégiale Notre-Dame**, an outstanding Gothic building with a magnificent rose window and tall, slender, lancet windows in the apse. The third church to occupy this site, it was begun in 1311 but only completed in 1536. There are several good statues inside, including a 15C St Christopher and the 14C Notre Dame de Huy in the north transept.

The **Treasury** contains **four exquisite shrines**, the oldest of which are the Châsse de St Marc of c 1200, and the Châsse de la Vierge of 1240.

The Treasury also contains the shrine of St Domitian made by Godefroid de Huy in 1173. It commemorates a Christian evangelist who converted many of the settlements along the Meuse. Later Bishop of Tongeren, he died c 560. The fourth shrine, made by Godefroid de Huy in 1175, commemorates St Mengold (fl. 892), who may have been a nobleman of Huy of English origin. He spent seven years doing penance for all the blood he had shed. However, there was also a hermit with the same name living in Huy at the time and it may well be that the two have become confused. The Treasury also has a small silver chalice of c 1100 from the grave of Bishop Dietwin of Liège.

A splendid gate known as the **Porte de Bethléem** stands next to the church. Formerly the cloister entrance, it is decorated with 14C reliefs of the Nativity. The columns are carved with bizarre animals and grotesque faces. The cobbled lane beyond the gate is lined with old gravestones. The lane runs along the south wall of the church to the former canons' entrance and the Hospice d'Oultrement where the tourist office is located.

Now cross the Avenue des Ardennes to reach the intimate Grand-Place, a good place for coffee. The **Bassinia** fountain in the middle of the square is considered one of the four wonders of Huy. It has a bronze basin of 1406 surmounted by the figures of four saints: Mengold, Domitian, Catherine and Ansfrid. The last Count of Huy, Ansfrid gave the town to Bishop Notger of Liège in 985. The Hôtel de Ville was built in 1766. A narrow lane leads to the Place Verte, where the 14C **Eglise Saint Mengold** contains the tomb of Saint Mengold.

A crooked lane flanked by high stone walls leads from the church to the **Musée Communal** at Rue Vankeerberghen. This interesting museum of local history occupies one wing of an attractive Franciscan friary built in Mosan renaissance style between 1664 and 1687 (see the wall anchors in the courtyard). The museum has an interesting **collection of wine presses** and other objects connected with the local vineyards that once flourished on the slopes of the Meuse. The most celebrated work in the museum is an oak figure of 1240 known as Le Beau Dieu de Huy. Other exhibits include Gallo-Roman and

Frankish archaeological finds, local engravings, coins minted in Huy for the prince-bishopric of Liège, Huy ceramics, furnished interiors, toys and glass.

Now return to the Meuse and turn right along the quay to reach a park on the Quai d'Arona. This contains the scanty remains of the **Abbey of Neufmoustier**, founded by Peter the Hermit. A 19C statue commemorates Peter, whose preachings inspired the First Crusade. He led an army which was defeated by the Turks at Nicaea. He later fought at the siege of Antioch and died in Huy in 1115.

There is a choice of routes to reach the **Citadel**. It is possible either to climb a steep path that begins on the quay beyond the tourist office or, if it is operating, take the **cable car** which begins on the opposite bank. The cable car offers a splendid view of the town and surrounding countryside. It continues to La Sarte where there is a good children's playground (open daily from Easter to mid-October).

The Citadel stands on the site of the first bishops' castle, built in the 11C or perhaps earlier. The present austere building was built by the Dutch between 1818 and 1823. It was used by the Germans as an internment camp during the Second World War. The camp cells have been preserved. There is also a small military museum.

The north bank is reached across a bridge built in 1956 to replaces one blown up in 1944. Here is an interesting old quarter with several historic buildings. To the left over the bridge is the **Maison Batta** built on the waterfront in 1575 as a refuge for the abbey of Val Saint Lambert. To the right is the **Hôtel de la Poste** which once served as a staging post for passenger bargers to Liège. Back at the bridge, go down Rue Neuve and turn right along Rue Saint Pierre to reach a 13C church with a 12C Romanesque font.

Huy environs

The abbey of **Val Notre-Dame**, 3km north of Huy, was founded c 1210 by Count Albert of Moha, whose only two sons killed each other during a friendly joust. Suppressed in 1796, the abbey was reoccupied in 1901 by nuns of the Order of the Assumption. The entrance, flanked by towers, and the attractive dovecot just inside, date from 1629. The farm buildings are mainly 16C. The rest, apart from the church which was rebuilt after a fire in 1932, was constructed from 1741 to 1745. The ruins of the 11C castle of the Counts of Moha lie just to the north of the attractive village of **Moha**, 3km west of the abbey.

The attractive château of **Modave** lies c 10km south of Huy, 1km from the Pont de Bonne. A long avenue of trees leads to the castle, which is perched precariously on a cliff 80m above the little Hoyoux river. The walls of the keep are 12C but the rest of the building mainly dates from c 1649. The remarkable stucco ceilings were made by Jean-Christian Hansche. The grounds contain a replica of an ingenious 17C hydraulic wheel built by Rennequin Sualem in 1667 to raise water from the river to the château. Sualem's invention was copied at Marly, near Versailles, to provide water for the fountains. (The castle is open daily from Apr–mid-Nov from 09.00–18.00.)

The village of **Bois-et-Borsu**, c 5km south of Modave, has a late 9C church containing 14C carvings and frescoes. The frescoes, which are in the nave, illustrate the histories of St Lambert and St Hubert. The Romanesque church at **Ocquier**, 2km to the east, dates from 1017. It stands on the foundations of perhaps three earlier churches.

The village of **Villers-le-Temple**, 5km east of Huy, has an impressive 13C church containing the tomb of a Templar, Gerard de Villiers, who died in 1273. De Villiers was the founder of the local commandery. The church was much altered in the 18C when it was given its Baroque apse. The ruins can still be seen of the fortified house of the Knights Hospitallers, who took over the Templars' properties when the latter were suppressed for heresy in 1312.

The church at **Saint Séverin,** c 12km east of Huy, is attractively set above the village green beside several old farm buildings. Once part of an abbey, the church was built c 1140. It has a curious 12C font with multiple supports.

From Huy to Liège

Leave Huy by the north bank to reach **Amay**, 7km east of Huy. The Romanesque **Collégiale Sainte Ode** occupies a site where archaeologists have uncovered evidence of prehistoric and Roman occupation. The church is dedicated to a French princess who married a Duke of Aquitaine. After his death, St Ode devoted her time and wealth to the care of the sick and needy. She died in 723. The nave of the church dates from 1098, the towers from 1525. Other parts were added in the 17C and 18C. It contains various treasures including a reliquary of c 1230 of St Ode and St George. This gilt and enamelled copper work is decorated with reliefs of the Apostles and silver plaques depicting scenes from the lives of the two saints.

A short detour leads to the **Château de Jehay**, 4 km north of Amay. Dating mainly from the 16C, this turreted building has curious chequered walls and a moat. Excavations here have revealed mesolithic remains and evidence that the château stands on the site of a Castrum Romanum. The interior is hung with several fine 15C–17C **tapestries**. These include Brussels, Aubusson and Gobelins tapestries based on designs by Teniers.

The castle also has **paintings** by Adriaen van Ostade, Frans Snyders, Murillo, Luca Giordano, the school of Rubens, Dominichino, Peter Lely (a *Portrait of Nell Gwynn*) and Cornelis de Vos. The furniture includes examples of Louis XIII–XVI and Queen Anne styles. Other treasures include lace (including pieces which belonged to the Prince-Bishops of Liège), porcelain, Celtic gold ornaments from Ireland, Gothic statues of the Virgin, a 15C St Anne, and bronzes by Guy van den Steen (including a unique study of Marsyas tortured by the Nymphs). A room devoted to the **Duke of Marlborough** contains manuscript maps, orders of battle and other militaria. An archaeological museum in the cellar has a large collection of objects found locally. (Open in Jul–Aug at weekends 14.00–18.00.)

A monument in **Jehay** village commemorates Zénobe Gramme (1826–1901), a physicist born here who invented the dynamo.

Now return to the Meuse and continue to Engis, where the château of **Aigremont** stands high above the river. The present building, which dates mainly from the early 18C, replaced a fortress of William de la Marck, the Wild Boar of the Ardennes. It is furnished in the style of the 18C. The entrance hall and staircase are decorated with striking wall and ceiling paintings by the Huy artist Jean Delloye. (Open Jul–Aug 10.00–12.00 and 14.00–18.00.)

Cross the river again to visit the **Grottes de Ramioul**, which were discovered in 1911. The caves are on two levels. A small **Museum of Prehistory and**

Speleology is attached (open Apr to early Nov at weekends and public holidays 13.00–18.30).

Continue on the north bank to **Chokier**, where the 18C château above the town has kept one of its medieval towers. The road soon reaches the sprawling industrial suburbs of Liège. The city and its environs are described in a separate chapter.

Liège to the Dutch border

The E25 motorway from Liège to Maastricht follows the Meuse as far as the Dutch border. It passes the port area, where a large statue of King Albert I marks the beginning of the Albert Canal. The industrial district of **Herstal**, 6km north-east of Liège, was the birthplace of Pepin of Herstal. The Fabrique Nationale arms factory is now the main industry. An elegant suspension bridge called **Le Pont de Wandre** cresses the Meuse and the Albert Canal at Herstal.

The château at **Oupeye**, 4km northeast of Herstal, dates from the 17C or 18C. It was originally built by the merchant Jean de Corte, who also owned the splendid mansion in Liège now occupied by the Musée Curtius. The château contains a **museum** of local archaeology.

The churchyard at **Haccourt**, 4km north of Oupeye, is enclosed by a restored medieval wall. It was probably built using stones hewn by the Romans.

The border town of **Visé**, on the east bank of the Meuse, grew up around a bridge built here during the 8C. The town has been frequently sacked over the centuries, most recently in 1914 when it was burnt down by the invading Germans. The 16C **Eglise Saint Martin** contains an outstanding silver and gold coffin-reliquary of the 11C or 12C decorated with scenes from the life of St Hadelin. Born in Gascony, he accompanied St Remaclus to Maastricht and Stavelot and founded a Benedictine monastery at Celles. Known as the Châsse Saint Hadelin, the reliquary came from Celles where Hadelin died in 690. It contains the saint's remains and some of his vestments. The adjacent silver bust dates from 1650.

The **Hôtel de Ville**, rebuilt in the original style of 1612, contains a local museum (open Thur 10.00–12.00).

The Voerstreek

The Voerstreek, east of Visé, is a narrow enclave of Flanders bordering the Netherlands. Known in French as the Fourons, this quiet pastoral district is plagued by linguistic quarrels. Historically linked to Liège and mainly French-speaking, it was annexed to the Flemish province of Limburg in 1963. Rarely visited by tourists, this district of gentle hills comprises six attractive villages on the rivers Berwijn, Voer and Gulp. The villages of Sint Martens-Voeren and Sint Pieters-Voeren have 11C churches.

The church at **Warsage**, 5km east of Visé, has a Romanesque tower. The Cistercian **Abbaye Val Dieu**, 8km southeast of Warsage, is built in a beautiful setting. Founded c 1216, the abbey was closed in 1798 during the French occupation. The Cistercians returned in 1844 and have remained here ever since. The choir of the abbatial church, the fourth on the site, probably dates from the 13C. Parts of the nave and transepts are 14C and 15C, the remainder is a rebuilding of 1870. The church has a fine 12C statue of St Bernard. The attractive 18C domestic buildings are reached through the gateway beside the church. The abbey **museum** has some outstanding works of Mosan art including a *Christ of the Cross* carved from Carrara marble in 1340.

A large tourist complex at **Blégny**, 7km southwest of Van Dieu, incorporates a disused **coal mine and museum** of 19C rural life (open daily Apr–mid-Sept 10.00–16.30, also weekends from Mar–Nov). Former miners give guided tours of the mines lasting about 2 hours. Boats run from Liège to Blégny in the summer. The complex includes a café and an adventure playground.

A large **Second World War cemetery** lies in open countryside 3km east of the village of **Aubel**, which is 2km east of Val Dieu. It contains the graves of American and German soldiers who mainly died in the attack on Aachen in September and October 1944. An American memorial colonnade was designed by Holabind, Root and Burgee. It incorporates a chapel.

The tiny district of **Moresnet**, c12km northeast of Val Dieu, has important zinc calamine mines. It once formed the north tip of the Cantons de l'Est, but, unlike the Cantons, it was not given to Prussia in 1815. It remained under the joint administration of Prussia and the United Kingdom of the Netherlands. The Belgian state took over from the Netherlands after the revolution of 1830, and the area became fully Belgian in 1920.

The **Drielandenbos**, north of Neu-Moresnet and spreading into Germany and the Netherlands, was once a Carolingian hunting forest. It is now a popular walking area with signposted paths. The frontiers of the three countries meet at the 322m high **Drielandenpunkt**. The site is a popular tourist attraction with Belgian and Dutch cafés and a labyrinth (on Dutch soil). It can be reached from the Dutch town of Vaals or the Belgian village of Gemmenich.

THE VALLEY OF THE OURTHE

The winding River Ourthe is one of the most attractive rivers in the Ardennes. It flows through the picturesque towns of La Roche-en-Ardenne and Durbuy before joining the Meuse at the Liège suburb of Angleur.

Tourist information

The Luxembourg Province tourist information office, Quai de l'Ourthe 9, La Roche-en-Ardenne, ☎ 084.41.10.11, covers most of the river.

Beginning in **Liège**, follow the river south to **Tilff**, 12km south of Liège. The attractive town of **Esneux**, 7km south of Tilff, stands on the river in a steep wooded valley. The Parc du Mary has walking trails and an arboretum.

Now follow the winding valley to reach the small town of **Comblain-au-Pont**, 10km south of Esneux. The stump of an old tower stands above the town. The confluence of the Ourthe and the Amblève is just north of the town. A 14C tower survives at **Comblain-la-Tour**, 2km south of Comblain-au-Pont.

The **Musée Régional de la Pierre** at Sprimont, 10km northeast of Comblain, occupies a former generator-house which once supplied the local quarries. The museum covers the mining of the local stone (open during the week between Easter and 1 Nov 09.00–17.00; on Sun 14.00–17.00).

The ruins of the **Château d'Amblève**, 7km east of Comblain, stand on a cliff above the River Amblève. According to a local legend, this was once a stronghold of the Quatre Fils Aymon. It later belonged to William de la Marck, the Wild Boar of the Ardennes. The castle was demolished by the Duke of Parma in 1587.

The **Château de l'Avouerie** at Anthisnes, 5km west of Comblain, has a 13C keep and residential buildings added in 1648. The keep is now occupied by a beer museum and tavern (open from Apr–Oct, Tues–Sun from 12.00–18.00).

A monument at **Hamoir**, 8km southwest of Comblain-la-Tour on the Ourthe, commemorates the baroque sculptor Jean Del Cour, who was born here in 1627.

The lively town of **Barvaux**, 6km east of Durbuy, is a popular resort on the Ourthe. A 7km path used by walkers and cyclists follows a beautiful meandering stretch of the river to Durbuy. Kayaks can be rented in Barvaux to make the descent to Durbuy. A crop maze is planted every year at the Labyrinthus park outside Barvaux (open daily from early July to Aug and at weekends in Sept from 10.30–19.30).

The area around **Wéris**, 5km southeast of Barvaux, is dotted with prehistoric stones and tombs. A curious dolmen with a massive roof slab stands beside the road northwest of Wéris, and a menhir can be seen just to the southwest of the village. The church at Wéris dates in part from the 11C. It has a 13C stone tabernacle.

A Romanesque church at **Tohogne**, 5km north of Barvaux, dates from the 11C. The hamlet of **La Bouverie**, just to the west, has an attractive farm built in 1570 by the monks of Stavelot-Malmédy. The small town of **Bomal**, 6km east of Tohogne, is twinned with Beaujolais in France. It celebrates the link by holding wine-tasting festivals.

The ruined castle of **Logne**, 6km northeast of Tohogne, occupies a site settled by prehistoric peoples and later by the Romans. During the 15C, it was a stronghold of William de la Marck, the Wild Boar of the Ardennes. It was destroyed by Henry of Nassau in 1521 on the orders of Charles V.

The village of **Sy**, 3km north of Logne via Vieuxville, stands at the head of one of the most picturesque ravines on the Ourthe.

Durbuy

Durbuy is an attractive small town built beside a narrow ravine whose rocks were tortured into bizarre shapes by a primeval cataclysm. Originally a Roman settlement, Durbuy was granted the status of a town in 1331, leading to the local claim that it is the smallest town in the world. Durbuy is now a busy tourist centre with forest walks, a cycle trail along the Ourthe and kayaks for rent.

Practical information

Where to stay
Clos des Récollets, Rue Prévôté 9, ☎ 086.21.29.69, is an attractive small hotel with an old-fashioned character. *Sanglier des Ardennes*, Rue Comte Th. d'Ursel 14, ☎ 086.21.32.62, is a large hotel from 1904 with restaurant overlooking the Ourthe. *Vieux Durbuy*, Rue Jean de Bohême 6,

☎ 086.21.32.62, is a rustic hotel in the old town.

Eating out
The *Sanglier des Ardennes* (see above) has a good restaurant with a view of the river.

Tourist information
Place aux Foires 25, ☎ 086.21.24.28.

There are many attractive buildings in the narrow cobbled streets of the old town, such as the half-timbered 16C **Halle aux Blés**, which once contained the corn exchange. The turrets and steep roof of the **Château des Comtes d'Ursel** dominate the town. Begun in the 9C, the castle was frequently besieged. The present building dates almost entirely from the 19C, but one 11C turret survives. The **Parc des Topiaires** (open daily 10.00–18.00, closed Jan) is a small park next to the Ourthe with several hundred box trees pruned in exotic shapes. The **Belvédère** to the south offers a panoramic view of the river.

The **Château of Deulin**, 8km southwest of Durbuy, dates from 1760. It is now used for concerts and exhibitions.

The riverside town of **Hotton**, 12km south of Durbuy, is overlooked by an escarpment occupied by prehistoric man and later fortified by the Romans. Discovered in 1958, the **Grottes de Hotton** (open daily Apr–Oct 10.00–17.00) are known as the 'Thousand and One Nights' because of their exotic formations. Visitors can look down on the river, some 30m below, roaring in the Stygian darkness.

An antiquated rural tram known as the **Tramway Touristique de l'Aisne** runs 10km from Erezée, 9km east of Hotton (on Sun from Easter to mid-Oct, and daily except Fri in Jul–Aug 10.30–17.00).

The village of **Marcourt**, 8km southeast of Hotton, was until the 11C the seat of the Counts of Montaigu. A chapel built in 1637 stands above the village on the site of count's castle. Marcourt was the birthplace of Anne-Josèphe Terwagne (1762–1817), the Amazon of the French Revolution who adopted the name Théoigne de Méricourt.

La Roche-en-Ardenne

The small town of La Roche-en-Ardenne lies in a steep wooded valley on a bend in the Ourthe. Most of the town was destroyed during the Battle of the Ardennes in December 1944. La Roche is now a popular tourist centre with an impressive ruined castle. It makes an excellent base for forest walks and canoe trips.

Practical information

Where to stay
Le Chalet, rue Chalet 61, ☎ 084.41.24.13, is a traditional Ardennes hotel with a panoramic view of the Ourthe.
Claire Fontaine, Route de Hotton 64, 2km west of La Roche, ☎ 084.41.24.70, is an attractive Ardennes inn on the banks of the Ourthe.
Hostellerie Linchet, Route de Houffalize 11, ☎ 084.41.13.27, is a comfortable hotel just outside the town.

Tourist information
Place du Marché 15, ☎ 084.41.13.42.

Local walks
Several walks are signposted from La Roche. The best walk is the **Promenade des Chapelles** (no. 4), which passes the 17C Chapelle Sainte Marguerite, the Belvédère du Deister, the Parc à Gibier, and the Diable-Château, where the rock formations are said to resemble a ruined castle.

Children
The Parc à Gibier, 2km east of La Roche, is a large wooded reserve with wild boar, deer, wolves and farm animals.

Opening times
The **castle** is open Apr–Jun and Sept–Oct daily 10.00–12.00 and 14.00–17.00; Jul–Aug 10.00–19.00; Nov–Mar on Mon-Fri 13.30–16.30, and weekends 10.00–12.00 and 14.00–16.00. It is closed when there is snow or ice.
Le Grès de la Roche craft centre is open daily except Mon in winter. It is closed Jan–mid-Feb.
Musée de la Bataille des Ardennes is open daily 10.00–18.00.
Parc à Gibier is open Thur–Tues 11.00–18.00. It is closed Weds in winter and from mid-Jan to mid-Feb.

The **castle** is an impressive medieval ruin with a double wall, turrets and an oubliette. It was once the seat of Henri, Count of La Roche.

The earliest fortification was probably built on this site in the 9C. The castle was later occupied by the Dukes of Burgundy. Louis XIV rebuilt its defences, but surrendered it after the Peace of Utrecht. It was dismantled in the 18C on the orders of Joseph II. The ruins are said to be haunted by the ghost of Countess Berthe, a beautiful local woman who threw herself from the castle walls after her fiancé was killed in a tournament. It turned out later that he was killed by a jealous woman who had entered the lists disguised as a knight. A useful free folder explains the different features of the castle. A tavern is open in the summer.

The **Grès de la Roche** craft centre at Rue Rompré 28 demonstrates the production of La Roche's coarse blue-grey pottery known as Grès. The adjoining Musée du Jambon d'Ardennes describes the production of local smoked ham. A shop sells Grès pottery, local ham and Belgian beers.

The **Musée de la Bataille des Ardennes à La Roche** in the town centre evokes the Battle of the Ardennes in December 1944 through a collection of photographs, uniforms, military vehicles and dioramas.

La Roche environs
Some of the finest scenery in the Ourthe Valley lies close to La Roche. The **Belvédère de Nisramont**, 11km southeast of La Roche, offers a fine view of the Ourthe and its dam. The **Belvédère des Six Ourthe**, 10km southeast of La Roche, near Nadrin, stands on a rocky ridge high above the river. It takes its name from the six loops in the Ourthe which can be seen.

The town of **Houffalize**, 26km southeast of La Roche, derives its name from *haute falaise* (high cliff). Sprawled over both sides of the steep valley of the upper Ourthe, the town was largely destroyed during the Battle of the Ardennes. It was here that the counter-offensives led by Patton and Montgomery joined forces. The **Eglise Sainte Catherine** has a 13C tower. It was formerly the church of a priory founded in 1248 by Thierry, Lord of Houffalize. His tomb is in the church. There is also a fine brass lectern of 1372 by Jehans Josès of Dinant.

An interesting fortified farm can be seen at **Tavigny**, 4km southeast of Houffalize.

The **Baraque de Fraiture**, 15km north of Houffalize, is a bleak area of heathland popular with skiers. The 636m summit is the second highest spot in Belgium.

THE VALLEY OF THE VESDRE

The River Vesdre rises in the Hautes Fagnes and flows through Eupen, Limbourg, Verviers and Chaudfontaine before joining the Ourthe in the Liège suburb of Angleur. The pure moorland water of the Vesdre has been used by the local cloth industry since the 14C.

Leave Liège by the right bank of the Ourthe and follow signs to the suburb of **Chênée** where a bridge crosses the Vesdre. The road then follows the winding river valley, passing below the hill of **Chèvremont** on the north bank, which is surmounted by a pilgrimage-church of 1697.

The river town of **Chaudfontaine**, 10km southeast of Liège, is a little spa resort which greatly appealed to Victor Hugo but is now virtually forgotten. The local mineral water can be sampled at a spring, just behind the large car park. This water, which reaches a temperature of 36.5°C, is rich in minerals. It has been used since 1676 for treating rheumatism. The **tourist office** occupies the old thermal establishment, the Maison Sauveur, in the Parc des Sources. An attractive footpath leads to a summit south of the town.

Verviers

Verviers, 32km east of Liège, is an important industrial town on the Vesdre, with handsome 18C and 19C buildings and three good museums.

History

An important textile town in the Middle Ages, Verviers was granted the right to sell cloth in Liège in 1480, though it only gained official status as a town in 1651. Verviers was the first town in Belgium to experience the industrial revolution after John Cockerill, a Lancashire industrialist, settled here and persuaded local manufacturers to use his patent spinning machine. The town has several handsome 19C flights of steps linking different levels of the town. Luc Sante's biographical *The Factory of Facts* describes a Verviers childhood in the 1950s.

Practical information

Where to stay
The Amigo, Rue Herla 1, ☎ 087.22.11.21, is an elegant hotel on the edge of a park in an interesting 19C district.

Tourist information
The tourist office occupies a handsome building at Rue Xhavée 61, ☎ 087.33.02.13. Closed Sunday.

Opening times
Musée des Beaux-Arts et de la Céramique (fine art and ceramics), Rue Renier, is open Mon, Wed and Sat 14.00–17.00, on Sun 15.00–18.00.
Musée d'Archéologie et Folklore Rue des Raines 42, is open Tues, Thur, 14.00–17.00, Sat 09.00–12.00, Sun 10.00–13.00.
Centre Touristique de la Laine (history of textiles), Rue de la Chapelle 30, is open daily 10.00–18.00.

A walk around verviers

Begin at Verviers station, an impressive 19C building with good ironwork in the booking hall. Local buses leave from the station forecourt for the Hautes Fagnes and Malmédy. Turn left down the Rue de la Concorde, and enter a little park with an Oriental bandstand and a Neo-classical concert hall built for the Société Royale d'Harmonie in 1835. Continue down the Pont du Chêne, cross the Vesdre, and turn right along Quai Jacques Brel. At the next bridge, go left up a narrow flight of steps to reach a promontory with a good view of the town. Now go back down to the river by another flight of steps, then continue along the wooded Promenade des Récollets.

Cross by the Pont d'Andrimont to reach the **Musée des Beaux-Arts et de la Céramique**, which occupies a late 17C home for old men in the Rue Renier, beside the river Vesdre. It is open Mon, Wed and Sat 14.00–17.00; on Sun 15.00–18.00. The museum has an important collection of **ceramics** and **Dutch and Belgian paintings** from the 16C to the 20C. These include a *Landscape* and *St Christopher* by Joachim Patinir; a *Punishment of Annanias* by Pieter Pourbus the Elder; a *Landscape* by Jan van Goyen; two portraits by Nicolas de Largillière; two landscapes with animals by Roelant Savery; a *Portrait of a Child* by Cornelis de Vos; an *Adoration of the Magi* by Gerrit Dou; *The Virgin among Flowers* by Daniel Seghers; a *Portrait of Admiral van Heemskerk* by Jan Weenix; *The Council of the Gods* by Gerard de Lairesse; the *Head of a Child* by Joshua Reynolds; a *Self-Portrait* by Marie Louise Vigée-Lebrun; an *Inn by a Lake* by Henri de Braekeleer; and *Skaters* and *A Canal Bridge* by Johann Barthold Jongkind.

The **first floor** has a collection of carved and sculpted 15C and 16C religious figures. There are also **modern paintings** here, including works by Gustave Courbet, Jacob Smits, Constantin Meunier, Hippolyte Boulenger, René Magritte, Paul Delvaux, Edgard Tytgat and Emile Claus. A collection of architectural fragments and gravestones is displayed in the passage leading to the basement.

Continue along Rue Renier and turn left down Rue des Raines to visit the **Musée d'Archéologie et Folklore** at no. 42, which occupies a handsome Rococo mansion built in 1737. It is open Tues and Thur 14.00–17.00, Sat 09.00–12.00, Sun 10.00–13.00. The **ground and first floors** are devoted to 17C and 18C furniture, paintings by local artists, and objets d'art. The museum also has a collection of memorabilia of the violinist Henri Vieuxtemps (1821–81), who was born in Verviers. He has given his name to the Place Vieuxtemps in the south part of the town. The **second floor** has a collection of weapons and local archaeological finds, including some Roman coins found near the museum. The museum also has a good collection of porcelain.

On leaving the museum, return to the Rue Renier and turn left to reach the Place du Marché, where the elegant Neo-classical **Hôtel de Ville** was built by J.B. Renoz in the 18C. Turn right down Rue Crapaurue and right on Rue Ortmans, where an impressive fountain honours Burgomaster Jean-François Ortmans.

Now turn left along Rue du College to reach Place du Martyr, where a statue commemorates **Grégoire Chapuis**, a local magistrate who was executed in 1794 by order of the Prince-Bishop of Liège after he carried out a civil marriage according to French Revolutionary law. This was construed by the Prince-Bishop—briefly back in power after the Austrian defeat of Dumouriez at

Neerwinden—as a seditious act. Chapuis was beheaded with a saw after the executioner had made six unsuccessful attempts with an axe.

The **Eglise Notre-Dame de Récollets** stands at the far end of the square. The present church was built in the 19C on the site of a 17C church which burnt down. The interior contains good 18C woodwork and a blackened statue of the Virgin that survived the blaze.

The Pont Saint-Laurent (once a bridge over a vanished waterway) leads to Place Verte, a lively square with several cafés. The Rue Xhavée leads from here to the **Théâtre**, built in 1892 in Neo-classical style. The station is nearby, but a short detour might be made into the upper quarters where Verviers' factory owners built handsome white villas in eclectic styles. Go through the small park and cross Rue du Palais, then turn left to reach an impressive flight of steps built in 1871–79. At the top, continue straight ahead, then turn right at a fork. This leads to the Place Henri Vieuxtemps, named after the 19C violinist and composer born in Verviers. A statue of Vieuxtemps holding his violin stands in the middle of the square.

One final museum deserves a mention. The **Centre Touristique de la Laine** occupies a former 19C factory and two adjacent 18C mansions to the west of the centre in the Rue de la Chapelle. Converted in 1999 into a museum, the centre uses the latest technology to illuminate the history of textiles from the middle ages to the 19C. The collection includes working looms, spinning machines and 18C engravings.

Verviers environs

The attractive walled town of **Limbourg**, 10km northeast of Verviers, stands on a ridge 275m above the Vesdre. A former fortress, the town was the capital of the duchy of Limburg from feudal times until 1648. Its present air of provincial tranquillity belies its history which was often savage and bloody. The town was besieged many times and frequently sacked. The ruined defences provide the only hint of these traumatic events. The church has a tower from 1300, though most of the building dates from the 15C and 16C.

The **Barrage de la Gileppe**, 4km southeast of Limbourg, is a peaceful lake enclosed by wooded hillsides. There is a good view from the Belvédère of the lake and its surroundings. A footpath marked **Sentier Touristique** descends to the dam, which was built between 1869 and 1878 to form a reservoir for Verviers. Further work to increase its height was undertaken from 1967 to 1971.

The village church at **Baelen**, 2 km northeast of Limbourg, has a curious spiral steeple of 1773.

Eupen

Eupen is an attractive German-speaking town on the Vesdre, 40km east of Liège. Using water from the Vesdre (known here by its German name of Weser), Eupen has produced textiles since the 14C. The industry received a substantial boost in the 17C and 18C when a number of French Calvinists settled here, but it was eclipsed in the 19C by Verviers. The town is capital of the small German-speaking Community of Belgium.

Practical information

Tourist information
Marktplatz 7, ☎ 087.55.34.50. Closed Sunday.

Carnival
Eupen is famous for its flamboyant Carnival celebrations which, following Germanic custom, culminate in a parade on Rosenmontag. The following day (Shrove Tuesday), women take to the streets with scissors to snip off men's ties.

Opening times
The **Eupener Stadtmuseum** is open on Mon and Fri 09.00–12.00 and 13.00–16.00, Wed 18.00–20.00, Sat 14.00–17.00, and Sun 10.00–12.00 and 14.00–17.00.

The Baroque **Eglise Saint Nicolas**, built from 1721–1726, has a striking Rococo interior. Its altar of 1744 is particularly remarkable. The **Eupener Stadtmuseum** at Gospert 52 occupies a handsome house of 1697 built by a cloth merchant. It contains an 18C interior, a collection of Raeren pottery and several rooms devoted to local history.

Eupen environs
The impressive **Barrage de la Vesdre**, 5km upstream, was completed in 1950 to provide Liège with water. The 410m-long dam is the largest in Belgium. A lift ascends the panoramic tower which affords a superb view of the reservoir and the great forest of the **Hertogenwald**. There are good forest walks, a children's playground and a restaurant. The N67 cuts through the Hertogenwald to the attractive German town of Monschau.

Raeren, 8km northeast of Eupen, was a flourishing pottery town from the 15C–19C. Raeren pottery was sold as far away as Ireland and Sweden. The castle, 14C in origin, now contains a fascinating **Pottery Museum**. The museum contains a reconstructed kiln and a collection of pottery from the 12C to the 19C (open Tues–Sun 14.00–16.45).

Spa and the Cantons de l'Est

The 18C aristocratic health resort of Spa is located in the eastern Ardennes, 38km southeast of Liège. Though now somewhat faded, it still has a certain elegant allure. Not far away, the Cantons de l'Est is a curious German-speaking region which once belonged to Prussia. The region has many good country hotels and local restaurants offering smoked Ardennes ham and delicious game in the autumn.

Spa

The attractive little resort of Spa, deep in a wooded valley, has given its name to health resorts throughout the world. Though slightly run-down now, there are still traces of Spa's former grandeur in the monumental architecture, grand hotels and spacious parks. The town is still visited for its mineral springs and baths. The surrounding woods and moorland make it an excellent centre for country walks.

Practical information

Where to stay

Almost all the grand old hotels have closed down. The only survivor is the *Doint Spa Balmoral*, Route de Balmoral 33, 3km from Spa, ☎ 087.77.25.81, a recently restored 19C hotel in the woods with an indoor pool.

Eating out

Brasserie du Grand Maur, Rue Xhrouet 41, ☎ 087.77.36.16, offers excellent brasserie cooking in a handsome 18C mansion.

Several attractive taverns are located next to the springs:

Fontaine de Tonnelet, Route du Tonnelet 82, ☎ 087.77.26.03, is an attractive restaurant in an 1884 conservatory.

Source de Barisart, Route de Barisart 295, ☎ 087.77.09.88, is a bright modern tavern in the woods.

Tourist information

Pavillon des Petits Jeux, Place Royale 41, ☎ 087.79.53.53.

Cures

A traditional thermal cure can be booked at the Thermes de Spa, ☎ 087.77.25.60.

Tours

Tourist trains with open carriages make a tour of the springs beginning at the Place Royale daily Jul–Aug 09.00–19.00. Also weekends May–Jun and Sept–Oct.

Opening times

Musée de la Ville d'Eau, Avenue Reine Astrid 77, is open daily between mid-June and mid-Sept 14.30–17.30; at other times only open at weekends and public holidays (same hours).

Pouhon Pierre-le-Grand and **Pouhon Prince de Condé** are open Apr–Oct, daily 10.00–12.00 and 13.30–17.00; Nov–Mar Mon–Fri 13.30–17.00 and weekends 10.00–12.00 and 13.30–17.00.

History of the springs

The springs at 'Sparsa fontana' have been celebrated since Roman times. **Pliny the Elder** wrote of the springs in his Natural History. Its fame spread throughout Europe in the 16C after Augustino, the Venetian physician of Henry VIII of England, published a book containing case histories of people cured by the mineral waters.

The resort was later visited by Henry III of France, Marguerite de Valois, Charles II of England, Christina of Sweden and Peter the Great of Russia. Not all the visitors were equally enchanted. 'We arrived at the nasty Spa, and have now begun to drink the horrid sulfur water,' Sir Ralph Verney grumbled in his 17C memoirs.

The long list of distinguished visitors led Joseph II to decribe Spa as the 'Café of Europe'. By the 18C, many people came here for the **casino** founded in 1763 as much as the waters. The visitors became known as bobelins from the Latin word bibulus (a heavy drinker). The first modern-style horse races on the Continent were held at the Hippodrome outside Spa in 1773, and the **first car rally** in Belgium was run in 1896 on a course near Spa. By the end of the 19th century, the town was mobbed by 15,000 visitors a year. The numerous 19C British visitors led to street names such as the Boulevard des Anglais, the Avenue du Lawn Tennis and the Route de Balmoral.

Spa was briefly the scene of dramatic events in 1918 as the **First World War** drew to a close. The German General Headquarters was established in the Hôtel Britannique in March. The Kaiser moved into the Château de Neubois, 2km east of Spa. It was here that he ordered Ludendorff's dismissal on 26 October. The Kaiser later moved to La Fraineuse, where he learned on the afternoon of 9 November that the chancellor Prince Max von Baden had on his own initiative announced the Kaiser's abdication in Berlin. Early the next morning, the Kaiser left for the Netherlands from Spa station. After the Armistice was signed, a German military mission remained in Spa for a few months to confer with the Allies.

A walk in the town

Begin at the Pouhon Pierre-le-Grand in the town centre. The second oldest spring in Spa, it has been known since at least the 16C.

Pouhon Pierre-le-Grand

It was originally a simple open niche. The present grand octagonal pavilion was built in 1880. The medallion inside, which bears the arms of Russia, was presented by Peter the Great of Russia in gratitude for a successful cure here in 1717. The Livre d'Or was created in 1894 by the local artist Antoine Fontaine. It portrays 93 of Spa's best known visitors of earlier centuries. A cup of the water can be sampled for 7 BF.

A memorial on the outside wall of the building records the gratitude of the people of Spa to the US 1st Army which liberated the town on 10 September 1944. The names of the most famous visitors from the 16C to the 19C are inscribed on a semicircular monument nearby.

The former **Grand Hotel** was built in 1768 by J.B. Renoz in the Rue de l'Hôtel de Ville. Gustavus Adolphus stayed in the hotel in 1780. Following the Armistice in 1918, Allied leaders held peace talks here with the German military command. The building was later occupied by a factory and the municipal library. It is now a school. The **Pouhon Prince de Condé** nearby has been meticulously restored to its 19C grandeur.

The **Casino** was rebuilt in a grand Neo-classical style in 1919. It has gaming tables, gardens, a restaurant, theatre, reception rooms and an exhibition area. The rather sober **Etablissement des Bains** next door was built in 1862–68.

The waters of Spa

Rich in iron and bicarbonate of soda, the waters of Spa are prescribed for heart and respiratory problems and rheumatism. The springs are known as **pouhons**, from the Walloon word for a healing spring. The chief springs are Pouhon Pierre-le-Grand in the town centre, and the Tonnelet, Sauvenière, Groesbeek, Géonstère and Barisart springs. The Spa Monopole water bottling plant is near the station.

The **Parc de Sept Heures** was laid out to the west of Place Royale in 1758 by the Archbishop of Augsburg. It takes its name from the custom of strolling there in the evenings. An iron arcade known as the Galérie Leopold II allowed visitors to take their habitual seven o'clock stroll when it rained. A flea market is held here on Sundays (08.00–14.00).

The **Villa Royale** at Avenue Reine Astrid 77 was a favourite residence of Queen Marie-Henriette, a dedicated curist who died at Ostend in 1902. Several rooms in the villa are now occupied by the **Musée de la Ville d'Eau**. This local museum displays an interesting collection of *jolités*. These painted wooden boxes made by Spa craftsmen are covered with up to 16 layers of lacquer. The former stables are occupied by a **Museum of the Horse**.

Return to the Pouhon Pierre-le-Grand and climb the Rue de la Sauvenière to reach the former **Hôtel Britannique**, now a boarding school, where German generals pored over maps of the Western Front in the final desperate months of the First World War.

The Tour des Fontaines

One of the highlights of a 19C trip to Spa was to take a carriage on a tour of the springs. The same route can be followed now by tourist train, or on foot supplied with a map from the tourist office. The **Tonnelet** spring, which became popular in the early 17C, takes its name from the fact that the water was once piped into a small barrel. The **Sauvenière** is the oldest spring. Women wanting to become pregnant have been encouraged since 1300 to sip the waters of this spring with one foot placed on the imprint of St Remaclus. An arboretum has been planted nearby. The **Groesbeek** spring is named after Baron Groesbeek who paid for a marble niche in 1651. The **Géonstère**, with rather sulphurous water, was visited by Peter the Great of Russia to alleviate his indigestion. The **Barisart**, although known since at least 1559, was not in popular use until 1850.

Spa environs

The attractive **Lac de Warfaaz**, 2km northeast of Spa, was created by a dam built in 1890. Surrounded by wooded hills, it has boating and fishing. The lake is reached from the Boulevard des Anglais, which skirts the estate of **Fraineuse** where the Kaiser lived in 1918. It is now a large sports complex.

The wildlife park at **La Reid**, 6km west of Spa, has over 200 deer, wild boar and bears (open daily 09.00–17.00).

The attractive town of **Theux**, 7km northeast of Spa, traces its origin to a Roman settlement. It was later controlled first by the Carolingian kings and then the prince-bishops of Liège. Theux was granted a charter as a town in 1456. The walls and nave of the **church**, which has a fortified tower, date from 1000 or earlier. It contains an interesting 12C font with a middle section thought to be Roman.

The town square has several 17C and 18C houses. The **Hôtel de Ville** dates from 1770. The perron was installed in 1769. An older perron dating from 1456 was destroyed by Charles the Bold in 1468.

The ruins of **Franchimont** stand on the hill above Theux. A pentagonal fortress with corner towers, it mainly dates from the 14C. A small **museum** next to the castle contains an exhibition of local history. (The castle and museum are open daily 09.00–dusk, but closed on Tues Oct–Mar.)

This castle was one of the strongholds of William de la Marck, the Wild Boar of the Ardennes. After William was executed in Maastricht, his brothers held the castle successfully against a siege mounted by the Bishop of Liège.

The 600 men of Franchimont

The castle at Franchimont is linked with a famous episode in Walloon history when 600 men set out from here in 1468 to attack the army of Charles the Bold and free King Louis XI of France. They tried unsuccessfully to storm the Burgundian army as it camped on a hill above Liège. Charles exacted his revenge by sacking Theux and destroying the perron. The Montagne de Bueren in Liège is named after the leader of the men of Franchimont.

A small chapel at **Tancrémont**, 2km northwest of Theux, contains an unusual 11C robed figure of Christ.

The town of **Banneux-Notre-Dame**, 6km west of Theux, became an important pilgrimage centre after the Virgin appeared eight times to a local girl in 1933. The Chapel of the Appearances is near the entrance. A fragment of stone from the grotto at Lourdes is incorporated into a nearby spring.

The village of **Francorchamps**, 9km southeast of Spa, derives its name from Francorum Campus where Charles Martel, the grandfather of Charlemagne, won a battle. It is now more famous for its 14km **Formula One circuit**. The race track is also used as a public highway. A museum in Stavelot charts the history of the Francorchamps circuit.

The **Amblève river** follows an attractive winding route to the west of Spa. The attractive riverside resort of **Remouchamps**, 16km west of Spa, sits in a wooded valley. The impressive **caves** were created by a tributary of the Amblève known as the Rubicon. They were inhabited by Palaeolithic hunters some 8000 years ago. **Guided tours**, lasting about an hour, take in the huge Salle de la Cathédrale and an underground boat ride. (Open daily from the spring Carnival to mid-Nov 09.00–18.00; other periods 09.30–17.00. Last tour begins one hour before closing time.)

The **Vallon des Chantoirs**, northeast of Remouchamps on the N666, takes its name from the many *chantoirs* or holes in the limestone rock.

The village of **Sougné**, just north of Remouchamps, sits at the foot of a rock called the Heid des Gattes from which the French dislodged the Austrians in 1794.

The village of **La Gleize**, 12km south of Spa, was where Kampfgruppe Peiper made its last stand during the Battle of the Ardennes. The local museum contains a German Tiger tank and other military relics. The village of **Cheneux**, 3km southwest of La Gleize, has a memorial to the American 509th parachute

Infantry Regiment, which stormed and retook La Gleize.

The Amblève flows in a loop of c 4km at **Coo**, c 20km south of Spa. The rocky neck was breached by the monks of Stavelot in the 18C to form a 17m cascade. The area is now a popular tourist attraction, with several cafés, an amusement park and a wildlife reserve. A chair-lift ascends to the summit of the 450m **Montagne de Lancre**, which offers a good view of the winding Amblève. (The lift runs daily from mid-Mar–mid-Nov 09.00–20.00.)

The small resort of **Trois-Ponts**, 3km south of Coo, is a popular walking centre.

Battle of the Ardennes

During the Battle of the Ardennes, Trois Ponts was the scene of a heroic action which stopped the advancing Kampfgruppe Peiper. Just before midday on 18 December, the German advance guard tanks, which had come from Stavelot, clattered under the railway viaduct to swing left for the vital Amblève bridge. They found themselves confronted by a lone American anti-tank gun which immediately destroyed the first tank. There followed a brief, uneven contest which ended inevitably with the destruction of the gun and the death of its crew of four. Yet the gallant stand of these American soldiers gave sufficient time for the demolition of the bridge and the destruction of Peiper's hopes of a dash to the Meuse. He was forced instead to turn north to La Gleize, where he was defeated.

Stavelot

Stavelot is a charming little town with narrow, winding streets. It has some handsome 17C and 18C houses which were mainly built after the town was razed to the ground by Louis XIV in 1680.

Tourist information
Ancienne Abbaye.
☎ 080.86.27.06.

Opening times
The **Musée Regional d'Art Religieux et de l'Ancienne Abbaye**, the **Musée Circuit de Spa-Francorchamps**, both in the abbey, and the **Musée Guillaume Apollinaire**, in the Hôtel de Ville, are open daily from 10.00–12.30 and 14.00–17.30 (all close one hour early in winter).

History

Stavelot and Malmédy owe their origins to abbeys founded in 650 and 648 respectively by St Remaclus, a nobleman born in Aquitaine who became a Benedictine monk. The twin abbeys remained up to the French Revolution the centre of a principality ruled by a succession of powerful prince-abbots. Politically these prince-abbots owed allegiance to the Holy Roman Empire, but ecclesiastically there was a division between Malmédy, which fell under juris-diction of Cologne, and Stavelot, which was subject to Liège. This division had important consequences when the Congress of Vienna awarded the Cantons de l'Est to Prussia in 1815. Stavelot was excluded and thus became part of the United Kingdom of the Netherlands, while Malmédy passed to Prussia.

The Battle of the Ardennes

Stavelot was the scene of bitter fighting during the Battle of the Ardennes. On 18 December 1944, the Allies failed to demolish the Amblève bridge below the abbey, possibly because of sabotage by German commando groups wearing American uniforms. This enabled the spearhead of the German attack, the Kampfgruppe Peiper, to cross the river. Despite the Americans successfully holding the Place Saint Remacle for about two hours, the Germans were able to swing to the southwest and head for Trois Ponts. It was in Stavelot and Trois Ponts, and at hamlets and farms in between like Ster, Renardmont, Parfondruy and Hurlet that the worst of the atrocities against civilians were committed. These were largely the crimes of SS youths who were enraged by their inability to advance in the face of American artillery and hysterically convinced that every house sheltered Belgian and American snipers.

A walk around the town

Begin at the **abbey**, whose church was destroyed during the Napoleonic period. All that survives are two 18C quadrangles approached through a huge 16C archway. This is in fact the lower part of the tower-arch of the now demolished church. Enter a garden and descend some steps to reach the main quadrangle, which contains the Hôtel de Ville and three museums.

The **Musée Regional d'Art Religieux et de l'Ancienne Abbaye** contains local religious art from the 14C to the 19C including church plate, statues, vestments and liturgical books. It also has sections on the history of the abbey, the local tanning industry, and modern Belgian ceramics. The **Musée Circuit de Spa-Francorchamps** occupies the Romanesque cellars of the abbey house. It has a collection of gleaming vintage cars, old posters and other material on the Francorchamps circuit dating back to 1907.

The **Musée Guillaume Apollinaire** in the Hôtel de Ville contains memorabilia of the Franco-Polish poet (1880–1918), who spent the summer of 1899 in Stavelot while his mother gambled in Spa casino. His stay is commemorated by a plaque on the wall of the Hôtel Mal-Aimé at Rue Neuve 12. It fails to mention that he decamped without paying his bills.

Now climb to the sloping Place Saint Remacle, an 18C market square with a **perron** of 1769. A stone memorial commemorates the halting of Von Rundstedt's offensive in December 1944. The **Eglise Saint Sébastien** of 1751 has a pulpit and medallions from the abbey. The church Treasury contains several richly decorated shrines and reliquaries, including the **Shrine of St Remaclus** of 1263 in gilt and enamelled copper; a 1626 reliquary bust by Jean Gossin of St Poppo (an abbot of Stavelot-Malmédy who died in 1048); a reliquary holding a part of the skull of St Poppo; and a 19C reliquary with the skull of St Remaclus.

The Cantons de l'Est

The largely German-speaking Cantons de l'Est occupy an upland forested region with numerous lakes and reservoirs. The region has several attractive small towns such as Eupen, Malmédy and Sankt Vith, which have a definite German atmosphere.

Tourist information
Cantons de l'Est Tourist Information

Office, Mühlenbachstrasse 2, Sankt-Vith, ☎ 080.22.76.64.

History

Bounded to the east by Germany and to the west by a line running roughly from Eupen through Baraque Michel and Malmédy to the border of the Grand-Duchy of Luxembourg near Beho, this region was divided between several rulers before the French Revolution. Eupen was a district of the duchy of Limburg, while Malmédy belonged in part to the ecclesiastical principality of Stavelot-Malmédy and in part to the duchy of Luxembourg. Sankt Vith was also partly in the duchy of Luxembourg, but the communes of Schönberg and Manderfeld were ruled by the prince-bishop of Trier (Trèves in French).

This complex situation ended when Belgium was absorbed into republican France. Following the French defeat at Waterloo, the Congress of Vienna gave the Cantons, minus the district of Moresnet and the town of Stavelot, to Prussia. A vigorous Germanisation policy was pursued until the First World War. The League of Nations transferred the Cantons to Belgium in 1920, but Hitler declared them a part of Germany in 1940. The Cantons now belong to the province of Liège, though they retain some political autonomy. The administrative capital of Eupen is described in the chapter on the Valley of the Vesdre.

Malmédy

The town of Malmédy is attractively situated at the confluence of the rivers Warche and Warchenne. It suffered considerable damage from Allied bombing in December 1944. Encircled by wooded hills, the town makes a good centre for forest walks.

Tourist information
Place Albert I 29, ☎ 080. 33.02.50.

The main building of interest is the **Cathedral**, dedicated to St Peter, St Paul and St Quirinus. Constructed in 1775–84, it stands on the site of a succession of churches. It has a somewhat austere interior with a lofty domed crossing and half-domed transepts, but the Louis XVI pulpit is exceptionally ornate, as are the carved stalls and cathedra. The four silver busts of Roman soldiers on the altar are reliquaries of martyred members of the Theban Legion. The domestic buildings of the abbey of c 1701 are now occupied by a school. The **Maison Villers** of 1724 (off Place Albert I in Chemin-Rue) survived the bombing of 1944.

Christian martyrs

According to early chroniclers, the **Theban Legion** formed part of the army of Maximinian Herculeus. The soldiers were Christians recruited in Upper Egypt. Commanded by the primicerius Maurice, the legion was sent to northern Italy and then to Switzerland c 287. Ordered to offer sacrifice to pagan deities before battle, the soldiers refused and were slaughtered at Agaunum, now St Maurice-en-Valais, in Switzerland. A basilica was erected there to enshrine their relics in c 369. A company, detached to Cologne, suffered the same fate. The relics in Malmédy probably belong to these martyrs.

Malmédy environs

The town of **Ligneuville**, 9km south of Malmédy on the Amblève, is mentioned in documents of the 9C and 10C. A memorial by the Hôtel du Moulin commemorates American prisoners of war shot there.

The Hautes Fagnes

The Hautes Fagnes is a fascinating upland region between Eupen and Malmédy. Rising to the Signal de Botrange, this region of peat bogs and sphagnum moss holds reserves of very pure water which feed the springs at Spa. The plant-life is of low Alpine and Nordic types, together with beech, oak, birch and alder trees. Some spruce plantations have been introduced recently. The ancient paths that cross this bleak region are often marked with pillars and crosses to guide travellers in blizzards.

The **Signal de Botrange**, 20km northeast of Malmédy, stands on a windswept forest plateau. The highest point in Belgium (694m above sea level), it has an observation tower and a rustic tavern. The **Baraque Michel**, 3km northwest, is a bleak spot on the Hautes Fagnes where a statue commemorates the local writer Albert Bonjean (1858–1939). An attractive **country tavern** serves local dishes.

The resort of **Robertville**, 8km northeast of Malmédy, is close to a reservoir formed by the Barrage de la Warche. The nearby castle of **Reinhardstein** was built in 1354. It was owned by the Metternich family for three centuries. A major restoration was begun in 1969 (open from mid-June to mid-Sept on Sun and on Easter Sunday, Ascension Day and Whit Sunday from 14.15–17.15. Guided tours are compulsory. Also in Jul–Aug on Tues, Thur and Sat, tours begin at 15.30).

A memorial known as the **Croix des Américains** stands at a crossroads at Baugnez, 4km southeast of Malmédy. It recalls a notorious massacre perpetrated by the ruthless SS Lieutenant Colonel Joachim (Jochen) Peiper.

The American Cross

The snow was thick on the ground as the Kampfgruppe Peiper advanced north along the minor road from Thirimont soon after noon on 17 December, 1944. At the same time, B Battery of 285th Field Artillery Observation Battalion, having just left Malmédy, reached Baugnez. They were directed south along what is now the N62. Almost at once, and taken wholly by surprise, the Americans came under tank fire. German infantry stormed across the open fields between the two roads, which are more or less parallel, while their tanks swung the short distance west and then south through Baugnez. It was very quickly obvious that the American situation was hopeless. Their only protection was the roadside ditch, which can still be seen. Their rifles useless against tanks and machine guns, the Americans surrendered. Marched back the few yards to the road fork, they were lined up in rows in the open field, now partly built over, immediately to the south of the café. They were then mown down by machine gun fire from two tanks. Of the 150 soldiers captured, 43 miraculously survived. The monument incorporates plaques with the names of the victims and a chapel shrine.

The small town of **Bütgenbach**, 12km east of Malmédy, has an attractive fortified farm. The Barrage de la Warche to the east is a reservoir with boating and fishing. A memorial on the N632, southeast of Bütgenbach, commemorates the American 1st Infantry Division.

The town of **Büllingen** (Bullange in French), 4km southeast of Bütgenbach, is an ancient settlement which grew up at the crossing of the Roman roads from Maastricht to Trier (the Via Mansuerisca), and from Rheims to Cologne. A Carolingian royal villa once stood here.

The town of **Sankt Vith**, 26km southeast of Malmédy, derives its name from an episode in c 836, when the relics of St Vitus, who had died 500 years earlier, were being carried from Paris to Corvey in Westphalia. The party halted here, leading to the construction of a chapel.

The old town was virtually obliterated by bombing in 1944. The **Büchelturm**, a relic of the old fortifications, was rebuilt in 1961 on a base dating in part from 1350. The small regional museum **Zwischen Venn und Schneifel** at Heckingstrasse 7 (open Sun 09.00–12.00) displays typical local interiors, sculpture and documents relating to the history of Sankt Vith.

The ruined castle at **Burg Reuland**, 12km south of Sankt Vith, dates from the 11C. It stands on the site of a stronghold first mentioned in 963. A minor road winds from here along the valley of the Our. This leads to a narrow pocket of Belgium which lies between the Grand-Duchy of Luxembourg and Germany. The village of **Ouren**, 10km south of Burg-Reuland, has some vestiges of a medieval castle. The three frontiers of Belgium, Luxembourg and Germany meet just south of here.

Off the beaten track

WALLOON BRABANT

The province of Walloon Brabant is an attractive French-speaking region to the south of Brussels. It has a distinctive landscape with vast open fields, large fortified farms and wayside shrines. This new administrative region of Walloon Brabant was created when Brabant province was split between Flanders and Wallonia. The main attractions are Waterloo battlefield and the ruined abbey of Villers-la-Ville. Places linked to the battle of Waterloo, including Wavre and Genappe, are covered in a separate chapter.

Tourist information
Walloon Brabant tourist information

office, Chaussée de Bruxelles 218, Waterloo. ☎ 02.351.12.00.

Villers-la-Ville

The ruins of a great Cistercian **abbey** stand in a peaceful wooded valley near the small town of Villers-la-Ville, 36km south of Brussels.

Practical information

Eating out
The *Chalet de la Forêt*, next to the abbey gate, is a rustic Belgian tavern with a good beer list.

Tourist information
A small tourist office opposite the abbey is opened limited hours Mon–Fri. The abbey shop is a better source of information, ☎ 071.87.95.55.

Walks
The abbey is located in a beautiful rural setting. The tourist office and abbey shop sell a useful **guide** to local walks, which take in wayside shrines, the abbey farm and a little stream. The trails, which are numbered, begin from the tourist office, east of the abbey.

Opening times
The abbey is open Apr–Oct Wed–Mon 10.00–18.00; it closes one hour earlier Nov–Mar.

History of the abbey

Originally established in 1146 on a nearby hill, the abbey was moved the following year to its present site beside the river. The site was apparently recommended by St Bernard during a visit to the new foundation. The oldest ruins date from 12C–14C. A second phase of construction was carried out in the 17C and 18C. The abbey was sacked by French revolutionaries in 1794 and suppressed two years later. This was followed by a long period of neglect, during which time the central nave of the church collapsed and part of the estate was acquired to build a railway line. The site was bought by the Belgian government in 1893; it is now managed by the French Community of Belgium. The abbey grounds occasionally provide a dramatic setting for French drama and classical concerts.

A track leads from the ticket office to a group of domestic buildings to the left. These include the 14C Romanesque warming room, the refectory built in Transitional style, and the kitchen which dates from the 12C and 13C.

The **cloisters** are almost completely in ruins. Originally Romanesque, they were later rebuilt in Gothic style. All that now survives from the Romanesque period are the twin 12C windows in the east walk. The south walk contains a collection of gravestones. The east walk has a staircase which connected with the dormitory, and doors that once led to the parlour, chapter house and mortuary. The tomb of Gobert d'Aspremont, a crusader knight, is in the northeast corner. He joined the order here, and died in 1263. The crypt, which is dark and often flooded, is in the northwest corner where there is also a Transitional style doorway with a three-cusped arch.

The huge ruined **church** adjoins the north walk of the cloisters. Despite neglect, plundering and the collapse of the nave in 1884, this remains an outstanding example of Gothic architecture. The large 13C brewhouse lies to the northwest of the church. The area immediately to the east of the apse was the burial ground. Now unrecognisable as such, it is cut through by the railway line.

The 17C and 18C buildings lie to the southeast of the church and cloisters together with the ruins of the Abbot's Palace. The formal landscaped gardens to the east stand on the site of the kitchen garden. A flight of worn stone steps leads under the railway line to a little Baroque chapel of 1615.

The Cistercians

The Cistercian order was founded in 1098 by **Robert of Molesmes**, a monk dissatisfied with the laxity of Benedictine life. He migrated with twenty followers to Cîteaux, near Dijon, where the Count of Burgundy provided a monastery. The energetic and popular **St Bernard** (1090–1153) joined the community in 1112, infusing it with new life. By the time of his death, there were 280 Cistercian houses. The number had grown to over 500 by the end of the 12C. Inspired by the teachings of St Bernard, the monks often settled in beautiful locations in wooded valleys. The Cistercian rule involved a strict adherence to the guidelines laid down by St Benedict. One of the main rules of the order was the emphasis on manual labour. Cistercians as a result became renowned as farmers; they built large farms and granges in the Low Countries and carried out much of the country's early land clearance.

Outside the abbey, the **Hôtel des Ruines**, opposite the abbey entrance, occupies the former abbatial mill. A medieval herb garden has been planted near the west gate. The **parish church** of Villers-la-Ville, 1km south of the abbey, contains two impressive retables with exquisite detailing. One dates from the early 15C, while the other is from the late 16C. Both were originally in the abbey church.

A cobbled lane runs east from the abbey under the railway line to the Baroque **Chapelle Notre-Dame des Affligés**. A French soldier who passed this site on his way to war vowed to build a chapel if he survived. His prayer was answered; he returned in 1731 carrying a medieval wooden statue he had rescued from a burning church. According to a local legend, the statue helps toddlers take their first steps provided that they are brought here on three successive Fridays and led three times round the chapel.

Villers-la-Ville environs

The village of **Tilly**, 3km southeast of Villers-la-Ville, has a 12C keep. This was the birthplace of the austere Jean 't Serclaes, Comte de Tilly (1559–1632). He led the Catholic League against the army of Gustavus Adolphus during the Thirty Years War.

The château at **Gentinnes**, 5km east of Villers-la-Ville, was given in 1903 to the **Order of Saint Esprit** as a centre for training missionaries to the Congo. It still belongs to the Order. A striking sculpture in front of the building was carved by Raf Mailleux. It commemorates missionaries killed during the troubles leading to the independence of the Congo in 1960. The façade of a beautiful chapel designed by Charles Jeandrain in 1967 is inscribed with the names of 181

Catholic missionaries and 30 Protestant victims. The altar in the chapel was made from Congo granite and the benches carved using timber from the Congo.

The village of **Baisy-Thy**, 4km west of Villers-la-Ville, was the birthplace of Godfrey of Bouillon (1060–1100). A leading figure in the First Crusade, he played a heroic role in the siege of Jerusalem. After its capture, he was chosen as ruler of the city. Famed for his pious and simple life, Godfrey generated many legends and *Chansons de Geste*. He is commemorated by a monument erected in 1855 in the church.

Genval

The Lac de Genval, 21km southeast of Brussels, is surrounded by picturesque villas and lakeside restaurants. A nearby spring is the source of Schweppes mineral water.

Practical information

Where to stay
Several attractive hotels are located near the lake:
Château du Lac, Avenue du Lac 87, ☎ 02.655.71.11, a grand country hotel with an indoor pool.
Le Lido, Rue Limalsart 20, ☎ 02.654.05.05, a country house hotel with an attractive garden.

Eating out
Lido (see above) has an attractive family restaurant.
Trefle à Quatre, in the Château du Lac (see above), is a distinguished restaurant looking out on the lake.

Genval environs
The town of **La Hulpe** (Terhulpen in Dutch), 2km west of Genval, has a church with a Romanesque tower and a 13C nave. The church contains the gravestone of Charles Baillie (1542–1625), a secretary of Mary Queen of Scots who died at La Hulpe. The **Château de la Hulpe** was built in 1842 by the Marquis of Béthune-Hesbigneul and bought in 1893 by the industrialist Ernest Solvay. Its landscaped gardens and woodlands are open to the public.

The **Château de Merode** is in **Rixensart**, 4km southeast of Genval. Built between 1631 and 1662, it has belonged to the De Merode family since 1787. The attractive court is laid out in the form of a cloister with galleries of flattened arches. The château contains tapestries, family portraits and a collection of Arabic weapons. The weapons were brought back from Egypt by Gaspard Monge, who directed archaeological and scientific studies during Napoleon's Egyptian campaign. The château also owns the lance-pennon of Frédéric de Merode, who died during the 1830 revolution. His memorial stands in the Place des Martyrs in Brussels. The Château is open Easter–Oct on Sun and public holidays 14.00–18.00.

Nivelles

Nivelles, 28km south of Brussels, is the main town of the French-speaking region of Brabant known as the *Roman Pays*. Although its centre was virtually destroyed by bombing in May 1940, the town retains much of its old character. It still has a number of handsome buildings dating from the 17C to the 19C. Its Dutch name is Nijvel.

Tourist information
Waux-Hall, Place Albert I,
☎ 067.21.54.13.

Opening times
Collégiale Sainte Gertrude is open daily 09.00–17.00. Guided tours are given Mon–Fri at 14.00 and weekends at 14.00 and 15.30.
Musée d'Archéologie, Rue de Bruxelles, is open Wed–Mon 09.30–12.00 and 14.00–17.00.

Collégiale Sainte Gertrude
The origins of Nivelles are linked to the impressive Collégiale Sainte Gertrude, which stood on the ancient pilgrimage route to Santiago de Compostella.

A convent was founded on this site in c 650 by Blessed Itte, the widow of Pepin of Landen. She brought her husband's remains to the convent and appointed her daughter, St Gertrude, as the first abbess. The convent church, which was originally dedicated to St Peter, changed its name after Gertrude was buried there.

Construction work on the present church began at the end of the 10C, but the building has been substantially altered since then, mainly due to the fact that the church was burnt down 19 times. The last occasion was during the bombing of Nivelles in May 1940. The restoration of the church, including the reconstruction of the upper part of the Romanesque tower, was finally completed in the mid-1980s.

The church is an outstanding example of a double-ended **Rhenish-Roman** structure. This style features transepts and choirs at both ends of the church. A 12C addition on the west side once had an apse, but this was demolished in 1619 and replaced in 1664 by a somewhat incongruous Baroque portal. The west tower is flanked by two 12C turrets. The south turret contains the tall figure of an armed knight known as Jean de Nivelles. This 15C jacquemart originally struck the hours on the former town hall (demolished in the 18C). It was moved to the church even before the town hall was demolished, in the early 17C. The other turret is known as La Tour Madame as it was close to the palace of the abbess.

Enter the church through one of two aisle doors with ornate carved lintels at the west end. The **Portail de Samson** on the north is the more elaborate. The beautifully-proportioned **nave** contains a fine Rococo pulpit carved in 1772 by Laurent Delvaux. The magnificent 13C shrine of St Gertrude is in the east choir. It was meticulously restored after virtually melting away during the furious fire in 1940.

Guided tours take visitors into the large **crypt** of c 1100, with its three aisles and six vaulted bays, and the even more ancient **Archaeological Cellar** where traces have been identified of no fewer than five earlier churches. The oldest of these is a 7C funerary chapel. There are also the remains of the first church, built in the late 7C and containing the tomb of St Gertrude; the first Carolingian church built in the late 9C; the second Carolingian church (10C) and the third Carolingian church (also 10C).

A 7C mystery

A fascinating mystery surrounds some of the ancient material found here. It establishes a vague link with **St Foillan**, a 7C Irish saint who left his native country accompanied by his brothers Fursey and Ultan. He eventually became abbot of Burgh Castle near Great Yarmouth. When the abbey was destroyed by the Mercians, he moved to the Low Countries and established the abbey of Fosses-la-Ville on land given to him by the Blessed Itte in c 650. St Foillan and three companions were murdered by robbers near Le Roeulx c 665.

A stone found in the Archaeological Cellar bears the inscription *Hic +Re/Quiescunt Mem/Bra Inlata Bea/Ta Memoria/Sin/ E (or Q) Vvaloni Qui Fu/ (I)t Interfec(tus) No(nis) IV(niis or liis)*. This is sometimes translated as: 'Here lie the remains of Sinewalon or Sinqualon of blessed memory. He was murdered on the ninth of June (or July)'. Some historians have suggested substituting 'S(ancti) M(artyri) Fvvaloni' for 'Sine(q)vvaloni'. This reading would establish a connection, tenuous perhaps, with St Foillan. The case for such an interpretation was strengthened by the discovery near the inscription of a sarcophagus, dated to the 7C, which contained the bones of four people.

The **cloister** is entered from the north aisle of the church. The northeast corner dates from the 11C or 12C, while the north walk is from the 13C. The remainder was rebuilt in 1846.

The **Musée d'Archéologie** in the Rue de Bruxelles occupies the 18C refuge of the abbey of Orval. Its collection, some of which comes from the Collégiale Sainte Gertrude, includes artefacts from prehistoric to Merovingian times and statues from the 15C to the 18C. Some of the statues are by the 18C sculptor Laurent Delvaux. A collection of Flemish paintings includes several works attributed to Rubens. The museum also has furniture, Brussels tapestries, ancient locks and keys, historic weapons and musical instruments.

A plaque on the wall of a house opposite the museum recalls a Gestapo atrocity. There is a medieval tower at Rue Seutin 38. Known as the **Tour Simone**, it is the only survivor of the 11 towers which formed part of the 12C ramparts of the town. The attractive Renaissance tower **La Tourette** in the Avenue de la Tour de Guet was built in 1620 as a country retreat for the Jesuits.

Nivelles environs

The Premonstratensian abbey at **Bois-Seigneur-Isaac**, 4km north of Nivelles, was rebuilt in 1903 on old foundations. The entrance dates from 1764. The richly decorated chapel, built betwen 1550 and 1580, is beside the road.

Louvain-la-Neuve

The university town of Louvain-la-Neuve, 28km southeast of Brussels, was founded in 1970 following a protest movement by Flemish students at Leuven University.

Marching in 1968 under the slogan 'Walloons go home', the Flemish students forced the government to create a new university town in Walloon Brabant for French students. Built on an attractive rolling site near Ottignies, the campus features imaginative town planning and inspiring architecture. The planners introduced some utopian notions to the site such as restricting the upper street level to pedestrians and cyclists, with roads and car parks kept below ground or on the perimeter. To enhance the sense of community, they decided that no district should be more than ten minutes on foot from the centre. The architects' use of light brick and narrow paved streets adds to the charm.

Two old Brabant farmhouses have been preserved on the campus. A plaque on the wall of the **Ferme de Blocry** has a quote from Gaston Bachelard's *Poetics of Space* advocating the use of the curve in architecture. The attractive **town museum** on Place Blaise Pascal contains an interesting collection of ethnography and modern art (open Mon–Fri 10.00–18.00 and Sun 14.00–18.00; closed at weekends in Jul–Aug). The **railway station** is decorated with a mural by Thierry Bosquet depicting an ideal Renaissance city and spot-lit copies of 25 paintings of Belgian railway stations by Paul Delvaux.

Louvain-la-Neuve environs

The village of **Corbais**, 2km southeast of Louvain-la-Neuve, has the remains of a 12C or 13C defensive keep known as the **Tour Griffon**. A better preserved keep of 1324, which once formed part of a manor house, is on an islet at **Alvau**, 3 km south of Louvain-la-Neuve.

Jodoigne

Jodoigne (Geldenaken in Dutch), c 36km southeast of Brussels, was an important trading centre in Roman times, when it was known as Geldonia. It grew into a fortress in the Middle Ages which controlled the road to Leuven and was therefore frequently attacked. The funnel-shaped Grand-Place was deliberately designed for defensive purposes. The **Hôtel de Ville**, on the site of the 13C corn-market, dates from 1733. The Chapelle Notre-Dame du Marché was built in the 14C.

The mixed Romanesque and Gothic **Eglise Saint Médard** is dedicated to a Frankish nobleman who lived c 470–568 and was Bishop of Tournai. Like St Swithin, his name was connected with the weather. He was also invoked by sufferers from toothache. The church is the oldest building in Jodoigne. It was built in the 12C on the site of a 7C chapel. Burned down in 1568 and again in 1578 by the soldiers of William of Orange, it was rebuilt in 1606. The French revolutionaries converted it into a Temple of Reason, but it was returned to the church authorities in 1802. It contains a chalice, part of which is attributed to Hugo d'Oignies, a painting of the *Virgin and Child* by Cornelis Schut and a triptych ascribed to Otto Venius.

Jodoigne environs

The village of **Gobertange**, 2km northwest of Jodoigne, gives its name to the white stone used in many local buildings. Gobertange stone is also used in the town halls at Brussels and Leuven, and in Brussels Cathedral.

There is a former 18C Premonstratensian abbey built by Laurent Dewez near the village of **Opheylissem**, 8km northeast of Jodoigne. The buildings are now used by the provincial government.

The impressive vestiges of the **Abbey of La Ramée** are near Jauchelette, 3km south of Jodoigne. Founded in the 13C by Cistercian monks, the abbey burned down in 1650, but was rebuilt soon afterwards. It was used as a field hospital for Marborough's wounded troops during the Battle of Ramillies in 1706. The church was destroyed by French Revolutionaries, but the enormous barn (the largest in Belgium), the stables, and a small chapel have survived. The buildings, which surround a vast cobbled courtyard, are being sensitively restored to create a restaurant, conference centre and possibly a hotel.

The village of **Glimes**, 6km southwest of Jodoigne, has one of the largest tumuli in Belgium. Located just south of the village, it is 12m high and 50m in diameter. There are other tumuli and traces of earthworks from a prehistoric settlement at the **Bois de Chaumont**, just northwest of Chaumont-Gistoux, 8km west of Glimes. Several more tumuli can be seen between here and the village of **Bonlez** to the northwest. This village has a château which dates in part from 1230. The hamlet of Dion Valmont, west of Bonlez, is mentioned in a document of 987.

The town of **Orp-le-Grand**, 10km east of Jodoigne, has a Romanesque church which dates mainly from the end of the 12C. It was badly damaged by fires in 1356, 1485 and 1637. After it was again damaged in a German attack in 1940, the foundations of two older churches and a large crypt were revealed. The earliest church on the site has been dated to the 8C or 9C. A small **museum** in the Maison Communale contains a collection of jewellery and weapons from the neolithic period to Merovingian times (open Mon–Fri 13.00–17.00).

The village of **Folx-les-Caves**, 4km southwest of Orp-le-Grand, has underground quarries which date back to Roman times or even earlier. Some of the caves are used for growing mushrooms. Open at weekends 10.00–18.00. Closed in Jan.

The hamlet of **Ramillies**, 3km southwest of Folx-les-Caves, is the site of a famous battle in which an allied army led by Marlborough defeated a French army commanded by Villeroi on Whit Sunday 1706. The forces were evenly matched. The French, facing northeast, occupied a line through the hamlets of Autréglise, Offus, Ramillies, Francqnée and Taviers. Their flanks were protected by small, marshy streams. Marlborough made a feint against the French left, then concentrated his attack against Ramillies, while his Dutch troops attacked Francqnée and Taviers. Both attacks were successful, though Marlborough himself was unhorsed. The French retired in disorder to Leuven. The Allied casualties, mainly Dutch, were some 5000 while the French lost 15,000 men.

Braine-le-Château

The small town of Braine-le-Château, c 18km southwest of Brussels, still has the pillory erected in 1521 by Maximilian de Hornes, chamberlain to Charles V. His impressive tomb can be seen in the church. The entrance to the **Château Robiano** is opposite the pillory. An old **water mill** at Rue des Comtes de Robiano 4 has been restored and reopened as a **museum**.

Braine-le-Château environs
The secluded village of **Ittre**, 4km south of Braine-le-Château, has a **forge** which dates from 1701 (open Easter–Oct Sun 14.00–18.00).

The village of **Saintes** (Sint Renelde in Dutch), 8km northwest of Braine-le-Château was the scene of a grisly martyrdom in 680. St Renelde (the sister of St Gudule) and her priest Grimoald, were both beheaded. Their servant was killed with nails driven into his skull. The **church** was built in 1553. It contains a wooden figure of St Renelde of c 1500 which may be by Jan Borman and also her silver shrine and a curious painting on wood depicting her family tree.

A small steam train runs in the summer on a 6km stretch of track at **Rebecq-Rognon**, 5km southwest of Saintes. The local **museum** occupies an old mill which straddles the Senne. The mill was rebuilt after a fire in 1858. The museum covers the history of the area and the mining of porphyry.

The town of **Tubize** (Tubeke in Dutch), 5km west of Braine-le-Château, lies close to the language border. The **Musée de la Porte** has an interesting display of Gallo-Roman artefacts, religious art, fossils and coins (open Tues–Sun 10.00–12.00 and 15.00–18.00.

The industrial town of **Clabecq**, on the River Senne 3km west of Braine-le-Chateau, is dominated by the ailing steelworks which line the Charleroi canal. They were founded in 1828 by Edouard Goffin, whose statue stands in the Grand-Place.

NAMUR PROVINCE
• • • • • • • • • • • • • • • • • • •

Namur province covers a large area of the Ardennes, including the popular caves at Han-sur-Lesse. The towns of Namur and Dinant, and the attractive Meuse valley, are covered in separate chapters.

Tourist information
Namur Province tourist information office, Avenue Reine Astrid 22, 5000 Namur, ☎ 081.74.99.00.

Han-sur-Lesse

The small Ardennes town of Han-sur-Lesse, c 24km southeast of Dinant, has been a busy tourist centre since the discovery in 1814 of an extensive network of grottoes.

Practical information

Where to stay

££ *Beau-Séjour*, Rue Platanes 16, Villers-sur-Lesse, 18km northwest of Han, ☎ 084.37.71.15, is a charming country hotel with a garden and an outdoor swimming pool.

£ *Ardennes*, Rue des Grottes 2, ☎ 084.37.72.20, is a traditional Ardennes hotel in the village centre. *Le Ry d'Ave*, Sourd d'Ave 5, Ave-et-Auffe, 4km southwest of Han, ☎ 084.38.82.20, is an attractive country hotel located in a former 19C tram station. It has an open-air pool and an extensive garden.

Eating out

Han has several Ardennes-style restaurants offering local game specialities in season. The *Taverne Ardennaise*, Rue des Grottes 2, is a traditional hotel restaurant offering local dishes and Rochefort Trappist beers.

Tourist information

For information on the caves and wildlife reserve, ☎ 084.37.72.12.

Opening times

The **caves and wildlife park** are open daily from late Feb–early Nov. Guided tours of the caves (compulsory) begin in the village at set times which vary according to the season. **Musée du Monde Souterrain** (admission free for visitors to the caves) is open daily Easter–Oct 12.00–18.00. Combined tickets are sold for the caves and safari park. Allow two hours to visit the caves or four hours for both the caves and wildlife park.

The caves are reached by an antiquated **rural tram** which leaves from the terminus next to the ticket office. Visitors are led through the caves by experienced guides who give a commentary in Dutch or French. The caverns consist of Devonian limestone below carboniferous rock. The River Lesse flows through the caves far below the walkways.

Some 8km of passages have been discovered, but the guided tour covers only a small section. The 20m high **Salle du Trophée** has the largest stalagmite, while the 250m long Galerie Lannoy leads to four caves with elaborate limestone formations known as the Mystérieuses. The **Salle d'Armes** is a circular cave 50m across which is used as a theatre for an impressive sound and light show. The lower part of the vast **Salle du Dôme**, 129m high, is filled by a small lake. Visitors are ferried out of the caves on the underground River Lesse. A small canon is fired at the exit to demonstrate the impressive echo.

There is a rustic **café** beside the river near the exit. A footpath leads back to the village, passing an adventure playground and a modern building occupied by a restaurant and the **Musée du Monde Souterrain**, which has an exhibition on the geology of the caves and some archaeological finds.

The **Safari Park** is a large nature reserve devoted to the vanished wildlife of the Ardennes forests. Visitors are taken on tours by safari cars to look at bison, tarpan, wild ox and brown bears.

Han-sur-Lesse environs

The **Belgian Space Communications Centre** at Lessive, 4km northwest of Han-sur-Lesse, has a museum with a replica communications satellite. It is open daily May–Oct 09.30–17.00. Visits are by guided tour. The centre has a café.

The moated château of **Lavaux-Sainte-Anne**, 7km west of Han-sur-Lesse, has massive squat round towers. Built from 14C–17C, it is occupied by a **museum of hunting**. It is open daily 09.00–18.00 (closes 17.00 from Nov–Feb and 19.00 Jul–Aug).

The town of **Beauraing**, 14km west of Han-sur-Lesse, has been an important pilgrimage centre since 1932–33 when the Virgin appeared several times to five children. The **Sanctuaire Marial** incorporates the Jardin de l'Aubépine (Hawthorn Garden), where the apparitions took place. The pilgrimage centre includes a large crypt, an upper church and a museum. The 12C castle nearby has 16C towers. It is now used by pilgrims.

Rochefort

Rochefort is a pleasant little town on the river Lomme, 24km southeast of Dinant. Its Trappist monastery brews dark Rochfort ales.

Tourist information
Rue Behogne 5, ☎ 084.21.25.37.

Opening times
The Grotto is open daily Apr–Oct

10.00–11.30 and 12.30–17.00.
Guided tours (compulsory) begin roughly every hour. The Castle is open daily mid-May–mid-Sept 10.00–18.00.

The **Grotte de Lorette-Rochefort** has a wild and menacing atmosphere. Discovered in 1865, it features marble and limestone rock formations. A *son et lumière* show is staged in the huge **Salle du Sabbat**, 125m by 65m by 85m high and a hot air balloon is released to demonstrate the impressive height of the cavern.

The ruins of the **feudal castle** stand opposite the grotto, next to a 19C mansion. A monument at the roadside commemorates the arrest here in 1792 of La Fayette by the Austrians. He had commanded one of the three French revolutionary armies formed to attack Austria, but secretly intended to use this force to restore the French monarchy. Proclaimed a traitor, he fled from France.

Floreffe

Floreffe is a small town on the Sambre, c 8km west of Namur, with grottoes and an important abbey.

Eating out
The Moulin restaurant occupies a 13C abbey mill. It is open Mon–Fri 11.00–18.00 and 11.00–20.00 at weekends.

Opening times
The caves are open daily Easter–mid-Oct 09.00–19.00.
The abbey is open daily Easter–Sept 13.30–17.00, Jul–Aug 10.30–18.00.

A slender 16C tower beside the main road marks the position of the **grottoes**, which are the only dolomitic caverns in Belgium. A small **museum** displays various finds, including human and bear bones, and other evidence of occupation during prehistoric times.

The imposing **Floreffe Abbey**, now a school, overlooks the green water meadows of the Sambre. Below the main complex, the **Moulin-Brasserie** of 1250 contains a restaurant which offers bread, beer and cheese made in the abbey.

The abbey was established here in 1120 by St Norbert, the founder of the Premonstratensian Order. The story goes that he was passing through Namur on his way back from Cologne when a local nobleman invited him to set up an abbey. It was sacked in 1188 by the Count of Hainaut, and again in 1232 and 1237 by the Counts of Flanders. Troops of Louis XIV attacked it again in 1683; it was finally suppressed by the invading French at the time of the revolution.

The existing domestic buildings date mainly from the 18C. The small vaulted **Salle des Frères Convers** of c 1150, next to the church entrance, is the oldest surviving part of the abbey. The **abbey church**, which has 12C murals, is a complex mixture of styles. The choir, transepts and nave are 12C or 13C, the tower is 16C, the eastern extension of the choir dates from 1638 and the Baroque west front was added during the 18C. Laurent Dewez faced the walls with stucco in the 18C. The elaborate Baroque stalls were carved from 1632–48 by Peter Enderlin, a German living in Namur. His carved signature appears on the stalls.

Floreffe environs

The ancient town of **Fosses-la-Ville**, 9km southwest of Floreffe, dates back to Celtic times when the place was called Biberona, the valley of the beavers. It became known by the Latin name of Fossa, presumably because of its fortifications, during the Gallo-Roman period. The widow of Pepin of Landen gave land to the Irish monk St Foillan (or Feuillen), for the foundation of an abbey here in c 650. This was later sacked by the Norsemen.

Bishop Notger of Liège built fortifications around a new abbey church in c 974. The present **Collégiale Saint Feuillen** stands on the site of the earlier churches. It dates mainly from the 18C, but parts of the foundations are 9C and 10C, and the Romanesque tower and crypt are slightly later. The stalls and pulpit are early 16C, while the marble choir screen has brass gates of 1756.

Several houses in the pleasant **Place du Chapitre** were formerly occupied by the canons. The largely 16C **Maison du Doyen du Chapitre** incorporates part of the old ramparts.

The industrial town of **Tamines**, 7km northwest of Fosses-la-Ville, was the scene of one of the worst German massacres of the First World War. On 20 August 1914, 384 civilians were mowed down by machine gun and rifle fire in front of the church. The victims were buried beside the church where they died. A monument recalls the atrocity.

The famous medieval goldsmith, Brother Hugo d'Oignies, was a member of the community of the abbey of **Oignies**, which stands on the other side of the river from Tamines. The abbey is now a glassworks. Hidden from the French Revolutionaries for 35 years in a barn, the Treasury of Hugo of Oignies is now kept in Namur.

The village of **Malonne**, 2km east of Floreffe, occupies a steep wooded valley. The mainly 17C church replaced an abbey church founded here before 698 by the Anglo-Saxon monk and missionary St Bertuin.

Philippeville

Philippeville, c 28km west of Dinant, was built as a fortress in 1555 by Charles V one year after the French captured Mariembourg, 12km to the south. Charles named it after his son Philip II. This is recalled by a commemorative stone in the church (on the first pillar on the left). Civilians were not allowed to live here until 1620. The town retains its **star-shaped fortress plan** and defensive galleries, the *souterrains* (open daily Jul–Aug 13.00–18.00). The former powder magazine is now occupied by the Chapelle des Remparts.

Tourist information
Rue des Religieuses 2, ☎ 071.66.89.85.

Philippeville environs
The Place de la Poste in the pleasant little town of **Walcourt** 10km northwest of Philippeville, was once occupied by a Gallo-Roman camp. A medieval castle was later built on the site.

The Basilique Saint Materne
The 4C St Maternus of Tongeren, incensed at finding a pagan altar, is said to have built the first Christian church here. This was replaced by the Basilique Saint Materne, the choir and transepts of which are 13C, while the rest was completed by 1477. The base of the tower and the narthex belong to an earlier church which was constructed between 990 and 1026. The upper part of the tower, with its strange 17C steeple, dates from c 1200. The marble rood-loft of 1531 is an exquisite example of the Flamboyant Gothic style. It was presented by Charles V when he made a pilgrimage to the miraculous Virgin of Walcourt, a wooden figure thought to date from the 11C, though local people insist that it is much older, even claiming that it may have been made by Maternus. The silver plating on the image dates from 1626. The Treasury displays some works attributed to the medieval goldsmith Hugo d'Oignies, who was a native of Walcourt.

The hamlet of **Thy-le-Château**, 3km north of Walcourt, has a castle of 1188 with a fine hall which was drastically restored 1920–39. The castle contains a collection of paintings by the 20C artist Charles Delporte.

The town of **Florennes**, 8km northeast of Philippeville, claims to be the birthplace of Arletta. The daughter of a tanner, she was the mother of William the Conqueror of England. The 18C **Eglise Saint Gangulphe** rests on foundations laid down in 1001. It is dedicated to a Burgundian nobleman who became a recluse. He was murdered c 760 by his wife's lover.

The hamlet of Senzeille, 5km southwest of Philippeville, contains a remarkable astronomical clock built by a local craftsman at the beginning of the 20C.

The village of **Roly**, 9km south of Philippeville, has a fortified farm which dates in part from the 12C. The estate has been converted into a nature reserve with signposted walks.

Couvin

The attractive town of Couvin, 44km south of Charleroi, stands on on the Eau Noire. It is a popular centre for rambles in the nearby wooded hills.

Tourist information
Rue de la Falaise 3, ☎ 060.34.01.40.

Opening times
Cavernes de l'Abîme are open daily Jul–mid-Sept 10.00–12.00 and 13.30–18.00 and weekends Apr–Jun

and Oct (same hours). The tour takes 45 minutes.
Grottes de Neptune are open daily Apr–Sept 10.00–12.00 and 13.30–18.00. They are also open at weekends in Oct. Tours last 45 minutes.

Couvin environs
The **Cavernes de l'Abîme** have been inhabited since prehistoric times. The inhabitants of Couvin took shelter here in 1940. One of the caves contains a museum of prehistory. A *son et lumière* show is staged in another cavern.

The town of **Mariembourg**, 6km north of Couvin, was built as a fortress in 1542 by Charles V and named after his sister Mary of Hungary. Believed to be impregnable, it was nevertheless taken by the French in 1554. The loss of Mariembourg led to the construction of Philippeville. Little trace now remains of the town's military past. The **Chapelle Notre-Dame de la Brouffe** belonged to a priory built in 1134.

A **steam train** runs between Mariembourg and Treignes to the east in the valley of the Viroin. (Trains run at weekends from Apr–Oct, and daily Jul–Aug. The round trip takes about two hours.)

An interesting region to the east of Couvin runs along the valley of the Viroin. The **Grotte de Neptune** at Petigny, 4km northeast of Couvin, was discovered at the end of the 19C. The visit includes a boat ride on the underground Eau Noire and a *son et lumière* performance near a waterfall.

Further along the valley, the small resorts of Nismes, Olloy and Dourbe on the Eau Blanche, have ruined castles, unusual rock formations and signposted walks.

The forest extends to the south of Couvin. The **Abri d'Hitler** near the village of Brûly-de-Pesche, 6km southwest of Couvin, was the site of Hitler's headquarters in 1940. (**Open** Easter–Sept daily 09.00–12.00 and 13.00–18.30; open Sun in Oct.)

The **Barrage du Ry de Rome**, 5km southeast of Couvin, is a large reservoir of 24 hectares in a forest setting.

The Condroz

The Condroz is a pastoral upland region in the northwest Ardennes, between the Ourthe and the Meuse.

The town of **Ciney**, 14km northeast of Dinant, is the capital of the Condroz. Its church, which is said to have replaced one founded by the 4C St Maternus, was badly damaged in a storm in 1618. The Romanesque tower and crypt survive.

The hamlet of **Chevetogne**, 8km south of Ciney, has an **Orthodox monastery** whose monks follow the Benedictine rule. Established in 1925, it is dedicated to the promotion of Christian unity. Its Eastern-style church of 1957 has some modern frescoes of the Cretan and Macedonian schools.

The attractive village of **Crupet**, 12km northwest of Ciney, has a beautiful **manor house** built from 14C–16C. The tower, standing on its own, is surrounded by water. Its only link to the house is by a small bridge. The 14C **church** contains some interesting funerary monuments. A tomb immediately to the left of the entrance depicts the formal dress of the period. The curious St Anthony grotto next to the church was built by a local priest in the early 20C.

The château at **Spontin**, 5km southeast of Crupet, claims to be the oldest feudal residence in Belgium (open daily 09.00–18.00). It was occupied by the Beaufort-Spontin family from 13C–19C. The building is an interesting example of a feudal stronghold combined with a manorial home. The lower keep was built in the 11C, but the building was largely destroyed in 1466 and again in 1555. It was rebuilt in a fortified style, though it served only as a manor house.

The château of **Jannée** near Pessoux, 5km east of Ciney, occupies the site of a 12C keep. It was built in an unusual horseshoe shape from 17C–19C. The castle has an interesting collection of furniture, paintings, porcelain and hunting trophies. The extensive park contains a wild boar reserve (open at weekends Apr–Sept and daily Jul–Aug 10.00–18.00)

Some of the furnishings in the **church** at **Sorinnes**, 7km east of Dinant, come from the abbey of Leffe near Dinant. The building was restored in 1777 and enlarged in 1890. The church at **Thynes**, 2km north of Sorinnes, has an 11C Romanesque crypt.

Gembloux

Gembloux, 18km northwest of Namur, is an important agricultural and sugar-refining centre. Its once powerful and learned **Benedictine Abbey** is now an agricultural college. The abbey was founded in 940 by St Guibert, a Lotharingian military leader who became a hermit on his estate here. It was rebuilt by Laurent Dewez from 1760–1779. A substantial section of the old wall is still standing beside the main entrance. The parish church, was built by Dewez in 1779 as the abbey church. It has an 11C crypt. A restored 17C chapel in the Rue de Mazy commemorates a victory of Don John of Austria in 1577 over the Dutch Sea Beggars.

The great castle of **Corroy-le-Château**, 3km southwest of Gembloux, was begun in c 1270. It comprises seven solid round towers linked by massive walls. Formerly topped with crenellations, the towers are now roofed over. The feudal structure remains otherwise virtually intact. It contains some interesting portraits, good furniture, a painting by Antoon van Dyck and a collection of dolls. The castle is now the residence of the Marquis de Trazegnies (open May–Sept at weekends and public holidays 10.00–12.00 and 14.00–18.00).

The well-preserved **village church** dates from the early 12C. St Norbert, the founder of the Premonstratensians, preached here in 1119.

The **Château de Mielmont**, 5km south of Corroy-le-Château, dates from 1160, but has been much rebuilt. It has a collection of paintings illustrating episodes in Belgian history (open Easter–Sept at weekends and public holidays 14.00–18.00).

HAINAUT PROVINCE

The province of Hainaut was heavily industrialised in the 19C along the valley of the Sambre. Many of its towns are now suffering from the decline of Wallonia's traditional steel and coal industries. The province retains many interesting relics from the Industrial Revolution including boat lifts, coal mines and former factories. It also has several impressive châteaux with landscaped gardens. The Hainaut towns of Tournai, Mons and Charleroi and described in separate chapters.

Tourist information
Hainaut tourist information office,

Rue des Clercs 31, Mons,
☎ 065.36.04.64.

Antoing

The town of Antoing, 5km southeast of Tournai in the southwest corner of the province, has an Hôtel de Ville dating from 1565. The imposing **château** (open mid-May–Sept on Sun and public holidays, guided tours at 14.30, 15.30 and 16.00) is largely a late 19C reconstruction, but it retains its 12C walls, 15C keep and a 16C tower. A corner tower contains some fine gravestones of the Melun and Ligne families. A number of these monuments are Tournai work from the 11C–16C.

The Château

Formerly the home of the Melun family, princes of Epinoy, the château passed by marriage to the princes of Ligne. The wedding ceremonies of Floris de Montmorency held here in 1565 initiated the nobles' rebellion against Spain. Count Egmont and Count Hoorn (who was brother of the bridegroom) were present, as was Jean de Glymes. By 1568, the Spanish authorities had executed or assassinated the two counts, De Gyymes and the bridegroom.

The battle of Fontenoy

The village of Fontenoy, 2km east of Antoing, has given its name to a battle fought nearby in May 1745. Ably assisted by the Irish Brigade, a French army led by the ailing Marshal Saxe defeated a British, Hanoverian, Austrian and Dutch force under the Duke of Cumberland. The main French line faced south between Antoing and Fontenoy, with an important fortified redoubt to the rear. After early attacks failed to defeat the French, Cumberland decided to attack between Fontenoy and the redoubt. He led the army, while the troops followed with drums beating and colours unfurled.

As the two armies met, Captain Lord Charles Hay of the Grenadier Guards ran forward, drank to the French and called for three cheers. Astonished, the French soldiers cheered in reply. They then called out: 'messieurs les anglais, tirez les premiers'. The English did so, then advanced deep into the French lines, believing that they were close to victory. Although deserted by his courtiers, Louis XV stood firm while Marshal Saxe brought his artillery into action. This shattered the allied square which, still fighting, was forced to fall back on Vezon. A Celtic cross erected in 1907 commemorates the part played by the Irish Brigade in this battle.

A 4.4m high menhir known as the **Pierre Brunehault** stands near Hollain, 2km south of Antoing.

Pays Blanc

The dusty Pays Blanc takes its name from the limestone which has been quarried here since at least Roman times. The village of **Calonne**, 1km north of Antoing, has a château in which Louis XV lodged at the time of the Battle of Fontenoy.

Péruwelz-Bon-Secours

The town of Péruwelz-Bon-Secours, 12km southeast of Antoing, is the centre of a marble quarrying industry. The Château de L'Hermitage stands close to the French frontier in the south part of the town. It was built by Marshal de Croy in 1749.

A large **Basilica** was built from 1885–92. According to an old legend, a 16C girl was accustomed to pray on this spot before a figure of the Virgin Mary which she had placed on an oak tree. Threatened by the plague in 1636, the people of Péruwelz pleaded with the Virgin to save them. Their prayers were answered and in gratitude they built a chapel. This was enlarged in 1642 and replaced in 1885 by the present building. It is said that the high altar stands on the site of the oak. The statue of the Virgin is carried in procession through the town on the first Sunday in July in fulfilment of a vow made by the townspeople in 1648.

Péruwelz environs
The village of **Bernissart**, 4km southeast of Péruwelz, was the scene of a major archaeological find in 1878 when fossil iguanodons 250 million years old were found here. They are now displayed in the Institut des Sciences Naturelles at Brussels.

A Romanesque church at **Blaton**, 2km north of Bernissart, dates from c 1183.

Beloeil

The **château at Beloeil**, 13km southeast of Ath and 18km northwest of Mons, dates back to the 12C. It has been occupied by the princes of Ligne since the 14C. The wings of the present building were constructed from 1682–1695, but the central section was rebuilt after a fire in 1900. The château (open at weekends Easter–May and daily Jun–Sept 10.00–18.00) has an important art collection, with works dating from the 15C to the 19C, fine tapestries, Louis XVI furniture, a valuable library of 25,000 volumes and the family archives from the 12C. The magnificent **gardens** (open daily 09.00–dusk) were laid out after 1711 in the style of Le Nôtre. The formal design features a great water basin, secret enclosed garden 'rooms' surrounded by tall clipped hedges, fountains and a ruin. The Orangery contains a **restaurant**.

Three families

The familes of **Ligne**, **Arenberg** and **Croy** have played an important role in the history of Belgium. All three families own extensive estates in various parts of the country. Arenberg was originally a 12C duchy to the west of Cologne. The lordship of Arenberg passed in 1547 to Jean de Brabançon, of the house of Ligne, through his marriage to the sister of the childless Robert d'Arenberg. Jean's son Charles was created Prince de Ligne in 1576. He married Anne de Croy, the heiress of Croy and Chimay. This alliance greatly increased the wealth and extended the estates of the family. Prince Charles Joseph (1735–1814) was a distinguished soldier and author who cynically said of the Congress of Vienna: '*Le Congrès danse mais ne marche pas*'.

Beloeil environs

The **Archaeosite** at Aubechies, 4km northwest of Beloeil, is a reconstructed prehistoric village with eight replica buildings from the Stone Age, Iron Age and Gallo-Roman period. The houses are furnished with exact copies of furniture and tools found by archaeologists. Demonstrations are given of weaving, pottery-making and other ancient skills. (Open Mon–Fri 09.00–17.00 and weekends Easter–11 Nov 14.00–18.00.)

Ath

The busy little town of Ath, c 24km northwest of Mons, has a **Hôtel de Ville** in the Grand-Place constructed from 1614–24 by Wenceslas Coeberger. The **Eglise Saint Julien**, founded in 1393, was struck by lightning in 1817. Only the east end and the tower escaped damage. A tower called the **Tour de Burbant** in the narrow Rue du Gouvernement is the last vestige of a castle dating from c 1150. It is the oldest surviving example of military architecture in Hainaut. The tower is surrounded by an attractive group of 15C buildings.

Ath environs

The village of **Chièvres**, 6km southeast of Ath, dates back to the 9C. The 16C late Gothic **Eglise Saint Martin** has a 12C chapel. The 15C Tour de Gavre in the churchyard is flanked by vestiges of the 15C ramparts. The **Chapelle de la Ladrerie** was built in 1112 as part of the leper house. A military airfield near the town was used by German bombers during the Second World War.

The 1777 basilica of **Tongre Notre-Dame**, 2km west of Chièvres, contains a miraculous 11C statue of the Virgin. It is visited by pilgrims in September and February. The Virgin is venerated here as the patron of universities, poets and writers.

There is a small red-brick 14C keep of the lords of Egmont at **Herchies**, 8km south of Chièvres. It is surrounded by attractive gardens. The château nearby, which dates from 1511, was built by Charles de Berlaymont.

The **Château d'Attre**, 5km southeast of Ath, was built in 1752 near the site of a medieval castle built by the Count de Gomegnies. It retains its original decoration and furnishings, including fine silver, ivory and porcelain. There are paintings by Watteau and Snyders. The remains of the 10C **Tour de Vignon** are in the park. According to a popular local legend, this was the lair of a brigand named Vignon who, masquerading as a hermit, robbed and murdered his visitors. There is also the former village pillory, a 17C dovecot, and a 19C man-made hill with a Swiss chalet. A strange artificial rock was built by De Gomegnies as a pavilion for the Archduchess Marie-Christine of Saxe-Teschen, who was Marie Theresa's governor in the southern Netherlands. The château is **open** Jul–Aug Thur–Tues 10.00–12.00 and 14.00–18.00; at weekends and public holidays Apr–Jun and Sept–Oct (same hours).

The town of **Leuze**, 13km southwest of Ath, has a 13C Collegiate Church which was rebuilt in 1745 in Louis XV style. The 16C château of **Anvaing**, 10km north of Leuze, was where Leopold II signed the Belgian capitulation on 27 May 1940. The village of **Moulbaix**, 7km east of Leuze, has a windmill of 1624 which is still in use.

The small town of **Lessines**, 11km northeast of Ath, is famous for its porphyry quarries, which were first exploited in 1707. The ancient **Hôpital Notre-Dame à la Rose** was founded in 1242 by Alix du Rosoit, widow of one of the lords of Lessines, and restored in the early 17C. It contains a hospital ward, an ancient pharmacy and a collection of paintings. (Open for guided tours Sun and public holidays Apr–Oct 15.00.)

The **Eglise Saint Pierre** was badly damaged in 1940 and largely rebuilt. A section of the central nave dates from the late 12C, while much of the choir is from the 14C. A small medicinal herb garden has been planted near the town centre.

A tree next to the church in **Bois de Lessines**, 4km southeast of Lessines, was planted in 1793 as a symbol of liberty. The village of **Deux-Acren**, 2km north of Lessines, lies in a district famous for its herbal gardens. The church has a 12C tower. The baptismal font is a fine example of 12C Tournai stonework.

Parc Paradisio

The estate of **Cambron Casteau**, 4km southeast of Attre, contains the ruins of a Cistercian abbey founded in 1148 and suppressed in 1797 by the French Revolutionaries. Renamed **Parc Paradisio**, the estate has been turned into the largest bird sanctuary in Europe, with some 2500 exotic birds kept in large enclosures open to visitors.

Beyond the entrance gate of 1722 are some 18C farm buildings and an octagonal dovecot. The ruined church, which was built from 1190–1240, contains fragments of ancient columns, parts of a 14C cloister and a number of recumbent effigies in the style of the Tournai school set in niches in the cloister wall. The tower, which is 56m high, was built in 1774. The undercroft dates from the 12C. There is also a grand balustraded stairway and a bridge of 1776. The **River Blanche** flows through the grounds. The park has several restaurants, a children's farm and an adventure playground. (Open Easter–early Nov 10.00–18.00. Latest entry at 16.00. Allow at least 3 hours to visit.)

Soignies

Soignies (Zinnik in Dutch) is an attractive old town, 20km northeast of Mons, with an ancient Romanesque collegiate church. The town was famous from 15C–18C for its **Song School**. Several renowned musicians served here, including the Englishman Peter Philipps, born in 1560, who was a canon here in 1610. The town still has a flourishing song school.

The **Collégiale Saint Vincent** is dedicated to St Vincent Madelgar, governor of Hainaut and husband of St Waudru of Mons.

St Vincent Madelgar

After the birth of his fourth child, he became a monk and founded a Benedictine abbey here. He died in Soignies in 677. The abbey was destroyed by Vikings in the 9C, but rebuilt soon afterwards. The choir and part of the cloister, built c 960, are the oldest parts of the church. The transepts and central tower were built in the 11C. The nave with its plain arcades was added a century later. The narthex and west tower are a 13C rebuilding. The main portal was added c 1620 and the vaulting in the transepts is 17C.

The 60 superb Renaissance **choir stalls** were carved in 1576 by Jacques Laurent and David Mulpas. The south side of the choir contains an impressive 15C *Entombment* with terracotta figures. There is also an outstanding French 14C polychrome statue of the Virgin below the roof-loft. The **Shrine of St Vincent** (reconstructed in 1803), is above the high altar. The original 13C shrine was buried for safekeeping in a nearby garden at the time of the French Revolution. When it was recovered in 1799, it was so damaged that it had to be reconstructed. The Chapel of St Vincent houses the **Treasury**, which contains the 13C crozier of St Landry (the son and successor of St Vincent Madelgar), and a 13C reliquary of St Vincent.

The east walk of the 10C **cloister** can be entered from the church, or from the Rue de la Régence, where a plaque beside the church with a Latin inscription commemorates the safeguarding of the Shrine of St Vincent. A short walk north leads to the old cemetery chapel, which dates partly from the 9C or 10C. It contains a small **archaeological museum**.

Soignies environs

The town of **Braine-le-Comte** ('s Gravenbrakel in Dutch), 7 km northeast of Soignies, has an interesting church. The **Eglise Saint Géry** is named after the saint who founded Brussels. Mainly built in the 16C, it has a Renaissance high altar of 1577 and a 3.40m-high 15C statue of St Christopher. Carved from a single piece of walnut, it stands on an octagonal base of Ecaussinnes bluestone. A section of the town's 12C fortifications is preserved opposite the church. Ruined ramparts of the same period have survived in the Ruelle Larcée behind the 17C Hôtel de Ville.

The town of **Enghien**, 13km north of Soignies, lies just south of the language frontier. Its name in Dutch is Edingen. Long an appanage of the Bourbon family, Henry IV of France sold it in 1607 to the Count of Arenberg. The 17C **Chapelle des Capucins** contains an alabaster tomb of Guillaume de Croy, Archbishop of Toledo, who died in 1521. It was carved by Jean Mone. The archives of the Arenberg family are kept in the chapel. The Arenberg château was destroyed by the French at the time of the Revolution, leaving just the 15C chapel and the stables.

Ecaussinnes

The attractive town of Ecaussinnes, 8km east of Soignies, is divided into Ecaussinnes-Lalaing on the east side of the Senne valley and Ecaussinnes d'Enghien on west side. Each takes the name of its former feudal lord. Ecaussinnes d'Enghien is mainly industrial, while the more picturesque Ecaussinnes-Lalaing is dominated by a large **castle**. This dates from the 12C, but was altered several times up to the 18C. It was owned by the Roeulx family in the 12C, the Lalaings in the 14C and 15C and the Croys in the 16C. The interior has several striking interiors including a 15C kitchen and a 15C chapel with a 14C statue of the *Madonna* attributed to the school of André Beauneveu. The hall and armoury contain two early 16C chimneypieces, some fine furniture and cabinets of glass and Tournai porcelain. (Open Jul–Aug Thurs–Mon; Apr–Oct weekends and public holidays 10.00–12.00 and 14.00–18.00.)

The 15C **Eglise Sainte Aldegonde** is dedicated to the sister of St Waudru of Mons. It contains the tomb of Blandine Rubens, sister of Pieter Paul Rubens. An *Assumption* by Gaspard de Crayer hangs in the church. The **Château de la Folie** on the northern edge of the town derives its name from *feuillie* (leafy). Built from 16C–18C, it stands on the site of a 14C castle of the lords of Enghien. The attractive 16C courtyard can be seen from the road.

Ecaussinnes environs

The village of **Arquennes**, 6km east of Ecaussinnes, has a Renaissance chapel from 1622. A moated château in the village of **Feluy**, 2km southwest of Arquennes, incorporates the vestiges of a medieval castle. The town of **Seneffe**, 4km south of Feluy, is famous as the scene of two decisive battles. Condé defeated William of Orange at Seneffe in 1674, and the French defeated the Austrians here in 1794. The **Château de Seneffe** was designed from 1763–68 by Laurent Dewez. It contains an outstanding **Museum of Jewellery** (open Tues–Sun 10.00–18.00). The 18C landscaped gardens contain an orangery and an attractive Palladian theatre.

> ### Ecaussinnes bluestone
> The region between Ecaussinnes and Soignies contains several quarries where bluestone (or *petit granit*) has been obtained since at least the 8C. This beautiful smooth stone was used by masons in buildings such as the Collégiale Sainte Waudru at Mons and several of the guild houses in the Grand-Place in Brussels.

La Louvière

La Louvière is a large 19C industrial town mid-way between Mons and Charleroi which has been badly hit by factory closures. The town has some impressive 19C industrial buildings.

Tourist information
Place Jules Mansart 17,

☎ 064.21.51.21. Information on the Canal du Centre.

La Louvière environs

The **Musem of Mining** in Bois-du-Luc, 1km east of La Louvière, occupies a former 19C mine which has been preserved by a group of local enthusiasts. The guided tour takes in a miner's house, a school classroom of c 1900 and a mine shaft. It is open Mon–Fri 09.00–12.00 and 13.00–17.00; weekends and public holidays 14.00–17.00.

A ruined 17C castle built on 12C foundations survives at **Havré**, 7km west of La Louvière. Jean Dunois, the 'Bastard of Orleans' and companion of Joan of Arc, was lord of Havré from 1452–68. The estate later belonged to the family of Croy-Havré. The Duke of Marlborough and Prince Eugene were entertained here in 1709.

The château of **Le Roeulx**, 7km northwest of La Louvière, was built from 14C–15C, but was given a new façade in 1713–60. Owned by the Croy family since the 15C, it contains family possessions accumulated over five centuries. According to a local legend, St Foillan and his companions were murdered here in the 7C. The park has a fine rose garden and magnificent trees.

The outstanding **Musée Royal de Mariemont**, 3km south of La Louvière, takes its name from Mary of Hungary, sister of Charles V and regent of the Netherlands, who built a hunting lodge on the edge of the Morlanwelz woods in 1546.

Mariemont

The builiding was destroyed by Henry II of France just eight years later. The Archdukes Albert and Isabella restored Mariemont as a château in the early 17C and created formal gardens inspired by Aranjuez in Spain. Charles de Lorraine built a new château here in 1756 and laid out the gardens in French classical style. Charles' château was burnt by French revolutionaries in 1794, though the ruins of the wings survive in the park. A new château was built in 1831 for the industrialist Nicolas Warocqué. It was bequeathed to the nation in 1917 by the art lover Raoul Warocqué, who also left a vast collection of decorative art. The château was badly damaged by fire in 1960 but most of the collection survived. An airy modern museum opened in 1975 to display the collection.

The museum has sections devoted to the **archaeology of Hainaut** and the history of Mariemont. But it is most famous for the magnificent collections of European, Asiatic and Oriental antiquities. The collection of **Tournai porcelain** is the finest in Belgium. It includes an outstanding service *aux oiseaux de Buffon* made for the Duke of Orleans in Tournai in 1787.

Other treasures include classical Greek funerary monuments; black and red-figure vases; Hellenistic statuettes; European jewellery; Egyptian statuary; wall-paintings from Pompeii; Han and Tang ceramics; Ming porcelain, and a 16C commemorative stele from Peking. The Merovingian section displays a magnificent lead sarcophagus and a variety of finds from sites in Belgium and Germany. The museum also has more than 12,000 books and ancient manuscripts. A bronze version of Rodin's *Burghers of Calais*, cast in Brussels for Raoul Warocqué, stands in the entrance hall.

The **park** contains the ruins of Charles de Lorraine's château, an orangery, a rose garden and some magnificent old cedars. The grounds are dotted with 19C Belgian statues and Japanese bronzes, including a serene Buddha seated cross-legged on a lotus blossom. The museum has a **café**. Open Tues–Sun 10.00–18.00. Admission free.

Canal engineering

There are several impressive examples of canal engineering on the **Canal du Centre**, west of La Louvière, off the E19 motorway at exit 21.

Opening times

Plan Incliné (inclined plane) at Ronquières is open daily Apr–Oct 10.00–19.00. Allow an hour to visit the tower. Last admission 17.00.

The **Visitors' Centre** at the Strépy-Thieu lock is open daily 10.00–18.00. **Cantine des Italiens** is open May–Oct daily 10.00–16.00 (Jul–Aug until 18.00).

Boat trips

Excursions by *bateau-mouche* run on the Ronquières lock May–Sept Tues and Thur–Sun at 12.00, 14.00, 15.30 and 17.30.

Boat trips through the **Hydraulic Lifts** on the Canal du Centre are run every day in Jul–Aug, and at weekends May–June, and Sept–Oct. Advance booking is required, ☎ 064.84.78.31.

The remarkable inclined plane boat-lift at **Ronquières**, c 14km north of La Louvière, was opened in 1963 on the Charleroi to Brussels canal. It has two large tanks which can lift large barges (up to 1350 tonnes) a distance 1432m and a height of 68m. Each tank has 236 rollers, runs on rails and is 91m long, 12m broad and has a water depth of between 3m–4m. At the upper end of the slope, a bridge dock (300m long by 60m broad) stands on 70 pillars, each nearly 20m high and 2m in diameter. This lock has cut the average time for barge journeys from Charleroi to Brussels from 25 hours to 18. You can climb a 150m **tower** for a view of the surrounding countryside. A film is screened in the tower on Hainaut province.

The Canal du Centre has a series of four impressive 19C **Hydraulic Locks** between Thieu and Houdeng-Goegnies, west of La Louvière. The locks are located at **Thieu** (where the road crosses the canal at the lock), Bracquegnies, Houdeng-Aimeries and Houdeng-Goegnies. Built from 1885 to 1919, each lift can raise a barge of 380 tonnes a height of 17m using water power alone. A group of enthusiasts hopes to preserve the redundant lifts as an industrial monument. The four locks were listed by Unesco in 1998 as World Heritage Sites.

A single giant lock is being built at **Strépy-Thieu**, between Mons and La Louvière. The world's largest lock, it will be able to lift 1350-tonne barges a height of 73m.

The **Cantine des Italiens** at Houdeng-Goegnies is a former settlement occupied in the 1950s by Italian miners. It contains an interesting exhibition on Italian migrants in Belgium.

Binche

The old fortified hill town of Binche, 14km east of Mons, has been famous for its exuberant annual Carnival celebrations since the 16C. Despite its ailing economy, the town still devotes enormous energy to its festivities on Shrove Tuesday and the preceding two days.

Tourist information
Hôtel de Ville, Grand-Place,
☎ 064.33.67.21.

Opening times
The **Musée International du**

Carnaval et du Masque is open Sat 13.30–18.00 and Sun–Thur 09.30–12.30 and 13.30–18.00. It is closed on Ash Wednesday and for a week after Christmas.

Carnival in Binche
The origins of Binche's Carnival have been traced back to the 14C, but the present celebrations are derived from Mary of Hungary's festival of 1549. The locals begin preparing for Carnival in January with various balls and processions. The celebrations reach a climax on Shrove Tuesday when the Gilles dance in the main square dressed in flamboyant costumes found nowhere else in the world. The costumes are thought to be derived from those worn by nobles who dressed as Peruvian Incas in 1549.

History of Binche
Binche was first fortified in c 1150 by Count Baldwin IV of Hainaut. Its walls were considerably improved in 1491 by Margaret of York, the English widow of Charles the Bold. A section of the defences was demolished in 1545 by Mary of Hungary, regent of the Netherlands and sister of Charles V, to allow her to build a palace within the town. It was in this palace in 1549 that she organised a great festival in the presence of Charles V to celebrate the Spanish conquest of Peru. Five years later Henry II of France, at war with Charles V, destroyed the palace and most of the town. Louis XIV razed a large part of the ramparts in 1675.

This walk begins in the **Vieille Ville** to the south where some of the oldest and most interesting buildings are found. The **Hôtel de Ville** in Grand-Place was begun by Jacques du Broeucq in 1555 on the site of an older town hall destroyed the year before by the French. Further alterations, including the stucco façade, were carried out by Laurent Dewez in 1735.

The **Collégiale Saint Ursmer**, south of Grand-Place, is dedicated to the architect of the Benedictine abbey at Aulne. Of the original 12C church, only the base of the tower and the Romanesque main portal survive. A statue of a *Gille* was unveiled next to the church in 1952. The outstanding **Musée International du Carnaval et du Masque** occupies the 18C Collège des Augustins at Rue Saint Moustier 10. The museum owns a fascinating collection of masks and Carnival costumes from far-flung regions. An interesting section covers the history of Carnival in Binche.

A small park beyond the church contains the foundations of the Renaissance **palace** built by Mary of Hungary. The palace was partly rebuilt by Jacques du Broeucq after its destruction in 1544. The building was used by the town for various functions until the 18C, when it was finally abandoned. A memorial in the park commemorates René Legaux, a local poet who died in a Nazi concentration camp. The park ends at a stretch of the ancient ramparts which are perched high above the river.

A lane leads past the Collégiale to the little 16C mortuary **Chapelle Saint**

André, which contains some finely carved stalls and interesting sculptures. The old cemetery behind the chapel was in use from the 14C to the 19C. It contains a stretch of the ramparts.

The 13C **ramparts** have survived virtually intact. An attractive landscaped walk was created around the walls in 2000. A small historical museum is due to open in the former refuse of the Abbaye de Bonne Espérance, in the Parc Communal.

Binche environs

The former abbey of **Bonne Espérance**, 3km south of Binche, dates mainly from the 17C and 18C. A church built by Laurent Dewez in 1770–76 incorporates a 15C tower and a cloister in which there is some 13C work. The abbey is now a seminary.

The Hôtel de Ville in **Fontaine-l'Evêque**, 9km to the east of Binche, occupies a former château of 1558, with a chapel and towers of the 13C and 14C. Exhibitions by local artists are organised in the chapel in the summer months. The towers are linked by an underground gallery which has been converted into an imaginative **Musée de la Mine**. This includes an extensive section of a coal-mine complete with working machinery. (Open 15 Mar–Oct daily 10.00–12.00 and 14.00–18.00. Closes at 15.00 on Fri.)

Thuin

The attractive town of Thuin, 18km southwest of Charleroi, occupies a summit above the winding Rivier Sambre. An outpost of the bishops of Liège, it was once strongly fortified. The town's walls were razed to the ground in 1408 on the orders of John the Fearless of Flanders and Luxembourg after he had crushed the Liégeois at the battle of Othée.

The **Belfry** of 1638 in the Place du Chapitre is all that remains of the former collegiate church. The base of the **Tour Notger** across the road is a relic of the fortifications erected c 1000 by Bishop Notger of Liège. A short distance up the main street, the post office occupies the early 16C refuge of the abbey of Lobbes. The 16C refuge of the abbey of Aulne is on the opposite side of the street. A striking 300m concrete viaduct carries the main road across the Sambre.

Thuin environs

The ruins of the abbey of **Aulne**, 6km northeast of Thuin, are in a beautiful wooded setting beside the Sambre. The abbey's name is derived from the alder (*aulne*) grove in which it was established in 657 by monks from Lobbes, led by St Ursmer and possibly St Landelin. It adopted the Cistercian rule in 1144 and prospered sufficiently under the protection of the prince-bishops of Liège to be called 'Aulne-la-Riche'. Its fortunes then waned. After being sacked in the 15C and 16C, it was almost completely burned down by French revolutionaries in 1794.

Some domestic buildings, mainly dating from the 18C, survived the attacks. These have been restored as a home for the elderly. The great abbey church, now in ruins, was built from 1214–1250. The 16C apse remains together with vestiges of the transepts, and something of the west front of 1728. (Open Mon–Sat 10.30–12.00 and 13.30–18.00; on Sun and public holidays 10.30–12.00 and 13.30–19.00. Closed Mon from Oct–Mar.)

There is a Benedictine abbey at **Lobbes**, 2km northwest of Thuin. It was founded c 654 by St Landelin, a repentant brigand of noble birth, who was also associated with Aulne. Destroyed by the French in 1794, all that survives of the mainly 18C domestic quarters are a gateway and part of a farm building near the railway station.

The Romanesque **Abbey Church of St Ursmer** stands on the hilltop above Lobbes. Dedicated to the architect of Aulne who was a monk here, it dates in part from c 825. It is an outstanding example of pre-Romanesque and Romanesque building style. The east crypt, chancel and west tower are all 11C, but the central tower and the roof of the west tower are rather unfortunate additions of 1865.

The town of **Ham-sur-Heure**, 8km east of Thuin, has an imposing castle. Dating from the 11C, this was virtually rebuilt in the 18C and 19C. It now belongs to the municipality. The **Eglise Saint Martin** contains a 12C font, a 15C retable and, in the porch, the 15C *poutre aux apôtres* (a carved 'Apostles beam').

The Botte du Hainaut

The Botte de Hainaut south of Beaumont is a narrow strip of land bordered by France to the west and south, and by the province of Namur to the east. The straight N53 road from Charleroi to Beaumont was originally a Roman road. The village of Strée, 8km south of Thuin, derives its name from the Latin *strata*. Just south of Gozée, the road passes a menhir known as the **Pierre de Zeupire**.

The small town of **Beaumont**, 12km south of Thuin, occupies a striking location on a hilltop. Some stretches of 11C and 12C fortifications are still standing. The **Tour Salamandre**, near Grand-Place, is all that remains of a castle built by Richilde, Countess of Hainaut c 1051. The rest was demolished in 1691. The tower contains a small **museum** of local history (open daily May, June and Sept 09.00–17.00; Jul–Aug 10.00–19.00; and in Oct on Sun 10.00–17.00).

Beaumont environs

The hamlet of **Montignies-Saint-Christophe**, 7km northwest of Beaumont, lies on the French border. An attractive Roman bridge in a quiet setting south of the village spans the little river Hantes. This is virtually the last trace of the ancient Roman road that ran from Bavai to Trier.

The town of **Solre-sur-Sambre**, 11km northwest of Beaumont, has one of the finest feudal strongholds in Hainaut. The moated castle comprises a 12C keep, which was the original fortified house, and a square court enclosed by walls with 14C cylindrical towers at the corners.

The **Barrages de l'Eau d'Heure**, southeast of Beaumont near Boussu-lez-Walcourt, is an extensive area of dams and reservoirs with a total capacity of 47 million cubic metres of water. The complex is designed to supply water to the Brussels to Charleroi canal, dilute urban and industrial pollution, and maintain the flow of the Meuse. The main dams are the **Eau d'Heure** in the north and the **Plate Taille**, where there is a power generating station, to the south.

The lakes have been turned into a sports centre with sailing, boat trips, walking trails, cycle routes, picnic sites, and adventure playgrounds. The **Information Centre** near the Plate Taille dam (open daily Easter–Oct 10.00–18.00) has a

107m observation tower reached by lift. The dam at Eau d'Heure (open the same hours) has an aquarium and a small exhibition on the history of the dams.

There are two menhirs just southwest of **Sautin**, 8km south of Beaumont. They are known locally as **Les Pierres-qui-tournent**. The 1572 church at **Renlies**, 3km northeast of Sautin, has a beautiful retable of 1530.

The village of **Sivry**, 3km west of Sautin, has a **Museum of Natural History and Toys** (open Mon–Fri 10.00–12.00 and 13.00–17.00; at weekends and on public holidays from Easter–Sept 14.00–18.00; closed 15 Dec–15 Jan). A Nature Study Centre aimed at schools is located in a former station in the village.

The town of **Rance**, 12km south of Beaumont, is famous for the red marble quarried nearby. Marble from Rance is used in the chimneypieces at Versailles and some of the columns in St Peter's at Rome.

Chimay

Chimay, in the south of the 'boot', is a pleasant town built above the River Eau Blanche. The chronicler Froissart was canon and treasurer of the collegiate church. He died here in 1410. A statue of the chronicler stands in Place Froissart.

Tourist information
Vielle Tour, Rue de Noailles,
☎ 060.21.18.46.

Opening times
The **château** is open daily Easter–1Nov 10.00–12.00 and 14.00–18.00.

The **Collégiale Saints Pierre et Paul** in Grand-Place was built over several centuries. The three east bays of the choir date from the 13C, the remainder of the church is largely 16C, while the tower was added in 1732. The church contains the tomb of Charles de Croy, first Prince of Chimay, who died in 1525. It also has the gravestone of Mme Tallien (see château below). A monument in Grand-Place commemorates the princes of Chimay.

A stone arch in the Grand-Place leads to an attractive narrow lane, which ascends to the **château** perched high above the river. Dating from the 15C, the building was altered in 1607, badly damaged by fire in 1935, and later rebuilt in its original style.

A revolutionary heroine

The château passed to the De Croy family at the start of the 15C. Charles de Croy was created Prince de Chimay in 1486 by Emperor Maximilian. A woman known as Madame Tallien died here in 1835. Born Jeanne Marie Ignace Thérèse Cabarrus in 1773, Madame Tallien played an important role in the French Revolution. The daughter of a Spanish banker, she married the Marquis de Fontenay and then divorced him. While being held a prisoner at Bordeaux awaiting execution in 1793, she met the revolutionary Jean Tallien who had suppressed all opposition by his ruthless use of the guillotine. Tallien fell in love with her and they were soon married. She then became involved in revolutionary affairs and helped Tallien's Thermidor coup against Robespierre, whom she detested. Notorious for her harsh and dissolute conduct, Madame Tallien was dubbed 'Notre-Dame de Thermidor' and became a leading figure in the revolutionary salons. Tallien divorced her in 1802; she married the Prince de Chimay three years later.

Most of the valuable objects in the château were saved from the fire of 1935. There are some interesting family portraits, including one of Madame Tallien, period furniture, and antiquities of the 18C and 19C. The small Rococo theatre, which is still used during Chimay's summer festival, was built for Madame Tallien by her son Prince Joseph. There are some Louis XI banners in the chapel.

Chimay environs
The abbey of **Notre-Dame de Scourmont** stands on a hill near Forges, 4km south of Chimay. Founded in 1850, it brews several outstanding Trappist beers under the Chimay label.

The **Etang de Virelles**, 3km northeast of Chimay, is the largest lake in Belgium. It is a popular centre for boating and picnics.

LUXEMBOURG PROVINCE

Luxembourg province is an upland region of forests and small towns of grey stone houses. Arlon is the provincial capital. La Roche en Ardenne, Durbuy and Bouillon are lively tourist towns with good hotels. The River Ourthe, which passes through La Roche and Durbuy, is covered in a separate chapter.

Tourist information
Luxembourg Province tourist information office, Quai de l'Ourthe 9,

La Roche-en-Ardenne.
☎ 084.41.10.11.

Vielsalm

Vielsalm, in the northeast corner of the province, was an American headquarters during the Battle of the Ardennes. A memorial immediately below a church on the road from Trois Ponts commemorates the members of the Ardennes Secret Army. At a road junction in the south part of the town, a small fountain and a rough, dark stone commemorate the American 7th Armoured Division. A memorial on the road from Vielsalm to Salmchâteau recalls the many people of this region who fought against slavery in the Congo.

Vielsalm environs
The village of **Salm Château**, 3km south of Vielsalm, has the ruins of the castle of the counts of Salm, which dates back to the 9C. The **Musée de Coticule** (open from Apr–Oct from Tues–Sat from 10.00–12.00 and 13.00–17.00, Sun from 14.00–17.30) displays hone stone or razor stone from quarries in this district. This was greatly sought after in the 19C and early 20C, but reduced demand led the quarries to cut output and finally close down in 1980.

The village of **Beho**, 13km southeast of Vielsalm on the Ardennes plateau, was where the British vanguard crossed into what was then German territory on 1 December 1918. The **church** at Beho has a 12C tower. The rest is a rebuilding of 1712. It has some good Baroque furnishings.

Marche-en-Famenne

The town of Marche-en-Famenne, on the western border of the province 46km southeast of Namur, owes its name to its position on the march, or border, of Luxembourg and Liège.

Tourist information
Rue des Brasseurs 7, ☎ 084.31.21.35.

Don John of Austria signed the **Perpetual Edict** with the States General here in 1577. To mark the event, the town was awarded the Order of the Golden Fleece. The Perpetual Edict, which accepted many of the demands of the Dutch, was soon ignored. The Catholic nobles, alarmed by the spread of Calvinism, regrouped and in 1579 signed the Union of Arras. This was followed by a similar declaration, the Union of Utrecht, by the Protestant provinces. By then, all prospects of reaching a compromise had vanished.

A tower called the **Rempart des Jésuites** is all that survives of the town's fortifications. It contains a small **museum of lace**. (Open daily from 09.00–12.00 and 13.30–17.30. Closed on Sun and Mon Nov–June.) Contact the tourist office to arrange a visit.

The village of **Waha**, 2km south of Marche, merits a visit for its 11C **Romanesque church** which is striking in its simplicity. Built by the local village masons, it has a consecration stone of 1050 on the outside wall. There are several curious 11C wooden figures inside the church. The **commemorative stone of the Perpetual Edict**, which bears the arms of Philip II, and the blazons of Luxembourg and of Marche, is kept in the church.

Redu

Redu is a small village of stone houses in the heart of the Ardennes. It lies just off the E411 motorway, c 40km west of Bastogne. Inspired by Hay-on-Wye in Wales, about 20 antiquarian book dealers have settled in the old houses to create a **book village**. Most books are French or Dutch, but some dealers sell a few English books. The village also has art galleries, craft shops, restaurants and cafés. Most bookshops are only open at weekends. There are attractive walks in the nearby woods.

Practical information

Where to stay
££ *Le Moulin*, Rue de la Lesse 61, Daverdisse, 3km northwest of Redu, ☎ 084.38.81.83, is an attractive country hotel in a restored 18C mill. It has a good restaurant.

Eating out
££ *Le Col-Vert*, Rue de Libin 75, Neupont 5km north of Redu, ☎ 084.38.81.35 is a comfortable country restaurant with excellent Ardennes regional cooking. Rooms available.

La Gourmandise, Rue de St-Hubert 16, Redu, ☎ 061.65.63.90 is a friendly tavern restaurant with Belgian specialities. Rooms available.

Tourist information

Place de l'Esro 63, ☎ 061.65.65.16. Publishes a free leaflet listing all the bookshops, galleries and restaurants in Redu. Good for maps of local walks in the nearby woods.

Walking and cycling

Several walks are signposted from Redu church. Other attractive trails follow the River Lesse between Redu and Daverdisse. A track for hikers, cyclists and horse riders runs beside the Lesse from Daverdisse to Halmo.

Redu environs

The village of **Maissin**, 4km south of Redu, has a war cemetery with a 16C Breton Calvary. It commemorates 3000 Bretons and over 200 Germans killed here on 22 and 23 August 1914.

The village of **Paliseul**, 8km southwest of Maissin, was the childhood home of the poet Verlaine. Once known as 'Palatidum', it was a hunting-seat of the first Merovingian kings.

The **Euro Space Centre** at Transinne, 4km east of Redu, is a centre on space exploration. The exhibits include a full-size replica of a space shuttle and detailed scale models of several rockets. A film with special effects is screened in the cinema. The centre runs residential courses on space exploration. (Open mid-June–Aug from 10.00–17.00.)

Saint Hubert

The small town of Saint Hubert is named after a saint who had a vision in a forest outside the town.

Saint Hubert

Born into a noble family in c 656, Hubert was out hunting on Good Friday in 683 when his hounds cornered a stag. When the animal turned, Hubert saw that it bore the Cross between its antlers. He also heard a voice reproaching him for hunting on such a solemn day. Hubert immediately renounced the world and entered the abbey of Stavelot. During a visit to Rome in 705, he learnt of the murder at Liège of Bishop Lambert of Maastricht and Tongeren. The Pope then offered Hubert the bishopric. He at first refused on the grounds that he was unworthy, but later accepted when an angel appeared to him in a dream and draped a white episcopal stole around his neck.

St Hubert died in 727, but it was not until 823 that his remains were brought from Liège to the 7C abbey which stood near the site of his conversion. He acquired such a reputation for sanctity that it was believed a shred of his mantle could cure madness and hydrophobia. The abbey and town became known as Saint Hubert from the 9C. Hubert later became the patron of hunters; hunting dogs are still brought to the church on his feast day, 3 November, to be blessed. His remains disappeared long ago, but the abbey remains a place of pilgrimage.

Tourist information
Rue St Gilles 12, ☎ 061.61.30.10.

Opening times
Fourneau Saint Michel is open from Mar–Dec daily from 09.00–17.00 (or 18.00 in Jul–Aug).

Musée de la Vie Rurale en Wallonie is open from Mar to mid-Nov daily from 09.00–17.00 (or 18.00 in Jul–Aug).

The **abbey**, which was rebuilt in 1729, survived until the French Revolution. Its domestic buildings on the main square are now a cultural centre. The abbey church, the **Basilique Saint Hubert**, was built in Flamboyant style from 1526–1560. The Italianate west façade was added in 1702. A relief of St Hubert can be seen between the towers.

The lofty brick vaulting inside was constructed in 1683 to replace the shingle vaulting destroyed by Protestant fanatics in 1568. The **crypt** below the choir is partly 11C. The **stalls**, Liège work of 1733, are carved with the stories of St Hubert and St Benedict. The south ambulatory contains an impressive retable with Limoges enamels of 1560, after Dürer's *Small Passion*. This is one the few furnishings which survived, albeit damaged, the destructive fury of the Protestants. The saint's tomb of 1847 by Willem Geefs was a gift from King Leopold I, who was a keen huntsman.

St Hubert environs
The spot where St Hubert had his vision is marked by a **chapel**, c 8km northeast of the town on the N89.

There is a **wildlife park** on the N849, 2km northwest of St Hubert. Deep in the forest, a squat pyramid set in a lonely clearing recalls that King Albert was deeply attached to this spot. He came here for the last time shortly before his death in 1934.

The **Fourneau Saint Michel**, 8km northwest of Saint Hubert, is a reconstructed 18C ironwork complex. It includes an 18C forge built by the last abbot of Saint Hubert, and a barn containing an impressive collection of firebacks. Tools and other equipment are displayed in a museum. It is open from Mar–Dec daily from 09.00–17.00 (or 18.00 in Jul–Aug).

The outstanding **Musée de la Vie Rurale en Wallonie**, open from Mar to mid-Nov daily from 09.00–17.00 (or 18.00 in Jul–Aug), occupies an extensive estate nearby. This open air museum illustrates Walloon rural life from the 16C to the 18C. It features reconstructed farmhouses, schools, chapels, cottages, tobacco halls and wash-houses.

Napoleon III stayed at **Recogne**, 15km south of St Hubert, in 1870 after his defeat at Sedan. The poet Verlaine claimed descent from the lords of Verlaine, 3km southeast of Recogne.

Bastogne

First mentioned in 634, Bastogne has been attacked countless times in its history. It was sacked in 1236 by the Liégeois, attacked unsuccessfully in 1318 by Louis of Nassau, and had its ramparts torn down by the troops of Louis XIV in 1688. Despite its antiquity, little remains from the past. The most interesting buildings are the 13C **Porte de Trèves** and the **Eglise Saint Pierre**, which has a 12C tower and a 15C Gothic Mosan style nave with elaborate and colourful vaulting.

Bastogne has been famous since the 15C for its smoked hams. In modern times it is known for the heroic stand made here by the Americans during the Battle of the Ardennes in December 1944.

Tourist information
Place MacAuliffe 24, ☎ 061.21.27.11.

Opening times
The **Bastogne Historical Centre** is open Mar, Apr and Oct 10.00–16.00; May, Jun and Sept 9.30–17.00; Jul and Aug 09.00–18.00.

'Nuts'

Bastogne was encircled by the Germans in December 1944 during the Battle of the Bulge. The town was defended by the American 101st Airborne Division commanded by General MacAuliffe. When the German commander invited him to surrender, MacAuliffe's laconic reply was 'Nuts'. Despite heavy bombardment, Bastogne held out until Allied pressure on both flanks forced the Germans to withdraw.

The main square, renamed Place MacAuliffe, contains a tank and a bust of MacAuliffe. The impressive **American Memorial**, made by Georges Dedoyard in 1950, stands on the Mardasson hill, 2km northeast of the town. It is designed in the form of a five-pointed star, with colonnades and an upper gallery surrounding a central opening. The story of the battle is related in gold letters on the memorial's pillars. The star-shaped **Bastogne Historical Centre** nearby gives an interesting insight into the Battle of the Bulge using old film, weapons, maps and battlefield dioramas.

Bastogne environs
The curious town of **Martelange**, 21km south of Bastogne, has the border between Belgium and the Grand-Duchy of Luxembourg running down the centre of the road. As petrol is cheaper in Luxembourg, its side of the road is lined with petrol stations. The small **Musée de l'Haute Sûre** contains a reconstruction of the interior of a slate worker's house.

Bouillon

Bouillon is a historic town on a loop of the River Semois in the southwest corner of the province with steep winding streets and attractive waterside walks. The town is dominated by a magnificent castle perched on a rocky summit high above the river.

Practical information

Where to stay
Bouillon has several attractive hotels situated close to the river or on the heights facing the castle.

££ *Feuillantin*, Rue au Dessus de la Ville 23, ☎ 061.46.62.93, is an elegant hotel on the high ground facing the castle.

££ *Hôtel de la Poste*, Place St-Arnould 1, ☎ 061.46.51.51, is a historic waterfront hotel of 1730 where Napoleon III was held prisoner in 1870. Most rooms have a view of the castle.

££ *Pommeraie*, Rue Poste 2, ☎ 061.46.90.17, occupies an ancient mansion with a garden in the old town.

Eating out

Hôtel de la Poste, Place St-Arnould 1, has an elegant restaurant looking out on the river. The bar serves sandwiches. *Pâtisserie Michels*, Place St-Arnould 8, is a rustic Ardennes tea room.

Tourist information

A pavilion at the Porte de France is open in the summer, ☎ 061.46.62.57.

Opening times

Bouillon castle is open Jul–Aug from 09.30–22.00 (to 19.00 on Mon and Thur); Dec and Feb from Mon–Fri from 13.00–17.00, and weekends from 10.00–17.00; other months, daily from 10.00–17.00 (to 18.00 Apr–Jun and Sept). Closed 25 Dec and 1 Jan. Guided visits with flaming torches are organised in Jul–Aug at 22.00 (not Mon or Thur). **Musée Ducal** (local history), opp. castle entrance, is open from Easter–11 Nov daily from 10.00–13.00 and 14.00–18.00.

Archaeoscope Godefroid de Bouillon (modern museum with multimedia historical reconstructions), in the former Couvent des Sépulcrines, is open Jul–Aug daily from 10.00–17.30 (to 17.00 May–Jun, and to 16.00 in Mar–Apr and Sept). Opening hours are shorter at other times of the year. It is closed on Mon in Oct–Dec, and in Jan.

History of Bouillon

The first castle was built at Bouillon in the 8C by the Counts (later Dukes) of Lower Lorraine. **Godfrey, the fifth duke**, was one of the leaders of the First Crusade in 1096. After the capture of Jerusalem by the Crusaders in 1099, he was elected king of Jerusalem, but he declined the title, preferring to be called 'Advocate of the Holy Sepulchre'. He reigned for one year only, dying probably from a disease caught during his campaigns in Palestine, though the chronicler Matthew of Edessa relates that he was poisoned by his Muslim adversaries during a visit to Caesarea of Philippi. 'Godfrey accepted (the supplies brought by the Muslims) and unsuspectingly ate the dishes they prepared, which were poisoned. He died several days later ... and was buried in Jerusalem ... on the hill which is called Golgotha,' he wrote.

Before leaving for the Holy Land, Godfrey had sold or mortgaged his ancestral lands, including Boulillon Castle, to the prince-bishop of Liège to buy equipment for himself and some of the poorer Crusaders. The prince-bishops ruled the duchy through local lords, who enjoyed virtual independence, and later styled themselves princes. Members of the La Marck family once fulfilled this role. They were succeeded by the La Tour d'Auvergne family.

Bouillon was granted to **Louis XIV** in 1678 under the terms of the Peace of Nijmegen. The last of the direct line of the princes of Bouillon adopted Philippe d'Auvergne (1754–1816), who came from Jersey in the Channel Islands. He reigned at Bouillon from 1814 until the duchy was ceded to the Netherlands by the Treaty of Vienna.

Prince Charles Edward, the Young Pretender, lived in Bouillon with Clementina Walkinshaw from 1755 to about 1760. **Napoleon III** spent the night of 3 September in 1870 at the Hôtel de la Poste as a prisoner of the Prussians.

A walk in the town

The **castle** dominates the rocky outcrop above Bouillon. With its warren of passages and damp dungeons, it is the most impressive medieval fortification in Belgium. Most of the surviving buildings date from the 15C or later, though the site had been occupied by a fortress for many centuries before. The fortifications were altered considerably by the French military engineer **Vauban** after Bouillon was ceded to France in 1678.

The most dramatic approach is to climb the steep footpath that begins behind Le Chalet in **Rue du Petit**. The castle is entered by a series of three bridges that span deep defensive ditches. A small booklet in English is sold at the ticket office that describes the main features of the castle. The **third ditch** (labelled no. 3) was paved in 1686; the moat could be filled with water from inside the castle. An impressive vaulted room (no. 5) called **Godfrey de Bouillon's Room** is hewn out of solid rock. The age of the ancient wooden cross on the floor, which was uncovered by accident in 1962, is not known.

Pass **two cells** (no. 6) from the Dutch period, then descend into the main **courtyard** (no. 7), where the duke's residence once stood. A bell on the left dates from 1563. The unusual twin-level loopholes with triple slits were probably the work of Vauban. He is known to have designed the **rampart walk** (no. 10) and the **semicircular tower** (no. 11). The clock-tower at the end of the rampart walk is a rebuilding by Vauban of an earlier watch-tower. The present clock was given by Napoleon in 1810, though the hour bell belongs to a clock of 1606.

The **Austrian Tower**, to the right of the clock-tower, is named after George of Austria, Prince-Bishop of Liège, who converted it into a caponier c 1551. In its earlier form, the tower was designed to protect this part of the castle. A curious double lookout hewn from the rock (no. 12) is known as **Godfrey de Bouillon's Chair**. It is one of the oldest parts of the castle (it could only have fulfilled its function before the clock-tower was built).

A good view of the town is afforded from **no. 13**, the top of the Tower of Austria, 75m above the river. The room **no. 14** in the basement of the Austrian Tower was once a guard-room. A small room (no. 20) is popularly known as the **Torture Room** though it was probably in fact the armourer's workshop. It contains several medieval torture instruments. The next two rooms (nos 21 and 22) were **dungeons**. A padlocked door (no. 24) leads to a **stairway of 396 steps** which descended to a 15C water mill on the Semois. The steps can be seen through the holes in the door; the last vestiges of the mill disappeared during the Second World War, but the weir across the Semois still survives.

Other steps descend to an impressive 90m-long underground gallery with a large **cistern** at one end (no. 25). This corridor is lined with former storerooms. The **well** (no. 27) was widened and deepened by Vauban.

The **Musée Ducal** occupies an 18C house opposite the castle entrance. It is open from Easter–11 Nov daily from 10.00–13.00 and 14.00–18.00. This interesting museum of local history was established in 1947. It covers the history of the duchy and local life in Bouillon, including hunting, clogmaking, carding, lacemaking and weaving. The exhibits include a reconstructed 16C living-room and kitchen, and a model of Bouillon in 1690.

The **Musée Godefroid de Bouillon** occupies a 19C mansion next door. It contains exhibits on the Crusades, works of art from medieval Europe and the

Near East, weapons and furniture. There are several interesting models of war engines and weapons, medieval ecclesiastical objects (including fine Limoges work of the 13C), ivories of the 13C and 14C, a remarkably well-preserved 14C belt and a 14C Shrine of the Virgin.

Descend to the town and cross the Pont de France. Once over the bridge, go back along the riverside walk to reach the **Archaeoscope Godefroid de Bouillon**. Located in the former 17C Couvent des Sépulcrines, this striking new historical centre is devoted to Godfrey of Bouillon. The visit begins with an impressive multimedia show on Godfrey and the First Crusade (screenings approximately every 30 minutes). Commentary is provided in English on headphones. Other sections cover Arab culture, European fortifications and local history. A corridor of the former convent has been reconstructed. It is open Jul–Aug daily from 10.00–17.30 (to 17.00 May–Jun, and to 16.00 in Mar–Apr and Sept). Opening hours are shorter at other times of the year. It is closed on Mon in Oct–Dec, and only open at weekends in Jan.

Bouillon environs

The Semois river winds between steep cliffs west of Bouillon and fine panoramic views can be obtained from various points. One of the best spots is south of Botassart, 8km northwest of Bouillon, where the **Tombeau du Géant,** a large natural mound enclosed by a sharp bend in the river, can be seen across the Semois.

The **Château des Fées**, 4km southwest of Bertrix, a village 14km northeast of Boullon, is a defensive work which seems to have been in use from the 4C until perhaps the 11C.

There are traces of a 1C BC Gallic camp and grottoes traditionally associated with St Remaclus near the village of **Cugnon**, 8km east of Bouillon. It is said that Remaclus was offered land here for a monastery; he then dug the grottoes to serve as a chapel.

Perched high above the river at **Herbeumont**, c 12km east of Bouillon, are the ruins of the 12C castle of the local counts. The castle was destroyed by Louis XIV in 1658, but it is worth climbing up from the village for the view from the crumbling ramparts. A hotel next to the River Semois south of Herbeumont occupies the site of the 18C **abbey of Conques**.

A viewpoint near **Chassepierre**, 21km southeast of Bouillon, attracts many artists. It is claimed that the village existed in prehistoric times and that primitive fishermen used its grotto. During the period of the Roman occupation it was known as 'Casa Petra'. The nearby village of **Azy**, 3km to the north within a loop of the Semois, has a dolmen.

The valley of the Semois

A winding road follows the beautiful valley of the Semois northwest from Bouillon to the French frontier (where the river becomes the Semoy). The road passes through attractive villages such as Membre, Vresse and Alle, which once had a flourishing tobacco industry. There are drying houses and a **tobacco museum** at **Vresse** (open daily from Mar–Dec). The museum contains a collection of pipes, tobacco jars, snuffboxes, and old tools used in the tobacco industry. It also contains a typical Ardennes kitchen and an old steam locomotive called 'Le Belge'. Kayaks and mountain bikes can be rented at Vresse.

Florenville

Florenville, 20km southeast of Bouillon, is an attractive frontier town on a hill which commands a wide view across the valley of the Semois. The view is best enjoyed from a terrace behind the church which has an orientation table, or from the top of the church tower. The church, rebuilt in 1950 after the destruction of much of the town in 1940, has a modern carillon of 48 bells. One of these was presented by No. 1 Fighter Wing, Royal Canadian Air Force, in gratitude for the hospitality they received from the people of Florenville.

Florenville environs
The town of **Lacuisine**, 1km north of Florenville, is a summer resort nestling in a loop of the Semois. Boats can be rented in **Chiny**, 4km north, to make the descent of **Le Défile du Paradis** (daily from Apr–Sept from 09.00–18.00). The château at **Epioux**, 6km north of Florenville, was built in 1650. It was the home of Pierre Bonaparte, nephew of Napoleon, from 1862–71.

The Tour Griffon at **Neufchâteau**, 23km northeast of Florenville, is a relic of a castle destroyed in 1555.

Virton

Virton, in the far southeast of the province, occupies the site of a Roman settlement known as Vertunum.

A stronghold was built here in about 1060 by one of the Counts of Chiny. The oldest known document to mention Virton is a bull of Pope Lucius II of 1133. The County of Chiny was sold in 1340 to **John the Blind**, King of Bohemia and Count of Luxembourg. This change of suzerainty brought four centuries of misery and unrest to the area. Virton was captured, sacked and burned several times. It suffered at the hands of mercenaries employed by its powerful neighbours, and was raided frequently by the sans-culottes during the **French Revolution**. An Indian totem pole at the entrance to the municipal park was a gift from Canadian forces stationed at a nearby NATO base.

Tourist information
Rue des Grasses Oies 2b, ☎ 063.57.89.04. The tourist office produces a useful guide to the town in English and a pamphlet describing walks around the town.

Opening times
The **Musée Gaumais** is open from Apr–Nov from 09.30–12.00 and 14.00–18.00. It is closed on Tues in Apr–May and Sept–Oct.

The **Musée Gaumais** in the Rue D'Arlon occupies a former Franciscan Récollet convent built at the end of the 17C. A jacquemart dressed as a Récollet friar strikes the hours on a clock. A reconstructed Gallo-Roman pottery stands opposite the entrance. The museum has an interesting collection of **local archaeology** from the prehistoric and Gallo-Roman periods; 15C to 19C decorated firebacks made in Gaume founderies; period furniture and local folklore.

The museum also has a small collection of paintings including works by

Brother Abraham of Orval, Camille Barthélemy and Nestor Outer. A diorama shows the adventures of the fiddler Djan d'Mady, who met a wolf in the woods near Virton and killed it with one blow of his umbrella.

Virton environs

The Gaume

The Gaume (or Belgian Lorraine) is a compact region in the remote southern corner of the country, southwest of Arlon. Geographically an extension of the Ardennes, it is a melting pot in which Walloon, Lorraine and Luxembourg dialects and customs mingle. The language of the inhabitants closely resembles that of Lorraine. The name of the area is believed to come from the 'Gaumains', the porters who carried iron products produced here to Liège and other towns. Ironworking—for centuries the principal industrial activity of the area—has left its mark in the form of many abandoned forges. Some excellent examples of the ironwork of long-dead craftsmen can be seen in the Musée Gaumais at Virton. The region also has many caves, known locally as Trous des Nutons (or Trous des Fées), which are said to be the homes of gnomes and fairies.

The attractive village of **Torgny**, 6km southwest of Virton, is the most southerly village in Belgium. Protected by a ridge, la Montagne, from the cold north winds, it has a mild, sunny climate. Flora and fauna not found in any other part of the country flourish here. The small cicada, the praying mantis, eight different orchids and the rare Wild Candytuft *Iberis amara* have all been found in this area. A **vineyard** was planted in 1951 with 2000 Riesling vines. Since then other varieties have been added, including Müller Turgau, Pinot Noir and Pinot Gris. The six vineyards currently cover 3 hectares of land, creating the largest vine growing area in Belgium. Wines from Torgny, accompanied by good local dishes, can be sampled in the village.

An 18C farm at **Montquintin**, 6km southwest of Virton, has been turned into a museum of country life (open in Jul–Aug daily from 14.00–18.00; for details of visits at other times contact the Musée Gaumais at Virton). The farm was built in 1765 by Monseigneur de Hontheim, bishop, author and one of the last squires of Montquintin. The kitchen and main room have 18C furnishings. The museum also has photographs from the turn of the century, and a collection of 18C and 19C head-dresses. The barn contains farming tools from the Gaume.

A small **museum of local history** at Latour, 4km east of Virton, charts the history of a Walloon regiment known as the Latour Dragoons. It also has exhibits on Gaume life, the aristocratic family of Baillet-Latour, and the two World Wars in the Gaume. (Open from Easter–Nov on Sun from 15.00–18.00; Jul–Aug daily from 15.00–18.00.)

The **Archaeological Park of Montauban**, is near Buzenol, 16km northeast of Virton. A 10-minute climb leads to a quiet, wooded spur occupied by this extensive site. An Iron Age earth rampart of c 500 BC was replaced in the 2C BC by a stone wall. Part of the wall is still visible together with the outline of some huts. A Gallo-Roman wall was built in the 4C as a defence against the Franks. A castle constructed on this site in the Middle Ages had links with the legend of Les Quatre Fils Aymon. A section of the keep is still standing.

The **Gallo-Roman wall** is the most important feature of the site. This was strengthened at some time with carved Roman funerary stones and stelae which, archaeologists believe, may have been hurriedly collected from abandoned settlements in the neighbourhood. Most of the blocks have been replaced by replicas. The originals, with other Gallo-Roman stonework, are on display in the nearby museum.

The most interesting of the carved blocks is the incomplete representation of a **Roman harvesting appliance**. Discovered in 1958, this depicts an agricultural machine which is described by Pliny the Elder in his *Historia Naturalis*. Another damaged stone block found in Arlon in 1854 and now in the Musée Luxembourgeois, which shows the same device, was not identified until the Montauban discovery. The machine was operated by a donkey which pushed a wheeled container, edged with teeth. These teeth tore off the ears of corn and dropped them into the container. A wooden reconstruction of the device stands near the museum. (The park is open throughout the year. Contact the Musée Gaumais at Virton for information on visiting the museum.)

The **Abbey of Orval** is sited in a beautiful wooded valley, 24km northwest of Virton. It comprises the ruins of an old abbey and modern buildings completed in 1948.

> The abbey is said to have been founded by **Matilda of Lorraine** (1046–1115), who was sitting beside a spring in this spot when she lost her gold ring in the water. After praying at a nearby oratory, she returned to the spring and a fish swam up with her ring in its mouth. This gave the place its name, which is an inversion of Val d'Or.
>
> Benedictine monks founded an abbey here in 1020. When they abandoned it in c 1132, it was taken over by **Cistercians**. Orval soon became one of the richest Cistercian houses in Europe, famed for the quality of its ironwork. The abbey was largely rebuilt by Dewez in his 18C Neo-classical style, only to be virtually destroyed by French revolutionaries in 1794. The estate was acquired by Trappists, a reformed branch of the Cistercian order, in 1926. The new buildings were consecrated in 1948.

The 12C and 13C ruined church is part Romanesque and part Gothic. The splendid **rose window** and pillars with Romanesque capitals are particularly attractive. The foundations of a late 11C church and an earlier **oratory**, perhaps the place where Matilda prayed, can be seen near the ambulatory. A 20-minute film on modern monastic life is screened in the former guest-house, which preserves a 13C gable. Other features include Matilda's Fountain, the remains of the cloisters, the museum, the modern church and a garden of medicinal plants used by the monks. The abbey shop sells excellent brown bread, cheese and dark Orval beer, which is one of only six real Trappist beers brewed in the world. Services are held in the abbey church. (**Guided tours** daily from the Sunday before Easter to the end of Sept from 09.00–12.00 and 13.30–18.00; at other times daily from 10.00–12.00 and 13.30–17.00.)

Arlon

Arlon, in the southeast of the province, is one of the oldest towns in Belgium. It has various Roman remains and an outstanding archaeological museum. The local cafés serve a summer aperitif known as Maitrank, made from dry white wine and woodruff.

Practical information

Where to stay
££ *Hostellerie du Peiffeschof*, Chemin du Peiffeschof 111, 3km northeast of Arlon, ☎ 063.22.44.15, is an attractive country hotel with a good restaurant.

Tourist information
Rue des Faubourgs 2, ☎ 063.21.63.60.

Opening times
Musée Luxembourgeois, Rue des Martyrs 13, is open Tues–Sat 09.00–12.00 and 13.30–18.00. It is also open Sun from mid-Apr to mid-Sept (same hours).
Archaeological Park is open daily.

History

The town originated in the 2C as the Roman trading post of Orolaunum Vicus on the route from Rheims to Trier. Walled in the 4C, it stood on the frontier of an area where the invading Franks were not absorbed by the Gallo-Romans. A Germanic dialect still survives in the surrounding villages.

The Marquessate of Arlon was attached to the County (later Duchy) of Luxembourg in 1226 by the marriage of Marquess Waleran IV with Ermesinda of Luxembourg. The town was badly damaged by the French from 1552–1554 and again in 1558. The ramparts were torn down in 1671, but the French fortified the town again during their occupation from 1681–1697. Much of Arlon was destroyed by a fire in 1785. General Patton chose the town as a base for the American counter-offensive that relieved Bastogne at the end of 1944.

A walk in Arlon
Begin on **Place Leopold**, the main square, where a tank has been preserved as a memorial to the American liberation of Arlon on 10 September 1944. A short walk leads to the **Musée Luxembourgeois** at Rue des Martyrs 13. This interesting archaeological museum contains a collection of Gallo-Roman sculpture and stone monuments. Most of the material in the museum comes from Arlon and the surrounding area. Supplemented by models and drawings, it provides a clear and detailed picture of the life and customs of the people in this part of northwest Europe during the first centuries of the Christian Era.

Several impressive **sculptures** depict Roman cavalry, an officer making a sacrifice, and the late 2C column of a Celtic cavalry deity (with representations of the four seasons on the capital). A touching memorial to the children Vervicius Modestinus and Vervicia Modesta features a sculptured frieze of scenes from the Iliad, the Odyssey and the Aeneid. The inscription reads: 'To the shades of the departed Sextus Vervicius Modestinus and Vervicia Modesta, their parents have erected this monument'.

Other **funerary monuments** include the late 2C pillar of Attianus, and the striking stele which shows a nude female dancer.

The museum displays a large collection of ceramics, statues, coins, seals and objects from daily life. One of the most interesting objects is a relief showing one of the first agricultural machines ever made, the **harvester of Trévires**. The subject of this relief remained a puzzle until the discovery of a similar carved stone at Montauban in 1958.

The **upstairs rooms** contain prehistoric and Frankish artefacts, together with an instructive description of Roman building methods. The museum also has a collection of religious art, including a good 16C retable of the Antwerp school.

Return to Place Leopold and climb the hill to Grand-Place. The summit beyond was once occupied by a castle. This was succeeded by a Capuchin convent of 1626, and a citadel built for Louis XIV. The site is now occupied by the **Eglise Saint Donat**. Once the 17C chapel of the Capuchins, it became the parish church in 1825. It was altered considerably in 1858 and 1900. The chapel of St Blaise is decorated with 17C or 18C frescos which illustrate the story of a Roman legion commanded by **Donat**, which was saved from thirst after its Christian members prayed for rain. There is a fine view of the town and the surrounding area from the church tower. An orientation table indicates places in Belgium, France and Luxembourg.

Outside the church are some relics of the medieval parish church which stood in the Grande Rue until it was torn down in 1935. A doorway below dates from 1634. There is also a gate from 1700 next to the church. This comes from the convent of Clairefontaine, 4km southeast of Arlon.

Now return to Grand-Place where the remains of a 4C **Roman wall and tower** stand at no 18. The key is kept in the Café d'Alby at Grande-Place 1. These defences seem to have been erected in haste to protect the town from Germanic invaders; old tombstones were used for the base. Go down the Grande Rue, where a 16C vaulted passage and some cellars below are all that survive of medieval Arlon. A tablet in the passage recalls a visit by Goethe in 1792.

The remains of the 1C **Roman Baths** are in the grounds of an elusive **archae-ological park**, off the Rue des Thermes Romains. Most of the complex was destroyed at the beginning of the century, but it is still possible to see the outline of the caldarium and of the urinals. The site of the **Roman Basilica** is nearby. Used by the Christians during the 5C and 6C, the ruins mark the position of the oldest church in Belgium. The Franks buried their dead here in the 6C and 7C. Objects found in the baths and basilica are displayed in the Musée Luxembourgeois.

Arlon environs

The road from Arlon to Luxembourg passes the **Source of the Semois**. A replica of a Roman statue displayed in the archaeological museum stands next to the spring.

Acknowledgements

Much of this book relies on painstaking work carried out by previous authors, including Russell Muirhead, John Tomes, Bernard Mc Donagh, Joanna Woodall and Tania Jones. I hope that I have managed to preserve the best of their work for future readers to enjoy while adding something of the contemporary spirit of Belgium. Local and regional tourist offices in Belgium have been consistently helpful in answering questions and sending information, and colleagues on *The Bulletin* magazine, particularly Cleveland Moffett, Clare Thompson and Lisa Johnson, have helped to reveal many hidden aspects of the country. The book has benefitted greatly from the diligent editing of Sue Harper and Kim Teo, and from the attractive new layout of Eric Drewery. Finally, I would like to thank my wife and children for joining me on many of my trips and waiting patiently while I poked around yet another dusty old church.

Glossary

Art Nouveau
Late 19C artistic style characterised by flowing lines resembling twisted plant tendrils. The main Belgian exponents of the style were Victor Horta, Henry van de Velde and Paul Hankar.

Art Deco
Artistic style which developed between the two world wars. It strived for a modern look through the use of a sober geometrical style.

Begijnhof (Béguinage in French)
An enclosed religious community without vows for lay single women. The earliest Begijnofs were founded at the time of the Crusades. The most impressive Begijnhofs are at Bruges, Ghent, Kortrijk, Leuven and Lier.

Belfry (Belfort in Dutch, Beffroi in French)
A tall tower built in the middle ages as a symbol of urban prestige. The city charters were often kept in a strong room in the Belfry. Good examples can be seen in Bruges, Ghent and Mons.

Brabançonne, La
The national anthem of Belgium. The music was written by the French actor Jenneval after the Belgian revolution of 1830. The words were rewritten in 1860 by Charles Rogier.

Carillon
A set of bells hung in a church tower or belfry. The cathedrals at Mechelen and Antwerp, and the Belfry at Bruges are famed for their carillons.

Cobra
A post-war art movement which began in Copenhagen, Brussels and Amsterdam. The most prominent Belgian members of the group were Corneille and Alechinsky.

Facility Communes
A regulation of 1963 allows for the use of two languages in 21 Flemish and Walloon communes located along the language frontier. The regulation has led to bitter fighting in the Flemish communes that encircle Brussels, the Voeren (or Les Fourons) in Limburg province, and Comines (Komen) in Hainaut province.

Flemish Baroque
An ornate version of Italian Baroque architecture which developed in 17C Flanders under the influence of Pieter Paul Rubens. The guild houses on Grand-Place in Brussels were built in this style in the late 17C.

Flemish Renaissance
An ornamental version of Italian Renaissance architecture which emerged in Flanders in the 16C. Many of the details were based on illustrations in books of Italian architecture published in the Netherlands.

Golden Fleece, Order of the
A chivalric order founded by Philip the Good, duke Burgundy, in Bruges on 10 January 1430 on the occasion of his marriage to Isabella of Portugal. the order takes its name from the ancient Greek legend of the golden fleece, which was removed from the winged ram Chrysomallus, and later recovered by Jason and the Argonauts after many adventures. Fourteen official meetings of the order were held in the great cities of Flanders, Brabant and Burgundy in the 15C. The knights wore a chain with a pendant in the form of a sheep.

Gothic
Artistic style which flourished in Europe from the 12C to the 16C, characterised by elongated figures and pointed arches.

Grisaille
A painting done in a series of grey tones, without the use of colour.

Language frontier
The border that devides the Dutch-speaking north of Belgium (Flanders)

from the French-speaking south (Wallonia).

Late Gothic

Flamboyant and often fanciful artistic style which flourished at the end of the Gothic period. The style flourished in Belgium in the late 15C and early 16C.

Neo-classicism

Late 18C artistic movement which revived the art of ancient Greece and Rome. The important French Neo-classical painter Jacques Louis David spent his final years in Brussels.

Neo-Gothic

a 19C revival of medieval Gothic architecture promoted in Belgium by the Catholic establishment. Most 19C buildings in Bruges adopt this style.

Neo-Renaissance

A 19C revival of 16C Renaissance architecture promoted in Belgium by the liberal establishment.

Neo-Romanesque

A 19C revival of Romanesque architecture.

Perron

A column erected in medieval Walloon towns as a symbol of liberty.

Retable

A large wooden altarpiece orginally attached to the wall behind the altar, with elaborate carved and painted figures representing biblical scenes. Most Belgian retables were made in Antwerp and Brussels in the 15C and 16C.

Rococo

Flamboyant style which developed in France under Louis XV, characterised by shell-like ornamentation.

Romanesque

A sober style of architecture which emerged in the 11C and reached its peak in the 12C. It was named Romanesque because of its revival of Roman elements such as round arches and barrel vaults.

Surrealism

An artistic movement which developed in the early 20C under the influence of Guillaume Apollinaire and André Breton. Artists often relied on dreams and the unconsious mind to create unexpected and disturbing images. René Magritte was the leading Belgian surrealist.

Transitional

An art style which emerged in the early 16C in which elements of Gothic and Renaissance are combined.

Belgian contributions to civilisation

Belgians are often too modest to boast about their achievements, yet this small country has produced a considerable number of scientists, musicians and writers. Unfortunately, they are quite often mistakenly assumed to be French or Dutch.

The list of famous Belgians includes:
Emperor Charles V, born in Ghent, or possibly in Eeklo, in 1500
Godfrey of Bouillon, crusader, born in Baisy-Thy in 1060
Jacques Brel, singer, born in Brussels in 1929
Jacques Feyder, film director, born in Brussels in 1887
Hergé, cartoonist, creator of Tintin, born in Brussels in 1907
René Magritte, painter, born in Lessines in 1898
Georges Simenon, writer, born in Liège in 1903
Simon Stevin, mathematician, born in Bruges in 1548
Antoon van Dyck, painter, born in Antwerp in 1599
Jan van Eyck, painter, probably born in Maaseik c 1390

Some Belgian contributions to civilisation include:
Anatomy, founded by Andreas Vesalius of Brussels, author of the first complete textbook of human anatomy.
Atlas, collection of maps first published in book form by Abraham Ortelius of Antwerp.
Average man, statistical concept invented by Lambert Adolphe Quetelet of Ghent.
Bakelite, plastic invented in 1913 by Leo Hendrik Baekeland of Ghent.
Big bang theory of the universe, which argues that the universe began as a single atom that exploded, proposed by Georges Lemaître, a Belgian astrophysicist.
Chicory, or Belgian endive, a blanched vegetable developed by accident in Belgium in the 19C.
Dynamo, invented by Zénobe Gramme of Jehay-Bodegnée.
Hydrostatics, the study of liquids, founded by Simon Stevin of Bruges.
Maigret, fictional detective created by Georges Simenon of Liège.
Mercator projection, method of mapping the earth invented by Gerardus Mercator of Rupelmonde.
Paris Metro, largely built by a company established by Baron Edouard Empain, an engineer from Hainaut.
Phenakistoscope, an early form of motion pictures, invented by Joseph Plateau of Ghent.
Praline, a filled chocolate invented by Jean Neuhaus of Brussels.
Roller skates, invented by Joseph Merlin of Huy.
Saxophone, invented by Adolphe Sax on Dinant, born 1814.
Solvay process, an industrial method of producing soda, invented by Ernest Solvay of Brussels.
Spa, town in the Ardennes which gave its name to health resorts.
Whooping cough vaccine, developed by Jules Bordet, a Belgian bacteriologist.

Index to Artists

A

Abraham of Orval, Brother 465
Aertsen, Pieter 97, 208
Appelmans, Pieter 210, 211
Artan, Louis 100
Aubé, M. 352
Aubroeck, Karel 287
Audenaerde, Robert van 225

B

Backer, Jacob de 212
Bacon, Francis 101
Baer, Jan de la 224
Baeren, Joost van den 244
Baker, Herbert 308
Balat, Alphonse 94
Balen, Hendrik van 224, 225
Baudin, Jacques 375
Baurscheit, Jan Peter van, the Elder 221, 227
Baurscheit, Jan Peter van, the Younger 204, 238, 261, 323
Bayart, Denis 376
Beaugrant, Guyot de 146, 257
Beauneveu, André 271, 449
Beckere, Pieter de 152
Benson, Ambrosius 148, 208
Bergé, Jacques 106, 243, 348
Berghe, Frits, van den 101, 196
Béthune, Jean, Baron 165
Beuckelaer, Joachim 232
Biesbroeck, Jules van 190
Binche, Arnulf de 275
Bles, Henri met de 208, 405
Blockx, Frank 347
Blomfield, Sir Reginald 303
Blondeel, Lancelot 146, 148, 161
Blootacker, Melchior van 166
Boeckel, L. van 261
Boeckhorst, Jan van 164, 206
Bol, Hans 208
Bonaventure de Lannoy 159

Bondt, J.A. de 191
Bonnard, Pierre 101
Bonnecroy, Jan Baptist 228
Borchman, Jan 333
Borcht, Pieter van der 216
Borman, Jan 336, 437
Borremans, Pasquier 324
Bosch, Hieronymus 96, 117, 148, 189
Bosschaert, Thomas 215, 217
Boulenger, Hippolyte 418
Boullain, Sylvanus 292
Bourla, Pierre Bruno 207
Bouts, Albert 115
Bouts, Dirk 95, 147, 188, 243
Braekeleer, Henri de 116, 391, 418
Bril, Paul 399
Broeucq, Jacques du 397, 452, 453
Brouwer, Adriaen 98, 273, 274
Bruegel, Pieter, the Elder 79, 97, 107, 121, 207, 208
Brueghel, Ambroos 224
Brueghel, Jan 208, 210, 232, 262, 390
Brueghel, Pieter, the Younger 98, 189, 209, 262
Brusselmans, Jan 149, 190
Bruyn, Willem de 83
Brys, Arno 298

C

Camp, Camille van 146
Campin, Robert, (the Master of Flémalle) 42, 384, 393
Cantré, Joseph 281
Capronnier, J.B. 88, 211
Caravaggio, Michelangelo Merisi da 153, 221
Cels, Cornelis 221, 255
Champaigne, Jean-Baptiste de 88, 181
Champaigne, Philippe de 99
Charlier, Guillaume 386, 390, 391

Index

Z

If you would like more information about
Blue Guides please complete the form below
and return it to

Blue Guides
A&C Black (Publishers) Ltd
Freepost
Eaton Socon
Huntingdon
Cambridgeshire
PE19 8EZ

or fax it to us on 020 7831 8478
or email us at travel@acblack.co.uk

Name ....

....

Address ....

....

....

....

Index to maps

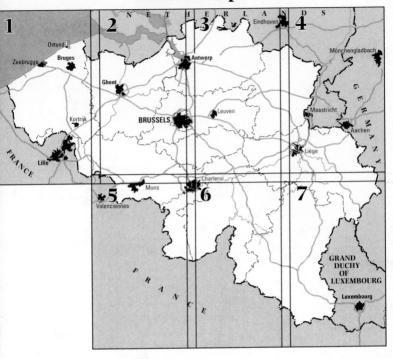

Key to maps

⊞	Ancient or religious building
☐	Feature of interest
◓	Caves
▲	Sight
✛	International Airport
▒	Forest / woodland
▬▬▬	Motorway
══════	Motorway under construction
─────	Major Road
─────	B Road
┄┄┄┄┄	C Road
┈┈┈┈┈	Minor Road
▬▬▬▬	Railway
··········	Canal
〰〰〰	River
─ ─ ─ ─	Ferry

Scale to maps

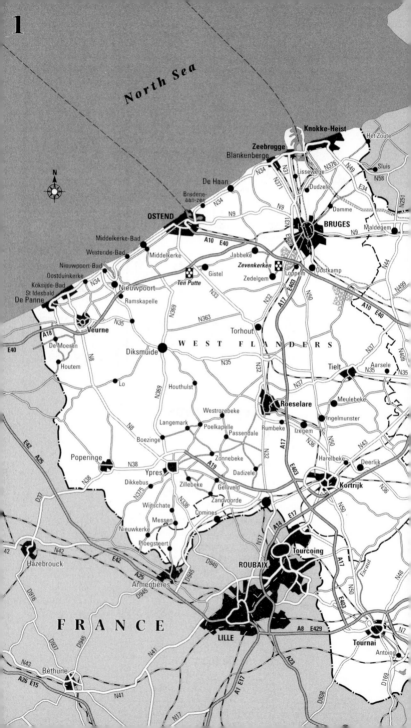

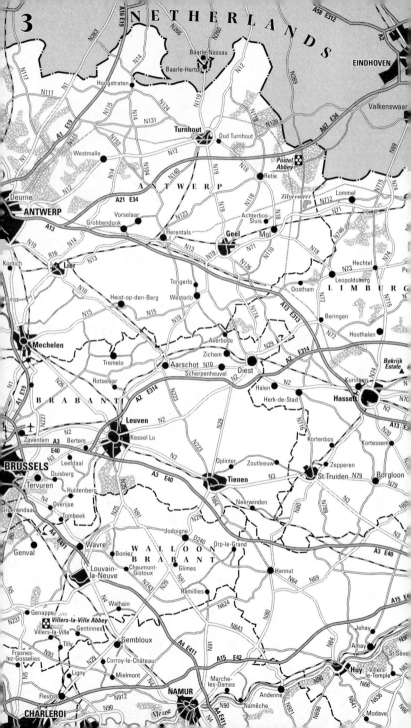

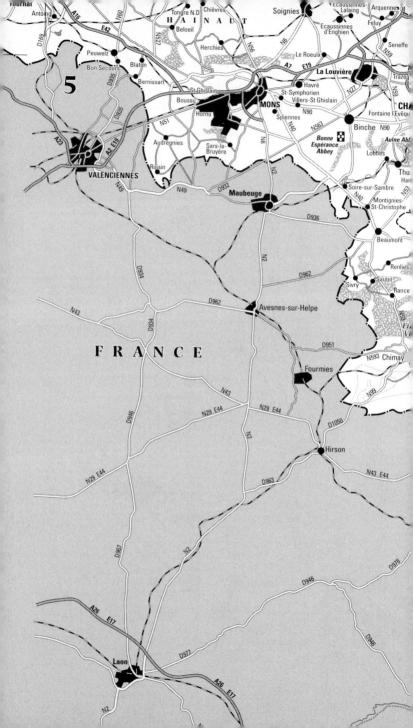

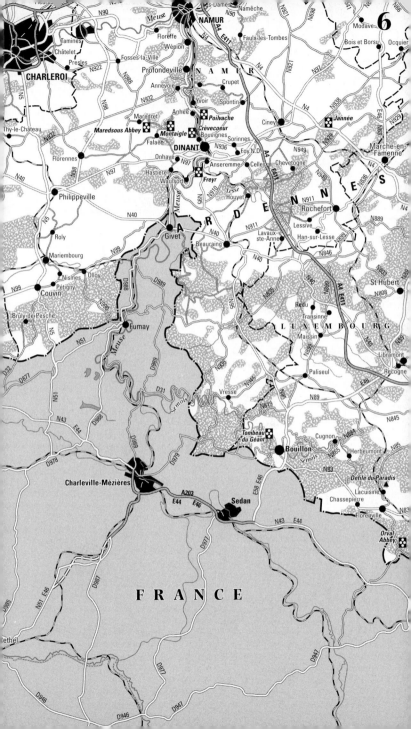

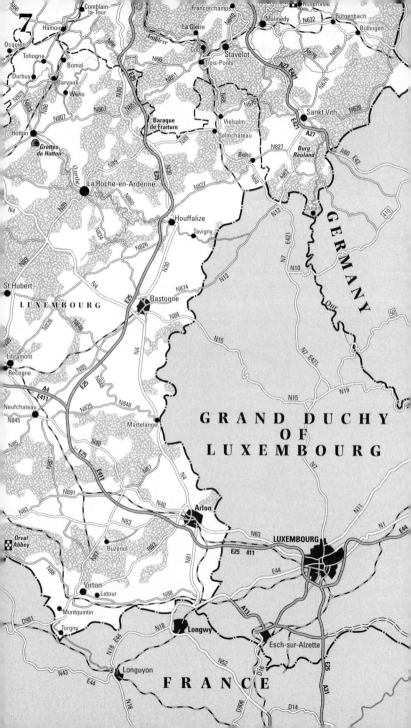